THE ARCHAEOLOGY OF DIFFERENCE

THE ANNUAL OF
THE AMERICAN SCHOOLS OF ORIENTAL RESEARCH

Volume 60/61

Series Editor
Nancy Serwint

THE ARCHAEOLOGY OF DIFFERENCE

GENDER, ETHNICITY, CLASS AND THE "OTHER" IN ANTIQUITY

STUDIES IN HONOR OF ERIC M. MEYERS

edited by Douglas R. Edwards and C. Thomas McCollough

AMERICAN SCHOOLS OF ORIENTAL RESEARCH • BOSTON, MA

ANNUAL OF THE AMERICAN SCHOOLS OF ORIENTAL RESEARCH
VOLUME 60/61

ISBN-10: 0-89757-070-7
ISBN-13: 978-0-89757-070-1

The archaeology of difference : gender, ethnicity, class and the "other" in antiquity : studies in honor of Eric M. Meyers / edited by Douglas R. Edwards and C. Thomas McCollough.

p. cm. -- (The annual of the American schools of oriental research ; v. 60/61)
Includes bibliographical references and index.
ISBN 978-0-89757-070-1 (alk. paper)
1. Social archaeology--Middle East. 2. Ethnoarchaeology--Middle East. 3. Ethnicity--Middle East--History. 4. Sex role--Middle East--History. 5. Social classes--Middle East--History. 6. Middle East--Antiquities. 7. Meyers, Eric M. I. Meyers, Eric M. II. Edwards, Douglas R. III. McCollough, C. Thomas.

CC72.4.A7347 2007
939'.4--dc22

2007038420

Printed in the United States of America on acid-free paper

CONTENTS

SECTION II —HELLENISTIC THROUGH BYZANTINE PERIODS

LIST OF FIGURES

Chapter 3

Chapter 4

Chapter 7

Chapter 14

Chapter 17

CHAPTER 33

CHAPTER 34

LIST OF TABLES

SETTING THE STAGE

Chapter 1

The Archaeology of Difference: Setting the Stage

by C. Thomas McCollough and Douglas R. Edwards

Human artifacts and texts that connote difference have long intrigued interpreters of the ancient world. Notably in the last century, efforts to elucidate religious, ethnic, social, and even gender boundaries have expanded dramatically. Many attempts have had their staunch critics. Disinterest, even disaffection, grew in no small measure from the sinister uses some approaches played in nationalistic reconstructions prior to and after World War II. Moreover, the rise of "New Archaeology," with its apparent rejection of "empiricist culture-history" and increased emphasis on "economic and subsistence strategies, exchange networks and social or economic organization," made ethnicity, in particular, seem for some an "outmoded and unfashionable archaeological paradigm" (Jones 1997: 5).

Near Eastern archaeology still retains its strong ties to "New Archaeology" or, better, processual archaeology (Renfrew and Bahn 2000). Indeed, Eric Meyers and several contributors to this volume were early proponents of its use. As evidenced in this collection of essays, interpreters have not remained stuck in some processual mud. Many contributors to this volume have participated in the clarion call to develop more useful models to understand the role difference played in the ancient world as well as its on-going significance, even in areas not easily accessible to the modern interpreter. Many depict a marriage of processual archaeology with careful consideration of the way artifacts (including texts) display ideas, symbols and elements of difference, a kind of cognitive-processual archaeology (Renfrew and Bahn 2000: 491–96). The ongoing significance of such analysis is evident in Neal Silberman's insightful study of the "archaeology of outsiders," where he demonstrates the importance of continuing to monitor the significant contributions of minority groups, such as Jews and Muslims, in Europe and their role in the formation of complicated societies.

Steven Fine examines how menorahs have influenced both ancient and modern sensibilities, most notably, the menorah taken by the Romans after the sack of Jerusalem and the destruction of the Temple in 70 C.E. An entire mythology has developed about its possible storage in a Vatican museum basement. Indeed, Fine observes that Jewish pilgrims (primarily Jewish Americans) go to the Vatican, a central Christian pilgrim site, with the hope of seeing the menorah. Such "pilgrimages," Fine argues in persuasive detail, reflect long-standing traditions that venerate the menorah.

On a related front, Volkmar Fritz suggests that current research indicates that the location of the altar and the central shrines of the First and Second Jewish Temples were not located over the bedrock now associated with the Dome of the Rock. Indeed, he argues, the tradition that marked the Dome as the location of the First Temple only developed during the Islamic period at the time of the building of the Dome in order to lend the site greater prominence and venerability. The modern implications for this thesis should be evident.

Rodney Sadler's nuanced study of Cushite imagery in the Biblical text illustrates how important clear discussions of race in antiquity are to discerning the nature of difference in the past. Moreover, it leaves aside the negative overtones of the "other," as so often happens today. William Dever in his essay is certainly correct that efforts to discern ethnic identities in antiquity need not fall *a priori* into some post-modernist and relativist strait jacket and merit reasoned and careful discussion. The strength of the essays in this collection rests in the cumulative effort to use material culture and texts to address what persons and societies presumed about difference in areas such as social *mores*, cultural expectations, gender definitions, or ethnic identities.

ARCHAEOLOGY IN A NEW AGE

The growing dissatisfaction with aspects of the "New Archaeology" brought about a renewed interest in the "archaeology of difference." The critiques of New Archaeology highlighted both the limitations of its positivist epistemology and the many problems associated with developing an adequate "middle range theory." Ian Hodder (1985) and a growing cadre of archaeologists concluded that cultures could not be viewed as purely adaptive to an external environment. This new approach reiterated how material culture was "actively manipulated by people" and thus expressive of social strategies, religious convictions, ethnicity, and gender. Material culture, as well as texts, had embedded within them such social constructions. This made fertile soil for a growing interest in engagement with the "archaeology of difference." As Foucault observed in his classic work, *The Archaeology of Knowledge*, perceived differences between groups often convey such symbolic power that whole societies structure their laws, gender roles, ethnic identities, and views toward the "other" in light of these perceptions.

Ascertaining the expressions of and the forces governing difference in the ancient world is a demanding task. The decision to use the phrase "archaeology of difference" as the conceptual guide for this book was intended to facilitate discussions that bear on core issues and questions regarding the interpretation of ancient texts and of the sparse material remnants we have of ancient people and their communities. Many of the issues that arise in the contributions are ones that Eric Meyers has long reflected upon, argued about, and even changed the direction of our thinking. In a career that has spanned over three decades, his contributions to the fields of Judaic studies, Biblical studies, and archaeology have been substantive and multifarious. The breadth and quality of the contributions to this work on the "archaeology of difference" reflect the vibrancy of the approach, as well as the challenges and opportunities for future work.

THE DIALOGUE BETWEEN TEXT AND ARTIFACT

What interpretive relation should exist between text and artifact? When gender, ethnicity, or race enter the conversation there seems a natural move toward debate regarding method. Discourses surrounding issues of identity that arise in the reading of texts have often shaped the understanding of the material culture without themselves being subject to critical analysis. On the other hand, the profound distrust of the subjective nature of the text has led some to a mistaken sense of the "objective" nature of the archaeological record. As this collection of studies makes evident, the study of ethnicity, gender, and cultural differentiation cannot go forward without careful and critical engagement with the historical sources as well as artifacts and the persistence of dialogue between text and artifact.

Enriching the dialogue between text and artifact depends not only on critical analysis, but also relies on an infusion of new ways of conceptualization and practice entailed in the study of difference. Eric Meyers has long championed the dialogic paradigm of text and artifact, most notably placing "Biblical archaeology" in conversation with related disciplines, such as anthropology and sociology. With Carol Meyers, he proposed a paradigm shift that would result in Biblical archaeology being "subsumed into the emerging discipline of social world studies" (Meyers and Meyers 1989: 143). Such a shift has dramatically broadened the conversation, since it involved "the integrative use of archaeology with all its ecological facets, of Biblical materials, and of comparative sociological and anthropological information and models" (Meyers and Meyers 1989: 143).

A number of contributors to this volume draw explicitly on theoretical models, often using the insights of other disciplines. Ofer Bar-Yosef illustrates the character of Neolithic villages through an astute analysis of ethnographic parallels and close study of the archaeological record. Alysia Fischer attempts a similar exercise in discerning glass makers in the Byzantine period, drawing on her study of traditional glass making techniques, notably in modern day Jordan and Egypt. John Dominic Crossan argues that the use of studies of ceramic manufacture in a variety of settings provides clues to the nature of social systems and exploitation during the time of the Galilean Jesus, while Carol Selkin Wise shows the value of ritual theory for unpacking the thorny issues surrounding the study of *miqwāʾôt*.

To be sure, interdisciplinary approaches can be perilous. As Ofer Bar-Yosef remarks, "Searching the anthropological literature is like crossing a stormy sea, and in ethnographic records one can always find the desired analogy." The articles in this volume demonstrate the fruitfulness of such disciplinary boundary crossings, with the *caveat* that the interpreter must demonstrate through careful, cautious, and critical analysis what is borrowed or used as analogous.

John Crossan, Carol Meyers, William Dever, and Gary Rendsburg in their respective articles demonstrate well Eric Meyers' call to archaeologists and textual scholars alike that one needs an "archaeological-literary approach for the study and reconstruction of ancient culture" (Meyers and Meyers 1989: 143). From the side of the archaeologist, the approach demands that the data be made available in a timely manner. It also means that it must be accessible to the non-specialist and is open to and conversant with the range of forces that impact communities or individuals. Eric Meyers' own excavations of and publications on towns and synagogues in northern Galilee (known collectively as the Meiron Excavation Project) are sterling examples of timeliness, accessibility, and a broadened archaeological approach (Meyers et al. 1981). The volume on the synagogue of Gush Halav (Volume 5 of the Meiron Excavation Project Reports), in particular, offers a paradigm of how close and technically astute analyses of loci and related data can lead to well-documented historical reconstructions (Meyers et al. 1991).

The text scholar, as Crossan notes, seeks insight from the archaeological record while noting its limitations in offering a full portrait of narrative traditions that reflect particular periods. As Meyers has argued, however, the absence of a true interchange between text and artifact can lead to acrimonious debate of the sort that swirls around the historicity of Israelite beginnings. Here, "revisionists" are seen to be pitted against conservative "Biblical archaeologists" (Meyers 2000: 350; see also Dever and Crossan in this volume). Gary Rendsburg provides an instructive example of a text scholar following closely the results of archaeological excavations as a check on, or corrective to, Biblical portraits of ancient Israel. Did ancient Israelite kings really avoid the practice of constructing stelae to display royal inscriptions? Were there no queens in ancient Israel, as the texts suggest? In each case, the search for counterevidence in the archaeological material proves fruitless. Nevertheless, this sort of serious and careful effort at "interchange" results in a conclusion that cannot be readily dismissed.

The dialogue between text and artifact has been richest and most productive in the field of ancient Near Eastern and Biblical studies. It has developed more slowly in the study of Judaism and early Christianity. As Meyers has noted, "The archaeological discoveries of the past decades have had little effect on the disciplines of Jewish history and New Testament scholarship" (Meyers 1988: 71). While Jewish scholarship had given "modest recognition of the discipline of archaeology as it relates to the period of the Hebrew Bible," it had little interest in archaeology "as it relates to the beginning of the common era (which witnessed, in connection with the creation of the Mishnah and Talmud, the development of rabbinic Judaism)" (Meyers 1988: 72). Likewise, "New Testament scholarship has been slow to take archaeology seriously..." (Meyers 1988: 72), something that has changed somewhat during the last decade, although with mixed results (e.g., Crossan in this volume; Moreland 2004; Horsley 1996; Chancey 2002; Reed 2000; Stegemann and Stegemann 1999). All too often social and historical reconstructions become reduced to images drawn from texts and that critical period of Jewish-Christian interaction and interdependence is left unrecovered. Only when texts are joined with artifacts can there be a "process of historical reconstruction" that produces "a reliable picture of these historic religions..." (Meyers 1988: 78).

The dialogue between text and artifact as a means for broadening the base of analysis beyond ancient Israel is evident in Meyers' work on early Judaism (or what, at one point, Meyers called "Talmudic Judaism"). As he noted in a programmatic article on the value of archaeology for studying rabbinic materials:

> In light of the ever-increasing sophistication in archaeological field methods, ceramic typology, numismatic analysis, environmental studies...etc., it is quite possible that these mute stones might speak with a far greater clarity than many of the texts...Indeed, the Talmud is a document of everyday life. It can lend itself uniquely to clarification through the use of archaeology... (Meyers 1975: 34).

Cynthia Baker (2004) and Miriam Peskowitz (2004) have illustrated the fruits of such an approach as they draw on Mishnaic and Talmudic material as well as archaeological remains to illustrate the character of gendered space in this period. In this volume, Barbara Geller draws on Mishnaic and Talmudic as well as classical Greek and Roman texts to illustrate the role rabies played within a theological framework conceived by the rabbis. She notes that medicine and magic interchange frequently in the ways rabbis (and others) discerned the nature (and healing) of rabies, although the rabbis always addressed it through the lenses of the law. Stuart Miller's utilization of Mishnah and Tosefta in regard to the question of the use of the "stepped pools" at Sepphoris offers a fine example of the ways in which these texts can at once shed light on practice and at the same time inhibit naive correlations between idea and artifact. The rich discussion of water and purity in the rabbinic sources certainly makes it reasonable to presume these pools were for ritual purity purposes. But, as Miller cautions, "...we should not believe for a moment that we know all of the possible uses of the stepped pools." The attempt to restrict these pools to either ritual or profane use is made problematic, if not unwarranted.

Within the range of material evidence that could be investigated for such "clarification," Meyers has often focused his efforts on synagogues. This was, one might say, an obvious choice given Meyers' argument that "everywhere in the classical world the main vehicle for the transmission of ancient Judaism was the synagogue" (Meyers et al. 1972: 28). This conviction about the value of the synagogue led Meyers not only to excavate synagogues and villages of northern Galilee, but also to assess the entire range of archaeological evidence for synagogues and its bearing upon the reconstruction of early Judaism. As one of the leading interpreters of ancient synagogues has noted, interest in the ancient synagogue has grown enormously in the last decades (Levine 2004: 70), and this is in no small measure owed to the formative work of Meyers and his colleagues. The article by Ze'ev Weiss offers substantive evidence for how careful study of synagogues and the features associated with them provide a glimpse of the diverse world of Judaism.

ETHNIC MARKERS

Meyers' search for the material evidence of early Judaism did not end with synagogue excavations. His more recent work centered on the ancient city of Sepphoris. A large urban site in lower Galilee, Sepphoris represents an important site to be put alongside of the reports from northern Galilee. Beginning in 1985, Meyers (initially in collaboration with Hebrew University—until 1989—and later under the rubric of the Sepphoris Regional Project) excavated a large portion of the acropolis of the ancient city, exposing a now well-known *triclinium* and its beautiful mosaic floor. The excavation of the domestic area also exposed numerous stepped pools, the interpretation of which raises one of the most critical and controversial aspects of the "archaeology of difference:" the validity and interpretation of the material correlates—ethnic markers—of identity.

Siân Jones has been an influential critic of the way in which archaeology and historical archaeology in particular has identified the material manifestations of ethnicity. Distortions in the interpretation of the material culture arise, she argues, when

> attempts to seek out the archaeological correlates of historically known ethnic groups...often ignore the situated and subjective nature of the historical sources, and also...disregard qualitative differences in the manifestation of ethnicity in written sources and material culture...the description and interpretation of material remains within historical archaeology is positively saturated with discourses of identity derived from written sources (Jones 1999: 220–21).

As regards the archaeology of ancient Israel and Roman Palestine, she quotes Tessa Rajak's remarks on studies of Jewish sites in ancient Palestine:

> To determine in advance what is Jewish and what is not (or even "probably" not) is to operate with a pre-conception of Jewish identity when our task is, precisely, to seek to define that identity (Rajak 1994: 239).

Jones' critique points the search for ethnicity away from a dependence on preconceived categories of difference and argues instead for a recovery of "the praxis of ethnicity." Working from Pierre Bourdieu's notion of *habitus*, ethnic difference becomes objectified in particular contexts, especially in contexts of contestation or opposition. A striking example of transient and confrontational expressions of ethnicity is to be found in Sepphoris. As James Strange's study of Sepphoris in the early Roman period and Thomas McCollough's s article on the city in the Byzantine period make evident, context may very well be the determinate of ethnic or cultural expression. As Strange notes, this city was "nestled between non-Jewish territories," which meant that "the citizens of Sepphoris and all Galilee faced daily the problem of maintaining Jewish identity...the Galileans used certain elements of the material culture to maintain their identity, namely stone vessels and ritual baths."

Ze'ev Safrai and Ofer Sion provide another case of context conditioning the modality of expression of identity. The value of a typology of settlement patterns is tested against the archaeological evidence of nomad settlement in the Late Byzantine–Early Moslem period in Palestine. What they found was that the "typical" nomadic settlement was not followed consistently and thus could not be effectively used to locate nomadic incursions. At particular times and in certain locales this type appears, while at other points it is evident that a centralized type of settlement pattern was adopted. In these cases, Jones' evocation of the notion of the praxis of ethnicity is relevant and, in fact, offers a challenge to the "seemingly coherent ethnic categories which are produced at a discursive level" (Jones 1999: 229).

But this challenge is not new. Eric Meyers has long urged caution in assigning ethnic identity based on ceramic, structural, or even faunal remains. What often appeared to be easy markers of identity at one point (e.g., glazed ceramic wares as evidence of the onset of Islamic occupation) can turn out to be less helpful, as further excavations reveal the errors of clear delineation of identity according to a particular artifact or structure. Indeed, for the Graeco-Roman period the challenge is, as he notes, "particularly great" (Meyers 1993: 743). The Greek and later Roman domination of Palestine produced a cultural complexity that often defies clear linkages between artifact or structure and ethnicity or gender. As Adam Porter's analysis of texts relating to the identification of the Tobiads indicates, this is a cautionary tale that must be taken seriously not only by those who study artifacts but also by those whose scholarly world is defined by ancient texts.

William Dever finds elements of Jones' agenda troubling. Notably, he argues that ethnicity is based on careful attention to assemblages of material remains. Contrary to revisionist approaches, Dever contends that ethnic constructs are not simply social constructions driven by current nationalistic or scholarly agendas, although he recognizes that such misconstructions can occur. Rather, ethnic identity evolves through recognition of patterns that appear in assemblages. He proposes an important set of criteria, an "archaeological trait-list," for determining ethnic differences, especially in roughly contiguous and contemporary societies. For later periods, the articles by Carol Selkin Wise, Katharina Galor, and Stuart Miller offer detailed and persuasive discussions that draw on textual and material remains at Sepphoris to discern the nature and function of *miqwā'ôt* or "stepped pools," the more neutral term Galor prefers. She analyzes the context of the stepped pools, often of varying sizes and construction, to determine if they had a ritual character. She concludes that many did, although they were not always used for ritual purposes. Here one finds a sophistication of analysis that achieves a dynamic relationship between text, artifact, and identity. Likewise, in Bill Grantham's study of the faunal remains at Sepphoris, one finds convincing evidence based on literary, epigraphic, and archaeological grounds that butchers at Sepphoris during the Roman period followed ritual observance in cutting their meat, indicating it was intended for Jewish consumption. Standardized cutting patterns suggest an active commercial enterprise and offer important clues to particular ethnic practices. Moreover, there is a remarkable absence of pig bones in the Roman period. This contrasts with increased amounts of pig bones in the Byzantine period, coinciding with a decrease in standardized butchery practices, which Grantham suggests denotes a change in culture, probably as the result of an increase in Christian population.

Even clearer markers, such as the menorah, can have multiple meanings, as Eric Lapp demonstrates in his study of the marketing of clay oil lamps with religious symbols. Economic concerns may govern the makers and distributors of oil lamps that have a menorah as a design. Indeed, he argues, the maker and distributor may not be Jewish at all. Promoters of their ceramic ware seek to attract religious audiences with admonitions to purchase their products to dedicate to the gods. Lapp argues that products found in shops indicate the sellers marketed their products to a religiously diverse audience. But lamp makers also apparently targeted particular groups, as indicated by crosses on some lamps and menorahs on others. Complications occur in determining how the symbols were viewed by those who bought them, since some lamps with menorahs were found in Christian burials.

But significant inferences regarding such symbols can often be drawn. In her article, Anna de Vincenz uses ceramic evidence, including lamps, inscriptions, and other material remains to argue that Jews and Christians coexisted at En-Gedi. Notably, two lamps had clear Christian symbols: one a bejeweled cross and the other an aedicule, indicating Christian presence in what literary sources and material remains suggest was largely a Jewish village in the fifth and sixth centuries C.E.

GENDER AND THE ARCHAEOLOGY OF DIFFERENCE

Feminist readings of the Bible and feminist critiques of Biblical scholarship have made us aware of how both ancient texts and the studies of those same texts are replete with complex and sometimes troubling issues relating to women and women's roles in the ancient world. One cannot hope to fully appreciate and address these issues without a dialogue between text and artifact. This volume brings together studies of both sorts to illustrate the value of such a dialogue.

From the side of text studies, Julia O'Brien's study of Nahum illumines the way in which the Biblical text, using female imagery, attempts to make Nineveh radically "other" over against Judah. The boundaries between the two are, however, rendered problematic when the text employs sexual assault as the means by which Yahweh vanquishes Nineveh. As O'Brien observes, "Nahum's feminizing of Nineveh allows feminist readers to see in the face of Nineveh their own faces, as well as those of rape victims around the world. No longer the abject other, the foe becomes Victim like me."

This sort of "reading against the text" has its archaeological corollary in studies of material culture that argue against assumptions and biases which are embedded in the readings of the archaeological record. Archaeological literature continues, for example, to give credence to a notion of progressive change from matrilineal to patrilineal society, to definitions of women in terms of their reproductive capacity (as opposed to men in their social capacity), and to simplistic notions of the domestic/public split. Overcoming such biases and assumptions has been slow, but the last decade or so has seen important advances in the study of gender and archaeology.

Roberta Gilchrist noted that one can trace a pattern of evolution that shows a strong correlation between "gender studies in archaeology and the progression of feminism" (Gilchrist 1999: 2). Breaking down the march of feminism into three waves, she notes the first wave, with its basic concerns for securing public emancipation of women, resulted in, among other things, a call for the recognition of the contributions of female archaeologists. The second wave of feminism focused on how patriarchy led to the subordination of women. This "second wave" manifested itself in archaeological studies by exposing the ways in which archaeological studies had perpetuated a "gender mythology." Citing the work of Margaret Conkey and Janet Spector, Gilchrist notes how this feminist critique made it apparent that archaeological studies drew implicitly "on contemporary gender stereotypes…" and in so doing legitimized "a long-standing continuity of gender roles, a linear evolution connected intrinsically with the biological functions of women and men" (Gilchrist 1999: 4). This second wave's call for attention to transitions in gender relations and the cultural specificity of gender opened the third wave with its postmodernist emphasis on the creation of subjectivity and the rejection of universal laws of female (or, for that matter, human) experience. The third wave led archaeologists to give more attention to symbolic and cultural manifestations of gender and to identify and accentuate expressions of *différence* in the material culture.

This evolving conversation between archaeology and feminist studies has stimulated, among other things, a call for a shift in focus to more micro-scale analyses of architecture and artifacts and a greater attention to the "traces of everyday occurrences and relations between people, on subtle shifts in power and relations of production" (Gilchrist 1999: 29). Carol Meyers exemplifies this in her examination of archaeological and textual evidence to determine the intertwining character of gender and the production of bread. She observes that interpreters have been "seduced into viewing archaeology primarily as the means to trace—or even verify—the large-scale social and political process involving tribes and nation states" and, therefore, have neglected the "primary units of society, family households." Meyers' article on bread production in Iron Age Israel is an impressive example of this shift in focus. Her approach illustrates how one can illumine the "everyday occurrences" and "read against" long held presumptions and perceptions of ancient society. Drawing on ethnography, ethnohistory, and iconography, Meyers argues that the material evidence we have available on bread production reveals "the female monopoly of the technology and the quasi-communal nature of the labor." This conclusion, in turn, challenges "the conventional wisdom that viewed women as passive and powerless," the private/public separation of sphere of influence, and male dominance in a hierarchical structured society.

THE ARCHAEOLOGY OF DEATH

Early in his career, Eric Meyers studied artifacts related to burials as a means of reconstructing the ancient world and its convictions. One of Meyers' earliest publications analyzed Jewish use of ossuaries for burials and showed how such use fits with the larger ancient Near Eastern pattern of funerary practice (Meyers 1971). Archaeological investigation of burial sites and practices has, indeed, proved fruitful, yielding not only spectacular finds (e.g., the bones of a victim of crucifixion at Giv'at ha-Mivtar or the ossuary inscribed with the name Caiaphas) but, perhaps more importantly, critical data for the reconstruction of ordinary life ways in the ancient world. The study of skeletons and grave goods, as well as the geography and architecture of burial have brought to light rich data that bears upon a host of questions relevant to this collection of studies. The archaeology of death has given us vital evidence relating to gender, to social status, to the interaction between culture and religion (e.g., Hellenism and Judaism), and to linguistic practice.

The contributors to this volume have surely proven the value of the archaeology of death. Joe Seger's study of the skeletal remains and grave goods in a Late Bronze Age tomb at Gezer provides a fascinating example of the way in which both status and "gender distribution patterns of work activity" can be teased out of the artifacts associated with death and burial. Similarly, the work of Zvi Gal, Howard Smithline and Dina Shalem on a Chalcolithic burial cave in Upper Galilee yields insights into "social hierarchy within this Chalcolithic society and gender aspects…," also enriching the discussion of iconography by way of its unusual mortuary figures.

In the articles by Byron McCane (Jewish ossuaries) and Peter Richardson (the tombs of Khirbet Qana), burial practices and tomb design are investigated for evidence of the extent of cultural intrusions and incorporation (notably, Hellenistic and Phoenician cultures) in shaping identity. The article by Rachel Hachlili reveals the convergence of magical formulae and structural configurations from Jewish tombs, coffins, and ossuaries for the sake of avoiding desecration. The archaeology of death is replete with data that bears upon identity formation and expression. As McCane has remarked, "rituals of death and burial, then, are culturally specific symbolizations that represent the culture's most basic norms and values for life. Death ritual, in other words, is an artifact of culture" (McCane 2003: 18).

SITE AND REGIONAL STUDIES

Eric Meyers has long called for the discernment of distinctive regional attributes in the study of particular sites or a large empire (Meyers 1979; cf. Millar, who has issued a similar call [1983, 1987]). A regional analysis means, among other things, being sensitive to the data as it comes to us and avoiding generalizations. While common forces may be in play (e.g., Roman imperialism, Hellenization), the interchange with these forces can be quite distinctive. At one point, it may call forth aggressive expressions of difference, at another, absorption and symbiosis. Meyers' archaeological reports on the synagogues and villages of northern Galilee, for example, make evident the importance of addressing such influences as regional economic forces, geology, architectural styles, and religious sensibilities that define synagogue construction in regional terms. There are a number of articles in this volume that have benefited from the paradigm established by these reports.

Ofer Bar-Yosef draws on core/periphery analysis and other anthropological insights to create a social history of the Holocene period in southwest Asian complex hierarchical villages, especially as they relate to larger regional patterns. He notes that at an early stage long-range trade existed, as evidenced by obsidian from Anatolia and shells from the coast. Moreover, complex systems, often hierarchical and reflecting distinctive status changes, developed in villages and their surrounding areas during the PPNB period, including structures and statuary devoted to ritual and cultic activity. His analysis extends to determining the causes of abandonment of villages within large areas at the end of the PPNB period, offering an astute discussion of what can occur to complex societies in the face of dramatic climate changes (his proposal) or environmental degradation, conflict, economic, or social changes.

In terms of historical archaeology, Melissa Aubin's study of two terracotta figurines from Sepphoris reveals the caution necessary in using artifacts to argue for the impact or even the reality of trade and importation. While both figurines show stylistic signs of influence outside of lower Galilee (i.e., Cypriot and western Roman Empire), one cannot assume these figurines are evidence of import without further "provenience testing." Aubin agrees with Ora Negbi (1966) "that one cannot determine place of production on stylistic grounds alone." Moreover, as Aubin notes, "Sepphoris would have provided a hospitable environment for producing crafts that were suitable for distribution within the city and region."

Rami Arav and Vassilios Tzaferis broaden the canvas to consider the architecture, coins, and faunal remains of the town of Bethsaida and the city of Caesarea Philippi/Paneas. In the case of Bethsaida, Arav has led an excavation that has exposed evidence which allowed him to trace the evolution of the identity of the town's population from the Iron Age into the early Roman period. The early Roman settlement turned out to be one of modest size (likely "several hundred" inhabitants) and, based primarily on numismatic evidence, largely Jewish in makeup. The elevation of the town to the status of a *polis* in 29/30 C.E. appears to have led to the building of a Roman temple, but this did not lead to a "thoroughly Hellenistic presence at the site…There are no remains of Hellenism in the architecture of the houses, not one single Greek capital and any Hellenistic fashion in the way it is represented at the nearby site of Tel Anafa and no mosaic floor." Bethsaida offers an important example of a local population in tension with, rather than absorbed by or absorbing, the Roman imperial culture.

Tzaferis' excavations of Caesarea Philippi/Paneas reveal a city whose architectural plan as well as structural elements were initially designed to continue a pattern of Hellenization and control over the regions of Gaulanitis (Golan), Ituraea (northern Golan Heights), and Ulatha (northern Hula and southern Beka'a valleys) begun by Antiochus III. This urban administrative center, imposed on the landscape by the tetrarch Phillip, son of Herod the Great, grew and flourished in the 2nd and 3rd centuries. The archaeological evidence suggests that the city prospered by way of its favorable location on trade routes and its association with various pagan deities. This is an urban space in a region of Roman Palestine that not only retained its Greco-Roman identity but prospered as a consequence. Indeed, as Tzaferis notes, "…all the available sources, archaeological, epigraphic, numismatic, and literary clearly confirm that Caesarea Philippi was actually replete with sanctuaries, temples, and cult statues."

In a more standard literary study, Stephen Goranson argues that identifying the region from which Celsus wrote, which he believes is Pergamum in Asia Minor, lends insight into the images and inclinations of the author. Indeed, the confluence of the Second Sophistic with increased concern to interpret Roman power through the lens of Greek ideals make Celsus' concern regarding Christian disruptive activities all the clearer. There were more appropriate ways to address Roman power (Swain 1996: 87–89).

The essays in this collection offer a variety of ways to discern the nature and character of difference as understood through the archaeological and textual record. They represent a small slice of a large topic and are intended to stimulate ongoing discussion in areas that Eric Meyers has championed over many years.

A TRIBUTE

This book, along with essays in an earlier work dedicated to Eric, *Religion and Society in Roman Palestine* (Edwards 2004), testifies to the respect for and profound influence of the long career of Eric M. Meyers as a leader, a teacher, and a scholar. As a member of the faculty of Duke University since the outset of his career, he continues as the Bernice and Morton Lerner Professor of Judaic Studies and Archaeology. He has been a visiting professor at a number of institutions, such as Brandeis University, Williams College, Jewish Theological Seminary, and the Free University of Berlin, and served as the director of the Albright Institute of Archaeological Research in Jerusalem, the Annenberg Research Institute, and the Center for Judaic Studies at Duke University. His long and faithful service to ASOR, most notably as its president, as well as his long tenure as scholar and teacher has brought many important contributions to scholarship and has resulted in a wealth of friends and students eager to honor him. The studies in this book stand as tribute to his leadership, his work, and his friendship. At the same time, they continue to widen the path of Meyers' insightful and often pioneering ways of gathering and assessing both the literature and material culture of the religions (and Judaism in particular) of the ancient Mediterranean. The editors and contributors to this volume dedicate it to honor the significant contributions that Eric M. Meyers has made and continues to make.

May 1, 2006

REFERENCES

Baker, C.

2004 Imagined Households. Pp. 113–28 in *Religion and Society in Roman Palestine: Old Questions, New Approaches*, ed. D. Edwards. New York, NY: Routledge.

Chancey, M. A.

2002 *The Myth of a Gentile Galilee*. Cambridge: Cambridge University.

Edwards, D. R., ed.

2004 *Religion and Society in Roman Palestine: Old Questions, New Approaches*. New York, NY: Routledge.

Foucault, M.

1972 *The Archaeology of Knowledge*. London: Routledge.

Gilchrist, R.

1999 *Gender and Archaeology*. London: Routledge.

Hodder, I.

1985 Postprocessual Archaeology. Pp. 1–26 in *Advances in Archaeological Method and Theory* 8, ed. M. Schiffer. New York, NY: Academic.

Horsley, R. A.

1996 *Archaeology, History, and Society in Galilee: The Social Context of Jesus and the Rabbis*. Valley Forge, PA: Trinity International.

Jones, S.

1997 *The Archaeology of Ethnicity: Constructing Identities in the Past and the Present*. London: Routledge.

1999 Historical Categories and the Praxis of Identity: The Interpretation of Ethnicity in Historical Archaeology. Pp. 219–32 in *Historical Archaeology: Back from the Edge*, eds. P. Paulo, A. Funari, M. Hall and S. Jones. London: Routledge.

Levine, L.

2004 The first-century Synagogue: Critical Reassessments and Assessments of the Critical. Pp. 70–102 in *Religion and Society in Roman Palestine: Old Questions, New Approaches*, ed. D. Edwards. New York, NY: Routledge.

McCane, B.

2003 *Roll Back the Stone: Death and Burial in the World of Jesus*. Harrisburg, PA: Trinity International.

Meyers, E. M.

1971 *Jewish Ossuaries: Rebirth and Reburial*. Rome: Pontifical Biblical Institute.

1975 The Use of Archaeology in Understanding Rabbinic Materials. Pp. 28–42 in *Texts and Responses: Studies Presented to Nahum N. Glatzer on the Occasion of His Seventieth Birthday by His Students*, eds. M. Fishbane and P. R. Mendes-Flohr. Leiden: Brill.

1979 The Cultural Setting of Galilee: The Case of Regionalism and Early Judaism. Pp. 686–702 in *Aufstieg und Niedergang der Römischen Welt: Geschichte und Kultur Roms Im Spiegel der Neueren Forschung*, vol. II.19.1, eds. H. Temporini and W. Haase. Berlin: de Gruyter.

1988 Early Judaism and Christianity in the Light of Archaeology. *Biblical Archaeologist* 51: 69–79.

1993 Identifying Religious and Ethnic Groups Through Archaeology. Pp. 738–46 in *Biblical Archaeology Today. Proceedings of the Second International Congress on Biblical Archaeology, Jerusalem, June 1990*. Jerusalem: Israel Exploration Society.

2000 Ceramics Chronology and the Historical Reconstruction. Pp. 344–50 in *The Archaeology of Jordan and Beyond: Essays in Honor of James A.*

Sauer, eds. L. E. Stager, J. A. Greene and M. D. Coogan. Winona Lake, IN: Eisenbrauns.

Meyers, E. M.; Kraabel, A. T.; and Strange, J. F.
1972 Archaeology and the Rabbinic Tradition at Khirbet Shema': 1970 and 1971 Campaigns. *Biblical Archaeologist* 35: 2–31.

Meyers, E. M., and Meyers, C. L.
1989 Expanding the Frontiers of Biblical Archaeology. *Eretz Israel* 20: 140–47.

Meyers, E. M.; Meyers, C. L.; and Strange, J. F.
1981 *Excavations at Ancient Meiron, Upper Galilee, Israel, 1971–72, 1974–75, 1977*. Meiron Excavation Project, vol. 3. Cambridge, MA: American Schools of Oriental Research.
1991 *Excavations at the Ancient Synagogue of Gush Halav*. Meiron Excavation Project, vol. 5. Winona Lake, IN: Eisenbrauns.

Millar, F.
1983 The Phoenician Cities. A Case Study of Hellenisation. *Proceedings of the Cambridge Philological Society* 209: 55–71.
1987 Empire, Community and Culture in the Roman Near East: Greeks, Syrians, Jews and Arabs. *Journal of Jewish Studies* 38: 143–64.

Moreland, M.
2004 The Galilean Response to Earliest Christianity: A Cross-cultural Study of the Subsistence Ethic. Pp. 37–48 in *Religion and Society in Roman Palestine: Old Questions, New Approaches*, ed. D. Edwards. New York, NY: Routledge.

Negbi, O.
1966 A Deposit of Terracottas and Statuettes from Tel Sippor. *'Atiqot (English Series)* 6: 1–22.

Peskowitz, M.
2004 Gender, Difference, and Everyday Life: the Case of Weaving and its Tools. Pp. 129–45 in *Religion and Society in Roman Palestine: Old Questions, New Approaches*, ed. D. Edwards. New York, NY: Routledge.

Rajak, T.
1994 Inscription and Context: Reading the Jewish Catacombs of Rome. Pp. 226–41 in *Studies in Early Jewish Epigraphy*, eds. J. W. van Henten and P. W. van der Horst. Leiden: Brill.

Reed, J. L.
2000 *Archaeology and the Galilean Jesus: A Re-Examination of the Evidence*. Harrisburg, PA: Trinity International.

Renfrew, C., and Bahn, P.
2000 *Archaeology: Theories, Method and Practice*, third ed. London: Thames and Hudson

Swain, S.
1996 *Hellenism and Empire: Language, Classicism, and Power in the Greek World, AD 50–250*. Oxford: Oxford University.

Stegemann, E. W., and Stegemann, W.
1999 *The Jesus Movement: A Social History of Its First Century*, trans. O. C. Dean, Jr. Minneapolis, MN: Fortress.

Chapter 2

Jewish and Muslim Heritage in Europe: The Role of Archaeology in Defending Cultural Diversity

by Neil Silberman

In today's ever-unifying Europe, cultural heritage has always been an important tool in fostering a sense of European identity. In that task, archaeology's role has been central. From the pioneering excavations of the 18th and 19th centuries to today's new techniques and ongoing research we now possess a rich and complex record of material life in Europe, extending from the Paleolithic, through the long succession of cultures and conquests, all the way to the battlefields and industrial sites of the late 19th and early 20th century. And in enhancing public consciousness of the scope and variety of European material heritage, archaeologists have not only discovered and scientifically documented technology, architecture, and artistic expression; they have helped to physically integrate the archaeological sites and monuments of the past into the European landscape of today.

Unfortunately, Europe has now also become a society of strangers. The multi-ethnic landscapes of 21st-century European cities are a growing source of social tension, occasional violence, and the main targets for demagogues of nationalistic nostalgia who hark back to images and slogans of ancient cultural "purity." Many of those images and monuments of nationalistic significance have been unearthed or illustrated by archaeological excavations and have been preserved as cultural heritage sites. Yet, as we all know, archaeology produces much more than national icons. At construction sites in busy cities, in wide-ranging surveys of settlement patterns, and in new analyses of ancient foodways and trading connections, the European past has proved to be anything but static or pure. Waves of immigration, trading connections, and shifting networks of military alliances and commerce through the millennia have left a complex and multifaceted record of human interaction—and new understandings of what "European" identity might have meant in each historical period.

When we refer to European material heritage, however, where should the boundaries be drawn? The nation-state has until recently been the main point of reference; antiquities services and preservation agencies have been largely focused on presenting to their various publics a national patrimony. Now, with the increasing influence of the European Union, efforts have been made to incorporate formerly distinct national heritage traditions into a shared European cultural and historical legacy. But is European material heritage just the sum of its various national parts? What is the responsibility of archaeologists and cultural heritage managers in Europe to study and present the material culture of groups that have always been depicted as outsiders? This chapter is about the public presentation of Muslim and Jewish heritage in Europe, though there are of course other heritages from Africa and Asia that would represent the same phenomenon. Yet, it could be argued that no two other groups of "outsiders," if we call them that, have left such a deep material record and were so deeply involved in the formation of European civilization and identity.

Muslim material heritage in Europe is divided into two main geographical areas and is confined to two main periods of time. The earlier is of course the period of Muslim rule over al-Andalus, Andalusia, in Spain. From the time of its conquest by the Umayyad general Tariq in 711 C.E. to the final expulsion of the Nasrids from the city of Grenada in 1492, this area was the home to a unique and creative civilization, known not only for its literary and scientific achievements, advanced agricultural technology, and urbanism, but also for the splendor of its architecture and decorative arts. The other area of significant Muslim material heritage in Europe lies at the other end of the Mediterranean and encompasses the islands of Cyprus and Crete and most of the Balkan Peninsula. It was incorporated into the Ottoman Empire beginning in the late 15th century; a significant Muslim population remains there today. Its monuments consist of a wide range of mosques, marketplaces, and other public structures. Archaeological excavations and surveys have been conducted throughout the Balkans, but their presentation to the public and even more so their preservation as cultural heritage sites remains entirely dependent on issues of modern warfare and ethnic tension, sadly far beyond the power of either archaeologists or cultural heritage managers to control.

The material heritage of the Jews presents an entirely different picture. The presence of historical Jewish communities is recorded in every European country, with the earliest mentions beginning in the Roman period and continuing to the present, punctuated by tragic interludes of expulsion and massacre. Jewish museums throughout Europe preserve significant collections of ritual objects, artworks, and artifacts of daily life. Of Jewish monuments in Europe, the best known are synagogues and cemeteries. In some places, the former ghetto or Jewish Quarter of a city is identified and protected. Since the 1990s, detailed architectural surveys have been undertaken throughout Central and Eastern Europe to document and systematically describe the remains that were damaged or neglected during the Holocaust and in the years of Communist rule. And in at least three notable cases, in France, Germany, and Austria, archaeological excavations have been conducted in medieval Jewish Quarters whose remains were exposed in the course of modern urban development.

How is this heritage presented to the public? For the most part, it remains somewhat out of the mainstream, both historically and administratively. In Spain, extensive efforts have been made by national and regional administrations to incorporate both Muslim and Jewish contributions into a shared cultural tradition. But elsewhere, Jewish and Muslim heritage is all too often seen as something grafted onto the main flow of national historical traditions: useful to mention, but still something of an exotic, ethnic curiosity. The impetus for public presentation of sites and monuments is steadily growing, but it is largely unofficial, sponsored by international bodies or local communities. Cultural heritage routes have been established to link important Muslim sites in Spain and in the Balkans and the Council of Europe's annual European Day of Jewish Culture, which now offers public open admission to hundreds of Jewish sites and monuments in twenty-three countries, attracted almost 100,000 visitors last year. Elsewhere, unfortunately, heritage is a matter of dispute. Many of the important sites of Muslim heritage in Bosnia, Serbia, and Kosovo were destroyed or badly damaged in the recent years of ethnic fighting, but the restoration of the Mostar Bridge between the Christian and Muslim Quarters of Sarajevo, scheduled to be completed this summer, offers a note of hope.

What role does archaeology have to play in contributing to an understanding of Europe's historical diversity and appreciating the value of cultural diversity today? I have already mentioned archaeological work in the former areas of the Ottoman Empire and in medieval Jewish Quarters, and I would suggest that archaeology has great potential for addressing some important historical questions about Jewish and Muslim roles in the shaping of European civilization. And its public presentation can, I believe, constructively expand the definition of European heritage itself.

The archaeological work already undertaken has provided new insights into the nature of Muslim and Jewish communities in medieval and early modern Europe. The excavations beneath the Palace of Justice in Rouen, for example, have revealed the existence of a large and impressive 12th-century Romanesque building in the heart of the medieval Jewish Quarter. Its architectural form is similar to chancellery chambers in contemporary Norman castles. Latin and Hebrew graffiti were scratched on the walls of the main hall. And its tentative identification as a Talmudic Academy has provided the first material evidence of the emergence of a Jewish communal institution that was deeply affected by the surrounding culture and, in turn, deeply influenced the institutions of world Jewry. Excavations in the medieval Jewish Quarter of Frankfurt have revealed a wide range of material culture connections that offer additional insight on the role of the Jews in commerce and trade. And the elaborate virtual reconstruction of the Jewish Quarter of Vienna in the late 13th century, based on the recent excavations, has offered a new perspective on medieval urban life and culture, in which the Jews are seen as neither marginal nor entirely alien, but as an integral part of life in medieval Vienna. Through their incorporation into a new branch of the city's Jewish Museum, the archaeological remains and a multimedia presentation offer an enlightening perspective and an effective public education tool.

In the coming years, archaeology's contributions can be even more substantial. The traditional understanding of Jewish settlement history in Europe has always been straightforward: these communities are the descendents of Roman Jewish populations from around the Mediterranean, themselves with a direct connection to Jerusalem. Following the Roman troops northward, they gradually established communities in the major cities of Gaul. The archaeological evidence is rare but suggestive, such as the oil lamps ornamented with the distinctive seven-branched candelabra or "menorah" found in the excavations of Roman Trier. But after the end of the Empire, even that faint material trail suddenly disappears. Traditional historiography and scattered references in early medieval texts suggest that Jewish communities existed in France, the Low Countries, and in the Rhine and Danube Valleys — only to push eastward to Eastern Europe in the wake of the Crusades. But even this basic scheme is now under question. Only in the 11th century does there appear a significant corpus of Hebrew inscriptions and dated tombstones, particularly in the Rhine Valley. What happened to the Jews of Western Europe from the 4th to the 11th centuries? And why did they appear in the archaeological record so suddenly?

Archaeology has proved its value in uncovering material traces of ancient cultures that were unknown or only incompletely known from the written record. In this respect, it is possible that archaeology can play a role in solving the great mystery of the "missing centuries" of European Jewish history. Finds such as the single, isolated Hebrew gravestone discovered by chance in the 19th century in Tienen, Belgium, on the main trade route from Cologne and the Rhine valley to Brussels and Bruges, may hint at the existence of still unknown early medieval Jewish communities. More intensive surveys and continued archaeological study of Jewish material culture are essential tools to a possibility of filling in the historical gap. Does the apparent absence of Hebrew inscriptions and other obvious indicators before the 11th century suggest that a massive population explosion took place in that period, or were more subtle processes of ethnic self-definition occurring at that time?

These are essential questions for understanding the role of Jews within European society.

Islamic archaeology has also shown great potential. It has already supplemented the traditional art historical approach with new insights on technology and agricultural systems introduced into Europe from the Muslim world. Excavations and surveys of irrigation systems in Andalusia and Ottoman plantation farming and sugar refining in Crete and Cyprus provide evidence of far-reaching social and economic changes that would affect Europe for centuries to come. Beyond the carefully preserved confines of the Alhambra Palace and the mosques and elaborate public fountains and caravanserais of the Balkans is the still-to-be explored archaeological evidence of communities deeply involved in the process of change. The continuing impact of Islamic town forms and the pattern of distribution of such simple artifacts as decorated clay tobacco pipes throughout the Ottoman territories offer fascinating insights not only into the interaction of Muslims with Europeans, but also about their shared interaction with the discovery of the New World. In sum, it is already apparent that the archaeological heritage of Muslims and Jews in Europe is not merely a passive reflection of entirely external cultural influences, but represents dynamic networks of social, economic, and artistic connections that contributed both to the development of a distinctively European culture and to the emergence of specific Jewish and Muslim cultural expressions as well.

The cultural identity of Europe is not and never has been static; today it is changing with unparalleled speed. New immigrants, new social landscapes, new economic and political tensions, and the continuing ideal of European unification force all of us to discard restrictive definitions of separate national legacies and to redefine what kind of a society a multi-national, multi-cultural Europe of the 21st century will be. For archaeologists across Europe, it is now evident that old, essentialist definitions of "Romans," "Barbarians," "Franks," "Celts," "Teutons," and all the others do not represent distinctive and unchanging groupings but a creative mixture of preexisting cultures and developing social forms. Such is also true of minority groups long seen on the periphery of European history. Indeed, the periphery is no longer so easy to distinguish. The incorporation of many voices and perspectives in our emerging scientific picture of the past provides a stark contradiction to the modern voices of discord and separation. Archaeology can continue to show us that Europe's national and regional cultural traditions have always been enriched by the continent's turbulent, ever changing mix of peoples, connections, and ideas.

Two objectives must be sought to place minority heritage in the mainstream of European heritage: the first is for Jewish, Muslim, and other ethnic minority sites to be recognized by antiquities services throughout Europe as an essential part of the historical and cultural landscape, as potentially significant for official preservation as monuments and periods of more traditional "national" interest. The other is for archaeological research agendas and heritage policies to recognize that the definition of Europe's common heritage is a dynamic field for reflection and reconsideration in which the story is far from being completely told. The public presentation of archaeology, in this respect, is not a matter of merely conveying scientific knowledge to the general public. It is a two-way process, in which the involvement of minority communities—both of the past and of the present—in the study and preservation of material remains can potentially widen and deepen modern discussions of history and identity. If given adequate support and scholarly attention, the archaeology of "outsiders" has a great potential for encouraging a constructive public appreciation of the complexity and diversity of Europe's material and archaeological record. Sites and artifacts long overlooked and still to be discovered can demonstrate that the vibrant interaction of ideas, cultures, and peoples is a fundamental part of Europe's cultural legacy.

SECTION I

NEOLITHIC THROUGH PERSIAN PERIODS

Chapter 3

The Emergence of Social Complexity in the Neolithic of the Near East

by Ofer Bar-Yosef

Applying social interpretations to archaeological remains is far from being an easy task. Our success is dependent upon perceived models of the evolution of social institutions, the formulation of relevant questions, and, with the available data, testing the suggested interpretations. Archaeologists rarely worry about the sources of their inferences. Searching the anthropological literature is like crossing a stormy sea, and in the ethnographic records one can always find the desired analogy. The tendency is to rely on known studies. For example, the Khoisan (San bushmen) served for several decades as the living representatives of Palaeolithic people. When the sample of modern hunter-gatherers was enlarged, a more balanced picture emerged and the amount of socioeconomic variability increased considerably (Kelly 1995).

THE ANTHROPOLOGICAL INFERENCES: A FEW ECLECTIC REMARKS

In the following pages, I will address several aspects of the social complexity of Neolithic village society. Pursuing this line of investigation, analogies to past farmers can be derived from a larger sample of living populations (Wolf 1966; Johnson and Earle 2000). Although traditional agricultural techniques are quickly disappearing during the twentieth century, we still live in a world where peasants' lifeways can be observed.

The difficulties in interpreting early Neolithic societies in the Levant is due to the need to understand how the first transition from hunting and gathering to incipient farming occurred. This major socioeconomic shift, which apparently affected the basic lifeways of people in the Near East some eleven millennia ago, is known as the Neolithic Revolution. By studying later, historical technological revolutions, we know that the process is initiated in a particular area within a certain group of people. Hence, as archaeologists, we face the uncertainties of identifying the population or populations of foragers who became farmers in a core area (Price and Gebauer 1995; Harris 1996; B. Smith 1998; O. Bar-Yosef 1998a; 1998b).

Current social determinations refer to societies such as the Natufian culture in the Levant as complex hunter-gatherers, a term which requires a more explicit, detailed definition (Bettinger 1991; Kelly

1995; Hayden 1995; Johnson and Earle 2000). This societal category is generally regarded as non-egalitarian and, in an archaeological sample, we suppose that one can trace the material attributes for social ranking. Commonly, the sources of information for such an inquiry are grave goods and/or body decorations, the variable dimensions of domestic structures, and evidence of public buildings. On the basis of ethno-history, it is assumed that members of such a society often reside in permanent villages or hamlets and that seasonal dispersals are part of their annual schedule. Craft specialization eventually emerges, thereby creating a particular niche for artisans within the social structure. Ceremonies or rituals are carried out as public events or performed within closed places by certain members of the group. Within the territory of each population, sacred sites, monuments, or worshiped geographic features are noticeable. Annual aggregations of the entire population in a holy place are expected as acts that enhance social cohesion. The meeting often serves for communal feasts, mating, political and other social negotiations.

As archaeologists, we compose the social interpretations by incorporating the data from particular sites and considering the region as a whole. While one large village may inhabit an entire viable biological entity where mating arrangements do not violate the incest taboo (O. Bar-Yosef 1998a; 1998b), relationships with other social units (whether in neighboring villages or a few hamlets) require a regional approach to the archaeological information. We, therefore, cannot escape the historical lesson that there are differences between a "core area" and a "periphery," and for analyzing prehistoric records we do not necessarily need to resort to a world system model. The concept of "core" and "periphery," as used by the author, can be applied to the prehistoric past, but this approach is not uniformly accepted. However, as will be shown below, the evidence from the early Neolithic of the Near East strongly suggests the presence of a "core area" as well as marginal spaces, all incorporated within larger interaction spheres.

Each investigation that advances the desirable goals of social archaeology stems, in part, from the advances made in the anthropology of technology. It is the improved understanding of the role of human agency in the past technologies and daily actions that facilitates the analysis of silent artifacts, houses, and lithic and bone assemblages (Lemonnier 1992; Pfaffenberger 1992; Dobres 2000; Dobres and Hoffman 1994; Clark 1999). While adopting an anthropological view of the material remains, we pretend, either explicitly or implicitly, to identify social entities or particular populations. However, resolutions concerning "ethnicity," language, gene drift, or gene flow remain elusive. While the research of material culture may seem tedious and unrewarding, the incorporated scientific techniques produce new insights. Among these are the organization of subsistence systems (e.g., identifying seasonality, patterns of hunting and butchering, herding wild species, cultivation, and the like), the manufacture and implementation of stone tools (e.g., tracing raw material sources, identifying core reduction techniques, curation of selected artifacts, hafting, recognizing specific stone tools employed in rituals, and so on), and finally the techniques employed in building houses.

The following pages aim to demonstrate, based on the available evidence, how modes of production, spatial distribution of sites and their hierarchies, societal structures, and certain environmental fluctuations intertwined in forming the social history of the early Holocene in the Levant. In spite of missing data, by employing a radiocarbon calibrated time scale the documented and interpreted data may indicate how in Southwest Asia complex hierarchical villages emerged, heralding the emergence of chiefdoms. In this narration I will follow the periodization as used by most writers (fig. 1).

The Neolithic of the Levant is traditionally subdivided either into two main periods (Pre-Pottery Neolithic A and B, coined by Kenyon, and abbreviated as PPNA and PPNB) or by Periods 1 through 5, as designated by the Lyon school (Aurenche et al. 1981). The basic definitions of the PPNA and PPNB rely on the techno-typological characteristics of the lithic industries. The periodization by numbers is based on radiocarbon chronology, recently calibrated (Aurenche and Kozlowski 1999). A further, more anthropologically oriented subdivision is that following the polythetic definition of archaeo-

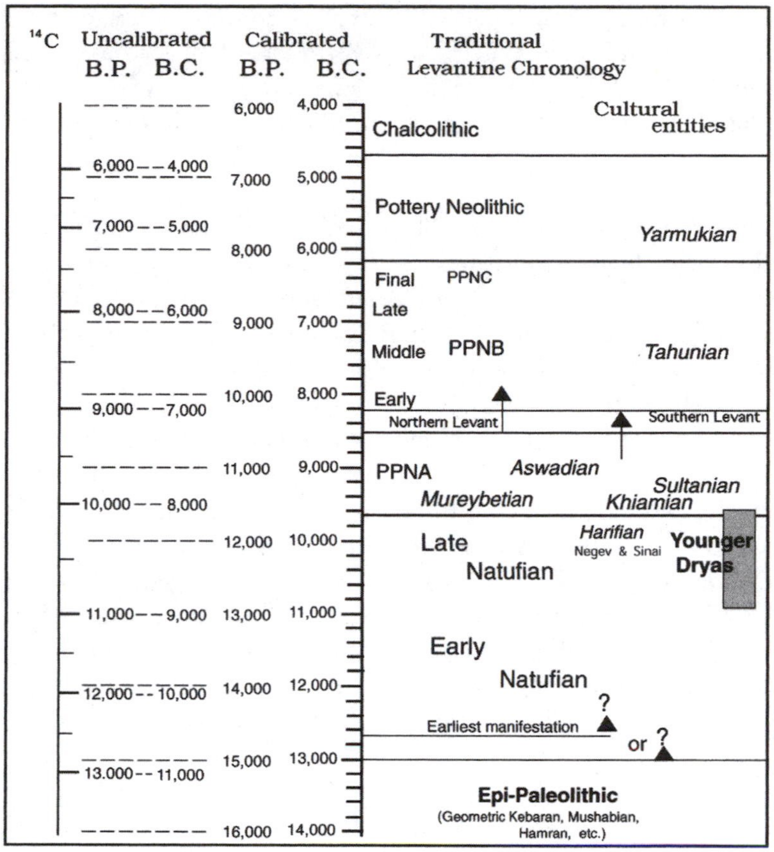

Fig. 1 *Chronological chart based on calibrated and uncalibrated radiocarbon dates with the periodic subdivision of the Neolithic sequence and a few of the cultural entities.*

logical cultures as proposed by Childe (1929) and elaborated by Clarke (1978). Examples are the Mureybetian and the Sultanian (both generally of PPNA age), identified on the basis of geography, tool-kits, imagery, types of buildings, and dated by radiocarbon. The use of the latter possibly indicates, for example, that the Sultanian lasted longer than the Mureybetian, and, therefore, does not comfortably fit with the periodic subdivision.

Finally, the finds from the early Neolithic sites are generally well-described and summarized in several recent publications (J. Cauvin 2000a; Aurenche and Kozlowski 1999; Kozlowski 1999; Kozlowski and Gebel 1996; Guilaine 1999; Kuijt 2000a). Numerous preliminary and interim site reports complete the broadly painted picture, although much that was discovered awaits the detailed accounts (Gebel and Kozlowski 1994; Gebel et al. 1997). Radiocarbon dates from the various sites increase rapidly, and calibrated dates are more often cited. Calibration chronology is employed in this paper through the use of CALIB 4.1 (Stuiver et al. 1998).

INITIAL VILLAGES OF CULTIVATORS AND HUNTERS

The first Neolithic entity in the Levant is known as the Khiamian. Unfortunately, due to the paucity of excavated samples and radiocarbon dates, it is still poorly defined (J. Cauvin 2000a). The small exposures in the various soundings make the identification of possible mixtures with earlier assemblages a difficult task. The time span of the Khiamian seems to have lasted for a few centuries, ca. 9,700–9,200 B.C.E. (Kozlowski 1999; Kozlowski and Gebel 1996; Aurenche and Kozlowski 1999; Gopher 1994a; 1994b; Goring-Morris and Belfer-Cohen 1997), although J. Cauvin (2000a) views it as a cultural horizon that encompasses the entire Levant with longer duration.

The aerodynamically shaped el-Khiam projectile points, asphalt-hafted sickle blades, some microliths, and high frequencies of perforators — a typical Neolithic tool — characterize the lithic industry of the Khiamian. Bifacial or polished celts, considered Neolithic "markers," are absent from the Khiamian contexts, although with further excavations they may turn up.

The Khiamian period was probably the time when the mode of food production changed from harvesting cereals in natural fields to intentional cultivation. Archaeobotanical remains indicate that the first strides toward achieving stable sources of staple food were probably made during the Younger Dryas or immediately after (Hillman 2000; Colledge 1998). One may hypothesize that the population that took this crucial step had survived on exploiting cereals that grew in natural stands. With the continuing cold and dry conditions, cereals as C_3 plants were affected by the decreasing atmospheric CO_2 (Monnin et al. 2001), which apparently resulted in declining yields of einkorn, emmer, rye, and barley in their natural environment. Witnessing the change and having, as common among pre-literate societies, the knowledge of plants and their life cycles, a social decision had to be made. The options were increased mobility and time to search for resources, residential movements into the northern neighboring territories while risking physical conflicts, or to start cultivating naturally wetted soils such as alluvial fans, river overbanks, or shallow lakeside shores. In addition, as marginal areas became drier, we may expect that kin-related groups moved and caused population densities to mount within the fertile, coastal-hilly belt of the Levant.

The evidence for incipient farming began to accumulate in recent years. Colledge (1998) analyzed the relationship between the occurrence of the various plant taxa (as published earlier by van Zeist and Bakker-Heeres 1986). By applying correspondence analysis to the assemblage from PPNA Mureybet, which takes into account the ecological classification of the various species, Colledge concluded that cultivation of wild cereals was practiced near the site. Hillman (2000) noted that the rise of weedy grasses, which characterizes cultivated fields in a dry land such as in Abu Hureyra, occurred at about 11,200–10,400 B.C.E. and was accompanied by the first appearance of charred domesticated rye grains. This botanical evidence is one of the clearest indications for the first attempts to intentionally cultivate plants. Similar conclusions concerning the growth of wild barley were reached by Kislev (1997) in reporting the plant assemblage from Netiv Hagdud, a PPNA site in the Jordan Valley. Genetic studies of einkorn and barley support the contention that their oldest progenitors were present across the Levant (Heun et al. 1997; Badr et al. 2000).

In sum, the initiation of cultivation took place within what is archaeologically defined as the Late Epi-Palaeolithic entity (such as in Abu Hureyra 1). There is yet no comparable archaeobotanical evidence from the Late Natufian in the southern Levant. Overall similarities between the lithic assemblages of Abu Hureyra 1, Mureybet 1B and the Late Natufian sites of the southern Levant were noted by various scholars (M.-C. Cauvin 1980; 1981; Valla 1995; Olszewski 2000), although the differences in the details resulted in incorporating all within one "culture" or as two neighboring entities. The distinct differences are expressed in the ground stone tools. While the Natufian is characterized by deep mortars and pestles, in the northern Levantine sites the shallow grinding slabs and dishes dominate (Moore 2000).

The early Neolithic settlements are better known from the Jordan Valley and the neighboring hilly ranges on both sides. The main sites (fig. 2) are Jericho (Kenyon 1981), Gilgal (Noy 1989), Netiv Hagdud (Bar-Yosef and Gopher 1997), Gesher (Garfinkel and Nadel 1989), Dhra (Kuijt 1995), and in the hilly region Nahal Oren (Noy et al. 1973), Hatoula (Lechevallier and Ronen 1994), 'Ain Darat (Gopher 1995), Iraq ed-Dubb (Kuijt 1994), and WF16 in Wadi Feinan (Mithen et al. 2000). Other groups of sites include Tel Aswad in the Damascus basin, Jerf el-Ahmar (Stordeur et al. 2001) and Mureybet

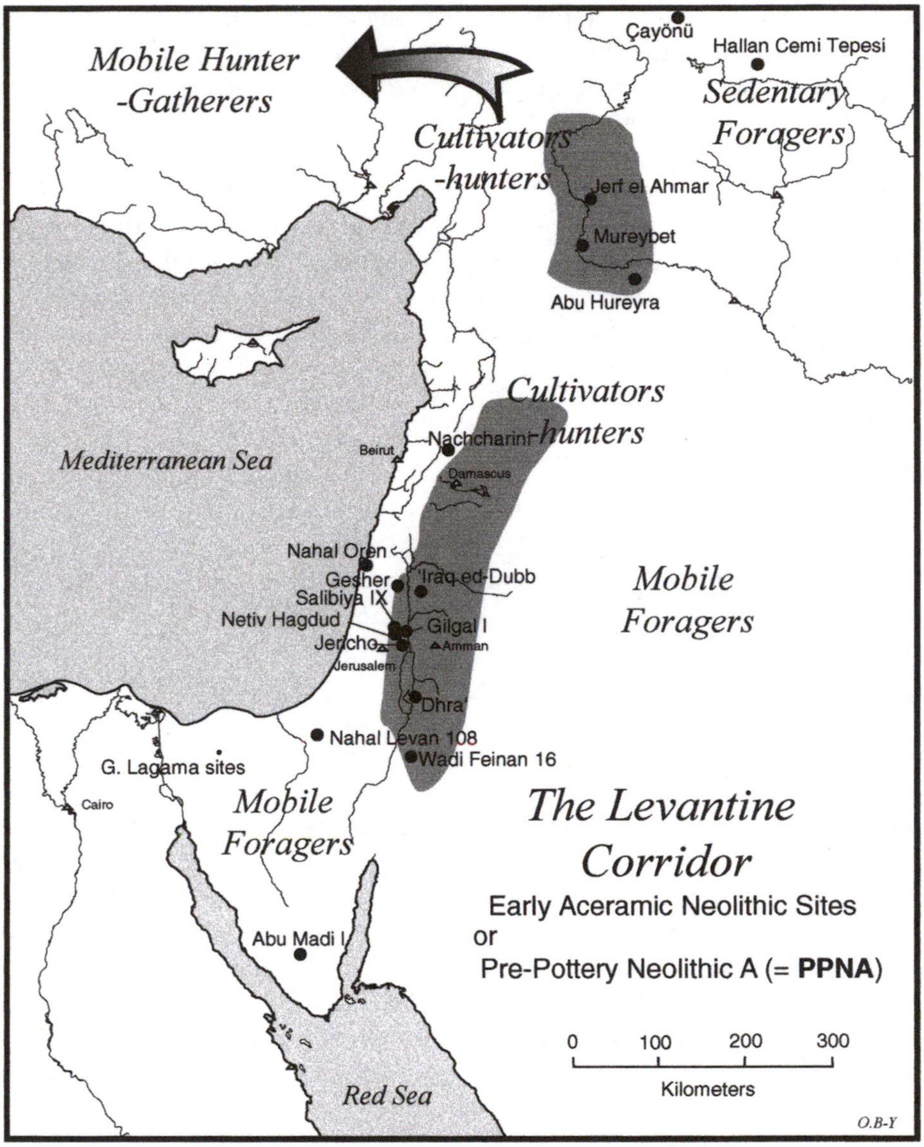

Fig. 2 Map of the Levant with PPNA (aceramic Neolithic) sites mentioned in the text indicating the geographic position of the Levantine Corridor.

II (J. Cauvin 1977) on the Euphrates, and Qermez Dereh (Watkins et al. 1989) as well as the lower level at Çayönü (A. Özdoğan 1999). Most but not all of these hamlets and villages are three to eight times larger than the largest Natufian sites (Bar-Yosef 1998a; 1998b). Their actual area varies from 0.2 to 2.5 ha and deserves a separate cultural definition.

On the basis of the typological characteristics of the lithic industries and their geographical variability, three cultural entities are identified in the Levant: the Mureybetian in the north, the Aswadian in the center, and the Sultanian in the south (J. Cauvin 2000a; Aurenche and Kozlowski 1999; Gopher in Kozlowski 1999). This subdivision does not take into account the material remains of hunter-gatherers who continued to survive in semi-arid areas.

The lithic technology exhibits continuity from the Khiamian, with small blades or bladelets for making the el-Khiam points (M.-C. Cauvin 1974; Nadel et al. 1991), blades used with or without retouch as sickle elements, and other cutting objects. Perforators are frequent in most PPNA sites. Bifacially chipped axes/adzes are common in the southern Levant and were made with a working edge formed by a transverse removal. Polished celts from limestone and basalt made their first appearance. In the Mureybetian, the common types are adzes (*herminettes*), which were shaped as unifaces from large and thick flakes. The limited amount of microwear studies suggests that most axes/adzes were employed in woodworking. These tools were, therefore, required in the course of activities such as building, creating furniture, and even boat construction, which probably began during the early millennia of the Holocene when Cyprus was first colonized (Peltenburg et al. 2000).

The shift in kitchen techniques from the Natufian is clearly expressed in the common types of ground stone tools. The previously abundant pounding tools gave way to the PPNA flat slabs with cupholes, rounded shallow grinding bowls, and hand stones, often loaf-shaped (Wright 1994; Bar-Yosef and Gopher 1997). Their distribution, when found *in situ,* is both in open courtyards and indoors.

With an increasing number of excavated sites and larger exposures, domestic and public architecture is becoming better known. Rounded to almost squarish pit-houses with stone foundations and walls built of plano-convex unbaked mudbricks or adobe are reported from various sites. Hearths are oval and sometimes possess cobble floors. The use of heated rocks in cooking resulted in abundant fire-cracked rocks in most sites. Storage facilities are found in every site, either as small, stone-built bins or larger, built-up mudbrick structures (J. Cauvin 1977; Bar-Yosef and Gopher 1997).

The best examples, as yet, of communal building efforts are the walls and the tower of Jericho. Originally interpreted by Kenyon (1957) as a defense system against raids by human groups, her conclusion disregarded plans of historical town walls. To fortify a town, towers are built as protruding structures from the outer face of the walls. This design facilitates shooting sideways at climbing attackers. The alternative interpretation, which did not advocate the absence of conflicts either personal or among groups (Bar-Yosef 1986), suggests that the PPNA wall was erected on the western side of the site to protect the settlement against mudflows and flash floods. In spite of the limited areas exposed in Jericho, by tracing the thickness of the PPNA layers across the mound it seems that there was only one tower in this settlement. The function of this 8.5 m high structure with interior steps is unknown, but it could have accommodated a small mudbrick shrine on the top. Although unequivocal evidence for public ritual is missing, the open space north of the tower (area M) may have been similar to the "plaza" in Çayönü (Turkey), which served for public gatherings (A. Özdoğan 1999).

Clear evidence for public rituals was provided by the excavations at Jerf el-Ahmar on the middle Euphrates River (Stordeur 2000; Stordeur et al. 1997; 2001; Stordeur and de Margueron 1998). Two major discoveries were recently reported. First, a communal building that is a "round house with cells," similar to the one uncovered in Mureybet IIIA (house 47; J. Cauvin 1977), encircled by what seems to be a series of family houses. Apparently, this type of settlement plan began at an earlier time when the communal building was the "house with slabs" (*le bâtiment aux dalles*), a pit-house with a bench encircling the walls with six column bases spread at equal distances at its edge. The outer face of the bench was shaped by a series of upright slabs incised with a zigzag pattern. Both the decoration on the slabs and the grooved objects (shaft straighteners?) connect Jerf el-Ahmar imagery with the Mureybetian world of symbols (J. Cauvin 2000a) as well as with the later PPNB sites in this region.

Mortuary practices and figurines are considered as indications of belief systems and rituals. In the Sultanian, most burials are single with no grave goods. Skull removal was performed only on adults, while child burials were left intact. Isolated crania are sometimes found in domestic areas or special purpose buildings. The entire array and sequence of mortuary practices in this period is interpreted as efforts in keeping an egalitarian social structure (Kuijt 1996). However, the differentiated treatment along age lines reflects changes in attitudes toward the dead. It seems that by differentiating between children and adults, the latter carried a higher social value evidenced by the conservation of their skulls in domestic contexts. This is one of the clear markers for additional ranking, which stress the departure from the Natufian tradition.

An exception to most PPNA burials in Jericho and Netiv Hagdud is the group of a dozen complete skeletons buried inside the lower passage in the Jericho Tower (Cornwall 1981). One may wonder whether these skeletal relics are not a group of PPNB humans or people killed in the course of a conflict, although the stratified deposits that accumulated following this phase were attributed by the excavators to the PPNA (Kenyon 1981).

Human figurines are more frequent in PPNA contexts, especially in the Mureybetian, when compared to earlier Levantine periods. They are shaped from limestone and clay and depict either standing or kneeling females. The figurines classified as representing the "seated woman" may herald the elaborate manifestations of the same image in the succeeding PPNB civilization. This explicit expression of gender, which was not evident in the Natufian culture, may indicate the emerging role of women in a society of farmers. Some suggest that this shift brought about the cult of the "mother goddess" in later centuries (J. Cauvin 2000a; 2000b).

The economy of PPNA settlements within the belt of early villages, as mentioned above, was based on hunting, trapping, gathering wild seeds and fruits, and cultivation of cereals and legumes. The common game animals in the middle Euphrates area were equids and cattle, while in the Jordan Valley people hunted wild cattle, gazelle, fox, fallow deer, and wild boar (Tchernov 1994; Peters et al. 1999; Horwitz et al. 1999). The broad spectrum exploitation that started earlier continued with the trapping of large numbers of birds, especially ducks. Lizards and tortoises were also gathered, probably by women and children.

Within the large PPNA interaction sphere there is ample evidence for long-distance exchanges. Obsidian from central Anatolia was found in Jericho, Netiv Hagdud, Nahal Oren, and Hatoula in the southern Levant. Marine shells were brought from the Mediterranean coast, with fewer from the Red Sea. Their selection differs from the Natufian culture. *Glycymeris* sp. and cowries became important, but *Dentalium* shells (yielded where excavated deposits were sieved) were still in use (D. E. Bar-Yosef 1991; Reese 1991).

Economic and social competition expressed in various ways is expected as part and parcel of the relationships between groups or even tribes. One way is physical conflict. It would be naïve to assume that there were no conflicts within sedentary communities, either on an individual basis or along extended family and clan lines. Disagreements concerning territorial subdivision, exploitation of suitable land plots, control over sources of water away from the perennial rivers are all expected in a farming society. With the declining use of natural resources such as game animals, obtaining meat in marginal areas could have been the trigger to the use of bows and arrows not just for hunting. Such events, along with the relative depletion of non-manured fields in addition to the natural population growth due to the availability of weaning foodstuff, as well as reduced mobility of females, may have led to the establishment of new villages. More serious could have been clashes between villages, a phenomenon well-known among peasant societies. Unfortunately, the archaeological evidence for such conflicts is rare until the first appearance of true defensive walls such as Tel as-Sawwan (Abu Es-Soof 1968; Al-A'dami 1968).

In sum, the archaeology of PPNA sites clearly demonstrates the emergence of a non-egalitarian society of cultivators-hunters that continued to rely on gathering. The public buildings in Mureybet and Jerf el-Ahmar indicate signs of ranked social organization. In the latter site, the pit-house with benches all around resembles later temples or shrines such as in PPNB Nevalı Çori and Göbekli Tepe (Hauptmann 1988; 1999). The tower of Jericho, except for having been the results of communal building efforts, probably functioned as a center for public gatherings. Social ranking is also expressed in mortuary practices (different treatment of adults and children). Indeed, the entire suite of data sets from all PPNA villages and hamlets does reflect the emerging social complexity, but the picture is as yet blurred, due to the small number of excavated sites. It becomes clearer with the proliferation of archaeological evidence from PPNB sites.

THE PPNB CIVILIZATION

The newly discovered archaeological aspects of PPNB sites demand a social definition different from previous references as to a world of supposedly egalitarian farmers (Kuijt 1996). While the term "civilization" has declined in use, except in general summary volumes (e.g., Lamberg-Karlovsky and Sabloff 1979; Redman 1978), historians often use the term "civilization" when discussing cultural manifestations in Mesopotamia, the Nile Valley, and later in Greece and Rome. The current accumulated field evidence and preliminary analyses of material elements, as briefly presented below, justify the use of the term "civilization" when we refer to the PPNB Levantine-Upper Mesopotamian interaction sphere. Characterized by a complex regional social structure, variable economic bases, elaborate cosmologies, and geographic social subunits (tribes?), this civilization, without a writing system but with markers of personal property and long-distance trade routes, survived successfully during about two and a half millennia. Its collapse around 6,400–6,200 B.C.E. raises intriguing questions concerning the capacity of a complex social structure to adapt itself in the face of abrupt climatic change. However, the subsequent record of the region demonstrates that the ensuing social formations could fall under the category of a pre-chiefdom or chiefdom level (Hassuna, Samarra), paving the way to the emergence of the Halafian chiefdom (Flannery 1999).

The assignment of assemblages, layers, and sites to the PPNB period is done on the basis of lithic techno-typological attributes. The common Levantine core reduction strategy was named after the shape of the discarded cores, i.e., the "naviform core technique" (Nishiaki 1994; Wilke and Quintero 1994; Quintero and Wilke 1995). The blades obtained by this particular method are often long with flat profiles and were suitable for shaping arrowheads and sickle elements. The recurring types of projectile points were named after sites such as Jericho, Byblos, and Amuq (J. Cauvin 1978; 1998; O. Bar-Yosef 1981; Gopher 1994a; 1994b), and their large size led Kozlowski (1999) to suggest the term Big Arrowhead Industry (abbreviated as BAI; Aurenche and Kozlowski 1999). Finally, the geographic distribution and radiometric ages of the arrowheads were interpreted as marking the advent of PPNB communities westward into the Anatolian plateau. Hence, the difference between the spread of the stone tools and the agricultural systems delineates the boundaries between the Levantine-Anatolian interaction sphere and the one of the Zagros foothills (figs. 3–4). In the latter region, also known as the Eastern Wing of the Fertile Crescent, the production of microliths continued through most of the Early Neolithic times. The suggestion that the process of "neolithization" or adoption of agriculture was achieved by diffusion and not through population expansion was proposed for the Zagros foothills and the intermontane valleys (Hole 1994; 1998; Kozlowski and Gebel 1996; Kozlowski 1999; O. Bar-Yosef 2001; Aurenche and Kozlowski 1999).

The variance in material culture across the Levant (on a north–south cross axis) gave rise to the ongoing controversy regarding the subdivision of the PPNB period, which according to the calibrated chronology lasted about 2,200–2,500 years. One subdivision recognizes the four phases of Early, Middle, Late, and Final PPNB. Several scholars do not accept the "Early PPNB" phase as a valid distinction. Other scholars defer to a proposal naming the last phase as PPNC on the basis of the uppermost PPN assemblage at ʿAin Ghazal (Rollefson et al. 1992; Rollefson and Köhler-Rollefson 1993). The increasing number of calibrated radiocarbon dates has generated a practical solution that defines cultural entities chronologically and geographically, regardless of their present attribution to a PPNB "phase."

Radiocarbon dated assemblages in the northern Levant and Upper Mesopotamia indicate that the PPNB lithic technology emerged first in this subregion, which can be defined as the "core area" of the Neolithic Revolution. The typical Sultanian assemblages continued to dominate the southern Levant for a few additional centuries (Aurenche and Kozlowski 1999; J. Cauvin 2000a; Gopher 1994a; 1994b). This conclusion is based on the new discoveries in the earliest layers at Göbekli Tepe (Schmidt 1999a; 1999b; 2001), Gopher's analysis of the arrowheads (Gopher 1989), Cauvin's interpreta-

Fig. 3 *Map of Levantine, Upper Mesopotamian, and Eastern Anatolian PPNB sites indicating the interaction zones between mobile foragers and farming communities.*

tion of the symbolic data including architectural remains, figurines, and bovid skulls (J. Cauvin 2000a; 2000b), and the chronological continuity of the Sultanian in the Southern Levant. Cauvin suggested the core area was located in the middle Euphrates Valley. Excavations of sites such as Nevalı Çori (Hauptmann 1988; 1999) also point to the area between the upper Euphrates and the valley of the Balikh, or the western portion of Upper Mesopotamia, as part of the core area (M. Özdoğan 1997; 1999; Özdoğan and Balkan-Atlı 1994; A. Özdoğan 1999). If this conclusion is sustained by additional discoveries, it will greatly assist in tracing the emergence of early chiefdoms in this region, a topic beyond the scope of this paper.

The economy of the PPNB settlements was based on the full suite of annual crops, such as barley, wheat, rye, flax, and legumes (including broad beans and chick peas), that were already domesticated (Garrard 1999; Anderson 1998; Aurenche and

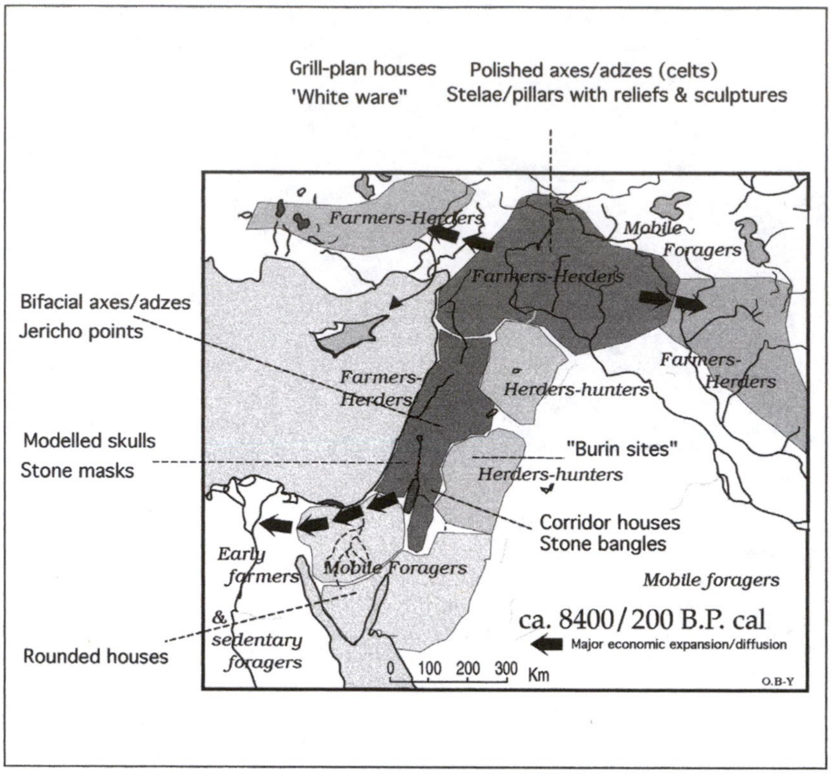

Fig. 4 *Map indicating the geographic spread of PPNB entities, "tribes," with the main material culture characteristics of each territory.*

Kozlowski 1999). Storage facilities were common (Kuijt 2000b). Animal bones reflect the herding and later the domestication of goat and sheep, which were the predominant game of foragers in the Taurus–Zagros ranges. At least in the first millennium, goat and sheep bones do not demonstrate the change in size that was previously seen as a morphological marker of domestication (Hesse 1984; Legge 1996; Zeder and Hesse 2000; Vigne et al. 2000). Following the penning and herding of these two species, both were introduced into villages of the central and southern Levant (Martin 1999; Garrard et al. 1996; O. Bar-Yosef 2000). It was only during the Pottery Neolithic period that herding was adopted by the inhabitants of the steppic belt and not before the early Chalcolithic that full-fledged pastoral nomadism became a common way of life in the Near Eastern deserts.

The domestication of cattle and pigs followed that of goat and sheep. It appears that attempts were made to pen pigs earlier at Hallan Çemi (Rosenberg et al. 1998), but not until the Middle and Late PPNB does the faunal evidence indicate intentional pig farming, and even then mostly in the more humid areas of the north (such as Çayönü) and the coastal Levant (Bar-Yosef and Meadow 1995).

By contrast, the domestication of cattle, at least in the case of Southwest Asia, was motivated by religious reasons more than by basic dietary needs (J. Cauvin 2000a; 2000b). This interpretation is based on the contexts in which cattle remains were uncovered at various sites in the northern Levant and Anatolia. Skulls with horns were found intact in dwellings and pits and are known from the by now famous examples of the Çatalhöyük buildings (Mellaart 1967; Hodder 1999). As with goats and sheep, it does seem that domesticated cattle were herded southward, although wild oxen are known from Epi-Palaeolithic assemblages from this region (Tchernov 1993; Horwitz et al. 1999).

PPNB farming communities were flourishing and expanding. In the Levantine region this is manifested in the increased size of sites, which range from 2.5 ha to 12 ha. Similar sizes were recorded on the Anatolian plateau. Among the sites themselves there is a clear size hierarchy (Kramer 1983; Bar-Yosef and Meadow 1995; Kuijt 2000c). Ethnoarchaeological studies (Kramer 1982; 1983; Watson 1979) demonstrate that exact surface areas cannot be translated by a simple formula into number of inhabitants. However, if we consider the measure of hectares as providing a relative scale and taking into account the "life history" of every site, then differences in population size can be shown. The assumption is that the largest tested sites accommodated a viable biological unit of about 400–500 people (Bar-Yosef and Belfer-Cohen 1989), while smaller villages or hamlets had only 50–100 people. Given the average occupation length of each major village as about 300–400 years, it is cautiously estimated that a "tribal" territory (fig. 4) was inhabited by about 1,000–2,500 people.

In each large village, domestic buildings reflect the basic social units. Thus, nuclear families probably occupied the rectangular houses of various types (Hole 2000; M. Özdoğan 1996) that were later subdivided into smaller rooms, while extended families shared accommodations in compounds such as seen in Bouqras (P. A. Akkermans et al. 1983) and in a more complex pattern in Aşıklı (Esin 1998). Houses with two storeys were more common in the later part of the PPNB. Among these are the "corridor houses" in Beidha (Byrd 1994) and the well-preserved two-storey houses of the "cell" type in Basta (Nissen et al. 1987). It seems that house size reflected family wealth and unequal social status. Examples are only known from sites where the excavated area is large, such as in Çayönü, where ca. 4,500 m^2 were exposed (Özdoğan and Özdoğan 1998; A. Özdoğan 1999).

An attribute of complex social structures is the presence of ceremonial areas, special buildings for rituals, and shrines. Such architectural components are recognized in sites where large exposures are available and in some cases where the edge of the village was uncovered. Examples include Aşıklı Höyük, Çayönü, Nevalı Çori, and Beidha (Esin 1996; Kirkbride 1968; Byrd 1994; Özdoğan and Özdoğan 1998). In addition, within each of the "tribal territories" we may expect a sacred settlement for annual or seasonal pilgrimage. Göbekli Tepe (Hauptmann 1999; Schmidt 1999a; 1999b), Kfar HaHoresh (Goring-Morris et al. 1995), possibly Ba'ja (Gebel and Hermansen 2000), and Çatalhöyük, or a certain portion of it, could have served for that purpose (Hodder 1999). In each of these sites, the archaeological context reflects a mixture of domestic as well as ceremonial and ritual activities, forming a continuum from the sacred to the mundane.

The complexity of symbols from both animal and human realms exemplified by the inventory of the sculptures at Göbekli Tepe and Nevalı Çori, as well as the reconstructed buildings at Çatalhöyük and the numerous mobile imagery objects from various sites are not easy to decipher (J. Cauvin 2000a; 2000b; Voigt 2000; Schmidt 2001). Scholars agree that the various suites of images demonstrate regional particularities as well as common themes within the PPNB interaction sphere.

Jacques Cauvin (2000a; 2000b) views the figurines and bucrania in the earlier Khiamian context of Mureybet and Jerf el-Ahmar as marking the first appearance of "the Woman and the Bull" images that become the emblems of the new religion. Hence, in order to fully understand the new cosmology, Cauvin employs the artistic expressions from Çatalhöyük, which represents the westward diffusion of later times, to explain the conceptual structure. The woman, a mother-goddess, is seen as giving birth to the bull, and the two remain the major deities during the ensuing millennia. The continuity over time and geographic space is testified, according to Cauvin, by their images on Halafian pottery. He interprets the emergence of the new symbolic system as signifying a change in collective psychology, which preceded the advent of the veritable Neolithic village society (J. Cauvin 2000a). In the materialistic world, he ties the shift expressed by PPNB imagery to the transition from rounded (representing "female," natural rounded lines) to rectangular (representing "male" desire to control) architecture.

Voigt (2000) warns that the demonstrable linkage between economic and political changes, on one hand, and Neolithic ideology and ritual, on the other hand, are limited. In her analysis of the Çatalhöyük figurines, she stresses the aspect of "abundance" rather than the aspect of "fertility," when domesticated plants and animals ensured the survival and wealth of village inhabitants.

No less important are the caches of human plaster statues uncovered in Jericho and 'Ain Ghazal (Rollefson 1983; 2000). Their archaeological context testifies to the intentional burial of used cultic objects (Garfinkel 1994). The breakage of such holy items prior to their interment is a well-known phenomenon from later historical periods in the Near East. The interpretation of the plastered statues, some of which are only busts, is not easy. According to the position of their hands, those holding the lower part of the belly are considered female representations (Aurenche and Kozlowski 1999). All have eyes encircled with asphalt lines and stripes of red color on their bodies. By employing an archaeological analogy to later millennia, the statues seem to represent a pantheon of deities, in which the human figure represents both the real and the mythological image. Amiran (1962) suggested that the mode of production of these statues—constructed from reeds, cloth, and plaster—resembled the creation of Man as depicted in the Gilgamesh epic. Hence, it is quite probable that the cosmology of the PPNB civilization, orally transmitted in the Near Eastern world, found its written expression several millennia later.

The territories of what seem to have been kinship-based entities were marked by sacred localities that symbolize ownership of the land, similar to Sheikh tombs in southern Sinai (Marx 1977). Such a special locality is the dark cave filled with ritual paraphernalia in Nahal Hemar. The location of this site marks the geographic boundary between the Judean desert and the northern Negev. Among the objects are skulls modeled with asphalt (mixed with collagen), stone masks, small human figurines, remains of plastered statues, special lithic tools, and various other objects (Bar-Yosef and Alon 1988; Bar-Yosef and Schick 1989; Schick 1989; Goren et al. 1993).

In sum, when the evidence for public ceremonial and domestic ritual activities is compiled with information about the variable mortuary practices, the comprehensive data set can serve as a basis for evaluating the social complexity of the PPNB civilization within its various tribal territories. The presence of special shrines, open spaces for social and ceremonial activities, human statues and stelae (with or without animal carvings), human and animal figurines (some of which could have been just temporary teaching devices), and the special locales that symbolize ownership of a certain landscape reflect a dynamic ranked society with elite cohorts in the largest villages.

THE COLLAPSE OF THE PPNB CIVILIZATION

Observations concerning site abandonment and stratigraphical gaps are common among PPNB villages. Very few settlements survived for many centuries, as the clusters of C^{14} dates demonstrate. Ethnoarchaeological studies indicate that the presence of deserted houses and courtyards is a common attribute of village life (Kramer 1982; Cameron and Tomka 1993).

Various reasons account for the abandonment of houses in a living village, from the death of the head of the family to the outcome of verbal and physical conflicts. However, when the entire village is deserted, the reasons could be more complex, ranging from over-exploitation of the immediate environment and successful aggression by a neighboring village to the impact of consecutive droughts. Examples for conflicts that ended in burning the entire village are rare during the PPNB period (Ganj Dareh; P. Smith 1976), although their paucity does not necessarily reflect the endurance of peaceful lifeways. On the contrary, data concerning physical conflicts is accumulating as more skeletal collections are published. Under any circumstances, the abandonment of one and/or several sites may precipitate societal restructuring, especially among farming communities. It is, therefore, necessary to first document the timing of abandonment and to ascertain whether it is only a local phenomenon or a regional event. Second, we need to search for the reasons, which among scholars inspire both lively debates and disagreements.

The stratigraphic gap between the latest PPNB deposits and the Pottery Neolithic pits was noticed by Garstang and Kenyon in Jericho. Similar phenomena, including rare cases of rebuilding on the site, were documented across the Levant (Banning and Byrd 1984; Gopher and Gophna 1993; M. Özdoğan 1996; A. Özdoğan 1999). Further support for observations concerning the abandonment of PPNB villages was gleaned from the subsequent establishment of new hamlets and farmsteads in various parts of the Levant. The better known cultural entity in the southern part is the Yarmukian (Banning and Siggers 1997; Stekelis 1972; Garfinkel 1993). Recent excavations at the type-site at Shaar HaGolan uncovered large built-up compounds (Garfinkel 1999).

In the early days of archaeological research, when radiocarbon measurements were rare, relative chronology was based on ceramics and lithics. The presence of pottery production in late PPNB contexts in the northern Levant reached the southern Levant, only to be found in Pottery Neolithic sites that do bear certain cultural attributes of the PPNB. This observation served as a basis for recognizing a cultural gap of unknown duration. The maximal guess was of a thousand years and a lesser one suggested five centuries (Gopher and Gophna 1993 and references therein). Perrot (1968) regarded this major change as the result of a climatic crisis that caused the desertion of most populated areas of the southern Levant. Subsequent field research and dating demonstrates that the cultural gap in this region essentially reflects a major shift in settlement pattern without a distinctive time gap. It is also evidenced in the northern Levant, for example in the Balikh valley (P. M. M. G. Akkermans 1993; Akkermans and Duistermaat 1996) and further north at the site of Çayönü (A. Özdoğan 1999), as well as in sites across the Anatolian plateau.

Other proposals for explaining the collapse of the PPNB were derived from contemporary ecological awareness of environmental deterioration caused by the Industrial Revolution and the ensuing rapid development and population increase during the nineteenth and twentieth centuries. Thus, the change within the sequence of 'Ain Ghazal was interpreted as a consequence of over-exploitation of pastures by herding goats and tree felling for plaster production and building elements (Rollefson 1990; Rollefson and Köhler-Rollefson 1989; Rollefson et al. 1992). To expect that the same processes took place in both Anatolia and the Levant is to advocate that the same destructive mechanism operated across every ecological belt within the entire eastern Mediterranean. As this seems unlikely, another cause or, more likely, causes need to be exposed to account for a geographically wide-ranged change.

Another perspective would be to see the collapse as motivated by societal over-exploitation. Unfortunately, we have no evidence for the presence of a Big Man or another kind of chief, in spite of intricate exchange systems or the enslaving of smaller communities by larger, richer ones. This is not to say that there is no evidence for social ranking or clear signs for the existence of personal property marked by stamps. Perhaps future excavations will record the presence of slaves, a known phenomenon from the sedentary villages of the Northwest coast of North America (Ames and Maschner 1999).

Today, as the image of the PPNB civilization is fuller than before, its collapse through the entire region should lead us to examine the possibility that an abrupt climatic change was responsible for the rapid worsening of environmental conditions. It is proposed that the climatic crisis around 6,400–6,200 B.C.E., as recorded in ice cores, was the culprit (Alley et al. 1997). The impact of the change is reflected in various terrestrial and marine pollen in the eastern Mediterranean from Greece (Rossignol-Strick 1995), Anatolia (van Zeist and Bottema 1991), and the Levant (Baruch and Bottema 1999). In addition, it is clearly marked in the palaeo-climatic curve of the $O^{16/18}$ sequence in Soreq cave (Bar-Mathews et al. 1997; 1999).

In the event of a series of droughts, a complex society that subsisted on farming and herding, where the demands of more affluent individuals (or families) drove the flow of foreign goods, could not continue to accumulate surplus. The shift in the pattern of seasonal precipitation imposed the search for pastures further away and resulted in lower yields of summer harvests. Finally, the economic deterioration resulted in a societal change expressed in the disappearance of previously large villages and the establishment of smaller villages, hamlets, or farmsteads. The new conditions probably enhanced the reliance on the more flexible subsistence strategy of pastoral nomads.

The events in Anatolia could have triggered another wave of colonizers moving westward into temperate Europe. Other colonizers brought the agricultural system to the Nile delta or into the regions of the Caucasus and beyond. Perhaps more important was the "push" given to societies that had already developed irrigation control during the PPNB in Upper Mesopotamia. With the hierarchical social structure in place, establishing "hydraulic civilization" all over Mesopotamia was the step that heralded the emergence of chiefdoms and city states.

REFERENCES

Abu Es-Soof, B.

1968 Tell es-Sawwan Excavations of the fourth Season (Spring 1967). Interim Report. *Sumer* 24: 3–16.

Akkermans, P. A.; Boerma, J. A. K.; Clason, A. T.; Hill, S. G.; Lohof, E.; Meiklejohn, C.; le Mière, M.; Molgat, G. M. F.; Roodenberg, J. J.; Waterbolkvan Rooyen, W.; and van Zeist, W.

1983 Bouqras revisited: Preliminary Report on a Project in Eastern Syria. *Proceedings of the Prehistoric Society* 49: 335–72.

Akkermans, P. M. M. G.

1993 *Villages in the Steppe: Later Neolithic Settlement in the Balikh Valley, Northern Syria.* Ann Arbor, MI: International Monographs in Prehistory.

Akkermans, P. M. M. G., and Duistermaat, K.

1996 Of Storage and Nomads. The Sealings from Late Neolithic Sabi Abyad, Syria. Commentaires de R. Bernbeck, S. Cleuziou, M. Frangipane, A. Le Brun, H. Nissen, H. T. Wright et réponse des auteurs. *Paléorient* 22, no. 2: 17–44.

Al-A'dami, K. A.

1968 Excavations at Tell es-Sawwan (second season). *Sumer* 24: 54–94.

Alley, R. B.; Mayewski, P. A.; Sowers, T.; Stuiver, M.; Taylor, K. C.; and Clark, P. U.

1997 Holocene Climatic Instability: A Prominent, Widespread Event 8200 yrs ago. *Geology* 25, no. 6: 483–86.

Ames, K. M., and Maschner, H. D. G.

1999 *Peoples of the Northwest Coast: Their Archaeology and Prehistory.* New York, NY: Thames and Hudson.

Amiran, R.

1962 Myths of the Creation of Man and the Jericho Statues. *Bulletin of the American Schools of Oriental Research* 167: 23–25.

Anderson, P. C.

1998 History of Harvesting and Threshing Techniques for Cereals in the Prehistoric Near East. Pp. 145–59 in *The Origins of Agriculture and Crop Domestication,* eds. A. B. Damania, J. Valkoun, G. Willcox and C. O. Qualset. Aleppo: ICARDA.

Aurenche, O.; Cauvin, J.; Cauvin, M.-C.; Copeland, L.; Hours, F.; and Sanlaville, P.

1981 Chronologie et organisation de l'espace dans le Proche Orient de 12000 à 5600 avant J.C. Pp. 571–78 in *Préhistoire du Levant,* eds. J. Cauvin and P. Sanlaville. Paris: CNRS.

Aurenche, O., and Kozlowski, S. K.

1999 *La Naissance du Néolithique au Proche Orient ou Le Paradis Perdu.* Paris: Editions Errance.

Badr, A.; Müller, K.; Schäfer-Pregl, R.; El Rabey, H.; Effgen, S.; Ibrahim, H. H.; Pozzi, C.; Rohde, W.; and Salamini, F.

2000 On the origin and domestication history of barley *(Hordeum vulgare). Molecular Biology and Evolution* 17, no. 4: 499–510.

Banning, E. B., and Byrd, B. F.

1984 The architecture of PPNB 'Ain Ghazal, Jordan. *Bulletin of the American Schools of Oriental Research* 225: 15–20.

Banning, E. B., and Siggers, J.

1997 Technological Strategies at a Late Neolithic Farmstead in Wadi Ziqlab, Jordan. Pp. 319–32 in *The Prehistory of Jordan, II. Perspectives from 1997,* eds. H. Gebel, Z. Kafafi and G. Rollefson. Studies in Early Near Eastern Production, Subsistence and Environment. Berlin: Ex Oriente.

Bar-Mathews, M.; Ayalon, A.; and Kaufman, A.

1997 Late Quaternary Paleoclimate in the eastern Mediterranean Region from Stable Isotope Analysis of Speleothems at Soreq Cave, Israel. *Quaternary Research* 47: 155–68.

Bar-Mathews, M.; Ayalon, A.; Kaufman, A.; and Wasserburg, G. J.

1999 The Eastern Mediterranean Paleoclimate as a Reflection of Regional Events: Soreq Cave, Israel. *Earth and Planetary Science Letters* 166: 85–95.

Bar-Yosef, D. E.

1991 Changes in the Selection of Marine Shells from the Natufian to the Neolithic. Pp. 629–36 in *The Natufian Culture in the Levant,* eds. O. Bar-Yosef and F. R. Valla. Ann Arbor, MI: International Monographs in Prehistory.

Bar-Yosef, O.

1981 The "Pre-Pottery Neolithic" Period in the southern Levant. Pp. 551–70 in *Préhistoire du Levant,* eds. J. Cauvin and P. Sanlaville. Paris: CNRS.

1986 The Walls of Jericho: An alternative Interpretation. *Current Anthropology* 27: 157–62.

1998a On the Nature of Transitions: the Middle to Upper Palaeolithic and the Neolithic Revolution. *Cambridge Archaeological Journal* 8, no. 2: 141–63.

1998b Introduction. Pp. 39–94 in *Last Hunters – First Farmers: New Perspectives on the Prehistoric Transition to Agriculture,* eds. T. D. Price and A. B. Gebauer. School of American Research Advanced Seminar Series. Santa Fe, NM: School of American Research.

2000 The Context of Animal Domestication in Southwestern Asia. Pp. 184–94 in *Archaeozoology of the Near East IVA. Proceedings of the Fourth International Symposium on the Archaeozoology of Southwestern Asia and Adjacent Areas,* eds. M. Mashkour, A. M. Choyke, H. Buitenhuis and F. Poplin. Centre for Archaeological Research and Consultancy Publication 32. Groningen: ARC.

2001 From Sedentary Foragers to Village Hierarchies: the Emergence of Social Institutions. Pp. 1–38 in *The Origins of Human Social Institutions,* ed. W. G. Runciman. Proceedings of the British Academy 110. Oxford: Oxford University.

Bar-Yosef, O., and Alon, D.

1988 Excavations in the Nahal Hemar Cave. *'Atiqot* 18: 1–30.

Bar-Yosef, O., and Belfer-Cohen, A.

1989 The Origins of Sedentism and Farming Communities in the Levant. *Journal of World Prehistory* 3, no. 4: 447–98.

Bar-Yosef, O., and Gopher, A. (eds.)

1997 *An Early Neolithic Village in the Jordan Valley, Part I: The Archaeology of Netiv Hagdud.* Peabody Museum of Archaeology and Ethnology. Cambridge, MA: Harvard University.

Bar-Yosef, O., and Meadow, R. H.

1995 The Origins of Agriculture in the Near East. Pp. 39–94 in *Last Hunters, First Farmers: New Perspectives on the Prehistoric Transition to Agriculture,* eds. T. D. Price and A. B. Gebauer. School of American Research Advanced Seminar Series. Santa Fe, NM: School of American Research.

Bar-Yosef, O., and Schick, T.

1989 Early Neolithic organic Remains from Nahal Hemar Cave. *National Geographic Research* 5, no. 2: 176–90.

Baruch, U., and Bottema, S.

1999 A New Pollen Diagram from Lake Hula: Vegetational, Climatic, and Anthropologenic Implications. Pp. 75–86 in *Ancient Lakes: Their Cultural and Biological Diversity,* eds. H. Kawanabe, G. W. Coulter and A. C. Roosevelt. Belgium: Kenobe Productions.

Bettinger, R. L.

1991 *Hunter-Gatherers: Archaeological and Evolutionary Theory.* Interdisciplinary Contributions to Archaeology, The Language of Science. New York, NY: Plenum.

Byrd, B. F.

1994 Public and Private, Domestic and Corporate: The Emergence of the Southwest Asian Village. *American Antiquity* 59, no. 4: 639–66.

Cameron, C. M., and Tomka, S. A.

1993 *Abandonment of Settlements and Regions: Ethnoarchaeological and Archaeological Approaches.* New Directions in Archaeology. New York, NY: Cambridge University.

Cauvin, J.

1977 Les fouilles de Mureybet (1971–1974) et leur signification pour les origines de la sédentarisation au Proche-Orient. *Annual of the American Schools of Oriental Research* 44: 19–48.

1978 *Les premiers villages de Syrie-Palestine de IXème au VIIème millénaire avant J.C.* Lyon: Maison de l'Orient.

1998 La néolithisation de l'Anatolie. Pp. 207–14 in *Light on Top of the Black Hill. Studies Presented to Halet Çambel,* eds. G. Arsebük, M. Mellink, J. and W. Schirmer. Istanbul: Ege.

2000a *The Birth of the Gods and the Origins of Agriculture,* trans. T. Watkins. Cambridge: Cambridge University.

2000b The Symbolic Foundations of the Neolithic Revolution in the Near East. Pp. 235–51 in *Life in Neolithic Farming Communities: Social Organization, Identity, and Differentiation,* ed. I. Kuijt. New York, NY: Plenum.

Cauvin, M.-C.

1974 Flèches à encoches de Syrie: Essai de classification et d'interprétation culturelle. *Paléorient* 2, no. 2: 311–22.

1980 Du Natoufien sur l'Euphrate? Pp. 11–20 in *Le Moyen Euphrate: Zone de Contacts et d'Échanges,* ed. J. C. Margueron. Leiden: Brill.

1981 L'Epipaléolithique de Syrie d'après les premiers recherches dans la cuvette d'el-Kowm (1978–1979). Pp. 375–88 in *Préhistoire du Levant,* eds. J. Cauvin and P. Sanlaville. Paris: CNRS.

Childe, V. G.

1929 *The Danube in Prehistory.* Oxford: Oxford University.

Clark, J. E.

1999 Comments – On "Stone Tools" by G. Odell. *Lithic Technology* 24, no. 2: 126–35.

Clarke, D. L.

1978 *Analytical Archaeology,* 2nd ed. London: Methuen.

Colledge, S.

1998 Identifying Pre-domestication Cultivation using Multivariate Analysis. Pp. 121–31 in *The Origins of Agriculture and Crop Domestication,* eds. A. B. Damania, J. Valkoun, G. Willcox and C. O. Qualset. Aleppo, Syria: ICARDA.

Cornwall, I. W.

1981 The pre-pottery Neolithic Burials. Pp. 395–406 in *Excavations at Jericho, Vol. III: The Architecture and Stratigraphy of the Tell,* eds. K. M. Kenyon and T. A. Holland. London: British School of Archaeology in Jerusalem.

Dobres, M.

2000 *Technology and Social Agency.* Oxford: Blackwell.

Dobres, M., and Hoffman, C.

1994 Social Agency and the Dynamics of Prehistoric Technology. *Journal of Archaeological Method and Theory* 1, no. 3: 211–58.

Esin, U.

1996 Aşıklı, Ten Thousand Years Ago: A Habitation Model from Central Anatolia. Pp. 19–30 in *Housing and Settlement in Anatolia: A Historical Perspective.* Istanbul: The Economic and Social History Foundation of Turkey.

1998 The Aceramic Site of Aşıklı and its Ecological Conditions based on its Floral and Faunal Remains. *Turkish Academy of Sciences Journal of Archaeology (TUBA-AR)* 1: 95–103.

Flannery, K. V.

1999 Chiefdoms in the early Near East: Why it's so hard to Identify them. Pp. 44–61 in *The Iranian World: Essays on Iranian Art and Archaeology,* eds. A. Alizadeh, Y. Majidzadeh and S. M. Shahmirzadi. Teheran: Iran University.

Garfinkel, Y.

1993 The Yarmukian Culture in Israel. *Paléorient* 19, no. 1: 115–34.

1994 Ritual Burial of Cultic Objects: The Earliest Evidence. *Cambridge Archaeological Journal* 4, no. 2: 159–88.

1999 Radiometric Dates from Eighth Millennium B.P. Israel. *Bulletin of the American Schools of Oriental Research* 315: 1–13.

Garfinkel, Y., and Nadel, D.

1989 The Sultanian Flint Assemblage from Gesher and its Implications for Recognizing Early Neolithic Entities in the Levant. *Paléorient* 15, no. 2: 139–51.

Garrard, A. N.

1999 Charting the Emergence of Cereal and Pulse Domestication in South West Asia. *Environmental Archaeology* 4: 67–86.

Garrard, A. N.; Colledge, S.; and Martin, L.

1996 The Emergence of Crop Cultivation and Caprine Herding in the "Marginal Zone" of the Southern Levant. Pp. 204–26 in *The Origins and Spread of Agriculture and Pastoralism in Eurasia,* ed. D. Harris. London: University College London.

Gebel, H. G., and Hermansen, B. D.

2000 The 2000 Season at Late PPNB Ba'ja. *Neo-Lithics* 2000, no. 2–3: 20–22.

Gebel, H. G., and Kozlowski, S. K.

1994 Remarks on Taxonomy and Related Questions of Neolithic Chipped Stone Industries in the Fertile Crescent, as Related to their Contemporaries in the Adjacent Regions. Pp. 453–60 in *Neolithic Chipped Stone Industries of the Fertile Crescent: Proceedings of the First Workshop on PPN Chipped Lithic Industries,* eds. S. K. Kozlowski and H. G. Gebel. Berlin: Ex Oriente.

Gebel, H. G.; Kafafi, Z.; and Rollefson, G. O. (eds.)

1997 *The Prehistory of Jordan, II. Perspectives from* 1997. Studies in Early Near Eastern Production, Subsistence, and Environment 4. Berlin: Ex Oriente.

Gopher, A.

1989 Neolithic Arrowheads in the Levant: Results and Implications of a Seriation Analysis. *Paléorient* 15, no. 1: 57–64.

1994a *Arrowheads of the Neolithic Levant: A Seriation Analysis.* Dissertation Series 10. Winona Lake, IN: Eisenbrauns.

1994b Southern-central Levant PPN Cultural Sequences: Time-space Systematics through Typological and Stylistic Approaches. Pp. 387–92 in *Neolithic Chipped Stone Industries of the Fertile Crescent: Proceedings of the First Workshop on PPN Chipped Lithic Industries,* eds. H. G. Gebel and S. K. Kozlowski. Berlin: Ex Oriente.

1995 'Ain Darat, a PPNA Site in the Judean Desert. *Neo-Lithics* 1995, no. 1: 7–8.

Gopher, A. and R. Gophna

1993 Cultures of the eighth and seventh Millennium BP in Southern Levant: A Review for the 1990's. *Journal of World Prehistory* 7, no. 3: 297–351.

Goren, Y.; Segal, I.; and Bar-Yosef, O.

1993 Plaster Artifacts and the Interpretation of the Nahal Hemar Cave. *Journal of the Israel Prehistoric Society* 25: 1201–31.

Goring-Morris, A. N., and Belfer-Cohen, A.

1997 The Articulation of Cultural Processes and Late Quaternary Environmental Changes in Cisjordan. *Paléorient* 23, no. 2: 71–94.

Goring-Morris, A. N.; Goren, Y.; Horwitz, L. K.; Bar-Yosef, O.; and Hershkovitz, I.

1995 Investigations at an Early Neolithic Settlement in the Lower Galilee: Results of the 1991 Season at Kefar HaHoresh. *'Atiqot* 27: 37–62.

Guilaine, J. (ed.)

1999 *Premiers paysans du monde: Naissances des agricultures.* Paris: Editions Errance.

Harris, D. (ed.)

1996 *The Origins and Spread of Agriculture and Pastoralism in Eurasia.* London: University College London.

Hauptmann, H.

1988 Nevalı Çori: Architektur. *Anatolica* 15: 99–110.

1999 The Urfa Region. Pp. 65–86 in *Neolithic in Turkey: Cradle of Civilization. New Discoveries,* eds. M. Özdoğan and N. Başgelen. Istanbul: Arkeoloji ve Sanat.

Hayden, B.

1995 Pathways to Power: Principles for Creating Socioeconomic Inequalities. Pp. 15–86 in *Foundations of Social Inequality,* eds. T. D. Price and G. M. Feinman. Fundamental Issues in Archaeology. New York, NY: Plenum.

Hesse, B.

1984 These are our Goats: The Origins of Herding in West Central Iran. Pp. 243–64 in *Animal and Archaeology, 3. Early Herders and Their Flocks,* eds. J. Clutton-Brock and C. Grigson. BAR International Series 202. Oxford: BAR.

Heun, M.; Schäfer-Pregl, R.; Klawan, D.; Castagna, R.; Accerbi, M.; Borghi, B.; and Salamini, F.

1997 Site of Einkorn Wheat Domestication Identified by DNA Fingerprinting. *Science* 278: 1312–14.

Hillman, G. C.

2000 Abu Hureyra 1: The Epipalaeolithic. Pp. 327–99 in *Village on the Euphrates: From Foraging to Farming at Abu Hureyra,* eds. A. M. T. Moore, G. C. Hillman and A. J. Legge. Oxford: Oxford University.

Hodder, I.

1999 Renewed Work at Çatalhöyük. Pp. 157–64 in *Neolithic in Turkey: Cradle of Civilization. New Discoveries,* eds. M. Özdoğan and N. Başgelen. Istanbul: Arkeoloji ve Sanat.

Hole, F.

1994 Interregional Aspects of the Khuzestan Aceramic–Early Pottery Neolithic sequence. Pp. 101–16 in *Neolithic Chipped Stone Industries of the Fertile Crescent: Proceedings of the First Workshop on PPN Chipped Lithic Industries,* eds. H. G. Gebel and S. K. Kozlowski. Berlin: Ex Oriente.

1998 The Spread of Agriculture to the Eastern Arc of the Fertile Crescent: Food for the Herders. Pp. 83–92 in *The Origins of Agriculture and Crop Domestication,* eds. A. B. Damania, J. Valkoun, G. Willcox and C. O. Qualset. Aleppo: ICARDA.

2000 Is Size Important? Function and Hierarchy in Neolithic Settlements. Pp. 191–209 in *Life in Neolithic Farming Communities: Social Organization, Identity, and Differentiation,* ed. I. Kuijt. New York, NY: Plenum.

Horwitz, L. K.; Tchernov, E.; Ducos, P.; Becker, C.; von den Driesch, A.; Martin, L.; and Garrard, A.

1999 Animal Domestication in the Southern Levant. *Paléorient* 25, no. 2: 63–80.

Johnson, A. W., and Earle, T.

2000 *The Evolution of Human Societies: From Foraging Group to Agrarian State.* 2nd ed. Stanford, CA: Stanford University.

Kelly, R.

1995 *The Foraging Spectrum: Diversity in Hunter-Gatherer Lifeways.* Washington, DC: Smithsonian Institution.

Kenyon, K. M.
1957 *Digging Up Jericho.* London: Benn.
1981 *Excavations at Jericho, Vol. III: The Architecture and Stratigraphy of the Tell.* London: British School of Archaeology in Jerusalem.

Kirkbride, D.
1968 Beidha: Early Neolithic Village Life south of the Dead Sea. *Antiquity* 42: 263–74.

Kislev, M. E.
1997 Early Agriculture and Paleoecology of Netiv Hagdud. Pp. 209–36 in *An Early Neolithic Village in the Jordan Valley, Part I: The Archaeology of Netiv Hagdud,* eds. O. Bar-Yosef and A. Gopher. Cambridge, MA: Peabody Museum of Archaeology and Ethnology.

Kozlowski, S. K.
1999 *The Eastern Wing of the Fertile Crescent: Late Prehistory of Greater Mesopotamian Lithic Industries.* British Archaeological Reports International Series 760. Oxford: Archaeopress.

Kozlowski, S. K., and Gebel, H. G. K. (eds.)
1996 *Neolithic Chipped Stone Industries of the Fertile Crescent and Their Contemporaries in Adjacent Regions: Proceedings of the Second Workshop on PPN Chipped Lithic Industries, Warsaw 1995.* Berlin: Ex Oriente.

Kramer, C.
1982 *Village Ethnoarchaeology.* New York, NY: Academic.
1983 Spatial Organization in Contemporary Southwest Asian Villages. Pp. 347–68 in *The Hilly Flanks and Beyond,* eds. T. C. Young, Jr., P. E. L. Smith and P. Mortensen. Studies in Ancient Civilization 36. Chicago, IL: The Oriental Institute.

Kuijt, I.
1994 A Brief Note on the Chipped Stone Assemblages of Iraq ed-Dubb, Jordan. *Neo-Lithics* 1994, no. 2: 2–3.
1995 Pre-Pottery Neolithic A Settlement Variability: Evidence for Sociopolitical Developments in the Southern Levant. *Journal of Mediterranean Archaeology* 7, no. 2: 165–92.
1996 Negotiating Equality through Ritual: A Consideration of Late Natufian and Prepottery Neolithic A Period Mortuary Practices. *Journal of Anthropological Archaeology* 15: 313–36.
2000a *Life in Neolithic Farming Communities: Social Organization, Identity, and Differentiation,* ed. I. Kuijt. New York, NY: Plenum.
2000b People and Space in Early Agricultural Villages: Exploring Daily Near Eastern Neolithic Research: Directions and Trends. Pp. 311–22 in *Life in Neolithic Farming Communities: Social Organization, Identity, and Differentiation,* ed. I. Kuijt. New York, NY: Plenum.
2000c People and Space in Early Agricultural Villages: Exploring Daily Lives, Community Size, and Architecture in the Late Pre-Pottery Neolithic. *Journal of Anthropological Archaeology* 19, no. 1: 75–102.

Lamberg-Karlovsky, C. C., and Sabloff, J.
1979 *Ancient Civilizations: The Near East and Mesoamerica.* Menlo Park, CA: Benjamin/Cummings.

Lechevallier, M., and Ronen, A.
1994 *Le gisement de Hatoula en Judée occidentale, Israël.* Paris: Association Paléorient.

Legge, T.
1996 The Beginning of Caprine Domestication in Southwest Asia. Pp. 238–62 in *The Origins and Spread of Agriculture and Pastoralism in Eurasia,* ed. D. Harris. London: University College London.

Lemonnier, P.
1992 *Elements for an Anthropology of Technology.* Anthropological Papers, Museum of Anthropology, 88. Ann Arbor, MI: University of Michigan.

Martin, L.
1999 Mammal Remains from the Eastern Jordanian Neolithic, and the Nature of Caprine Herding in the Steppe. *Paléorient* 25, no. 2: 87–104.

Marx, E.
1977 Communal and Individual Pilgrimage: The Region of Saints' Tombs in South Sinai. Pp. 29–51 in *Regional Cults,* ed. R. P. Werbner. The Hague: Mouton.

Mellaart, J.
1967 *Çatal Hüyük, a Neolithic Town in Anatolia.* London: Thames and Hudson.

Mithen, S.; Finlayson, B.; Pirie, A.; Carruthers, D.; and Kennedy, M.
2000 New Evidence for Economic and Technological Diversity in the Pre-Pottery Neolithic A: Wadi Faynan 16. *Current Anthropology* 41, no. 4: 655–63.

Monnin, E.; Indermuhle, A.; Dallenbach, A.; Fluckiger, J.; Stauffer, B.; Stocker, T.; Raynaud, D.; and Barnola, J.-M.
2001 Atmospheric CO_2 Concentrations over the Last Glacial Termination. *Science* 291: 112–14.

Moore, A. M. T.
2000 The Excavation of Abu Hureyra 2. Pp. 327–99 in *Village on the Euphrates: From Foraging to Farming at Abu Hureyra,* eds. A. M. T. Moore, G. C. Hillman and A. J. Legge. Oxford: Oxford University.

Nadel, D.; Bar-Yosef, O.; and Gopher, A.
1991 Early Neolithic Arrowhead Types in the Southern Levant: A Typological Suggestion. *Paléorient* 17, no. 1: 109–19.

Nishiaki, Y.
1994 The Naviform Method at Houara Cave II, Palmyra, Syria. Pp. 363–78 in *Neolithic Chipped Stone Industries of the Fertile Crescent: Proceedings of the First Workshop on PPN Chipped Lithic Industries,* eds. H. G. Gebel and S. K. Kozlowski. Berlin: Ex Oriente.

Nissen, H. J.; Muheisen, M.; Gebel, H. G.; Becker, C.; Neef, R.; Pachur, H. J.; Qadi, N.; and Schultz, M.
1987 Report on the first two Seasons of Excavation at Basta (1986–1987). *Annual of the Department of Antiquities of Jordan* 31: 79–119.

Noy, T.
1989 Gilgal 1: A Pre-Pottery Neolithic site, Israel. *Paléorient* 15, no. 1: 11–18.

Noy, T.; Legge, A. J.; and Higgs, E. S.
1973 Recent Excavations at Nahal Oren, Israel. *Proceedings of the Prehistoric Society* 39: 75–99.

Olszewski, D. I.
2000 The Chipped Stone. Pp. 133–54 in *Village on the Euphrates: From Foraging to Farming at Abu Hureyra,* eds. A. M. T. Moore, G. C. Hillman and A. J. Legge. Oxford: Oxford University.

Özdoğan, A.
1999 Çayönü. Pp. 35–64 in *Neolithic in Turkey: Cradle of Civilization. New Discoveries,* eds. M. Özdoğan and N. Başgelen. Istanbul: Arkeoloji ve Sanat.

Özdoğan, M.
1996 From Huts to Houses: "Firsts" in Architecture. Pp. 19–30 in *Housing and Settlement in Anatolia: A Historical Perspective.* Istanbul: The Economic and Social History Foundation of Turkey.
1997 Anatolia from the Last Glacial Maximum to the Holocene Climatic Optimum: Cultural Formations and the Impact of the Environmental Setting. *Paléorient* 23, no. 2: 25–38.
1999 Concluding Remarks. Pp. 225–36 in *Neolithic in Turkey: Cradle of Civilization. New Discoveries,* eds. M. Özdoğan and N. Başgelen. Istanbul: Arkeoloji ve Sanat.

Özdoğan, M., and Balkan-Atlı, N.
1994 South-east Anatolian Chipped Stone Sequence. Pp. 205–6 in *Neolithic Chipped Stone Industries of the Fertile Crescent: Proceedings of the First Workshop on PPN Chipped Lithic Industries,* eds. H. G. Gebel and S. K. Kozlowski. Berlin: Ex Oriente.

Özdoğan, M., and Özdoğan, A.
1998 Buildings of Cult and the Cult of Buildings. Pp. 581–601 in *Light on Top of the Black Hill. Studies Presented to Halet Çambel,* eds. G. Arsebük, M. Mellink, J. and W. Schirmer. Istanbul: Ege.

Peltenburg, E.; Colledge, S.; Croft, P.; Jackson, A.; McCartney, C.; and Murray, M. A.
2000 Agro-Pastoralist Colonization of Cyprus in the 10th Millennium BP: Initial Assessments. *Antiquity* 74, no. 286: 844–53.

Perrot, J.
1968 La préhistoire palestinienne. Cols. 286–446 in *Supplément au Dictionnaire de la Bible,* vol. 8. Paris: Letouzey and Ane.

Peters, J.; Helmer, D.; von den Driesch, A.; and Segui, M. S.
1999 Early Animal Husbandry in the Northern Levant. *Paléorient* 25, no. 2: 27–47.

Pfaffenberger, B.
1992 Social Anthropology of Technology. *Annual Review of Anthropology* 21: 491–516.

Price, T. D., and Gebauer, A. B. (eds.)
1995 *Last Hunters – First Farmers: New Perspectives on the Prehistoric Transition to Agriculture.* School of American Research Advanced Seminar Series. Santa Fe, NM: School of American Research.

Quintero, L. A., and Wilke, P. J.
1995 Evolution and Economic Significance of Naviform Core-and-Blade Technology in the Southern Levant. *Paléorient* 21, no. 1: 17–33.

Redman, C.
1978 *The Rise of Civilization.* San Francisco: Freeman.

Reese, D. S.
1991 Marine Shells in the Levant: Upper Paleolithic, Epipaleolithic, and Neolithic. Pp. 613–28 in *The Natufian Culture in the Levant,* eds. O. Bar-Yosef and F. R. Valla. Ann Arbor, MI: International Monographs in Prehistory.

Rollefson, G. O.
1983 Ritual and Ceremony at Neolithic 'Ain Ghazal (Jordan). *Paléorient* 9, no. 2: 29–38.
1990 The Uses of Plaster at Neolithic 'Ain Ghazal, Jordan. *Archeomaterials* 4, no. 1: 33–54.

2000 Ritual and Social Structure at Neolithic 'Ain Ghazal. Pp. 165–90 in *Life in Neolithic Farming Communities: Social Organization, Identity, and Differentiation,* ed. I. Kuijt. New York, NY: Plenum.

Rollefson, G. O. and Köhler-Rollefson, I.
1989 The Collapse of Early Neolithic Settlements in the Southern Levant. Pp. 73–89 in *People and Culture in Change: Proceedings of the Second Symposium on Upper Palaeolithic, Mesolithic and Neolithic Populations of Europe and the Mediterranean Basin,* ed. I. Hershkovitz. British Archaeological Reports, International Series 508. Oxford: British Archaeological Reports.
1993 PPNC Adaptations in the First Half of the 6th Millennium B.C. *Paléorient* 19, no. 1: 33–42.

Rollefson, G. O.; Simmons, A. H.; and Kafafi, Z.
1992 Neolithic Cultures at 'Ain Ghazal, Jordan. *Journal of Field Archaeology* 19: 443–70.

Rosenberg, M.; Nesbitt, R.; Redding, R. W.; and Peasnall, B. L.
1998 Hallan Çemi, Pig Husbandry, and Post-Pleistocene Adaptations among the Taurus–Zagros Arc (Turkey). *Paléorient* 24, no. 1: 25–41.

Rossignol-Strick, M.
1995 Sea–Land Correlation of Pollen Records in the Eastern Mediterranean for the Glacial–Interglacial Transition: Biostratigraphy versus Radiometric Time-Scale. *Quaternary Science Reviews* 14: 893–915.

Schick, T.
1989 Early Neolithic Twined Basketry and Fabrics from the Nahal Hemar Cave in Israel. Pp. 41–52 in *Tissage, Corderie, Vannerie: Actes des IXèmes Rencontres Internationales d'Archéologie et d'Histoire d'Antibes, 20–22 Octobre 1988.* Juan-les-Pins: APDCA.

Schmidt, K.
1999a Boars, Ducks, and Foxes – the Urfa-Project 99. *Neo-Lithics* 1999, no. 3: 12–15.
1999b Frühe Tier- und Menschenbilder vom Göbekli Tepe – Kampagnen 1995–98: Ein Kommentierter Katalog der Großplastik und der Reliefs. *Istanbuler Mitteilungen* 49: 5–21.
2001 Göbekli Tepe, Southeastern Turkey: A Preliminary Report on the 1995–1999 Excavations. *Paléorient* 26, no. 1: 45–54.

Smith, B. D.
1998 *The Emergence of Agriculture,* 2nd ed. New York, NY: Scientific American Library.

Smith, P. E. L.
1976 Reflections on Four Seasons of Excavations at Tapeh Ganj Dareh. Pp. 11–22 in *Proceedings of the IVth Annual Symposium on Archaeological Research in Iran,* ed. F. Bagherzadeh. Teheran: Iranian Centre for Archaeological Research.

Stekelis, M.
1972 *The Yarmukian Culture.* Jerusalem: Magness/Hebrew University.

Stordeur, D.
2000 Jerf el-Ahmar et l'émergence du Néolithique au Proche Orient. Pp. 31–60 in *Premiers paysans du monde: Naissances des agricultures,* ed. J. Guilaine. Collection des Hesperides. Paris: Editions Errance.

Stordeur, D.; Brenet, M.; der Aprahamian, G.; and Roux, J.-C.
2001 Les bâtiments communautaires de Jerf el-Ahmar et Mureybet horizon PPNA (Syrie). *Paléorient* 26, no. 1: 29–44.

Stordeur, D., and de Margueron, T.
1998 Espace naturel, espace construit à Jerf el-Ahmar sur l'Euphrate. Pp. 93–108 in *Espace Naturel, Espace Habité en Syrie du Nord (10e–2e millénaires av. J-C.). Actes du colloque tenu à l'Université Laval (Québec) du 5 au 7 mai 1997,* eds. M. Fortin and O. Aurenche. Toronto: Canadian Society for Mesopotamian Studies.

Stordeur, D.; Helmer, D.; and Wilcox, G.
1997 Jerf el-Ahmar: un nouveau site de l'horizon PPNA sur le moyen Euphrate syrien. *Bulletin de la Societé Préhistorique Française* 94, no. 2: 282–85.

Stuiver, M.; Reimer, P. J.; Bard, E.; Beck, J. W.; Burr, G. S.; Hughen, K. A.; Kromer, B.; McCormac, G.; van der Plicht, J.; and Spurk, M.
1998 INTCAL98 Radiocarbon Age Calibration, 24,000–0 cal BP. *Radiocarbon* 40, no. 3: 1041–84.

Tchernov, E.
1993 From Sedentism to Domestication: A Preliminary Review for the Southern Levant. Pp. 189–233 in *Skeletons in her Cupboard: Festschrift for Juliet Clutton-Brock,* eds. A. Clason, S. Payne and H.-P. Uerpmann. Oxbow Monograph 34. Oxford: Oxbow.
1994 *An Early Neolithic Village in the Jordan Valley II: The Fauna of Netiv Hagdud.* American School of Prehistoric Research Bulletin 44. Cambridge, MA: Peabody Museum of Archaeology and Ethnography.

Valla, F. R.
1995 The First Settled Societies – Natufian (12,500–10,200 BP). Pp. 169–89 in *The Archaeology of Society in the Holy Land,* ed. T. Levy. London: Leicester University.

van Zeist, W., and Bakker-Heeres, J. A. H.
1986 (1984) Archaeobotanical Studies in the Levant 2. Neolithic and Halaf Levels at Ras Shamra. *Palaeohistoria* 26: 151–70.

van Zeist, W., and Bottema, S.
1991 *Late Quaternary Vegetation of the Near East.* Beihefte zum Tübinger Atlas des Vorderen Orients, Reihe A (Naturwissenschaft) Nr. 18. Wiesbaden: Reichert.

Vigne, J.-D.; Carrère, I.; Saliège, J.-F.; Person, A.; Bocherens, F.; Guilaine, J.; and Briois, F.
2000 Predomestic Cattle, Sheep, Goat, and Pig during the late 9th and the 8th Millennium cal. BC on Cyprus: Preliminary results of Shillourokambos (Parekklisha, Limassol). Pp. 83–106 in *Archaeozoology of the Near East IV A: Proceedings of the Fourth International Symposium on the Archaeozoology of Southwestern Asia and Adjacent Areas,* eds. M. Mashkour, A. M. Choyke, H. Buitenhuis and F. Poplin. Centre for Archaeological Research and Consultancy Publication 32. Groningen: ARC.

Voigt, M. M.
2000 Çatal Höyük in Context: Ritual at Early Neolithic Sites in Central and Eastern Turkey. Pp. 253–93 in *Life in Neolithic Farming Communities: Social Organization, Identity, and Differentiation,* ed. I. Kuijt. New York, NY: Plenum.

Watkins, T.; Baird, D.; and Betts, A.
1989 Qermez Dere and the Early Aceramic Neolithic in Northern Iraq. *Paléorient* 15, no. 1: 19–24.

Watson, P. J.
1979 *Archaeological Ethnography in Western Iran.* Tucson, AZ: University of Arizona.

Wilke, P. J., and Quintero, L. A.
1994 Naviform Core-and-Blade Technology: Assemblage Character as Determined by Replicative Experiments. Pp. 33–60 in *Neolithic Chipped Stone Industries of the Fertile Crescent: Proceedings of the First Workshop on PPN Chipped Lithic Industries,* eds. H. G. Gebel and S. K. Kozlowski. Berlin: Ex Oriente.

Wolf, E. R.
1966 *Peasants.* Foundations of Modern Anthropology. Englewood Cliffs, NJ: Prentice-Hall.

Wright, K. I.
1994 Ground Stone Tools and Hunter-Gatherer Subsistence in Southwest Asia: Implications for the Transition to Farming. *American Antiquity* 59, no. 2: 238–63.

Zeder, M. A., and Hesse, B.
2000 The Initial Domestication of Goats (*Capra hircus*) in the Zagros Mountains 10,000 Years Ago. *Science* 287: 2254–57.

Chapter 4

Gender Features and Social Hierarchy in the Chalcolithic Period in the Light of the Peqi'in Cave, Israel

by Zvi Gal, Howard Smithline and Dina Shalem

During the course of road construction in the village of Peqi'in, in Upper Galilee (fig. 1), a unique Chalcolithic burial cave was revealed (Gal et al. 1997)[1]. The cave is located on the lower western fringe of the Mt. Meiron massif, the highest mountain west of the Jordan River, and remote from any of the known regional cultural spheres related to this period: the Golan Heights, the Jordan Rift Valley, the Judean Desert, the northern Negev and the Coastal Plain. The finds in the cave, however, reflect for the first time artifactual aspects of all of these dispersed regional cultures combined in a single site.[2] It is, as yet, the most northern Chalcolithic mortuary site discovered in Israel. The cave, a geologically impressive environment of stalagmites and stalactites, was originally utilized as a domestic habitation in the early stage of the Chalcolithic period, at the beginning of 5th millennium B.C.E., but experienced its definitive use during the Ghassul phase (mid-5th–mid-4th millennium B.C.E.). It was at this time that the cave was transformed into a major burial site or necropolis.

PEQI'IN BURIAL CUSTOMS AND THE HUMAN MOTIF

As is common in Chalcolithic burial caves, predominantly found on the coastal plain, the burials are all secondary. Unusual here, however, is that alongside the great variety of ossuaries and jars utilized for the reinternments are reburials in the cave soil, outside any receptacle. The cave contains the richest assemblage of ossuaries yet found. These, together with the other vessels found in the cave, indicate the existence of a technologically advanced culture with highly artistic, creative, and spiritual aspects and expressions. Both social hierarchy within this Chalcolithic society and gender aspects may be interpreted through a study of the cave and its finds.

The ossuaries, all ceramic, were found in a variety of types, shapes, and models, some of which are unique. The largest group consists of rectangular boxes with a flat base or four or six legs and a separate gable lid (figs. 2–3). A series of small horizontal handles was placed diametrically on

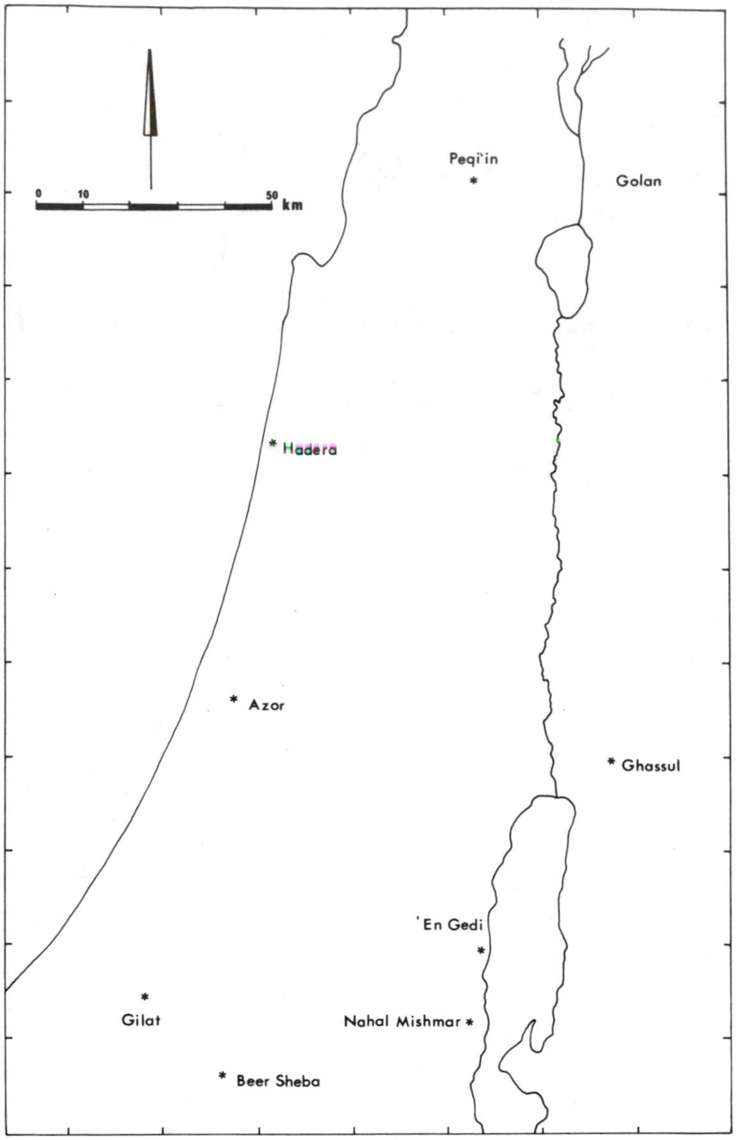

Fig. 1 *Map showing the location of Peqi'in and other sites mentioned.*

the boxes and the lids in order to facilitate their being tied together. Often the façades of these lids are decorated with portrayals of anthropomorphic facial features in a variety of fashions: symbolic faces (fig. 3), painted faces (fig. 4), applied features (figs. 2, 5–6), and three-dimensional sculpted human heads (fig. 7).

Another ossuary type is a closed box, sometimes with four or six legs (figs. 4, 6). Each is equipped with an opening, either on its front or on the rear side, to enable the placing of bones inside the box and a façade with a prominent nose and eyes, either sculpted or painted.

A few classes of ossuaries are outside the scope of this study but, nevertheless, require mentioning. Numerous ossuaries are modeled as zoomorphic portrayals. An additional group consists of shallow, open, rectangular boxes with large horizontal handles or a series of pierced holes along the rim. It is assumed that they were covered by a sheet made of an organic material that was fastened to the handles or tied to the holes and which long

Fig. 2 An ossuary with a lid and applied human features.

Fig. 3 An ossuary with a lid, six legs and symbolic face.

Fig. 4 An ossuary made of a closed box with painted face.

ago decomposed, leaving no trace. Red geometric patterns, perhaps imitating clothing, are commonly found painted on the sides of all the different ossuary types. The heavy nature of the ossuaries left on their base the impressions of the variety of mats upon which they were constructed and left to dry before firing.

Secondary burial in jars, though less common than ossuary reinterment, was practiced as well. Most of the jars have large pierced handles for carrying and transporting, and similar smaller handles for attaching a cover. Some of the jars have applied human features, female breasts, or painted human features (fig. 8). Many were painted red or decorated with red-painted linear, circular, or other geometric patterns.

The outstanding artistic innovations from the Peqi'in cave are the three-dimensional sculpted and painted ceramic heads. This is the first time that various natural human features are composed to express a fully human portrayal on ossuaries. Together with the large applied plastic nose and sculpted female breasts, already known as features

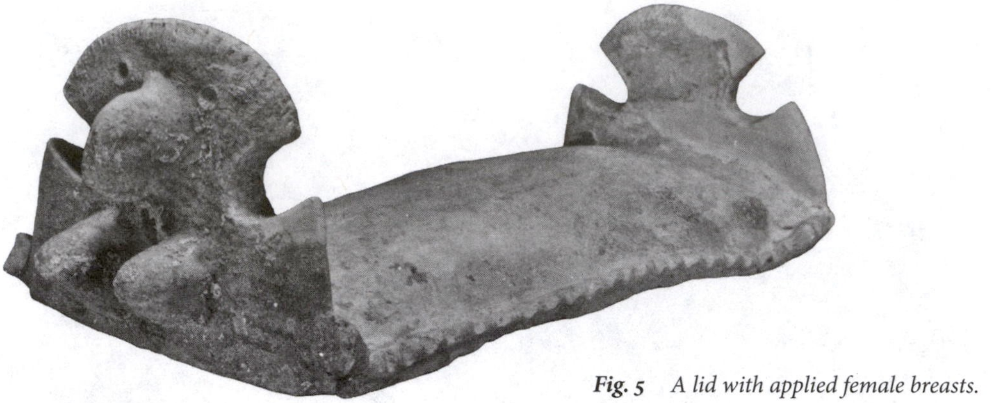

Fig. 5 *A lid with applied female breasts.*

Fig. 6 *An ossuary made of a closed box with six legs and applied human features.*

on some Chalcolithic ossuaries, are nostrils, eyes, ears, mouths, teeth, and beards (figs. 2, 5–7). The previously interpreted symbolic anthropomorphic representations have, with the discovery of this cave, suddenly become complete and more complex. Anthropomorphic features such as these were found painted or molded on ossuaries, jars, and even high-footed bowls.

Secondary burial in ossuaries was common in the Chalcolithic culture, however, the evidence from the Peqi'in cave shows that secondary burial without ossuaries was also practiced. In some of the natural niches along the walls of the cave were orderly bundles of bones, mostly long bones of arms and legs. One of the niches contained nineteen disassociated skulls. It is possible that in order to reuse ossuaries the skeletal remains and skulls were removed from their ossuaries and subsequently reburied in these niches. However, the fact that they were rather orderly placed in the niches, even imitating the ordered placement of the long bones in the ossuaries, makes this less likely and suggests that these individuals were intentionally reinterred in the soil within the cave. Multiple reinterments in a single ossuary have been found previously (Perrot and Ladiray 1980: 68–69, figs. 114–15); in Peqi'in there is also at least one ossuary that contained two skulls.

As mentioned above, iconographic art in Chalcolithic culture has been essentially symbolic, appearing on both ossuaries and basalt pillar figures. Its representation has been limited to the prominent nose (e.g., Perrot and Ladiray 1980: 113; Epstein 1998: 230, pls. 30–33) and painted eyes (Perrot and Ladiray 1980: figs. 32–33). In addition, there are some artifacts with portrayals of full complementary facial features: the Be'er Sheva ivory figurines (Perrot 1959) and the Gilat ceramic statue (Alon 1976). Facial and other physical human features have been generally considered as attributes of deities and, as such, served in a purely cultic function (Epstein 1982).

Fig. 7 *A three-dimensional, sculpted human head.*

Fig. 8 *A burial jar with female breasts.*

In contrast, the human sculpted heads and other iconographic expressions on the Peqi'in ossuaries and other vessels present an array of full human facial characteristics within a mortuary environment (Gal et al. 1999). Numerous ossuaries have the typical nose and/or painted or relief eyes — all in symbolic presentations. More elaborate vessels are decorated with the typical prominent nose formed with nostrils and accompanied by eyes, mouth, ears, beard, painted or applied hair representation, breasts, and — in some instances — also hands (fig. 2). Some of these vessels were carefully designed and produced as individual, one of a kind items. In these cases there was no single pattern or standard facial representation used as the basis for these artifacts; each head was molded or painted according to a particular model or idea. Most of the ossuaries, nonetheless, including those that are apparently unique, may be grouped into a number of definable types. The ability to produce these complex vessels demonstrates the advanced technological ability of the Chalcolithic pottery workshops.

The widespread use of such a variety of anthropomorphic faces demonstrates that, in contrast to already known Chalcolithic burial sites either on the coastal plain or in the northern Negev, the anthropomorphic motif played a central role in the mortuary ritual at Peqi'in. During the preceding Neolithic period the anthropomorphic motif, although rarely found, is evident in certain aspects of society, not restricted to mortuary practices: plastered skulls (e.g., Jericho: Kenyon 1957: 60–65, Beisamon: Lechevallier 1978: 179–81, Kefar Hahoresh: Goring-Morris 1995: 47–48, figs. 8–10), masks (Bar-Yosef and Alon 1988), and the 'Ain Ghazal statuary (Schmandt-Besserat 1998). Plastered skulls have been interpreted as relating to ancestor worship (e.g., Kenyon 1957: 85; Cauvin 1972; Goring-Morris 2000: 127; Kuijt 2001; for a different opinion see Bonogofsky 2003), while the 'Ain Ghazal statuary is believed to personify deities (Schmandt-Besserat 1998: 13).

GENDER FEATURES

The anthropomorphic ossuaries, lids, and jars depict both male and female gender aspects that may be identified, at first glance, by the presence of breasts or a beard (figs. 5–7). Several of the ossuaries and lids are also styled with an unusual fan-shaped façade (e.g., fig. 5) whose shape, as Yadin (1976) pointed out in regard to previously discovered ossuaries, is reminiscent of the Chalcolithic "violin figurines." Violin figurines are considered as an expression of female aspects (Alon and Levy 1989: 185–87) usually related to fertility. Unfortunately, no *in situ* skeletal remains were found in these ossuaries[3] and, thus, any correlation between the gender of the deceased and the ossuary type is impossible to determine. Nevertheless, it is clear that the ossuaries bear gender characteristics, which apparently were significant in certain aspects of the mortuary practice. Due to the centrality of the Peqi'in cave, it seems that this phenomenon reflects some aspects of the Chalcolithic belief.

Gender specific artifacts are among the objects accompanying the burials. The previously mentioned violin figurines may be interpreted as being abstract representations of more recognizable female figurines. This interpretation is enhanced by the uncommon violin figure modeled with breasts. Male reinterment may be identified by the presence of flint adzes apparently specially prepared for burial. They are traditionally associated with either masculine activities performed during the lifetime of the deceased or as representing the male sexual organ (Barkai 2000: 88–94, 244–49). In this vein then, could the many mysterious flint discs with a central piercing be interpreted as being representative of either unspecified feminine aspects or, more specifically, the female sexual organ?

SOCIAL HIERARCHY

The Chalcolithic period has been classed as a pastoral egalitarian society (Levy 1995). However, the variety of burial practices revealed at Peqi'in — outside ossuaries, within ossuaries, and, most notably, in the richly diverse and imaginative ossuary types themselves — reflects different degrees of attention applied to the individuals reinterred in the cave. It may be conjectured that those who were buried in ossuaries were of a higher social status than those whose bones were placed in the wall niches reserved for common reburial. To carry this analogy a step further leads us to suggest that those who were reinterred in more complex ossuaries with anthropomorphic attributes were of a higher status than those whose bones were placed in simple and less expressive ossuaries. We can tentatively enumerate at least seven socio-hierarchical groups of the deceased, as interpreted through each specific reburial. The following groups also contain subgroups and are not listed in any hierarchically relevant ascending or descending order.

- Individuals reburied outside ossuaries
- Individuals reburied in open boxes
- Individuals reburied in "simply designed" ossuaries
- Individuals reburied in sculpted ossuaries
- Individuals reburied in plain jars
- Individuals reburied in Golan-type jars (cf. Note 2)
- Individuals reburied in sculpted jars

The mere existence of this cave itself is an indication of a structured and hierarchical society operating in the northern Chalcolithic cultural sphere. A number of factors are to be taken into account. This major necropolis was isolated from the known, densely occupied regions of the Chalcolithic period,[4] necessitating the existence of an organized system that maintained the cave's functioning and determined the order of the placing of the ossuaries and jars in this very cramped environment. This necessity is amplified by the difficulty created by the darkness that apparently permeated the cave. The final placing of each individual ossuary was probably determined by the status attained by the deceased during his/her lifetime, or by his/her status determined after his/her death. It should be pointed out that no children under the age of three were buried in the cave (Nagar and Eshed 2001). They were buried somewhere else, most likely as determined by the excepted hierarchical structure of the society. Most probably the reburials were accompanied by cultic activities, either prior to or at the time of reburial, which would require the functioning of a group of individuals — a priestly class — versed in performing these activities. It would possibly be these people who were required to maintain the memory of this unique burial site within the collective consciousness of the society and upon whom it was required to incorporate the secondary burial into seasonal cultic activities.

CONCLUSIONS

The unique iconography applied to the Peqi'in ossuaries raises the question of its purpose and meaning. Many scholars who have studied 7th–4th millennium B.C.E. Near Eastern iconography concur that its source is to be found in the divine world of gods and goddesses (e.g., Kenyon 1957: 84; Epstein 1982; Beck 1989; Tadmor 1989; Merhav 1993; Schmandt-Besserat 1998). There are, however, major differences between the circumstances and functioning of the Peqi'in iconography and comparable iconography from other Chacolithic sites: the metal hoard from Nahal Mishmar, the Golan basalt figures, the Gilat figurine, the Be'er Sheva ivory figurines, the violin shaped figurines, as well as the Neolithic 'Ain Ghazal statues. All of these objects originate from either domestic or cultic contexts and not from a burial context. The Peqi'in mortuary iconography thus presents a new direction for interpreting the expression of iconography. A number of suggestions may be offered. A simple, personal one-on-one representation relevant to each deceased individual may be possible in some cases, but does not appear to be the rule. The practice of ancestor worship, where both male and female ancestors play an influential role, is strongly implied within the context of secondary burial and as a manifestation of the early state of communal organization of the Chalcolithic period.

Anthropological study of the skeletal remains shows that the minimum number of individuals buried in the cave was ca. 600, with the maximum number being possibly twice as much. The grave goods accompanying the reburials clearly represent the various regional Chalcolithic cultures of the southern Levant, while the cave functioned as a central burial site for an extended population of several villages or, perhaps, several regions. In the light of the diversity of artifacts and the large anthropological sample, the cave may be considered as a paradigm of the Chalcolithic period wherein social status and gender definition were already defined.

NOTES

1 The excavation was carried out on behalf of the Israel Antiquities Authority.

2 Along with ossuaries and burial jars, the cave yielded several other ceramic vessel types of which the most common were the low- and high-footed bowls. Deserving of mention are the numerous Golan-type jars, rich in basalt inclusions, that are considered characteristic of the Golan Chalcolithic subculture. Among the finds were a number of bronze objects, an ivory figure, an assortment of stone 'violin figures,' and flint tools and artifacts.

3 The cave was extremely disturbed and apparently had been subject to robbing and destruction, most possibly within the Chalcolithic period. Most of the burial receptacles were overturned or broken and the bones were randomly strewn around (Gal et al. 1997: 147).

4 A Chalcolithic site was recently discovered within the boundaries of the village of Peqi'in, across the wadi (Getzov, forthcoming). Shalem's study (2003) shows more than twenty villages in the mountains of the Upper Galilee, most of them small (ca. 5 *dunam*).

REFERENCES

Alon, D.
1976 Two Cult Figurines from Gilat. *'Atiqot* 11: 116–18.

Alon, D., and Levy, E. T.
1989 The Archaeology of the Cult and the Chalcolithic Sanctuary at Gilat. *Journal of Mediterranean Archaeology* 2: 163–221.

Bar-Yosef, O., and Alon, D.
1988 Nahal Hemar Cave. *'Atiqot* 18: 1–30.

Barkai, R.
2000 Flint and Stone Axes as Cultural Markers: Socio-economic Change as Reflected in Holocene Flint Tool Industries of the Southern Levant. Unpublished Ph.D. thesis, Tel Aviv University.

Beck, P.
1989 Notes on the Style and Iconography of the Chalcolithic Hoard from Nahal Mishmar. Pp. 39–47 in *Essays in Ancient Civilization Presented to Helen J. Kramer,* eds. A. Leonard and B. B. Williams. Chicago, IL: Chicago University.

Bonogofsky, M.
2003 Neolithic Plastered Skulls and Railroading Epistemologies. *Bulletin of the American Schools of Oriental Research* 331: 1–10.

Cauvin, J.
1972 *Religions néolithiques de Syro-Palestine.* Librairie d'Amérique et d'Orient. Paris: Maisonneuve.

Epstein, C.
1982 Cult Symbols in Prehistoric Palestine. *Bolletino del Centro Camuno dei Studi Preistorici* 19: 63–82.
1998 *The Chalcolithic Culture of the Golan.* IAA Reports 4. Jerusalem: Israel Exploration Society.

Gal, Z.; Smithline, H.; and Shalem, D.
1997 A Chalcolithic Burial Cave at Peqi'in, Upper Galilee. *Israel Exploration Journal* 47: 1–12.
1999 New Iconographic Aspects in the Chalcolithic Art – Preliminary Observations on Finds from Peqi'in. *'Atiqot* 37: 1–17.

Getzov, N.
Forthcoming Peqi'in, in *Excavations and Surveys in Israel.*

Goring-Morris, N.
1995 Investigations at an Early Neolithic Settlement in the Lower Galilee: Results of the 1991 Season at Kefar HaHoresh. *'Atiqot* 27: 37–62.
1998 The 1997 Season of Excavations at the Mortuary Site of Kfar Hahoresh. *NeoLithics* 3: 1–4.
2000 The Quick and the Dead: The Social Context of Aceramic Neolithic Mortuary Practices as seen from Kfar Hahoresh. Pp. 103–36 in *Life in Neolithic Farming Communities, Social Organization, Identity, and Differentiation,* ed. I. Kuijt. New York, NY: Kluwer Academic.

Kenyon, K. M.
1957 *Digging up Jericho.* New York, NY: Praeger.

Kuijt, I.
2001 Place, Death and the Transmission of Social Memory in Early Agricultural Communities of the Near East Pre-Pottery Neolithic. Pp. 80–89 in *Social Memory, Identity and Death: Anthropological Perspectives on Mortuary Rituals,* ed. M. Chesson. Archaeological Papers of the American Anthropological Association 10. Arlington, VA: American Anthropological Association.

Lechevallier, M.
1978 *Abou Gosh et Beisamoun – Deux gisements du VII millénaire avant l'ère chrétienne en Israël.* Paris: Association Paléorient.

Levy, T.
1995 Cult, Metallurgy and Rank Societies – Chalcolithic Period (ca. 4500–3500 BCE). Pp. 226–44 in *The Archaeology of Society in the Holy Land,* ed. T. Levy. London: Leicester University.

Merhav, R.
1993 Scepters of the Divine from the Cave of the Treasure at Nahal Mishmar (in Hebrew). Pp. 21–42 in *Studies in the Archaeology and History of Ancient Israel,* ed. M. Helzer, A. Segal and D. Kaufman. Haifa: Haifa University.

Nagar, Y., and Eshed, V.
2001 Where are the Children? Age-Dependent Burial Practices in Peqi'in. *Israel Exploration Journal* 51: 27–35.

Perrot, J.
1959 Statuettes en ivoire et autres objets en ivoire et en os provenant des gisements préhistoriques de la region de Beersheba. *Syria* 36: 8–19.

Perrot, J., and Ladiray, D.
1980 *Tombes à ossuaries de la region côtière palestinienne au IV millénaire avant l'ère chrétienne.* Paris: Association Paléorient.

Schmandt-Besserat, D.
1998 'Ain Ghazal "Monumental" Figures. *Bulletin of the American Schools of Oriental Research* 310: 1–18.

Shalem, D.
2003 The Chalcolithic Period Sites in the Mountains of the Galilee – Settlement Distribution and Ceramic Characteristics. Unpublished MA thesis, University of Haifa (Hebrew with English summary).

Tadmor, M.
1989 The Judean Desert Treasure from Nahal Mishmar: A Chalcolithic Traders' Hoard? Pp. 249–61 in *Essays in Ancient Civilization Presented to Helen J. Kantor,* eds. A. Leonard Jr. and B. B. Williams. Chicago, IL: Chicago University.

Yadin, Y.
1976 Note on the Violin-Shaped Figurine from Gilat. *'Atiqot* 11: 121.

Chapter 5

Ethnicity and the Archaeological Record: The Case of Early Israel

by William G. Dever

Can a specific "ethnic identification" of an ancient people be determined on the basis of material culture remains unearthed by archaeology? That question poses one of the most fundamental, most urgent, yet most difficult issues in archaeology. The author of the most recent book on the subject,[1] *The Archaeology of Ethnicity*, begins with a statement of Olivier and Coudart (1995: 365) that "the crucial theoretical question of archaeology today is that of national identity, or more specifically that of the relationship archaeology enjoys with the construction (or the fabrication) of collective identities" (Jones 1997: 1).

This chapter will use the case of early Israel — or the question of "Israelite origins" — as a test-case in addressing the issue of ethnicity in the archaeological record. It is offered as a tribute to Eric M. Meyers, a colleague and friend of more than thirty-five years, who has been a pioneer in confronting similar methodological concerns in his efforts to identify early Jewish and Christian ethnicity in the archaeology of the Galilee.[2]

ETHNICITY AND "ISRAELITE ORIGINS" IN RECENT SCHOLARSHIP

In the wake of Israeli archaeological surveys in the West Bank in the 1980s, first reported to the wider world in 1988 by Israel Finkelstein in *The Archaeology of the Israelite Settlement*, the discussion of "Israelite origins" in Canaan has burgeoned.[3] The basic archaeological evidence has been widely discussed and summarized by several archaeologists, including myself, and by now should be well known to most biblical scholars and historians.[4] This extensive complex of many types of diverse but related data constitutes what archaeologists call an "assemblage." And such an assemblage is *always* assumed to have cultural, and therefore what I would call "ethnic," significance. The aspects of this Iron I or 12th–11th centuries B.C.E. assemblage that are relevant for our discussion here will be discussed presently.

Prior to the availability of the recent archaeological data, scholars have had as their only source for the history of the formative era of early Israel (the biblical "period of the Judges") the narratives of the "exodus and conquest" in the Hebrew Bible.

Yet there has been increasing skepticism in recent years among scholars of all schools, "maximalists" as well as "minimalists," as to whether much, if any, genuine historical information can be derived from the biblical texts.[5] These texts are all later literary compositions, highly selective in content, idealist and elitist in perspective, and, above all, theologically tendentious.

The current, pervasive historiographical crisis in biblical studies has brought us to the point where leading scholars can assert that there *was* no "early Israel" in the 12th–11th centuries B.C.E., indeed not even an Israelite Monarchy before the 9th century B.C.E., and no Judean (or southern) kingdom worthy of the name before the 7th century B.C.E.[6]

For adherents of the "revisionist" schools of Sheffield and Copenhagen—the most radical of the current schools of biblical criticism—the skepticism rests not only on a minimalist (if not nihilist) view of the biblical texts, but upon two other *theoretical assumptions*. Unfortunately, these are rarely advanced as rigorous intellectual constructs, merely what I would call "notions," and, as I shall show, uninformed notions at that. These assumptions are: (1) that the Iron I hill-country archaeological assemblage that we now have, although well documented, cannot be confidently associated with any known ethnic group because of the limitations of all archaeological evidence; and (2) that, in any case, "ethnicity" is a modern "social construct," and therefore it is illegitimate to project it back upon the ancient textual or archaeological record. Thus, the "revisionists" simply "write early Israel out of history" (Halpern 1995).

Here are some typical "revisionist" statements. Niels Peter Lemche concludes his 1998 book, *The Israelites in History and Tradition,* with this statement:

> The Israel of the Iron Age proved to be most elusive, in historical documents as well as in material remains, where hardly anything carries an ethnic tag that helps the modern investigator to decide what is Israelite and what is not (1998b: 166).

Thomas L. Thompson simply disposes of the issue:

> Ethnicity, however, is an interpretive historiographical fiction.... Ethnicity is hardly a common aspect of human existence at this very early period.... Ethnicity is only a modern attempt to describe societal relationship and collective decisions...the physical effects of such collective decisions are often arbitrary and are, indeed, always accidental (1997: 175).

It is no wonder then that in his 1999 book, *The Mythic Past: Biblical Archaeology and the Myth of Israel*, Thompson concludes that

> ...so much of the Bible deals with the origin traditions of a people that never existed as such. This metaphorical nation's land and language, this imagined people's history, moreover, is an origin tradition that belongs to the 'new Israel' (i.e., much later Judaism: WGD), not the 'old' (1999: 34).

Elsewhere, Thompson broadens his skepticism to include other ancient peoples. Thus, Philistines, Canaanites, and Israelites are all "peoples writ large in tradition for purposes fictional."[7]

Keith W. Whitelam's position in his *The Invention of Ancient Israel: The Silencing of Palestinian History* goes to the point of absurdity. The "biblical Israel" is a fiction, concocted by ancient Judaism as a tortuous exercise in self-identity, and perpetuated by all later Jewish and Christian scholars (especially Zionist Israelis). There was no ancient or Iron Age "Israel" in an ethnic sense. Yet the "Palestinians" as a people—a distinct *ethnoi*—flourished already in the Bronze Age; historians and archaeologists biased by the Judaeo-Christian tradition have simply written them out of history.[8]

A recent collection of essays by biblical scholars, *Ethnicity and the Bible* (Brett 1996), does not deign to include any archaeologists, presumably because the editors did not consider their data relevant. Yet one of them, Diana V. Edelman (now with the Sheffield group), draws up a "trait list" of the sort that has been used by some archaeologists in the past to identify "ethnicity." Nevertheless, she concludes that attempting to identify any of the Iron I–II peoples of Palestine ethnically, based on material culture remains, "is to wish upon a star" (1996: 55).[9] As she puts it in the very first sentence of her chapter: "Given the present state of textual and artifactual evidence, nothing definitive can be said about the ethnicity of premonarchical Israel" (1996: 25).

Most of the above statements scarcely need refutation. For Lemche, Thompson, and Whitelam, as well as Philip R. Davies, there cannot have been an "ancient Israel," because that would not suit their presuppositions (for that is what they are).[10] And Thompson's incredible notions that ethnic markers are all "arbitrary, accidental," if taken seriously, would put *all* the social sciences out of business, since these disciplines proceed on the essential principle that culture is "patterned," i.e., intentional, and thus diagnostic for describing culture and cultural change (below). As for Edelman, her survey of some of the archaeological data is typical of the selective, cavalier, and amateurish use of archaeology by most of the other "revisionists."[11]

Unfortunately, the "anti-positivist" bias of some biblical scholars — in my judgment largely a reflex of the naïve, belated borrowing of "post-modernist" epistemology — has affected a few Palestinian archaeologists (below).[12] Most archaeologists until recently have been comfortable and confident in applying to typical Bronze or Iron Age assemblages in Palestine such ethnic labels as "Canaanite," "Egyptian," "Philistine," "Aramaean," "Phoenician," and, of course, "Israelite."

Now, however, it seems suddenly fashionable to call such ethnic identifications into question and even to impute to scholars still using them improper motives — in the case of the term "Israelite," a theological or biblicist bias (as Whitelam 1996). Ironically, the most outspoken current opponent of the "Israelite" terminology, or even my cautious term "Proto-Israelite," is Israel Finkelstein. He had originally "written the book" on the subject, *The Archaeology of the Israelite Settlement* (1988). But since 1991, Finkelstein has denied that we can use the ethnic label "Israelite" for the Iron I hill-country assemblage that he did so much to put on the map. In 1996, specifically attacking my more optimistic treatments of early Israel (Dever 1992a; 1995a), Finkelstein argues that the distinctive material culture traits that we both acknowledge on the LB/Iron I horizon are more the result of environmental and socioeconomic factors than reflective of any new "ethnic" elements in the population. To support his views, Finkelstein minimizes the importance of a unique, new combination of agricultural technologies — terraces, silos, cisterns — even denying that they are innovative. Finally, he misrepresents my reconstruction as based either on Gottwald's "peasant revolt" model or on theories "too wedded to the Biblical story." He concludes that an ethnic identification based even on texts, such as those of the Hebrew Bible, is an "illusion." Yet in his most recent popular book, Finkelstein speaks throughout quite glibly about an "early Israel." All this, in my opinion, is *ideology*, not reasoned, well-documented, balanced scholarship.[13]

On the other hand, I have consistently maintained a more positive view, presumably one in line with mainstream archaeological scholarship, although I have not defended this view explicitly until now (but cf. 1998). Nor is there much other treatment of the subject of "ethnicity" in the literature of Palestinian archaeology.[14]

One of the few explicit treatments of archaeology and the problem of "Israelite ethnicity," although focused on Iron II rather than the more problematic Iron I period, is that of a young Tel Aviv archaeologist, Avraham Faust (2000a; 2000b), with excellent general bibliography. Faust concentrates on the rural areas of 9th–8th century B.C.E. northern Israel, where he persuasively identifies an "Israelite" as well as a regional "Canaanite-Phoenician" archaeological assemblage, coinciding with both geographical and socioeconomic or cultural "boundaries."

Of particular significance here is Faust's utilization of McGuire's (1982) postulate that it is not the totality of cultural traits that identifies ethnic differences, but rather "those traits that the groups utilize as symbols of their identity separate from other groups." These traits, McGuire holds, "may be behavioral or material in form" (1982: 160). Furthermore, "ethnic boundaries" may be most readily recognized (1) when they are not connected with factors such as ecology, wealth, social status, or setting; and (2) when the focus is on simpler, supposedly more monolithic rural groups. Faust's consequent look at rural areas in Iron II is closely comparable to our look at the overwhelmingly rural "Israel" in Iron I.

A similar attempt to identify "Judean ethnicity" in Iron II has been made recently by another young Tel Aviv archaeologist, Raz Kletter. Kletter analyzes two distinctive classes of southern artifacts of the late 8th–7th centuries B.C.E.: (1) "pillar-base" (Asherah) figurines, and (2) stone shekel-weights. Not surprisingly, Kletter's detailed distribution maps of both (1999: 31, 35) coincide almost exactly with the *political* boundaries of Judah as reflected in texts of the 7th century B.C.E. Deuternomistic history in II Kings. Thus, a sense of "Judean ethnicity" must have actually prevailed in late Iron II and was not simply "invented" by the biblical writers and later editors, as the "revisionists" fatuously proclaim.[15]

GENERAL THEORETICAL CONSIDERATIONS ON "ETHNICITY"

None of the theoretical objections noted above to the use of the concept of "ethnicity" stands up to close scrutiny. Let us analyze them in order.

(1) "Ethnicity" is a modern "social construct." This, of course, is simply one of the typical slogans of post-modernism, borrowed mindlessly here. The point is that *all* intellectual formulations are "social constructs," as, indeed, culture itself is — unless one supposes that the phenomena are handed down from heaven. Religion is a "social construct." Does that mean that it is not a significant factor in cultural change or that it is too elusive to be analyzed?

The question is only the degree to which such "constructs" reflect facts, i.e., reality. In the case of "ethnicity," the construct *is* the reality. "Ethnicity" means simply "a sense of peoplehood" (Greek *ethnos*, "a community of people"). And if a certain group thinks itself a distinctive "people," then they *are* by that very fact. Finally, such a sense of peoplehood is not a modern phenomenon, as claimed by the "revisionists," but has characterized every known human community in every time and circumstance. A sense of unique *selfhood* is fundamental to human nature, not a mere epiphenomenon, an arbitrary and flimsy "social construct."

(2) What may be called "ethnic boundaries" are flexible, constantly changing. No doubt; but again that does not mean that they do not exist in reality or cannot be subjected to rigorous scrutiny and systematic analysis. Here, too, the analogy with culture in general, as well as with certain aspects of culture such as religion, is appropriate.

(3) Specific markers, or "ethnic traits," either cannot be adequately characterized or will turn out not to be reflected in material culture. If this were true, however, archaeology as a discipline would be impossible, since archaeology is widely acknowledged to be essentially the study of the *material correlates* of behavior, i.e., of culture in all its dimensions, including a sense of ethnic identity. If there *are* no "material correlates," then human thought, behavior, and culture are all arbitrary, inscrutable, and not susceptible to any systematic analysis. Yet that is not the case, as I shall show presently. Culture is "patterned" social behavior or it is nothing; and archaeology seeks to comprehend those patterns, as they are inevitably reflected in material culture remains as well as in ideology.

(4) Finally, "revisionists" and others assert that without texts, material culture is "mute" and thus cannot be said to reflect any specific ethnic identity. Yet if the arguments above are valid, it is evident that archaeology *can* characterize distinctive material culture assemblages and then can legitimately assume that they do reflect various ethnic groups. It is only the specific ethnic *label* that texts necessarily supply. And in the case of ancient "Israel," we have the requisite texts, both biblical and non-biblical (below).

If one examines the currently faddish negative rhetoric about "ethnicity," as in Sían Jones' *The Archaeology of Ethnicity* (1998; above), it soon becomes evident that much of the skepticism is due to the confusion of attempts to identify "ethnicity" with *racism*, which is and should be politically incorrect. Thus, Jones' principal case study in the abuse of the concept of "ethnicity" is the program of the Nazis to use archaeology to document the superiority of their "super race." But that is surely a monstrous caricature. Such a distorted concept of "race" has long been repudiated by archaeologists and anthropologists everywhere. But that does not invalidate the category of "ethnicity," which was never really based on supposed racial characteristics and still remains both valid and useful.

Ironically, the call of many post-modernist social scientists for "multi-cultural" approaches presupposes our ability to *identify* distinctive individual "ethnic groups." And if we can do so in modern times, why not in antiquity, as long as we have adequate evidence? Instead of denying the existence of "ethnic identity," archaeologists are engaged in recognizing and indeed celebrating it. *We* are the true "multi-culturalists," and instead of using archaeology as a tool of cultural imperialism, as sometimes charged, we archaeologists are the real champions of cultural diversity.[16]

TOWARD A WORKING ARCHAEOLOGICAL MODEL OF "ETHNICITY"

Much of the current frustration and apparent failure in recognizing "ethnicity in the archaeological record" is due, I believe, to (1) inadequate or unrealistic definitions of "ethnicity;" and (2) the lack of an appropriate analytical methodology, especially in assessing "ethnic traits" in material culture remains.

Elsewhere I have drawn on the work of the eminent anthropologist and ethnographer Fredrik Barth (1969) in order to define an "ethnic group" as a population that is (1) biologically self-perpetuating; (2) shares a fundamental, recognizable, relatively uniform set of cultural values, including language; (3) constitutes a partly independent "interaction sphere;" (4) has a membership that defines itself, as well as being defined by others, as a category distinct from other categories of the same order; and (5) perpetuates its sense of separate identity by developing rules for maintaining ethnic boundaries, as well as for participating in interethnic social encounters (Dever 1995a: 201).

However heuristically valuable the methodology of Barth and other ethnographers may be, it is best suited to the analysis of modern, not ancient, cultures. Our primary task here is to identify a list of distinctive and specifically *archaeological* "ethnic traits" that may realistically be expected to be preserved and capable of being identified in the archaeological record of typical sites. Yet few archaeologists, and none in the field of Palestinian or biblical archaeology, have developed such an archaeological trait list (Table 1).[17] I offer the following as a tentative step in the right direction. After long reflection, it seems to me that we ought to be able to discern "ethnic differences" in comparing the following material culture traits in different assemblages and cultures, especially when they are contiguous or roughly contemporary:

(1) Environmental setting
(2) Settlement type and pattern
(3) Demography
(4) Technology, adaptation, and subsistence, especially food systems
(5) House type
(6) Burial customs
(7) Dress
(8) Language
(9) Social organization
(10) Political structure
(11) Religion and cult
(12) External relations

These are, of course, modern analytical categories, which ancient peoples would not have comprehended in the same way that we do or of which they may not even have been consciously aware. But nevertheless, I would argue, they did understand the "differences" that such traits reflect, especially when comparing themselves with other groups. In short, the "ancient Israelites" of the Iron Age in Palestine surely knew who they were; and it is up to us to find that out, even when they have not always candidly revealed themselves in the biblical texts. It is archaeology that may be our best clue.

THE ARCHAEOLOGICAL EVIDENCE FOR EARLY "ISRAELITE" ETHNICITY

In summarizing the archaeological data now available that might bear upon each of the above "ethnic markers" for identifying an "early" Israel, I must be brief, referring to more extensive documentation elsewhere.[18]

Table 1 Comparison of "cultural traits" exhibited in the Iron I archaeological record, by ethnic group; numbers refer to the list in the text. If these other Iron I groups in Palestine can be distinguished by an ethnic label, as they are in contemporary scholarship, so can our highland peoples.

Trait	Canaanite	Egyptian	Philistine	"Proto-Israelite"
1	Central	Strategic	Coastal	Marginal; hill-country
2	Declining urban	Forts; garrisons	New urban foundations	Village/Rural
3	LB urban tradition	"Residencies"	Non-specific	"Four room"/courtyard
4	Long-term decline	Penultimate collapse	Slow growth	Rapid growth
5	Mixed, local	Subsidized	Mixed	Agrarian
6	—	—	—	—
7	Stagnant	Egyptian	Foreign, innovative	Local, innovative
8	Long-term Canaanite	Bi-lingual	Unknown	"Canaanite" dialect
9	Stratified	Hierarchal	Elitist	Egalitarian
10	Declining city states	Imperial	City state	Segmentary
11	LB Canaanite	Egyptian (?)	Aegean	"Canaanite"
12	Isolated; some Egyptian	Egyptian	Aegean, Mycenaean	

1 – *Environmental Setting*

The more than 300 small Iron I or 12th–11th century B.C.E. villages, which constitute our best evidence for what I have designated a "Proto-Israelite" population, are all located in marginal areas. They are found in the heretofore sparsely occupied central hill-country, principally in Samaria and Judea, but also extending into the northern Negev and probably into lower Galilee. The environmental setting in these regions, with ample rainfall, is conducive to dry farming, stock breeding, and pastoralism, but only with the development of new technologies (below). The isolation and scarcity of resources, however, do not encourage larger-scale industry, much less trade or international connections. This is in sharp contrast to both the Late Bronze Age Canaanite city states and the contemporary Philistine establishments along the coast and in the riverine valleys.

2 – *Settlement Type and Pattern*

The basic features have been noted above. The essential point here is that the settlements and their distribution mark again a sharp and relatively sudden shift from the prevailing urban pattern of the Late Bronze Age Canaanite society, as well as a contrast to the coastal Philistine sites. None of the 300 or so "Proto-Israelite" sites is larger than a few acres, has a population in excess of about 300, exhibits monumental architecture, or boasts city defenses. This is a decidedly *rural* culture, which, as we saw above, may provide our best test case.

3 – *Demography*

The demographic data, based on recent surveys of the hill-country sites, show another radical change accompanying the transition from Late Bronze Age Canaanite society into the early Iron Age. The estimated population of the central hill-country, for instance, grows dramatically from ca. 12,000 in the 13th century B.C.E., to ca. 50,000 in the 12th century B.C.E., to ca. 75,000 in the 11th century B.C.E.[19] Such a "population explosion" cannot possibly be explained by natural increase alone, but points to a large-scale in-migration of new peoples, whom it is not unreasonable to designate as an "ethnic group," especially when other evidence points in the same direction. The only questions are who and from where.

4 - *Technology, Adaptation, and Subsistence*

The evidence adduced above shows that the Iron I hill-country assemblage reflects a society and economy that are fundamentally village-based and agrarian. A major agricultural component is visible, of course, in the society and economy of every era in ancient Palestine, from the Neolithic onward. Yet, in scarcely any other period does the "rural" aspect dominate so *exclusively* as it does in the Iron I hill-country assemblage. Nearly all the new technology is geared to adapting to the challenges of setting the hill-country frontier and opening it for agricultural development: extensive terracing of the hillsides; the hewing out of cisterns in the bedrock; stone-lined silos for grain storage; large "collar-rim" jars for storage of various foodstuffs; the introduction of heavy iron implements (although limited at first); and the proliferation of stereotyped courtyard houses especially well suited to farming families. Some aspects of these technologies go back to the Bronze Age, but the peculiar and standardized *combination* is new in Iron I and also peculiar to the hill-country settlements.[20]

One aspect of food production is now widely acknowledged to be significant, even by skeptics: the almost complete absence of pig bones in the presumed hill-country "Proto-Israelite" sites of Iron I, whereas they are common in other periods and areas. This phenomenon suggests that one of the most conspicuous "ethnic markers" of the later, well-documented Israelite (or biblical) culture — the prohibition of pork — was in fact an early distinction from Canaanite religion and culture.[21]

5 - *House Type*

The typical Iron I hill-country village house has been mentioned above. These houses are very stereotyped in plan, with three banks of rooms surrounding a central courtyard (thus the common name, "four-room house") and usually a second story. The ground floor provides animal stables, ample storage facilities, and food-preparation areas. The second story, with its six to ten rooms, would accommodate a large, multi-generational family of perhaps as many as 20–25 people. These are obviously ideal farmhouses, and with rare exceptions they are unattested in the preceding Late Bronze Age. Despite the fact that this was formerly dubbed "the Israelite type-house," similar structures have recently been brought to light in Transjordan, which may or may not have been part of the "Proto-Israelite" territories. These distinctive houses do, however, characterize later and undisputedly Israelite sites in Western Palestine in the 10th–6th centuries B.C.E. If the house type provides one of the most instructive commentaries on ethnicity, as most archaeologists and anthropologists would maintain, then these unique courtyard houses of the Iron Age reflect a distinctive "mentality" — in this case, one that enshrines an agrarian, family-based lifestyle and its social and communal values.[22]

6 - *Burial Customs*

Unfortunately, thus far we have discovered no cemeteries associated with the hill-country settlements and only an occasional individual 12th–11th century B.C.E. burial elsewhere.[23]

7 - *Dress*

Manner of dress is another well-recognized "ethnic marker," but again our evidence is scant or non-existent, due to the fact that textiles are well preserved in the archaeological record only under exceptional circumstances. Dress is sometimes indicated in tomb or wall paintings, where, for instance, in earlier periods we can clearly distinguish between Egyptians, Canaanites, Assyrians, and others. But we have no such evidence for the 12th–11th centuries B.C.E. and no surviving portraits of Israelites at all, until much later in the Iron Age.[24]

8 – Language

Language is, without doubt, one of the most critical and sensitive indicators of ethnic affiliation and has been so regarded since Herodotus' discussion of the Greek *ethnos*. Currently we have only a handful of putative "early Israelite" inscriptions, including a Hebrew personal name on a jarhandle from Khirbet Radanna and an abecedary (or list of alphabetic characters in order) from 'Izbet Ṣarṭa. The form of the letters is demonstrably Old Canaanite, and this plus other linguistic data from later periods demonstrates that Israelite Hebrew of the Iron Age derived directly from Late Bronze Age Canaanite. But by the 10th century B.C.E. at latest, Hebrew had diverged sufficiently in vocabulary, syntax, orthography, and script so as to constitute a separate, well-developed "national" language. By the Iron II period, Hebrew was distinguished as well from Aramaic, Phoenician, and such languages of Transjordan as Ammonite, Moabite, and Edomite, by both language and script.[25]

9 – Social Organization

Social organization is not nearly as elusive as many non-archaeologists suppose, and it can be inferred from several of the categories of material culture already discussed. In keeping with small-scale agrarian societies in general, the social structure of our hill-country assemblage may best be characterized as kin-based, centered on extended family and clan units, relatively unstratified and with strong "egalitarian" tendencies. Lawrence Stager (1985) has shown that the typical clusters of courtyard houses reflect almost exactly the Biblical ideal of the *mišpāḥa* or "extended multi-generational family," of the Books of Joshua, Judges, and Samuel (later compositions, but set in the Iron I period). This correspondence can scarcely be fortuitous and suggests that later traditions of what I have called the "domestic mode of production" had ancient roots.[26]

10 – Political Structure

Political organization has already been hinted at above. There can be little doubt that the 12th–11th centuries B.C.E. complex represents not only a "pre-urban," but a "pre-state" level of political organization, probably even a "pre-chiefdom" level in the typical parlance of the literature on state-formation processes. Later biblical traditions recall the formative period nostalgically as "tribal" not entirely without reason, but perhaps "segmentary" best describes the early system of political organization.[27] In any case, it contrasts sharply with the Late Bronze Age Canaanite system of city states and also with the contemporary Philistine "feudal" system.

11 – Religion and Culture

Religion, like language, is one of the most fundamental indicators of ethnic identity. The archaeological data for religious belief and practice in the 12th–11th century B.C.E. highland villages consists, on the one hand, of negative evidence: the complete absence of the temples and their impressive paraphernalia that characterized the previous Late Bronze Age Canaanite civilization. Nor is there any trace of the mythological and liturgical literature so well attested from Canaan in this period, much less the organized priesthood and cult personnel who could have produced such a literature.[28]

On the other hand, we do have at least one open cult place, Mazar's "Bull Site" in the tribal territory of Ephraim (Mazar 1982). It is a small hilltop shrine with a low enclosure wall, a standing stone reminiscent of the biblical *māṣṣēbā*, and a few scraps of metal and Iron I pottery. The only outstanding find is a fine bronze bull figurine, almost identical to a Late Bronze example from Hazor and best understood in the light of the iconography of "Bull El," the principal male deity of the old Canaanite pantheon.

Again, we have both elements of continuity and discontinuity with Late Bronze Age Canaan. It is noteworthy that the El cult continues into later Israelite society, the name itself and typical El epithets being common in the older strands of the biblical literature. Thus, what little we can say of the religion of our hill-country settlements suggests that it grew out of the Late Bronze Age Canaanite cult, but it was more in keeping with the simple character of the new settlements, yet on its way toward becoming a new and unique religious syncretism, "Yahwism."[29]

12 – External Relations

By "external relations," I refer to those relationships of a community with outsiders, or "others," that help to define who "we" are. The notions of "us" and "them" will always be, of course, partly subjective, but they are, nonetheless, real as perceptions and thus subject to analysis. In the case of the Iron I hill-country assemblage, it is the relative isolation of the peoples in question that strikes us. Part of this isolation was due to the natural setting of the dozens of small villages in a region that had long been on the somewhat remote frontier of Canaanite civilization, hitherto sparsely settled. It was not so much a matter of physical distance, since the hill-country, at least the foothills, lies in fairly close proximity to the lowlands, but rather a matter of difficulty of access. The new settlements constituted a "mountain redoubt," much like the small Christian enclaves in the mountains of Lebanon today.

There is little evidence of outside trade of any kind. There are none of the Syrian, Egyptian, Cypriot, and Mycenaean imports so characteristic of the previous Late Bronze Age, and scarcely any trace of even the contemporary Philistine "Bichrome" pottery. The overwhelming impression one has is that of an entirely self-sufficient economy and society, one moreover that is not interested in outside contacts, perhaps even hostile to them. The transitional Late Bronze Age/Iron I culture might be said to represent a new group of people in the marginal zones, whose ethnic self-identification is based partly on its sense of being "displaced," both geographically and ideologically.[30] This group's isolation was relatively short-lived, however, in the 12th–11th centuries B.C.E., but it was nevertheless formative — indeed, if I am right, later mythologized in the Hebrew Bible as a "golden age," the *ideal* Israel.

THE IRON I HILL-COUNTRY ASSEMBLAGE: "PROTO-ISRAELITES"?

It is time now to draw together the principal arguments in favor of labeling the Iron I hill country archaeological assemblage as "Israelite" or — as I prefer, on the side of caution — "Proto-Israelite." There are, in my opinion, two arguments that taken together are conclusive.

A Distinctive Iron I Archaeological Assemblage and Ethnos

The first argument is based on analyzing the cultural traits reflected in the archaeological record as outlined above, in order to compare and contrast a putative "early Israel" with *other* Iron I ethnic groups, whose existence and identity is beyond reasonable doubt. The results of such an analysis are tabulated for brevity's sake in Table 1. It will hardly be sufficient to dub these the "X-people," if for no other reason than the well-known reference to "Israel" on the "Victory Stele" of the Egyptian Pharoah Merneptah. Dated closely to 1207 B.C.E., this inscription refers to several ethnic groups in Palestine identified by Egyptian intelligence and sufficiently well-known to be perceived as a threat, among them "Hurrians," the common Egyptian term for the Canaanite population in New Kingdom times (the texts also mentions "Canaanites" directly), and "Israelites," the term followed by the determinative sign for "people," rather than nation-state, the whole phrase being a plural gentilic, thus designating "the Israelite peoples."[31]

The reading "Israel" has never been seriously questioned, and the date of ca. 1207 B.C.E. is fixed within the margin of a very few years. Furthermore, the location of the Egyptian strongholds, of sites like Ashkelon and Gezer, of the "Hurrian" or Canaanite population, and the "Shasu" or nomadic populations of other Egyptian texts can easily be charted on a map of Palestine, and the only area *left* for Merneptah's "Israelites" is in the central hill-country north and south.[32] Thus, we have in the Merneptah inscription a firm extra-Biblical reference to "Israelite peoples" in Palestine, precisely *when* and *where* the recently discovered late 13th–early 12th century B.C.E. settlements are located — and furthermore in what was the heartland of later "biblical Israel," which is even better textually documented (below).

The Merneptah datum *alone* would seem to be sufficient textual warrant for designating the Iron I settlements "Israelite." How do the "revisionists," who as we have seen are skeptical of the very concept of Israelite ethnicity, confront this "inconvenient" datum? Lemche is the most sanguine, although he refers to the inscription as the "so-called Israel-stele." He does concede that the entity in question is to be located somewhere in the central highlands, but he concludes that this evidence has little to do with later, *biblical* "Israel."[33]

Whitelam concedes that the Merneptah stele mentions an entity called "Israel," but he argues that "the term 'Israelite' when applied to these (Iron I) settlements is meaningless" (1996: 228). Apparently that is to be understood as "meaningless" to Whitelam, since it does not meet *his* expectations of significant information. Yet the Merneptah datum tells us all that we *need* to know at this point—that a late 13th-century B.C.E. "Israelite" *ethnic* group exists in the highlands. The archaeological data, which the "revisionists" all refuse to connect with this Israel and scarcely appreciate anyway, reveal much of the rest, such as socioeconomic structure and political organization and even origins, if I am correct.

Thompson, as usual, is the most radical. He simply dismisses the reference to "Israel," declaring that "it does not correspond with the highland Israel or any biblical Israel" (1999: 79). Elsewhere, he contends that the Egyptian term "Israel" is to be paired with the term "Canaan" as a spouse, and that the two are "metaphorical parents of three towns destroyed by the Egyptian army" (1999: 81).[34] What is a sensible person to make of such "scholarship"?

Edelman's treatment of the Merneptah stele is equally tortured. Not only does it yield "almost no firm data about this unit or entity," but the reading "Israel" is suspect and "could just as well be Jezreel," i.e., the Jezreel Valley (1996: 36).

Finkelstein, an archaeologist now virtually in the "revisionist" camp, does somewhat better. In his latest work, he acknowledges that the reference to "Israel" does indicate that some group by that name was in Canaan at the time and that this group is probably to be linked with the highland settlements of the period (Finkelstein and Silberman 2001: 57). But elsewhere, Finkelstein continues to deny that any of the textual or archaeological data distinguishes an *ethnic* group. Thus, he declares that the evidence gives "no sign...of a clearly defined ethnic group. Instead, it seems to be a revolution in lifestyle" (Finkelstein and Silberman 2001: 107). Finkelstein does not seem to understand that "ethnicity" *is* lifestyle! The fact that we moderns do not know all we wish to know about the Israelites' lifestyle or perceptions of themselves in Iron I does not mean that they had no such perceptions. Finkelstein's reluctance to use specific ethnic terms is reminiscent of Lemche's dictum that "the Canaanites of the ancient Near East did not know that they were themselves Canaanites" (Lemche 1991: 152). Yet somehow Lemche "knows" that they were *not*. This elevates "creeping skepticism" from simply a proper critical attitude to an overarching scholarly method.[35]

The Continuity of "Early Israel" and "Biblical Israel"

Even the most doctrinaire of the "revisionists" are forced to concede that there was an "Israel" in Palestine by the mid-9th century B.C.E.—but *only* because a series of Neo-Assyrian records dealing with military campaigns in the west now mentions such an entity (The biblical narratives, of course, are all dismissed as late and unhistorical). For instance, in the Neo-Assyrian annals describing their very first encounter with a coalition of western kings following the battle of Shalmaneser III at Qarqar in central Syria in 853 B.C.E., the text refers to one of the kings as "Ahab of Israel."[36]

Even this explicit reference to Israel, however, is not sufficient to dispel the "revisionists'" doubts (or predilections?). They consistently prefer the later Neo-Assyrian term "house (dynasty) of Omri," or the still later usage "province of Samarina." As Lemche puts it, "there can be no doubt that in the eyes of the Assyrians, after they obtained a firsthand knowledge of the territories of Palestine, Israel was not the name of the Northern Kingdom" (1998b: 53). The extraordinary lengths to which the "revisionists" go to delegitimize even the *name* "Israel" suggests to me that it is ideology, not scholarship, that is at work here. There cannot have *been* an "ancient Israel," because that is a biblical concept (read "social construct" or "fiction").

Despite rather desperate recent attempts to "erase ancient Israel from history" (Halpern

Table 2 Elements of continuity/discontinuity in cultural traits in the archaeological sequence from Iron I to Iron II.

Cultural trait	Mostly continuous	Discontinuous
1 – Settlement Type or Pattern		×
2 – House Type	×	
3 – Demography	×	
4 – Subsistence, Economy	×	
5 – Technology	×	
6 – Pottery	×	
7 – Social Structure	×	
8 – Political Organization		×
9 – Ideology, Art, Religion	×	
10 – Language, Literature	×	
11 – External Relations		×

1995), it should be obvious to any honest and well-informed person that an "Israelite" state (or biblical divided monarchy) did exist in Palestine throughout the era that archaeologists designate the Iron II period, ca. 900–600 B.C.E.[37] The point here is that if it can be shown that the fundamental material culture of this *Iron II* "Israel" is in direct continuity with and derives from that of the Iron I assemblage, then the latter may be legitimately known as "Israelite," or better "Proto-Israelite," as well. Yet virtually no scholar seems to have seen the force of such an argument, which I would regard as impeccable in principle and certainly founded now on ample archaeological evidence.[38] Again, in the interest of brevity, a chart will be used to summarize a mass of data (Table 2).

Note that the only elements of discontinuity in the entire Iron I–II sequence of central Palestine over the span of some 600 years are those three (nos. 1, 8, 11) that have to do with *urbanization* and *centralization* — precisely those traits that in the comparative and cross-cultural literature define "statehood."[39] And the emergence of the state — whether in the conventional 10th century B.C.E. or in the minimalist 9th century B.C.E. — is not only well attested by extensive archaeological evidence, but it also fits remarkably well with the biblical scheme of "tribe to nation," however artificial that may seem to some. Elsewhere, I have argued that when the "core history" of the biblical narratives is isolated, stripped of its mythical and propagandistic elements, it coincides closely with archaeological "facts on the ground," then historians are on reasonably solid ground (Dever 2001a).

Why, then, do I continue to favor the term "Proto-Israelite" for the Iron I assemblage? I do so principally to err on the side of caution — both because "ethnicity" *is* difficult to define archaeologically and also because the objection of some that this "Israel" is not the *same* as the later, biblical "Israel" is sound (as far as it goes). Thus in my view, the conglomerate of peoples of the Iron I highland settlements, although they were neither homogeneous nor constituted anything like a modern nation-state, nor were even conscious of all the implications of the ethnic term "Israelite," were nevertheless the *authentic progenitors* of later biblical Israel in the Iron II period.

Several other scholars, even Finkelstein at times, have adopted the term "Proto-Israelite," while others have objected to it as too cautious or even arbitrary.[40] But archaeologists are familiar and comfortable with various "proto"-terminologies, especially in attempting to define transitional periods like the Late Bronze II–Iron I horizon, where cultural changes are gradual and complex. The "Israelite" peoples and states did exist. But they did not spring into existence overnight: they had a long prehistory. Much later biblical writers and editors knew that.

CONCLUSION

The current ideologically driven trend to deny the earliest Israelites their ethnic identity is ominous—the first step in an agenda that would erase ancient and biblical Israel from history, from memory, and from any claim to moral authority. Fortunately, there is ample empirical evidence from archaeology to frustrate this scheme and to discredit its perpetrators.

NOTES

1 This chapter was written in 2001 and was only slightly updated in 2003. Later literature cannot be discussed now but would include my own *Who Were the Early Israelites, and Where Did They Come From?* (Grand Rapids, MI: Eerdmans, 2003), as well as, specifically on the question of archaeology and "Israelite ethnicity," the following: E. Bloch-Smith, "Israelite Ethnicity in Iron I: Archaeology Preserves What Is Remembered and What Is Forgotten in Israel's History," *Journal of Biblical Literature* 122 (2003): 401–25; R. Miller, "Identifying Earliest Israel," *Bulletin of the American Schools of Oriental Research* 333 (2004): 55–68; A. E. Killebrew, *Biblical Peoples and Ethnicity: An Archaeological Study of Egyptians, Canaanites, Philistines and Early Israelites* (Leiden: Brill, 2005); R. Kletter, "Can a Proto-Israelite Please Stand Up?" Pp. 573–86 in *"I Will Speak the Riddles of Ancient Times:" Archaeological and Historical Studies in Honor of Amihai Mazar on the Occasion of his Sixtieth Birthday,* eds. A. M. Maeir and P. de Miroschedji (Winona Lake, IN: Eisenbrauns, 2006); A. Faust, *Israel's Ethnogenesis: Settlement, Interaction, Expansion and Resistance* (London: Equinox, 2006).

2 For representative works of Meyers on Jewish and early Christian ethnicity, see Meyers and Chancey 2000; Meyers 1993.

3 For the basic survey data, see the original report and brief synthesis in Finkelstein 1988; and cf. the final report in Finkelstein and Lederman 1997. See also the review of the latter in Dever 1999b.

4 Full references to the literature will be found conveniently in Dever 1995a; 1995b; 1997b; 1998. The response from biblical scholars other than those of the "revisionist" or "minimalist" school has been scant, but see Gottwald 1993; Stager 1998; McNutt 1999: 64–103; Miller and Callaway 1999 for balanced, centrist interpretations of the data. For the "revisionists," see n. 5, below.

5 See, for instance, Grabbe 1997. The basic literature and a summary of various schools of thought will be found in Dever 1999a. See also my own later treatments in Dever 2001a; 2001b, and add now Lemche 1998a; 1998b; Thompson 1999. For an authoritative survey of contemporary scholarship on the Hebrew Bible in general, with a critique of "revisionist" ideology similar to my own, see now Barr 2000 (and cf. Lemche's response in 2000).

6 See references in works cited in nn. 4–5 above, especially essays in Fritz and Davies 1996; and cf. Lemche 1998a; 1998b; Thompson 1999 for the latest "revisionist" treatments.

7 Thompson 1997: 177. Thompson's entire chapter (in Grabbe 1997) consists of a vicious, often slanderous attack on my early, positivist views of "Israelite ethnicity," such as Dever 1993; 1995a; 1995b. Thompson's nihilism regarding any historical "Canaanites" is undoubtedly borrowed from Lemche 1991; but see the decisive refutation of Rainey 1996. Thompson's similar skepticism regarding the archaeological identification of "Philistines" (as 1997: 173 reveals his complete ignorance of archaeological scholarship of the past 15 years); cf., for example, Stager 1995; 1998 and references there. On archaeological data and the "ethnicity" of Canaanites, Philistines, and the peoples of Transjordan, see further Dever 1995a; 1998.

8 See Whitelam 1996: *passim*; and cf. my critique of Whitelam's ideological biases and his distortion of the archaeological data in Dever 1998; 1999a. Even Whitelam's fellow-"revisionist" Lemche (1997: 151) has pointed out the absurdity of his attempt to identify

the *Iron Age* population of Palestine as "Palestinians;" cf. also Thompson 1997: 179. This is simply ideological cant. Lately Thompson has even refused to use the term "Israelite," preferring to see the people (not an *ethnos*) in question as something like "the Iron Age population of southern Syria's marginal fringe;" cf. 1997: 176–77, 184; 1999: 168, 190, 235.

9 Edelman, to her credit, has done some archaeological fieldwork, and she is currently one of the staff of Mazar's excavations at Tel Rehov. And, despite her recent affiliation with Davies, Whitelam, and other "revisionists" at Sheffield, she is not as radical as they are. Nevertheless, her basic "minimalist" position is revealed in such statements as "there are no *artifactual* remains that can consistently be used to understand a group's ethnicity" (1996: 26; italics hers).

10 See references in nn. 4–6 above, especially Dever 1998; 1999a; 2000; 2001a.

11 See Edelman 1996: 39–54. Despite some reference to the archaeological data and literature, this entire discussion lacks authority. It is typical of the "monologues" that result when most biblicists resort on their own to archaeology; cf. Halpern 1997.

12 On the post-modernist background of much "revisionist" discourse, see Dever 1998; 2000; 2001a. Ironically, "post-modernism's" overriding emphasis on "multi-culturalism" ought to have stimulated a renewed appreciation of the ethnic distinctiveness of many cultures. It is we archaeologists who are the real multi-culturalists, as the astute social critic Camille Paglia has pointed out (1999). On Finkelstein's flirtation with the "post-Zionist" version of post-modernism, see below.

13 See Finkelstein 1996: *passim*; and cf. his further attack on my views in Finkelstein 1997. These articles actually go back to an ideological shift in the early 1990s, which Finkelstein rarely acknowledges or cites. For his latest reversion to using the term "Israel," see Finkelstein and Silberman (2001: for instance, throughout Chapter 4, 97–122). The popular book referred to here is Finkelstein and Silberman 2001; cf. the review in Dever 2001b.

14 In addition to Finkelstein 1996; 1997, discussed above; my 1995a; 1998; Kletter 1999; and Faust 2000b, I can cite only Bunimovitz and Yasur-Landau 1996, and Bunimovitz and Faust (2001; 2003).

15 See Kletter 1999. Note the overweening use of the terms "invention" by Whitelam (1996), and "myth" by Thompson (1999). Whitelam and Thompson insist that the ancient Israelites and Judeans did not know who they were; but *they* know.

16 See n. 12, above.

17 Oddly enough, only Edelman (1996)—a Biblical scholar—has employed such a "trait list," although superficially; cf. n. 11 above. The scant works of other biblicists, such as Sparks (1998), ignore the archaeological data completely and focus on texts, with predictably minimal and quite unrealistic results. On Finkelstein's fundamental skepticism regarding "ethnic traits," see, for instance, 1996: 202–6. He sees only diet—i.e., the statistically significant absence of pig bones in early Iron Age hillcountry sites—as a valid "ethnic marker;" cf. Finkelstein 1996: 206; 1997: 227–30; and further below. Obviously, I think that there we have many other ethnic markers. On pottery, for instance, see Bunimovitz and Yasur-Landau 1996 ("Philistine ethnicity").

18 The fundamental evidence, on which all reconstructions necessarily rest, are first the survey data, for which see Finkelstein 1988; Finkelstein and Na'aman 1994; Finkelstein and Lederman 1997. The few excavated sites would include 'Ai (Callaway 1993); Radanna (Callaway and Cooley 1971; Callaway 1983); 'Izbet Ṣarṭa (Finkelstein 1989); Shiloh (Finkelstein 1993a); and Giloh (Mazar 1981). One might add Tel Masos (Fritz and Kempinski 1983; cf. Dever 1990); the "Bull Site" (Mazar 1982); and the Mt. Ebal installation (Zertal 1986–87). A convenient, semi-popular summary of the evidence is Dever 1992b; cf. also Stager 1985; 1998.

19 For the figures, see Finkelstein 1988: 296–97, 330–35; 1994: 154. Cf. Stager 1985: 3, 21, 23, with slightly different results (ca. 17,000 in LB; ca. 48,000 in early Iron I). Elsewhere, Stager (1998: 135) documents an increase in the number of individual sites from 36 in LB to 319 in early Iron I, most of the latter newly founded in the 12th century B.C.E.

20 On these aspects of technology, cf. Finkelstein 1988: 202–4, 264–69; Stager 1985: 5–10, and full references in both. I have argued strongly that it is not a single, innovative technology that characterizes the new hill-country archaeological assemblage in Iron I, but rather the distinctive *combination* (Dever 1992b: 38, 79; 1995a: 207–8). Finkelstein's criticisms (1993b: 64–65; 1996: 201–2; 1997: 222–23) are a distortion of my views. Originally, he himself had emphasized the importance of such technologies as terracing, the hewing of cisterns, and the construction of silos—at least for the Iron I settlements west of the central ridge, i.e., the majority (1988: 202–4; 264–69). One aspect of technology—ceramics—has been omitted here, since the discussion is very technical; but see Dever 1995a, and contrast Finkelstein 1996: 204.

21 Cf. Finkelstein 1996: 206; 1997: 227–30; Hesse and Wapnish 1997. At least Finkelstein and I agree on the ethnic significance of this particular datum.

22 On the early Iron Age courtyard houses, cf. Stager 1985: 11–17; Finkelstein 1988: 254–59; 1996: 204–6. On its development and diffusion in Iron II, see the extensive treatment of Holladay 1992. In a forthcoming paper, Bunimovitz—originally a skeptic regarding "ethnicity" in the archaeological record—has demonstrated convincingly that the ubiquitous courtyard or "four-room" house in the Iron II period reflects precisely an "Israelite" cultural ideal; cf. Bunimovitz and Faust 2003.

23 See Bloch-Smith 1992: 60, 64. It has even been suggested that the "Proto-Israelites" typically cremated their dead, but that is extremely unlikely. On mortuary customs and ethnicity, see Brown 1971.

24 For perhaps the only real portraits we have on the famous Neo-Assyrian depictions of the fall of Lachish in 701 B.C.E. see Ussishkin 1982: 84, 88, 100, 113.

25 For the ʿIzbet Ṣarṭa abecedary, see Demsky 1977; for the Radanna jarhandle, see Callaway and Cooley 1971: 20–21. On the related Iron Age West Semitic languages and scripts in general, see Naveh 1982.

26 See further Dever 1991a: 201; the model is adapted from Sahlins (1972). This is in some ways similar to Gottwald's "communitarian" model (1993).

27 The issue of whether Israel's "tribal" origins were historical or simply one aspect of the nationalist ideology of the later literary traditions is vexed. For my own view, with references to the wider literature, see Dever 1997a. Cf. also the exhaustive but rather ideological discussion of Gottwald 1979: 224–28, 429–76.

28 For a general discussion of the archaeological evidence for early Israelite religion, see Dever 1997b and references there.

29 For the latest treatments of the development of Yahwism, see Day 2000; most other standard treatments by biblical scholars are deficient, because they fail to utilize the archaeological and art historical data. For my own synthesis, see Dever 1992b; 1997b.

30 The term "displaced" owes much to Norman Gottwald's pioneering study (1979), although I would place less stress on the *ideological* aspects—simply because the archaeological evidence is scant and ambiguous.

31 The latest, exhaustive treatment is that of my student Michael Hasel (1999).

32 For the best map locating the peoples referred to on the Merneptah stele, see Yurco 1990: 34; note the obvious lacuna in the central hill-country, where I would place the "Proto-Israelites."

33 See Lemche 1998a: 75; 1998b: 35–38, 42, 57. Lemche concedes that the stele does refer to "some sort of ethnic (*sic*) unity, which was identifiable as far as it had its own name, Israel" (1998b: 36). But he thinks that what this is not "easy to ascertain" (1998b: 36). Perhaps not easy—but possible.

34 In a session of the Second International Congress on Ancient Near Eastern Archaeology in Copenhagen in May 2000, where Thompson and I presented papers opposite each other, he went so far as to suggest that the Egyptian scribe may have simply invented the name "Israel," and that its being identical with the biblical "Israel" is coincidental. Leading Egyptologists with whom I have consulted consider all of Thompson's opinions absurd.

35 On "creeping skepticism", see Hallo 1990; and cf. my expansion of this as part of my critique of the "revisionists" in the conclusion of Dever 2001a.

36 See, for example, the reference in Lemche 1998b: 52. Nevertheless, Lemche and Thompson both regularly ignore this clear extra-biblical reference to a 9th-century B.C.E. "Israel"; see below.

37 Note that standard recent archaeological handbooks devote hundreds of pages to this Iron Age "Israel," never once supposing that it is not consonant in many or even most ways with "biblical Israel;" cf. Weippert 1988 (264 pages); Mazar 1990 (127 pages); and Ben-Tor 1992 (71 pages). Why is this evidence never cited by the "revisionists"?

38 Even Finkelstein, who has reservations about my term "*Proto*-Israelite (see n. 40 below), agrees unequivocally with the argument based on Iron I–II continuity, which he says "is doubtless correct" (1996: 200). For details, see Dever 1995a: 207–10.

39 See the full exposition in Dever 1997c. The "revisionists," while vociferously denying that there was an early Israelite state, never really define "statehood," nor do they show familiarity with any of the extensive anthropological and archaeological literature on what are called "state formation processes."

40 For the introduction and rationale of the term "Proto-Israelite," see Dever 1991b: 87 and subsequently 1992a; 1993; 1995a: 208–10; 1997b: 42–45. Finkelstein initially accepted the term, then rejected it, and now (1996) uses it without comment. Mazar (2003), on the other hand, argues that it should be abandoned as needlessly hesitant. Similarly, Stager (1998) speaks without qualification of an early "Israel" in the 12th–11th century B.C.E.

REFERENCES

Barr, J.
2000 *History and Ideology in the Old Testament: Biblical Studies at the End of a Millennium.* Oxford: Oxford University.

Barth, F. (ed.)
1969 *Ethnic Groups and Boundaries: The Social Organization of Culture Difference.* Boston: Little, Brown and Company.

Ben-Tor, A. (ed.)
1992 *The Archaeology of Ancient Israel.* New Haven: Yale University.

Bloch-Smith, E.
1992 *Judahite Burial Practices and Beliefs About the Dead.* Sheffield: Sheffield Academic.

Brett, M. G. (ed.)
1996 *Ethnicity and the Bible.* Leiden: Brill.

Brown, J. A. (ed.)
1971 *Approaches to the Social Dimensions of Mortuary Practices.* Washington, DC: Society of American Archaeology.

Bunimovitz, S., and Faust, A.
2001 Chronological Separation, Geographical Segregation or Ethnic Demarcation? Ethnography and the Iron Age Low Chronology. *Bulletin of the American Schools of Oriental Research* 322: 1–10.
2003 Building Identity: The Four Room House and the Israelite Mind. Pp. 411–23 in Symbiosis, Symbolism and the Power of the Past: Canaan Ancient Israel and Their Neighbors, eds. W. G. Dever and S. Gitin. Winona Lake, IN: Eisenbrauns.

Bunimovitz, S., and Yasur-Landau, A.
1996 Philistine and Israelite Pottery: A Comparative Approach to the Question of Pots and People. *Tel Aviv* 23: 88–102.

Callaway, J. A.
1983 A Visit With Ahilud. *Biblical Archaeology Review* 9, no. 5: 42–53.
1993 Ai. Pp. 39–45 in *New Encyclopedia of Archaeological Excavations in the Holy Land*, ed. E. Stern. Jerusalem: Israel Exploration Society.

Callaway, J. A., and Cooley, R. E.
1971 A Salvage Excavation at Radanah, in Bireh. *Bulletin of the American Schools of Oriental Research* 201: 9–19.

Day, J.
2000 *Yahweh and the Gods and Goddesses of Canaan.* Sheffield: Sheffield Academic.

Demsky, A.
1977 A Proto-Canaanite Abecedary Dating from the Period of the Judges and Its Implications for the History of the Alphabet. *Tel Aviv* 4: 1–13.

Dever, W. G.
1990 Archaeology and Israelite Origins: Review Article. *Bulletin of the American Schools of Oriental Research* 279: 89–95.
1991a Unresolved Issues in the Early History of Israel: Toward a Synthesis of Archaeological and Textual Reconstructions. Pp. 195–208 in *The Bible and the Politics of Exegesis: Essays in Honor of Norman K. Gottwald on his Sixty-Fifth Birthday*, eds. D. Jobling, P. L. Day and G. T. Sheppard. Cleveland, OH: Pilgrim.
1991b Archaeological Data on the Israelite Settlement: A Review of Two Recent Works. *Bulletin of the American Schools of Oriental Research* 284: 77–90.
1992a Archaeology and the Israelite "Conquest." Pp. 545–58 in *Anchor Bible Dictionary*, vol. 3, ed. D. N. Freedman. New York, NY: Doubleday.
1992b How to Tell a Canaanite from an Israelite. Pp. 27–56 in *The Rise of Ancient Israel*, ed. H. Shanks. Washington, DC: Biblical Archaeology Society.
1993 Cultural Continuity, Ethnicity in the Archaeological Record, and the Question of Israelite Origins. *Eretz-Israel* 24: 22*–33*.
1995a Ceramics, Ethnicity, and the Question of Israel's Origins. *Biblical Archaeology Review* 58, no. 4: 200–13.
1995b Will the Real Israel Please Stand Up? Archaeology and Israelite Historiography: Part I. *Bulletin of the American Schools of Oriental Research* 279: 61–80.
1997a Philology, Theology, and Archaeology: What Kind of History Do We Want, and What Is Possible? Pp. 290–310 in *The Archaeology of Israel: Constructing the Past, Interpreting the Present*, eds. N. A. Silberman and D. Small. Sheffield: Sheffield Academic.
1997b Archaeology and the Emergence of Early Israel. Pp. 20–50 in *Archaeology and Biblical Interpretation*, ed. J. R. Bartlett. London: Routledge.
1997c Archaeology and the "Age of Solomon:" A Case-Study in Archaeology and Historiography. Pp. 217–51 in *The Age of Solomon: Scholarship at the Turn of the Millenium*, ed. L. K Handy. Leiden: Brill.

1998 Archaeology, Ideology, and the Quest for an "Ancient" or "Biblical" Israel. *Near Eastern Archaeology* 61, no. 1: 39–52.

1999a Histories and Nonhistories of Ancient Israel. *Bulletin of the American Schools of Oriental Research* 316: 89–195.

1999b Review of I. Finkelstein and Z. Lederman, eds., Highlands of Many Cultures: The Southern Samaria Survey, The Sites, Tel Aviv: Institute of Archaeology, 1997, *Bulletin of the American Schools of Oriental Research* 313: 87–88.

2000 Save Us from Postmodern Malarkey. *Biblical Archaeology Review* 26, no. 2: 28–35, 68.

2001a *What Did the Biblical Writers Know, and When Did They Know It? What Archaeology and the Bible Can Tell Us About Ancient Israel.* Grand Rapids, MI: Eerdmans.

2001b Excavating the Hebrew Bible, Or Burying It Again? *Bulletin of the American Schools of Oriental Research* 322: 67–77.

Edelman, D. V.

1996 Ethnicity and Early Israel. Pp. 25–55 in *Ethnicity and the Bible*, ed. M. G. Brett. Leiden: Brill.

Faust, A.

2000a The Rural Community in Ancient Israel during Iron Age II. *Bulletin of the American Schools of Oriental Research* 317: 17–39.

2000b Ethnic Complexity in Northern Israel During Iron Age II. *Palestine Exploration Quarterly* 132: 2–27.

Finkelstein, I.

1988 *The Archaeology of the Israelite Settlement.* Jerusalem: Israel Exploration Society.

1989 *'Izbet Sartah: An Early Iron Age Site near Rosh Ha'ayin, Israel.* British Archaeological Reports International Series 299. Oxford: British Archaeological Reports.

1993a *Shiloh: The Archaeology of a Biblical Site.* Tel Aviv: Institute of Archaeology, Tel Aviv University.

1993b Response. Pp. 63–69 in *The Rise of Israel*, ed. H. Shanks. Washington, DC: Biblical Archaeological Society.

1994 The Emergence of Israel: A Phase in the Cyclic History of Canaan in the Third and Second Millennia BCE. Pp.150–78 in *From Nomadism to Monarchy: Archaeological and Historical Aspects of Early Israel*, eds. I. Finkelstein and N. Na'aman. Jerusalem: Israel Exploration Society.

1996 Ethnicity and Origin of the Iron I Settlers in the Highlands of Canaan: Can the Real Israel Stand Up? *Biblical Archaeologist* 59, no. 4: 198–212.

1997 Pots and Peoples Revisited: Ethnic Boundaries in the Iron Age. Pp. 216–37 in *The Archaeology of Israel: Constructing the Past, Interpreting the Present*, eds. W. A. Silberman and D. Small. Sheffield: Sheffield Academic.

Finkelstein, I., and Na'aman, N. (eds.)

1994 *From Nomadism to Monarchy: Archaeological and Historical Aspects of Early Israel.* Jerusalem: Israel Exploration Society.

Finkelstein, I., and Lederman Z. (eds.)

1997 *Highlands of Many Cultures: The Southern Samaria Survey, The Sites.* Monographs of the Institute of Archaeology, Tel Aviv University, 14. Tel Aviv: Institute of Archaeology, Tel Aviv University.

Finkelstein I., and Silberman, N. A.

2001 *The Bible Unearthed: Archaeology's New Vision of Ancient Origin of Its Sacred Texts.* New York, NY: Free Press.

Fritz, V., and Davies, P. R. (eds.)

1996 *The Origins of the Ancient Israelite States.* Sheffield: Sheffield Academic.

Fritz, V., and Kempinski, A. (eds.)

1983 *Ergebnisse der Ausgrabungen auf der Hirbet el-Mšāš (Tel Māśōś) 1972–1975.* Wiesbaden: Harrassowitz.

Grabbe, L. L. (ed.)

1997 *Can a "History of Israel" Be Written?* Sheffield: Sheffield Academic.

Gottwald, N. K.

1979 *The Tribes of Yahweh: A Sociology of Liberated Israel, 1250–1050 B.C.E.* Maryknoll, NY: Orbis.

1993 Method and Hypothesis in Reconstructing the Social History of Early Israel. *Eretz-Israel* 24: *77–*82.

Hallo, W. W.

1990 The Limits of Skepticism. *Journal of the American Oriental Society* 110: 187–99.

Halpern, B.

1995 Erasing History: The Minimalist Assault in Ancient Israel. *Bible Review* 11, no. 6: 29–35, 47.

1997 Text and Artifact: Two Monologues. Pp. 311–41 in *The Archaeology of Israel: Constructing the Past, Interpreting the Present*, eds. N. A. Silberman and D. Small. Sheffield: Sheffield Academic.

Hasel, M. G.

1999 *Domination and Resistance: Egyptian Military Activity in the Southern Levant, 1300–1185 B.C.* Leiden: Brill.

Hesse, B., and Wapnish, P.
1997 Can Pig Bones Be Used for Ethnic Diagnosis in the Ancient Near East? Pp. 238–70 in *The Archaeology of Israel: Constructing The Past, Interpreting the Present*, eds. N. A. Silberman and D. Small. Sheffield: Sheffield Academic.

Holladay, J. S., Jr.
1992 House, Israelite. Pp. 308–18 in *Anchor Bible Dictionary*, vol. 3, ed. D. N. Freedman. New York, NY: Doubleday.

Jones, S.
1997 *The Archaeology of Ethnicity: Constructing Identities in the Past and Present*. London: Routledge.

Kletter, R.
1999 Pots and Polities: Material Remains of Late Iron Age Judah in Relation to Its Political Borders. *Bulletin of the American Schools of Oriental Research* 314: 19–54.

Lemche, N. P.
1991 *The Canaanites and Their Land*. Sheffield: Sheffield Academic.
1997 Clio Is Also Among the Muses! Keith W. Whitelam and the History of Palestine: A Review and a Commentary. Pp. 123–55 in *Can a "History of Israel" Be Written?*, ed. L. L. Grabbe. Sheffield: Sheffield Academic.
1998a *Prelude to Israel's Past: Background and Beginnings of Israelite History and Identity*. Peabody, MA: Hendrickson.
1998b *The Israelites in History and Tradition*. Library of Ancient Israel. Louisville, KY: Westminster /John Knox.
2000 Ideology and the History of Ancient Israel. *Scandinavian Journal of the Old Testament* 14, no. 2: 165–93.

Mazar, A.
1981 Giloh: An Early Israelite Settlement Site near Jerusalem. *Israel Exploration Journal* 31: 1–36.
1982 The "Bull Site" – An Iron Age I Open Cult Place. *Bulletin of the American Schools of Oriental Research* 247: 27–42.
1990 *Archaeology of the Land of the Bible 10,000–586 B.C.E.* New York, NY: Doubleday.
2003 Remarks on Biblical Traditions and Archaeological Evidence Concerning Early Israel. Pp. 85–98 in *Symbiosis, Symbolism and the Power of the Past: Canaan Ancient Israel and Their Neighbors*, eds. W. G. Dever and S. Gitin. Winona Lake, IN: Eisenbrauns.

McNutt, P. M.
1999 *Reconstructing the Society of Ancient Israel*. Library of Ancient Israel. Louisville, KY: Westminister/John Knox.

McGuire, R. H.
1982 The Study of Ethnicity in Historical Archaeology. *Journal of Anthropological Archaeology* 1: 159–78.

Meyers, E. M.
1993 Identifying Religious and Ethnic Groups Through Archaeology. Pp. 738–46 in *Biblical Archaeology Today, 1990: Proceedings of the Second International Congress on Biblical Jerusalem, June 1990*, eds. J. Aviram and A. Biran. Jerusalem: Israel Exploration Society.

Meyers, E. M., and Chancey, M.
2000 How Jewish Was Sepphoris in Jesus' Time? *Biblical Archaeology Review* 26, no. 1: 18–33, 61.

Miller, J. M., and Callaway, J. A.
1999 The Settlement in Canaan: The Period of the Judges. Pp. 55–89 in *Ancient Israel: From Abraham to the Roman Destruction of the Temple*, ed. H. Shanks. Revised and expanded edition. Washington: Biblical Archaeological Society.

Naveh, J.
1982 *Early History of the Alphabet: An Introduction to West Semitic Epigraphy and Paleography*. Leiden: Brill.

Olivier, L., and Coudart, A.
1995 French Tradition and the Central Place of History in the Human Sciences: Preamble to a Dialogue Between Robinson Crusoe and His Man Friday. Pp. 363–81 in *Theory in Archaeology: A World Perspective*, ed. P. J. Ucko. London: Routledge.

Paglia, C.
1999 The Right Kind of Multiculturalism. *The Wall Street Journal*, September 30, 1999: 2.

Rainey, A.
1996 Who is a Canaanite? A Review of the Textual Evidence. *Bulletin of the American Schools of Oriental Research* 304: 1–15.

Sahlins, M. D.
1972 *Stone Age Economics*. Chicago, IL: Aldine.

Sparks, K. L.
1998 *Ethnicity and Identity in Ancient Israel: Prolegomena to the Study of Ethnic Sentiments and Their Expression in the Hebrew Bible*. Winona Lake, IN: Eisenbrauns.

Stager, L. E.

1985 The Archaeology of the Family in Ancient Israel. *Bulletin of the American Schools of Oriental Research* 260: 1–35.

1995 The Impact of the Sea Peoples (1185–1050 BCE). Pp. 332–48 in *The Archaeology of Society in the Holy Land,* ed. T. E. Levy. London: Leicester University.

1998 Forging an Identity: The Emergence of Ancient Israel. Pp. 123–75 in *The Oxford History of the Biblical World*, ed. M. D. Coogan. New York, NY: Oxford University.

Thompson, T. L.

1997 Defining History and Ethnicity in the South Levant. Pp. 166–87 in *Can a "History of Israel" Be Written?,* ed. L. L. Grabbe. Sheffield: Sheffield Academic.

1999 *The Mythic Past: Biblical Archaeology and the Myth of Israel.* New York, NY: Basic Books.

Ussishkin, D.

1982 *The Conquest of Lachish by Sennacherib.* Tel-Aviv: Institute of Archaeology, Tel-Aviv University.

Weippert, H.

1988 *Palästina in vorhellenistischer Zeit.* Munich: Beck.

Whitelam, K. W.

1996 *The Invention of Ancient Israel: The Silencing of Palestinian History.* London: Routledge.

Yurco, F. J.

1990 3,200-Year-Old Picture of Israelites Found in Egypt. *Biblical Archaeology Review* 16, no. 5: 20–38.

Zertal, A.

1985 Has Joshua's Altar Been Found on Mt. Ebal? *Biblical Archaeology Review* 11, no. 1: 26–45.

1986–87 An Early Iron Age Cultic Site on Mount Ebal: Excavation Seasons 1982–1987. *Tel Aviv* 13–14: 105–65.

Chapter 6

From Field Crops to Food: Attributing Gender and Meaning to Bread Production in Iron Age Israel*

by Carol Meyers

Decades ago, the field projects carried out in Upper Galilee by Eric Meyers and his colleagues had as their goal the recovery of the village context as well as the monumental (synagogue) architecture present at those sites.[1] Similarly, his team working in Lower Galilee at Sepphoris, while uncovering or exploring stunning public buildings — the palatial Roman building with Dionysos mosaic and the Roman theater — also conducted extensive excavations in the residential quarter on the western acropolis.[2] In attending to the remains of domestic as well as communal activity, Meyers and his associates have recovered the kind of data that allow for the understanding of household life and, consequently, of the gendered aspects of that life.

Although this chapter deals with an earlier period — the Iron Age rather than the Roman–Byzantine era — its focus on households acknowledges and celebrates the fact that by his holistic approach to ancient Jewish sites Eric Meyers has contributed in important ways to the possibility for studying households and their activities. And, on a more personal note, this essay about food production is dedicated to him also because he has contributed bountiful intellectual and emotional, as well as edible, food to our marital table for over four decades.

HOUSEHOLD ARCHAEOLOGY AND GENDER

The processes involved in converting a major nutritional source — cereal crops — into edible forms were carried out in social units designated as households. Except for the most elite sectors of the population, daily grain-processing activities played a central role in the survival of virtually all families in Syria-Palestine in the Iron Age. Because households have left substantial traces in the archaeological record, the investigation of this set of household activities can draw upon material remains recovered by field projects. Using those archaeological data must take into account, first and foremost, the nature of households.

As has long been understood by social anthropologists, arriving at a definition of a household that is universal across cultures is virtually impossible. However, certain features of a household in premodern societies can be identified. For one thing, households involve groups of people but are not coterminous with families. Although they overlap, households and families are distinct social phenomena (Bender 1967: 495; Wilk and Netting 1984: 3). Similarly, despite considerable overlap, households and domiciles are not the same, the latter being structural configurations that constitute living places for certain groups of people. In short, a household is a built environment consisting of not only persons and their "hardware" (their material culture, including their domicile and all its associated artifacts) but also their activities and other aspects of their daily lives (Rapoport 1994: 461). Thus, demographic and architectural aspects of Syro-Palestinian households in the Iron Age were intertwined with economic ones (see Goody 1972: 106).

More specifically, a household in premodern agrarian societies consists of three elements. First, as a demographic or social unit it comprises varying configurations of affinals and consanguinals as well as, sometimes, unrelated servants or sojourners. Also, as a demographic unit it encompasses human reproductive functions. Second, it has material components, namely, a residential structure along with the items — artifacts — that enable its inhabitants to meet their physical and social as well as spiritual or ideological needs. These material aspects make it possible for households to be recovered archaeologically. The third element is behavioral; it is the set of activities carried out in the household context to meet the needs of its residents.

Seen this way, a household emerges as a fundamental organizing feature of human society because it is the level at which premodern social groups articulate directly with the environment in order to survive. That is, a household can be conceptualized as a strategy that both participates in and utilizes material culture in order to meet the productive and reproductive needs of humans (Wilk and Rathje 1982: 618). The economic dimension of this conceptualization is based on the simple premise, going back to Polanyi (1944: 53), that people produce for their own sake and/or for that of the group(s) to which they belong (Henshaw 1999: 79). Because it is the site of fundamental and essential activities that are embedded in material culture, the household is susceptible to analyses of how people organize their economic production and of the social interactions rooted in productive activities (Whitridge 1998: 2).

Near Eastern archaeologists, especially those of us working in the so-called historical periods, have rarely, if ever, been willing to venture into the business of analyzing the social context of the material culture of everyday life. Part of the reason for this is that such analysis is difficult; complex interpretative processes are required in order to move from physical remains to theories about social dynamics among household members. But more likely, the availability of written documents from the Bronze and Iron Ages has made it seem, perhaps falsely, that we have access to more direct and reliable sources of information about the past than the silent artifacts themselves. This notion persists even though material remains (unlike most documents) possess contemporaneity with the societies that interest us, especially for the periods of the Hebrew Bible, and, even more important, are not subject to the distortions and biases of written records.

Another factor that has virtually precluded consideration of households and their inhabitants is that the information in written sources, notably the "historical" books of the Hebrew Bible, has seduced us into viewing archaeology primarily as the means to trace — or even verify — the large-scale social and political processes involving tribes and nation-states that are presumably recorded in Scripture. The text-driven agendas of the archaeology of the Iron Age of Syria-Palestine have thus, in their focus on polities and ethnicities, neglected the primary units of society, family households. The tribe or city state or kingdom has been labeled the primary unit of social organization (as by Gottwald 1979: 237–92). Yet, it may be more appropriate to consider the household, which is the basic unit of production and reproduction, as the primary unit. As the social and physical spaces in which all members of a culture experience their daily lives, households are the necessary foundations for the more complex socio-political structures of any society.

In redressing the archaeological emphasis on diachronic issues that have characterized Syro-Palestinian archaeology from the outset (C. Meyers 1997b: 273–74), we would do well to learn from archaeologists examining prehistoric cultures. Prehistorians have long been aware of the centrality of households; and for several decades they have been quite explicit in their practice of "household archaeology," by which is meant a micro-scale investigation of the spatial components and organizations of the built environment in order to understand the economic activities and the social relations of this basic unit of society (Steadman 1996). By using the excavated architectural and artifactual remains as the main data base, the nature of diverse subsistence tasks and of divided task performance can be ascertained, the relations of production and consumption can be inferred, and even associated ideologies can be theorized. The investigation of households clearly holds the promise of providing information available in no other way about human behavior. Households have too often been neglected by Syro-Palestinian archaeologists intent on recovering the monumental architecture — temples, palaces, fortifications — of the elites (C. Meyers 1988: 17-18). It is now time to acknowledge that the ubiquity and abundance of households signify the availability of information about how life in the Iron Age was experienced by most of the population, not just the military, political, and cultic leadership.

In thinking of the household as the locus of peoples' lives, the potential of household archaeology for learning about women as well as men becomes apparent (C. Meyers 2003a). Males may have been dominant in military, political, and cultic leadership, but females were present in approximately the same proportions as males in family households. If archaeology can, in fact, situate household architecture and artifact assemblages within an economic and social context, then the gendered relations of production, present in all known human societies, can be explored (Lawrence 1999: 121–23). Too often, human behavior is equated with males. The examination of the gendered behavior of household members allows us to redress this androcentric tendency; it makes it possible to "identify or assert the presence of the activities of women" (Conkey and Gero 1997: 414–15), some of which can be differentiated from the activities of men in the archaeological record.

Identifying the activities of either gender involves the gender attribution of sets of behaviors constituting productivity. In premodern agrarian societies, both women and men must contribute substantially, perhaps in nearly equal measure, to the subsistence tasks of a household unit (C. Meyers 1983; cf. C. Meyers 1988: 168–73). However, for reasons of efficiency and for strengthening group life through cooperation and interdependence (Lenski and Lenski 1987: 44–45), not everyone performs all the same tasks. Although there is some overlap, with women and men and even children working together at the same operations (such as harvesting) at certain times, most household labor is divided into tasks carried out more often or even exclusively by one gender rather than the other. Even in the simplest societies, gender is a key factor in the allocation of subsistence tasks (Brown 1970; Costin 1996: 112; Kent 1990: 148).

The division of labor by gender has long been recognized and recorded by social scientists. Consequently, evaluating the contributions of women or men to household life as a prelude to reconstructing gender relations is contingent upon identifying women's work as distinct from men's work. Virtually no tasks, however, are universally ascribed to a single gender, whereby women and men of all cultures always perform certain household jobs. To be sure, some tasks are linked more strongly with one gender rather than another, as will become clear below. Yet, because the gender of those who perform specialized tasks in any society cannot be assumed, identifying the gender of major household activities is a necessary step in understanding the role of women and men in the household and in the larger communities in which households are embedded. Because bread (or, more generally, food made from grains) was a critical staple of the diet of Iron Age agrarians, the gender attribution of bread production is an appropriate test case for examining the daily activities of Israelite households and the power dynamics that played out in the relationships of household members.

BREAD PRODUCTION

The preparation, distribution, and consumption of a cereal—wheat and barley in the case of the biblical world—probably consumed a considerable portion of household activity in terms of time and space. Because only the seeds of cereals but not the outer husks are edible and because the nutritional starch in the seeds cannot be easily digested in raw form, a complex series of processing activities—parching or soaking, milling or grinding, heating, and/or leavening—is essential in order to transform the grain into an edible form, whether it be porridge, gruel, or more commonly bread. In fact, bread itself was so important as to frequently represent "food" in the Hebrew Bible (Reed 1992: 778; Dommershausen 1995: 523–24).

The growing of grain as a field crop is a necessary preliminary to bread production and itself requires multiple operations: plowing, sowing, reaping, threshing, winnowing (Borowski 1987: 47–70). Those activities, however, are not part of daily life. Rather, they are limited to two periods of several months each, as is clear from the Gezer Calendar and other ancient sources (Borowski 1987: 31–38, fig. 2, tables 1–3), as well as from agronomic data. Sowing of both wheat and barley would have taken place in two winter months (*yrḥw zrʿ* = "two months of sowing"), with harvesting and ingathering, followed by threshing and winnowing, taking place in the spring—probably April for barley (*yrḥ qṣr śʿrm* = "a month of harvesting barley") and May for wheat (*yrḥ qṣr -l-*, probably = "a month of harvesting and measuring" [Cassuto 1954]). Thereafter, grain was stored in bulk or in jars in a variety of subterranean (pits, silos, cellars) and above-ground (granaries, storerooms, storehouses) storage facilities for availability for conversion to edible form during the entire year (Borowski 1987: 71–83).

Bread production, in contrast, was a daily activity in virtually every household. Even in urban or elite settings, where grain might be procured in markets or as income from tenant farmers, individual households were the sites of the multiple operations involved in transforming grain into bread or gruel. The archaeological record preserves several kinds of evidence attesting to the location of bread production in virtually all household settings. Ovens (*tanurs* or *tabuns*), baking trays, and various stone grinding tools are the principle artifactual witnesses to the processing of grains.

Although such artifacts are widely found in Syro-Palestinian sites of the Iron Age, they are not always available in the publications of excavated sites in ways that allow for their find-spots and their architectural context to be determined, as is necessary in order to establish household use. That is, archaeological publications commonly illustrate ceramic and artifactual materials in stylistic groupings, or typologies, rather than in locus groups (Daviau 1993: 26–27). This publication strategy is a function of the diachronic interests of the excavators, who seek to trace change over time in relation to socio-political history. Moreover, ovens are not always depicted on schematic building plans, which are meant to show architectural form more than functional space. Valuable data have undoubtedly been lost because of excavation and record-keeping techniques, as well as publication goals, that have not been sensitive to the possibility of recovering archaeological materials in ways that allow for the reconstruction of household economies and, ultimately, of gendered activities (Steadman 1996: 3).

Nevertheless, some information can be salvaged from past projects. This information is typically embedded in discussions of the so-called "four-room house," apparently a type of structure formed in the Iron Age to fill the functional needs of agrarian settlements in the hill-country and Negev highlands (Holladay 1992; 1997; Stager 1985: 11–17) and eventually—although this remains somewhat controversial—becoming associated with Israelite ethnogenesis (Bunimovitz and Faust 2003). Although the use of certain spaces in those highly standardized dwellings is still debated, inferences based on ethnography have established these structures as functional adaptations to dry-farming mixed with horticulture and animal husbandry in Iron Age hamlets, villages, and towns, largely in sites considered Israelite or Judean.[3] The large central space in the four-room house probably served as the major work area for a variety of activities, including the pounding of grain into flour and the kneading of flour with water to produce dough and, ultimately, cakes or loaves.

Large shallow limestone or basalt objects, variously called grindstones, grinding slabs, slabs, querns, or saddle querns,[4] are often recovered in the large space of four-room houses (Mazar 1992: 488; Holladay 1997: 339). These tools have a concave work surface, a flat back, and are generally twice as long as they are wide. They serve as lower grinding stones and have as their counterparts upper grinding stones, sometimes called grinders or handstones. The length of the typically convex upper stones is usually somewhat less than the width of the associated lower grinding stones; the former were held with two hands and moved forward and backward over the latter (see Pritchard 1954: fig. 149). Most grain was probably crushed in such sets of upper and lower grinding stones, which presumably were located in each household. At ʿIzbet Ṣarṭah, for example, the thirteen grinding stones of Stratum II–IV (late eleventh–early tenth century) were evenly distributed, with one to three in every four-room building unit and none found outside the living areas (Finkelstein 1986: 93–94). The fact that sometimes three grinding stones were found in one household is noteworthy, for it indicates that two or three people were processing grain at the same time, an example of simple task simultaneity (Wilk and Rathje 1982: 622), which is a useful way of organizing labor when time-consuming procedures are involved.

Mortars (round, concave stone artifacts, usually made of limestone or basalt and smaller than grinding stones) together with pestles (conical or cylindrical pounding stones with slightly rounded bases), probably used mainly for grinding small grains such as herbs, spices, or pigments, may also have been used as supplemental tools for grinding small quantities of cereal grains (see Num 11:8; cf. Prov 27:22). These tools are also sometimes reported in archaeological publications, but the lack of illustrations and the confusion of terminology make it difficult to assess locations or quantity. The hammerstone or pounder was also a common grinding tool, but it is often overlooked because of artifact collection strategies that favor more recognizable ground stone tools (Ebeling 2002). Kneading troughs are even harder to identify in the archaeological record, perhaps because they may sometimes have been wooden slabs or simply pieces of fabric laid upon the cobbled or dirt surface of the workspace.[5]

The mention of ovens in the archaeological literature contains conflicting or, rather, variant information. Baking ovens made of clay, usually with foundations of small stones, are sometimes found in the main workspace of four-room houses; in other instances they appear outside the structure in an open area (courtyard space) or special structure (Mazar 1992: 488). Indeed, they are not necessarily found in every household, but rather may be positioned in outdoor spaces accessible to several households (as at Tell el Far'ah, North; see Holladay 1997: 339), suggesting communal use. Bread could also be baked in bread pans or on griddles (see Lev 2:5, 7; 7:9), both of which would have entailed the use of hearths (see 1 Kgs 19:6 and Isa 44:19). These are notoriously difficult to locate in the archaeological record, let alone in archaeological publications, possibly because, as ethnographic evidence suggests, hearths, unlike ovens, were often situated in second-story rooms or, in the hot months, outside the domestic structures in exterior courtyards (Kramer 1979: 147–48).

Although archaeological publications do not always provide easy access to them, it seems certain that the implements and installations used in transforming grains into edible form can be located in or near households, in interior or exterior workspaces. What is not readily apparent, however, is the identity of those who used these tools and structures. The artifacts and ovens or hearths are not intrinsically gender noisy. Precisely because the gender attribution of responsibility for specific household subsistence tasks is not universal, one cannot simply assume that the archaeological assemblages associated with bread-making in Syro-Palestinian households can be assigned to one gender or the other. In order to assess the experiential world of the Iron Age and interrogate any household activity for information about human behavior, hierarchies, and power differentials, the practitioners of that activity must first be identified. Prehistorians doing the archaeology of gender (as Gero and Conkey

1991; Wright 1996; Nelson 1997) have devised strategies for determining with reasonable certainty the gendered use of artifacts; those strategies can be employed effectively in ascertaining the gender of bread-producers in Iron Age Israel.

Gender attribution analysis utilizes three major sources: ethnography, texts, and iconography (see Costin 1996: 117–20). All of these are frequently used in the interpretation of the material remains recovered by Syro-Palestinian archaeology. Ethnography, for example, has been heavily utilized for studies of Iron Age dwellings and their various functions. Indeed, the most important studies of the four-room house (such as Stager 1985; Holladay 1992; 1997) have been ethnoarchaeological; that is, they have depended on several classic ethnographic analyses of agrarian Iranian villages (Kramer 1982; Watson 1979). Although some would question the value of recent behavior patterns observed by ethnographers for understanding archaeological remains, analogical interpretation is arguably essential for all archaeological work, especially if the ethnographic information comes from the same general geographic region as the excavations and thus bears the possibility of cultural continuity (see Carter 1997). Textual sources — written documents of the populations producing the artifact assemblages in question — are also *de rigueur* for the interpretation of Iron Age remains from Syria-Palestine.[6] The Hebrew Bible is the written source *par excellence* and also the one most notoriously attacked as ideologically biased and therefore unreliable, but that judgment may be less relevant for the biblical allusions to household life than they are for the assessment of the political or religious issues that are the *raison d'être* of the biblical corpus. Other ancient written sources, such as those from Mesopotamia and Ugarit, may be relevant, although their focus on urban elites means they, too, must be used cautiously. Finally, iconographic materials, though relatively scarce for Syria-Palestine in comparison with Mesopotamia and Egypt, are occasionally available. Artistic representations of household activities from nearby societies may also be useful if used critically, given the differences as well as similarities between Israelite and other Near Eastern cultures.

GENDER ATTRIBUTION OF BREAD PRODUCTION

Ethnography

The ethnographic evidence for engendering bread-production comes, first and foremost, from the large cross-cultural data base amassed by George Murdock (see Murdock and White 1969), developer of the Human Relations Area Files (HRAF). Using information on 185 sample societies, Murdock and Provost (1973; cf. Murdock 1937) identified 50 technological activities or tasks and arranged them according to the ratio of male and female participants, beginning with those mostly, or even exclusively, associated with men (e.g., smelting ores, hunting large aquatic fauna) and ending with those predominantly assigned to women. Although a few activities are exclusively performed by males in all 185 societies, none is done by females alone.[7] Nevertheless, some activities appear within women's domain in a high percentage of societies; and the one most associated with women is the preparation of vegetal, as opposed to animal, foods (Murdock and Provost 1973: tables 1 and 5). In 145 societies such work *was* exclusively female, and in only 3 was it exclusively male. In the other 27 cases (with data unavailable for 11 more) vegetal food preparation was performed by both genders.

Many individual anthropological studies across cultures corroborate those findings. They also provide some additional relevant information about grain-processing tasks, namely, their social aspect. Ethnography shows that tedious sets of activities, such as grinding grain and kneading dough, are often performed in gendered work groups. Women of one household — and there can be several adolescent or adult women in the extended family households that probably were typical for Iron Age agrarian settlements (Stager 1985; C. Meyers 1997a; Faust 2000)[8] — and even of neighboring households frequently gather together to grind, knead, and bake (Friedl 1991: 208; Sweely 1999: 168). The last operation has an ecological and labor-saving motivation as well as a social one; that is, where fuel is relatively scarce, firing an oven to produce multiple loaves for several households may reduce the amount of fuel that would otherwise have been required for individual household ovens.

Ethnographic data from regions close to Syria-Palestine, including Turkey and Iran, invariably depict women controlling bread production and other food-processing activities (Kramer 1979; Watson 1979). Palestinian examples may be even more relevant. Ironically, studies of local domestic architecture and related activity patterns have been rather under-utilized by "biblical" archaeologists intent in many other ways in interpreting the results of their excavations. Following in the footsteps of the few explorers (such as Canaan 1933; Dalman 1942) who documented Palestinian dwellings, a late 1970s survey, sponsored by the Center for the Study of Eretz Israel and Its Yishuv, investigated in great detail fifteen Ottoman-period houses in the Hebron district (Hirschfeld 1995). The survey team interviewed older family members and also studied the architecture and the installations for food preparation. Although primarily interested in construction techniques, the researchers nonetheless recorded several kinds of ethnographic information relevant to bread production. In particular, they ascertained the occupancy levels of dwellings and also certain aspects of household activities, including location and gender.

To their surprise, they discovered that the maximum number of inhabitants averaged sixteen (Hirschfeld 1996: 135, table 5). This figure, representing three to four generations, is consonant with notions of the Israelite extended family as the basic social unit. Another feature is that bread ovens were often built in outdoor spaces and courtyards, sometimes thereby serving several households, whereas hearths were usually not permanent structures (Hirschfeld 1995: 133, 140–41, 166). Finally, interviews with both female and male occupants revealed that women were the ones who determined the allocation of space for objects and activities in the household (Hirschfeld 1995: 148–49, 152, 182). The communal nature of bread production, as well as the female control of the artifacts and space in which bread was prepared, thus emerge as salient features of Palestinian ethnography.

Texts

Iron Age textual information from Syria-Palestine is in accord with the ethnographic data. First, with respect to grinding, a number of passages in the Hebrew Bible mention millstones or the grinding of grain. Most of them provide no information about the gender of those using the grinding stone, NRSV "hand-mill" (*rēḥayim*, a Hebrew dual form probably representing a grinding artifact consisting of two parts: upper and lower grinding stones). For example, in Jer 25:10, the sound of grinding stones is indicative of happy family life; in Deut 24:6, neither a "handmill" nor part thereof, i.e., an "upper millstone," is to be taken as collateral; and in Num 11:8, the "people" — probably a gender-inclusive term — collectively gather manna and grind it with millstones or in a mortar. The two passages in which the gender of those grinding is apparent both denote women. In Exod 11:5, Egyptian slave girls work the millstones; and in Isa 47:1–2, Babylon is personified as a woman who loses her royal status, becomes a peasant woman, and takes the hand-mill to produce flour.

Similarly, the Hebrew word for the upper grinding stone (*rekeb*, from the root *rkb*, "to ride," as a stone "riding" on the lower grinding stone) is found three times in the Hebrew Bible, once in a gender neutral passage (Deut 24:6, where it appears with the dual "handmill" = pair of grinding stones) and twice in reference to a woman (the woman of Thebez), who rescues her city and its population by seizing an "upper millstone" and throwing it from a tower onto the upstart Abimelech and killing him (Judg 9:53–54; 2 Sam 11:21; see C. Meyers 2000d). Because large, stationary, rotary mills with fitted turning stones for grinding were probably not introduced until the Persian or Hellenistic period (Amiran 1956; cf. Frankel 2003), the "upper millstone" used by the woman of Thebez would have been the portable upper grinding stone, usually labeled a grinder or rubbing stone in the archaeological literature; that is, she used one part, the upper part of the dual *rēḥayim*, as her deadly weapon.

Also relevant is the use of the verb *ṭḥn*, "to grind," in the Hebrew Bible. Sometimes this term denotes the crushing of substances other than grain, as when Moses pulverizes the idolatrous golden calf (Exod 32:20; cf. Deut 9:21), or when First Isaiah (3:15) bemoans the way the poor are being crushed by the elite. However, whenever the verb mentions the grinding of grain in a way that links it with one gender, women are specified. The reference to maiden Babylon transformed to a woman at work has her grinding meal (Isa 47:2). In Job 31:10, Job insists that if he has been unfaithful, then his wife will "grind for another," which may be a double entendre denoting a sexual as well as a milling activity. And, although it probably dates to the Persian period and not the Iron Age, Eccl 12:3 seems relevant in its reference to "women who grind," which epitomizes strong women doing household labor, in parallel with a reference to the strong men of the house (C. Meyers 2000e); the diminution with age of strength to grind will mean that the sound of handmills will diminish (Eccl 12:4). The only two texts in which males are linked to grinding stones maintain the association of those tools with females, because both texts depict abnormal situations. In Judg 16:21, an emasculated and sightless Samson, without hair or eyes, is relegated to working a grindstone (*wayĕhî ṭôḥēn*) in a Philistine prison; and in Lamentations 5, the destruction of Jerusalem is expressed by a lengthy catalogue of ways in which the "normal" order has been reversed — slaves now rule (v. 8) and young men hold millstones (*baḥûrîm ṭĕḥôn nāśā'û*, v. 13).

The various passages in the Hebrew Bible that refer to bread-baking contain similar gender information. One of them, Gen 19:3, implies that a man (Lot) baked bread for "two angels;" but the Lot narrative is fraught with difficulties about sex and gender roles and perhaps can, therefore, be discounted. And another (Gen 40:1) refers to a foreigner — an Egyptian administrator in charge of bread-baking — and can likewise be discounted; or, it can be compared to Lev 24:5, which implies that (male) priests prepared the bread for the golden table in the Tent of Meeting. This would conform to the notion of specialized or elite bread production being taken over by men (Goody 1982: 101). Similarly, commercial production of bread in the truly urban setting of the royal capitals of Jerusalem or Samaria might have involved men (Jer 37:21; Hos 7:4).

However, biblical texts indicate that women in family households produced bread in the non-urban contexts in which most Israelites lived in the Iron Age. Among the covenant curses at the end of the Book of Leviticus, one of the disasters that will result if the people disobey God will be a great reduction in the availability of food. This paucity is indicated by a scenario in which "ten women shall bake your bread in a single oven" (Lev 26:26). The image is that of a bread shortage — the bread of ten households can be baked in an oven usually serving fewer households. The idea of households sharing an oven is noteworthy. So, too, is another aspect of this text, in which the task of allotting bread to others belongs to the women who have baked it: the women "shall dole out your bread by weight." Women, in other words, control food portions; they allocate life-sustaining resources (C. Meyers 2000b). Another text depicts a woman, the medium of Endor, providing unleavened cakes as well as meat from a stall-fed calf that she herself slaughters in order to provide psychological and physical sustenance for Saul (1 Sam 28:24).

Cultic preparation of bread in the central sanctuary may have been a male priestly task; but household religious practice, which was arguably dominated by women (C. Meyers 2005), involved women as producers of loaves for the Queen of Heaven. Jeremiah 7:18 reports that fathers build fires and children gather kindling, but that "mothers knead dough, to make cakes for the Queen of Heaven." Jeremiah's emphasis (see also Jer 44:15–19, 25) on women as makers of these cereal offerings, along with libations and the burning of incense, may indicate that the worship of the Queen of Heaven was particularly attractive to women (Ackerman 1989). Men did participate too, however, and in making fires they may have been sharing a predominantly female role, which appears as woman's work in First Isaiah's portrait of the demise of normal life (27:11; see C. Meyers 2000c). Starting fires and keeping them going in a world without matches probably involved the cooperative efforts of neighbors and nearby kin; tending fires embodies the cooperative aspect of the communal world of women more than that of men (Goody 1982: 70).

One other gendered reference to bread production is the famous passage in 1 Samuel, in which the prophet Samuel tries to dissuade the people of early Israel of their demand for monarchic rule. He asserts that a king may, indeed, provide stability and justice but that there will be a cost: heavy taxation and the conscription of both young women and men to menial positions in the military and palace bureaucracies. The tasks listed for these young people probably reflect Israelite patterns of division of labor by gender: males will become soldiers, makers of ornaments, and workers in the king's fields; and females will serve as "perfumers and cooks and bakers" (8:13). Usually, when tasks performed by women in domestic settings become specialty occupations or professions connected with courts or temples, they are taken over by men, as was apparently the case in ancient Israel for the production of cultic bread, as mentioned above. But, according to the Samuel text, Israelite women retained bread-making, along with two other female tasks, even when those jobs became linked with the political elites (C. Meyers 2000a).

The existence of a Syro-Palestinian source, the Hebrew Bible, containing references to women grinding grain and producing bread precludes the necessity of looking to other ancient Near Eastern cultures. Yet it is worth noting that Mesopotamian and Egyptian texts also link women with the preparation of bread. Mesopotamian sources indicate that women spent much time in carrying out the processes required for producing loaves or cakes; indeed, millstones might even be part of a woman's dowry (Harris 1992: 949). Similarly, Egyptian documents suggest that women of all classes were responsible for a variety of household technologies, especially those associated with baking (Robins 1993: 100–102, 117–19, 126).

Iconography

Late Iron Age iconographic materials, chiefly small terracotta figurines, consistently depict women, rather than men, grinding or kneading. Most of these artifacts, part of a large corpus of *genre* scenes, come from Cyprus. However, because several have been recovered from Syria-Palestine and because the production of those terracottas in general is thought to have been introduced to Cyprus from Syria-Palestine via Phoenician coroplasts (Vandenabeele 1986), examining Cypriot as well as Levantine examples is appropriate. A terracotta from Ahzib (Pritchard 1954: 152), dating to the late Iron Age, shows a female figure bending over a bread trough and kneading dough. The plethora of similar Cypriot pieces includes a number of examples in which two women are performing this task in tandem (Karageorghis 1998: fig. 24, pls. 29:9, 30:1–2). Similar figural compositions appear in ancient Greece, and a Boeotian terracotta showing four women kneading dough together in a communal trough led the excavators of Tel Dor to interpret an installation in an Iron I context as a bread-kneading trough (Stern et al. 1997: 52–56, figs. 10–12).

Iconographic materials from ancient Egypt, largely from periods preceding the Iron Age, depict women grinding grain or carrying out some other step in the process of producing baked goods. A famous tomb model from the Middle Kingdom (Robins 1993: fig. 32; see also Pritchard 1954: 149), for example, shows a kneeling woman rubbing grain by pressing an upper stone or grinder on a lower grinding stone. Such depictions suggest that bread production was one of the few activities that usually involved exclusively women, in elite households as well as in those of workers (Robins 1993: 102, 118).

DISCUSSION

Taken together, these sources make it reasonably certain that the various steps in the daily production of cereal foods can be attributed to women. In addition, several features of these data suggest an important aspect of female bread-making, namely, that some or all of the requisite procedures were done by women working together (cf. Matt 24:41 for similar information from the New Testament).The sources for gender attribution fit with the archaeological picture, in which several grindstones appear within single households and in which ovens serve several households. In addition, the notion of women within and across households working together on a series of tedious tasks makes sense in light of the significant amount of time — two hours or more per day — required for bread production (Bossen 1989; cf. Brumfiel 1991: 238). Ethnographic literature abounds with descriptions of women lightening the hard and time-consuming process of grinding by working together, singing and chatting (Goody 1982: 69).

For this study, the two salient emerging features of bread-production in Iron Age agrarian households, thus, are the female monopoly on the technology and the quasi-communal nature of the labor. That is, bread production involved women's group work. Based on this information, a number of inferences, again using ethnographic analogy, can be made about women's lives and about gender dynamics in Iron Age agrarian communities. However, the implications of identifying bread production as women's group work cannot be fully grasped without first acknowledging several conceptual obstacles.

Perhaps the most significant obstacle to understanding the importance of women's contributions to household life in biblical antiquity is present-mindedness. The meaning and value of women's work cannot be ascertained on the basis of our experience in contemporary middle-class western culture (Nelson 1997: 13–21, 88). Despite the objections of many second-wave American feminists, women's household activities are tacitly considered supportive and secondary, and are thereby trivialized and marginalized, while activities historically or traditionally associated with men tend to be imbued with power and/or prestige. These negative perspectives of women's work are rooted in the identification of women with the home in western ideologies of the last two centuries (Lawrence 1999: 121), which in turn is the result of the removal of significant economic processes from the household as part of the industrial revolution. Women's unpaid housework became seen as simply the performance of housekeeping chores. As a result, it became increasingly difficult to acknowledge the economic value and the attendant social power and prestige of women's labor in premodern households (C. Meyers 1999a: 154–58).

The traditional view of women as passive and powerless in virtually all premodern societies is now known to be deeply flawed. Women's productive activities in such societies have major economic value (Brumfiel 1991: 224–25), and newer ethnographic studies show that women's household economic roles, in craft production as well as in subsistence tasks, functioned in ways that challenge our persistent and often unexamined notions of female dependence and patriarchal dominance. It is now clear that the work patterns and authority structures in premodern societies meant that daily life was rarely organized along hegemonic, male-dominated, gendered lines. To put it another way, women's technologies have been rescued from their degraded status, and the prestige or even power they have accorded to women is now recognized.

A second and equally powerful obstacle to reaching an emic, or insider's, perspective on Iron Age society is the set of values associated with the so-called public/private dichotomy. This dichotomy is an analytical construction, also stemming from changes brought about by industrialization, that views the public (political and economic institutions and activities) and the private (family or domestic life) as separate domains. This private/public binary was popular several decades ago in assessing women's roles in traditional societies (as Rosaldo 1974; Sanday 1974), but it is no longer considered a useful or even accurate analytical framework (Sharistanian 1987; C. Meyers 1988: 32–36, 175–76; Helly and Reverby 1992; cf. Rosaldo 1980; Lamphere 1993; Gilchrist 1999). A more integrated approach now sees that "public" and "private" are overlapping domains in premodern societies. *All* household activities have significance for both the household and the larger community in which it is embedded—the domestic *is* political and the private *is* public (Hegland 1991: 216–18, 228–29).

Women's productive activities in Iron Age households, as in other premodern societies, must, therefore, be perceived as dynamic elements of the social and political fabric of their communities (Yanagisako 1979: 191; Hendon 1996: 47). Ethnographic research has demonstrated that gender-associated artifacts signify gender-associated economic activities, which in turn signify gender-linked power. Approaches to power in the modern west tend to focus on formal institutions, whereas informal power relations in traditional societies are the concomitant of the control of productive activities (Sweely 1999: 155–56). Because people in premodern communities exercise power in ways that are related to their productive tasks, the identification of bread-making as a women's activity has significance for household power differentials. Three kinds of female power can be identified for woman as bread-producers.

First, female control of the complex technologies for transforming the raw into the cooked—grain into bread—likely signified *social power* within households. Ethnographers have documented, across cultures, that important household decision-making powers accrue to women by virtue of their dominance of essential household processes (Counihan 1998: 2, 4). The virtual exclusivity in Israelite households of women as producers and distributors of the fundamental nutritional source, which cannot be obtained in any other way, thus denotes female power. Note that a general notion of female provision of all food for Israelite households appears in the passage describing the strong female household manager in Prov 31:15—the woman of that acrostic provides nourishment (Hebrew *ṭerep*; see Wagner 1986: 253) for her entire household. Women produced bread (and probably most other cooked foodstuffs), allotted portions, and thereby exercised control over critical aspects of household life.

The control by Israelite women of activities that provided sustenance cannot be compared to western domestic patterns, with women as traditional "gatekeepers" of food into the home and onto the tables. In the modern world, where food can easily be obtained outside the home and without technological expertise, provisioning food can even sometimes be linked to female subservience (DeVault 1991). Not so in premodern societies, where providing food is linked with power. To be sure, the total effort for supplying nourishment in ancient Israel involved both female and male labor. Tasks associated with growing field crops were probably allocated to males, according to textual data: plowing (Isa 28:24; 1 Kgs 19:19; Job 1:14), sowing (Gen 26:12; Isa 28:25; 32:20), and harvesting (2 Kgs 4:18; Isa 28:28; Jer 9:21; Amos 9:13; but cf. Ruth 2:2, 8–9). This complementarity of food production is likely to have equalized gendered power in household life (C. Meyers 1988: 168–73; cf. Kahn 1986). Still, food-processing activities within or near the domicile itself were daily, female-controlled activities; and they were also the final stages of the chain of activities required to make field crops edible. Both these features may have privileged women in terms of internal household power differentials (C. Meyers 1991: 49–51).

A second kind of power in relation to food production must also be considered: the *personal power*, or valued sense of self, that is contingent upon the importance of a set of tasks and the gratification derived from performing them. Two aspects of women's work are relevant to assessing gratification (C. Meyers 1997a: 26–27). First, female tasks in the aggregate in premodern agrarian households require more technological skills than those of males and, thus, for Israelite women would have been qualitatively different in their ability to produce a sense of accomplishment. Second, women's tasks produce items that are immediately useful or consumable. The products of male labor—the growing of crops—were assessed in amounts that were dependent on unmanageable nature, whereas women's work produced usable/edible items that were dependent on manageable technology. Again, satisfaction and an attendant sense of personal worth may, thus, have been more consistently part of women's daily experience than of men's.

A third kind of power—*socio-political* power—is implicated in the communal aspect of bread-producing activities. The gathering of women in groups to perform repetitive, labor-intensive tasks signals the formation of women's networks. Women working together over extended periods of time on a daily basis not only share information and techniques relevant to the tasks they are performing but also share information about each other and each other's families. They know each other intimately, and this social knowledge creates a sphere of female relationships. Women in such social contexts obtain information that is unavailable to men and that may often be critical for forging supra-household political connections. At the least, such information is essential for solving sporadic economic problems, such as the differential need for field labor among households, and for assisting with difficulties such as illness or death in individual households (C. Meyers 1999a: 176–77, 182–83; cf. Ardener 1993: 9; Sirman 1995). More simply, women's social knowledge and the concomitant solidarity meant that women would know if a given household was short of field labor at a critical time in the agricultural calendar and would also know which household might have enough older unmarried children to be able to provide temporary assistance to a struggling household. Or it meant that women would know if a neighboring woman was too ill to carry out her household tasks, and they could deploy labor resources to compensate.

These informal alliances among women, which are probably signified by the term *šĕkēnôt* ("female neighbors") or other similar terms (see C. Meyers 1999b), were hardly casual affairs. They may represent a more diffuse and, thus, less visible form of powerful female agency than do more visible male social groups. Yet, especially in communities with limited material and human resources, such informal women's networks are essential for the viability of the community as a whole (Strathern 1979; March and Taqqu 1986; Marcus 1992; Zonabend 1996). They constituted the informal but important mediating group that forged households into larger "kin" groups. Those groups are likely the equivalent of biblical *mišpaḥôt*, which are understood as a "protective association of families" that extended social, economic, and military aid to its constituent households (Gottwald 1979: 257–67; cf. Lamphere 1993: 70). Furthermore, because Israelite women married into one household while still retaining ties with their natal households, they had structural links with two descent groups, whereas men had connections with only one such group. These marital and consanguinal ties, along with their daily communal labor, meant that women were often better positioned than men, socially and spatially, to mediate community relations (Lamphere 1993: 70). Female household members typically channel and regulate many interactions among households. This overlapping of "domestic" and "public" realms is visible even today in third world countries, where the state does not always reach into rural areas. Politics in such communities are typically conducted through kin relationships.[9]

In conclusion, I want to suggest that this understanding of female power has implications for understanding the social structure of ancient Israel. Because the household was the primary social and economic unit of society, and because women's economic tasks made them part of a web of social roles essential to community life, the conventional wisdom about male dominance in pervasive hierarchical structures affecting all domains of human interaction in Iron Age agrarian communities must be contested. It may be more accurate to consider the gendered spheres of those settlements as interconnected and complementary, rather than discrete and hierarchical. The concept of *heterarchy*, an organizational structure in which "each element possesses the potential of being unranked (relative to other elements) or ranked in a number of different ways depending on systemic requirements" (Crumley 1979: 144), may be more appropriate than that of hierarchy for acknowledging the variability, context, and fluctuation of social relations in peasant societies (Levy 1995: 17).

In this perspective, women's activities and networks along with those of men are considered sub-systems that together constitute the heterarchical whole. Such sub-systems are recognized as relating laterally to each other, rather than vertically. This seems to be an especially useful model in which to situate the social power accruing to Iron Age women, because of their dominance of critical aspects of household life (C. Meyers 2006).[10] They worked in female cohorts to produce life-sustaining food, they produced other essentials such as textiles and even the tools themselves (Ebeling 2002), and they controlled critical aspects of household religious life. Their daily lives were thus replete with intricate and subtle opportunities for contributing to household and communal well-being and for experiencing the attendant aspects of social and personal power. It is time to deconstruct the notion of male-dominated hierarchies in our reconstructions of ancient Israelite society. Acknowledging the reality and significance of women's economic, socio-political, and also religious roles renders gender hierarchy a problematic and inappropriate model and allows for a more nuanced and accurate understanding of gender as difference.

NOTES

* A limited treatment of bread production appeared along with a discussion of textile production in C. Meyers 2003b; and a different version of this paper is found in *Nashim* 5 (2002). The editors of both those publications, as well as of the present one, graciously agreed to these overlapping studies.

1 These projects were Khirbet Shemaʿ (E. Meyers et al. 1976), Meiron (E. Meyers et al. 1981), Gush Ḥalav (E. Meyers et al. 1990), and Nabratein (Meyers and Meyers, forthcoming). Only at Gush Ḥalav did restrictions on the excavation permit preclude adequate exploration of domestic structures.

2 Among the many reports on Sepphoris, see Nagy et al. 1996.

3 The usual translation of the Hebrew word *ʿārîm* as "cities" is misleading (C. Meyers 2003b: 425–26, n. 1). Villages and towns, some of the latter walled, rather than cities, dominated in the Iron Age as in virtually all past agrarian societies (Lenski 1984: 199–200).

4 That many terms are used for grinding stones indicates that the classification of ground stone tools lacks the refinement in terminology that characterizes ceramic typologies. Prehistorians, however, have provided useful descriptive categories (Milevski 1998: 61–62).

5 See the discussion of iconography, below, for a possible interpretation of stone troughs as kneading basins.

6 Documentary evidence is routinely used, wherever possible, even for studying prehistoric cultures or those that have not produced written sources. For example, anthropologists who study Northern, Southern, or Meso-American cultures sometimes depend on the probability of cultural continuity and thus value reports from early colonial eyewitnesses; see Conkey and Gero 1991: 18 and many of the studies in Gero and Conkey 1991.

7 Note that breast-feeding and caring for newborns, which *are* exclusively female tasks, are not considered technological and thus were not included in the Murdock and Provost study.

8 Holladay (1995: 387–89) claims that the nuclear family was the basic social and domestic unit in Iron II agrarian groups, but his claim should be modified by the fact that unrelated servants might be attached to the nuclear family, by the realization that the nuclear family is part of a segmentary structure with the extended family as the next level of complexity, and by the possibility that certain activities were performed jointly by family members from beyond the nuclear unit.

9 Not long ago, ethnographic observation in Alaiabad in Iran revealed that "personal and domestic relations were also public and political relations" (Hegland 1991: 215).

10 Definitions of power vary among social scientists. One possible understanding of power is that it is the "net ability or capability of action to produce or cause intended outcomes or effects, particularly on the behavior of others, or on others' outcomes" (Szinovacz 1987: 652). Issues of household power are typically resource based, with significant labor output and control of technology—both aspects of women's lives in premodern agrarian societies—thus signifying the presence of female power.

REFERENCES

Ackerman, S.

1989 "And the Women Knead Dough:" The Worship of the Queen of Heaven in Sixth-Century Judah. Pp. 109–24 in *Gender and Difference in Ancient Israel,* ed. P. L. Day. Minneapolis, MN: Fortress.

Amiran, R.

1956 The Millstones and the Potter's Wheel. *Eretz Israel* 4: 46–49 (Hebrew).

Ardener, S.

1993 Ground Rules and Social Maps for Women: An Introduction. Pp. 1–30 in *Women and Space: Ground Rules and Social Maps,* ed. S. Ardener. Providence, RI: Berg.

Bender, D. R.

1967 A Refinement of the Concept of Household: Families, Co-residence, and Domestic Functions. *American Anthropologist* 69: 493–504.

Borowski, O.

1987 *Agriculture in Iron Age Israel.* Winona Lake, IN: Eisenbrauns.

Bossen, L.

1989 Women and Economic Institutions. Pp. 318–50 in *Economic Anthropology,* ed. S. Plottner. Stanford, CA: Stanford University.

Brown, J.

1970 A Note on the Division of Labor. *American Anthropologist* 72: 1073–78.

Brumfiel, E. M.

1991 Weaving and Cooking in Aztec Mexico. Pp. 224–51 in *Engendering Archaeology: Women and Prehistory*, eds. J. Gero and M. Conkey. Oxford: Blackwell.

Bunimovitz, S., and Faust, A.

2003 Building Identity: The Four-Room House and the Israelite Mind. Pp. 411–23 in *Symbiosis, Symbolism, and the Power of the Past: Canaan, Ancient Israel and Their Neighbors from the Late Bronze Age through Roman Palaestina*, eds. W. G. Dever and S. Gitin. Winona Lake, IN: Eisenbrauns.

Canaan, T.

1933 *The Palestinian Arab House. Its Architecture and Folklore.* Jerusalem: Palestine Oriental Society.

Carter, C. W.

1997 Ethnoarchaeology. Pp. 280–84 in *The Oxford Encyclopedia of Archaeology in the Near East*, vol. 2, ed. E. M. Meyers. New York, NY: Oxford University.

Cassuto, M. D.

1954 Gezer, the Gezer Calendar. Cols. 471–74 in *Encyclopaedia Biblica*, vol. 2, ed. E. L. Sukenik. Jerusalem: Bialik Institute (Hebrew).

Conkey, M. W., and Gero, J. M.

1991 Tensions, Pluralities, and Engendering Archaeology: An Introduction to Women and Prehistory. Pp. 3–30 in *Engendering Archaeology: Women and Prehistory*, eds. J. M. Gero and M. Conkey. Oxford: Blackwell.

1997 Program to Practice: Gender to Feminism in Archaeology. *Annual Review of Archaeology* 26: 411–37.

Costin, C. L.

1996 Exploring the Relationship between Gender and Craft in Complex Societies: Methodological and Theoretical Issues of Gender Attribution. Pp. 111–40 in *Gender and Archaeology*, ed. R. P. Wright. Philadelphia, PA: University of Pennsylvania.

Counihan, C. M.

1998 Introduction – Food and Gender: Identity and Power. Pp. 1–10 in *Food and Gender: Identity and Power*, eds. C. M. Counihan and S. L. Kaplan. Food in History and Culture 1. Amsterdam: Harwood Academic.

Crumley, C.

1979 Three Locational Models: An Epistemological Assessment of Anthropology and Archaeology. Pp. 141–73 in *Advances in Archaeological Method and Theory*, vol. 2, ed. M. B. Schiffer. New York, NY: Academic.

Dalman, G.

1942 *Arbeit und Sitte in Palästina, VII: Das Haus.* Gütersloh: Bertelsmann.

Daviau, P. M. M.

1993 *Houses and Their Furnishings in Bronze Age Palestine.* JSOT/ASOR Monograph Series 8. Sheffield: Sheffield Academic.

DeVault, M. L.

1991 *Feeding the Family: The Social Organization of Caring as Gendered Work.* Chicago, IL: University of Chicago.

Dommershausen, W.

1995 *leḥem.* Pp. 521–29 in *Theological Dictionary of the Old Testament* VII, eds. G. J. Botterweck, H. Ringgren and H.-J. Fabry. Grand Rapids, MI: Eerdmans.

Ebeling, J.

2002 Bread Making as Women's Technology in Ancient Israel. Paper presented at the Annual Meeting of the American Schools of Oriental Research. Boulder, CO.

Faust, A.

2000 The Rural Community in Ancient Israel in Iron Age II. *Bulletin of the American Schools of Oriental Research* 317: 17–39.

Finkelstein, I.

1986 *ʿIzbet Ṣarṭah: An Early Iron Age Site near Rosh Haʿayin, Israel.* British Archaeological Reports International Series 299. Oxford: British Archaeological Reports.

Frankel, R.

2003 The Olynthus Mill, Its Origin, and Diffusion: Typology and Distribution. *American Journal of Archaeology* 107: 1–22.

Friedl, E.

1991 The Dynamics of Women's Spheres of Action in Rural Iran. Pp. 195–214 in *Women in Middle Eastern History: Shifting Boundaries in Sex and Gender*, eds. N. R. Keddie and B. Baron. New Haven, CT: Yale University.

Gero, J. M., and Conkey, M. W. (eds.)

1991 *Engendering Archaeology: Women and Prehistory.* Oxford: Blackwell.

Gilchrist, R.
1999 *Gender and Archaeology: Contesting the Past.* New York, NY: Routledge.

Goody, J.
1972 The Evolution of the Family. Pp. 103–124 in *Household and Family in Past Times,* eds. P. Laslett and R. Wall. London: Cambridge University.
1982 *Cooking, Cuisine, and Class.* Cambridge: Cambridge University.

Gottwald, N. K.
1979 *The Tribes of Yahweh: A Sociology of the Religion of Liberated Israel, 1250–1050 B.C.E.* Maryknoll, NY: Orbis.

Harris, R.
1992 Women. Mesopotamia. Pp. 947–51 in *Anchor Bible Dictionary,* vol. 6, ed. D. N. Freedman. New York, NY: Doubleday.

Hegland, M. E.
1991 Political Roles of Aliabad Women: The Public-Private Dichotomy Transcended. Pp. 215–30 in *Women in Middle Eastern History: Shifting Boundaries in Sex and Gender,* eds. N. R. Kiddie and S. Baron. New Haven, CT: Yale University.

Helly, D. O., and Reverby, S. (eds.)
1992 *Gendered Domains: Rethinking Public and Private in Women's History.* Ithaca, NY: Cornell University.

Hendon, J. A.
1996 Archaeological Approaches to the Organization of Domestic Labor: Household Practice and Domestic Relations. *Annual Review of Anthropology* 25: 45–61.

Henshaw, A.
1999 Location and Appropriation in the Arctic: an Integrative Approach to Historic Innuit Household Economies. *Journal of Anthropological Archaeology* 18: 79–118.

Hirschfeld, Y.
1995 The Traditional Palestinian House: Results of a Survey in the Hebron Hills. Pp. 109–215 in *The Palestinian Dwelling in the Roman-Byzantine Period,* by Y. Hirschfeld. Studium Biblicum Franciscanum, Collectio Minor 34. Jerusalem: Franciscan Printing and Israel Exploration Society.

Holladay, J. S., Jr.
1992 House, Israelite. Pp. 308–18 in *Anchor Bible Dictionary,* vol. 3, ed. D. N. Freedman. New York, NY: Doubleday.
1995 The Kingdoms of Israel and Judah: Political and Economic Centralization in the Iron II A–B (ca. 1000–750 BCE). Pp. 368–98, 586–90 in *The Archaeology of Society in the Holy Land,* ed. T. E. Levy. New York, NY: Facts on File.
1997 Four-room House. Pp. 337–42 in *The Oxford Encyclopedia of Archaeology in the Near East,* vol. 2, ed. E. M. Meyers. New York, NY: Oxford University.

Kahn, M.
1986 *Always Hungry, Never Greedy: Food and the Expression of Gender in a Melanesian Society.* New York, NY: Cambridge University.

Karageorghis, V.
1998 *The Coroplastic Art of Ancient Cyprus, V. The Cypro-Archaic Period: Small Female Figurines, A. Handmade/Wheelmade Figurines.* Nicosia: Leventis Foundation.

Kent, S.
1990 A Cross-cultural Study of Segmentation, Architecture, and the Use of Space. Pp. 127–52 in *Domestic Architecture and the Use of Space: An Interdisciplinary Cross-cultural Study,* ed. S. Kent. Cambridge: Cambridge University.

Kramer, C.
1979 An Archaeological View of a Contemporary Kurdish Village: Domestic Architecture, Household Size, and Wealth. Pp. 139–63 in *Ethnoarchaeology: Implications of Ethnography for Archaeology,* ed. C. Kramer. New York, NY: Columbia University.
1982 *Village Ethnoarchaeology: Rural Iran in Archaeological Perspective.* New York, NY: Academic.

Lamphere, L.
1993 The Domestic Sphere of Women and the Public Sphere of Men: The Strengths and Limitations of an Anthropological Dichotomy. Pp. 67–77 in *Gender in Cross-Cultural Perspective,* eds. C. B. Brettell and C. F. Sargent. Englewood Cliffs, NJ: Prentice Hall.

Lawrence, S.
1999 Towards a Feminist Archaeology of Households: Gender and Household Structure in the Australian Gold Fields. Pp. 121–41 in *The Archaeology of Household Activities,* ed. P. M. Allison. London: Routledge.

Lenski, G. E.
1984 *Power and Privilege: A Theory of Social Stratification.* Chapel Hill, NC: University of North Carolina.

Lenski, G., and Lenski, J.
1987 *Human Societies: An Introduction to Macrosociology*, 5th ed. New York, NY: McGraw-Hill.

Levy, J. E.
1995 Heterarchy in Bronze Age Denmark: Settlement Patterns, Gender, and Ritual. Pp. 41–53 in *Heterarchy and the Analysis of Complex Societies*, eds. R. M. Ehrenreich, C. L. Crumley and J. E. Levy. Archaeological Papers of the American Anthropological Association 6. Arlington, VA: American Anthropological Association.

March, K. S., and Taqqu, R. L.
1986 *Women's Informal Associations in Developing Countries*. Women in Cross-Cultural Perspective. Boulder, CO: Westview.

Marcus, J.
1992 *A World of Difference: Islam and Gender Hierarchy in Turkey*. London: Allen and Unwin.

Mazar, A.
1992 *Archaeology of the Land of the Bible, 10,000–586 B.C.E.* New York, NY: Doubleday.

Meyers, C.
1983 Procreation, Production, and Protection: Male-Female Balance in Early Israel. *Journal of the American Academy of Religion* 51: 569–93.
1988 *Discovering Eve: Ancient Israelite Women in Context*. New York, NY: Oxford University Press.
1991 'To Her Mother's House'—Considering a Counterpart to the Israelite *Bêt 'āb*. Pp. 39–51, 304–7 in *The Bible and the Politics of Exegesis: Essays in Honor of Norman K. Gottwald on His Sixty-Fifth Birthday*, eds. D. Jobling, P. Day and G. T. Sheppard. New York, NY: Pilgrim.
1997a The Family in Early Israel. Pp. 1–47 in *Families in Ancient Israel*, by L. G. Perdue, J. Blenkinsopp, J. J. Collins and C. Meyers. Louisville, KY: Westminster John Knox.
1997b Recovering Objects, Re-Visioning Subjects: Archaeology and Feminist Biblical Study. Pp. 270–84 in *A Feminist Companion to Reading the Bible: Approaches, Methods, and Strategies*, eds. A. Brenner and C. Fontaine. Sheffield: Sheffield Academic.
1999a Guilds and Gatherings: Women's Groups in Ancient Israel. Pp. 154–84 in *Realia Dei: Essays in Archaeology and Biblical Interpretation in Honor of Edward F. Campbell, Jr.*, eds. P. M. Williams, Jr., and T. Hiebert. Atlanta, GA: Scholars.
1999b 'Women of the Neighborhood' (Ruth 4.17): Informal Female Networks in Ancient Israel. Pp. 110–27 in *Ruth and Esther: A Feminist Companion to the Bible*, 2nd series, ed. A. Brenner. Sheffield: Sheffield Academic.
2000a Daughters as Perfumers, Cooks, and Bakers (1 Sam 8:13). P. 255 in *Women in Scripture: A Dictionary of the Named and Unnamed Women in the Hebrew Bible, the Apocryphal-Deuterocanonical Books, and the New Testament*, eds. C. Meyers, T. Craven and R. S. Kraemer. Boston, MA: Houghton Mifflin.
2000b Women as Bread Bakers (Lev 26:26). Pp. 213–14 in *Women in Scripture: A Dictionary of the Named and Unnamed Women in the Hebrew Bible, the Apocryphal-Deuterocanonical Books, and the New Testament*, eds. C. Meyers, T. Craven and R. S. Kraemer. Boston, MA: Houghton Mifflin.
2000c Women Making a Fire (Isa 27:11). Pp. 320–21 in *Women in Scripture: A Dictionary of the Named and Unnamed Women in the Hebrew Bible, the Apocryphal-Deuterocanonical Books, and the New Testament*, eds. C. Meyers, T. Craven and R. S. Kraemer. Boston, MA: Houghton Mifflin.
2000d Woman of Thebez (Judg 5:53–54; 2 Sam 11:21). Pp. 241–42 in *Women in Scripture: A Dictionary of the Named and Unnamed Women in the Hebrew Bible, the Apocryphal-Deuterocanonical Books, and the New Testament*, eds. C. Meyers, T. Craven and R. S. Kraemer. Boston, MA: Houghton Mifflin.
2000e Women Who Grind (Eccl 12:3). P. 310 in *Women in Scripture: A Dictionary of the Named and Unnamed Women in the Hebrew Bible, the Apocryphal-Deuterocanonical Books, and the New Testament*, eds. C. Meyers, T. Craven and R. S. Kraemer. Boston, MA: Houghton Mifflin.
2003a Engendering Syro-Palestinian Archaeology: Reasons and Resources. *Near Eastern Archaeology* 66: 185–97.
2003b Material Remains and Social Relations: Women's Culture in Agrarian Households of the Iron Age. Pp. 425–44 in *Symbiosis, Symbolism, and the Power of the Past: Canaan, Ancient Israel, and Their Neighbors from the Late Bronze Age through Roman Palaestina*, eds. W. G. Dever and S. Gitin. Winona Lake, IN: Eisenbrauns.
2005 *Households and Holiness: The Religious Culture of Israelite Women*. Facets. Minneapolis, MN: Fortress.
2006 Hierarchy or Heterarchy? Archaeology and the Theorizing of Israelite Society. Pp. 245–54 in *Confronting the Past: Essays in Honor of William G. Dever*, eds. S. Gitin, J. E. Wright and J. P. Dessel. Winona Lake, IN: Eisenbrauns.

Meyers, E. M., and Meyers, C. L.
forthcoming *Excavations at Ancient Nabratein.* Meiron Excavation Project VI. Winona Lake, IN: Eisenbrauns.

Meyers, E. M.; Kraabel, A. T.; and Strange, J. F.
1976 *Ancient Synagogue Excavations at Khirbet Shema', Upper Galilee, Israel 1970–72.* ASOR Annual 42. Durham, NC: American Schools of Oriental Research.

Meyers, E. M.; Meyers, C. L.; with Strange, J. F.
1990 *Excavations at the Ancient Synagogue of Gush Ḥalav.* Meiron Excavation Project V. Winona Lake, IN: Eisenbrauns.

Meyers, E. M.; Strange, J. F.; and Meyers, C. L.
1981 *Excavations at Ancient Meiron, Upper Galilee, Israel, 1971–72, 1974–75, 1977.* Meiron Excavation Project III. Cambridge, MA: American Schools of Oriental Research.

Milevski, I.
1998 The Groundstone Tools. Pp. 61–72 in *Villages, Terraces, and Stone Mounds: Excavations at Manahat, Jerusalem, 1987–89,* eds. G. Edelstein, I. Milevski and S. Aurant. Jerusalem: Israel Antiquities Authority.

Murdock, G. P.
1937 Comparative Data on the Division of Labor by Sex. *Social Forces* 51: 551–53.

Murdock, G. P., and Provost, C.
1973 Factors in the Division of Labor by Sex: A Cross-Cultural Analysis. *Ethnology* 12: 203–25.

Murdock, G. P., and White, D. R.
1969 Standard Cross-cultural Sample. *Ethnology* 8: 329–69.

Nagy, R.; Meyers, E. M.; Meyers, C. L.; and Weiss, Z. (eds.)
1996 *Sepphoris in Galilee: Crosscurrents of Culture.* Raleigh, NC: North Carolina Museum of Art.

Nelson, S. M.
1997 *Gender in Archaeology: Analyzing Power and Prestige.* Walnut Creek, CA: AltaMira.

Polanyi, K.
1944 *The Great Transformation.* Boston, MA: Beacon.

Pritchard, J. B.
1954 *The Ancient Near East in Pictures Relating to the Old Testament.* Princeton, NJ: Princeton University.

Rapoport, A.
1994 Spatial Organization and the Built Environment. Pp. 460–502 in *Companion Encyclopedia of Anthropology,* ed. T. Ingold. London: Routledge.

Reed, S.
1992 Bread. Pp. 777–800 in *Anchor Bible Dictionary,* vol. 1, ed. D. N. Freedman. New York, NY: Doubleday.

Robins, G.
1993 *Women in Ancient Egypt.* Cambridge, MA: Harvard University.

Rosaldo, M. Z.
1974 Women, Culture, and Society: A Theoretical Overview. Pp. 17–42 in *Women, Culture, and Society,* eds. M. Z. Rosaldo and L Lamphere. Stanford, CA: Stanford University.
1980 The Use and Abuse of Anthropology: Reflections on Feminism and Cross-cultural Understanding. *Signs* 5: 389–417.

Sanday, P. R.
1974 Female Status in the Public Domain. Pp. 189–206 in *Women, Culture, and Society,* eds. M. Z. Rosaldo and L Lamphere. Stanford, CA: Stanford University.

Sharistanian, J. (ed.)
1987 *Beyond the Public/Private Dichotomy: Contemporary Perspectives on Women's Lives.* Contributions to Women's Studies 78. Westport, CT: Greenwood.

Sirman, N.
1995 Friend or Foe? Forging Alliances with Other Women in a Village of Western Turkey. Pp. 199–218 in *Women in Modern Turkish Society: A Reader,* ed. S. Tekeli. London: Zed Books.

Stager, L. E.
1985 The Archaeology of the Family in Ancient Israel. *Bulletin of the American Schools of Oriental Research* 260: 1–35.

Steadman, S. R.
1996 Recent Research in the Archaeology of Architecture: Beyond the Foundations. *Journal of Archaeological Research* 4: 51–93.

Stern, E.; Berg, J.; Gilboa, A.; Sharon, I.; and Zorn, J.
1997 Tel Dor, 1994–1995: Preliminary Stratigraphic Report. *Israel Exploration Journal* 47: 29–56.

Strathern, M.
1979 *Women in Between: Female Roles in a Male World.* Seminar Studies in Anthropology 2. New York, NY: Seminar.

Sweely, T. L.
1999 Gender, Space, People, and Power at Cerén, El Salvador. Pp. 155–71 in *Manifesting Power: Gender and the Interpretation of Power in Archaeology,* ed. T. L. Sweely. London: Routledge.

Szinovacz, M.
1987 Family Power. Pp. 276–307 in *The Sociology of Gender,* eds. B. Hess and M. Susman. New York, NY: Plenum.

Vandenabeele, F.
1989 Has Phoenician Influence Modified Cypriot Terracotta Production? Pp. 266–71 in *Early Society in Cyprus,* ed. E. Peltenburg. Edinburgh: Edinburgh University.

Wagner, S.
1986 *ṭārap̱; ṭerep̱; ṭerep̱â; ṭārāp̱.* Pp. 350–57 in *Theological Dictionary of the Old Testament*, vol. 5, eds. G. J. Botterweck and H. Ringgren. Grand Rapids, MI: Eerdmans.

Watson, P. J.
1979 *Archaeological Ethnography in Western Iran.* Viking Fund Publications in Archaeology 57. Tucson, AZ: Wenner-Gren Foundation for Anthropological Research and the University of Arizona.

Whitridge, P.
1998 Gender, Labor, and the Division of Space in Thule Society. Paper (revised) presented at the 30th Annual Meeting of the Canadian Archaeological Association, 1997, Saskatoon, Saskatchewan.

Wilk, R. R., and Netting, R. McC.
1984 Households: Changing Forms and Functions. Pp. 1–28 in *Households: Comparative and Historical Studies of the Domestic Group,* eds. R. McC. Netting, R. R. Wilk and E. J. Arnould. Berkeley, CA: University of California.

Wilk, R. R., and Rathje, W. L.
1982 Household Archaeology. *American Behavioral Scientist* 25: 617–39.

Wright, R. P. (ed.)
1997 *Gender and Archaeology.* Philadelphia, PA: University of Pennsylvania.

Yanagisako, S. J.
1979 Family and Household: The Analysis of the Domestic Group. *Annual Review of Anthropology* 8: 161–205.

Zonabend, F.
1996 An Anthropological Perspective on Kinship and Family. Pp. 25–39 in *Distant Worlds, Ancient Worlds: A History of the Family,* vol. 1, eds. A. Burghiere, C. Lapisch-Zuber, M. Segalen, and F. Zonabend, trans. S. H. Tenison, R. Morris, and A. Wilson. Cambridge, MA: Belknap.

Chapter 7

Queen or Crone? Gendered Archaeology in an LB Tomb at Gezer

by Joe D. Seger

Analysis of human remains is an important path by which to research gender roles in past cultures. From burial styles and burial goods, inferences can be made regarding gender treatment. Details regarding sex differentials in respect to workloads, diseases, physical risks, stresses, and rates of mortality can all be assessed. Similarly, the skeletal remains themselves often preserve patterns of trauma, disease, and/or workload stress that lead to better comprehension of gender specific conditions and cultural circumstances (Nelson 1997: 59; Cohen and Bennett 1993: 273–78).

An interesting case study in this regard is provided by remains in an LB IB–IIA (1450–1300 B.C.E.) tomb, excavated by the author during several seasons between 1969 and 1971 in Cave I.10A at Tell Gezer in central Israel (Seger 1988). Of special interest is the status and character of the last individual to be buried in the chamber, a tall, gracile female, whose complement of associated grave goods suggests a status that seems to conflict with evidence derived from the analysis of her physical remains. Was she a queen, as may be inferred from associated artifacts? Or was she a more humble crone on testimony of the condition of her skeleton?

Discovery of the Cave I.10A chamber occurred at the conclusion of the summer season of the Hebrew Union College Excavations at Tell Gezer in 1969. The team in Area 10 at the southern end of Field I had reached bedrock everywhere and was cleaning for final photography, when an opening under a ledge was observed. Excavation was resumed at this point for two weeks in October 1969 and again for three weeks in the spring of 1970. As the spring work progressed, it became clear that workers were clearing a large bell-shaped cistern. The entry point was shown to be fortuitous, provided for by the antique collapse of a weakened section of the chamber's roof. Adjacent to the access opening, but beyond the limits of the excavation area above bedrock to the west, the shaft leading up through the chamber ceiling to the original cistern head was discovered. During week two of the spring excavations, however, after removal of almost six meters

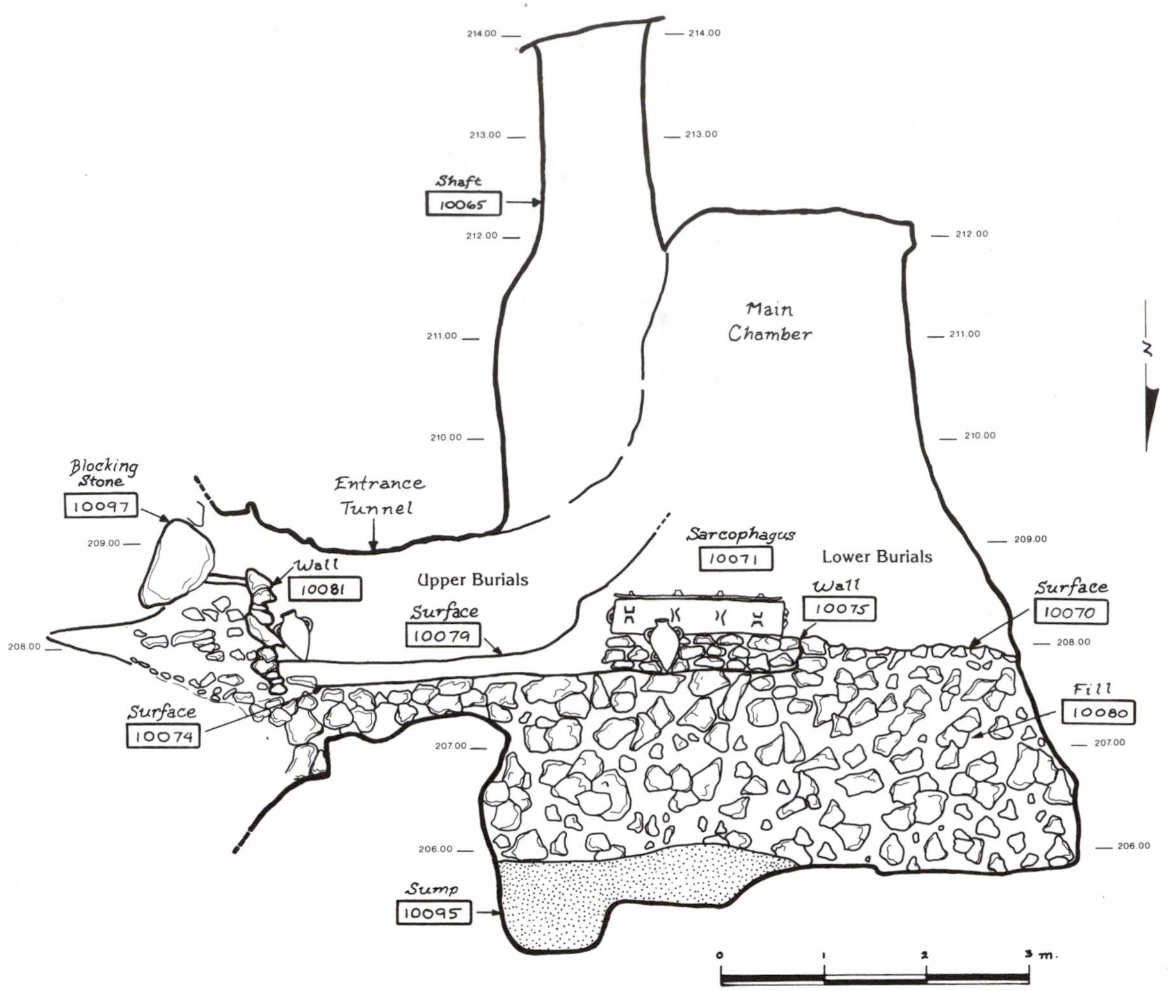

Fig. 1 *Cave I.10A east–west profile.*

of accumulated soil and debris from the cistern chamber, a level of burial remains was reached.

Excavation continued during the succeeding week and also for additional six-week seasons in the summers of 1970 and 1971. These efforts demonstrated that the original cistern chamber had been converted into a tomb at the start of the LB IB period. This had been accomplished by the cutting of a horizontal tunnel from its south side, through bedrock, and out to the slope of the hill below the tell. It was also shown that the collapse of the chamber ceiling had occurred in the early decades of the 14th century B.C.E., at a mid-point in the history of the use of the tomb. This collapse had admitted a deposition of soil and stone debris that entirely covered the early, "lower phase," burial materials and put the main chamber area out of use (fig. 1). However, in a subsequent "upper phase," the entryway tunnel was partly re-cleared and prepared for continued use. The chronological profile of the ceramic and artifact assemblage associated with the upper phase of burials places them comfortably in the LB IIA period. The tomb's use clearly extended through the post-Amarna age of the mid-14th century, but it most certainly was not functioning after 1300 B.C.E. (Seger 1988: 52).

The disposition of burial remains in the upper phase was typical of the tomb in both phases, i.e., with bones, skulls and grave goods from earlier interments moved into casual heaps along the

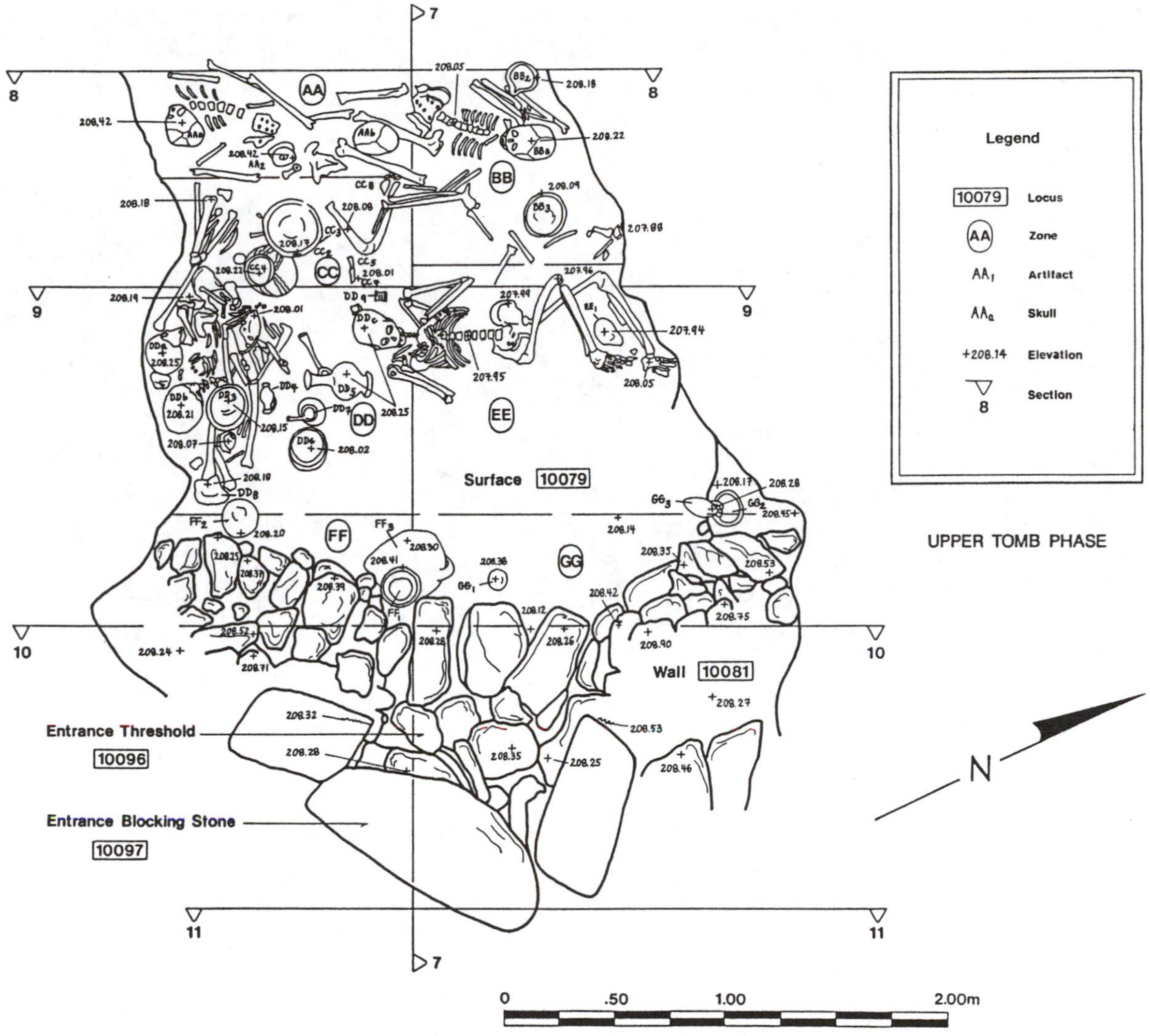

Fig. 2 *Plan of upper-phase burials in tomb I.10A.*

wall to the side and back of the tunnel chamber (figs. 2–3). To judge from the arrangement of the last *in situ* burial, referenced as Individual #1, or more colloquially by the dig team as "Sarah," such clearance in the upper tomb level did not quite provide enough space for the proper prone extended placement of the corpse (fig. 2: Sections DD–EE, Skull DDc). Both Sarah and Individual #88, the only other articulated skeleton found among these upper remains (fig. 2: Section BB, Skull Bba), appear with knees semi-flexed. However, evidence of articulated remains from the lower tomb phase makes it clear that the fully extended prone posture was preferred (Finkel 1988: 129). The orientation of the bodies, on the other hand, seems to be wholly random. Lower-level articulated Individuals #1 and #2, contained in the ceramic sarcophagus designated as Locus 10071, had heads to the south, while the head of articulated Individual # 39 from Sections F and I of Locus 10070.P was to the north. Upper-level Individuals #1 and #88 were oriented in opposite directions; #1 south–southwest and #88 north–northeast. The inference, overall, is that the rituals of burial were regularly accommodated to the practical constraints of available space.

Fig. 3 Individual #1, "Sarah," the last person buried in Tomb I.10A in situ *upper-phase deposits. Meter stick rests on the already cleared lower-phase burial surface.*

The burial of Sarah is notable, not only because she was the last individual to be admitted to the tomb, but because of the character of her associated grave goods. These included an assemblage of seven items, consisting of a Cypriot Base Ring II jug (DD5); three items of local ware: a pitcher (EE1), a bowl (DD6) and a bowl base (DD7); a set of bone tubes and beads (CC1 and CC7); a bronze knife (CC5); and an Egyptian glass vase (DD9; fig. 4). While the pottery group includes an imported Cypriot jug, this is not exceptional, since numerous imported Cypriot items are represented in each of the burial phases. The repertoire of local ware is also quite ordinary. However, the other artifacts suggest that Sarah may have been a woman of some prestige and wealth.

That Sarah enjoyed an elevated status is most specially witnessed by the presence of the rare imported Egyptian glass vase (fig. 5). This vase was found alongside of her skull, next to her left ear. When first found, its color was a deep blue with yellow and turquoise blue wavy threads around the neck. But once exposed, these colors rapidly faded to light grey and white. *In situ,* the vase lay broken cleanly into two pieces. The fracture was across the main body and the form was easily mended.[1] The restored form was 95 mm in height. Traces of fine, light reddish brown sand adhered to the inner surface of the small jar, testifying to the sand-core method of manufacture.

The vessel shape is typical for such mid-second-millennium B.C.E. sand-core molded glass jars, with a tall wide neck, a bulbous body with horizontal handles on two opposing sides, and a flaring foot. Egyptian examples from chronologically secure contexts provide a range in dates that extends from the reign of Thutmose IV (1413–1405 B.C.E.) to that of Amenhotep IV (Akhenaten; 1367–1350 B.C.E.). During this era, the shape was popular not only in Egypt, but such glass jars (with and without handles) were also exported to Palestine, Cyprus, Rhodes, and Crete (Barag 1988; Nolte 1968: 184–85).

The Gezer Cave I.10A vase is one of only six intact examples found in Palestine, and is the only one of these found in a closely dated context con-

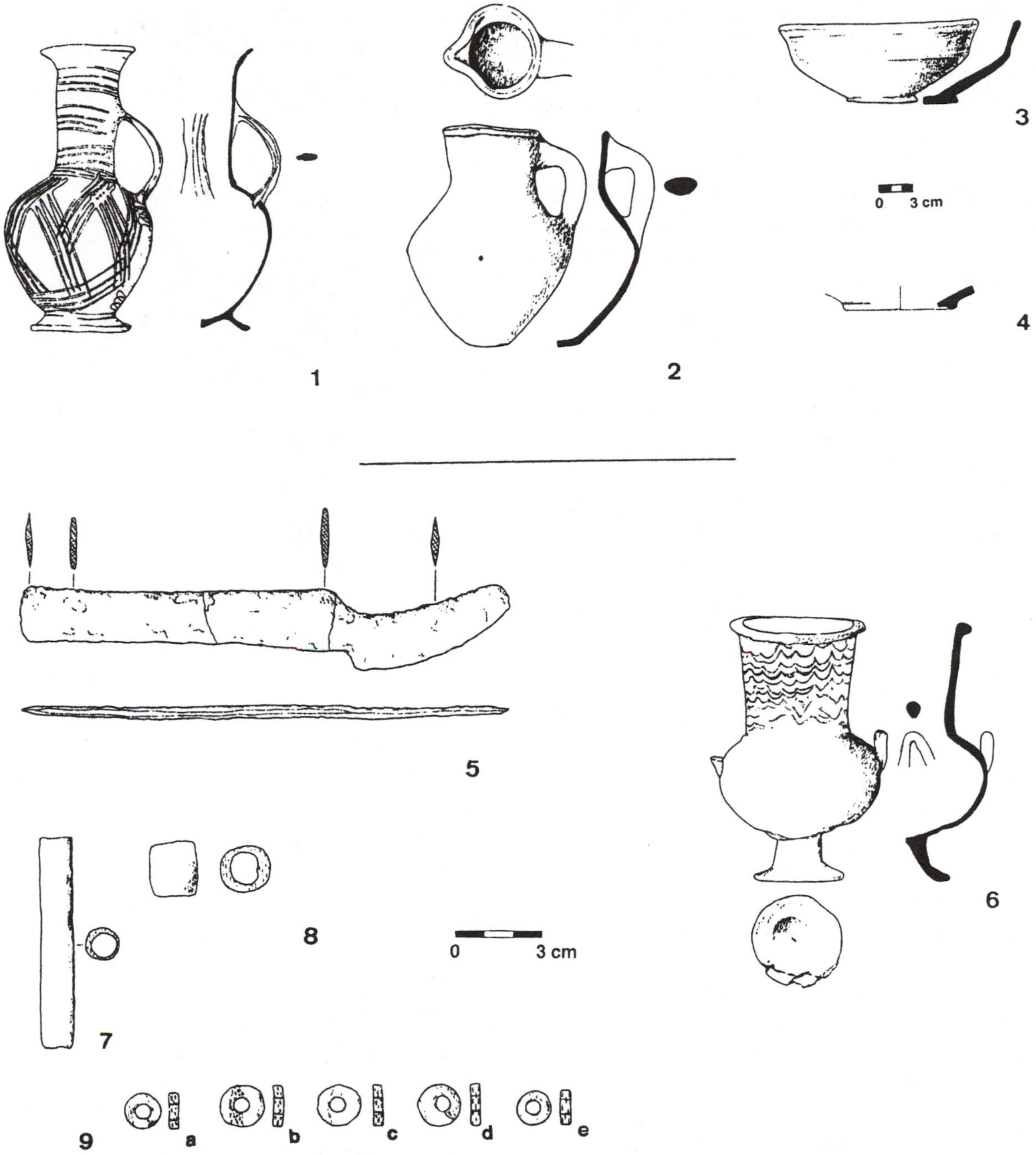

	ITEM	DESCRIPTION		ITEM	DESCRIPTION
1	DD5	Cypriot BR II jug	5	CC5	Bronze knife
2	EE1	Trefoil mouth jug; local ware	6	DD9	Egyptian glass vase
3	DD6	Flaring carinated bowl; local ware	7	CC7a	Bone tube bead
4	DD7	Bowl base; local ware	8	CC7b	Bone tube bead
			9	CC1a–e	Bone beads

Fig. 4 *Burial objects associated with Individual #1, "Sarah." All objects stem from Locus 10079.P.*

temporary with parallels from Egypt. Three such jars were found at Tell el-Ajjul (Petrie 1932: 10, pl. 26:139–140; 1934: 11, pl. 36:2); one came from the Fosse Temple II at Lachish (Tufnell et al. 1940: pl. 24:78); and one from Tomb 11 at Beth-Shemesh (Grant 1938: 24, no. 825, pl. 50:1) The possession of such a rare imported vessel, otherwise associated with the Egyptian noble classes and royalty, readily promotes the argument that Sarah was a person of some high status within the population at Gezer. As suggested by Barag, the vase "may very well have been among presents sent by the Egyptiam monarchs to the kings of Gezer" (Barag 1988: 100).

Fig. 5 *Egyptian sand-core molded glass vase (DD9).*

In a more modest way, the other objects found with Sarah likewise suggest some prestige. The collection of seven bone beads (CC7a–b; CC1a–e), found just next to the glass vase, likely are from a special necklace. Individual bone tubes and discs of similar type can be cited from contemporary deposits in Tomb 216 at Lachish (Tufnell 1958: pl. 28:11, 54:5 and 7) and from the Dominus Flevit burials in Jerusalem (Saller 1964: 183–84, fig. 63:25–26), but no other such full assemblage is documented. Bronze knife CC5, found in the same artifact cluster, is a sickle-style blade of Egyptian type. Of its total length of 175 mm, only 55 mm represent the cutting blade. The remaining 120 mm served as a handle and are straight and rectangular in section. It is likely that the knife was prepared to receive some additional hafting. Petrie described this type of implement as a "cutting-out knife" and suggested that it was used by women to cut linen (Petrie 1917: 51 and Pl. 62:18). Linen cloth, one can postulate, was a luxury product found more commonly among the upper class. It can, accordingly, be presumed that Sarah enjoyed a place within the leading circles at Gezer during her life.

This picture, however, stands in some contrast to the study of Sarah's skeletal remains carried out by physical anthropologist David Jonathan Finkel (Finkel 1988). The skeleton was completely articulated and was in excellent condition when it was removed. Sex was determined from the sacrum and innominate bones and from the general gracility of the skeletal structure. Sarah was a female. Her age was estimated at 30 ± 3 years (Finkel 1988: 132). This estimate was based on completed tooth eruption and condition of the teeth, and on evidence that epiphyseal union had begun to take place in the skeleton, including the clavicles. Sarah was also rather tall: estimates made from all long bones suggest a mean of 169.7 cm (5 feet, 7 inches). Only one small artificial contusion was observed on the left front of the skull near the coronal suture. However, Sarah had suffered from severe osteoarthritis. Her vertebrae were all badly lipped, especially the lumbar. There was also deterioration of thoracic and cervical vertebrae (Finkel 1988: 132).

Within the larger Cave I.10A population, Sarah's physical state was not exceptional. A minimum population of 88 individuals has been estimated (Finkel 1988: 130). As a group it is extremely young, with 31 individuals of less than 10 years and only 7 individuals older than 35 years. Among the 57 adults, gender distinctions could be made for 37 individuals. Of these, 17 were males and 20 females. Excepting the nature of associated grave goods, no evidence was found to suggest any separation or differentiation of burials or burial practices in relation to gender. For 7 individuals within the adult group, a specific age could not be ascertained. Of the remaining 45, the average age at death was 27.5 years, with the median at 24 years. Just over half died between the ages of 14 and 24, another third by 35 years, with the oldest individuals reaching only 55 years. Given the high incidence of infant mortality, it is clear that the life expectancy of this tomb population was extremely low.[2]

At the same time, most of the other adults, like Sarah, were also found to have suffered from osteoarthritis. Almost half of the lumbar vertebrae recovered were severely arthritic, and the rest showed at least slight lipping around the vertebral bodies:

> Thoracic and cervical vertebrae show varying degrees of osteoarthritis as well; and phalanges, metatarsals, and metacarpals reveal lipping and irregular faceting. There is one case of the lower lumbar vertebrae being fused at the top of the sacrum (Finkel 1988:130).

The presence of such severe arthritic conditions, focused especially in the lumbar region, suggests that this population was engaged in work that required continuous stooping or similar postures that regularly placed stress on their lower backs. That this condition was endemic among a population so young is quite notable.

Overall, the population studied is reasonably homogeneous, with characteristics such that they can be considered members of an extended family group.[3] There was considerable sexual dimorphism in the population. The females appear to have been tall and gracile. Finkel notes that with the females, extensive development of ridges and tuberosities for muscle attachments is rare (Finkel 1988: 131):

> On the other hand, the males are distinguished by their robusticity. The occipital tori are large, often with deep median fossae. The brow ridges are pronounced, and some are continuous rather than divided. Supramastoid crests and zygomatic processes are generally well developed. The long bones also show pronounced robusticity. The linea aspera form a large pilaster, and the third trochanters are generally large (Finkel 1988: 131).

Degenerative arthritis and robusticity of bones are suggestive of physical stresses and heavy workloads (Cohen and Bennett 1993). It thus seems clear that this Gezer population was engaged in some form of intensive subsistence labor. The most ready explanation is that these conditions resulted from agricultural practices, where the long hours of work in the fields, plowing, sowing, hoeing, and reaping, required extensive bending, placing severe stress on backs and limbs. The earlier idea that it is normative for women to function as "gatherers," while men hunt and otherwise are the primary initiators of plant and animal domestication has now been effectively challenged (Watson and Kennedy 1991). In small-scale food-producing societies, the whole population, men, women, and children share the agricultural burdens, and such would fit the case of this group at Gezer. However, the lack of robusticity among the females in the group suggests involvement at a lesser scale, at least as far as any "heavy lifting" is concerned. It can also be noted that there were no agricultural tools among the grave goods, but since tombs of the period rarely, if ever, contain this type of object, this is not of much significance.

Before returning to the question of Sarah's probable role within the group, comment must be made with respect to implications that can be drawn from the overall character of the tomb's grave goods. There is a fairly broad sample of local ceramic vessels, but, as noted previously, there are also large numbers of imported wares, mostly of Cypriot origin. In addition, however, there are numerous other imported objects and vessels from origins scattered widely around the eastern Mediterranean. Of special note is the already mentioned L.10071 ceramic sarcophagus. This coffin, though locally made, has parallels only among the repertoire of *larnakes* with multiple handles that are common in Middle Minoan II and Late Minoan I tombs on Crete (Seger 1988: 52). Only one other fragmentary form of such a coffin has been found so far in Palestine. This was in Tomb C2 of the so-called Persian Garden cemetery at Akko (Ben-Arieh and Edelstein 1977). Also possibly from Crete, or otherwise from northern Canaan near Ugarit, is a flanged hilt dagger (item H6). Similar connections or influences reflective of north Canaanite metal working centers can also be proposed for other bronze objects, including daggers, arrowheads, and toggle pins. A more certain import from this northern area is one example of a tall, red burnished "Syrian" bottle (item C2), for which type neutron activation tests have now confirmed the northern coastal provenance. Finally, in addition to the glass vase and the "linen-cutting" knife previously cited, there are numerous other objects of Egyptian export. Among other items, these most notably include several scarabs, four with prenomina of Eighteenth-Dynasty pharaohs; two carved limestone kohl vessels with baboons holding baskets; and an alabaster *tazza* or pedestal dish made of Egyptian calcite (Seger 1988: 50–52).

From this repertoire of imported goods it can be inferred that the early LB community at Gezer was in full contact with the trade networks of the period and that it held sufficient residual wealth to be able to partake extensively in the broad-ranging exchange system. Stratigraphic evidence indicates that, after languishing for almost a century following the rout of the Hyksos by the Egyptians in the late sixteenth century, Gezer recovered and by about 1425 B.C.E. supported a fairly sizeable population. Within early LB IIA, recovery was sufficient to provide occasion for the addition of a substantial wall system (Seger 1988: 57). The Amarna letters testify that just after this time, during the reign of Akenaten (Amenhotep IV; 1467–1350 B.C.E.), one Milkilu, prince of Gezer, respected the Pharaoh as overlord and was actively involved in exchanges of concubines and materials for Egyptian goods (Pritchard 1955: 487). It thus seems likely that the Gezer community at this time may have included some immigrants and traders, but, as we have seen, the population of Tomb I.10A appears to represent more exclusively an extended family of local character, albeit somewhat susceptible to international influences.

How then do we finally assess the role played by Sarah within the Gezer community? Was she a queen, even possibly an ancestor of Milkilu? While there is, in fact, no certain evidence to substantiate such a claim, the presence of such a rare item of Egyptian trade as the glass vase, be it as a direct gift or heirloom, is a clear indicator of some special status. At the same time, on evidence of her arthritic condition, she would seem to have participated in the same regimens of work stress as did others in the clan group, at least to the same extent as did the other females. What implications should be drawn from the fact that the men within the group appear to be more robust? Does this indicate further that Sarah and the other women were of a more favored group? Probably not. While division of labor by gender is rarely absolute, and while gendered work is likewise not necessarily sex-segregated work (Nelson 1997: 111), there is no reason to suppose either that some gender distribution in patterns of work activity might not normally apply (Hamlin 2001). Although exact details of the nature and character of the work in which the Tomb I.10A people were involved can not be specified, some assignment by gender to ordinary and to heavier work activities does seem to have pertained.

We can, however, postulate that the women at Gezer, like women in other small-scale food-producing societies, did a great deal of the productive agricultural work, including gathering and harvesting, along with much of the maintenance, food preparation, caring for children, sewing, and cleaning. Such daily toil would easily account for the physical stresses displayed by their physical remains. Whatever status Sarah held, she apparently was not exempt from these rigors. Yet, at 30 or so years of age, she was much too young to be considered a crone. Given the overall assemblage of burials and tomb goods, along with the obvious economics involved in the preparation and maintenance of the tomb itself, it may be concluded that the extended tomb family in Tomb I.10A represented a somewhat elite, if not upper-class, part of the Gezer LB population. Sarah, it would seem, was one of the most highly regarded among them.

NOTES

1 The restored vessel was complete, with the exception of some small chips that were missing off of the body, the base and one handle. The wavy thread decoration was wound around the neck and marvered into the surface in the final stages of preparation of the upper body and rim. The workmanship is less than excellent (see Barag 1988).

2 It can be noted, however, on evidence supplied by contemporary tomb populations at Megiddo, that such a low estimate of life expectancy is not unusual for this mid-second millennium B.C.E. period. See Guy and Engberg 1938: 111–13, table 6.

3 DNA analysis would help to confirm such an association. However, Finkel's study of these materials was completed in an era before such analysis became an option.

REFERENCES

Barag, D.

1988 An Egyptian Glass Jar. Pp. 100–101 in *Gezer V: The Field I Caves,* ed. J. D. Seger. Annual of the Hebrew Union College. Jerusalem: Nelson Glueck School of Biblical Archaeology.

Ben-Arieh, S., and Edelstein, G.

1977 Akko Tombs near the Persian Garden. *'Atiqot* (English Series) 12: 1–15.

Cohen, M., and Bennett, S.

1993 Skeletal Evidence for Sex Roles and Gender Hierarchies in Prehistory. Pp. 273–96 in *Sex and Gender Hierarchies,* ed. B. Miller. Cambridge: Cambridge University.

Finkel, D. J.

1988 Human Skeletal Remains. Pp. 129–46 in *Gezer V: The Field I Caves,* ed. J. D. Seger. Annual of the Hebrew Union College. Jerusalem: Nelson Glueck School of Biblical Archaeology.

Grant, E.

1938 *Ain Shems Excavations IV: Pottery.* Haverford, PA: Haverford College.

Guy, P. L. O., and Engberg, R. M.

1938 *Megiddo Tombs.* Oriental Institute Publications 33. Chicago, IL: University of Chicago.

Hamlin, C.

2001 Sharing the Load: A Study of Gender and Task Division at the Windover Archaeological Site (8BR246). Pp. 119–35 in *Gender and the Archaeology of Death,* eds. B. Arnold and N. Wicker. Walnut Creek, CA: AltaMira.

Nelson, S. M.

1997 *Gender in Archaeology: Analyzing Power and Prestige.* Walnut Creek, CA: AltaMira.

Nolte, B.

1968 *Die Glasgefässe im Alten Ägypten.* Berlin: Hessling.

Petrie, W. M. F.

1917 *Tools and Weapons.* British School of Archaeology in Egypt 30. London: Quaritch.

Pritchard, J. B. (ed.)

1955 *Ancient Near Eastern Texts Relating to the Old Testament.* Princeton, NJ: Princeton University.

Saller, S. J.

1964 *The Excavation at Dominus Flevit (Mount Olivet, Jerusalem), Vol. II: The Jebusite Burial Place.* Jerusalem: Franciscan Printing.

Seger, J. D. (ed.)

1988 *Gezer V: The Field I Caves.* Annual of the Hebrew Union College. Jerusalem: Nelson Glueck School of Biblical Archaeology.

Tufnell, O.

1958 *Lachish IV (Tell ed-Duweir): The Bronze Age.* New York: Oxford University.

Tufnell, O.; Inge, C. H.; and Harding, L.

1940 *Lachish II (Tell ed-Duweir): The Fosse Temple.* New York: Oxford University.

Watson, P. J., and Kennedy, M. C.

1991 The Development of Horticulture in the Eastern Woodlands of North America: Women's Role. Pp. 255–75 in *Engendering Archaeology: Women and Prehistory*, eds. J. M. Gero and M. W. Conkey. Oxford: Blackwell.

Chapter 8

No Stelae, No Queens: Two Issues Concerning the Kings of Israel and Judah

by Gary A. Rendsburg

This chapter treats two independent issues relevant to the study of the kings of Israel and Judah: (a) the lack of royal inscriptions from these kings, and (b) the lack of queens in the royal courts of Samaria and Jerusalem. The treatment will be relatively short — after all, we are dealing here with "lack," not with evidence — but I hope that in the end the reader will agree that the issues are of major significance for our understanding of ancient Israelite society and religion.

It gives me extreme pleasure to dedicate this chapter to Eric Meyers, the person who introduced me to the academic study of Judaism during my undergraduate career more than thirty years ago.[1] I fondly refer to Eric as "my first teacher," and it is heartwarming to have an enduring friendship after more than three decades.[2]

NO STELAE

The question of whether or not Israelite kings erected royal inscriptions has received considerable attention from a variety of scholars utilizing a variety of approaches in recent years. The answer to this question, however, regardless of the approach employed, has been the same: yes, the kings of Israel and Judah did erect such monuments. I would like to propose a different answer: no, they did not.

The flurry of recent scholarly activity absolves me of having to present a full examination of the state of the question, especially in light of Parker's (2000) fine and detailed contribution. Instead, only a brief review of the literature is necessary, after which I shall pass to my own analysis of the issue, including, most importantly, my reasons for a conclusion contrary to that posited by others.

The most eloquent statement in favor of the view that (at least) the kings of Judah erected royal inscriptions was put forward recently by Na'aman (1998). His basic argument, anticipated by others in a minor way (see, e.g., Montgomery 1951: 35 and Van Seters 1983: 301), runs as follows: selected passages in the book of Kings evoke the language of West Semitic dedicatory inscriptions, either the building type or the military type; therefore, these passages in Kings most likely are based on stelae read by the author(s) of Kings, or perhaps by the authors of the sources cited by the author(s) of Kings, that is, the Chronicles of the Kings of Israel (1 Kgs 14:19, etc.) and the Chronicles of the Kings of Judah (1 Kgs 14:29, etc.).

Parker (2000) agrees, in theory, that the Israelite and Judahite kings could have erected inscribed stelae, but he demurs on the issue of the passages from Kings. He argues that the passages are sufficiently different from the kind of inscriptions one finds on West Semitic stelae, and, therefore, believes that the author of Kings did not make use of such epigraphs, even if they existed.

An idiosyncratic view is that of Wesselius (1999a; 1999b), who posits that the Aramaic inscription from Tel Dan is the work of Jehu, which is to say that we now possess our first ancient Israelite royal inscription. But this analysis is not convincing, for it leaves unexplained such questions as to why the text is written in Aramaic (and not in Hebrew), and why the same individual credited by the Bible as eradicating Baal worship should twice evoke Hadad (= Baal) in a positive vein. Wesselius anticipated such criticisms and attempted to counter them in his article, but I suspect that few scholars will be persuaded by his argument.

I would like to propose a new approach altogether: the kings of Israel and Judah did *not* produce royal monumental inscriptions because of the social, political, and theological controls specific to Israel in the ancient Near Eastern world. That is to say, Parker is correct that the author(s) of Kings (and/or the sources of Kings) did not utilize royal inscriptions;[3] but Parker, Na'aman, and others are incorrect in positing the existence of such inscriptions.

It seems to me that after 150 years of excavation in the land of Israel and its environs, especially given the variety of places excavated and the range of discoveries made, if Israelite, Israelian, and Judahite royal inscriptions existed, then we would have found them by now.[4] The evidence is as follows. In close proximity to Israel, archaeologists have uncovered royal inscriptions erected by Mesha, king of Moab, at Dibon and at El-Kerak (the latter extremely fragmentary), by Hazael, king of Aram, at Dan (at least he is the most likely candidate for the author of this document), and by Akkayush, king of Ekron, at Ekron.[5] Less dramatic and not quite a royal inscription, but nevertheless the work of a neighboring king or his scribe, is the Tel Siran bottle inscription of Amminadav, king of Ammon. Further afield we have the stelae of various Aramean kings found throughout Syria, and, of course, we have some relevant Phoenician documents such as the inscription of Yeḥawmilk, king of Byblos, and various tomb epitaphs.

It is not that archaeologists simply have not excavated Israelite royal centers and other major cities to the same extent that they have excavated such sites in neighboring lands. Indeed, after more than a century of exploration, we can point to the palace of Omri and Ahab at Samaria, major public works at Megiddo and Hazor, a large altar site at Dan, the remains of Shechem and Tirzah, fortifications and other structures at Lachish, a temple at Arad, and numerous buildings in Jerusalem in the excavated portions of the City of David and the Ophel. And yet we have nothing, not a single royal inscription. We have inscriptions from almost all of the aforementioned sites, but none of them can be identified as a royal inscription.

Single fragments of two display inscriptions have been found, one in Samaria and one in Jerusalem, but the extremely fragmentary nature of these two finds prevents any conclusion as to their authors, contents, or purpose. The Samaria find includes only one word, apparently the word אשר, presumably the relative pronoun (Sukenik 1936),[6] but no further statement can be made. The Jerusalem find is the Ophel inscription (Naveh 1982; Ben-Dov 1994; Ahituv 1992: 17–18), in which only two or three complete words can be read. The subject appears to be waterworks of some sort, but we can say nothing further about this text. I certainly would not jump to the conclusion of Ben-Dov (1994: 75):

> This fragment…indicate[s] that it was not uncommon for stelae, inscriptions and plaques bearing texts in praise of rulers…to be installed in the capital of the kings of Judah.

We are left, accordingly, with lack of evidence. This silence is most notable in the case of Hezekiah's tunnel, the most sure correlation between a building project undertaken by a king of Israel or Judah mentioned in the Bible and a known archaeological site.[7] Indeed, we have an inscription from this site, but it is noteworthy that the words are conspicuously not by the king but rather by a workman or foreman. One need only contrast this situation with the boasts of other kings about their waterworks. Most famous are the boasts of the Assyrian kings, including statements familiar to Isaiah as demonstrated by Machinist (1983). But we need not travel so far to read such texts, because Mesha of Moab describes comparable activities (Mesha Stele, especially line 23), and the aforementioned Tel Siran bottle inscription refers to Amminadav's similar effort (line 5). I believe we may ask rather forthrightly: if other Near Eastern kings, great and small, took credit for the construction of major water resource management projects, and if the dominant view that Israelite kings also wrote royal inscriptions is correct, should we not expect to find such a text at the site of Hezekiah's tunnel?

In the current debate between the maximalists and the minimalists, the latter claim that the lack of evidence described above indicates that the kings mentioned in the Bible either did not exist at all or were minor petty rulers. But such an approach is misdirected in the extreme. There plainly is enough evidence from Assyrian records, in particular, to establish the basic historicity of the record presented in the book of Kings (see Halpern 1995: 30 for a convenient summary). But to return to the specific issue at hand, as suggested above, I believe we will not find royal inscriptions, because there were social, political, and theological controls that operated to prevent the kings from producing and displaying monumental stelae and other, lesser epigraphs.

One of the main teachings of the Bible, repeated in a variety of contexts, is the emphasis on humility. The most famous passage, of course, is Micah 6:8 in which the prophet states that one of the three basic items required by God is הצנע לכת עם אלהיך "to walk humbly with your God." The only other attestation of the root צנע in the Bible, Prov 11:2, reads as follows: בא זדון ויבא קלון ואת צנועים חכמה "arrogance comes, then disgrace comes, but with the humble is wisdom."[8] Other pertinent passages from the prophets and poetic books, all using the root ענו, include Isa 11:4 והוכיח במישור לענוי ארץ "and he shall decide with justice for the humble of the earth;" Zeph 2:3 בקשו ענוה "seek humility;" Ps 25:9 ידרך ענוים במשפט וילמד ענוים דרכו "he leads the humble with justice, and he teaches the humble his way;" Ps 37:11 וענוים יירשו ארץ והתענגו על רב שלום "and the humble shall inherit the earth, and they shall have pleasure in abundant peace;" Ps 149:4 יפאר ענוים בישועה "he adorns the humble with victory;" and Prov 3:34 ולענוים יתן חן "and to the humble he grants grace." The historical books, using the root כנע, praise various kings for having humbled themselves before God, e.g., 2 Kgs 22:19, where Huldah says to Josiah, ותכנע מפני יהוה "and you humbled yourself before YHWH" (see also 2 Chr 12:6–7, 12:12 concerning Rehoboam and his men humbling themselves before God in the wake of Shishak's invasion; 2 Chr 33:12 where Manasseh humbles himself before God while held captive by the king of Assyria; etc.). Even Ahab is accorded such a remark, as God says to Elijah in 1 Kgs 21:29 הראית כי נכנע אחאב מלפני "have you seen how Ahab has humbled himself before me?"

The Bible's constant emphasis on humility, I submit, was taken seriously by the people of Israel to such an extent, it appears, that the kings of both kingdoms refrained from following the practices of neighboring monarchs in erecting stelae boasting of their accomplishments. Indeed, one can go further and note that in other matters, the kings of Israel and Judah differed from neighboring kings. A classic example concerns Ahab, of all people. In a famous episode in the Bible, we read how this monarch observed the moral teachings of Israel, even as he violated the most basic of Israel's cultic practices. I refer to Ahab's acceptance of Naboth's response in 1 Kings 21, without attempting to obtain the vineyard through illegal methods. Ahab appears to be guided by the principle of לא תחמד "you shall not covet" (Exod 20:17, Deut 5:21), so that he was unable to take further action. Jezebel, by contrast, was raised in a different cultural milieu — in fact, in her culture the gods are portrayed as covetous (see *CTU* 1.12.I:38, 1.92:29 for Baal, *CTU* 1.92:6 for Athtart, *CTU* 1.17.VI:13–14 for Anat) — and, therefore, she did not feel constrained by Israel's teachings (see Gordon 1963; 1996: 59–61). It is striking that Ahab's lack of action in this story runs counter to Samuel's description of monarchy in 1 Samuel 8. There we read that among the king's abuses will be ואת שדותיכם ואת כרמיכם וזיתיכם הטובים יקח, "and your fields and your vineyards, and your good olive-groves he will take" (v. 14), and yet Ahab refrained from such action. When we recall further that Samuel's denunciation of kingship was based on the reality of royal actions attested in the ancient Near East (see Mendelssohn 1956), among them the appropriation of property,[9] Ahab's lack of action is even more remarkable.

But to return to the issue of humility, a most instructive text appears in 2 Chr 32:24–26 concerning Hezekiah. Here the Chronicler, in what appears to be an attempt to explain why this glorious king suffered from an unspecified disease, refers to Hezekiah's hubris, though in the end he amended his behavior and thereby saved both himself and the nation from God's wrath. The specific wordings are כי גבה לבו "for his heart was haughty" (v. 25), and ויכנע יחזקיהו בגבה לבו "and Hezekiah humbled himself for the haughtiness of his heart" (v. 26). It is not quite clear which action by Hezekiah is criticized here, but most likely the text refers to the king having shown his treasury to the emissaries from Babylon. True, this is referred to only in the older sources of 2 Kgs 20:13–15 = Isa 39:2–4, and the Chronicler (2 Chr 32:31) does not relate the visit by the Babylonian ambassadors directly to Hezekiah's pride. But in both Kings (/Isaiah) and Chronicles, the two episodes of Hezekiah's illness and the visit by the Babylonian delegation are juxtaposed and intertwined, so most likely it is this display of hubris that the Chronicler has in mind when he refers to Hezekiah's גבה לבו "haughtiness of heart" (for discussion see Williamson 1982: 386–87; Japhet 1993: 992–93).[10] It is important to add that Chronicles does not object to the wealth of the king. In fact, the description of Hezekiah's wealth in 2 Chr 32:27–29 is much grander than that noted in 2 Kgs 20:13 (= Isa 39:2). The message is clear: there is nothing wrong with riches and success, only in boasting about it.

Now one might argue that the Chronicler's critique of arrogance represents only post-exilic theology, with closer links to the moralizing of post-biblical Jewish texts than to pre-exilic thought in Israel and Judah. But in light of the panoply of texts pertaining to humility presented above — and I did not even cite perhaps the most famous of all texts: Numb 12:3 והאיש משה ענו מאד מכל האדם אשר על פני האדמה "and the man Moses was very humble, more so than any man on the face of the earth" — clearly one must recognize this point as a basic tenet of Israelite thinking throughout the biblical period. The passage in 2 Chr 32:24–26 provides our best example relevant to a king of Israel or Judah, but the theology reflected there is not an innovation of the post-exilic period.[11]

Another instructive text is Isa 22:15–16, where the prophet admonishes Shevna, the king's majordomo, for having prepared such an elaborate tomb. It is our good fortune that we most likely have uncovered the actual tomb of this individual in Silwan.[12] Assuming the tomb in Silwan is that of Shevna, this discovery represents another excellent correspondence (along with Hezekiah's tunnel discussed above) between a biblical passage and an archaeological site. Shevna's burial site is among the most elaborate ever found in Israel; it is one of only four above-ground monolithic tombs found in the country (the other three are in close proximity of Silwan), and it has several unique traits, e.g., an outside installation apparently to allow offerings at all times (see Bloch-Smith 1992: 43, 209–10). Furthermore, the tomb includes an inscription that closely parallels the tomb inscription of Tabnit, king of Sidon, in contrast to other Israelite tombs, which either lack epitaphs altogether or have simpler inscriptions.[13] In light of this archaeological discovery, we gain a fuller understanding of Isaiah's critique of Shevna's tomb. This royal official contradicted the Israelite teaching of modesty, a point that led the prophet to single him out for disapproval.[14]

The above evidence demonstrates that humility played a special role in Israelite religion. Although we occasionally have such statements in other Near Eastern traditions (e.g., in the Egyptian Instruction of Ptahhotep),[15] the evidence demonstrates that kings in particular, as well as other officials, ignored this teaching; one need only consider the enormous size of the Old Kingdom pyramids, the New Kingdom mortuary temples, the Abu Simbel shrine, and similar monuments, all intended as boastful statements of the pharaohs. For a textual reference, one may point to a passage such as Ahiqar 107, מלך כרחמן אף קלה גבה ה[ו] "a king is like the Merciful [= El/God], indeed his voice is haughty," with no condemnation implied.[16] In Israel, by contrast, the kings followed the teaching of humility (and other basic teachings as well, as noted above in the case of Naboth's vineyard), a point which I believe explains the total absence of royal inscriptions from Israel and Judah.[17]

This contention is obviously an *argumentum e silentio*, and I will be the first to jump for joy if my suggestion is disproved by the discovery of a royal inscription from David, Solomon, or any of their dozens of successors in Israel and Judah. But, if after 150 years of digging we still have not found any, my working hypothesis is that they did not exist.

NO QUEENS

As is well known, the term מלכה "queen" is never applied to a royal woman in the court of Israel or Judah. This term may be used for a reigning monarch from Arabia, viz., the Queen of Sheba in 1 Kings 10, or for a Jewish woman married to the king of Persia, viz., Esther; but מלכה "queen" is never applied to any of the royal women within the constellation of the Israelite, Israelian, or Judahite royal families (see, e.g., Gordon 1988: 130).[18] This point extends even to individuals such as Jezebel in Samaria and Athaliah in Jerusalem, both of whom wielded considerable power, the latter, of course, even serving as regent (note the participle form מלכת in 2 Kgs 11:3).

In place of the queen in the royal court of Judah stood the *gevira*, best translated as "royal-lady," though "queen-mother" is the best functional equivalent in English. Probably the kingdom of Israel included the same position with the same title *gevira*, though the evidence is less forthcoming. In 2 Kgs 10:13, royal visitors from Judah travel to Israel to visit בני המלך ובני הגבירה "the sons of the king and the sons of the *gevira*;" since these words are in the mouth of the Judahite visitors, we cannot be sure whether their use of the word *gevira* reflects their native usage or attests to the same position in the kingdom of Israel. In any case, we can reaffirm the statement that no "queen" appears in the very detailed material concerning Saul, David, Solomon, and the dozens of kings of Israel and Judah who followed them after the split in the kingdom. As to my preferring the term "royal-lady" over "queen-mother," I would not use the latter because it includes the word "queen," thus running counter to the very point under consideration here.[19]

To the best of my knowledge, no one has offered an explanation for the lack of a queen in the courts of Israel and Judah. I will propose one below, but first let us review the evidence from Israel's neighbors.

In other cultures of the Near East, generally the wife of the king, that is, the queen, the king's consort, served as the chief royal female in the court. Famous examples include Tiy, wife of Amenhotep III, Nefertiti, wife of Akhenaten, Nefertari, wife of Rameses II (all of Egypt), Puduḫepa, wife of Hattušili III (of Hatti), and Šibtu, wife of Zimri-Lim (of Mari).[20] This is not to deny that on occasion the mother of the king served in an official capacity or wielded power in the court. For example, in Assyria, the mother of the king ruled the harem consisting of the king's wives and concubines (Leichty 1995: 949). Ugarit has yielded several letters written by the king to his mother regarding political and administrative issues (Heltzer 1982: 182),[21] and it is quite possible that the queen-mother played a role in the royal succession (Gordon 1988; for further discussion see Wiggins 1993: 65–66).[22] In Hatti, the title Tawananna, "queen," was retained by the individual who bore it until she died, even when she survived her husband the late king, and only then did it pass to the wife of the king (Gurney 1952: 66; Beckman 1995: 537).[23] In Egypt, Thutmose IV portrayed himself with his mother Tiaa more often than with his wives (Kozloff and Bryan 1992: 35–36), and Rameses II held a special place for his mother Tuya (Kitchen 1982: 97). The Bible portrays the mother of the king of Massa, a tribe of the Syrian desert (Eph'al 1984: 218–19), advising her son in

Prov 31:1–9. But side-by-side with these examples, certainly in the cases of Rameses II and Hattušili III, we also see the wife of the king (as noted above, Nefertari and Puduḫepa, respectively) functioning as the major female figure in the royal family. This pattern is clearly the general practice in the ancient Near Eastern monarchy.

By contrast, the Bible portrays the *gevira* as the dominant royal woman for the entire history of the kingdom of Judah. The first sign of this is the statement in 1 Kgs 2:19 that Bathsheba was seated to the right of Solomon on a throne reserved especially for her. We then read the numerous accession notices of the Judahite kings mentioning the name of the mother of the king, with no reference to the wife of the king (the first occurs in 1 Kgs 14:21). Towards the end of the Judahite kingdom, we gain a few more specific references. For example, when Jehoiachin, king of Judah, leaves the city of Jerusalem in 598 B.C.E. to meet Nebuchadnezzar, he is accompanied by his mother (2 Kgs 24:12; see also Jer 29:2), and when God commands Jeremiah to address the royal "couple," the wording is אמר למלך ולגבירה "say to the king and to the *gevira*" (Jer 13:18).

In light of this evidence, both biblical and extra-biblical, we may affirm that a significant difference existed between Israel and her neighbors. In Israel, the position of queen does not exist and the wife of the reigning king plays no public role in the realm. Elsewhere in the Near East, notwithstanding the evidence presented above regarding the queen-mother, the chief royal woman in the court was the queen, the wife of the king. Moreover, on occasion the queen wielded considerable power; most striking is the diplomatic correspondence of Puduḫepa of Hatti (for samples, see conveniently Beckman 1996: 123, 125–31).

We now are in a position to ask the important question: Why? Why did Israel alone in the ancient Near East not provide a position of prominence for the wife of the king?

As is well known, the king and queen in the typical ancient Near Eastern society had religious responsibilities. Most importantly, they served as the earthly representatives of the chief god and chief goddess of the pantheon. An up-to-date survey of the various cultures of the ancient Near East relevant to this point would be a welcome addition to the scholarly literature.[24] For our present purpose, it suffices to point out only a few celebrated facts in the most general of terms. In major empires such as Egypt, Hatti, and Assyria, the king served as high priest of the chief god, if not all the gods, at least in a *de jure* fashion, for naturally *de facto* specially trained priests administered the cult on a regular basis. The melding of king and deity can be illustrated by the annual (re-)coronation of the Assyrian king at which the assembled shouted "Assur is king!" referring, that is, to the chief god of the realm (Oppenheim 1964: 99). A similar ceremony existed in Egypt (Frankfort 1948: 129–32), though, of course, in this case one can expand upon the point because the pharaoh was viewed as the god Horus incarnate. The Hittite king is referred to as "the Sun," and the Hittite queen has a special relationship with the sun-goddess (Gurney 1952: 140–41). An important Hittite ritual text describes how the king and queen together exit the palace, proceed to the temple of Zababa, kneel, and then sit upon the throne (Gurney 1952: 154–55). In sum, although Kozloff and Bryan (1992: 43) refer specifically to Egypt in noting that "the theological paradigm by which the king's family relationships were patterned after those of the great gods," the same words could be applied to the ancient Near East in general.

The system of governance in ancient Israel, by contrast, was designed to prevent such an understanding of the king and his wife. First of all, the king could not serve as high priest, or as priest at any rank, because the classical system demanded that the king stem from the tribe of Judah and the priests from the tribe of Levi. Even in the northern kingdom of Israel, where the king could stem from any of the northern tribes, we do not see the king performing a sacerdotal role. Jeroboam I appointed non-Levites as priests (1 Kgs 12:31), but the phrase מקצות העם "from among the people" implies non-royalty. There are exceptions to the above generalization, but mostly they follow a pattern. At an early stage in the Israelite monarchy, presumably before the Levite monopoly was firmly established, David's sons served as priests (2 Sam 8:18). The other instances of royal involvement in the sacrificial service are limited to dedications of temples and altars (see Hurowitz 1992: 292), thus with David (2 Sam 6:17), Solomon (1 Kgs 8:62–63),[25] Jeroboam I (1 Kgs 12:31–13:1), and Ahaz (2 Kgs 16:12–13). The singularity of these events is self-evident; note especially the manner in which Ahaz instructs the priest Uriah on how to perform the sacrifices henceforth (2 Kgs 16:15–16). In short, there is no sustained involvement in the cult by the king in either Israel or Judah.[26]

Even if the king could not serve in a priestly role, it is still very possible that he was viewed in some way as the representative of Yahweh on earth. After all, royal imagery is used for both God and king, the shepherd metaphor is applied to both, and the two appear parallel in various biblical statements (e.g., 1 Kgs 22:10, 22:13, Qoh 8:2, etc.; see also Exod 22:27, though here the word נשיא "ruler" is used). In addition, passages such as Ps 2:6–7, 89:26–27 demonstrate a close familial connection between the king and Yahweh.

Assuming that the average Israelite saw the king as God's agent on earth, there would be an inherent danger in elevating the wife of the king to the level of official consort. The official religion of ancient Israel viewed Yahweh alone as the ruler of the universe, with no attendant deities and, most importantly, no consort.[27] Obviously, on a popular level, such was not the case, as the presence of the expression ליהוה...ולאשרתה "Yahweh...and his Asherah" at Khirbet el-Qom and Kuntillet Ajrud clearly demonstrates. But the intellectuals responsible for the Bible believed otherwise, and we may assume that their convictions had influence over many aspects of Israelite society, including the manner of the king.

Against such background, one can understand that the presence of a queen as the official consort of the king would be considered theologically dangerous. One need only recall the Hittite ritual mentioned above, with king and queen present, or glance at the rock relief at Firatkin with Hattušili libating before the storm-god and Puduḫepa libating before the goddess Hepat (see van den Hout 1995: 1111) to realize how perilous it would be for ancient Israelite theologians, political theorists, and the like, to countenance a queen in the royal court of Israel or Judah.

There still is a need for a royal woman in the court, and this function is filled by the mother of the king. As we have seen, there were precedents for this royal female having some stature. It appears that Israel formalized this position in a way otherwise not encountered in the ancient sources. Exactly what the *gevira* did in the court cannot be determined with any specificity. We have one well-known account of Bathsheba receiving Adonijah and serving as a channel of communication to king Solomon (1 Kgs 2:13–18), but we do not know whether this was a regular occurrence or not. Another episode informs us that Maacah was involved with the cult of Asherah, an action which led (most likely) her grandson (see above, n. 22), King Asa, to dismiss her from the position of *gevira* (1 Kgs 15:13); but this seems to have been a singular event and we should not extrapolate from this that the *gevira* served as a religious functionary (see further below). I am content to assume that the *gevira* served the general role of "royal-lady" (my definition above), if for no other reason than to provide a female presence alongside the king, as presumably required by the rules of etiquette governing official occasions (see 2 Kgs 24:12).[28]

In short, I propose that the lack of a queen in the royal courts of Israel and Judah be seen as a direct reflection of Israel's unique theology in the ancient Near East.[29] Ironically, other scholars (for example, in a radical fashion Ahlström 1963: 57–88; and, less radically, Ackerman 1993; 1998: 138–54) have proposed a religious function for the *gevira*, to be more specific, as symbolizing "the virgin goddess in the *hieros gamos* ceremony," or as the "ideological replica" of Asherah in her role as mother of the gods (Ahlström 1963: 75–76). This understanding of the rank of *gevira*, however, imputes to Israel a ceremony not attested in the Bible,[30] and places far too much emphasis on the singular experience of Maacah. There simply is no evidence for this approach. Far from ascribing a religious function to the *gevira*, I am arguing for exactly the opposite: that the elevation of the mother of the king to "royal-lady" in ancient Israel was intended to dispel any suggestion that the king had a consort, thereby paralleling Israel's view of Yahweh, a deity who had no consort.

CONCLUSION

This essay takes an opposite approach to that offered in much of recent scholarship. The fashion among scholars today is to assume that the Israelites were in many ways indistinguishable from the Canaanites, and by extension shared the general theology of the polytheistic ancient Near East. I have charted a different course altogether. The biblical record — which once more I must emphasize is to be understood as an expression of the official teachings of ancient Israel, often at odds with popular currents in the society — reveals a religious tradition that charted a new course in the ancient world. The two items discussed herein, both relevant to the monarchy in ancient Israel, represent two aspects where Israel differed. The emphasis on humility preached by Israelite religious leaders prevented the kings from erecting boastful stelae, and the uniqueness of Yahweh among the gods of antiquity as a deity without a consort explains the absence of queens from the royal courts of Israel.[31]

NOTES

1 I was a student at the University of North Carolina at Chapel Hill during the years 1971–1975. At the time, the offerings in Jewish Studies on that campus were limited, so Eric Meyers was imported from Duke University to teach at UNC as well.

2 Indeed, not even the intense basketball rivalry between the two neighboring institutions of UNC and Duke has affected our amicable relationship!

3 For one possible quasi-exception, see below, n. 17, regarding 1 Kgs 6:1–2.

4 I use the term "Israelite" to refer to pan-Israel (in this particular case, this refers to the united monarchy under David and Solomon), the term "Israelian" to refer to the northern kingdom of Israel, and the term "Judahite" to refer to the southern kingdom of Judah. In a separate article, Na'aman (1999: 112–13) argues that West Semitic royal inscriptions appear suddenly in the second half of the 9th century B.C.E. in imitation of the Assyrian custom of erecting stelae, at the very time that Assyria began its westward advancement. If he is correct, then we should not speak of possible royal inscriptions of David and Solomon at all. It seems to me, however, that this argument denies any potential influence from Egypt in this regard. Of course, given my view expressed herein, these are moot points for me.

5 On the pronunciation of the name Akkayush, see Eph'al (1999: 5).

6 Though see also Garr 1985: 150, n. 55a.

7 The attempt by Rogerson and Davies (1996) to date the tunnel and the inscription to the Maccabean period has been refuted by a series of scholars in a follow-up article (Hackett et al. 1997).

8 Some have doubted that the root צנע means "be humble," especially in the Micah passage (see Andersen and Freedman [2000: 529–30] for recent discussion). But later Hebrew (Ben Sira and Mishnaic) and Aramaic usage shows this to be the meaning of the verb quite clearly (see the brief discussion in Vargon 1994: 182). Chen (2000: 109) has identified צנע as a northern lexeme, based on its two occurrences in the Bible, Mic 6:8 and Prov 11:2, in contrast to the standard terms כנע and ענו. On Proverbs as a northern compilation, see Chen (2000); on Micah 6–7 as a northern text, see Burkitt (1926), van der Woude (1971), and Ginsberg (1982: 25–26). The presence of צנע in Ben Sira is the result of direct influence from Proverbs, as per Chen.

9 See Mendelssohn (1956: 19–20) for this specific parallel.

10 The Chronicler uses the expression גבה לבו "his heart was haughty" in one other place, 2 Chr 26:16, concerning Uzziah. Quite unexpectedly, the phrase ויגבה לבו "his heart was high" predicated of Jehoshaphat in 2 Chr 17:6 carries a positive connotation (see Japhet 1993: 747).

11 My interest here is the critique of the kings of Israel and Judah, but it is important to note that foreign kings also are criticized for their boastful claims. See, for example, 2 Kgs 19:21–28 = Isa 37:22–29 (concerning Sennacherib, king of Assyria) and Isa 14:4–21 (concerning "the king of Babylon").

12 The tomb cannot be identified definitively as that of Shevna, because the deceased's name is broken in the inscription. Only three final letters remain, namely, -יהו, and of course this tells us very little. The typical

assumption is that the full name of this individual is שבניהו "Shevnayahu," of which the biblical Shevna is a hypocoristicon. Certainly, this is the conclusion of virtually every major scholar who has studied the text and who has pondered the point. See most importantly Avigad (1953) and Ahituv (1992: 27–29).

13 A second epitaph is found on the tomb of Zeraʿyahu adjoining that of Shevna/Shevnayahu; see Reifenberg (1948) and Ahituv (1992: 30–31).

14 Actually, even if the tomb discovered in Silwan is not that of the biblical Shevna, the point remains, for this individual "is attacked by the prophet in a bitter confrontation for having built himself a splendid private tomb. The prophet announces the divine judgment against this act of arrogance in the most violent language possible" (Childs 2001: 161). See also Hurowitz (2000–2001: 137–38), who noted the contrast between Isaiah's words מרום קברו "the height of his tomb" concerning Shevna (Isa 22:16), and Moses's burial בגי "in a ravine" (Deut 34:6) in line with the latter's aforementioned humility.

15 The Egyptian expression is *ʿ3 ib*, literally "big of heart," meaning "proud, arrogant," for which see Lichtheim (1973: 76 n. 6). The expression occurs in lines 52 and 178 according to the enumeration system of Dévaud (1916) and Žába (1956).

16 Though I admit that the exact sense of קלה גבה "his voice is haughty" is not clear. See further Lindenberger (1983: 93).

17 As Hurowitz (1992: 227–32) has noted, it is possible that 1 Kgs 6:1–2 is based on "some sort of building inscription or a votive inscription from the temple itself, written by one of the Tyrian or Byblian workmen involved in the project." This would be a quasi-exception to my main point, but to some extent it is the exception which proves the rule. The only passage in the Bible that may hark back to an inscription available to the author(s) of Kings (and/or his sources) is written not by an Israelite but by a Phoenician. Though, in any case, the presumed text would not be a royal inscription, which is our main concern here. On Phoenicianisms in the Temple building account of 1 Kings 6–8, see the brief treatment in Rendsburg (1990: 29–30). A full treatment of this topic remains a desideratum. At this point, I would note just two other examples of Phoenicianisms in these chapters, namely, פעם as a unit of measurement in 1 Kgs 7:4 (see further Mulder 1988), and זבול "exalted, princely" in 1 Kgs 8:13 (attested in Ugaritic and Phoenician).

18 In a delightful book written for children, *Cleopatra VII: Daughter of the Nile* (Gregory 1999), the 12-year-old future pharaoh is depicted as already learned, spending time in Alexandria's famed museum and library, having read the literature of many peoples, including the Bible (Septuagint, of course). As she realizes that one day she may be pharaoh of Egypt, she is inspired by these very two ladies: "That is why I study royals from the past, because I can follow their examples. The Queen of Sheba so desired in her heart to have knowledge, that she rode by caravan all the way to Jerusalem to meet King Solomon, the wisest man on Earth. Queen Esther of Persia saved her Jewish people from slaughter by bravely standing before King Xerxes" (p. 75). Note that no "queens" of Israel and Judah can be invoked for inspiration.

19 In addition, of course, גבירה derives from a different root than מלך "king," מלכה "queen," etc. Standard treatments of the *gevira* are Andreasen (1983) and Ben-Barak (1991). For more recent discussion on specific issues, see the series of articles by Spanier (1994a; 1994b; 2000).

20 For more details on these queens, see respectively: Kozloff and Bryan (1992: 41–43); Hornung (1999: 36); Kitchen (1982: 98–100); Otten (1975; for a brief summary see van den Hout [1995: 1112]); and Batto (1974: 8–23). For more general information on queens in ancient Egypt, see Troy (1986). I know of no similar study on the queens of Mesopotamia, a fact most probably due to the paucity of information; see Batto (1974: 8). For a brief statement on the situation in Hatti, see Hoffner (1995: 564–65).

21 Heltzer (1982: 184) concluded that the mother of the king had more influence than the wife of the king, but the evidence is not clear on this point, and he may have overstated the case. The problem lies in the fact that the word *mlkt* is used in both contexts, and we cannot be sure to which royal female it applies at all times. In a letter such as *CTU* 2.30:1 *lmlkt u*[*m*]*y* "to the queen, my mother," obviously the mother of the king is addressed. But in a letter such as *CTU* 2.21:2–3, [*l*]*mlkt u*[*grt*] [*a*]*ḫty* "to the queen of Ugarit, my sister," one should assume that the wife of the king is addressed. Heltzer (1982: 182), however, understood the latter as addressed to the queen-mother, and thus he may have exaggerated the influence of this individual.

22 This process could transcend generations, as demonstrated by the presence of Šarelli at the coronation of her grandson Ammurapi of Ugarit; see Singer (1999: 691). One should assume the same situation in Judah in 1 Kgs 15:10 where the name of Asa's "mother" is Maacah bat Abishalom, the same individual who was mother of Asa's father and predecessor Abijam in 1 Kgs 15:2 (though other scenarios are possible).

See further Arbeli 1985. For a documented case of a failed attempt to place one's son on the throne, by Tiy, a secondary wife of Rameses III, see de Buck (1937).

23 For a thorough study of this position, see Bin-Nun (1975).

24 Frankfort (1948) approached the data from the opposite end, that is, he began with the world of the divine and then turned to the world of man. Nevertheless, this classic study still may be consulted profitably.

25 Though in this instance the wording could be factitive. The Chronicler, to be sure, understood 1 Kgs 8:62–63 literally, for he omitted this passage from the book of Chronicles; see Gray (1970: 232).

26 2 Chr 26:16–21 relates how Uzziah attempted to offer incense in the Temple but was prevented from doing so by the priests. As is often the case when Chronicles includes information lacking from Kings, it is difficult to judge the historicity of this episode. This could be simply a matter of the Chronicler attempting to explain how an otherwise good king (see 2 Kgs 15:3) was stricken with leprosy (2 Kgs 15:5), thus the expanded account in Chronicles. On rabbinic explorations into this passage, see Aptowitzer (1931: 142–45; reference courtesy of Prof. Victor Hurowitz of Ben-Gurion University).

27 The term "official religion" is one which scholars prefer not to use nowadays. I still find it convenient, however, to use the term as the sum of Israel's religious beliefs as expressed in the Bible. See Weinfeld (1987: 481) and Rendsburg (1995: 2–3).

28 This would be more or less in line with Ben-Barak (1991: 34), who argued that the *gevira* had "no official political status in the kingdom."

29 For a succinct presentation of how Israel's understanding of Yahweh differed from the general ancient Near Eastern theology, see Weinfeld (1987: 481–82).

30 One will agree with Weinfeld (1996: 528): "In sum, there is a great difference between belief and practice in ancient Israel. The *hieros gamos* as a divine principle has been elaborated, especially in the mystic literature, which flourished in the Kabbalah. However, the religion of Israel prohibited the performance of any ceremony regarding the *hieros gamos*."

31 It is a pleasure to thank my colleague Jeffrey R. Zorn for his comments on an earlier draft of this article.

Note added in proof:

After this article was in press, I learned of the existence of a fragment of a second monumental inscription from Jerusalem, this one from the City of David excavations. Once more it is extremely fragmentary, with only four letters legible, and the text does not allow any major conclusions. For the *editio princeps*, see J. Naveh, Hebrew and Aramaic Inscriptions. Pp. 1–2 in *Excavations at the City of David, 1978–1985*, ed. D. Ariel. Qedem 41. Jerusalem: Institute of Archaeology, Hebrew University of Jerusalem, 2000. For additional remarks, see F. M. Cross, A Fragment of a Monumental Inscription from the City of David. *Israel Exploration Journal* 51 (2001) 44–47. Cross's suggestion that this inscription may be related to the story of Hezekiah's appeal for offerings (2 Chr 31:3–9) is most intriguing. Nevertheless, one still cannot claim this text to be a royal inscription.

REFERENCES

Ackerman, S.

1993 The Queen Mother and the Cult in Ancient Israel. *Journal of Biblical Literature* 112: 385–401.

1998 *Warrior, Dancer, Seductress, Queen: Women in Judges and Biblical Israel.* New York, NY: Doubleday.

Ahituv, S.

1992 *ʾAsufat Ketovot ʿIvriyyot.* Jerusalem: Mosad Bialik.

Ahlström, G. W.

1963 *Aspects of Syncretism in Israelite Religion.* Lund: Gleerup.

Andersen, F. I., and Freedman, D. N.

2000 *Micah.* Anchor Bible 24E. New York: Doubleday.

Andreasen, N.-E. A.

1983 The Role of the Queen Mother in Israelite Society. *Catholic Biblical Quarterly* 45: 179–94.

Aptowitzer, A.

1931 Bet ha-Miqdash shel Maʿala ʿal pi ha-ʾAggada. *Tarbiz* 2: 137–53.

Arbeli, S.

1985 Maʿakha ke-ʾEm ha-Melekh (ha-Gevira) bi-yme Malkhutam shel ʾAviya ve-ʾAsa ve-Hasaratah mi-Maʿamad Ram Zeh. *Shnaton* 9: 165–78.

Avigad, N.

1953 The Epitaph of a Royal Steward from Siloam Village. *Israel Exploration Journal* 3: 137–52.

Batto, B. F.
1974 *Studies on Women at Mari*. Baltimore, MD: Johns Hopkins University.

Beckman, G.
1995 Royal Ideology and State Administration in Hittite Anatolia. Pp. 529–43 in *Civilizations of the Ancient Near East*, vol. 1, ed. J. Sasson. New York, NY: Simon & Schuster Macmillan.
1996 *Hittite Diplomatic Texts*. Society of Biblical Literature Writings from the Ancient World Series. Atlanta, GA: Scholars.

Ben-Barak, Z.
1991 The Status and Right of the *Gĕbîrâ*. *Journal of Biblical Literature* 110: 23–34.

Ben-Dov, M.
1994 A Fragmentary First Temple Period Hebrew Inscription from the Ophel. Pp. 73–75 in *Ancient Jerusalem Revealed*, ed. H. Geva. Jerusalem: Israel Exploration Society.

Bin-Nun, S. R.
1975 *The Tawananna in the Hittite Kingdom*. Heidelberg: Winter.

Bloch-Smith, E.
1992 *Judahite Burial Practices and Beliefs about the Dead*. Journal for the Study of the Old Testament Supplement Series 123 = JSOT/ASOR Monograph Series 7. Sheffield: Sheffield Academic.

de Buck, A.
1937 The Judicial Papyrus of Turin. *Journal of Egyptian Archaeology* 23: 152–64.

Burkitt, F. C.
1926 Micah 6 and 7: A Northern Prophecy. *Journal of Biblical Literature* 45: 159–61.

Chen, Y.
2000 *Israelian Hebrew in the Book of Proverbs*. Unpublished Ph.D. dissertation, Cornell University.

Childs, B. S.
2001 *Isaiah*. Old Testament Library. Louisville, KY: Westminster John Knox.

Dévaud, E.
1916 *Les Maximes de Ptahhotep*. Fribourg: n. publ.

Eph'al, I.
1984 *The Ancient Arabs*. Jerusalem: Magnes.
1999 On the Pronunciation of Some Proper Names. Pp. 5–7 in *Eretz Israel, 26* (*Frank Moore Cross Volume*), ed. B. A. Levine. Jerusalem: Israel Exploration Society. (Hebrew)

Frankfort, H.
1948 *Kingship and the Gods*. Chicago, IL: University of Chicago.

Garr, W. R.
1985 *Dialect Geography of Syria-Palestine, 1000–586 B.C.E.* Philadelphia, PA: University of Pennsylvania.

Ginsberg, H. L.
1982 *The Israelian Heritage of Judaism*. New York, NY: Jewish Theological Seminary.

Gordon, C. H.
1963 A Note on the Tenth Commandment. *Journal of Bible and Religion* 31: 208–9.
1988 Ugaritic *rbt/rabītu*. Pp. 127–32 in *Ascribe to the Lord: Biblical and Other Studies in Memory of Peter C. Craigie*, eds. L. Eslinger and G. Taylor. Journal for the Study of the Old Testament Supplement Series 67. Sheffield: JSOT.
1996 The Background of Some Distinctive Values in the Hebrew Bible. Pp. 57–68 in *"Go to the Land I Will Show You": Studies in Honor of Dwight W. Young*, eds. J. E. Coleson and V. H. Matthews. Winona Lake, IN: Eisenbrauns.

Gray, J.
1970 *I & II Kings*. Old Testament Library. Philadelphia, PA: Westminster.

Gregory, K.
1999 *Cleopatra VII: Daughter of the Nile*. New York, NY: Scholastic.

Gurney, O. R.
1952 *The Hittites*. Harmondsworth: Penguin.

Hackett, J. A.; McCarter, P. K.; Yardeni, A.; Lemaire, A.; Eshel, E.; and Hurvitz, A.
1997 Defusing Pseudo-Scholarship. *Biblical Archaeology Review* 23, no. 2: 41–50, 68.

Halpern, B.
1995 Erasing History. *Bible Review* 11, no. 6: 26–35, 47.

Heltzer, M.
1982 *The Internal Organization of the Kingdom of Ugarit*. Wiesbaden: Reichert.

Hoffner, H. A.
1995 Legal and Social Institutions of Hittite Anatolia. Pp. 555–69 in *Civilizations of the Ancient Near East*, vol. 1, ed. J. Sasson. New York, NY: Simon & Schuster Macmillan.

Hornung, E.
1999 *Akhenaten and the Religion of Light*. Ithaca, NY: Cornell University.

Hurowitz, V. A.

1992 *I Have Built You an Exalted House: Temple Building in the Bible in Light of Mesopotamian and Northwest Semitic Writings*. Journal for the Study of the Old Testament Supplement Series 115 = JSOT/ASOR Monograph Series 5. Sheffield: JSOT.

2000 –2001 Ha-Qevura we-ha-ʾEvel ba-Miqraʾ. *Bet Miqraʾ* 45, no. 161: 121–45.

Japhet, S.

1993 *I & II Chronicles*. Old Testament Library. Louisville, KY: Westminster John Knox.

Kitchen, K. A.

1982 *Pharaoh Triumphant: The Life and Times of Rameses II*. Warminster: Aris & Phillips.

Kozloff, A. P., and Bryan, B. M.

1992 *Egypt's Dazzling Sun: Amenhotep III and His World*. Cleveland, OH: Cleveland Museum of Art.

Leichty, E.

1995 Esarhaddon, King of Assyria. Pp. 949–58 in *Civilizations of the Ancient Near East*, vol. 2, ed. J. Sasson. New York, NY: Simon & Schuster Macmillan.

Lichtheim, M.

1973 *Ancient Egyptian Literature*, vol. 1: *The Old and Middle Kingdoms*. Berkeley, CA: University of California.

Lindenberger, J. M.

1983 *The Aramaic Proverbs of Ahiqar*. Baltimore, MD: Johns Hopkins University.

Machinist, P.

1983 Assyria and Its Image in the First Isaiah. *Journal of the American Oriental Society* 103: 719–37.

Mendelssohn, I.

1956 Samuel's Denunciation of Kingship in the Light of the Akkadian Documents from Ugarit. *Bulletin of the American Schools of Oriental Research* 143: 17–22.

Montgomery, J. A.

1951 *A Critical and Exegetical Commentary on the Book of Kings*. International Critical Commentary. Edinburgh: T. & T. Clark.

Mulder, M. J.

1988 *Paʿam* as a Measure of Length in 1 Kings 7.4 and *KAI* 80.1. Pp. 177–81 in *Text and Context: Old Testament and Semitic Studies for F. C. Fensham*, ed. W. Claassen. Sheffield: JSOT.

Naʾaman, N.

1998 Royal Inscriptions and the Histories of Joash and Ahaz, Kings of Judah. *Vetus Testamentum* 48: 333–49.

1999 The Historical Background of the Aramaic Inscription from Tel Dan. Pp. 112–18 in *Eretz Israel* 26 (*Frank Moore Cross Volume*), ed. B. A. Levine. Jerusalem: Israel Exploration Society. (Hebrew)

Naveh, J.

1982 A Fragment of an Ancient Hebrew Inscription from the Ophel. *Israel Exploration Journal* 32: 195–98.

Oppenheim, A. L.

1964 *Ancient Mesopotamia: Portrait of a Dead Civilization*. Chicago, IL: University of Chicago.

Otten, H.

1975 *Puduḫepa: Eine hethitische Königin in ihren Textzeugnissen*. Akademie der Wissenschaften und der Literatur, Abhandlungen der Geistes- und Sozialwissenschaftlichen Klassen, 1975/1. Mainz: Steiner.

Parker, S. B.

2000 Did the Authors of the Books of Kings Make Use of Royal Inscriptions? *Vetus Testamentum* 50: 357–78.

Reifenberg, A.

1948 A Newly Discovered Hebrew Inscription of the Pre-Exilic Period. *Journal of the Palestine Oriental Society* 21: 134–37.

Rendsburg, G. A.

1990 *Linguistic Evidence for the Northern Origin of Selected Psalms*. Society of Biblical Literature Monograph Series 43. Atlanta, GA: Scholars.

1995 An Essay on Israelite Religion. Pp. 1–17 in *Approaches to Ancient Judaism*, New Series, vol. 8, ed. J. Neusner. Atlanta, GA: Scholars.

Rogerson, J., and Davies, P. R.

1996 Was the Siloam Tunnel Built by Hezekiah? *Biblical Archaeologist* 59: 138–49.

Singer, I.

1999 A Political History of Ugarit. Pp. 603–733 in *Handbook of Ugaritic Studies*, eds. W. G. E. Watson and N. Wyatt. Handbuch der Orientalistik. Leiden: Brill.

Spanier, K.

1994a The Queen Mother in the Judaean Royal Court: Maacah – A Case Study. Pp. 186–95 in *A Feminist Companion to Samuel and Kings*, ed. A. Brenner. Sheffield: Sheffield Academic.

1994b The Queen Mother in the Judaean Royal Court: Maacah and Athaliah. Pp. 75–82 in *Proceedings of the Eleventh World Congress of Jewish Studies*, Division A, *The Bible and Its World*. Jerusalem: World Union of Jewish Studies.

2000 The Northern Israelite Queen Mother in the Judaean Court: Athaliah and Abi. Pp. 136–49 in *Boundaries of the Ancient Near Eastern World: A Tribute to Cyrus H. Gordon*, eds. M. Lubetski, C. Gottlieb and S. Keller. Journal for the Study of the Old Testament Supplement Series 273. Sheffield: Sheffield Academic.

Sukenik, E.

1936 Note on a Fragment of an Israelite Stele Found at Samaria. *Palestine Exploration Fund, Quarterly Statement* 68: 156.

Troy, L.

1986 *Patterns of Queenship in Ancient Egyptian Myth and History*. Uppsala Studies in Ancient Mediterranean and Near Eastern Civilizations 14. Uppsala: n. publ.

van den Hout, T. P. J.

1995 Khattushili III, King of the Hittites. Pp. 1107–20 in *Civilizations of the Ancient Near East*, vol. 2, ed. J. Sasson. New York, NY: Simon & Schuster Macmillan.

van der Woude, A. S.

1971 Deutero-Micah: Ein Prophet aus Nord-Israel? *Nederlands Theologisch Tijdschrift* 25: 365–78.

Van Seters, J.

1983 *In Search of History: Historiography in the Ancient World and the Origins of Biblical History*. New Haven, CT: Yale University.

Vargon, S.

1994 *Sefer Mikha: 'Iyyunim u-Ferushim*. Ramat-Gan: Bar-Ilan University.

Weinfeld, M.

1987 Israelite Religion. Pp. 481–97 in *The Encyclopaedia of Religion*, ed. M. Eliade. New York, NY: Macmillan.

1996 Feminine Features in the Imagery of God in Israel: The Sacred Marriage and the Sacred Tree. *Vetus Testamentum* 46: 515–29.

Wesselius, J.-W.

1999a De eerste koningsinscriptie uit het oude Israël: Een nieuwe visie op de Tel Dan-inscriptie. *Nederlands Theologisch Tijdschrift* 53: 177–90.

1999b The First Royal Inscription from Ancient Israel: The Tel Dan Inscription Reconsidered. *Scandinavian Journal of the Old Testament* 13: 164–86.

Wiggins, S. A.

1993 *A Reassessment of 'Asherah'*. Alter Orient und Altes Testament 235. Neukirchen-Vluyn: Neukirchener.

Williamson, H. G. M.

1982 *1 and 2 Chronicles*. New Century Bible Commentary. Grand Rapids, MI: Eerdmans.

Žába, Z.

1956 *Les Maximes des Ptahhotep*. Prague: Editions de l'Académie Tchécoslovaque des Sciences.

Chapter 9

The Problem of the Other(ed) Woman in Nahum

by Julia M. O'Brien

In bold and striking tones, the book of Nahum celebrates Yahweh's destruction of Nineveh. After the deity's dramatic theophany as the Divine Warrior in chapter 1, chapters 2 and 3 narrate vivid scenes of battle: scarlet-clad warriors march into the city, chariots dart like lightning, hearts faint, knees tremble, and corpses line the street: "...piles of dead, heaps of corpses, dead bodies without end—they stumble over the bodies!" (3:2).

Scholars and people of faith have long wrestled with the ethical dimensions of this little book, whether it should be denigrated as jingoistic nationalism or embraced as the just resistance of the oppressed to colonial powers. Less attention, however, has been devoted to the rhetorical strategies Nahum employs in its attempt to convince the reader that such treatment of Nineveh is appropriate—indeed, demanded. Here, I will explore the ways in which Nahum renders Nineveh as the Other fit for annihilation, and the techniques by which the book attempts to distance Nineveh from the reader and the reader's sympathies. In the course of this discussion, I will consider, too, the ultimate success of Nahum's project. Might Nahum's multiple strategies undercut one another?

NAHUM'S TECHNIQUES

Nahum 1:1

The othering of Nineveh begins in Nahum's superscription where the book is labeled *maśśāʾ*. While scholarly debate continues about whether *maśśāʾ* should be translated as "oracle" (RSV, NRSV) or "burden" (ASV, KJV), the term clearly is a technical term for prophetic material of a threatening nature, as seen through a consideration of other prophetic materials labeled *maśśāʾ*.

In the *maśśāʾ* collections that begin at Hab 1:1, Zec 9:1, 12:1, and Mal 1:1, the deity appears in bold theophany to act decisively on Judah's behalf. In Habakkuk 3 and Zechariah 9, God bursts in as a Divine Warrior before whom mountains and enemies tremble, intent on saving the faithful. In Malachi 3, a messenger arrives to purify the Temple and its priests. In all of these collections, except Malachi, the salvation of the faithful requires the punishment of the nations: Habakkuk protests the wickedness of the Chaldeans, Zechariah 9 denounces Syrian and Philistine cities, and Zechariah 12 sharply distinguishes Judah from "all the nations of the earth" (12:3), envisioning a time in which

Jerusalem will become the cup of reeling for the nations, a heavy stone. While Malachi stands alone in directing judgment primarily toward Judah's own people and priests (after a short introductory slap at Edom), it nonetheless joins the other collections in drawing a sharp distinction between "them" and "us" (e.g., Mal 3:18) and in linking the salvation of God's people with the destruction of the wicked.

The term *maśśāʾ* also begins various oracles in Isaiah 13–23 (13:1, 15:1, 17:1, 19:1, 21:1, 21:11, 21:13, 22:1, 23:1, and 30:6). Erlandsson has argued that a strong anti-Assyrian thread runs throughout these oracles: all the nations here mentioned either already have been defeated by Assyria, are on the verge of being defeated by Assyria, or belong to anti-Assyrian coalitions. He further demonstrates that

> The threads which bind together 14.24–23.18 are primarily (1) Assyria's behavior, (2) the attempts through a policy of alliances to crush Assyria and (3) the proclamation that it is Yahweh who will crush Assyria and guarantee Zion's security (Erlandsson 1970: 102–3).

The corresponding salvation of Judah is less explicit in Isaiah 13–23 than in the other *maśśāʾ* texts, though still present. Isa 16:4b–15 suggests that only when oppressors are vanquished can a just king sit on the throne of David, and 14:2 casts the future as a time in which the house of Jacob will rule over those who once oppressed its people.

As a genre marker, then, the label *maśśāʾ* evokes a rhetorical world in which punishment for the wicked is necessary for the salvation of the righteous, and it clues its reader to expect harsh words for "them" and promises of salvation for "us." By designating Nineveh as the specific target of the *maśśāʾ* to follow, Nahum's superscription designates Nineveh as one whose punishment is necessary to Judah's salvation.

Nahum 1:2–10

While the opening theophany of Nahum may represent a redactional addition (for a discussion see Nogalski 1993), in its present placement it serves as a thematic introduction to the book. Here attention turns away from Nineveh toward an atemporal characterization of Yahweh, God of Israel. The reader first learns through a threefold repetition that Yahweh is *nōqēm*—vengeful, determined to assure that all persons reap the consequences of their actions. Yahweh then appears as the Divine Warrior, who comes to establish justice on earth and before whom the earth shakes.

In the course of describing Yahweh's commitment to justice and his ability to carry out his intentions, Nahum repeatedly mentions Yahweh's enemies (my use of masculine pronouns follows the book's consistent personification of the deity as male). The final clause of Nah 1:2 stresses that God's vengeance is against his enemies, and 1:3 adds that while Yahweh may be slow to anger he does not clear the guilty. The distinction is drawn between God's vengeance against enemies and his care for his own people most clearly in 1:7–8, where, as throughout the Psalms, "those who take refuge" stands as the antonym for "enemies" (Ps 17:7; 37:40).

God's character is revealed in this opening section of Nahum through the contrast between his treatment of his friends and his enemies. Yahweh is vengeful toward and rages against his enemies (1:2), he is a place of safety for those who take refuge in him (1:7), and he pursues his enemies into darkness (1:8). Read in light of other Divine Warrior texts, this discrimination response is seen to arise from God's justice: throughout the Hebrew Bible, such texts rely on the conviction that God's vengeance is warranted and just, a righting of wrongs (Hab 3:13, Deut 32:43, Ps 58:10).

Reading this section of Nahum together with its superscription bears important consequences. The indication that the book is a *maśśāʾ* against Nineveh gives specificity to the generic "enemies" of 1:2–10: Nineveh becomes the (or at least one of the) enemies against whom God rages and whose fate is contrasted with those who take refuge in Yahweh. The mythological nature of the Divine Warrior language in 1:2–10 also casts Nineveh as a suprahistorical enemy of Yahweh: Nineveh is not only a formidable military foe of Judah but also a threat to the cosmic order. Related mythological language serves the same function in 1:11, as Floyd notes:

> This masculine character is generally identified as an enemy of Yahweh and more specifically as the kind of enemy that threatens the moral order of creation, whom Yahweh therefore annihilates with an "overwhelming flood" and "pursues into darkness" (1.8; Floyd 2000: 48).

That the reader is to approve of God's activities is made clear by Nah 1:7. Its affirmation that "Yahweh is good" directs the reader to affirm a God who punishes Nineveh.

Nahum 1:11–14

This section continues and develops the "us/them" dichotomy so far established in the book. Two figures are directly addressed as "you"—one threatened with punishment, the other promised salvation. Problematically, however, these addressees remain unnamed.

Nah 1:11 speaks to a feminine singular "you." Many translators interpret the verse as chastising this figure, as reflected in the renderings of NRSV ("From you one has gone out, one who plots evil against the LORD, one who counsels wickedness") and NIV (which expands the Hebrew to read, "From you, O Nineveh, has one come forth…"). Floyd, however, argues that the feminine figure addressed here is Judah, who is not criticized but rather reminded of a past act of Yahweh's salvation. Translating the opening phrase as "from you has departed" rather than "from you has gone out," Floyd maintains that Judah is reminded of Sennacherib's departure from Jerusalem in 701 B.C.E. as the basis for believing in Yahweh's future graciousness (Floyd 2000: 50–51). Floyd's argument fits well with subsequent verses, in which Judah is liberated from the bonds of an oppressor. Though not yet identified as Judah, the feminine "you" of 1:11 clearly is the one whom God will save.

A second "you" is addressed in 1:14. The grammatical shift to masculine singular suggests a new referent, as does the change in the figure's fate. The masculine figure will be cut off and his grave will be set. In Floyd's rendering, he is the same masculine referent designated by the "plotter" of 1:11 and of "his rod" in 1:13 (Floyd 2000: 48). The one whose bonds once held the feminine "you" will now be punished himself.

In sum, like the previous theophany, 1:11–14 contrasts God's friends and enemies. The feminine singular "you" is promised salvation and protection, as were "those who seek refuge" in 1:2–10. "He," who remains unnamed, stands against God's purposes—God's adversary and enemy (1:8), who ultimately will fall.

Nahum 2:1–14

The announcement of salvation in 2:1, as in the previous unit, is addressed to a feminine singular "you," explicitly named for the first time as Judah. Nah 2:2 also addresses another feminine singular "you," but one whose fate is clearly opposite that of Judah: Judah was invited to celebrate (2:1), but this "you" is warned to mount a defense against an approaching "scatterer." This new "you" is the target of a military siege, the description of which dramatically builds in suspense and intensity through 2:11.

In 2:9, without fanfare, the reader receives a crucial piece of information: the feminine "you" about to undergo siege is Nineveh, mentioned for the first time since the superscription (though NIV adds the name of Nineveh to 1:8, 1:11, and 2:1). This identification of Nineveh with the target of Yahweh's attack has profound implications for the book as a whole. In the unit itself, it serves to contrast two named female characters, Judah and Nineveh—one who can rest from Evil (2:1) and one who is now experiencing destruction. That the fate of Nineveh is opposite that of Judah is made clear: Judah is called to rejoice because her oppression has ended, while Nineveh is described as under siege by Yahweh, the Divine Warrior; and Nah 2:1 opens with a messenger bringing good news to Judah, while 2:14 ends with the obliteration of Assyria's messengers.

When this unit is read in light of all that precedes it in the book, Nineveh's characterization as God's enemy is intensified. The explicit naming of Nineveh in 2:9 ties the book to its superscription, clarifying that the target of the vengeful and angry God 1:2–8 is the foreign city. She is the "adversary" and "enemy" of God (1:8), and the one who receives the threat of 1:14 must find common cause with her.

In turn, by announcing to Judah the time for celebration, 2:1 explicitly names the beneficiary of Yahweh's favor. Judah, then, is the "one who takes refuge," the one for whom God's vengeance is "good" (1:7), the one who will be "afflicted no more" (1:12). Throughout, Nahum remains a *maśśāʾ*, a book in which the fate of "us" is a mirror image of the fate of "them." Judah (the positive female) receives God's protection, while Nineveh (the negative female) receives his judgment. The rhetoric of the book casts Nineveh as Judah's antithesis and also equates Judah's enemy with God's enemy.

The first two chapters of Nahum not only stake a clear dichotomy between "us" and "them," one deserving Yahweh's comfort and the other his wrath. They also encourage the reader to identify with Judah. Such a rhetorical device is found in the structure of 2:1. The opening particle *hinnēh* arrests the attention of the reader, who is invited to gaze at the feet of an anonymous bearer of good news. The commands that immediately follow, however, address Judah. This easy slide from the perspective of the reader to that of Judah aligns their allegiances, inviting a reader to find comfort in the promise given to Judah of perpetual relief from the Evil that had threatened once before (1:11), and to rest assured that the wrath of the Divine Warrior is not directed against us (= Judah, 2:1 = those who take refuge in him, 1:7) but against the Other (Nineveh = his enemies, 1:2).

Nahum 3:1–19

In this unit the destruction of Nineveh is revisited, this time in greater detail and gore. Nineveh, still described as a woman, is sexually assaulted for her crimes. The first verb in 3:5 is usually translated as the "uncovering" of the skirt, although the verbal root *gālâ* is the same one used for "exile" in 2:8. The exposure of a woman's genitalia as a means of humiliation is well-known from the prophetic literature, as in Isa 47:2–3, where daughter Babylon is stripped and humiliated, and in Hos 2:2–3, where stripping is preliminary to the death of the woman. "Uncovering" often also carries the sense of sexual violation: in Lev 8:18 it is paralleled with taking a woman as rival to her sister; in the description of Israel's whoring in Ezek 16:36 it is paralleled with the outpouring of lust; and in Jer 13:22, Judah is not only exposed but also "violated."

Nah 3:5 is marked as divine speech, only the third indication of such in the book. Here, Yahweh not only announces Nineveh's punishment but also explains that he will carry it out himself. He will do the uncovering; he will throw filth on her and despise her; he will make others look upon her. Indeed, 3:5–7 expresses great concern about the gaze of others. Not only will nations and kingdoms see Nineveh's shame (3:5), but she will also be a "sight" (3:6) and all will recoil from seeing her (3:7). The deity is imaged as a man who sexually assaults Nineveh as other nations, imaged as men, gaze at her nakedness.

Nahum's portrayal of the fall of Nineveh is gender-specific: Nineveh is characterized as a woman who is exposed and raped. But to justify the brutal treatment of Nineveh, Nah 3:4 casts her not as any woman, but rather as a specific kind of woman: a *zônâ*, a prostitute. In the Hebrew Bible, *zônâ* refers both literally to a professional prostitute who receives money for sexual acts (e.g., Joshua, Genesis) and figuratively to any promiscuous woman (e.g., Deuteronomy, Ezekiel). As an extension of the figurative usage, *zônâ* is used frequently in the prophetic literature in the context of the marriage metaphor, in which God's relation Israel/Judah is compared to a man's relation to his wife and in which religious unfaithfulness is compared to adultery. Such usages suggest that *zônâ* refers to any woman who does not meet societal expectations of sexual conduct. It most often is a slur that demeans by equating the object of scorn with women who sell their sexual services.

By calling Nineveh *zônâ*, Nahum sets Nineveh as the ultimate Other. The city is not only female and foreign but also a woman on the boundaries of society. Nah 3:4 confirms her dual status: although she is filled with debaucheries, she is also appealing, "gracefully alluring." Rather than attribute agency to the one who finds her attractive, the text blames Nineveh's allure on her own sorcery; as in 2 Kgs 9:22 and Isa 57:3, the charge of *zônâ* is paired with that of witchcraft.

Nahum's *zônâ* slur against a personified female differs from that of other prophetic literature.

While Hosea, Jeremiah and other prophets slander their own people as *zônâ,* Nahum directs the punishment of the whore against a foreign nation. Although in Isaiah Tyre receives both Yahweh's punishment and the label of *zônâ,* Tyre is not punished for promiscuity, but rather the proceeds of her activities are dedicated to Yahweh (Isa 23:18). Nahum uses the sexually freighted language of his culture and of the prophetic genre to justify Nineveh's treatment, but, importantly, only in Nahum does Yahweh punish the promiscuity of one with whom he is not in covenant/marriage relationship.

The apparently rhetorical questions in 3:7 also strive to distance the reader's sympathy from the fate of Nineveh. Who will grieve Nineveh? Not the implied author, who began the chapter with a call to the reader of "woe!" From where will she receive comforters (the same verbal root as the name Nahum)? Not from Nahum, the character who authorizes this book. And, if the book of Nahum is successful, not the reader who witnesses her fate.

CONCLUSIONS ON NAHUM'S TECHNIQUES

In the course of its flow, Nahum uses various rhetorical strategies to convince the reader that Nineveh is the "Other," fit for annihilation. Multiple structural techniques attempt to align the reader's sympathies with Judah against Nineveh, who is cast as its opposite. The genre label of *maśśāʾ*, the decree that Yahweh is good for punishing the wicked in 1:7; the linkage of God's enemy with Judah's enemy which results from a synchronic reading of 1:2–10 and 1:11–14; the slide between Judah and the reader in 2:1; and the rhetorical questions in 3:7 all serve to set Nineveh apart from the reader.

Nahum also utilizes gender ideologies to cast Nineveh as the bad woman, over against the good woman Judah. Nineveh is the whore, promiscuous, the woman whose uncontrolled sexuality warrants sexual assault. In contrast, Judah is the ideal feminine. She is protected by Yahweh and follows his instructions (1:12; 2:1).

Judah is both contrasted with and threatened by the example of Nineveh, the one who did not take refuge in Yahweh. The example of Thebes, the already ravished woman (3:8), warns not only Nineveh but Judah as well: no physical surroundings were strong enough to protect her from devastation. The good woman with her male protector (Judah) is safe, unlike the promiscuous woman (Nineveh), and the woman who trusted her home for protection (Thebes). The brutal treatment afforded the promiscuous Nineveh and the futility of Thebes' self-defense communicate a clear, consistent point to Judah: to be safe, Judah must not act like these women, but instead depend on Yahweh's protection.

Throughout its diatribe against Nineveh, Nahum works hard to obscure the face of the enemy. In Nahum 1, Nineveh is a suprahistorical enemy, the nondescript "wicked;" in Nahum 2 and 3, the fallen of Nineveh are generic, unsexed bodies (2:10; 3:3); and in Nahum 3, the fall of the city is described metaphorically—"she" is the harlot who "naturally" deserves the punishment she receives. Moreover, the reality that (innocent?) children will die in the march of the Divine Warrior is never addressed directly, but only inferred when Nineveh is compared to Thebes, whose children (also) were dashed to pieces at the head of every street (3:10). Nahum does not give face or voice to the fallen; they remain Other, Enemy, Them.

COUNTERCURRENTS

Practioners of deconstructionist, ideological, and certain types of feminist criticism have long maintained that texts have a way of working against their own interests. In their heavy-handed efforts to persuade, texts often say more than they intend. Their various rhetorical techniques spill over into one another and into other texts, destabilizing the individual pieces of the argument and undermining the cumulative effect of the whole. Read from such angles, Nahum's efforts to cast Nineveh as Other are disrupted by the interplay of the book's own language and style.

Identifying the Enemy

As a rhetorical whole, Nahum depends on maintaining the dichotomy between Judah and Nineveh and their respective fates. This distinction, however, is rendered tenuous by the book's enigmatic use of pronouns. The problem is especially acute in 1:11–14, where the "you" who will receive punishment is not clearly named. After having established in 1:2–10 the awesome potential of the Divine Warrior to destroy, Nahum's failure to immediately identify the object of divine anger produces a reading anxiety: against whom is God angry? Similarly, Nahum does not identify the male character threatened at the end of chapter 1 until the last two verses of the book; only at the end does the reader learn the ultimate target of divine wrath. Although Nahum does eventually name all of its characters, the piecemeal style in which it does so requires a process of reading and rereading, the continual searching for clues. Such a style itself precludes any definitive reading. How can one read with any confidence and comfort a text that withholds the answers to so many questions: Is the enemy singular or plural? Masculine or feminine? "Us" or "them"?

The destabilizing function of Yahweh's admission that "I afflicted you" (1:12) scarcely can be overestimated. Nahum attempts to persuade its reader to see the world as divided into two camps: (1) Nineveh = God's enemy = one who plots against Yahweh; and (2) you = those who take refuge in him = the one about to be rescued. But the news that 1:12 delivers alters the equation that Nahum's rhetoric works so hard to formulate: "I afflicted you" suggests that, at least for a time, "you" were God's enemy. Was Assyria, then, God's friend?

Faced with this tension, the reader might retreat to Nahum's Isaiah intertexts, since Isaiah affirms that Assyria can be both used and punished by Yahweh in ways that do not compromise his justice. And yet, reading Nahum in light of Isaiah highlights what Nahum is lacking. Unlike Isaiah, Nahum never names Judah's crimes or the censure she might justly face. If Nahum agrees with Isaiah that guilty Judah has been punished by God through the means of Assyrian oppression, where is Nahum's judgment against Judah (cf. Isaiah 1–2)? Or if, as in Isaiah, God is now ready to punish the instrument he once used to humble Judah, to what changed conditions is he responding? Judah's repentance (cf. Isaiah 37)? Her destruction (cf. Isa 10:12)?

Behind every Bad Woman...

As noted above, Nahum's uses of *zônâ* to castigate Nineveh is unique in the prophetic literature. Nahum does not follow the prophetic marriage metaphor (in which the people's unfaithfulness to Yahweh is compared to a woman's unfaithfulness to her husband), since Nineveh is not imagined to be accused of violating an exclusive relationship with Yahweh.

Employing the *zônâ* charge in this new way wields great rhetorical weight in Nahum, immediately casting Nineveh as the worst kind of woman, but it also raises new questions for the reader (some of which prove problematic for Nahum's argument). For example, fundamental to the concept of *zônâ* is the absence of male to female legitimate sexual activity. According to Phyllis Bird,

> *zônâ* is not used for incest or other prohibited relationships, such as homosexual relations or bestiality. It focuses on the absence of a marriage bond between otherwise acceptable partners (Bird 1989: 90, n. 13).

That is, the defining mark of *zônâ* is the absence of a husband.

Nahum's use of *zônâ*, even if inadvertently, raises the issue of marriage and of legitimate partnership. Which males have been dishonored by Nineveh's promiscuity? While in the prophetic marriage metaphor Yahweh's own honor is at stake, what is Yahweh's interest in Nineveh's promiscuity? Or, perhaps, is another male's honor being challenged?

Other clues in the book suggest that, despite the explicit attention to feminine characterization in Nahum, the implicit and more pressing concern of the book is with male honor. Nahum 1 ends with threats to an unnamed male character, and the lion's den allegory of Nahum 2 focuses on the male's failure to provide for his female and his cubs. Nahum 3 also ends with a threat to a male character, who in an appositive is identified as the king of Assyria, implying that he is the previously unnamed male. As the conclusion to Nahum, it may also suggest that he, and not Nineveh, is the book's ultimate concern (For a fuller discussion of the gendered dynamics of reading Nahum, see O'Brien 2002).

In this reading, the sexual assault on Nineveh represents the public humiliation of her male protector. Brownmiller's classic study of the patriarchical ideology of rape insists that, especially in war, the rape of women is the ultimate means by which to humiliate the men who perceive themselves as protectors:

> Defense of women has long been a hallmark of masculine pride, as possession of women has been a hallmark of masculine success… The body of a raped woman becomes a ceremonial battlefield, a parade ground for the victor's trooping of the colors. The act that is played out upon her is a message passed between men—vivid proof of victory for one and loss and defeat for the others. (Brownmiller 1975: 31)

The rape of women in war is as much about men as it is about women themselves.

In classic patriarchal terms, Yahweh's rape of Nineveh in Nahum 3 is not punishment for her unfaithfulness to him (as in the prophetic marriage metaphor), but a means by which the Assyrian king is shamed in front of others. In a battle about honor between males, transacted on the bodies of their women, Assyria's king is, indeed, the lion who cannot protect his den. Yahweh's ability to vanquish Nineveh and to protect Judah, in turn, demonstrates his own power and potence. (In light of the book's concern with male honor, the supposedly parenthetical comment in 2:3 takes on new meaning: the good news proclaimed by the messenger is less about the comfort of Judah herself than the restoration of the honor of Jacob and Israel.).

Also in classic patriarchal fashion, Nahum's concern with male honor pits women against one another. Judah is warned not to follow the example of Nineveh (and Thebes), but to rely solely on Yahweh's protection. The logic of Nah 3:8–11, however, runs in a counter direction. Nineveh is expected to imagine herself as like Thebes: "Are you better than Thebes…? Even she [went] into exile…. Also, you will become drunk…." Nahum invites Nineveh (and Judah) to experience Thebes' pain, to care about her exile. By introducing the case of Thebes, Nahum invites identification among women.

In the service of Nahum's rhetoric, the mutual identification of the females helps reinforce their dependence (all women need male protection), and it also feeds female fear. Just as Nineveh is reminded that what happened to Thebes can happen to her too, so, as Brownmiller describes, stories of others' rape lead real-life women to control themselves and to reign in their own independence. And yet, in challenge to Nahum's rhetoric, the identification among women also challenges the good woman/bad woman dichotomy on which patriarchy depends. Any sympathy/empathy that the "good woman" feels for the "bad woman" erodes the distinction between them. Once Nineveh can empathize with Thebes, there is little to keep Judah from empathizing with Nineveh.

Nineveh's Face

The casting of Nineveh as a whore serves as an example of how language's "surplus of meaning" destabilizes ideological intent. On the one hand, by calling Nineveh a whore, Nahum effects a powerful Othering. She is not only Woman, but Bad Woman, deserving of whatever punishment she receives, with no one to sympathize with her plight. And yet, on the other hand, by giving the enemy the face of a woman, who is further described as beautiful, Nahum opens itself to the diverse responses that readers have to women, and to women punished for their sexual activities.

Feminist commentators, for example, deem the assault of Nineveh not the just punishment of a foreign nation's transgression, but rather as the threat that rape poses to all women. Judith Sanderson's treatment of Nahum in *The Women's Bible Commentary* asserts the dangers of Nahum's rhetoric to all women and girls:

> …What would it mean to worship a God who is portrayed as raping women when angry? …To involve God in an image of sexual violence is, in a profound way, somehow to justify it and thereby to sanction it for human males who are for any reason angry with a woman (Sanderson 1992: 221).

Sanderson further argues that in order to resist the contemporary mind-set that perpetuates rape, readers must refuse to perpetuate Nahum's language:

> No aspect of God's relationship with humankind can be represented in the modern world by an image that depends on a destructive view of women's bodied selves (Sanderson 1992: 220).

Ironically, it is only because Nahum has chosen a feminine face for Nineveh that feminists such as Sanderson are able to identify with the book's intended foe and resist its rhetoric. Nahum's feminizing of Nineveh allows feminist readers to see in the face of Nineveh their own faces, as well as those of rape victims around the world. No longer the abject Other, the foe becomes Victim Like Me.

CONCLUSION

I have suggested multiple fissures in Nahum's construction of the oppositional differences on which the identities of Nineveh and Judah depend. The distinctions between "us" and "them" do not hold steady throughout the book; antecedentless pronouns render difficult an easy identification of God's friend and God's enemy, and Nineveh's invitation to compare herself with Thebes spawns a web of identification among the feminine characters of the book that destabilize the abjection of Nineveh.

Psychoanalytic theory joins deconstruction in positing that, as a project, Othering is a slippery business. The work of Jacques Lacan and Luce Irigaray suggests that the construal of the Other is an attempt to shape one's own identity; as Beal discusses in his application of Irigaray to the book of Esther, the problem of the Other is always a problem of the self (Beal 1997: 60). The Other becomes the site of what is abjected in the self—that which the self cannot/will not own.

Such theory poses a troublesome question to the book of Nahum: What anxiety of Judah's identity drives Nahum's construction of Nineveh? Does, for example, the designation of Nineveh as whore belie a question of Judah's own fidelity? Is that same anxiety raised when God briefly comments, "I have oppressed you," without explaining why? Does Nahum really portray Judah as innocent (as commentators have suggested)? The concern with the king of Assyria's manliness—his ability to protect his female—likewise may suggest an underlying question of Yahweh's ability to protect his own. Read in the light of Lacan, the sheer energy the book devotes to contrasting the weakness of Assyria with the overwhelming might of Yahweh suggests the paradoxical power of Assyria to confirm—or not to confirm—Yahweh's might.

The recognition of Nahum's ultimate inability to cast Nineveh as Other has several consequences. First, it helps explain why contemporary readings of the book differ so greatly, how it is that feminist scholars recognize Nineveh not as "them" but as "us." Second, and perhaps more importantly, such recognition also offers one grounding for an ethical response to the book's violence. If, as Levinas maintains, "the epiphany of the face is ethical" (Levinas 1961:199), then conjuring the faces not only of oppressed Judeans but also of vanquished Ninevehites calls the reader to move beyond simple denigration or easy embrace of Nahum to a recognition of how blurry the distinction between "us" and "them" really is—not only in this little book, but also in a polarized world.

REFERENCES

Beal, T.

1997 *The Book of Hiding: Gender, Ethnicity, Annihilation and Esther*. New York, NY: Routledge.

Bird, P.

1989 "To Play the Harlot:" An Inquiry Into an Old Testament Metaphor. Pp. 75–94 in *Gender and Difference in Ancient Israel*, ed. P. L. Day. Minneapolis, MN: Augsburg Fortress.

Brownmiller, S.

1975 *Against Our Will: Men, Women and Rape*. New York, NY: Bantam.

Erlandsson, S.

1970 *The Burden of Babylon: A Study of Isaiah 13.2–14.23*. Coniectanea Biblica, Old Testament Series 4. Lund: Gleerup.

Floyd, M.

2000 *Minor Prophets, Part 2,* vol. 22. Forms of Old Testament Literature. Grand Rapids, MI: Eerdmans.

Levinas, E.

1961 *Totality and Infinity: An Essay in Exteriority*, trans. A. Lingis. Pittsburgh, PA: Duquesne University.

Nogalski, J.

1993 *Redactional Processes in the Book of the Twelve.* Beihefte zur Zeitschrift für die Alttestamentliche Wissenschaft 218. Berlin: de Gruyter.

O'Brien, J. M.

2002 *Nahum. Readings*. Sheffield: Sheffield Academic.

Sanderson, J.

1992 Nahum. Pp. 217–21 in *The Women's Bible Commentary*, eds. C. A. Newsom and S. H. Ringe. Louisville, KY: Westminster John Knox.

Chapter 10

Linguistic Variation Emphasized, Linguistic Variation Denied

by Raymond F. Person, Jr.

Developed from a combination of anthropology, sociology, and linguistics, sociolinguistics emerged as a separate discipline of study in the 1960s.[1] Sociolinguistics concern the interaction of language and social status, including such topics as language variability according to class, gender, and ethnicity and an individual's use of various registers in different social settings.[2] The 1966 article "On Sociolinguistically Oriented Language Surveys" by Charles Ferguson, the "principal architect" for sociolinguistics (Tucker 1997: 321), was reprinted in the 1967 volume of *Bible Translator* (Ferguson 1967). In his article, Ferguson mentions favorably the work of the ethnolinguist William Reyburn, who was the Translations Consultant for the United Bible Societies in Nigeria. This early relationship between sociolinguistics and Bible translation led to the widespread use of sociolinguistics by numerous leaders in Bible translation, especially Eugene A. Nida and his colleagues in the United Bible Societies (e.g., Nida 1979; Stine 1986). Until recently, sociolinguistically informed studies of the Bible were primarily limited to concerns of translation, and most of these studies concerned the New Testament. In the 1990s, sociolinguistics began to influence other aspects of biblical interpretation more widely, including linguistic topics (e.g., reported speech, dialect), social conflict, and discussions of gender and class.[3]

This essay joins these recent studies in using sociolinguistics to interpret the Hebrew Bible. First, I review recent studies that demonstrate how social differentiation is evident in ancient Hebrew. Second, I turn my attention to the way in which biblical narrative portrays the relationship between social differentiation and language, specifically concerning communication between speakers of different dialects or languages. Relatively few biblical narratives emphasize language as a marker of social differentiation (Gen 11; 2 Kgs 18:26–27; Jdgs 12:5–6); rather, as we will see in the Abraham narrative (Gen 12:1–25:11), biblical narratives generally gloss over linguistic variations, thereby denying their importance.

EVIDENCE OF LANGUAGE AND SOCIAL DIFFERENTIATION IN ANCIENT HEBREW

Recent studies of the Hebrew Bible and available epigraphic evidence have demonstrated that behind classical biblical Hebrew were a variety of Hebrew dialects. Although one must be cautious when using the Hebrew Bible to reconstruct ancient society, careful studies can reach well-nuanced conclusions about the culture that wrote and first read the Hebrew Bible. Below, I discuss several recent studies that provide strong evidence for linguistic variation according to social differentiation, including spoken versus written dialects, regional dialects, and the influence of gender on language.

In his 1980 New York University dissertation, Gary Rendsburg drew from the work of sociolinguist Charles Ferguson and borrowed Ferguson's term "diglossia" to refer to the existence of two varieties of ancient Hebrew, a spoken dialect and a written dialect (Rendsburg 1990). His observations were based primarily upon morphological evidence. Assuming that Mishnaic Hebrew was a spoken dialect and Qumran Hebrew its contemporaneous written dialect, he compared grammatical features that are considered unusual in relationship to the accepted norms of classical Hebrew to Mishnaic Hebrew. He also compared such grammatical features to the analogous diglossia in spoken and written Arabic and other living Semitic languages. In many cases, the uncommon grammatical features in classical Hebrew were common features in Mishnaic Hebrew and paralleled characteristics in spoken Arabic and other spoken Semitic languages. Therefore, Rendsburg concluded that classical Hebrew was the literary dialect of ancient Hebrew and that a popular, spoken Hebrew coexisted, sometimes influencing the language of the Hebrew Bible. This influence is evident in certain colloquialisms present in the Hebrew Bible.

In a later work, Rendsburg concluded that regional varieties of ancient Hebrew also existed (Rendsburg 1992). Whereas in his dissertation he explained some colloquialisms by referring to diglossia, he now explained some colloquialisms by referring to the differences between regional dialects, specifically southern Judahite Hebrew and northern Israelian Hebrew. As the literary Hebrew of the Judahite capital of Jerusalem, classical Hebrew was the written dialect of Judahite Hebrew. Rendsburg noted that certain sections of the Hebrew Bible, which other scholars had concluded were probably of a northern provenance, contained a higher percentage of the colloquialisms that he identified as features of Israelian Hebrew. Thus, Rendsburg argued that he had provided evidence that some of the uncommon grammatical features found in the Hebrew Bible were colloquialisms from Israelian Hebrew, preserved in literature that is predominantly Judahite Hebrew (= classical Hebrew).

Rendsburg's conclusions concerning Israelian Hebrew have been seriously challenged from a methodological perspective by both Daniel Fredericks and Ian Young (Fredericks 1996; Young 1993; 1997). However, Rendsburg's basic argument for linguistic diversity in ancient Hebrew—spoken versus written, standard versus non-standard—is now widely accepted, even by his critics. That is, the evidence that Rendsburg and others have presented convincingly suggests linguistic variations of ancient Hebrew according to social status and region; the disagreements concern which specific linguistic communities may be associated with the colloquialisms. For example, Fredericks and Young both argue that the evidence certainly points to the existence of a colloquial dialect of ancient Hebrew that has left some traces in the language of the Hebrew Bible; however, they disagree with Rendsburg's conclusion that we can reasonably locate this dialect in the north (Fredericks 1996; Young 1993; 1997). Thus, it is generally accepted that there was significant diversity among different speakers of ancient Hebrew, and that this diversity betrays social differentiation.

In his 1993 Vanderbilt University dissertation, Robert Johnson drew extensively from sociolinguistic studies of language variation to examine the dialogue in the book of Ruth, with special regard to the ways in which gender relates to language variation (Johnson 1993). Although he was careful not to draw conclusions concerning gender and language variation in ancient Hebrew in general,

Johnson demonstrated extremely well the influence that gender had upon the way the biblical author represented male and female characters in dialogue in the narrative. This is especially clear in his discussion of Boaz's conversational style in the narrative as compared to Ruth's. Boaz speaks more than any other character in the book. He always initiates the conversation, issues more commands, and uses fewer politeness strategies. In contrast, Ruth speaks less and, with one exception, only when she is spoken to by another character who initiates the conversation. She uses no declaratives, but does use various politeness strategies (Johnson 1993: 196–98). Although the characters of Boaz and Ruth speak the same Hebrew dialect, the pragmatic aspects of their dialogues differ significantly along the lines of gender. As Johnson demonstrates so well, this is also the case for other characters in the book of Ruth.

LINGUISTIC VARIATION EMPHASIZED IN THE HEBREW BIBLE

The studies of Rendsburg, Johnson, and others clearly demonstrate the influence of social differentiation upon linguistic variation in ancient Hebrew. These studies concern linguistic features that can be understood to occur "naturally"—that is, speakers generate such linguistically diverse features often without consciously reflecting on their speech patterns. For example, what might be considered a "colloquialism" by one speaker may simply be understood to be standard speech by another. Furthermore, a woman can easily change her mode of speech from a context with a male superior to a context with a good mutual female friend without having to consciously and intentionally note the change. Of course, this does not mean that speakers are always unconsciously generating such speech, but in most contexts we simply speak what comes "naturally" according to social conventions in that particular setting.

Although we might be able to make some good arguments for the intentional use of linguistic variation as a literary device (e.g., Rendsburg 1995; 1999; Gianto 1996; Fredericks 1998), I suspect that some (if not most) of the "colloquialisms" identified by Rendsburg and others occurred "naturally." Likewise, I suspect that much of the influence of gender on language variation in the book of Ruth occurred "naturally," as the author simply wrote how men and women "naturally" speak. That is, in most cases the biblical authors simply wrote what they perceived, consciously or unconsciously, as what "normal" people might "naturally" say in such situations. Below, I examine three biblical narratives (Gen 11; 2 Kgs 18:26–27; Jdgs 12:5–6) that may contain some of the "naturally" occurring evidence of linguistic variation as discussed by Rendsburg, Johnson, and others. However, these biblical narratives contain intentional and conscious reflections upon linguistic variation that are much more obvious in that each of them explicitly refers to diverse languages or dialects.

The most obvious biblical narrative concerning the relationship between language and society is the story of the tower of Babel (Gen 11:1–9). In fact, the first explicit biblical references to diverse languages are in Gen 10–11, because the narrative asserts that from Adam and Eve to the tower of Babel "the whole earth had one language and the same words'" (Gen 11:1). The narrative assumes that the existence of only one language allows humanity to cooperate, so that nothing is impossible. "And the Lord said, 'Look, they are one people, and they have one language; and this is only the beginning of what they will do; nothing that they propose to do will now be impossible for them'" (Gen 11:6). Note that here there is an explicit connection between being "one people" and having "one language"—that is, ethnicity and language are closely related. God's solution to this perceived problem is to confuse humanity by making them speak different languages: "Come, let us go down, and confuse their language there, so that they will not understand one another's speech" (Gen 11:7). This confusing of language divides humanity into different peoples, whom the Lord scattered "over the face of all the earth" (Gen 11:9). From the biblical narrative's perspective, the existence of different languages contributes to different ethnic identities and often to misunderstandings between ethnic groups that lead to social conflict.

From the tower of Babel onwards, the biblical narrative assumes that linguistic diversity is a reality in human history—that is, the Lord determined to confuse humanity at the tower of Babel and this confusion continues throughout the narrative. But humans were able to find some ways of overcoming such confusion, even if only imperfectly, and one such way was to learn multiple languages. Geographically situated between the ancient superpowers of Mesopotamia and Egypt, Israel's elite learned other languages. This is well represented in the account of Sennacherib's siege of Jerusalem (2 Kgs 18:13–19:37).

Both the Assyrian and Judean officials in the narrative speak at least two languages—Hebrew and Aramaic—that is, the political elite has devised ways around the confusion of Babel. With this knowledge also comes social power to control information for political means. When the Rabshakeh delivers the Assyrian threat in Hebrew, Hezekiah's officials say, "Please speak to your servants in the Aramaic language, for we understand it; do not speak to us in the language of Judah within the hearing of the people who are on the wall" (2 Kgs 18:26). Here the Judean bureaucrats want to use their linguistic skills to withhold from the common people the information that the Rabshakeh is there to deliver for Sennacherib, but they fail. The Rabshakeh's purpose is best served by speaking loudly and clearly in Hebrew, so that all the inhabitants of Jerusalem can hear and understand. "But the Rabshakeh said to them, 'Has my master sent me to speak these words to your master and to you, and not to the people sitting on the wall, who are doomed with you to eat their own dung and to drink their own urine?'" (2 Kgs 18:27). That is, the Rabshakeh also has the linguistic competence necessary to deliver his message, so that his foreign enemies, including the common people, understand the message directly from him without any meddling intervention on the part of the Judean bureaucracy. The Rabshakeh, therefore, continues with his threatening message "in a loud voice in the language of Judah" (2 Kgs 18:28).

The narratives of the tower of Babel and Sennacherib's siege of Jerusalem contain explicit references to linguistic variation in the form of different languages. However, the studies in the preceding section all concerned linguistic differences within the same language: ancient Hebrew. One biblical narrative contains an excellent example of this type of linguistic variation as a key element of the narrative itself, the story of Jephthah the judge (Jdgs 11:1–12:7). Jephthah leads the Gileadites to victory over the Ammonites and then over their fellow Israelites, the tribe of Ephraim. The Gileadites defeat the Ephraimites and the Ephraimites scatter. Whenever the Ephraimites cross the Jordan River, they believe that they can easily deceive the Gileadites and then safely pass through enemy territory to return home. However, the Gileadites come up with a foolproof linguistic test for identifying the Ephraimites, based on different regional pronunciations.

> Whenever one of the fugitives of Ephraim said, "Let me go over," the men of Gilead would say to him, "Are you an Ephraimite?" When he said, "No," they said to him, "Then say Shibboleth," and he said, "Sibboleth," for he could not pronounce it right. Then they seized him at the fords of the Jordan (Jdgs 12:5–6).

This narrative demonstrates clearly how one's linguistic diversity can be a matter of life or death in some circumstances.[4] In this narrative, 42,000 Ephraimites were killed because they did not pronounce one particular word in the same manner that their more powerful enemy did.

LINGUISTIC VARIATION DENIED IN THE HEBREW BIBLE

Above, we have seen evidence of linguistic variations not only occurring "naturally" in biblical narratives but occurring even in some explicit references to linguistic variation and its social consequences in the Hebrew Bible. In fact, the tower of Babel story suggests that the biblical narrative assumes that the existence of various languages determines, to some degree at least, diverse ethnic groups and that misunderstandings between these groups often lead to social conflict. Although some biblical narratives may contain some type of evidence for linguistic variation on the basis of dialect, gender, or social status, few biblical narratives contain any explicit reference to linguistic variation. Most biblical narratives containing interactions between people who speak different languages simply ignore this dimension of the narrative, denying that such linguistic variation could create any kind of difficulty in communication. In fact, when one reads most biblical narratives, one could easily get the impression that everyone in the ancient Near East spoke Hebrew.

Such a denial of linguistic variation is evident in the Abraham story, where it appears that everyone speaks the same language. The biblical narrative makes no speculations concerning the origin of Hebrew. As noted above, ethnicity and language are generally connected in biblical narrative, and this is certainly the case with Abram/Abraham. In Gen 14:13, he is referred to as "Abram the Hebrew," indicating his ethnicity and, indirectly, his language. However, nowhere in the dialogues of the narrative is there an explicit reference to the language Abram/Abraham and the other characters speak. When Abram and Sarai flee the famine by becoming "aliens" in Egypt (Gen 12:10–20), they seem to have no problem whatsoever communicating with the Egyptians. Abram tells Sarai, "Say you are my sister" (Gen 12:13), and Sarai presumably does so. In fact, the Pharaoh's question later implies that Abram also tells the Egyptians upon his arrival, "She is my sister" (Gen 12:19). This certainly leaves open the question of how these Hebrew-speaking aliens communicated with the Egyptians. Were Abram and Sarai bilingual and spoke in Egyptian? Did the Egyptians understand Hebrew? This question is even more obvious when Pharaoh is speaking with Abram (Gen 12:18–19). Does Abram understand Egyptian? Does Pharaoh speak Hebrew? Was an interpreter present? The narrative provides absolutely no information upon which to answer these questions, completely ignoring what must have been a language barrier between the characters of Abram and Pharaoh.

When Abram defeats the alliance of kings who had captured Lot, the priest-king Melchizedek blesses him, apparently with a Hebrew blessing (Gen 14:19–20). Does this imply that the Canaanites also speak Hebrew? Or is Melchizedek bilingual? Abram and the king of Sodom then speak concerning the spoils Abram gained (Gen 14:20–24). Again, does the Canaanite king speak Hebrew or Abram the Semitic language of the Canaanites? Was an interpreter present? Concerning these questions, the narrative remains silent.

Other places in the Abram/Abraham narrative raise similar questions, especially those in which Abraham interacts with King Abimelech of Gerar. Again, since ethnicity and language are generally assumed to be connected, one would think that Abram/Abraham would have some difficulty in communicating with the Egyptians, Canaanites, and other peoples in the narrative. However, there is nothing in the narrative to suggest this. It is as if all of the characters speak the same language, the language of the Hebrew narrative itself.

The same kinds of questions can be asked in regard to a variety of biblical narratives. How did the Ninevites understand Jonah's terse Hebrew oracle? How did David and Goliath communicate? How did the Israelite spies and Rahab communicate? Are we to assume that all of these characters were bilingual or multilingual? I think not.[5] The biblical narrative simply glosses over such details as it selects what is important to communicate to its readers. When linguistic variation is crucial to the development of the plot or characterization, specific references to the particular type of linguistic variation occur (e.g., Gen 11:1–9; 2 Kgs 18:26–28; Jdgs 12:5–6). Since this is rarely the case, biblical narrative simply ignores or denies such linguistic variation because, as with all narrative, telling a good story requires selectivity and in most biblical narratives linguistic variation simply does not count as something worthy of being selected for comment. As a result, it appears that all of the characters generally speak Hebrew, the language of the narrative itself and, in many cases, the same Hebrew dialect.

CONCLUSIONS

Although there is clear evidence that linguistic diversity was a reality behind the Hebrew Bible, the biblical narrative generally avoids any explicit references to such linguistic variations. Since sociolinguistics has repeatedly demonstrated that such linguistic variation is closely related to social differentiation and to issues of power and control in society, this narrative tendency to selectively ignore a source of potential social conflict is yet another instance of the perspective of the "other" being minimized in biblical narrative. Other studies concerning gender, ethnicity, and social class (including other essays in this volume) have examined analogous narrative tendencies of selectivity. Fortunately, new methods of interpretation of archaeological and textual evidence are offering new opportunities to recover some of the voices of the "other."

I am pleased to contribute this essay in honor of Eric M. Meyers, a teacher, scholar, and friend who has encouraged the exploration of new interpretive methods.

NOTES

1 For an excellent discussion of the history of sociolinguistics, see Shuy 1997 and other essays in Paulston and Tucker 1997.

2 For an excellent introduction to the principles, methods, and observations of sociolinguistics, see Holmes 1992.

3 For example, the Sociolinguistics and Biblical Studies Consultation met at the 1994, 1995, and 1996 Annual Meetings of the Society of Biblical Literature. Some related publications by participants in this consultation include the following: Blount 1995; Meier 1992; Miller 1996; Nida 1993; Hurtgen 1993; Aageson 1996; Fredericks 1996; 1998; Porter 1997; Person 1996 and 1999. Some other studies explicitly drawing from sociolinguistics include the following: Rendsburg 1990; Wilt 1996; Gianto 1996; Young 1997.

4 There are various ways to explain the difficulty of the Ephraimites' attempt to pronounce the word the same way as the Gileadites, but the point remains the same in each of the various explanations. For a discussion of some of the various explanations, see Young 1993: 188.

5 Another possible explanation may be that some of these speakers understood the other's language because some of the dialects were closely related on a continuum of Semitic languages in Syria-Palestine. For example, W. Randall Garr argues that Jer 27:3 suggests that Jeremiah's Hebrew was understood by others knowing Phoenician, Ammonite, Edomite, and Moabite (Garr 1985: 231). Although this may have been the case between speakers of some closely related ancient languages, the linguistic dissimilarities between other languages (e.g., Egyptian and Hebrew) would certainly limit the application of this argument to the general narrative practice of simply glossing over such details when they do not contribute directly to the development of plot or characterization. Moreover, this general narrative tendency calls into question the use of biblical narrative to support such an argument; therefore, Garr's assumption of historical accuracy here is probably using Jer 27:3 for purposes not imagined by the biblical author(s).

REFERENCES

Aageson, J. W.
1996 "Control" in Pauline Language and Culture: A Study of Rom 6. *New Testament Studies* 42: 75–89.

Blount, B. K.
1995 *Cultural Interpretation: Reorienting New Testament Criticism*. Minneapolis, MN: Fortress.

Ferguson, C. A.
1967 On Sociolinguistically Oriented Language Surveys. *Bible Translator* 18: 128–32.

Fredericks, D. C.
1996 North Israelite Dialect in the Hebrew Bible? Questions of Methodology. *Hebrew Studies* 37: 7–20.

1998 Diglossia, Revelation, and Ezekiel's Inaugural Rite. *Journal of the Evangelical Theological Society* 41: 189–99.

Garr, W. R.
1985 *Dialect Geography of Syria-Palestine, 1000–586* BCE. Philadelphia, PA: University of Pennsylvania.

Gianto, A.
1996 Variations in Biblical Hebrew. *Biblica* 77: 493–508.

Holmes, J.
1992 *An Introduction to Sociolinguistics*. London: Longman.

Hurtgen, J. E.
1993 *Anti-Language in the Apocalypse of John*. Lewiston, NY: Mellen.

Johnson, R. M., Jr.
1993 The Words in Their Mouths: A Linguistic and Literary Analysis of the Dialogues in the Book of Ruth. Unpublished Ph.D. Dissertation, Vanderbilt University.

Meier, S. A.
1992 *Speaking of Speaking: Marking Direct Discourse in the Hebrew Bible*. Vetus Testamentum Supplement 46. Leiden: Brill.

Miller, C. L.
1996 *The Representation of Speech in Biblical Hebrew Narrative: A Linguistic Analysis*. Harvard Semitic Monographs 55. Atlanta: Scholars.

Nida, E. A.
1979 Translating Means Communicating: A Sociolinguistic Theory of Translation. *Bible Translator* 30: 101–7, 318–25.
1993 *Breakthroughs in Bible Translating*. Philadelphia, PA: Trinity International.

Paulston, C. B., and Tucker, G. R. (eds.)
1997 *The Early Days of Sociolinguistics: Memories and Reflections*. Dallas, TX: Summer Institute of Linguistics.

Person, R. F., Jr.
1996 *In Conversation with Jonah: Conversation Analysis, Literary Criticism, and the Book of Jonah*. Journal for the Study of the Old Testament, Supplement 220. Sheffield: Sheffield Academic.
1999 A Reassessment of *Wiederaufnahme* from the Perspective of Conversation Analysis. *Biblische Zeitschrift* 43: 241–48.

Porter, S. E.
1997 Ancient Rhetorical Analysis and Discourse Analysis of the Pauline Corpus. Pp. 249–74 in *The Rhetorical Analysis of Scripture: Essays from the 1995 London Conference*, eds. S. Porter and T. Olbricht. Journal for the Study of the New Testament, Supplement Series. Sheffield: Sheffield Academic.

Rendsburg, G. A.
1990 *Diglossia in Ancient Israel*. American Oriental Series 72. New Haven, CT: American Oriental Society.
1992 Morphological Evidence for Regional Dialects in Ancient Hebrew. Pp. 65–88 in *Linguistics and Biblical Hebrew*, ed. W. R. Bodine. Winona Lake, IN: Eisenbrauns.
1995 Linguistic Variation and the "Foreign" Factor in the Hebrew Bible. *Israel Oriental Studies* 15: 177–90.
1999 Confused Language as a Deliberate Literary Device in Biblical Hebrew Narrative. *Journal of Hebrew Scriptures* 2: article 6 (http://www.arts.ualberta.ca/JHS/Articles/article_12.htm).

Shuy, R. W.
1997 A Brief History of American Sociolinguistics: 1949–1989. Pp. 11–32 in *The Early Days of Sociolinguistics: Memories and Reflections*, eds. C. B. Paulston and G. R. Tucker. Dallas, TX: Summer Institute of Linguistics.

Stine, P. C. (ed.)
1986 *Sociolinguistics and Communication*. UBS Monograph 1. New York, NY: United Bible Societies.

Tucker, G. R.
1997 The Development of Sociolinguistics as a Field of Study. Pp. 317–24 in *The Early Days of Sociolinguistics: Memories and Reflections*, eds. C. B. Paulston and G. R. Tucker. Dallas, TX: Summer Institute of Linguistics.

Wilt, T.
1996 A Sociolinguistic Analysis of *nāʾ*. *Vetus Testamentum* 46: 237–55.

Young, I.
1993 *Diversity in Pre-Exilic Hebrew*. Forschungen zum Alten Testament 5. Tübingen: Mohr.
1997 Evidence of Diversity in Pre-Exilic Judahite Hebrew. *Hebrew Studies* 38: 7–20.

Chapter 11

Representing the Cushite Other: The Use of Cushite Phenotypes in Numbers 12 and Jeremiah 13:23

by Rodney S. Sadler, Jr.

It is remarkable that phenotypic differences receive scant attention in the Hebrew Bible, even when those differences were as stark as we presume they were between the ancient Judeans and Cushites.[1] Cushites[2] were known through Egyptian[3] and Assyrian epigraphy (Snowden 1983: pl. 13) to be a dark-skinned people with features consistent with modern notions of "negroes." The Cushites, often deemed "Ethiopians" or "Nubians" in modern translations, have been commonly perceived by contemporary scholars as "black" or "African" (Hays 1996a: 399; 1996b; cf. Adamo 1986). Yet, though Cush-related terms[4] are employed more than fifty times in the Hebrew Bible, in only three instances do the Judean authors discuss Cushite phenotypes (Num 12; Isa 18; and Jer 13).

Two of these biblical texts appear to address the color of a Cushite's skin (Num 12 and Jer 13). However, in both of these instances, skin coloration is not explicitly described, only implied. It is only because Judean people (and subsequent exegetes) knew something about the distinctive coloration of Cushite skin that these implicit references to phenotypes are discernible in the pages of the Hebrew Bible. To the uninformed, the reference to הָאִשָּׁה הַכֻּשִׁית, "the Cushite woman (wife)" in Num 12:1 offers little more than the ethnic background of a woman Moses married. Further, the phrase כּוּשִׁי עוֹרוֹ, "a Cushite's skin," in Jer 13:23 provides limited information about what the reader should glean from this cursory reference. It is only when exegetes begin to understand the commonplace value the term כּוּשִׁי, "Cushite," had in ancient Israel/Judah that references to this ethnic term become significant for interpreting these biblical texts (Num 12:1 and Jer 13:23), and they can symbolically associate Cushites with the notion "dark skin."

Such an association pertains to another issue: how differences that moderns would perceive as racial were viewed in Judean society. Though recognition of distinctive human skin color alone does not characterize racial thought, phenotypic differences between Cushites and Judeans can be characterized as constituent elements[5] of racialist[6] thought. It is unlikely that there was an established system of racial othering in Judah during the Iron II or exilic periods, but Numbers 12 and Jer 13:23 provide valuable information about how constituent elements like phenotypic differences were perceived and the ideological significance ascribed to these differences.

NUMBERS 12 — MOSES' CUSHITE WIFE

Numbers 12 is a chapter requiring careful attention, because it is enigmatic for a variety of reasons. Initially, the reader notes that the cause of the conflict in this chapter is not apparent. According to verse 1, the reason Miriam[7] and Aaron complain against Moses seems to pertain to their brother's marriage to a Cushite woman.

Evidence from Jewish literature composed during the latter centuries B.C.E. and the first century C.E. illustrates how much of a problem this woman's identity caused early interpreters.[8] According to Exod 2:15–22, Moses married Zipporah, identified as a daughter of the Midianite priest Reuel,[9] while Jud 1:16 and 4:11 imply that Moses married a Kenite woman, daughter of Hobab. Though the question about whether Zipporah was a Midianite or a Kenite was seldom the cause of much contention,[10] whether Moses married a Cushite woman was a matter of significant interest. Did this mean that Moses had married a second wife? Or was this label — Cushite — consistent with this wife's identity as Zipporah, a Midianite? These two questions point to the two principle solutions early Jewish authors offered to this dilemma.

Demetrius the Chronographer and Ezekiel the Tragedian, both favoring the second solution, determined that Moses had only one wife and offered explanations of how Zipporah could properly be deemed Cushite (cf. Robertson 1985; Hanson 1985). Artapanus and Josephus chose the first solution, introducing legends of a military campaign into Ethiopia to the Moses narratives (cf. Collins 1985; Feldman 1993). Though Artapanus makes no explicit reference to the wife of Numbers 12, the Ethiopian campaign seems to provide a context for a resolution of the dilemma raised by this passage, as is expressed explicitly in Josephus' use of the campaign legend (*Ant.* 2.252). The introduction of this Cushite woman into the Moses narratives was apparently a reason for concern.

However, suggesting that the cause of contention was the Cushite wife raises another equally potent question: What was it about this wife that provoked Miriam (and Aaron), causing her (them) to complain? In theory, there are a number of compelling motivations for the complaint, not the least among these the issue of race. Cain Felder, in his 1989 text *Troubling Biblical Waters*, concludes that despite the "extraordinarily progressive racial values of the Bible," the complaint was based upon Miriam's assessment of Moses' wife's racial identity. Hence, in this paradigm, we should contrast Miriam's visceral reaction against this Cushite woman in verse 1 with the nature of YHWH's punishment of Miriam in verse 12 (Felder 1989: 42; cf. Waters 1991: 204).[11] We will say more about this conclusion below.

Felder, however, uncomfortable with the implication that "race" could cause such contention in Israelite/Judahite society, was later pleased to recant this initial assessment in his 1991 article, "Race, Racism and the Biblical Narratives" (Felder 1991: 127–45). In this article, persuaded by Randall Bailey's hypothesis (Bailey 1991: 179), he revised his earlier conclusions, suggesting that the complaint was not based upon the perceived racial inferiority of the Cushite wife, but upon her perceived social valuation. Hence, for Bailey and Felder what seemed to be a conflict stemming from a matter of racialist denigration of the Cushite Other is actually a matter of conflict over the elite social status associated with the Cushite Other (Felder 1991: 135–36).

Alice Bellis notes that there may be reasons for the objection beyond the racial and social status issues. Following Drorah Setel, she suggests that the issue of the Cushite wife may have been cultic. If this wife is, indeed, Zipporah, as Bellis contends (Bellis 1994: 103), the conflict may have to do with her status as a priestess (cf. Exod 4:24–26). Moses' union with a priestess then may have bestowed upon him a particular prophetic authority over that of Miriam (and Aaron), hence producing the tension between Moses and his sibling(s) (Bellis 1994: 104–5).

Bellis has also hypothesized that the reason the author introduced the conflict over the Cushite wife into the context of the Pentateuch may stem from an issue of contemporary relevance for the author. The purpose of the narrative may be to resolve the issue of Moses' marriage to a foreign wife, when this issue was becoming a problem in Israelite society (Bellis 1994: 104).[12] It is beyond contention that Moses married a foreign woman from the south,[13] and the redactor of Numbers to his or her specific ends employed this fact to achieve the purpose of the present passage (Bellis 1994: 255 n. 21). Presumably, each of the designations[14] could overlap in the minds of Judahites. The actual reason for the objection to the Cushite wife occurring in 12:1 may continue to be a matter of contention for exegetes; however, the lack of clarity regarding why the issue was raised in the first place should not distract from the fact that it was. This discussion will primarily address the existence of the complaint and only secondarily propose a reason for it.

Some initial comments about the composition of Numbers 12 are in order. Exegetes have not always perceived this chapter as a single coherent textual unit. In fact, Martin Noth sees two distinct literary strands interwoven in this complex, which can no longer be "disentangled" (Noth 1968: 93). Eryl Davies, who attempts to sort the two narratives, champions a modified version of Noth's position.

He does so as follows:

(1) Cushite Wife controversy—verses 1, 9a, 10ab, 13–16.

(2) Authority controversy—verses 2–5a, 6–8, 9b, 10aa.

His hypothesis posits that Miriam alone was the antagonist in the first story, while Miriam and Aaron act cooperatively in the second (Davies 1995: 114). In regard to the odd construction of the feminine singular verb ascribed to both Miriam and Aaron in verse 1, the anomaly is explained: it was never intended to have Aaron as its subject. Davies' interpretation runs contrary to that of Noth, who sees the unusual construction simply as another example of the predicate in first position assuming the form of the initial subject in a series (Noth 1968: 93). Davies takes the feminine singular predicate and the plural subjects as evidence that Aaron was not a character in the first narrative. Were he included, then he probably would have been mentioned first as the most recognizable character (Davies 1995: 117).

Davies' "two narratives" explanation clarifies a number of the problems in this chapter, since it provides a clear cycle of problem, confrontation, and resolution for both narratives. Further, though his solution perhaps oversimplifies the complex redactional process that gave rise to this narrative, it facilitates a discussion about the matter of the Cushite wife on its own grounds: it is a specific complaint raised by Miriam, then resolved by YHWH's disciplinary hand. The inclusion of the material from a subsequent intervening Aaron and Miriam story only serves to complicate matters.

However, as Gordon Wenham cautions, there are structural reasons to read the entire chapter as a coherent narrative unit. Wenham finds in the extant passage evidence of a pattern also repeated in Numbers 11, 14, 16 (twice), 17 and 21, which is as follows:

> (a) the people complain; (b) the Lord appears /hears; (c) the Lord is angry and punishes; (d) the people appeal to Moses; (e) Moses prays for people; (f) the judgment ceases (Wenham 1997: 51–52).

In this regard, the two narratives identified by Davies in chapter 12 fulfill the pattern found in the larger literary context only in their present intertwined state, suggesting that the redactor forfeited the unique themes of the independent units. Thus, while employing Davies' notion that two distinct complaints have been combined for analytical purposes, we should be careful not to disregard the symmetry of the complete extant passage.

These structural insights help to clarify the confusion most scholars encounter when confronting this passage. There may be two distinct concerns reflected in two distinct traditions, but they are conflated into one composite narrative. Though elements have been lost from the story of Aaron's and Miriam's complaint about Moses' authority, the Cushite wife was evidently a concern only for Miriam, which was resolved when YHWH punished her with a temporary case of skin disease and a period of banishment from the community.

We will return to the implications of this reading below.

As regards the Cushite wife, it is important to realize as we approach this text that it contains the only explicit reference to a Cushite woman in the Hebrew Bible.[15] That fact alone makes Numbers 12 significant, for the portrayal of Moses' wife provides the limited information we have about how Cushite women were viewed by Hebrew authors. Because the text does not provide adequate detail, we cannot be sure what it was about this woman's identity that offended Miriam, provoking her objection. Whether the objection was due to aesthetics or cultural otherness is unclear. One could argue that the principle objection was to the union of this prominent Levite with a non-Hebrew, hence othered, woman.[16] This would be true whether the Cushite woman was Zipporah or a subsequent bride (though if she is presumed to be Zipporah, she can then be associated with a priestly lineage, hence perhaps assuaging the problem). Had Moses married any non-Hebrew woman, it might have produced this reaction by the prophetic matriarch, Miriam.

Still, the repetition in verse 1 of the MT, confirming the Cushite identity of Moses' wife, emphasizes that because she is Cushite, she is Other, significantly unlike Moses. Reading the complete chapter as a single story, the contextual clues indicate the ambiguity with which the difference is valued. What is clear is that Miriam implies the Cushite woman was Other and that the difference mattered; Moses has somehow by this marriage elevated himself above his siblings. Hence, it is not likely that the Cushite wife was denigrated because of her Cushite identity; perhaps just the opposite: she stood as a symbol of Moses' status and authority, as Bailey suggests.[17]

However, following Davies' two-narrative hypothesis, the Cushite wife narrative remains paradoxical. Even though it cannot be said to prohibit Moses' union with this Cushite woman, the fact that it posits the partnering as a matter of contention implies that it raised a red flag for Miriam. In this regard, the passage is a double-edged sword. It both indicates by Miriam's complaint that the marriage challenged normative assumptions of who is marriageable, demonstrating that this union could be seen as unacceptable by certain members of the Hebrew community, and it affirms by YHWH's silence in response to Miriam's complaint that such unions could not be categorically proscribed.

This smaller narrative is further complicated by the way YHWH punished Miriam. The phrase מְצֹרַעַת כַּשָּׁלֶג, meaning "leprous as snow" in verse 10 adds to the text another layer of complexity. According to the narrative, after the cloud containing the presence of an angry YHWH departed from the tent "Miriam had become leprous, as white as snow" (v. 10 *NRSV*). Note the additional aspect of color present in the *NRSV* translation. Whether or not the notion of color is germane to מְצֹרַעַת כַּשָּׁלֶג is a matter of significance for this study, but the text is by no means unequivocal on this point.

It must be stated that no explicit color terms (i.e., לבן) are used in this chapter. However, מְצֹרַעַת כַּשָּׁלֶג cannot be deemed void of all color content. Athalaya Brenner, in her 1982 study of color terms in Hebrew, classified the root of the latter term in this construction, שֶׁלֶג, as a secondary color term or a term that functions in certain contexts "as specifications of לבן" (Brenner 1982: 42). In this manner, מְצֹרַעַת כַּשָּׁלֶג has often been understood as a simile for "whiteness" in Num 12:10, as well as in Exod 4:6 and 2 Kgs 5:27, as is apparent in the *NRSV*.

This being said, some scholars have argued against connoting color in these three aforementioned verses. Most notably, Brenner herself has suggested that the term as it is employed in Num 12:10 should not be understood as a simile for "whiteness," but for flakiness, reflecting the texture of snow.[18] Though considering the term a reference to the flaking associated with a psoriasis-like condition is entirely plausible, it would be arbitrary to preclude its connotation as a color term[19] in Num 12:10, Exod 4:6, and 2 Kgs 5:27, which each address similar stories of a skin disorder brought on by YHWH's activity. As stated above, Brenner herself recognizes the clear use of כַּשָּׁלֶג as a simile for "whiteness" in Isa 1:18, Ps 51:9, and Dan 7:9, and more directly she states "that 'white' can be signified by a comparison to snow" (Brenner 1982: 82). In addition, a psoriasis-like condition can be described as "shiny-silvery scales" (Brenner 1982:

90) or "raised, red patches or lesions covered with a silvery white build up,"[20] which by no means makes the simile "white as snow" implausible. Further, following Brenner's conclusion that כּוּשִׁי can have a connotation of "dark-skinned person," particularly in reference to Jer 13:23, it seems likely that the author of Numbers 12 intentionally employed two secondary color terms, כֻּשִׁית in 12:1 and כַּשָּׁלֶג in 12:10, knowing that the irony of the consequence of Miriam's complaint against Moses' marriage to the Cushite woman being a sickness that made her "as snow" would not be lost on his or her audience (Felder 1989: 42; Bailey 1991: 180).

Bellis has also offered a challenge to interpretations of this passage that presume the author's color consciousness in this narrative. Bellis suggests that the image of מֵת אֲשֶׁר בְּצֵאתוֹ מֵרֶחֶם אִמּוֹ, or the "stillborn infant" in 12:12, should govern our interpretation of this passage. In her estimation, it is not color that is being emphasized in this simile, but the leprosy-like condition of the corpse where its skin has been eaten away. She further argues that the color of the corpse would not be "white" but "gray and mottled" (Bellis 2000). Though this perspective does emphasize the debilitating effect of the leprous condition, it does not change the "color" aspect of this verse. If anything, it strengthens the notion of the contrast between the "pale" complexion of the infant and the "dark" complexion of the Cushite woman. Further, since the contrast is not between the distinct spectral opposites, "black" and "white", but between generally tanned to dark brown Mediterranean complexions, "dark" and "pale," the potency of Miriam's punishment remains intact. She has forfeited whatever natural skin coloration she had, and became like a corpse, not "white" as we think of it with its constituent ideological baggage, but a blotchy, perhaps even vitiligo-like[21] "whiteness" perceived as the absence of color.

The introduction of a color-laden concept into Miriam's punishment at the end of this pericope suggests another reason for the repetitive reference to Moses' union with a Cushite woman. There is a strange irony to the story of a woman who complains against a woman twice identified as Cushite, implicitly dark-skinned, whose skin is then transformed, as a result of YHWH's punishment, to be void of color (cf. Ashley 1993: 227; Felder 1989: 42; Waters 1991: 204). The author emphasized the Cushite woman's heritage to exploit the obvious contrast between her skin and Miriam's leprous skin. But instead of explicitly stating that YHWH punished Miriam for her prejudice against this female Other by "whitening" her skin, she or he employed the power of the commonplace terms כֻּשִׁית and כַּשָּׁלֶג, knowing that the audience would recognize the ironic contrast between these terms.

Despite her inactive role, the Cushite wife remains a significant character in this narrative because the cursory reference to her clarifies a number of issues. First, her presence in this narrative implies that the author presumed that there was a Cushite element in the initial migration from Egypt to Israel. Second, the lack of a negative response from YHWH to Miriam's complaint about Moses' marriage precludes the existence of a prohibition against such unions. Third, as the narrative affirms (vv. 2–3), a Cushite woman's connection with so significant a character in the unfolding historical narrative in no way diminished his stature and standing in subsequent generations. Fourth, following Bailey and reading the extant combined passage, it seems that Moses' association with this Cushite woman elevated his social standing, since the affirmation of Moses' humility in verse 3 would be irrelevant if the redactor of the text perceived the marriage as demeaning.

So what is the conclusion of the matter of the Cushite wife? Though far from any permanent solution to the issues raised by this chapter, it appears that Cushite phenotypic darkness was employed to ironic ends in Numbers 12. But as to whether the Israelites/Judahites viewed Cushites through a racialist lens certain qualified conclusions are in order. Accepting the contention that the author intended to contrast the color of the Cushite woman's skin with Miriam's after YHWH's punishment, then it follows that the color of a Cushite's skin was a prevalent feature in the mind of the audience. In this regard, to say "Cushite" could invoke images of dark skin (cf. Jer 13:23) in a manner similar to the way saying "snow" conjured images of "whiteness" or "paleness."

Though the association of an ethnic group with a prominent phenotypical trait is a constituent element of racialist thought, it does not necessarily follow that the author had a racialist mindset. As determined above, the *Tendenz* of the author definitively opposed Miriam's disdain for the union of Moses and his Cushite wife. It is even plausible that the chapter is anti-racialist in its orientation, seeking to combat the notion that Cushites were ontologically different from Hebrews, symbolically transcending perceived otherness by tacitly placing YHWH's seal of approval on Moses' union with a Cushite woman. Hence, this narrative may contain an early biblical author's strategy for addressing an emerging ethnic or color prejudice by highlighting YHWH's ironic response to Miriam's complaint.

JEREMIAH 13:23 — CAN A CUSHITE CHANGE HIS SKIN?

The reference to a Cushite in Jer 13:23 occurs in a riddle comprised of a rhetorical question soliciting a negative response from its audience.[22] The question posed is הֲיַהֲפֹךְ כּוּשִׁי עוֹרוֹ וְנָמֵר חֲבַרְבֻּרֹתָיו "Is a Cushite able to change his skin or a leopard his spots?" Of course they cannot. The answer to the question then forms the basis of YHWH's response to the people of Judah's query in verse 22. Why had an unpleasant fate befallen Judah? The answer: They were incapable of change! Jeremiah's response is more eloquent: גַּם־אַתֶּם תּוּכְלוּ לְהֵיטִיב לִמֻּדֵי הָרֵעַ "then you too will be able to do good, you who are taught evil." In a circuitous manner, Jeremiah declares that the people of Judah were unable to change their ways and were consequently destined to suffer a horrendous fate.[23]

Consider the phrase הֲיַהֲפֹךְ כּוּשִׁי עוֹרוֹ "Can a Cushite change his skin?"[24] What is it about the skin of the Cushite that is under consideration in this rhetorical question? Isaiah 18 provides the best ethnography for Cushites in the Hebrew Bible. It refers to a phenotype related to a distinctive quality of Cushite skin. The land of Cush is described as the home of "a nation tall and smooth" (*NRSV*). Thus, because of this recognized quality of Cushite phenotype, Jeremiah's question could be restated: "Can a Cushite change [the smoothness of] his skin?"

However, the purpose of these rhetorical questions is to present a scenario where change would be impossible. Though it would not be easy for a man with a hairless face to grow a beard, Cushites with facial hair were known in antiquity (e.g., Snowden 1970: pls. 43, 54–55, 71, 73, 93 and 95). Judean people probably knew of such Cushites, hence lack of hair is unlikely to satisfy the requirements of this riddle.

The other significant aspect of a Cushite's skin that had commonplace value in the ancient world was its color. Again, Brenner has classified the term "Cushite" as one of a series of Hebrew terms, like those for "snow" and "wine," that had idiomatic value and could replace specific color terms, particularly in poetry (Brenner 1982: 47). The verb יַהֲפֹךְ, "to turn or overturn," is used frequently in reference to color, particularly in relation to skin disease in Lev 13:3–4, 13, 20, and 55. In each of these instances, the root הפך is associated with turning "white;" hence, it is not beyond the realm of possibility that the transformation of the Cushite's skin to a "white" complexion is the paradox raised by Jeremiah. If this were the image Jeremiah intended to evoke in his audience, the startling contrast between "whiteness" (or paleness) and a Cushite's dark complexion would impress upon his audience the implausibility of Judah's repentance. However, though this contrast would strengthen the riddle, turning the Cushite's skin "white" is by no means the certain implication.[25]

Besides Isaiah 18, Jer 13:23 is the most obvious reference to a Cushite phenotypical trait in the Hebrew Bible, making it one of the only opportunities we have to examine how Judean authors viewed Cushite phenotypic skin coloration.[26] Because of the nature of the riddle, the only thing that was emphasized about the color of the Cushite skin was its inability to change (Drake 1990: 5). We find a similar proverb in Egyptian wisdom literature in the "Instructions of 'Onchsheshonqy" (Gemser 1960: 105–6). These instructions, thought to have been composed in the fifth century B.C.E., contain a series of lessons an imprisoned member of a failed assassination plot against an unknown pharaoh composed for his son. The proverb provides a fitting answer to the rhetorical question asked in Jeremiah 13:23.

As 'Onchsheshonqy declares, "(t)here is no Negro who lays off his skin" (Gemser 1960: 126). From this, we may conclude that the color of Cushite skin had commonplace value to the Judeans,[27] the Egyptians, and likely other peoples in the ancient Near East. Still, the limited emphasis on phenotypic difference in most references to Cush in the Hebrew Bible suggests that distinct appearance was not the characteristic aspect of Cushite identity most familiar to biblical authors (Sadler 2005: 149–51).[28]

At the same time, there also does not appear to be any clear value ascribed to skin color.[29] It would have been simple to equate darkness to evil in this passage, as has been done in subsequent Christian and Jewish post-biblical literature. Robert Hood, for example, notes that in his

> study of the images of blackness in the West…the following characteristics are associated with the color black: gloom, woe, darkness, dread, death, terror, horror, wickedness, mourning, defilement, annihilation. By contrast, the color white evokes the following traits: triumph, light, innocence, joy, purity, regeneration, happiness, gaiety, peace, femininity, delicacy (Hood 1994: 1–2).

He goes on to demonstrate that such associations of "blackness" and negative themes were common in the cultures of the Chinese, Arabs, Indians, and later Greeks and Romans to various degrees from the second millennium B.C.E. to the contemporary period (Hood 1994: 1–21). However, though other ancient societies appear to have correlated negative themes with concepts of "blackness" and dark skin color, such a contrast does not appear in the present instance, nor in general in the Hebrew Bible.[30] As stated above, YHWH in Num 12:1 seems to counter such prejudices against the color of the Cushites' skin by punishing Miriam for her disdain at Moses' marriage to a Cushite woman. This brief reference to Cush is incorporated not to disparage this Other, but to say something about Israel. Jeremiah's rhetorical question emphasizes Israel's stubborn refusal to repent of their deviant disposition (cf. Hos 5:3d–4; Holladay 1986: 415; Jones 1992: 203; Leslie 1954 : 75).

Other questions arise: Why does skin coloration, such an obvious means for Othering and a constituent element of racialist thought, play such a limited role in the Hebrew Bible? Further, why, once skin color was acknowledged, was it given so little attention? Could it be that such differences were neither remarkable nor off-putting in the ancient Judean context? Was the ancient Levant a region replete with people of various hues where a Cushite's complexion was a common feature? Suffice it to say here that even when Cushite coloration was acknowledged, the distinctiveness of Cushite skin was not granted ideological significance, as it would be under a racialist paradigm.

CONCLUSION

In the two instances where Cushite coloration is implied, there is no ideological value given to the color of Cushite skin. Though Cushites represent the quality "dark skin," in neither Numbers 12 nor Jeremiah 13:23 is there a hint of derision or condescension associated with the Cushites. The most that can be said is that because of their dark skin, Cushites could be employed in Hebrew literature to certain literary ends, establishing contrasts between their dark skin and lighter complexions or depicting its indelibility; it could not become "white."

The resulting portrait of Judean representation of the Cushite Other demonstrates that even presumably stark phenotypic differences, though constituent elements of racialist thought, were relatively unimportant in the Hebrew Bible. They were not employed as criteria for establishing human hierarchies or othering social groups, but were only incidental descriptive traits utilized to accomplish specific literary goals. Biblical authors' representations of Cushites did not depreciate their appearance. Ironically, when these differences are evoked, it is not to disparage the Other, but to correct the biblical audience.

NOTES

1 It was Dr. Eric M. Meyers who first suggested that I study the people of Cush, noting that it was essential to employ archaeology, anthropology, and all other applicable methodologies to understand this people rarely discussed in biblical scholarship. Under his watchful eye, I was encouraged to experiment with theories of race and othering, though they were beyond the traditional constraints of biblical scholarship. His constant support facilitated the completion of my research on Judean representation of the Cushite Other and his jovial nature buoyed my waning spirit on many occasions. It is with great joy that I submit this article in honor of an exemplary advisor, scholar, teacher, and friend.

2 Or "Kushites" as the term is transcribed in the literature of Egyptologists.

3 For example, see Snowden 1983: pls. 4, 6, 7a–b, 8a–b, and 9–10.

4 I.e., כּוּשׁ, כּוּשִׁי, כֻּשִׁית, and כּוּשַׁן.

5 Consider Smedley 1993: 26–27. She defines this term as the collection of "ideological ingredients" that, when perceived in concert, form "a singular paradigm constituting the racial worldview."

6 Social critic Kwame Appiah defines "racialism" as the acceptance of the proposition that

> there are heritable characteristics, possessed by members of our species, that allow us to divide them into a small set of races, in such a way that all the members of these races share certain traits and tendencies with each other that they do not share with members of any other race. These traits and tendencies characteristic of a race constitute, on the racialist view, a sort of racial essence (1990: 4–5).

Appiah would argue that a racialist view is not intrinsically immoral, like a racist posture. However, he would argue that racialism is a necessary, though not sufficient precondition for racism. See also Appiah 1999: 1576.

7 Actually, it looks like the text has been edited by a redactor who included Aaron at a later time, perhaps to vilify this leader and elevate the status of Moses (12:6–8). Note that the initial verb employed in this chapter (12:1) is feminine singular, though the extant text would seemingly call for a plural verb, since the subjects are Miriam and Aaron. Note that Miriam is the only recipient of YHWH's wrath (12:10). We will revisit this issue below. Also see Adamo 1990: 111.

8 For example, see Ezekiel the Tragedian, Demetrius the Chronographer, Artapanus, and Josephus.

9 Cf. Exod 3:1, where the priest father-in-law of Moses is identified as Jethro. This narrative clearly contains strains of numerous traditions.

10 This is due largely to the conflation of the stories about the Kenites and Midianites, both thought to be populations dwelling south of Judah and connected with Moses traditions. Cf. Halpern 1992, where he notes that the differences in the use of the ethnic terms Kenite and Midianite relate to differences in the literary sources and political interests of Mushite and Aaronid schools. In this regard, it is most significant that the many sources that mention Moses' wife and in-laws agree on two principal points: that he married a non-Israelite woman and that she came from the region south of Judah.

11 Though Felder thinks the Numbers 12 passage is an anomaly, Waters thinks it represents a "growing dislike for Africans."

12 Bellis also rehearses a number of other *raisons d'être* for this complex passage, such as it was an attempt to deal with Moses' adultery as he had married a second wife; the objection about the wife was a "pretext" for the actual dilemma: prophetic authority; or the matter was one of cultic purity. See 1994: 255–56, n. 27.

13 He married either a Midianite (Exod 2:11–22; 3:1; Num 10:29), a Kenite (Judg 1:16; 4:11), or a Cushite (Num 12:1). However we understand these various passages, it is clear that Moses had married a foreign woman from the south. It is possible to conflate each of these peoples. For example, Jud 1:16 would allow us to conclude that Midians and Kenites could be the same peoples. Hab 3:7 would suggest that Midian and Cushan could be conflated. Hence, we could determine the Cushite wife as actually Cush(an)ite, from the region to the south of Edom.

14 Midianite, Kenite, or Cushite, though we are by no means definitively arguing that Zipporah was the wife of Num 12:1.

15 There may also be others in the Bible, i.e., the Queen of Sheba in 1 Kings 10, following Charles Copher and the suggestion by Edward Ullendorff, who, based upon his reading of Josephus (*Ant.* 8.6, 5–6), would look for Sheba in South Arabia or in Cush–Egypt; or even Queen Candace in the New Testament (Acts 8:27). But the former is not an explicit reference to a Cushite woman and the latter is not in the Hebrew Bible. Cf. Copher 1993: 62; Ullendorff 1968: 131–45;

Felder 1989: 141. Also, if this woman is identified with Zipporah and deemed of Midianite/Kenite–Cush(an)ite heritage (cf. Hab 3:7), then other women (and men) so identified may merit our attention.

16 Cf. Exod 34:16; Deut 7:1–4; 23:1–7. However, we should note that Hamilton found that prohibitions of exogamous marriages are limited to few Others in the pre-exilic period and are only universal in the post-exilic writings of Ezra (9–10) and Neh (9:2; 10:30; 13:3, 23–28). See Hamilton 1992 and Bellis 1994: 255, n.21.

17 Bailey 1991: 179. Here Bailey argues that Miriam's complaint is not racist but a matter of status. Moses' marriage to an African woman bestows a higher status on him than on his siblings (his elevated status is implied in vv. 3–4 and marriage to an African was also a symbol of status for Solomon in 1 Kgs 3:1). Bailey's reading is significant because he argues, against conventional wisdom, that association with an "African" would serve to diminish one's status and is consistent with the arrogance Miriam appears to oppose. He concludes by noting the irony associated with the contrast between a Cushite woman in 12:1 (black) and Miriam's punishment (being "white as snow"), further stating that being "white as snow" is a matter of punishment, citing Isa 1:18, which he analyzes grammatically as a curse (cf. 2 Kgs 5:27).

18 Brenner 1982: 82, 90, 168. Brenner follows Hulse 1975: 87–105. See also Wenham 1981: 113.

19 This is particularly so for another reason. These texts were likely composed in Judah, a region not known for an excessive amount of snow. Though snow does fall occasionally in Judah, the intended audience would perhaps be most familiar with snow seen from a distance, i.e., upon Mt. Hermon or other high northern mountains. Hence, I suggest that the metaphorical value of snow evoked images of "whiteness," not the other proximately relevant qualities like "flakiness" or "wetness." See Davies 1995: 124.

20 http://www.psoriasis.org/about/psoriasis from the National Psoriasis Foundation website (May 2007).

21 Webster and McKechnie (1983: 2045) define vitiligo as "a disease characterized by the formation of smooth, white, pigmentless patches on various parts of the body."

22 Holladay notes that this rhetorical style was likely borrowed from the wisdom literature genre (1986: 414).

23 The horrendous nature of the fate is emphasized by the image of sexual assault in verse 26: "I myself will lift up your skirts over your face, and your shame will be seen" (*NRSV*). Their punishment would be a brutal violation and a source of shame.

24 Holladay (1986: 411 and 415) translates the phrase with a conditional or interrogative sense: "Does the [Cushite] ever change his skin, or the leopard his spots?"

25 For references to Cushite skin color see Blackwood 1977: 129; Carroll 1986: 305; Davidson 1983: 115.

26 Num 12:1 implies the same recognition of color, but Jer 13:23 is far more explicit.

27 Numbers 12 would lend further support to this hypothesis in regard to the Israelite/Judahite community.

28 I conclude that biblical authors most frequently employ Cushites to symbolize unparalleled military might.

29 Blackwood (1977: 129) notes that the "[Cushite's] skin pigment is under discussion, not his character," further noting the Cushite official Ebed-melech's role in rescuing Jeremiah.

30 There are a number of references to black in relation to skin color, but these are not associated with Cushite skin coloration. For example, Job 30:30 has עוֹרִי שָׁחַר "my skin is black," and Song of Songs 1:5 has the phrase שְׁחוֹרָה אֲנִי "I am black" and 1:6 has שְׁאֲנִי שֶׁאֲנִי שְׁחַרְחֹרֶת "because I am black." Similarly, Lam 5:10 contains the phrase עוֹרֵנוּ כְּתַנּוּר נִכְמָרוּ "our skin as an oven has been blackened." Each of these statements represents the effect of the sun that has darkened someone's skin. This darkening would likely not be deemed pleasing, less for aesthetic than for health reasons, for essentially the authors are saying that they have been sunburned. In Jer 8:21, the prophet proclaims קָדַרְתִּי, "I am black." This appears to be more a poetic assessment of his affective state, where "blackness" denotes mourning, than a description of his phenotypical traits. These are but a few of the instances where terms for blackness are used in description for people of Israel/Judah. A more thorough study of these terms is in order. However, a cursory review has revealed no racialist assessment when these terms are employed, nor any type of bias against Cushites where these or other color terms are used disparagingly. In fact, the term Cush never occurs in relation to any explicit Hebrew term for "blackness."

REFERENCES

Adamo, D.

1986 The Place of Africa and Africans in the Old Testament and Its Environment. Ph.D. dissertation, Baylor University.

Appiah, K.

1990 Racisms. Pp. 3–17 in *Anatomy of Racism*, ed. D. Goldberg. Minneapolis, MN: University of Minnesota.

1999 Race: An Interpretation. Pp. 1575–80 in *African: The Encyclopedia of the African and African American Experience*, eds. K. Appiah and H. Gates, Jr. New York, NY: Civitas.

Ashley, T.

1993 *The Book of Numbers*. Grand Rapids, MI: Eerdmans.

Bailey, R.

1991 Beyond Identification: The Use of Africans in Old Testament Poetry and Narratives. Pp. 165–86 in *Stony the Road We Trod: African American Biblical Interpretation*, ed. C. H. Felder. Minneapolis, MN: Fortress.

Bellis, A.

1994 *Helpmates, Harlots, Heroes: Women's Stories in the Hebrew Bible*. Louisville, KY: Westminster John Knox.

2000 Zipporah: Issues of Race, Religion, Gender and Power. Paper presented at the Duke Hebrew Bible Fall Seminar. Durham, NC.

Blackwood, Jr., A.

1977 *Commentary on Jeremiah*. Waco, TX: Word.

Brenner, A.

1982 *Colour Terms in the Old Testament*. Sheffield: Journal for the Study of the Old Testament.

Carroll, R.

1986 *Jeremiah: A Commentary*. Philadelphia, PA: Westminster.

Collins, J.

1985 Artapanus. Pp. 889–904 in *The Old Testament Pseudepigrapha*, vol. 2, ed. J. Charlesworth. Garden City, NY: Doubleday.

Copher, C.

1993 *Black Biblical Studies: An Anthology of Charles B. Copher*. Chicago, IL: Black Light Fellowship.

Davidson, R.

1983 *Jeremiah*. Philadelphia, PA: Westminster.

Davies, E.

1995 *Numbers*. Grand Rapids, MI: Eerdmans.

Drake, St. C.

1990 *Black Folk Here and There*, vol. 2. Los Angeles, CA: Center for Afro-American Studies, University of California.

Felder, C.

1989 *Troubling Biblical Waters: Race, Class, and Family*. Maryknoll, NY: Orbis.

1991 Race, Racism and the Biblical Narratives. Pp. 127–45 in *Stony the Road We Trod: African American Biblical Interpretation*, ed. C. H. Felder. Minneapolis, MN: Fortress.

Feldman, L

1993 Josephus' Portrait of Moses. *The Jewish Quarterly Review* 83: 301–30.

Gemser, B.

1960 The Instructions of 'Onchsheshonqy and Biblical Wisdom Literature. Pp. 102–28 in *Congress Volume, Oxford 1959*. Leiden: Brill.

Halpern, B.

1992 Kenites. Pp. 17–22 in *Anchor Bible Dictionary*, vol. 4, ed. D. N. Freedman. New York, NY: Doubleday.

Hamilton, V.

1992 Marriage (OT and ANE). Pp. 559–68 in *Anchor Bible Dictionary*, vol. 4, ed. D. N. Freedman. New York, NY: Doubleday.

Hanson, J.

1985 Demetrius the Chronographer. Pp. 843–54 in *The Old Testatment Pseudepigrapha*, vol. 2, ed. J. Charlesworth. Garden City, NY: Doubleday.

Hays, J.

1996a The Cushites: A Black Nation in the Bible. *Bibliotheca Sacra* 153: 396–409.

1996b The Cushites: A Black Nation in Ancient History. *Bibliotheca Sacra* 153: 270–80.

Holladay, W.

1986 *Jeremiah: A Commentary on the Book of the Prophet Jeremiah Chapters 1–25*. Philadelphia, PA: Fortress.

Hood, R.

1994 *Begrimed and Black: Christian Traditions on Blacks and Blackness*. Minneapolis, MN: Fortress.

Hulse, E.
1975 The Nature of Biblical 'Leprosy' and the Use of Alternative Medical Terms in Modern Translations of the Bible. *Palestine Exploration Quarterly* 107: 87–105.

Jones, D.
1992 *Jeremiah*. Grand Rapids, MI: Eerdmans.

Leslie, E.
1954 *Jeremiah: Chronologically Arranged Translated, and Interpreted*. New York, NY: Abingdon.

Noth, M.
1968 *Numbers: A Commentary*. Philadelphia, PA: Westminster.

Robertson, R.
1985 Ezekiel the Tragedian. Pp. 803–20 in *The Old Testament Pseudepigrapha*, vol. 2, ed. J. Charlesworth. Garden City, NY: Doubleday.

Sadler, R.
2005 *Can a Cushite Change His Skin? An Examination of Race, Ethnicity, and 'Othering'in the Hebrew Bible*. Journal for the Study of the Old Testament, Supplement Series 425. New York, NY: Clark.

Smedley, A.
1993 *Race in North America: Origin and Evolution of a Worldview*. Boulder, CO: Westview.

Snowden, F., Jr.
1970 *Blacks in Antiquity: Ethiopians in the Greco-Roman Experience*. Cambridge, MA: Harvard University.
1983 *Before Color Prejudice: Ancient Views of the Blacks*. Cambridge, MA: Harvard University.

Ullendorff, E.
1968 *Ethiopia and the Bible*. Oxford: Oxford University.

Waters, J.
1991 Who was Hagar? Pp. 187–205 in *Stony the Road We Trod: African American Biblical Interpretation*, ed. C. H. Felder. Minneapolis, MN: Fortress.

Webster, N., and McKechnie, J. (eds.)
1983 *Websters New Universal Unabridged Dictionary*. New York, NY: Dorset and Baber.

Wenham, G.
1981 *Numbers: An Introduction and Commentary*. Leicester: Inter-Varsity.
1997 *Numbers*. Sheffield: Sheffield Academic.

SECTION II

HELLENISTIC THROUGH BYZANTINE PERIODS

Chapter 12

What Sort of Jews were the Tobiads?

by Adam Porter

According to Benedict Anderson, ethnicity is an imaginary category (Anderson 1991). It has no biological basis. Indeed, the human genome project makes it clear that, genetically, humans are virtually identical to one another; we even have great affinities with mice. But the fact that race and ethnicity are imagined does not mean that they are insignificant or do not exist. Rather, it means that they are social constructs.

"Ethnicity" provides a way for groups to organize themselves. It allows communities to define boundaries, to determine who belongs to the group and who is outside. Boundaries change over time (A. Smith 1986). Jonathan Smith described them as "political" because what constitutes Us and Them changes depending on the needs of the group and its interactions with its larger contemporary society (J. Smith 1985).

Recognizing that "ethnicity" is pliant, scholars should hesitate before trying to classify ancient individuals or groups as belonging to one ethnic group or another. For archaeologists, this has begun. Eric Meyers noted the difficulty in determining "ethnicity" from archaeological remains (Meyers 1993), and attempts to correlate specific architectural designs (i.e., the so-called "four-room house") or pottery forms (i.e., the "collared-rim" jar) with "Israelites" have been rejected (Mazar 1990; 342, 346–47; Fritz 1997; Holladay 1997; Ibrahim 1997).

But archaeologists are not the only scholars who should be affected by the sociologists' argument that "ethnicity" is indeterminate and imaginary. Textual scholars should be similarly cautious in assigning individuals to a particular "ethnic" (or religious) group. I will illustrate this by examining the Tobiad family, whom scholars commonly identify as "Jews" (Mazar 1957), and showing that the evidence for "Jewishness" in this family is questionable. I will argue that they are no more "Jewish" than another geographically proximate group of Yahwists: the Samaritans.

That the Tobiads defy easy classification is suggested by the fact that many scholars who discuss the Tobiads issue caveats about their "Judaism." Thus, Grabbe notes their "broad-minded tolerance of the social conventions of Greek society" (Grabbe 1992: 196), Feldman describes the family as "highly assimilated — and truly exceptional" (Feldman 1993: 14), Tcherikover remarked of Toubias' use of a pagan formula ("Many thanks to the Gods!" = πολλὴ χάρις τοῖς θεοῖς) in a letter to Apollonios (*CPJ* 4) that "we do not expect to find this pagan formula in a letter written by a Jew" (Tcherikover and Fuks 1957: 127). Hengel said of the same phrase that it "shows a very lax view of the law" (Hengel 1974: 268). Nevertheless, the standard conclusion is that the Tobiads were Jewish.

But what evidence is there that the Tobiads were "Jews"? This question is difficult to answer, in part because it is difficult to define "Jew" or "Judaism" (and most scholars have not attempted to do so). Who was a Jew? Is it primarily an "ethnic" term and, if so, how does one define ethnic (Østergård 1992)? Or is it a "religious" term and, if so, what practices are considered the essential components of the religion, and when do they become normative? Between ca. 150 B.C.E. and 70 C.E., many different Jewish sects flourished, with different praxis and interpretation of biblical law; it is only with the destruction of the Temple that Rabbinic Judaism began, slowly, to become normative (Schiffman 1985). I suspect that Jewish sectarianism probably began before 150 B.C.E., but the sources are too limited to allow fruitful discussion of it (but see M. Smith 1987).

For this essay, I will use the definition of "Jew" offered by Shaye Cohen, who suggested that before the end of the second century B.C.E., all the terms translated as "Jew" (including Latin *Iudaeus*, Greek Ιουδαιος, and Hebrew יהודי) are more properly translated as "Judaean" (Cohen 1999: 69–103). He concluded, "'Judaean' is an ethnic[1]-geographic term" that is used of people living in Judaea[2] or who descended from a Judaean. It is *not* a religious term, as is the English "Jew."

According to Cohen, it is only late in the second century B.C.E. that *Ioudaios* gained two additional meanings, one political, the other religious. When Antiochus the Great conquered Judaea in 200 B.C.E., he saw its ancestral laws as its way of life (or *politeia*). The Hasmoneans accepted this definition, and when they incorporated Ituraea and Idumaea into their kingdom, they allowed (or compelled) the Ituraeans and Idumaeans to live according to (at least some of) the ancestral laws of the Judaeans. Because the Ituraeans and Idumaeans were observing the *politeia* of the Jews, they became Jews in a constitutional sense (they were observing the "law of the land"). Thus, the Hasmoneans split "citizenship" away from genealogy or geography and provided a political way to incorporate outsiders into kingdom of Judaea (Cohen 1999: 110–29).

In addition to this political definition, Cohen argues that during the Hasmonean period, the idea that one could religiously "convert" to Judaism developed. Again, the Greeks may have provided a model for this notion. According to Herodotus, four features define "Greekness:" (1) common blood, (2) common language, (3) common worship, (4) common way of life (*Herod.* 8.144). During the Hellenistic period, the genealogical component was de-emphasized and the latter three traits were emphasized, allowing anyone to be come a "Hellene." Jews shared the same four traits. For Jews, genealogy continued to be significant, but language was unimportant — Judaeans shifted from Hebrew to Aramaic in Palestine and adopted Greek in the diaspora. According to Cohen, during the Hasmonean period common worship and common way of life became emphasized and allowed people to "become" Judaeans. He describes this as a religious conversion (Cohen 1999: 129–35).

Significantly, all the evidence concerning the Tobiad family predates the Hasmonean period; the latest reference to the Tobiads is found in 2 Macc 3:11, before the beginning of the Maccabean revolt (167–164 B.C.E.). Thus, for this period, according to Cohen, "Jewish" meant residing in Judaea or having ancestors who were Judaeans. I will examine the references related to the Tobiads and demonstrate that they neither resided in Judaea, nor did they have Judaean ancestry (or their claims to such ancestry were rejected).

The earliest source is Zechariah, dating to 520–518 B.C.E. (Meyers and Meyers 1987: xlvi). In this prophetic text, Zechariah described an enthronement ceremony in which Heldai, Tobiah, and Jedaiah crowned the High Priest; another crown is to be kept in the Temple as a reminder to Helem, Tobiah, Jedaiah, and Hen ben-Zephaniah. Meyers and Meyers suggested that Heldai (= Helem) and Tobiah represent groups of non-Yehudite Yahwists, the former exiles in Mesopotamia and the latter Yahwists in Transjordan (Meyers and Meyers 1987: 340–43). The theophoric component in the name Tobiah makes it clear that Tobiah was a Yahwist, but this did not mean he was a Judaean. The genealogical lists in Ezra and Nehemiah cast doubts on his Judaean-ness.

Both Ezra and Nehemiah preserve lists of returned exiles; they both list the family of Tobiah as of questionable ancestry:

> The following were those who came up from Telmelah, Telharsha, Cherub, Addan, and Immer, though they could not prove their fathers' houses or their descent, whether they belonged to Israel: the sons of Delaiah, the sons of Tobiah, and the sons of Nekoda, six hundred and fifty-two (Ezra 2:59–60 / Neh 7:61–62).

Tobiah *claimed* to be a Judaean, but his claim was rejected, even though he was a Yahwist.

Tobiah is mentioned many times in Nehemiah (2:10, 3:35, 4:1, etc.), always as an opponent of Nehemiah and often working in league with "Sanballat the Horonite" and/or "Geshem the Arab" (Neh 2:10, 2:19, 4:7, 6:1, 6:12). Nehemiah's main goal was to rebuild the walls of Jerusalem (Neh 2:5, 17), but why this met with opposition from Tobiah, Sanballat, and Geshem has not been explained well. Grabbe suggested that Tobiah and Sanballat, the governors of Amman and Samaria, respectively, may have preferred a weak Jerusalem (Grabbe 1992: 134); Alt suggested that Yehud may have been a part of Samaria, so Nehemiah's activities, creating another province, would have reduced his territory (Alt 1953; Myers 1965: xxi); Alt's suggestion was bolstered by Stern, who cited archaeological evidence to argue for "a kind of renewed national pride" (Stern 1981: 14).

Scholars agree that Nehemiah's references to Tobiah as the "Ammonite slave" (טובה העבד העמוני) are sarcastic references to his official title as a servant of the king, but most label him an important Jewish leader (Grabbe 1992: 132–33; Mazar 1957: 143–44). They do not label Sanballet in the same manner, however—he is a "Samaritan governor" (Myers 1965: 100–101; Grabbe 1992: 135). But the similarities between Tobiah and Sanballat are numerous and significant:

(1) Both Tobiah and Sanballat were related to Eliashib, the High Priest (Neh 3:1) in Jerusalem. Eliashib's grandson was married to Sanballat's daughter (Neh 13:28). Tobiah's father-in-law was Shecaniah (Neh 6:18), the keeper of the East Gate. Tobiah's son, Jehohanan, married the daughter of Meshullam (Neh 6:18), who helped rebuild Jerusalem's walls (Neh 3:4, 30).[3] And Tobiah himself was related (although Nehemiah doesn't specify how) to Eliashib (Neh 13:4).

(2) Both of them were Yahwists. This is suggested by the names of their sons. Tobiah's son was named Jehohanan (6:18). Sanballat's sons are known from the Aramaic papyri from Elephantine in southern Egypt. The Jews[4] at Elephantine wrote a letter (ca. 407 B.C.E.), in which they refer to a prior letter (not preserved) written to "Delaiah and Shelemiah sons of Sanballat, governor of Samaria."[5]

(3) They had similar political interests; they were united in their opposition to Nehemiah's attempts to rebuild the walls of Jerusalem. In this, they perhaps reflect regional bias; the residents of Samaria requested that the Judaeans allow them to participate in the rebuilding of the Jerusalem Temple, since they worshipped the same God (and had done so for two centuries), but the Judahites rebuffed them, presumably because they saw them as impure (Myers 1965: 35). In response, according to the author of Ezra, Judah's neighbors sought to prevent the Temple from being built by writing letters to the Persian king (Ezra 4:11–16, 5:7–17) and suggesting that the rebuilding would prompt rebellion by the Judaeans. It is possible that a Tobiad also participated in opposing the building activity in Jerusalem:[6] one of the named opponents is *Tob'al* (טבאל, Ezra 4:7). Mazar suggested that Tob*el* is an older form of the name Tob*iah*(*u*).[7] If this was so, perhaps some continuity can be seen between opponents of rebuilding the Temple and opponents of rebuilding Jerusalem's city walls.

(4) They may both have claimed to be members of the community of exiles but were unable to prove their ancestry. This is certainly true for Tobiah, as mentioned above. However, it may also be true for Sanballat. One of his sons was

> named "Delaiah," and in the lists of rejected exiles "the sons of Delaiah" appear adjacent to "the sons of Tobiah" (Ezra 2:59–60 / Neh 7:61–62). Papponymy is known to have occurred with the name Sanballat,[8] and it is not unreasonable to assume that Sanballat named his son after his own father. If so, Sanballat might be the son of the Delaiah whose ancestry was rejected.

In short, if scholars want to label Tobiah a "Jew," then Sanballat should also bear this label. The split between the Samaritan community and the Judaean community, reflected strongly in first-century C.E. sources like the New Testament and Josephus, was not definitive before Hyrcanus' destruction of Samaria late in the second century B.C.E. (*Ant.* 13.280) and perhaps comes even later (Anderson 1992; Grabbe 1992: 502–7). But if one follows Cohen, there is little reason to label Tobiah a "Jew" — there is no evidence that he came from Judaea or traced his ancestry to Judaea. And the plain reading of Nehemiah suggests that Tobiah was not, in fact, a Jew. Nehemiah described him as an "Ammonite" and not a Judaean or Judahite. Tobiah acted against what Nehemiah (and many scholars) regarded as the best interests of Judaea — fighting to keep Jerusalem's walls in ruins and encouraging the local elite to oppose the activities of Nehemiah (Neh 6:17). Hengel suggested that Tobiah was a "Judaizing Ammonite," a suggestion that perhaps warrants further consideration.[9] In any case, using Cohen's criteria, it is hard to see Tobiah as a "Jew."

If there is little reason to see Tobiah the Ammonite slave as Jewish, there is even less reason to believe the Toubias in the Zenon Papyri was Jewish. The Zenon papyri date to ca. 259 B.C.E. They are a collection of letters written to and from Zenon, an agent of Apollonios, the finance minister of Ptolemy II Philadelphus. Of the approximately 1,200 documents, five relate to a Toubias, probably a descendant of Tobiah the Ammonite slave (Tcherikover and Fuks 1957: 115–30; Grabbe 1992: 172; Hengel 1974: 267). These documents show that Toubias had a close relationship to Apollonios and even Ptolemy II himself.[10]

Was this Toubias a Jew? Virtually all scholars believe he was, including the revised Schürer (Schürer et al. 1973: 140, n. 4) and Grabbe (Grabbe 1992: 192–98). Hengel thinks the "Ammonite" family "had become completely Judaized" (Hengel 1974: 267), and Tcherikover and Fuks include his correspondence in the *Corpus Papyrorum Judaicarum*. Yet there is no evidence in the Zenon papyri to suggest that Toubias was a Jew. None of the documents refer to Toubias as a Judaean, none indicate that he lived in Judaea. Rather, he was in charge of a military outpost in the territory of Amman (or Ammanitis; *CPJ* 1).

Josephus provides a connection to Jerusalem for Toubias (Τουβιας), when he says that Tobias (Τωβιας) married High Priest Onias' sister (*Ant.* 12.160). We noted above that both Sanballat and Tobiah were related to the High Priest Eliashib at the time of Nehemiah. Josephus reports that ca. 335 another Sanballat (III, according to Cross 1966), who was the governor of Samaria, gave his daughter, Nikaso, to Manasses (*Ant.* 11.302). Manasses and Jaddus, his brother, "shared" the office of High Priest until the "elders of Jerusalem" told Manasses "either to divorce his wife or not to approach the altar" (*Ant.* 11.307).

Since this occurred perhaps fifty years before Toubias, can we assume that prohibition of marrying "foreigners" was normative at his time (Grabbe 1998)? If so, it might be evidence that Toubias was Jewish. But the story about Manasses demonstrates that intermarriage took place at the highest levels of Judaean society. The punishment meted out by the elders — not being able to serve at the altar — would have been irrelevant to a woman, who would not have served at the altar. Hence, there would have been no reason not to have the *sister* of the High Priest marry a foreigner. Moreover, if these foreign marriages were "diplomatic" marriages, connecting the highest officials in Judaea to other governments, it would suggest that Toubias *was* foreign and that the marriage served to connect Judaea to Ammon politically and diplomatically. If there is nothing in the Zenon papyri to suggest that Toubias was Jewish, can the evidence of the *Tobiad Romance* be cited?

The *Tobiad Romance* (*Ant.* 12.156–222, 228–36)[11] relates the adventures of Joseph, the son of Tobias, the nephew of High Priest Onias. After borrowing money from his friends in Samaria, he traveled to Alexandria, charmed the king and queen, and won the rights to collect taxes for Coele-Syria, which he did for twenty-two years. On one trip to Alexandria, he lusted for an Egyptian dancing girl, but his brother substituted his own daughter for the dancing girl. From their union was born Hyrcanus, Joseph's youngest son.

After the birth of Hyrcanus, the focus of the story shifts to him. He is described as smarter and craftier than his elder brothers. He traveled to Alexandria, where he spent an enormous amount of money on presents for the king. Just as his father had done, Hyrcanus charmed the king and queen with his wit and his largesse. This angered his father and elder brothers, who attacked him when he returned home. The elder brothers dwelt in Jerusalem and Hyrcanus fled to Transjordan, where he built caves, a fortress, and a palace. Josephus' description of Hyrcanus' construction project closely corresponds to the archaeological finds from ʿArâq el-Amîr (Lapp and Lapp 1993; P. Lapp 1962; 1963; N. Lapp 1983; Will and Larché 1991; Will 1983; 1992). In 2 Macc 3:11 it is mentioned that Hyrcanus, whose father was "a man of very prominent position," deposited some money at the Temple in Jerusalem.

Are the Tobiads Jews according to Cohen's definition? Joseph resided in Jerusalem, but this is not attested until late in his career. He came from Phichola (Φιχοαν)[12] before going to "the city"[13] to meet with "the people" and become their envoy to Egypt. Hence, there is little to suggest that they resided in Judaea, and we have argued above that there is little reason to think Joseph's ancestors were Judaeans.

Could they be "political" or "religious" converts to Judaism (Cohen's second and third definitions of Judaism)? None of the Tobiads in the *Romance* show much regard for Jewish tradition. Both Joseph and Hyrcanus freely (and presumably frequently) dine with the Egyptian king and participate in his court activities. This is very different from Daniel, Judith, and Tobit, all of which exhibit a strong prohibition against eating the food of the gentiles (Daniel 1, Tobit 1:11, Judith 10:5, 12:2, 19). Remarkably, even the narrator of the story seems unfamiliar with Jewish law: Joseph wants to have intercourse with an Egyptian dancing girl, but the narrator says "Jews were prevented by law from having intercourse with a foreign woman" (*Ant.* 12.187). The law does not prohibit sex; it only prohibits marriage (Deut 7:3–4) and might not even apply to Egyptians (Cohen 1999: 241–62).

Finally, the archaeological evidence from ʿArâq el-Amîr (in Transjordan) shows complete disregard for aniconism (Lapp and Lapp 1993; P. Lapp 1962; 1963; N. Lapp 1983; Will and Larché 1991; Will 1983; 1992). The Qasr el-ʿAbd, a pleasure palace (Netzer 1999), which may have been built by Hyrcanus, was decorated with panther fountains that spouted water from their mouths and a frieze of lions that marched around its second story. Whether third- and second-century-B.C.E. Jews were aniconic or not,[14] this building is unique in its lavish use of figural art. In short, both Joseph and Hyrcanus appear to pay little attention to Jewish tradition and custom.

But elements of the *Romance* resemble other features of the family's earlier history. Joseph borrowed money from his friends in Samaria to finance his initial trip to Egypt (*Ant.* 12. 168). Evidently, the ties between the Tobiads and Samaria, prominent in the days of Nehemiah, continued. As mentioned above, Joseph was related to the High Priest by marriage, just as Tobiah the Ammonite slave had been. Tobiah the Ammonite tried to exert control over Jerusalem but was thwarted by Nehemiah. Joseph had no opponent and succeeded in becoming the administrator of not only Jerusalem and Judaea but all Coele-Syria.

In sum, there is no reason, according to Cohen's criteria for "Jewishness," to assume that the Tobiads were Jewish. There is no evidence that they lived in Judaea before just prior to the Maccabean revolt. Tobiah the Ammonite slave, Toubias, and Joseph all live outside Judaea: the first two in Transjordan, the last at Phichola, an unidentified city. According to Ezra and Nehemiah, the family claimed to be of Judaean ancestry, but they could not prove this and were rejected as belonging to Israel. There is no evidence that this stigma was erased over time and that they joined the community of Judaeans.

If we apply the political or religious definitions of Judaism that Cohen believes arose late in the second century B.C.E. (some 80 years after the last mention of the Tobiads), there is no more evidence to suggest that the Tobiads were Jews. The political criteria stipulate that they would observe (at least some of) the laws of the ancestors. Apart from circumcision, Cohen did not suggest what minimal observances were required in order to be considered "Jewish" (and circumcision was not only practiced by the Jews, as Jer 9:24–25 may suggest). And while it is clear that the Tobiads did not observe many traditions, it is hard to find any that they *did* observe (apart, perhaps, from using theophoric names, which is not stipulated by Torah). The religious criteria stipulate that converts would adopt the Jews' common worship and way of life. Again, there is no evidence that the Tobiads did this.

If the Tobiad family was not Jewish, why has the scholarly community traditionally viewed them as Jews? Probably the most important reason is that Josephus presumably regarded them as Jews,[15] as witnessed by his inclusion of the *Romance* into his *Jewish Antiquities*. Why Josephus considered them Jews is unclear. Goldstein admitted some surprise:

> Are these tales of bribery and wenching, which are romantic enough to suggest they are fiction, the sort of history one would expect from the pious Josephus? (Goldstein 1975: 88)

Unfortunately, Josephus does not describe why the Tobiads were Jews, nor does he describe what aspects of Jewish/Judaean law were required of the Idumaeans, Itureans, or other religious or political converts. Josephus' vagueness can be seen by looking at the famous example of the conversion of the Royal House of Adiabene (*Ant.* 20:34–54). Ananias, a Jewish merchant, taught the king's wives to worship God "after the manner of the Jewish tradition." Helena, the king's mother, had also "been brought over to their laws." The king wanted to convert, but hesitated about whether to be circumcised; Ananias said circumcision was not necessary if it would put the king's life in jeopardy. Being a "devoted adherent of Judaism…counted more than circumcision." Sometime later another Jew, Eleazar, told the king that circumcision was required, that he needed to "not merely read the law but also…to do what is commanded in it." The king was circumcised and, according to Josephus, God preserved him and caused his kingdom to prosper. From this story, it is apparent that Josephus thought circumcision necessary, as well as observation of the law. But there were different interpretations of the law, as the story itself demonstrates: Ananias thought circumcision unnecessary, while Eleazar required it.

However, even if Josephus considered the Tobiads to be Jews, he would be judging them by criteria that postdated their last appearance in history by 250 years. Since this period saw dramatic changes in Judaism and the way "Jew" was defined, accepting Josephus' evaluation is methodologically suspect.

A second reason for the assumption that the Tobiads were Jews is that, until recently, there has been little attempt to define "Jewishness." An (unspoken) assumption has been that "Jews" followed the Law in much the same way later Rabbinic Jews did. But this is anachronistic, as Barclay has argued in several articles (Barclay 1995; 1996: 82–124; 1998). He suggested that scholars should eschew terms like "orthodox," "classical," and "pure" when describing Judaism, because these terms presume there was an "orthodox" or "classical" model from which people could deviate.

Cohen's definition is not perfect; it appears to be fairly straightforward, but is, in fact, frustratingly vague, especially the "political" and "religious" definitions of Judaism (What constituted the core practices and beliefs of Judaism?). With regards to the Tobiad family, Cohen's lack of discussion regarding the geographic boundaries of "Judaea" is especially significant. One could make an argument that parts of Transjordan, perhaps the region later identified as Peraea, were considered part of Judaea. If this was the case, one might have found Judaeans east of the Jordan River, including perhaps the Tobiads. However, Cohen's work is important because it provides a basis for further discussion and attempts to define "Judaism" in the ancient world.

Such definitions, however, will be difficult for modern scholars to determine, because ethnic and religious groups define themselves by erecting imaginary boundaries. Since these boundaries are flexible and shift over time, we should expect them to be difficult for scholars to identify. This is especially true in times of rapid social change, which was the case for Palestine from 200 B.C.E. until 135 C.E. Recognition that ethnic boundaries are plastic will make it more difficult to assign ancient individuals to particular religious or ethnic groups, but it should prompt scholars to develop more complex and rigorous definitions of Judaism. Archaeologists may provide a model for textual scholars: having abandoned the (simplistic) notion that a four-room house indicates Israelite settlement, archaeologists have developed more complex and rigorous models of Israelite settlement in Canaan (Dever 1992). With the acceptance of the notion that "Judaism" is a flexible category, textual scholars will need to be more precise and clear about why certain people or groups are identified as "Jews" and, hopefully, provide detailed discussion to support their definition.

NOTES

1 One of the most frustrating aspects of Cohen's work is that nowhere did he define many important terms, including "ethnic" or "religion." He argued that the end of the second century B.C.E. saw a shift in the meaning of *Ioudaios* from "Judaean" to "Jew," a shift from an "ethnos" to an "ethno-religion." But, lacking definitions of either of these terms, it is unclear what the implications for this are. For more on this, see Avery-Peck 2000.

2 Cohen does not discuss the thorny issue of the geographic boundaries of "Judaea." The question is complex, because in the Persian period "Judaea" (or Yehud) included only the territory surrounding Jerusalem, but during the Hellenistic and Hasmonean periods it grew dramatically and the Hasmonean kingdom included territory from south of the Dead Sea (Idumaea and Moab) to territory north of the Sea of Galilee (Galilee and Gaulanitis). It extended from the coast to Transjordan. Josephus lists the "districts" of Judea and includes Idumaea and Gaulanitis as parts of Judaea (*War* 3.51–58). But Josephus differentiates between these districts and their inhabitants, suggesting that he saw a distinction between Judeans, who lived in the territory around Jerusalem, and those residing in other districts (*Ant.* 17:254). For discussion of the geography of Judaea, see Avi-Yonah 1966; Abel 1938.

3 Unfortunately, there are multiple Meshullams in Nehemiah. Two are provided with patroynms in chapter three: "Meshullam ben Berechiah" (vv. 4, 30: ברכיה) and "Meshullam ben Besodeiah" (vs. 6: בסודיה), but not in subsequent references. Thus, when listing the people who signed the book of the law, one Meshullam is listed with the priests (10:7) and another is listed with the leaders of the people (10:20, perhaps reappearing in 12:33). When listing the heads of the priestly houses, a Meshullam appears at the head of the house of Ezra (12:13) and another heads the house of Ginnethon (12:16). One of these helped Ezra read the law (8:4), but which one is unknown. There is also a Levitical gatekeeper (12:25) bearing this name. Lacking patronyms, it is imposible to know if any of these Meshullams was the father of Tobiah's daughter-in-law.

4 This military colony was populated by people from Judea and they are typically called Jews (see, for example, Porten 1968). This highlights the inconsistency and difficulty of labeling ancient peoples; the Elephantine colony had a temple for Yahweh and, thus, would have certainly been condemned by the Chronicler (as well as the Deuteronomistic historian). Who determines "proper" worship? And how do modern scholars describe it?

5 Cowley papyrus 30, ln. 29 and 31, ln. 28: סנאבלט פחת שמרין דליה ושלמיה בני.

6 The letter(s) to the king do not mention the rebuilding of the Temple and instead seem to focus on the rebuilding of Jerusalem (4:13). But the Chronicler explained the long delay in rebuilding the Temple by citing "foreign" opponents; this letter documents this opposition.

7 Mazar discussed this in reference to the "ben-Tab'al" mentioned by Isaiah (Isa 7:6), who Mazar believed was in league with Pekah, King of Israel, and Rezin, King of Aram, to try to replace Ahaz as King of Judah; see Mazar 1957: 236. Arguing against this is the

suggestion that during the Josianic reformation (ca. 622 B.C.E.) theophoric names shifted from *-el* to *-iahu*. Thus, the family name would have shifted from Tob*el* to Tob*iah(u)*. This might preclude the later Tabeel (ca. 535 B.C.E.) from being associated with Tobiah the Ammonite servant.

8 A Sanballat (II) is mentioned in the Wâdimam Dâliyeh papyri, ca. 380 B.C.E. Josephus mentioned a Sanballat (III) ca. 330 (*Ant.* 11.297–301). For more on this, see Cross 1966 and Williamson 1992.

9 Hengel 1974: 267. Unfortunately, Hengel does not explain why Tobiah would want to adopt "Jewish" mores.

10 *CPJ* 4 and 5 are both addressed to Apollonios; *CPJ* 5 refers to a letter Toubias wrote to the king. Additionally, Toubias supplied men and supplies to Apollonios for his journey through Coele-Syria (*CPJ* 2c and 2d).

11 The *Romance* bristles with historical problems. These include trying to fit the story into the chronology and history of the Ptolemaic and Seleucid empires, attempting to correlate the materials from Josephus with those of 1 and 2 Maccabees, creating plausible scenarios to explain the behavior of Onias, and so forth. For discussion of the various historical reconstructions, see Schwartz 1998. Other scholars have suggested that the *Romance* is completely unreliable as a historical source and should be regarded as historical fiction. They argue that the Tobiad clan and their settlement in Transjordan was well-known enough to generate a fictional story focused on them. For discussion, see Gera 1990; Gruen 1998: 100–106. The date that the story was composed is also unclear. Hengel suggested the second half of the second century B.C.E.; Goldstein dated it to Ptolemy VI (181–45 B.C.E.); see Hengel 1974: 269 and Goldstein 1975.

12 This city is unidentified. Mazar suggested it was in Wadi Fukin near Bethlehem, where the Tobiads "apparently had a family estate" (Mazar 1957: 137). Mazar does not make clear why he thinks there was a family estate near Bethlehem; as far as I know, there is no evidence to support this whatsoever. Marcus thinks Phichola was in Transjordan, a more reasonable suggestion, since all earlier evidence associates the Tobiad clan with Transjordan (Josephus 1986: 84, note c.).

13 What city Joseph goes to is unclear. Marcus and Whiston both add "Jerusalem" to the Greek text; this seems a reasonable assumption, since Joseph subsequently entered the temple to speak to the people.

14 The history of the idea of Jewish aniconism has recently been reviewed by Bland (Bland 2000), but he focused on later periods. For the Second Temple period, what little evidence there is seems to indicate that most Jews refrained from sculptured figural art. Geometric and floral motifs predominate in Herod's palaces and the Temple in Jerusalem. Herod installed a golden eagle over one of the entrances to the Temple and when he fell ill, some of the more pious Jews attempted to cut it down (*Ant.* 17.152). Similarly, when Pilate attempted to bring Roman standards into Jerusalem, huge crowds protested (*Ant.* 18.56–59). This view shifted over time, and in later periods synagogues were frequently decorated with eagles, lions, and figural art. The earliest of these is the Dura Europos synagogue (destroyed ca. 245 C.E.); most are much later. For discussion, see Fine 1996.

15 "Presumably," because Josephus does not label them "Jews." He praised Joseph for bringing the "Jewish people from poverty and a state of weakness to more splendid opportunities of life during the twenty-two years when he controlled the taxes of Syria, Phoenicia, and Samaria" (*Ant.* 12.224). Is this the reason Josephus thought them Jews?

REFERENCES

Abel, F. M.

1938 *Géographie de la Palestine*. Paris: Gabalda.

Alt, A.

1953 Die Rolle Samarias bei der Entstehung des Judentums. Pp. 316–37 in *Kleine Schriften zur Geschichte des Volkes Israel*, vol. 2. München: Beck.

Anderson, B.

1991 *Imagined Communities: Reflections on the Origin and Spread of Nationalism*. New York, NY: Verso.

Anderson, R. T.

1992 Samaritans [Heb Hashsho_mero_nîm]. Pp. 940–47 in *Anchor Bible Dictionary*, vol. 5, ed. D. N. Freedman. New York, NY: Doubleday.

Avery-Peck, A. J.

2000 Review of "The Beginnings of Jewishness: Boundaries, Varieties, Uncertainties." *Journal of the American Academy of Religion* 68, no. 4: 885–87.

Avi-Yonah, M.
1966 *The Holy Land: From the Persian to the Arab Conquests (536 B.C. to A.D. 640)*. Grand Rapids, MI: Baker.

Barclay, J. M. G.
1995 Deviance and Apostacy. Pp. 114–27 in *Modelling Early Christianity,* ed. P. Esler. London: Routledge.
1996 *Jews in the Mediterranean Diaspora - From Alexander to Trajan (323 BCE–117 CE)*. Edinburgh: Clark.
1998 Who Was Considered an Apostate in the Jewish Diaspora? Pp. 80–98 in *Tolerance and Intolerance in Early Judaism and Christianity*, ed. G. Stanton. Cambridge: Cambridge University.

Bland, K. P.
2000 *The Artless Jew: Medieval and Modern Affirmations and Denials of the Visual.* Princeton, NJ: Princeton University.

Cohen, S. J. D.
1999 *The Beginnings of Jewishness*. Berkeley, CA: University of California.

Cross, F. M.
1966 Aspects of Samaritan and Jewish History in Late Persian and Hellenistic Times. *Harvard Theological Review* 59, no. 3: 201–11.

Dever, W. G.
1992 Israel, History of: Archaeology and the Israelite "Conquest." Pp. 545–58 in *Anchor Bible Dictionary,* vol. 3, ed. D. N. Freedman. New York, NY: Doubleday.

Feldman, L. H.
1993 *Jew and Gentile in the Ancient World: Attitudes and Interactions from Alexander to Justinian.* Princeton, NJ: Princeton University.

Fine, S. (ed.)
1996 *Sacred Realm: The Emergence of the Synagogue in the Ancient World.* New York, NY: Oxford University.

Fritz, V.
1997 Israelites. Pp. 192–97 in *The Oxford Encyclopedia of Archaeology in the Near East*, vol. 3, ed. E. M. Meyers. New York, NY: Oxford University.

Gera, D.
1990 On the Credibility of the Histories of the Tobiads. Pp. 21–38 in *Greece and Rome in Eretz Israel*, eds. A. Kasher, G. Fuks and U. Rappaport. Jerusalem: Yad Izhak Ben-Zvi.

Goldstein, J. A.
1975 The Tales of the Tobiads. Pp. 85–123 in *Christianity, Judaism, and Other Greco-Roman Cults,* ed. J. Neusner. Leiden: Brill.

Grabbe, L. L.
1992 *Judaism from Cyrus to Hadrian*. Minneapolis, MN: Fortress.
1998 Triumph of the Pious or Failure of the Xenophobes? The Ezra-Nehemiah Reforms and Their *Nachgeschichte*. Pp. 50–65 in *Jewish Location Patriotism and Self-Identification in the Graeco-Roman Period,* eds. S. Jones and S. Pearce. Journal for the Study of the Pseudepigrapha Supplement Series 31. Sheffield: Sheffield Academic.

Gruen, E. S.
1998 *Heritage and Hellenism: The Reinvention of Jewish Tradition*. Berkeley,CA: University of California.

Hengel, M.
1974 *Hellenism and Judaism: Studies in Their Encounter in Palestine During the Early Hellenistic Period.* Philadelphia, PA: Fortress.

Holladay, J. S., Jr.
1997 Four-Room House. Pp. 327–42 in *The Oxford Encyclopedia of Archaeology in the Near East,* vol. 2, ed. E. M. Meyers. New York, NY: Oxford University.

Ibrahim, M.
1997 Sahab. Pp. 450–52 in *The Oxford Encyclopedia of Archaeology in the Near East,* vol. 4, ed. E. M. Meyers. New York, NY: Oxford University.

Josephus
1986 *Jewish Antiquities, Books XII–XIV*, trans. R. Marcus. Cambridge, MA: Harvard University.

Lapp, N. L.
1983 *The Excavations at Araq el-Emir*. Annual of the American Schools of Oriental Research. Winona Lake: IN: Eisenbrauns.

Lapp, P. W.
1962 Soundings at 'Araq el-Emir (Jordan). *Bulletin of the American Schools of Oriental Research* 165: 16–34.
1963 The Second and Third Campaigns at 'Araq el-Emir. *Bulletin of the American Schools of Oriental Research* 171: 8–38.

Lapp, P. W., and Lapp, N. L.
1993 Iraq el-Emir. Pp. 646–49 in *The New Encyclopedia of Archaeology in the Holy Land,* vol. 3, ed. E. Stern. Jerusalem: Israel Exploration Society and Carta.

Mazar, A.
1990 *Archaeology of the Land of the Bible: 10,000–586 B.C.E.* New York, NY: Doubleday.

Mazar, B.
1957 The Tobiads. *Israel Exploration Journal* 7: 137–45, 229–38.

Meyers, C. L., and Meyers, E. M.
1987 *Anchor Bible*, vol. 25B, *Haggai–Zechariah 1–8*. Garden City, NY: Doubleday.

Meyers, E. M.
1993 Identifying Religious and Ethnic Groups Through Archaeology. Pp. 738–45 in *Biblical Archaeology Today*, eds. A. Biran, J. Aviram and A. Paris-Shadur. Jerusalem: Israel Exploration Society.

Myers, J. M.
1965 *Anchor Bible*, vol. 14, *Ezra–Nehemiah*. Garden City, NY: Doubleday.

Netzer, E.
1999 Floating in the Desert: Jordan's Pleasure Palace. *Archaeology Odyssey* 2, no. 1: 46–55.

Østergård, U.
1992 What is National and Ethnic Identity? Pp. 16–37 in *Ethnicity in Hellenistic Egypt*, eds. P. Bilde, T. Engberg-Pedersen, L. Hannestad and J. Zahle. Aarhus: Aarhus University.

Porten, B.
1968 *Archives from Elephantine: The Life of an Ancient Jewish Military Colony*. Berkley, CA: University of California.

Schiffman, L. H.
1985 *Who Was a Jew?* Hoboken, NJ: Ktav.

Schürer, E.; Vermes, G; and Millar, F
1973 *The History of the Jewish People in the Age of Jesus Christ*. Edinburgh: Clark.

Schwartz, D. R.
1998 Josephus' Tobiads: Back to the Second Century? Pp. 47–61 in *Jews in a Græco-Roman World*, ed. M. Goodman. Oxford: Clarendon.

Smith, A. D.
1986 *The Ethnic Origins of Nations*. New York, NY: Blackwell.

Smith, J. Z.
1985 What a Difference a Difference Makes. Pp. 3–48 in *To See Ourselves as Others See Us*, eds. J. Neusner and E. S. Frerichs. Chico, CA: Scholars.

Smith, M.
1987 *Palestinian Parties and Politics That Shaped the Old Testament*. London: SCM.

Stern, E.
1981 The Province of Yehud: The Vision and the Reality. Pp. 9–21 in *Jerusalem Cathedra*, vol. 1, ed. L. I. Levine. Detroit, MI: Wayne State University.

Tcherikover, V., and Fuks, A.
1957 *Corpus Papyrorum Judaicarum*. Cambridge, MA: Harvard University.

Will, E.
1983 The Recent French Work at Araq el-Emir: The Qasr el-Abd Rediscovered. Pp. 149–53 in *The Excavations at Araq el-Emir*, ed. N. L. Lapp. Winona Lake, IN: Eisenbrauns.
1992 'Iraq el-Emir (M.R. 221147). Pp. 454–56 in *Anchor Bible Dictionary*, vol. 3, ed. D. N. Freedman. New York, NY: Doubleday.

Will, E., and Larché, F.
1991 *'Iraq al-Amir: Le Château Du Tobiade Hyrcan*. Paris: Geuthner.

Williamson, H.G.M.
1992 Sanballat (PERSON) [Heb Sanballat]. Pp. 973–75 in *Anchor Bible Dictionary*, vol. 5, ed. D. N. Freedman. New York, NY: Doubleday.

Chapter 13

The Relationship between Galilean Archaeology and Historical Jesus Research

by John Dominic Crossan

I recognize that, while an historical Jesus scholar cannot ignore early first-century Galilean archaeology, Galilean archaeologists may find the historical Jesus of little or no interest. I must read them and always do; they do not need to read me and sometimes do not. Archaeologists might assert quite accurately that there is more to Galilean archaeology than the first third of the first century and more to that first third than the historical Jesus. But, granted all that, I try in this chapter to consider what a mutually creative relationship would look like, at least from my side of the dialogue. How, in theory and practice, do we correlate the material remains from Antipas' Galilee and the textual remains about the historical Jesus?

IVORY AND POVERTY

As an example of interaction between material and textual remains, I go back about seven hundred years before Antipas' Galilee and Jesus' challenge. Nahman Avigad, introducing the 1908–1910, 1931–1935, and 1965–1967 expeditions excavating the city of Samaria, gave this summary of the textual evidence:

> In the days of the great Israelite king, Jeroboam II (784–748 B.C.E.), Samaria reached the zenith of its prosperity and expansion. Jeroboam conquered Damascus, extending the borders of his kingdom from Hamath to the sea of the Arabah (2 Kg 14:23–29). In the days of Samaria's greatness, a powerful aristocracy emerged that pursued a life of luxury. Instances of injustice appeared, causing the prophet Amos to protest strongly against the luxuries in the palaces and 'ivory houses' in Samaria and against the pomp of the cult at Bethel (Amos 3:9–15, 4:4).[1]

Imagine for the moment that we had no extant book of Amos, or worse, that we had never heard of Amos and never knew he existed. But imagine also that those first two expeditions had discovered both the Ostraca House with "records of shipments of oil and wine sent by various settlements in the district of Samaria to the royal household as taxes in kind" and the Ivory House with "the most important collection of miniature art from the Iron Age discovered in Israel." Imagine, in other words, that we had those material remains from that capital city but no textual remains about it from a prophet like Amos (I bracket for now any debates on the precise dating of both ostraca and ivories.).

My question is this: Could (should?) the archaeologists working within that imagined limitation have raised the issue of "instances of injustice" all by themselves and without any textual prompts from an Amos? And if they could (should?) have done so, from what source would they have derived such thoughts? Another way to put that question is this: Did Amos' textual indictment, which is not just against ivory, but against ivory causing poverty, not just against luxury and pomp, but against inequality and injustice, leave any traces on the ground and in the earth? If archaeologists were looking for such traces could (should?) they find them? If they did not or could not, should they at least mention that limitation in their discipline or, better, ponder ways to offset and remedy it?

I put that question another way. What general and/or specific presuppositions could archaeologists bring to Samaria's material remains that might raise in their minds the accusations Amos raised in his texts? For example, what about general cross-cultural anthropology or specific Israelite tradition? Either or both of those approaches would warn archaeology that, even in the total absence of an Amos, ivories and taxes might generate covert or overt resistance from Jeroboam's peasantry. My wider question, in other words, is this: Can archaeology dig justice or injustice out of the ground, or even raise questions about justice and injustice from material remains alone? Or, at least, from the general and/or specific presuppositions they bring to those material remains?

Finally, the main content of this chapter was first presented at a special session of the Society of Biblical Literature Annual Meeting on "The Historical Jesus and Galilean Achaeology in the Year 2000." Its organizer was Douglas Edwards and he asked, among other programmatic questions, "Was Galilee impoverished or was there a boom economy in Herod Antipas' reign?" If I rephrased that question in terms of my preceding example, I would ask: Was Israel impoverished or was there a boom economy in Jeroboam II's reign? But what if Jeroboam's boom *was* Amos' impoverishment? What, similarly, if Antipas' boom *was* Jesus' impoverishment? Ask not for whom the boom booms; it may not boom for thee.

MATERIAL REMAINS AND SOCIAL SYSTEMS

I do not presume any ascendancy of either archaeological or exegetical data over the other. I agree with the theoretical proposal of James Strange that "literary remains" and "material remains" should each be used separately to establish their "social systems," and that only then should those systems confront one another in "dialogue" to produce "combined social systems" and, finally, a "reconstructed social reality"'(Strange 1992b: 25, 31). That still leaves, of course, some very general questions about how one gets from data to systems, even or especially for Strange himself. Is it enough, for example, to speak of a Roman "urban overlay" over "local, Jewish culture"? Is that too abstract and too benign for the social system of a large and pagan empire and its small and Jewish colony? But, in any case, Strange's model suggests that both archaeologists and exegetes meet as equals in the reconstructed social world of early first-century Galilee. It will not do for exegetes to focus on the person of Jesus and reduce archaeology to background, and neither will it do for archaeologists to focus on the territory of Antipas and reduce Jesus to decoration. Each comes independently, separately, and sovereignly to reconstruct from its own data the social world of Antipas' rule and Jesus' life. It is, in my view, only this dialectic of projected social worlds, one derived from the archaeology of material remains and the other derived from the exegesis of textual remains, that can establish a powerful interaction between those twin disciplines.

I have tried myself to reconstruct the historical Jesus as a "Jewish Mediterranean peasant," that is, within interlocking social world(s) of Jewish traditional religion, Roman imperial commercialization, and peasant cross-cultural anthropology. What I expect from Galilean archaeologists are their own reconstructions of similar social worlds, but from material rather than textual sources. But sometimes I find first-class analyses of material remains combined with off-hand conclusions about the social world. I am especially interested when those archaeological conclusions about the social world are too easily dismissive of exegetical conclusions about the social world made by historical Jesus scholars (like myself). I am particularly conscious of social-world comments or dismissals made, and often made without references or footnotes, in the final paragraphs or sentences of otherwise detailed archaeological analyses.

Archaeology and Exegesis

I first mentioned this case in the 1994 dialogue between scholars of Galilean archaeology and the historical Jesus; it is still somewhat of a paradigmatic instance for me, and I use it here to raise important issues both inside and outside itself.[2] David Adan-Bayewitz's 1985 doctoral dissertation at Jerusalem's Hebrew University was first summarized in an article co-authored by his advisor, Isidore Perlman and then revised and expanded into a book (Adan-Bayewitz and Perlman 1990; Adan-Bayewitz 1992). His thesis is that "the majority of the common pottery used in Roman Galilee, [was] produced in town or village manufacturing centres, and not by the important cities of the Galilee" (Adan-Bayewitz and Perlman 1990: 170). That majority came from two villages, from Kefar Hananya due east of Acco-Ptolemais and Shikhin, identified by James Strange in 1988 with some ruins about a mile northwest of Sepphoris (Strange 1992a: 351). After a meticulous survey of the *material remains,* based on neutron activation analysis of the clay from which that pottery was made, the conclusion generalizes as follows about the *social world.*

First, from the article:

> The quantitative distribution of Kefar Hananya ware, on the one hand, and the direct marketing to the consumer of pottery at Kefar Hananya and Shikhin…on the other, do not seem consistent with the picture, common among some scholars, of the exploitation of the Galilean peasant by the urban wealthy. Finally, there seems to be a misconception among certain scholars that rural Galilee was exclusively agricultural in the early Roman period. The present evidence contributes toward a more accurate perspective of the Galilean economy (Adan-Bayewitz and Perlman 1990: 171–72).

Second, from the book:

> It may also be noted that the distribution pattern of Kefar Hananya ware does not seem consistent with the picture, common among scholars, of the exploitation in the early Roman period of the Galilean peasant by the urban wealthy (Adan-Bayewitz 1992: 219).

Those comments are extremely important and far-reaching, but they are also given in a somewhat off-hand and terminal manner, without footnotes to individual scholars or specific texts.

I have chosen Adan-Bayewitz' work quite deliberately to contrast the detailed excellence and persuasive evidence with which he has analyzed *material remains,* and the sweeping generality with which he proposed and opposed *social systems* in Galilee's early Roman period (to borrow Strange's terms once more). I understand that Adan-Bayewitz is making the following social conclusions from his pottery evidence. The arrival of two cities, rebuilt Sepphoris and newly-built Tiberias, was good news for (some? all?) Galilean peasants. They were simply an opportunity for increased trade, for larger markets. We should not imagine exploited peasants, but entrepreneurial potters, not oppressed farmers, but enhanced traders. Romanization, urbanization, commercialization, in other words, would be very good for such artisan villagers.

I focus specifically on those two points where he counters the social systems proposed by others. One is with what he terms the erroneous view "common among some scholars" (article) or "common among scholars" (book) about "the exploitation of the Galilean peasant by the urban wealthy" (article and book). The other is what he terms the erroneous view of "certain scholars that rural Galilee was exclusively agricultural" (article only).

Potter and Peasant

My argument is that "the exploitation of the Galilean peasant by the urban wealthy" is confirmed, rather than disconfirmed, by the evidence of a pottery village like Kefar Hananya. It is also ironic that my source for this argument is from a book mentioned several times by Adan-Bayewitz himself (Arnold 1985; Adan-Bayewitz 1992: 235–38).

The first thesis of Dean Arnold's 1985 study of *Ceramic Theory and Cultural Process* is that "that there are certain universal processes involving ceramics that are tied to ecological, cultural or chemical factors. These processes occur in societies around the world and can provide a solid empirical (as opposed to speculative) base for interpreting ancient ceramics." His book, in other words, attempts "to provide cross-cultural generalizations about the relationship which can be applied to many different societies in the present and the past."[3]

The second thesis of Arnold's cross-cultural anthropology of ceramic production is that population pressure and the concomitant loss of subsistence farming force peasant farmers to become peasant artisans. *They are not drawn to that change by entrepreneurial opportunity but forced to it by agricultural necessity*. That is the crucial point for me. It is, in other words, exploitation that pushes peasant farmers to become peasant artisans and, indeed, female household production to become male household or workshop industry. Here are a few key conclusions from his work.

He proposes as a "general principle" that "when a population exceeds the ability of the land to sustain it (and, thus, exceeds its carrying capacity), there is movement into other occupations like pottery making." In other words, "pottery making and other crafts are a secondary choice to agriculture and resorted to by people with poor quality, insufficient, or no land. While agriculture provides food directly to a family, craft production does not, but requires additional labor and greater risks than agriculture "... [so that] once there is a better living with agriculture or more secure or steady work, pottery making is abandoned."[4]

When I map Adan-Bayewitz' *material* remains atop Arnold's ceramic anthropology, I am forced to very different *social* conclusions. Those village ceramicists were not daring entrepreneurs but desperate farmers. I find nothing in their existence that argues against the general phenomenon of the urban aristocracy exploiting the peasant countryside. But there seem to be deeper misconceptions behind that first, and especially the second, of Adan-Bayewitz' social conclusions

Peasant and City

At this point I am moving within Adan-Bayewitz' second point ("Galilee is not exclusively rural"), but also expanding it into a wider consideration of where archaeologically based scholars talk against, but actually talk past, anthropologically based exegetes.

I myself use a term like "peasant" in its strictly cross-cultural anthropological meaning. I do not use it as some romantic or archaic equivalent for farmer or rural worker. But, as far as I can judge, very many archaeologists use "peasant" as a loose equivalent for "farmer," so that, for example, one could imagine peasants/farmers without cities (you could for farmers, but not for peasants) or an exclusively rural peasants/farmers environment (once more, you could for farmers, but not for peasants). But, against the anthropological background I am presuming, this is my thesis: *The phrase "an exploited peasantry" is a redundancy and the phrase "an exclusively rural peasantry" is an oxymoron*. That thesis is based on the following citations, which do not represent a tendentiously selective set of cross-cultural anthropological definitions of peasant or peasantry, but are representative of all that I have ever read.[5]

One example: Of the four characteristics that define a peasantry for Teodor Shanin, the final one is "the 'underdog' position. The domination of peasantry by outsiders.... The political economy of peasant society has been, generally speaking, based on expropriation of its 'surpluses' by powerful outsiders, through *corvee*, tax, rent, interest, and terms of trade." Shanin also lists "marginal groups of peasantry," and the first two such "major marginal groups" he mentions are: "(1) *agricultural labourers* who lack a family farm" and work on a large estate, and "(2) rural inhabitants who draw their main means of livelihood from *crafts and trades*, but who live in peasant environments and often work some land, e.g., rural craftsmen."[6] You could talk, in that understanding, not just of peasant farmers, but also of (marginalized) peasant laborers and peasant artisans. I suppose from that last category that Shanin would agree with Arnold's assessment of those Galilean village ceramicists.

Another example: George Foster also connects peasants, rural artisans, and even fishers within the same definition (Foster 1967: 4, 6, 9). He answers the question "What is a peasant?" while introducing the reader to peasant society by including in that term not only agriculturalists but "other small-scale producers, such as fishermen and rural craftsmen" as well. The reason is his insistence that "like most anthropologists, we agree that peasants are primarily agriculturalists, but we also believe that the criteria of definition must be structural and relational rather than occupational. For in most peasant societies, significant numbers of people earn their livings from nonagricultural occupations. It is not *what* peasants produce that is significant; it is *how* and *to whom* they dispose of what they produce that counts." And that structural relationship is not a very benign one. "Peasants are not only poor, as has often been pointed out, but they are relatively powerless.... Peasants know that control over them is held in some mysterious fashion by superior powers, usually residing in cities.... It is noteworthy, too, that whatever the form of control held by the elite, they usually drain off most of the economic surplus a peasant creates, beyond the necessity for a bare subsistence living and for local religious expenditures."

In a narrower sense, then, a peasant is an exploited farmer and, in the wider sense, a peasant is an exploited producer of any kind.[7] If you find my term "exploited" too morally judgmental, choose whatever word you prefer for a structural relationship wherein a producer is kept at subsistence level by having any surplus "expropriated" (so Shanin) or "drained off" (so Foster) by more powerful forces (cities, castles, states, or whatever).[8]

From all of that cross-cultural anthropological background, I draw two conclusions. First, a peasantry is by definition an exploited group (or, if you prefer, a surplus-expropriated group). Second, an exclusively rural or isolated peasantry is by definition impossible. What power or force exploits them or expropriates their surplus?

It may be possible for that expropriation to come from elsewhere than a city, but generally in both theory and practice, that extractive relationship is between rural peasantry and urban aristocracy. From Robert Redfield: "There were no peasants before the first cities. And those surviving primitive peoples who do not live in terms of the city are not peasants" (Redfield 1953: 31). From George Foster: "The primary criterion for defining peasant society is structural—the relationship between the village and the city (or the state)" (Foster 1967: 8). From Moses Finley: "The peasant was an integral element in the ancient city" (Finley 1977: 322).

It is necessary, once and for all, to stop confusing *isolated* with *rural* with *peasant* and to start taking the term *peasant* as it is used in cross-cultural anthropology—or, at least, to define how one is using it differently. Otherwise, exegetes who use cross-cultural anthropology and archaeologists who do not will simply talk past one another forever. *Peasants and cities go hand-in-hand. They are the necessarily twin sides of an oppressive or exploitive system (or of, if you prefer, a surplus-expropriative system).*

Archaeology and Empire

I acknowledge that Galilean archaeologists could assert that they are interested only in the disciplined discovery and precise description of material remains and that social worlds are not their business (I leave aside whether that position is theoretically credible, practically possible, academically respectable, or financially viable.). But such a position would make Galilean archaeologists rather different from other contemporary archaeologists working on different sites within that same Roman imperial system.

My first example is this prefatory comment from Susan Alcock on Roman Greece:

> To-day, instead of focusing upon the perquisites of the victor, archaeologists are engaging with the effects of imperialist ex-

> pansion upon subject peoples, generating a new kind of 'archaeology of imperialism.' A battery of archaeological techniques is being turned upon issues such as shifting levels of exploitation, changes in economic and social behavior, acculturation, and resistance. Settlement studies, often made possible for the first time as a result of archaeological survey, have in many cases proved particularly crucial indicators of the life of a conquered population (Alcock 1993: 5).

Alcock's terms emphasize the variety, diversity, and complexity of such interactions between colony and empire. In terms of content, her archaeology of "imperialism" is presumably the same as Marianne Sawicki's archaeology of "contact."[9] But I find the former a better term than the latter. All imperialism is contact, but not all contact is imperialism. The term "contact," like the term "urban overlay," mutes and even disguises the unequal power pressures between empire and colony (as distinct from, say, two cultures in contact on more or less equal terms). How would, and should, an archaeology of imperial contact project the social world of early first-century Galilee?

My second example is the way in which John Patterson studied "'Romanisation'—the effects that Roman rule had on the economics and societies of the ancient Mediterranean" (Patterson 1991: 147–48, 155). His focus was on two mountainous regions: Samnium in the central Italian Apennines and Lycia in southwestern Turkey. His plan was to test the hypothesis that there is a general structural relationship between "three important facets of town-country relations—public building in the towns, settlement change in the countryside, and the mobility shown by those members of elites who acquired their wealth in the countryside, but spent it principally in the towns." I focus here on his second element, that is, on rural settlement change, as small peasant freeholders yield before "the increasing agglomeration of rural estates" owned by urban elites. This is how he formulated his question: "The problem then arises of what this change actually meant in practice for the common people who owned or occupied these estates. Various possibilities could exist: that the peasants remained on the land as tenants of the larger proprietors, living in poor and squalid circumstances; or that they left the land to become bandits...or departed the land altogether to go to the city." I presume, speaking, of course, systemically rather than individually, that none of those three options is a particularly happy one for the peasants involved. In all of those options, the safety net of village membership, ancient kinship, and extended family is destroyed forever.

Could an archaeologist ask those questions for Sepphoris and Tiberias, as Patterson did for Samnium and Lycia? Is any relationship discernible between city growth and rural consolidation? And, if smaller rural plots are being unified into larger holdings, can one legitimately infer something about what the peasantry would have thought about such changes? Could and should one infer it from a general background in cross-cultural peasant anthropology? Could and should one infer it from earlier Jewish tradition, when God proclaims in Torah that "the land shall not be sold in perpetuity, for the land is mine; with me you are but aliens and tenants" (Lev 25:23)? Could and should one infer it from later Galilean history, when Josephus acknowledges in his *Life* that the Galilean peasantry hated, detested, and wanted to exterminate both Sepphoris and Tiberias?[10]

GROUND AND TORAH

In a preceding section I emphasized how cross-cultural anthropological expectations could (should?) influence the depiction of the social world drawn from material remains by archaeological scholars. That was, I suppose, suggested long ago and in another context by this challenge from William Dever:

> It would be an oversimplification to say that traditional Near Eastern *historical* archaeology was giving way to the more characteristic *anthropological* archaeology of prehistorians and New World archaeologists, but the *rapprochement* between orientations formerly thought antithetical

> is pertinent.... More fundamental still is the question of whether the archaeology of the ancient Near East should be historically or anthropologically oriented — or both.... This dichotomy is, of course, in many ways a false one, but at the very least the presuppositions of anthropological archaeology, drawn largely from prehistory, must be examined and applied both critically and selectively to the archaeology of the Near East, which has a *history*, based both on artifactual remains and an abundance of literary sources going back 5,000 years (Dever 1981: 15, 21).

But I particularly underlined how that lack led to misinterpretation of exegetical scholars, like myself, who use such terms, definitions, and presuppositions, by archaeological scholars who do not utilize them. I specifically criticized off-hand dismissals of historical Jesus conclusions, either in passing or at the end of otherwise excellent archaeological reports and surveys.

In this section I look at another example of terminal dismissal lacking citation or reference, but do so, once again, to raise wider questions on the relationship between Galilean archaeology and historical Jesus research. The titular question asked by Mark Chancey and Eric Meyers is "How Jewish was Sepphoris in Jesus' time?" but they concluded that, first, I denied "Jesus was an apocalyptic prophet proclaiming the end of the present age and the arrival of a new age where God's rule would be accomplished on earth — the traditional understanding of the 'kingdom of God' that he preached," that, second, "His followers were to abandon their possessions, 'storing up treasures in heaven' instead (Matthew 6:19)," and that, finally, I understood Jesus as "advocating Cynic-like values, wanting to bring about, not an apocalyptic kingdom, but a kingdom in which social barriers were eliminated and social outcasts and rejects were elevated" (Chancey and Meyers 2000: 32–33).

For my present purpose, I leave aside the accuracy or cogency of those criticisms[11] and focus on the significance and importance of certain material remains as ethnic markers of Jewish identity and their presence in Sepphoris (and elsewhere). Three major markers of Jewish identity are suggested by Chancey and Meyers: "the lack of pig-bones, the abundance of stone vessels and the presence, at least in our view, of many *mikva'ot* all support our conclusion that during Jesus' time Sepphoris was home to a significant Jewish community."[12] I find that argument and its supporting evidence to be utterly persuasive. Their conclusion, interpreting those material remains with textual data, is that "the evidence points to a Jewish population in the Hellenistic–Roman period that maintained at least some of the most important religious laws of the Bible and Mishnah" (Sawicki 2000: 27). That is, once again, quite persuasive but, recalling this article's inaugural clash between Jeroboam II and Amos, I ask a delicate and pointed question.

Torah, the covenantal law of Israel, included an integrated mandate of divine justice *and* divine ritual. Archaeologists can certainly find and have found the latter's traces in the ground, but how does one find the former's presence or absence? Torah is emphatically not *only* about ritual, although it is emphatically *also* about ritual.[13]

Put negatively, the absence of any ethnic markers indicating purity observance would have raised a very serious question about Jewish identity. After all, Josephus, describing the apostasy of Philo's nephew, Tiberius Julius Alexander, said simply that he "did not stand by the practices of his people" (*Ant.* 20.100). If all indications of ritual observance were gone, the ethnic markers of covenantal fidelity would be gone with them, and what then of Torah's injunctions to divinely mandated distributive justice for this earth?

Put positively, the question is much more difficult. Granted purity observances, what about divine justice and divine righteousness? I do not presume that the observance of ritual purity indicates the absence of distributive justice, but I ask how does the former's presence interact with the latter's presence or absence? For example, there are many *mikva'ot* (maybe excessive and even ostentatious?), stone vessels, and aniconic decorations among the high-priestly quarters of Jerusalem's Upper City. But despite such Torah observance, those high-priestly families underwent a Zealot class war, a peasant reign of terror, even when all should have been preparing for the Roman siege in the spring of 68 C.E.[14] And the four leading families were finally immortalized by a dismissive poem preserved in the *Babylonian Talmud,* which concluded its fourfold "woe is me" by noting that "they are the high priests, and their sons are treasurers, and their sons-in-law are trustees, and their servants beat the people with staves" (Pesahim 57a). To be Torah-observant certainly involved observance of ritual purity, but it demanded much else as well.

CONCLUSION

On the presumption that interaction between historical research on Jesus' life and archaeological research on Antipas' Galilee should be strongly interactive, I imagine three possible models for that process, the last two of which have been considered above. First, there is a neutral or *parallel* model, which was not discussed in this paper. One describes, for example, all the archaeological discoveries about Nazareth and then one summarizes all the textual mentions of Nazareth. Those twin data bases remain more parallel than interactive, but, of course, while archaeology must pay careful attention to stratification, that textual corpus often remains unstratified. One could say, for instance, that no early first-century synagogue *building* has been discovered at Nazareth without discussing whether Luke 4 is the Jesus-layer or the Luke-layer of textual stratification. Second, there is the *terminal* model of interaction criticized above. After a long archaeological book or article there is, at the end, a passing dismissal of certain historical Jesus research, given either without names or references, or with names but without references. Third, there is the *social* model, in which both archaeology and exegesis programmatically project social worlds from their respective data and do so first independently and then interactively with one another.

That, I hope, is the future for studying the historical Jesus in Galilee and archaeology in this century, and here is just one terminal example of how it might work (Crossan and Reed 2001). Archaeology can show very clearly how commercialization by Roman urbanization struck Judea forcibly through the expansion of Jerusalem's Temple and the creation of Casarea's all-weather port under Herod the Great, but only reached Galilee at Sepphoris and Tiberias under his son Herod Antipas. Urbanization has an immediate effect on the local peasantry in terms of both food and health. In terms of *food*: "As consumer centers with 8,000–12,000 inhabitants, Sepphoris and Tiberias did shift both the agricultural and commercial focus of Galilee onto themselves. Though not nearly as large as Scythopolis, Caesarea, or Tyre, nor as wealthy, in their Galilean context, they encapsulated Antipas' rule in terms of a shift from a traditional to a commercialized agrarian society. This placed an economic strain on Galilean peasants, added stress to families and challenged current values, and created new rural-urban dynamics."[15] In terms of *health* "the first and second centuries probably brought a relatively higher incidence of disease. One reason was the rapid urbanization in the first century," and again "the countryside was healthier than an urban metropolis for the reasons already discussed (e.g., higher population densities increase the incidence of infectious diseases)."[16] As Antipas focused the establishment of his miniature Kingdom of Rome around the urbanization of Sepphoris and Tiberias, so Jesus focused his counter-establishment of the Kingdom of God around the reciprocity of free healing and shared eating.

NOTES

1 Stern et al. 1993: 1301, 1304.

2 "Issues in the Integration of Material and Literary Remains." Paper read at a joint session of the Archaeology of the New Testament World Group and the Historical Jesus Section, Society of Biblical Literature Annual Meeting, Chicago, IL (19–22 November, 1994). The full version of that paper was later published as Crossan 1998: 223–30.

3 Arnold 1985: ix and 16. Or again, still on p. 16: "By deriving generalizations from modern cultures, it is

possible to understand and explain how ceramics articulate with the rest of culture and environment. By applying these generalizations to the past, it is possible to develop a more precise interpretation of how archaeological ceramics relate to an ancient environment and culture."

4 Arnold 1985:168, 193. Arnold distinguishes four levels of ceramic production, and I presume those Galilean villages would fall into his second and third categories. Notice, once again, that he emphasizes the agricultural pressure that forces farmers to become potters and female household production to become male household or workshop industry.

The first type is *household production*: "All adult females have learned the craft and have the same potential to make pots" (p. 226). Each home makes its own pottery for itself and, since females are tied to the home by children, they are the potters.

The second type is *household industry*:

> Population pressure forces men into the craft and the social position of the potters thus decreases because of their limited access to or ownership of agricultural land...(and it also) forces farmers to go further and further away to obtain suitable agricultural land.... At a distance of 7–8 kms...travel to their fields becomes uneconomic and people may prefer to exploit resources like ceramic raw materials closer to their homes.... Pottery making in the household industry mode of production is thus an adaptation of a population to specific kinds of non-agricultural resources; it is an adaptation to land which is limited or poor agriculturally, but which has ceramic resources (pp. 226–27).

The third type is *workshop industry*:

> Population pressure has largely, if not completely, eliminated agriculture as a subsistence base for the potters. Subsistence activities do not conflict with pottery making and thus males are potters since they have no alternative means of subsistence. Once direct food production ceases, the potter's family is dependent on the craft for a living, and the risks inherent in making pottery must be reduced in order to have a reliable income.... In order for the potter to realize increased control over the process, capital investment in innovations is necessary (such as constructing a shed for forming and drying pottery, building a kiln, and buying or making molds or a wheel). Because potters in the household industry [the second mode of production] are poor and economically marginal, most potters cannot afford the capital investment that these innovations require and are therefore forced to hire themselves out to those who have them.... This change removes pottery production from the household and thus totally eliminates women from the pottery making process.... Because of the low status of pottery making and the economic marginality of potters in a household industry [the second mode of production], potters do not often choose to develop a more intensive craft, but rather prefer to enhance their status. They may ultimately abandon pottery making for a more prestigious and lucrative occupation as a middleman or the owner of a pottery workshop. Thus, the development of a workshop mode of production with capital investment (needed for obtaining innovations and paying workers on a regular basis) is a pattern initiated by higher status individuals who are either outside of pottery making completely or socially and economically marginal to the craft (pp. 227–29).

The fourth type is *large-scale industry*. It is "characterized by substantial capital investment in production for a maximum output and minimal cost per unit. The regulating effects of weather and climate are totally eliminated...innovations have...maximized efficiency...production is full-time for the entire year...women are totally eliminated...potters are men...[and] full-time production requires extensive distribution of pottery to provide remuneration for the potter to buy food (p. 231).

5 Other examples are Lenski 1966: 271; Wolf 1966: 3–4, 11; Dalton 1972: 385–415, esp. 404, 406; Scott 1976: 173–74; and Kautsky (1982: 4, 6, 18, 24) about the aristocracy who "live off the peasantry."

6 Shanin 1971: 296–97. The other three characteristics of a peasantry are: "(1) the peasant family-farm as the basic unit of multi-dimensional social organization... (2) land husbandry as the main means of livelihood directly providing the major part of the consumption needs...(3) specific traditional culture related to the way of life of small communities" (pp. 294–96) The other five "marginal groups of peasantry" are: (1) frontier squatters, (2) free armed peasantry "along frontiers and in the mountains," (3) pastoral tribal peoples "on the borderline between the pre-peasant and the peasant," (4) peasant-workers who keep their farms "merely for consumption purposes and as a place to live while drawing the grater part of [their]

income from town-based wages," (5) member of Kolkhozes [Soviet collective farms] and communes (pp. 297–98).

7 That external definition does not in any way deny the importance of internal differentiation between upper and lower peasantry; see Landsberger 1973: 13–15; Roseberry 1989: 123; Cancian 1989: 152; and Dobrowolski 1971: 290–91, 293–94, n. 1.

8 Compare the comment of de Ste. Croix (1975: 26):

> Class, then, essentially a relationship, *is* above all the collective social expression of the *fact of exploitation* (and of course of resistance to it): the division of society into economic classes is in its very nature the way in which exploitation is effected, with the propertied classes living off the non-propertied. I admit that in my use of it the word 'exploitation' often tends to take on a pejorative colouring; but essentially it is a 'value-free' expression, signifying merely that a propertied class is freed from the labour of production through its ability to maintain itself out of a surplus extracted from the primary producers, whether by compulsion or by persuasion or (as in most cases) by a mixture of the two.

9 Sawicki 2000: 176–98 and 212–13; "'Contact' is the shorthand term for the complex and negotiated borders between two or more cultures when representatives of those cultures live together" (p. 212).

10 "I marched with such troops as I had against Sepphoris and took the city by assault. The Galilaeans, seizing this opportunity, too good to be missed, of venting their *hatred* on one of the cities which they *detested*, rushed forward, with the intention of *exterminating* the population, aliens and all. Plunging into the town they set fire to the houses, which they found to be deserted, the terrified inhabitants having fled in a body to the citadel. They looted everything, sparing their countrymen no conceivable form of devastation.... As, however, they refused to listen to either remonstration or command, my exhortations being overborne by their *hatred,* I instructed some of my friends to circulate a report that the Romans had made their way into another quarter of the city with a large force...that...I might check the fury of the Galilaeans and so save Sepphoris....Tiberias, likewise, had a narrow escape from being sacked by the Galilaeans...[who] loudly denounced the Tiberians as traitors and friendly to the king [Agrippa II], and requiring permission to go down and *exterminate* their city. For they had the same *detestation* for the Tiberians as for the inhabitants of Sepphoris" (*Life* 374–84, italics added).

11 For my actual views on Jesus and Cynicism, see Crossan 1998: 333–35. Across thirty years of research and publication, I have consistently maintained that Jesus was eschatological but not apocalyptic. Cynicism was also eschatological but not apocalyptic and was *at that time* a rebuttal of the realized eschatology of Augustan triumphalism. Whether Jesus knew anything of Cynicism may be accepted or rejected and, in any case, I find that conjunction comparatively useful rather than constitutively necessary. Fellow Jews hearing Jesus would presume an eschatological prophet (at least). Pagans hearing him (does one imagine that might ever have happened?) would presume some sort of philosophical cynic (at least). Finally, it is not prudent to separate or oppose even "an apocalyptic kingdom" to radical egalitarianism here below. Think, for example, of these lines from an Augustan-era Jewish full-service apocalypse: "The earth will belong equally to all, undivided by walls or fences. It will then bear more abundant fruits spontaneously. Lives will be in common and wealth will have no division. For there will be no poor man there, no rich, and no tyrant, no slave. Further, no one will be either great or small anymore. No kings, no leaders. All will be on a par together" (*Sibylline Oracles* 2:319–24). For the dating and translation see Collins 1983: 351, 353.

12 Chancey and Meyers 2000: 27. That article was followed by a debate on "The Pools of Sepphoris" in Meyers 2000 with an argument that "They're Not Ritual Baths" (Eshel), "Yes, They Are" (Meyers), and "We Need More Data" (Eshel). The clear conclusion was that *at least some* of those pools (the *mikveh-otzer* combinations) were *certainly* ritual pools and not hygienic bathtubs. From those pools (and other evidence) Meyers argues that Sepphoris was then a Jewish city. But even if we agree on that conclusion, what exactly are its implications? Sawicki argues that such Jewish ritual plumbing was an act of covert resistance to Roman bathing plumbing, the *mikveh* against the aqueduct as an act of fidelity to Torah (2000: 121–28). That surely helps to specify what "Jewish" meant in a "Jewish city" within an archaeology of imperial contact and colonial social world.

13 For a very good balance between Torah's demands as *both* distributive justice *and* ritual purity, see Reed 2000. For the four major markers of Jewish identity despite Roman urbanization (stepped, plastered pools as *mikva'oth*, stone vessels, absence of pig bones, *loculi/kokhim* body burial and pit or ossuary bone burial) see Reed 2000: 44–57 and for questions of distributive justice under Roman urbanization, see Reed 2000: 66–69.

14 For details and citations from Josephus see Crossan 1991: 210–18.

15 Reed 2000: 96. See also Reed's earlier comments: "We first turn to Sepphoris and Tiberias' impact on agriculture. In terms of food alone, the agricultural practices of Galilee were completely realigned and stretched with the foundation of these two cities. The picture of numerous self-sufficent farms or hamlets in Galilee radically changed. The entire agricultural focus turned to feeding Sepphoris and Tiberias" (1994: 70).

16 Avalos 1999: 4, 113. In the first case, Avalos refers to Stambaugh 1988. In the second, he refers to Shaw 1996.

REFERENCES

Adan-Bayewitz, D.
1992 *Common Pottery in Roman Galilee: A Study of Local Trade*. Bar-Ilan Studies in Near Eastern Languages and Culture. Ramat-Gan, Israel: Bar-Ilan University.

Adan-Bayewitz, D., and Perlman, I.
1990 The Local Trade of Sepphoris in the Roman Period. *Israel Exploration Journal* 40: 153–72.

Alcock, S. E.
1993 *Graecia Capta: The Landscapes of Roman Greece*. Cambridge: Cambridge University.

Arnold, D. E.
1985 *Ceramic Theory and Cultural Process*. New Studies in Archaeology. Cambridge: Cambridge University.

Avalos, H.
1999 *Health Care and the Rise of Christianity*. Peabody, MA: Hendrikson.

Cancian, F.
1989 Economic Behavior in Peasant Communities. Pp. 127–70, 443–46 in *Economic Anthropology*, ed. S. Plattner. Stanford, CA: Stanford University.

Chancey, M., and Meyers, E. M.
2000 How Jewish Was Sepphoris in Jesus' Time? *Biblical Archaeology Review* 26: 18–33.

Collins, J. J.
1983 Sibylline Oracles (Second Century BC–Seventh Century AD): A New Translation and Introduction. Pp. 317–472 in *The Old Testament Pseudepigrapha*, vol. 1, ed. J. H. Charlesworth. Garden City, NY: Doubleday.

Crossan, J. D.
1991 *The Historical Jesus: The Life of a Mediterranean Jewish Peasant*. San Francisco, CA: HarperSanFrancisco.
1998 *The Birth of Christianity: Discovering What Happened in the Years Immediately After the Execution of Jesus*. San Francisco, CA: HarperSanFrancisco.

Crossan, J. D., and Reed, J. L.
2001 *Excavating Jesus: Beneath the Stones, Behind the Texts*. San Francisco, CA: HarperSanFrancisco.

Dalton, G.
1972 Peasantries in Anthropology and History. *Current Anthropology* 13: 385–415.

de Ste. Croix, G. E. M.
1975 Karl Marx and the History of Classical Antiquity. *Arethusa* 8: 7–41.

Dever, W. G.
1981 The Impact of the 'New Archaeology' on Syro-Palestinian Archaeology. *Bulletin of the American Schools of Oriental Research* 242: 15–29.

Dobrowolski, K.
1971 Peasant Traditional Culture. Pp. 277–98 in *Peasants and Peasant Society: Selected Readings*, ed. T. Shanin. Baltimore, MD: Penguin.

Finley, M. I.
1977 The Ancient City: From Fustel de Coulanges to Max Weber and Beyond. *Comparative Studies in Society and History* 19: 305–27.

Foster, G. M.
1967 Introduction: What is a Peasant? Pp. 2–14 in *Peasant Society: A Reader*, eds. J. M. Potter, M. N. Diaz and G. M. Foster. Boston, MA: Little Brown.

Kautsky, J. H.
1982 *The Politics of Aristocratic Empires*. Chapel Hill, NC: University of North Carolina.

Landsberger, H. A.
1973 Peasant Unrest: Themes and Variations. Pp. 1–64 in *Rural Protest: Peasant Movements and Social Change*, ed. H. A. Landsberger. New York, NY: Barnes & Noble.

Lenski, G. E.
1966 *Power and Privilege: A Theory of Social Stratification*. New York, NY: McGraw-Hill.

Meyers, E. M.
2000 The Pools of Sepphoris – Ritual Baths or Bathtubs? *Biblical Archaeology Review* 26: 46–48, 60–61.

Patterson, J. R.
1991 Settlement, City, and Elite in Samnium and Lycia. Pp. 146–68 in *City and Country in the Ancient World*, eds. J. Rich and A. Wallace-Hadrill. New York, NY: Routledge.

Redfield, R.
1953 *The Primitive World and Its Transformation*. Ithaca, NY: Cornell University.

Reed, J. L.
1994 *Places in Early Christianity: Galilee, Archaeology, Urbanization and Q*. Ann Arbor, MI: University Microfilms International.
2000 *Archaeology and the Galilean Jesus: A Re-Examination of the Evidence*. Harrisburg, PA: Trinity International.

Roseberry, W.
1989 Peasants and the World. Pp. 108–26, 441–43 in *Economic Anthropology*, ed. S. Plattner. Stanford, CA: Stanford University.

Sawicki, M.
2000 *Crossing Galilee: Architectures of Contact in the Occupied Land of Jesus*. Harrisburg, PA: Trinity International.

Scott, J. C.
1976 *The Moral Economy of the Peasant: Rebellion and Subsistence in Southeast Asia*. New Haven, CN: Yale University.

Shanin, T.
1971 Peasantry: Delineation of a Sociological Concept and a Field of Study. *European Journal of Sociology* 12: 289–300.

Shaw, B. D.
1996 Seasons of Death: Aspects of Morality in Imperial Rome. *Journal of Roman Studies* 86: 100–138.

Stambaugh, J. E.
1988 *The Ancient Roman City*. Baltimore, MD: Johns Hopkins University.

Stern, E.; Lewinson-Gilboa, A.; and Aviram, J. (eds.)
1993 *The New Encyclopedia of Archaeological Excavations in the Holy Land*, vols. 1–4. Jerusalem: Israel Exploration Society and Carta.

Strange, J. F.
1992a Six Campaigns at Sepphoris: The University of South Florida Excavations, 1983–1989. Pp. 339–55 in *The Galilee in Late Antiquity*, ed. L. I. Levine. New York, NY: The Jewish Theological Seminary of America.
1992b Some Implications of Archaeology for New Testament Studies. Pp. 23–59 in *What Has Archaeology to Do with Faith?* eds. J. H. Charlesworth and W. P. Weaver. Faith and Scholarship Colloquies. Philadelphia, PA: Trinity International.

Wolf, E. R.
1966 *Peasants*. Foundations of Modern Anthropology Series. Englewood Cliffs, NJ: Prentice-Hall.

Chapter 14

Zum Standort des Tempels

by Volkmar Fritz

In seiner detaillierten Untersuchung *Vom Tempel zum Felsendom* hat Ernst Vogt nachgewiesen, dass der heute vom Felsendom überbaute Felsen nicht der Standort des Tempels gewesen sein kann (Vogt 1974). Vielmehr hat der Felsen erst seit omajjadischer Zeit die heutige Bedeutung erlangt. Erst mit dem Bau des Felsendomes durch den Kalifen Abd el-Malik (685–705 n.Chr.) hat der Felsen die verschiedenen Traditionen angezogen, die ihm Würde und Ansehen verleihen. Ausgangspunkt für die Aneignung des gesamten Tempelplatzes durch die Muslime war dabei die Übertragung der Tradition von der Himmelsreise des Propheten in Sure 17:1 auf den Felsen: „Die Himmelsreise wurde zum *Hieros Logos* des Felsens" (Vogt 1974: 50). Gleichzeitig sollte der Felsendom ein „Gegenstück" zur Kuppel der Anastasis bilden, die Jerusalem als wichtigstes christliches Heiligtum überragte. Scheidet damit der Felsen als ehemaliger Standort des Tempels aus (gegen Donner 1977; Ritmeyer und Ritmeyer 1998; Jacobson 1999), ist die Frage nach der Lokalisierung des Tempels erneut offen. Die Verbindung des Felsens mit dem Tempel gehört also in den Bereich späterer Traditionsbildung, die Lage des Tempels ist durch den Felsen nicht markiert. Der Tempel von Jerusalem gehört somit nicht zum Typ des umbauten Götterfelsens (gegen Noth 1968: 109), da der Fels nicht vom Allerheiligsten (*debir*) überbaut gewesen ist. Ursprünglich war das Allerheiligste ohnehin ein Einbau aus Holz (Schult 1964), so dass eine Überbauung des Felsens durch den Tempel auf jeden Fall ausscheidet.

In dem Bericht über den Bau des Tempels durch Salomo in 1 Kön 6–8 verlautet über den Standort des Tempels nichts. Es ist lediglich deutlich, dass er innerhalb des königlichen Palastes im Bereich einer Erweiterung der Stadt nach Norden gelegen hat. Insofern ist er als Heiligtum der von David begründeten Dynastie zu bestimmen und hat als irdischer Palast Jahwes gedient (1 Kön 8:12f.). Nach 2 Kön 21:5 und 23:12 können für den Tempel zwei Höfe unterschieden werden, die eine gewisse Abgrenzung gegenüber dem königlichen Palast nahe legen, doch ist ihre Lage nicht mehr zu bestimmen. Nach 1 Kön 6:2f. kann der Tempel als Langraum mit Vorhalle und einem Einbau als Allerheiligstes rekonstruiert werden (Busink 1970; Zwickel 1999), er hat vermutlich die Form eines Antentempels gehabt. Dieser Bautyp ist auch sonst im Vorderen Orient seit dem 2. Jt. weit verbreitet gewesen (Fritz 1980). Beim Wiederaufbau des Tempels in frühnachexilischer Zeit (sog. zweiter Tempel) wurden anscheinend die gleichen Maße wie beim Vorgängerbau verwendet. Das geht zwar aus dem

Text Esra 6:3 nicht eindeutig hervor, da die Stelle durch ein Schreiberversehen entstellt ist, doch lassen sich die Maßangaben mit einiger Sicherheit entsprechend denen des salomonischen Tempels wiederherstellen (Rudolph 1949: 54f.).

Der Standort dieses zweiten Tempels wird nicht näher beschrieben, so dass nicht zu entscheiden ist, ob er an der Stelle des ersten gestanden hat oder an anderer Stelle wiederaufgebaut wurde. Auf jeden Fall wurde der Palast der einstigen Könige von Juda nicht wieder errichtet, so dass der Tempel nun von großen Höfen umgeben war, was auf eine einigermaßen zentrale Stellung des Tempelgebäudes auf dem Tempelplatz schließen lässt. Die genaue Lage des Tempelgebäudes innerhalb dieser Höfe lässt sich nicht mehr feststellen, obwohl diese in dem sog. Verfassungsentwurf Ezechiels Ez 40–48 und im Mischnahtraktat Middot mit Maßangaben beschrieben werden. Deutlich markieren diese Höfe ein Gefälle abnehmender Heiligkeit, was sich auch in der Betretbarkeit durch unterschiedliche Personengruppen äußert. Weiterhin kann aus Ez 43:4 geschlossen werden, dass der zweite Tempel von West nach Ost orientiert war, was durch die Mischnah bestätigt wird. Ob diese Orientierung durch den ersten Tempel vorgegeben war, kann nicht mehr festgestellt werden, ist aber zumindest wahrscheinlich.

In nachexilischer Zeit ist der Tempel damit zu einem frei stehenden Gebäude geworden, das von mehreren Höfen umgeben war. Abgesehen von dieser Veränderung im Bereich der Umgebung scheint der Tempel in nachexilischer Zeit dem salomonischen Bau entsprochen zu haben, so dass mit einer gewissen Beharrungstendenz in der Gestaltung des Grundrisses zu rechnen ist. Ob der zweite Tempel auch den Standort des salomonischen Baus eingenommen hat, kann nicht mehr festgestellt werden, auch wenn eine solche Fortführung der Kulttradition als wahrscheinlich anzunehmen ist. Zu bedenken bleibt jedoch, dass der erste Tempel innerhalb des Palastes errichtet wurde, so dass eine Verlegung bei der Neugestaltung des Platzes nicht ausgeschlossen werden kann. Erst gegen Ende seiner Geschichte wurde er durch Herodes neu erbaut und umgestaltet. Dabei scheint das eigentliche Tempelgebäude in den gleichen Maßen wiedererrichtet worden zu sein, wie aus den Beschreibungen des Josephus (*Ant.* XV 11.1–7 und *Bellum* V 5.1–7) hervorgeht. Die Veränderungen betreffen abgesehen von den Säulenhallen auf dem Tempelplatz vor allem zwei Bereiche: eine Vergrößerung der Vorhalle und eine Erweiterung des Tempelareals. Während die Veränderung der Vorhalle in diesem Zusammenhang auf sich beruhen bleiben kann, wurde mit der Erweiterung des Tempelareals ein Eingriff vorgenommen, der bis heute die Ausmaße des Tempelplatzes bestimmt, wobei die Vergrößerung im Süden und Westen durch eine neue Umfassungsmauer markiert ist (Bahat 1994), während an der Nordseite die Begrenzung durch die erhaltene Nordostecke (Ritmeyer 2000) und die Abarbeitung des Felsens vorgegeben ist. Bei der Erweiterung des Tempelplatzes wurde die an der Nordwestecke gelegene Burg, die Herodes neu befestigt und in Antonia umbenannt hat (*Ant.* XV 11.4), offensichtlich teilweise abgetragen. Bereits unter Herodes hatte der Tempelplatz somit seine trapezoide Form. Erst mit dieser Neugestaltung rückte der Felsen in den Mittelpunkt des Tempelplatzes.

In seinen Untersuchungen hat Leen Ritmeyer (Ritmeyer und Ritmeyer 1998: 57–89) auch den vorherodianischen Tempelplatz rekonstruieren können. Dabei ist das hasmonäische (= vorherodianische) Tempelareal noch einmal von dem vorhasmonäischen Tempelplatz zu unterscheiden, da wahrscheinlich bereits in hasmonäischer Zeit eine Erweiterung des Areals nach Süden vorgenommen wurde. Ausgangspunkt für die Rekonstruktion ist die bis heute unverändert bestehende Ostmauer, die auf Grund der Gegebenheiten im Gelände bereits von Herodes teilweise übernommen und nicht versetzt wurde. Die noch heute an der Ostseite sichtbare Baufuge markiert den Ansatz der herodianischen Bautätigkeit. Aber in vorhasmonäischer Zeit umfasst der Platz nur die Erstreckung von einem Knick an, der etwa 40.6 m weiter nördlich dieser Baufuge bereits von Charles Warren festgestellt wurde, und der in einem weiteren leichten Knick in der Mauerführung etwa 262.4 m nördlich des ersten Knicks eine Entsprechung hat. Diese Erstreckung der Ostmauer zwischen zwei leichten Abknickungen in der Mauerführung stellt nach Ritmeyer die

Ostseite des vorhasmonäischen Tempelplatzes dar. Dieser Platz des zweiten Tempels wird dann auf Grund von weiteren Beobachtungen im Gelände als ein Quadrat von etwa 262.4 m Seitenlänge rekonstruiert. Dieser Platz wurde von den Hasmonäern zu einem Rechteck erweitert, dessen Schmalseite der vorhasmonäischen Abmessung entspricht, dessen Längsseite aber nun von Nord nach Süd (Ritmeyer und Ritmeyer 1998: 61) an der Ostseite etwa 303 m ausmacht. Bei dieser Rekonstruktion des Tempelplatzes in vorherodianischer Zeit bleibt zwar der in islamischer Zeit überbaute Felsen innerhalb des heiligen Bezirks, rückt aber aus dem Zentrum an den Rand des Areals. Diese Randlage ist jedoch für den zweiten Tempel insofern unwahrscheinlich, als die Beschreibung des Josephus in *Ant.* XV 11.3 eine eher zentrale Lage voraussetzt. Darauf weisen sowohl die Säulenhallen entlang der Außenmauern, als auch die verschiedenen Höfe, die den Tempel umgeben. Zudem berichtet Josephus „nichts von einem heiligen Felsen unter dem Tempel" (Vogt 1974: 40). Die Überbauung des Felsens durch den Tempel lässt sich durch Josephus gerade nicht belegen.

Bei der Eroberung Jerusalems durch die Römer im Jahre 70 n. Chr. wurde auch der Tempel zerstört. Obwohl im Zuge dieser Zerstörung auch die Umfassungsmauern teilweise auf die an ihnen entlang führenden Strassen im Westen und Süden herabgestürzt wurden, blieb der Tempelplatz als eigenes Areal immer intakt und als heiliger Bezirk erhalten bis das Gelände im 7. Jh. endgültig von den Muslimen übernommen wurde. Die von den Omajjaden errichteten Großbauten verliehen dem Platz neue Würde und Bedeutung. Der heilige Felsen unter dem Felsendom mit seiner Höhle wurde zum Haftpunkt zahlreicher Traditionen, die vom Islam aus demJudentum und Christentum übernommen wurden (Dalman 1912: 101–51). In römischer Zeit berichtet Cassius Dio (Vogt 1974: 42, n. 2) von der Errichtung eines Tempels für die kapitolinischen Götter Jupiter, Juno und Minerva auf dem Gelände des Tempelplatzes. Der Tempelbau unter Hadrian führte zunächst zum Bar Kochba Aufstand, in dessen Verlauf es auch zum Bau eines neuen Tempels kam. Erst nach der Niederschlagung des Aufstandes durch römische Truppen im Jahre 135 n. Chr. konnte der heidnische Tempel zusammen mit der neugegründeten Stadt errichtet werden. Nach einer Nachricht des *Chronicon Paschale* (Vogt 1974: 43) aus frühbyzantinischer Zeit wurde dabei der jüdische Tempel, den die Aufständischen neu erbaut hatten, erneut zerstört. Nach Cassius Dio wurde der römische Tempel an der Stelle des zweiten Tempels errichtet, und bewahrt somit die Tradition des Standorts des ehemaligen Tempels, wenngleich über den genauen Standort keine Angaben gemacht werden. Der Pilger von Bordeaux, der im Jahre 333 n. Chr. die Stadt besuchte, erwähnt zwei Statuen Hadrians, aber nicht den Tempel der kapitolinischen Götter, so dass zumindest vermutet werden kann, dass der heidnische Tempel im Zuge der Christianisierung der Stadt aufgegeben wurde. Jedenfalls ist beim Pilger von Bordeaux die Tendenz unverkennbar, die vorhandenen baulichen Überreste auf Salomo zurückzuführen und mit dem Leben Jesu in Verbindung zu bringen. Bei den beiden Statuen handelt es sich wohl um Standbilder der Kaiser Hadrian (117–138 n. Chr.) und Antonius Pius (138–161 n. Chr.), zumal letzterer den Adoptivnamen Aelius Hadrianus trug. Nach Hieronymus (Vogt 1974: 43) handelte es sich um Standbilder des Kaisers Hadrian zu Pferde. In jedem Fall scheinen Reste des römischen Tempels noch im 4. Jh. vorhanden gewesen zu sein, denn „Hieronymus konnte noch deutlich die Stelle des Tempelhauses und des Brandopferaltares unterscheiden" (Vogt 1974: 46f.). Im Verlauf der byzantischen Epoche wurde die Stadt weiter verchristlicht, wobei der Tempelplatz unbebaut blieb. Als Trümmerstätte sollte der Tempelplatz zur Demonstration der Ankündigung Jesu von der Zerstörung des Tempels in Mk 13:1 und parallel Mt 21:1f. und Lk 21:5f. dienen. Lediglich während der kurzen Herrschaft des Kaisers Julian (361–363 n. Chr.) kam es zu einem Versuch von Seiten des Judentums, den zerstörten Tempel wiederaufzubauen, doch hat der frühe Tod des Kaisers dieses Unternehmen zu einem vorzeitigen Ende kommen lassen. Bis zur Übernahme der Stadt durch den Kalifen Omar im Jahre 638 n. Chr. blieb der Tempelplatz somit eine unbenutzte Ruinenstätte. Die frühislamische Übernahme setzte mit dem Kalifen Omar ein und knüpfte bewusst an die jüdische Kulttradition der Stätte an.

Fig. 1 *Der Tempelplatz von Südosten mit den Resten der monumentalen Treppe (Photo von C. F. Tyrwhitt-Drake um 1870).*

In byzantischer Zeit war aber jüdischerseits diese Kulttradition niemals aufgegeben worden, wenngleich sie notgedrungen die Form der Ausübung von Klageriten angenommen hatte. Die Klagen über den zerstörten Tempel werden vom Pilger von Bordeaux an dem sog. durchbohrten Stein auf dem Tempelplatz verortet (Donner 1979: 56), der aber nicht näher bestimmt werden kann und von dem sog. Gründungsstein (Yoma 5:2) zu unterscheiden ist. Dieser Gründungsstein (*gtyh*) hat verschiedene Vorstellungen angezogen, die dann auch in der Grabeskirche und im Felsendom verhaftet wurden. Da beide Steine nicht zu lokalisieren sind, können diese Nachrichten nicht für die Lokalisierung des Tempels herangezogen werden. Aus den Quellen ist über den Standort des ersten wie des zweiten Tempels nichts zu entnehmen. Ebenso ist die Lage des römischen Tempels auf dem Gelände unbekannt, die Angaben bei Cassius Dio weisen lediglich darauf hin, dass das Heiligtum für die kapitolinischen Götter an der Stelle des zweiten Tempels errichtet wurde. Aus den Quellen ist die Lage der vorislamischen Heiligtümer somit nicht zu bestimmen, wahrscheinlich ist jedoch, dass der in omajjadischer Zeit vom Felsendom überbaute Felsen nicht der Standort der älteren Heiligtümer gewesen ist. Archäologisch hat der von Herodes geschaffene und von einer Mauer umschlossene Tempelplatz seit der Zerstörung Jerusalems durch die Römer 70 n. Chr. weiterbestanden. Das Gelände, in dem der Tempel gelegen hat, ist somit einwandfrei markiert. Auf Grund sorgfältiger Beobachtungen an der Ostmauer konnte Ritmeyer den Umfang des vorherodianischen Tempelplatzes erschließen, ohne dass damit die Lage des Tempels näher eingegrenzt werden könnte.

Nun haben Jacobson und Gibson (1995) ein Photo von Tyrwitt-Drake veröffentlicht, das zumindest einen Anhaltspunkt für die mögliche Lage des Tempels gibt, wenngleich es keine endgültige und eindeutige Entscheidung in dieser Frage zulässt. Das Photo (fig. 1) zeigt die Konstruktion von vier Stufen, die sich vor der Südseite der Plattform befinden, über die sich heute der Felsendom erhebt.

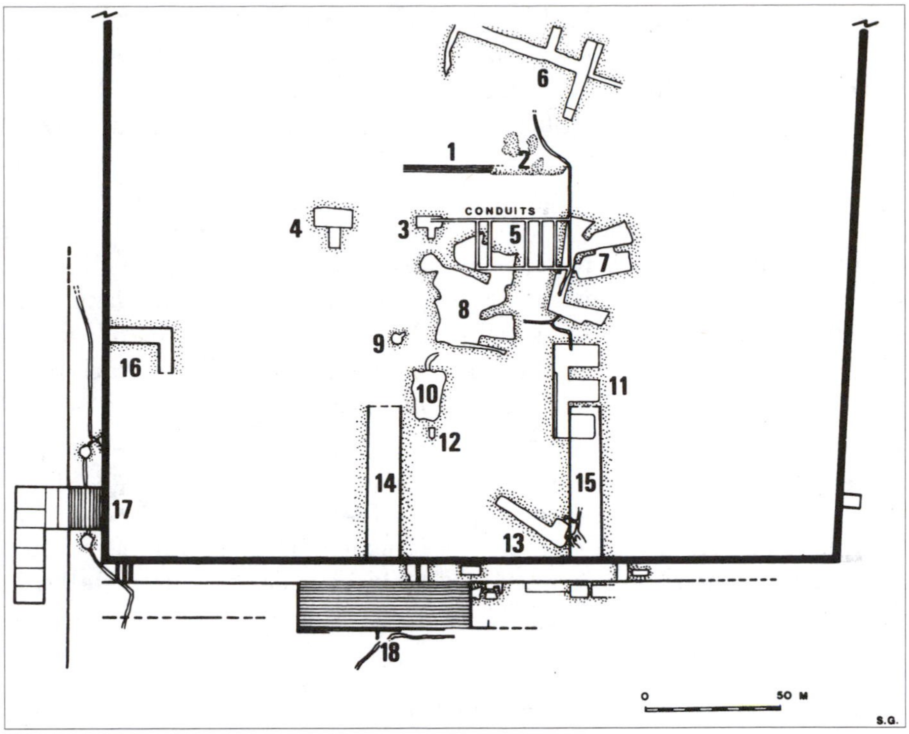

Fig. 2 *Der südliche Bereich des Tempelplatzes mit den Resten der monumentalen Treppe (1).*

Diese Konstruktion stellt ein Element dar, das älter als die Plattform mit ihren Stufenzugängen ist; sie wurde auch von Warren in seine Pläne des Tempelplatzes eingezeichnet (fig. 2). Obwohl die gegenwärtigen Treppen zu dieser Plattform erst aus dem 17. Jh. stammen, ist doch damit zu rechnen, dass die Plattform zur Einebnung des Geländes bereits in der omajjadischen Zeit zusammen mit dem Felsendom angelegt wurde (Rosen-Ayalon 1989: 30–32). Die wiederentdeckte Konstruktion, die bereits im Jahre 1887 verschwunden war, stellt somit wahrscheinlich ein vorislamisches Bauelement dar. Damit stellt sich das Problem der Bestimmung und Datierung dieser Konstruktion.

Nun ist für ein bauliches Element ohne Ausgrabung kein einigermaßen sicheres Datum zu gewinnen. Da aber archäologische Untersuchungen auf dem Tempelplatz wegen der Heiligkeit des Ortes für die Muslime bis auf Weiteres ausgeschlossen sind, muss die Zweckbestimmung dieser Konstruktion immer Vermutung bleiben. Auf Grund eines Größenvergleichs mit abgebildeten Personen haben Jacobson und Gibson (1995: 169) die Höhe dieser Stufen auf 45 bis 50 cm bestimmt. Damit ist deutlich, dass es sich bei dem erhaltenen Restbestand nicht um eine ältere Treppenanlage gehandelt hat. Jacobson (1999: 57) bestimmt die erhaltenen Überreste als Teil des Podiums, auf dem der herodianische Tempel gestanden hat. Die Umfassungsmauer dieses Podiums wird in der Mischnah (Middot 11:3) eigens erwähnt. Gegen diese Interpretation erheben sich jedoch erhebliche Bedenken. Zum einen geht Jacobson ohne weitere Begründung davon aus, dass der Tempel über dem Felsen erbaut war, und zum anderen folgt er für die Bestimmung dieser Plattform den Maßangaben in der Mischnah, ohne dass diese in irgendeiner Weise gesichert werden können. Die Konstruktion bestimmt Jacobson (1999: 60) als Unterbau (*erepidoma*) für eine Tempelanlage, wobei er als Parallele vor allem auf den Tempel von Didyma verweist, der aus hellenistischer Zeit stammt. Nun ist zwar nicht auszuschließen, dass bereits Herodes bei der Erneuerung des zweiten Tempels nach hellenistischem Vorbild eine solche Tempelplattform geschaffen hat, wie sie dann in der Mischnah (Middot) beschrieben wird. Wahrscheinlicher ist es aber, dass der von Hadrian erbaute römische Tempel auf einem solchen Unterbau gestanden hat. Bei der heute verschwundenen stufenförmigen Konstruktion südlich der heutigen Plattform könnte es sich somit um einen Rest des Podiums für den römischen Tempel handeln. Die Abmessungen dieses Podiums sind nicht mehr auszumachen, am ehesten ist mit einem von West nach Ost gerichteten rechteckigen Unterbau zu rechnen, mit dem gleichzeitig eine ebene Fläche für die Errichtung des Tempels in römischer Zeit geschaffen wurde. Diese rechteckige Plattform hat aber auf keinen Fall mehr den Felsen mit eingeschlossen, sondern südlich des Felsens gelegen. Damit wäre der Standort des heidnischen Tempels in römischer Zeit im Süden des heutigen Felsendomes eingegrenzt. Da aber der römische Tempel am Standort des zweiten Tempels errichtet wurde, ist mit dieser Lage auch die Lokalität des zweiten Tempels eingegrenzt. Der zweite Tempel hat südlich des Felsens gelegen, dieser war nicht überbaut, sondern hat in dem den Tempel umgebenden Hof frei gestanden. Die Lage des ersten Tempels bleibt weiterhin unbekannt. Erst Herodes hat den Tempelplatz zu seiner heutigen Größe erweitert und damit den Felsen in das Zentrum der gesamten Anlage gerückt. Bei der Übernahme des Platzes durch die Muslime im 7. Jh. n. Chr. wurde der Felsen nördlich des ehemaligen Tempelbereiches überbaut und damit zum neuen Mittelpunkt kultischer Traditionsbildung. Die Reste der alten Plattform blieben auch bei der Neugestaltung erhalten, bis sie aus unbekannten Gründen in der zweiten Hälfte des 19. Jh. endgültig verschwanden.

REFERENCES

Bahat, D.

1994 The Western Wall Tunnels. Pp. 177–90 in *Ancient Jerusalem Revealed*, ed. H. Geva. Jerusalem: Israel Exploration Society.

Busink, T. A.

1970 *Der Tempel von Jerusalem von Salomo bis Herodes I. Der Tempel Salomos*. Leiden: Brill.

Dalman, G.

1912 *Neue Petra-Forschungen und der Heilige Felsen von Jerusalem*. Leipzig: Hinrichs.

Donner, H.

1977 Der Felsen und der Tempel. *Zeitschrift des Deutschen Palästina-Vereins* 93:111.

1979 *Pilgerfahrt ins Heilige Land. Die ältesten Berichte christlicher Palästinapilger (4.–7. Jahrhundert)*. Stuttgart: Katholisches Bibelwerk.

Fritz, V.

1980 Der Tempel Salomos im Licht der neueren Forschung. *Mitteilungen der Deutschen Orient-Gesellschaft* 112: 53–68.

Jacobson, D. M.

1999 Sacred Geometry. Unlocking the Secret of the Temple Mount, Part 2. *Biblical Archaeology Review* 25, no. 5: 54–63.

Jacobson, D. M., and Gibson, S.

1995 A Monumental Stairway on the Temple Mount, *Israel Exploration Journal* 45: 162–70.

Noth, M.

1968 *Könige*. Neukirchen-Vluyn: Neukirchener Verlag des Erziehungsvereins.

Ritmeyer, L.

2000 Where was the Temple? Ritmeyer Responds to Jacobson. *Biblical Archaeology Review* 26, no. 2: 52–59.

Ritmeyer, L., and Ritmeyer, K.

1998 *Secrets of Jerusalem's Temple Mount*. Washington, DC: Biblical Archaeology Society.

Rosen-Ayalon, M.

1989 *The Early Islamic Monuments of al-Haram al-Sharif*. Jerusalem: Institute of Archaeology, Hebrew University of Jerusalem.

Rudolph, W.

1949 *Esra und Nehemia samt 3. Esra*. Tübingen: Mohr.

Schult, H.

1964 Der Debir im Salomonischen Tempel. *Zeitschrift des Deutschen Palästina-Vereins* 80: 46–54.

Vogt, E.

1974 Vom Tempel zum Felsendom. *Biblica* 55: 23–64.

Zwickel, W.

1999 *Der salomonische Tempel*. Mainz: Zabern.

Chapter 15

"When I Went to Rome… There I Saw the Menorah…" The Jerusalem Temple Implements During the Second Century C.E.

by Steven Fine

The interests of Eric M. Meyers stretch from the Bronze Age through the early Islamic period, from ancient Israel to the diaspora communities of late antique Italy, from literary to archaeological sources to the State of Israel and contemporary Jewish life in America. In celebration of Eric Meyers' interests and contributions, I offer this study of the menorah—which spans all of these sources, periods and locales.

From the earliest literary depictions of the Tabernacle and its implements in the Pentateuch to most recent times, concern for the Temple implements has held a central place in Jewish thought.[1] This is true of the implements described in Exodus 25 and 37, and, to a lesser extent, of the implements of the Second Temple. A poignantly contemporary example of this concern was reported on page one of the *Jerusalem Post* on January 18, 1996. The newspaper reports a personal meeting between then Israel Minister of Religious Affairs Shimon Shetreet and Pope John Paul II. After the meeting, Shetreet reported that

> …he had asked for Vatican cooperation in locating the 60-kg gold menorah from the Second Temple that was brought to Rome by Titus 70 C.E. Shetreet claimed that recent research at the University of Florence indicated the menorah might be among the hidden treasures in the Vatican's catacombs.[2] "I don't say it's there for sure," he said, "but I asked the Pope to help in the search as a goodwill gesture in recognition of the improved relations between Catholics and Jews (Palmieri-Billig 1996: 1).

The Israeli newspaper *Haaretz* discussed the responses to the incident in an article in May 1996. Witnesses to this conversation, reports *Haaretz*, "tell that a tense silence hovered over the room after Shetreet's request was heard" (Bergman 1996:

18–20, 22). Shetreet's request, and others that have followed,[3] are a fascinating extension of the Zionist hope that the Menorah taken by Titus be returned "home" by the Zionist movement (Mishory 2000: 165–99). This is expressed in literary and visual sources, most officially in the Israel Independence Day 1955 commemorative postage stamp showing the Arch of Titus menorah ablaze within the seal of the State of Israel (Mishory 2000; see Litzman 1978: 76).

The legends of the menorah at the Vatican have considerable currency among American Jews. I have heard it from Jews who are members of all synagogue movements, clergy and laity, many of whom take it to be a historical fact. I have heard three versions, though many others surely exist. According to the first, a certain American Orthodox rabbi entered the Vatican and saw the menorah.[4] According to a second, told to me by an Israeli Moroccan rabbi resident in the United States, it was a Moroccan rabbi known as "Rabbi Pinto." An American resident in Jerusalem recently told me a version that bears a distinctly Anglo-Israeli loading. This story recently embellishes the famous rescue mission of former chief Rabbi of Israel, Isaac Herzog, to rescue Jewish children in Europe, during which he visited with the Pope at the Vatican.[5] According to this embellishment, the Pope showed Rabbi Herzog the menorah and refused to return it! Father Leonard Boyle, former director of the Vatican Libraries, tells of Orthodox Jewish tourists from the United States entering the library during their visits to the Vatican and with all naiveté telling Father Boyle that their rabbi teachers had instructed them to go find the menorah during their visits (Bergman 1996). In this way, the most holy pilgrimage complex in Western Christendom is turned into a Jewish pilgrimage site (or at least a religiously amenable option for Jews uncomfortable with visiting Christian sites)! The folklore of the Vatican menorah is well deserving of a broader treatment.

Folklorist Dov Noy tells me that the myth of the menorah at the Vatican is not a part of traditional Jewish folklore, and was not recorded by the researchers of the Israel Folklore Archive. I would not be surprised if this is a distinctly American-Jewish urban myth, blending American anti-Papism with traditional Jewish fear and distrust of Christians (particularly Catholics). I mention elements that I have encountered casually over the last few years only to illustrate the contemporary interest and passion that the Temple menorah, plundered and taken to Rome by Titus, continues to engender.

Rabbinic literature is, of course, vitally interested in the Tabernacle/Temple vessels. Among the most fascinating evidence for this Rabbinic concern is a group of sources that suggest that the Sages actually visited Rome and there "saw" the menorah and other vessels of the Temple. The earliest appears in Tannaitic sources and the latest in Byzantine-period *midrashim* (Strack and Stemberger 1992: 119–244, 254–393). My purpose in this context is to assess the historicity of these sources against the background of Rabbinic literature and what we know about the whereabouts of the these vessels, especially the menorah, during the latter first and second century C.E. Parallel sources for this inquiry—from Josephus and the archaeology of Rome and Palestine—allow for the contextualization of these traditions: something rare for Rabbinic evidentuary traditions. The sources under discussion are as follows:

1. *Tosefta Kippurim* 2:16[6]
 —The Temple Veil (*parokhet)*

> He took the blood from the one who was stirring it.
> He entered the place into which he had entered [earlier] and stood in the place where he had stood, and sprinkled some of it on the Mercy Seat (*kapporet*)[7] toward the two cloths of the ark,
> One [sprinkle] upwards and seven downwards. But he did not intentionally sprinkle upwards or downwards. But he did it like one who swings a whip.
> And thus did he count: "One, one and one, one and two, one and three, one and four, one and five, one and six, one and seven."
> Rabbi Judah said in the name of Rabbi Lazer: "Thus did he count: 'One and one and one, two and one, three and one, four and one, five and one, six and one, seven and one.'"

He went to his left, along the veil (*parokhet*).
And he did not touch the veil.
But if he touched it, he touched it.
Said Rabbi Lazer son of Rabbi Jose, "I saw it in Rome and there were drops of blood on it. And they told me:[8] *'These are from the drops of blood of the Day of Atonement.'"*

2. *Sifre Zutta, Baalotekha* to Numbers 8:2[9]
— The Menorah

…And whence do I know that each lamp was pointed toward the middle lamp? Scripture says: "toward the lampstand (*menorah*)" (Num 8:2).
And thus it says: "and he dwells turned toward me" (*memuli;* Num 22:5).
Said Rabbi Simeon: When I went to Rome there I saw the menorah. All of the lamps were pointed toward the middle lamp.

3. *Jerusalem Talmud, Yoma* 4:1, 41c[10]
— The Priestly Frontispiece (*tsits*)

The priestly frontispiece, on it was written: "Holy to the Lord."
"Holy" was written below, and "to the Lord" was written above.
This is like a king who sits on his throne.
And similarly [for lots for the scapegoat].
Said Rabbi Eleazar son of Rabbi Jose: I saw it in Rome, and the name was written on it in a single line, "Holy to the Lord."

4. *Genesis Rabba* 10, 7 (Venice, 1545)[11]
— The Mosquito that Ate Titus' Brain

The wicked Titus entered the Holy of Holies, his sword drawn in his hand, slashed the two veils. He brought two harlots and performed sex on them on the altar, and his sword came out full of blood.
There are those who say that it was from the blood of the sacrifices, and there are others who say that it was from the blood of the he-goat of Yom Kippur.
He cursed and blasphemed and took all the Temple vessels and made them like a single net and began to curse and blaspheme Heaven, saying: "One who makes war with a king in the desert and vanquishes him cannot be compared with one who makes war against a king in his own palace and vanquishes him."
He then embarked on a ship. As soon as he had embarked a storm smote the sea.
Said he: "It appears that the power of the God of this nation is only on the sea. He punished the Generation of Enosh by water. He only exacted retribution from the generation of Enosh through water. He only exacted retribution from the generation of the Flood through water. He exacted retribution from Pharoah and his army through water. When I was in His house and His own domain He could not stand against me, but now I am beginning to think that he will kill me with water."
The Holy One, blessed be He said to him: "Villain! By your life, I will inflict punishment upon this villain using the most insignificant creature that I created during the six days of creation."
Immediately the Holy One, blessed be He, beckoned to his guardian angel of the sea and he ceased from his fury.
When he reached Rome all the dignitaries of Rome came out and lauded him.
When he arrived in Rome he entered to the bath house, and when he left they brought him a vial of spiced wine to drink.
A mosquito entered his nose and gnawed his brain until it became as big as a two pound dove. He screamed, saying: "Let them (the doctors) split open the brain of that man (that is, his own brain)."
Immediately the doctors were called.
They split his brain and removed it, being the size of a two pound dove.
Rabbi Eleazar son of Rabbi Jose said: I saw it in Rome (ברומי אנא חמיתיה). *There were two pounds on one side [of the scale] and the dove on the other, and the one weighed exactly the same as the other.*

> They took it [the pigeon] and placed it in one bowl. As the bird changed so did he [Titus] change, and when the mosquito fled, the soul of the wicked Titus fled.

5. *Esther Rabba* 1, 12[12] — The Throne of Solomon

> …It has been taught: Asa and all the kings of Judah sat upon it, and when Nebuchadnezzar came up and sacked Jerusalem he carried it off to Babylon.
> From Babylon it was taken to Media and from Media to Greece and from Greece to Edom. *Rabbi Eleazar son of Rabbi Jose said: I saw its fragments in Rome.*

Our sources in *Tosefta Sukkah, Sifre Zutta* and *Yerushalmi Yoma* have a reasonable chance at historicity, while the *Genesis Rabba* and *Esther Rabba* sources are wholly literary. In *Genesis Rabba* this literary convention is used to add veracity to the physical evidence of Titus' punishment. *Esther Rabba* reworks the "I saw" type in response to the travels of Solomon's throne. After passing through Babylonia, Media, and Greece, the throne arrives in Rome by force of Daniel's vision of the four kingdoms. Another Byzantine-period collection, *Avot de-Rabbi Nathan,* is aware of both Tabernacle artifacts that were "hidden away" and Second Temple artifacts taken to Rome. The objects taken to Rome include "the mortar of the house of Avtimas, the table, the menorah, the veil of the ark and the vestments of the anointed priest." This tradition assembles the artifacts that sources suggest Sages "saw" in Rome, adding to these "the mortar of the house of Avtimas."[13]

The traditions preserved in *Tosefta Yoma, Sifre Zutta* and *Yerushalmi Yoma* are, however, of another order. Each of the items described in these traditions, the *parokhet,* the menorah, and perhaps the priestly frontispiece, could well have been viewed in Rome by the second-century rabbis mentioned: Rabbi Simeon, son of Yohai, and the son of his Ushan compatriot Rabbi Eleazar, son of Rabbi Jose.[14] This evidence parallels the first-person Rabbinic verifications of the Temple service and structure that appear throughout Tannaitic literature. To cite just one example: In *Mishnah Middot* 1:2 we find the wonderfully piquant comment "Rabbi Eleazar son of Jacob says: Once they found the brother of my mother sleeping, and they burned his robe!" The Rome comments are the continuation of this sort of personal verification. In the sources under discussion, direct evidence of having "seen" these Temple vessels and other "historical" artifacts is taken at face value. It is privileged testimony that serves to conclude theoretical discussions of the vessels within the various pericopae.

Our evidence for the disposition of the Temple vessels after the destruction of the Temple comes from two complementary sources: Josephus' *Jewish War* (completed ca. 75 C.E.) and the Arch of Titus in the Roman Forum, completed ca. 90 C.E. Josephus Flavius reports that the table for showbread, the menorah, the Temple veil, and a Torah scroll from the Jerusalem Temple were among the booty brought to Rome in triumph by Titus and paraded through the streets of Rome (*War* 7:5, 132–61). This event was immortalized approximately a decade later in relief panels within in the Arch of Titus.[15]

Josephus describes in detail the manner in which many of the Temple vessels were turned over to the Romans. In *War* 6, 387–91 Josephus describes how a certain priest handed over to them "some of the sacred treasures," including

> two lamp stands similar to those deposited in the sanctuary, along with tables, bowls, and platters, all of solid gold and very massive; he further delivered up veils, the high-priests' vestments, including the precious stones, and many other articles for public worship. Furthermore, the treasurer of the temple, by the name of Phineas, being taken prisoner, disclosed the tunics and girdles worn by the priests, an abundance of purple and scarlet kept for necessary repairs to the veil of the temple, along with a mass of cinnamon and cassia and a multitude of other spices, which they mixed and burned daily as incense to God. Many other treasures also were delivered up by him, with numerous sacred ornaments; those services procuring for him, although a prisoner of war, the pardon accorded to the refugees.[16]

In Chapter 7, lines 148–52 of *The Jewish War,* Josephus Flavius describes Titus' triumphal return to Rome from his successful campaign in Judaea in great detail. His descriptions of the Temple vessels are relevant to our discussion:

> The spoils in general were borne in promiscuous heaps; but conspicuous above all stood those captured in the temple at Jerusalem. These consisted of a golden table, many talents in weight, and a lamp stand, likewise made of gold, but constructed on a different pattern than those which we use in ordinary life. Affixed to a pedestal was a central shaft, from which there extended slender branches, arranged trident-fashion, a wrought lamp being attached to the extremity of each branch, of these there were seven, indicating the honor paid to that number among the Jews. After these, and last of all the spoils, was carried a copy of the Jewish Law. They followed a large party carrying images of victory, all made of ivory and gold. Behind them drove Vespasian, followed by Titus; while Domitian rode beside them, in magnificent apparel and mounted on a steed that was in itself a sight.

Josephus continues in lines 158–62:

> The triumphal ceremonies being concluded and the empire of the Romans established on the firmest foundation, Vespasian decided to erect a Temple of Peace. This was very speedily completed and in a style surpassing all human conception. For, besides having prodigious resources of wealth on which to draw he also embellished it with ancient masterpieces of painting and sculpture; indeed, into that shrine were accumulated and stored all objects for the sight of which men had once wandered over the whole world, eager to see them severally while they lay in various countries. Here, too, he laid up the vessels of gold from the temple of the Jews, on which he prided himself; but their Law and the purple hangings of the sanctuary he ordered to be deposited and kept in the palace.

The descriptions of vessels taken to Rome fits well with the "inventory" provided by our Rabbinic traditions. The description of the golden table of the showbread and of the menorah parallels the prominent place afforded these objects on the Arch of Titus. This pairing of the menorah and the showbread table is based not just upon their proximity in the Temple, but also upon both their physical impressiveness and the large quantities of gold of which each was manufactured. The fact that Josephus felt obliged to describe the menorah as being "arranged trident-fashion" is indicative of the uniqueness of this object, which adds to its visual effectiveness. The artist of the Arch of Titus panel realized this, thus emphasizing the menorah in his bas-relief. The menorah and table were paired earlier on a *lepton* of Mattathias Antigonos, minted in 39 B.C.E. as an apparent propaganda tool to ward off the Roman-backed usurper Herod (Meshorer 1982: 94). The issue of proximity, which one would imagine would not have impressed the Roman artists, accounts for the apparent juxtaposition of the table and the menorah on a plaster fragment discovered in the Jewish Quarter excavations in Jerusalem (Avigad 1975: 47–49).

Many of the Temple vessels were eventually deposited, according to Josephus, in Vespasian's Temple of Peace. This temple was built to commemorate the Flavian defeat of Judaea. The Templum Pacis was begun in 71, completed in 75 C.E., and later rebuilt by Domitian. It was constructed on the southern side of the Argiletum, a road that connected the Subura to the Forum (Anderson 1982; Richardson 1992: 286–87; Ward-Perkins 1954; see now Millar 2005). Pliny the Elder includes the Temple of Peace among Rome's "noble buildings," listing it among "the most beautiful [buildings] the world has ever seen."[17] The square was surrounded by porticoes, which enclosed a pleasure garden. It also contained a library. The temple was integrated into the east portico. As described by Josephus (*War* 7, 158; quoted above), the Temple of Peace contained quite a collection of artifacts from throughout the Empire.

As Paul Zanker aptly suggests, "the opulence and variety of the furnishings stood as a symbol for Rome as the center of the world" (Zanker 1997: 187).

The Rabbinic viewing of the menorah and the veil would have taken place in this temple. One might suspect that many Jews, both natives of Rome and visitors, might have come to the Temple of Peace to view the Temple items—as Jews to this day still flock to the Arch of Titus.

Josephus has it that the Temple veil and the scroll of the Torah were placed in Vespasian's palace. The imperial palace was a partially public space, as the White House is in the modern United States. As Vitruvius suggests, in homes of the powerful "the common rooms are those into which, though, uninvited, persons of the people can come by right, such as vestibules, courtyards, peristyles and other apartments of similar uses."[18] Referring to the Palatine, Pliny notes that "Imperial mansions were often filled with excellent statues" (*NH* 39.4.38). Little is known of the Domus Vespasianus, where the Temple vessels were apparently displayed. It was probably the same building as the Domus Titus Flavius Vespasianus, later rebuilt by Domitian as the Templum Gentis Flaviae (Richardson 1992: 137–38, 140). Important artifacts were displayed in the Domus Titus. Pliny suggests the Laocoon was exhibited there, as well as Polykleitos of Sikyon's "...Two Boys Playing Dice, likewise in the nude, known by the Greek name of *Astragalizontes* and now standing in the atrium of the Emperor Titus (*Titi imperatorius atrio*)." Pliny adds that "this is considered the most perfect work of art in existence" (*NH* 34.19.55). Of the Laocoon Pliny writes: "...the Laocoon, [is] in the palace of General Titus, a work superior to any painting and any bronze. Laocoon, his children and the wonderful clasping coils of the snakes were carved of a single block" (*NH* 39.4.37). It is not inconceivable (though certainly beyond proof, owing to the sparseness of the evidence) that the Temple veil and the Torah scroll were part of the same public/private collection, displayed in the same palace. The Laocoon was discovered on that site January 14, 1506, and significantly impacted Renaissance and later art (Richardson 1992: 137–38; Bieber 1942: 1). The Temple vessels, of course, are lost.

Babylonian Talmud, Meilah 17b, places the *parokhet* in the personal and very private "treasury of the Emperor," though this text says more about late Babylonian Rabbinic storytelling than about the historical *parokhet*. The enigmatic statement in *Tosefta Yoma* that someone told Rabbi Eleazar, son of Rabbi Jose, that "these are from the blood of the Day of Atonement," suggests that many had seen the veil and that there was some sort of local tradition that existed before Rabbi Eleazar raised his question. One can almost imagine Rabbi Eleazar going to see the *parokhet*, perhaps in the Templum Gentis Flaviae, and discussing the spots with local Jews.[19] Whatever the context, what is certain from Josephus is that the sacred vessels were deposited and on view within Vespasian's palace during the later first century.

The Torah scroll that Josephus describes as having been deposited in Vespasian's palace finds an intriguing parallel in a tradition preserved in an 11th-century collection, *Bereshit Rabbati*.[20] According to this tradition, a scroll from the Temple was brought from Jerusalem and eventually deposited in a Rome synagogue:

> This is one of the words which were written in the scroll that was captured in Jerusalem and was brought to Rome and was stored in the synagogue of Severos.

The description of this scroll as using what later came to be called the medial *mem* and the final *mem* indiscriminately fits well with first-century Jerusalemite orthographic practice, as scholars have long noted (Lieberman 1940: 23–24). The disposition of Temple booty within a local synagogue is know from Seleucid times, when vessels of the Jerusalem Temple were placed in an Antioch synagogue by Antiochus IV. Such a dispersal of Jewish sacred artifacts is, thus, not beyond the imaginations of Roman Jews. In *War* 7, 44–45. Josephus writes that

> For, although Antiochus surnamed Epiphanes sacked Jerusalem and plundered the Temple, his successors on the throne restored to the Jews of Antioch all such votive offerings that were made of brass (*chalka*), to be laid up in the synagogue (*tan sunagogan*) and, moreover, granted them citizenship rights on equality with the Greeks. Continuing to receive similar

> treatment from later monarchs, the Jewish colony grew in numbers, and their richly designed and costly offerings formed a costly ornament to the temple (*to hieron;* Zeitlin 1964: 236; cf. McKay 1994: 81–82).

What is significant is that a Jewish community in Rome perceived itself as possessing such a relic of the Temple, transferred apparently by the Romans themselves to the Jewish community. Some scholars have associated the Synagogue of Severos with the second-century emperor Alexander Severus (Momigliano 1934; Leon 1960: 162–65). The Severan dynasty is presented in Rabbinic thought as having been particularly friendly toward the Jews, and a temple was even dedicated "to fulfill a vow of the Jews" to Marcus Aurelius at Qasion on the border of the Upper Galilee and Phoenicia.[21] If there is, indeed, an association between the synagogue of Severos and Alexander Severus, the transfer of a Torah scroll taken from Jerusalem for storage there would be all the more significant.

Let us return for a moment to *Sifre Zutta's* description of the Temple menorah. There we read that "all of the lamps were inclined toward the central lamp." This purportedly eyewitness evidence concludes an anonymous academic discussion of the Temple menorah's lamp arrangement and is the ultimate support for accepting the position that "all of the lamps were inclined toward the central flame...," interpreting Numbers 8:2–3:

> Speak to Aaron and say to him: When you raise up the lamps, opposite the face of the menorah (אל-מול פני המנורה) shall the seven lamps shine. And Aaron did thus opposite the face of the menorah he raised up its lamps just as Moses had commanded.

The attempt to focus all of the lamps toward the central one, as my somewhat stilted translation of אל-מול פני המנורה suggests, is well-known also outside the Rabbinic corpus, perhaps as early as the Jerusalem graffito from before 70 and certainly from late antique archaeological contexts. We see this, for example, in the Hammath Tiberias B synagogue mosaic (Dothan 1983: 37–38) and the Beth Shean small "synagogue" (more likely a study house) mosaic (Bahat 1981; Fine 1987: 100–101). At some level, it is a natural way to arrange the lamps such that the menorah (or images of the menorah) would be a self-contained and self-referential image. If this text merely reflects the Palestinian context, it supplies the "missing link" between these two pieces of visual evidence.

What, though, if Rabbi Simeon (or some other Sage) really did see the menorah, and its lamps were, in fact, directed toward the central lamp? In that case, then the visual *midrash* at Hammath Tiberias may reflect actual knowledge of the Temple menorah that goes beyond Rabbinic speculation. Significantly, images of the menorah from the Roman catacombs, which date to the fourth century, often depict the lamps atop the menorah's branches inclined toward the central stalk. We see this, for example, in wall paintings from the Villa Torlonia catacomb.[22] Is this based upon a Palestinian or even local interpretation of Num 8:2, or is this imagery drawn from actual observation of the Temple menorah? In addition, the shape of most menorah depictions from Rome is different from both the graffito and most later Palestinian depictions. In these depictions, the ratio of the height of the branches to the width of the branches approximates the depiction on the Arch of Titus. The inspiration for these branches could well be the arch, if not the menorah itself. Significantly, the base of the Arch of Titus menorah is nowhere to be found on later depictions. It is depicted as a tripod (as in Palestinian synagogue images). Our *Sifre Zutta* passage raises serious questions regarding the presence of the menorah in Rome, what was actually seen there, and Palestinian relations with the Jews of Rome. No conclusive answers are possible, of course, but the issues are too important to leave unexplored.

What, then, may we say about the Temple vessels in Rome after 70? Josephus' descriptions of the presence of the menorah and the showbread table are verified by the Arch of Titus reliefs. The presence of the menorah, the veil and a Temple Torah scroll is expressed in Rabbinic sources as well. Rabbinic sources describe Sages viewing these vessels, as well as the head plate of the high priest. This piece is not mentioned by Josephus, and thus its presence in Rome is not confirmed beyond the

Rabbinic corpus. While it would be easy to dismiss these Rabbinic sources as mere literary devices or as folklore, the external evidence, from Josephus, from the Arch of Titus, from the Jewish catacombs of Rome, and from Palestinian archaeology, do not facilitate a quick dismissal. The Sages clearly knew that the menorah and other vessels continued to exist in Rome long after the destruction of the Temple, and were on public view. For just this evidence regarding the century after Josephus, we should be grateful.

I should note that I am far from the first to ask how it is that the Sages could actually see the vessels. The Sages of the Babylonian Talmud, who were distant from the world of Roman palaces, pleasure gardens, and fora, were also bothered by this question. Their solution assumes a less public and considerably more nefarious deposition of the *parokhet*. A tale told in Meilah 17a–b focuses upon the Jewish presence in Rome and quickly turns to allege a Roman decree that forbade the Jews from keeping the Sabbath, from circumcising their sons, and required them to have sexual intercourse with menstruant women. The remainder of the pericope deals with ways that the Jews worked to reverse the decree. A sub-text to our narrative grafts Rabbi Eleazar, son of Rabbi Jose, and his comments on seeing the *parokhet* pertain to the present context. Simeon, son of Yohai, our text tells us, was sent as the emissary to the Emperor's house. In route he met a demon named Ben Temalion. Intending to help Rabbi Simeon, and with his assent, Ben Temalion "advanced and entered into the Emperor's daughter." When Rabbi Simeon arrived there, he demonstrably carried out an exorcism, calling out:

> "Ben Temalion leave her, Ben Temalion leave her!"
> and as he said this, he left her.
> He [the Emperor] said to them [to Rabbi Simeon and to Rabbi Eleazar son of Rabbi Jose]:
> Request whatever you desire.
> They were led into the treasure house (לגניזה) to take whatever they chose.
> They found the decree (איגרא), took it and tore it up.
> It was in reference to this that Rabbi Eleazar son of Rabbi Jose said:
> "I saw it in the city of Rome and there were on it several drops of blood"
> (Bacher 1897: 285–87; Bar-Ilan 1995: 17–31).

Benjamin of Tudela (second half of 12th century) describes the holy vessels of the Temple in Rome, using some similar terminology in his 12th-century travelogue. Benjamin suggests that medieval Romans had a tradition that the Temple vessels were in Christian hands:

> In the church of St. John in the Lateran there are two copper columns that were in the Temple, the handiwork of King Solomon, peace be upon him. Upon each column is inscribed "Solomon son of David." The Jews of Rome said that each year on the Ninth of Av they found moisture running down them like water. There also is the cave where Titus the son of Vespasian hid away (שגנז) the Temple vessels which he brought from Jerusalem (Adler 1967: 7).

While the supposed columns of "Solomon son of David" were in full sight, the vessels of the Second Temple, brought by Titus to Rome, were thought to be hidden away. Benjamin uses the verb *ganaz*, to hide, to describe the dispersal of the vessels by Titus. This parallels our Meliah passage, where the *parokhet* was hidden away with the decree against the Jews in the king's treasure house, his *genizah*. One wonders, therefore, whether Benjamin's account draws upon our tradition, or whether the linguistic parallel is accidental. In any event, Benjamin of Tudela provides important evidence that medieval Roman Jews did indeed believe that vessels of the Second Temple were in Rome, under Christian auspices. By the 13th century, Christians agreed. An apse mosaic laid in Saint John in the Lateran in 1291 proclaims the presence of not only the Ark of the Covenant but the menorah and columns: "…Titus and Vespasian had this ark and the candelabrum and…the four columns here present taken from the Jews in Jerusalem and brought to Rome." By the end of the 13th century, then, the Lateran was claiming to have the Temple booty of the Solomonic Temple, taken, anachronistically by "Titus and Vespasian," on display (or in a reliquary).[23] This is the same church where in modern times relics from the Jewish catacombs of Rome, especially inscriptions and images of menorahs, were displayed. According to other Christian sources—which do not appear to be any more reliable—the menorah was taken away to North Africa by the Visigoths, who sacked Rome in the 5th century, and from there to Constantinople, and perhaps back to Jerusalem after that.[24]

Benjamin of Tudela "knew" that the Temple vessels had been brought to Rome. He also knew that he could not see them, for they had been "hidden"—just as tractate Meliah said they had. The holy objects were present and non-present. They were visible in the Arch of Titus, yet invisible in a cave where Vespasian himself had placed them—under a church, no less. When contemporary Jews go to Rome, the menorah is no less present, yet non-present. They know that their holy vessels were brought to Rome, as commemorated in that open sore known as the Arch of Titus. They can also see the menorah in the remains of the Jewish catacombs of Rome, most of which are safely stored and displayed in the Vatican, and that until relatively recent times the Church had actively acquired Jewish books and artifacts—often in improper ways. As long as they can believe that the menorah is in Rome, awaiting return to Jerusalem, the hope of restoration is not yet lost—whether in a religious sense or in its secularized Zionist form. The modern rabbis whom I have mentioned—the American Orthodox rabbi, "Rabbi Pinto," and even Rabbi Herzog, whom some contemporary Jews earnestly believe entered the Vatican in search of the menorah—give life to this myth, to Jewish longing for the return of the Temple vessels, to lingering Jewish distrust of Christians, and, finally, to American anti-Papacism (as evidenced most vividly in the blockbuster popularity of Dan Brown's best-seller, *The Da Vinci Code*; Brown 2003). Contemporary Jews, particularly Orthodox Jews, have been known to reenact this myth on their own searches of the Vatican for the menorah—providing a Jewish overlay for their own touristic (and often emotionally conflicted) forays into the holiest site of Roman Christendom.[25] As we have seen, even the Israeli Minister of Religious Affairs participated in this myth, merging it with traditional Zionist imagery of returning the menorah home through the Zionist enterprise. With Rabbi Simeon, all of these contemporary searchers (and to be candid, not a few academic scholars) would like nothing more than to be able to say "When I was in Rome...there I saw the menorah."

NOTES

1 Meyers 1976, and the short essays collected by Y. Israeli 2000.

2 No one at the University of Florence whom I have contacted has knowledge of this research.

3 For more recent contacts between Israeli officials and the Vatican, see Kingsley 2006: 37–39. Parfitt (2006) responsibly reviews and contextualizes Kingsley's thesis.

4 Many thanks to Lawrence Schiffman for this information.

5 "Herzog, Isaac," *Encyclopedia Judaica* (Jerusalem: Keter, 1971), 422–25.

6 *The Tosefta,* ed. S. Lieberman, 2nd ed. (New York: Jewish Theological Seminary, 1992); *Tosefta Kifshutah,* ed. S. Lieberman (New York: Jewish Theological Seminary, 1955–1988), *ad. loc.*, for parallels.

7 See Lieberman's comment, *ibid.*

8 See *Midrash Tanhuma*, ed. S. Buber (Vilna: Romm, 1913), *Va-yakel* 10; Lieberman, *Tosefta Kifshutah.* Compare Jacob Neusner's translation, *The Tosefta* (New York: Ktav, 1981) 199.

9 *Sifre Zutta, Be-ha'alotkha* to Numbers 8:2, *Sifre D'Be Rab and Sifre Zutta on Numbers,* ed. H. S. Horowitz (Jerusalem: Wahrmann, 1966) = *Midrash ha-Gadol,* ed. Z. M. Rabinowitz (Jerusalem: Rav Kook Institute, 1967), *ad. loc.*

10 *Talmud Yerushalmi According to Ms. Or. 4720 (Scaql. 3) of the Leiden University Library with Restorations and Corrections* (Jerusalem: Academy of the Hebrew Language, 2001). See Sukkah 5a = B. Yoma 63b.

11 See the manuscript traditions and parallels cited in

Midrash Bereshit Rabba, eds. J. Theodor and C. Albeck (Jerusalem: Wahrmann, 1965), 1:84–85 and *Midrash Wayyikra Rabbah,* ed. M. Margulies (New York: Jewish Theological Seminary, 1993) 23:3.499–502.

12 Vilna edition.

13 Ed. S. Schechter (New York: Feldheim, 1967), version A, ch. 41, p. 67.

14 Strack and Stemberger 1992: 84–85. Attributions in Rabbinic literature are always difficult. See Strack and Stemberger 1992: 62–68; Green 1978; Kalmin 1992: 165–97, esp. 168–69.

15 On the Arch of Titus, in general, see Yarden 1991 and the bibliography cited there.

16 Translations of Josephus follow *Josephus Flavius, The Complete Works*, trans. H. St. J. Thackery, R. Marcus, A. Wikgren and L. Feldman (Cambridge, MA: Harvard University, 1961–1965).

17 Pliny, *NH* 36, 102, trans. D. E. Eichholz, *Loeb Classical Library* (Cambridge, MA: Harvard University, 1962).

18 Vitruvius, *On Architecture* 6.5.1, trans. F. Granger, *Loeb Classical Library* (Cambridge, MA: Harvard University, 1934).

19 The evidence is surveyed by Leon (1960: 46–74, 195–228, 263–346); Kraabel (1979: 497–500); Noy (1995); Rutgers (1995).

20 *Midrash Bereshith Rabbathi,* ed. C. Albeck (Jerusalem: Mekitse Nirdamim, 700, 1940). *Va-Yigash* 45:8, and Albeck's notes, pp. 210–11.

21 Roth-Gerson 1987: 125–29 and the bibliography cited there; Chiat 1982: 62–63; Ilan 1991: 57–59; Fine 1999: 226–30.

22 The illustrations are most conveniently arranged by Goodenough 1953: 3, nos. 769, 808, 810, 817, 973.

23 Many thanks to Prof. Dale Kinney, who brought this mosaic to my attention; Kinney 2005.

24 See Levy 1969: 255–58. Levy discusses Patristic sources for the disposition of the menorah through the eleventh century. See also Strauss 1960; Sperber 1965: 154–55; Harrison 1994.

25 A typical example of Jewish renarrativizing of Christian pilgrimage occurred on an eleven-day kosher tour of Italy that I co-led in 2001. Members of the group avidly discussed the permissibility and their personal comfort level in entering the Vatican and other Christian sites. A minority chose not to enter, while most did (including the wife of a deceased American ultra-orthodox rabbi). The Israeli guide and I narrated the visits to Christian sites in such a way as to highlight Jewish points of contact, providing a Jewish script for a distinctly Christian pilgrimage experience. At the Arch of Titus, this guide orchestrated a distinctly Jewish ritual event, singing with the group Psalm 126 to the tune of *Hatikvah,* the Israeli anthem. (Note that this psalm is recited before festive meals on Sabbaths and festivals. The tune of *Hatikvah* is used with Psalm 126 in nationalistic Jewish religious contexts in Israel and abroad, particularly on Israel Independence Day).

REFERENCES

Adler, M. N.

1967 *The Itinerary of Benjamin of Tudela: Critical Text, Translation and Commentary.* New York, NY: Feldheim.

Albeck, C. (ed.)

1940 *Midrash Bereshith Rabbathi.* Jerusalem: Mekitse Nirdamim.

Anderson, J. A.

1982 Domitian, the Argiletum and the Temple of Peace. *American Journal of Archaeology* 86: 101–10.

Avigad, N.

1975 Excavations in the Jewish Quarter of the Old City, 1969–1971. Pp. 47–49 in *Jerusalem Revealed: Archaeology in the Holy City, 1968–1974*, ed. Y. Yadin. Jerusalem: Israel Exploration Society.

Avot de-Rabbi Nathan

1967 Ed. S. Schechter. New York, NY: Feldheim.

Bacher, W.

1897 La Legende de l'Exorcisme d'un Démon par Simon B. Yohai. *Revue des Etudes Juives* 35: 285–87.

Bahat, D.

1981 A Synagogue at Beth-Shean. Pp. 82–85 in *Ancient Synagogues Revealed*, ed. L. I. Levine. Jerusalem: Israel Exploration Society.

Bar-Ilan, M.

1995 Exorcism by Rabbis: Talmudic Sages and Magic. *Da'at* 34: 17–31.

Bergman, R.

1996 Ha-Otzrot Ha-Yehudi'im Shel Ha-Apifior. *Mussaf Haaretz*, 15 May, 18–20, 22.

Bieber, M.
1942 *Laocoon: The Influence of the Group Since Its Rediscovery*. New York, NY: Columbia University.

Brown, D.
2003 *The Da Vinci Code: A Novel*. New York, NY: Doubleday.

Chiat, M. J.
1982 *A Handbook of Synagogue Architecture*. Chino, CA: Scholars.

Dothan, M.
1983 *Hammath Tiberias: Early Synagogues*. Jerusalem: Israel Exploration Society.

Fine, S.
1987 *This Holy Place: On the Sanctity of the Synagogue During the Greco-Roman Period*. Notre Dame, IN: University of Notre Dame.
1999 Non-Jews in the Synagogues of Palestine: Rabbinic and Archaeological Perspectives. Pp. 226–30 in *Jews, Christians and Polytheists in the Ancient Synagogue: Cultural Interaction During the Greco-Roman Period*, ed. S. Fine. London: Routledge.

Goodenough, E. R.
1953 *Jewish Symbols During the Greco-Roman Period*, ed. J. Neusner. Bollingen Series. Princeton, NJ: Princeton University.

Green, W.
1978 What's in a Name? The Problematic of Rabbinic Biography. Pp. 77–96 in *Approaches to Ancient Judaism: Theory and Practice*, ed. W. S. Green. Brown Judaic Studies 1. Missoula, MT: Scholars.

Harrison, M.
1994 From Jerusalem and Back Again: The Fate of the Treasures of Solomon. Pp. 239–48 in *Churches Built In Ancient Times: Recent Studies In Early Christian Archaeology*, ed. K. Painter. London: University of London.

Ilan, Z.
1991 *Ancient Synagogues in Israel*. Israel: Ministry of Defense.

Israeli, Y. (ed.)
2000 *By the Light of the Menorah*. Philadephia, PA: Jewish Publication Society of America.

Josephus
1965–1969 *Josephus Flavius, The Complete Works*, trans. H. S. J. Thackeray, R. Marcus, A. P. Wikgren and L. H. Feldman. London: Heinemann.

Kalmin, R.
1992 Talmudic Portrayals of Relationships Between Rabbis: Amoraic or Pseudepigraphic? *Annual of Jewish Studies Review* 17, no. 2: 165–97.

Kingsley, S.
2006 *God's Gold: The Quest for the Lost Temple Treasure of Jerusalem*. London: John Murray.

Kinney, D.
2005 Spolia. Pp. 16–47 in *St. Peter's in the Vatican*, ed. W. Tronzo. Cambridge, MA: Cambridge University.

Kraabel, A. T.
1979 The Diaspora Synagogue: Archaeological and Epigraphic Evidence. Pp. 477–510 in *Aufstieg und Niedergang der Römischen Welt*, vol. 19.1, eds. J. S. Ruebel and R. Scaife. Berlin: de Gruyter.

Leon, H. J.
1960 *The Jews in Ancient Rome*. Philadelphia, PA: Jewish Publication Society.

Levy, J. H.
1969 *Studies in Jewish Hellenism*. Jerusalem: Bialik Institute.

Lieberman, S.
1940 *Hellenism in Jewish Palestine: Studies in the Literary Transmission, Beliefs, and Manners of Palestine in the Century I* B.C.E.*–IV* C.E. New York, NY: Jewish Theological Seminary.

Litzman, G.
1978 *Gershon's 1978 Specialized Catalogue of Israel and the Holy Land*. New York, NY: Litzman.

McKay, H. A.
1994 *Sabbath and Synagogue: The Question of Sabbath Worship in Ancient Judaism*. Leiden: Brill.

Meshorer, Y.
1982 *Ancient Jewish Coins*. Dix Hills, NY: Amphora.

Meyers, C.
1976 *The Tabernacle Menorah: A Synthetic Study of a Symbol from the Biblical Cult*. Missoula, MT: Scholars.

Midrash Bereshit Rabba
1965 Ed. J. Theodor and C. Albeck. Jerusalem: Wahrmann.

Midrash Ha-Gadol
1967 Ed. Z. M. Rabinowitz. Jerusalem: Rav Kook Institute.

Midrash Tanhuma
1913 Ed. S. Buber. Vilna: Romm.

Midrash Wayyikra Rabbah
1993 Ed. M. Margulies. Jerusalem: Jewish Theological Seminary.

Millar, F.
2005 Last Year in Jerusalem: Monuments of the Jewish War in Rome. pp. 101–28 in *Flavius Josephus and Flavian Rome,* eds. J. Edmondson, S. Mason and J. Rives. Oxford: Oxford University.

Mishory, A.
2000 *Lo and Behold: Zionist Icons and Visual Symbols in Israeli Culture* (Hebrew). Tel Aviv: Am Oved.

Momigliano, A.
1934 Severo Alessandro Archisynagogus. *Athenaeum* 12: 151–53.

Noy, D.
1995 *Jewish Inscriptions of Western Europe, 2: The City of Rome*. Cambridge, MA: Cambridge University.

Palmieri-Billig, L.
1996 Shetreet: Pope Likely to Visit Next Year. *The Jerusalem Post*, 18 January, 1.

Parfitt, T.
2006 Where Is God's Gold? *World Jewish Digest* 12, mounted at http://worldjewishdigest.com, posted 1 December.

Pliny the Elder
1962 *Natural History*, trans. D. Eichholz. Loeb Classical Library 10. Cambridge, MA: Harvard University.

Richardson, L., Jr.
1992 *A New Topographical Dictionary of Ancient Rome.* Baltimore, MD: Johns Hopkins University.

Roth-Gerson, L.
1987 *Greek Inscriptions in the Synagogues in Eretz-Israel*. Jerusalem: Ben Zvi Institute.

Rutgers, L. V.
1995 *The Jews of Late Ancient Rome: An Archaeological and Historical Study on the Interaction of Jews and Non-Jews in the Roman-Diaspora*. Leiden: Brill.

Sifre D'Be Rab and Sifre Zutta on Numbers
1966 Ed. H. S. Horowitz. Jerusalem: Wahrmann.

Sperber, D.
1965 The History of the Menorah. *Journal of Jewish Studies* 16: 135–60.

Strack, H. L., and Stemberger, G.
1992 *Introduction to the Talmud and Midrash*, trans. M. Bockmuehl. Edinburgh: Clark.

Strauss, H.
1960 The Date and Form of the Menorah of the Maccabees. *Eretz Israel* 6: 122–29.

Talmud Yerushalmi According to Ms. Or. 4720 (Scaql. 3) of the Leiden University Library with Restorations and Corrections
2001 Jerusalem: Academy of the Hebrew Language.

The Tosefta
1981 Ed. J. Neusner. New York: Ktav.

The Tosefta
1992 Ed. S. Lieberman. New York: Jewish Theological Seminary.

Tosefta Kifshutah
1955–1988 Ed. S. Lieberman. New York: Jewish Theological Seminary.

Vitruvius Pollio
1934 *On Architecture*, trans. F. Granger. Loeb Classical Library 2. Cambridge, MA: Harvard University.

Ward-Perkins, J. B.
1954 Constantine and the Origins of the Christian Basilica. *Papers and Monographs of the British School at Rome* 22: 69–90.

Yarden, L.
1991 *The Spoils of Jerusalem on the Arch of Titus: A Re-Investigation*. Stockholm: Svenska Institutet i Rom.

Zanker, P.
1997 In Search of the Roman Viewer. Pp. 179–91 in *The Interpretation of Architectural Sculpture in Greece and Rome*, ed. D. Buitron-Oliver. Washington, DC: National Gallery of Art.

Zeitlin, S.
1964 Tefillah, the Shemoneh Esreh: An Historical Study of the Canonization of Hebrew Liturgy. *Jewish Quarterly Review* 54: 208–49.

Chapter 16

Miqwāʾôt and Second Temple Sectarianism

by Carol Selkin Wise

If there has been a *Leitmotiv* to the career and teachings of Eric Meyers, it has been the proposition that data requires context and interdisciplinary discussion (Meyers and Strange 1981). Religious groups should not be analyzed exclusive of their broader socio-cultural contacts (e.g., Meyers and White 1989), towns and cities must be considered dynamic units of interplay in a regional network (Meyers 1976), and, perhaps most fundamentally, archaeology and text should dialogue.

In that spirit, this chapter is an attempt to bring textual information and ritual theory to bear on a matter of current archaeological interest, namely the ritual immersion pool, or *miqweh* (pl. *miqwāʾôt*).[1] My aim is to decode the ritual regulations of *miqwāʾôt* to reveal the postulates of sectarian self-identity. I will commence with a discussion of some halakhic issues, proceed to a discussion of pertinent ritual theory, and conclude with a proposal for how specific legal/ritual positions may represent sectarian world views.

OUTLINES OF A HALAKHIC DEBATE

In a programmatic study on *halakhah* and 4QMMT, Sussmann indicated that the *mûṣāqôt* mentioned in MMT just might be relevant to the issue of the *miqweh*, but he added that the matter required further study (Sussmann 1989–90). Since then, there has been rebuttal of this notion (Elman 1996; Grabbe 1997: 93–95). I would argue that the text *does* relate to the subject of *miqwāʾôt*, specifically the issue of single pools vs. double pools.[2] There are actually three related halakhic issues that will be addressed in this section:

- The Purity Status of Streams of Water, with Reference to *mûṣāqôt*
- The Purity Status of Stone
- Physical Dirt or Stains as a Purity Issue

First, the matter of the *mûṣāqôt*. The relevant section of 4QMMT was previously entitled 4QMišn(ique)[a] and first appeared in print in some remarks made in 1962 by J. Milik about the Copper Scroll in DJD III (Baillet et al. 1962: 222, 225). I reproduce the Hebrew as it appeared in its official publication in DJD X (Qimron and Strugnell 1994: 52–53):

ואף על המוצקות אנאחנו אומרים שהם שאין בהם
טהרה ואף המוצקות אינם מבדילות בין הטמא
לטהור כי לחת המוצקות והמקבל מהמה כהם לחה אחת

And concerning *mûṣāqôt*, we say regarding them that they are not pure[3] [Or possibly:

> do not have the ability to transmit purity.]. Furthermore, *mûṣāqôt* do not constitute a separation between the impure and the pure, for the liquid of the *mûṣāqôt* and that which receives them is as one liquid.

First Yigael Yadin (1983: 213), and subsequently Joseph Baumgarten (1980: 163–64) observed that the *mûṣāqôt* should probably be identified with the *niṣṣôq* of rabbinic literature, a phenomenon specifically mentioned as a focal point of dissent in a sectarian controversy depicted in *M. Yadayim:*

> אומרים צדוקין קובלין אנו עליכם פרושים שאתם מטהרים את הנצוק
>
> The Sadducees say 'We protest against you, Pharisees, because you say a *niṣṣôq* is pure!'
>
> אומרים פרושים קובלין אנו עליכם צדוקים שאתם מטהרים את אמת המים הבאה מבית הקברות
>
> The Pharisees reply 'We protest against you, Sadducees, because you say a water channel running through a graveyard is pure!' (*M. Yadayim* 4:7)

The question then is, of course, what is the *niṣṣôq* at the center of this debate? As already explained by Baumgarten (1980: 163–64; see also Ginzberg 1976: 54; Guttmann 1970: 153–54; Finkelstein 1962: 716–18, 811–13), there are two mishnaic texts that have traditionally been used to clarify the *mishnah* in *Yadayim.* The first is *M. Ṭoharot* 4:4, which describes a particular circumstance, but which does *not* use the word *niṣṣôq:*

> המערה מכלי לכלי ונמצא שרץ בתחתון העליון טהור
>
> If someone was pouring from one vessel into another vessel and it turned out there was a creepie-crawly in the lower vessel, [even so] the upper vessel is [still] pure (*M. Ṭoharot* 4:4).[4]

The second text is *M. Makširin* 5:9, which does use the term *niṣṣôq* and is understood to be adding information to the preceding *mishnah:*

> כל הנצוק טהור חוץ מדבש הזיפין והצפחת בית שמאי אומרים אף המקפה שלגריסין ושלפול מפני שהיא סולדת לאחריה
>
> Every *niṣṣôq* is pure except one of *zif* honey or *ṣapaḥat.* The School of Shammai adds *miqpâ* [apparently a thick stew or paste] made from grits or fava beans, because it recoils backwards (*M. Makširin* 5:9).

The situation presented in these two *mishnayot* is one in which a person is pouring from an upper vessel, which is pure, to a lower vessel, which is impure. Does the interposing stream—the *niṣṣôq*—cause the impurity of the lower vessel to travel upwards to the upper vessel? The determination of the Mishnah is that it does not, unless the *niṣṣôq* is viscous, in which case the lower end of the stream, having been in contact with the impure receptacle, might rebound back into the pure container.

This matter of the *niṣṣôq* is then presented in *M. Yadayim* as the subject of a dispute between the Pharisees and Sadducees, with the Pharisees holding what would later be the rabbinic position, and the Sadducees apparently holding the view taken in MMT, namely, that the *niṣṣôq* / *mûṣāqôt* do indeed transmit impurity.

In passing, we note two points: (1) minimally, the apparent coincidence of subject matter raises the question of just which group was meant when rabbinic material used the term Zadokite—perhaps *not* Josephus' aristocratic Sadducees; and (2) the coincidence of legal positions is, of course, part of the argument that has led Schiffman to argue that the Dead Sea Sect is Zadokite rather than Essene (Schiffman 1990; 1992b), at least in its origins, and which has led Sussmann to conclude that there were two main schools of Jewish legal thought in antiquity—the Zadokite/priestly (to which *both* the Dead Sea Sect and Josephus' aristocratic Sadducees belonged) and the Pharisaic. I will be adopting the latter view as a working hypothesis, so that it makes little difference whether MMT belongs to the Qumran community or to its antecedent parent group, since both would have been part of the Zadokite/priestly legal school.

What does a liquid poured from an upper vessel into a lower vessel have to do with *miqwāʾôt*, especially when the Mishnah spends so much time establishing that the immovable *miqweh* is something different than a moveable vessel? In discussing the *mûṣāqôt* in MMT, Sussmann observed that *M. Miqwāʾôt* 6:8 deals with the case of an upper *miqweh* being purified by a lower one

מטהרים את-המקואות העליון מן-התחתון
והרחוק מן-הקרוב...

> Upper miqweh's can be purified from lower ones,
> and far ones ["those"] from near ones ["these"] *M. Miqwāʾôt* 6:8

The way in which this purification takes place is by siphoning. In this case it is not impurity but purity that travels upward via a stream of fluid. One assumes that Sussmann made the connection between MMT and the first part of this *mishnah* because the circumstance of higher and lower *miqwāʾôt* appears to be analogous to that of upper and lower vessels. Let us, however, emphasize the second half of the *mishnah*, the "near" and "far," which can be construed as demonstratives, i.e., "this" *miqweh* can be purified by "that" one, regardless of positioning, by drawing a stream of water through piping.[5] This indicates that the issue of *mûṣāqôt* may involve more than relative altitude.

The rabbinic position, as seen in the preceding *mishnah*, is that a pure pool can be used to purify an impure one. Stated succinctly, כל המעורב למקוה, כמקוה "Any [water] mingling with a *miqweh*, is like the *miqweh* [itself]" (*M. Miqwāʾôt* 6:1). *Sifra* defends this position by using Lev 11:36 (אך מעין ובור מקוה-מים יהיה מהור) as a prooftext:

מנין אם טמא יטהרנו

> Where does it say that if one [of these water sources] is impure, it can be purified?

ת"ל מקוה ומעין יהיה טהור

> Scripture says, a *miqweh* and a spring [together] will be pure.

אין לי אלא מעין את המקוה
מנין מקוה את המקוה מקוה את הבור בור את הבור
בור את המקוה מנין

> It only says a spring purifies a *miqweh*. Where does it indicate a *miqweh* purifies a *miqweh*, a *miqweh* [purifies] a cistern, a cistern another cistern, and a cistern a *miqweh*? (Where?)

ת"ל מעין יחיח טהור בור יהיה טהור ומקוה מים יהיה
טהור

> Scripture says, a spring will be pure, a cistern will be pure, and a *miqweh-mayim* will be pure (*Sifra, Šĕmînî, Parašah* 9 [2])

This last phrase is the functional equivalent of MMT's ואף על המוצקות אנאחנו אומרים שהם שאין *מהרה בהם* (we say *mûṣāqôt* do not have the capacity to transmit purity), that is, "we rabbis say regarding the spring, cistern, and *miqweh* (*שיש בהם טהרה*)" they *do* have the capacity to transmit purity. *M. Miqwāʾôt* Chapter 6 in its entirety is predicated on the assumption that pure and impure water can be safely mingled under the right circumstances (Neusner 1976–77: Part 22:93). One further *mishnah* will help illuminate just what those circumstances were.

M. Ṭoharot 8:9 clusters together several categories of water connections:[6]

הנצוק והקטפרם ומשקה טופח אינן חיבור לא לטמאה
ולא לטהרה
והאשברן חבור לטמאה ולטהרה

> The *niṣṣōq*, the *qaṭaprēs* [water on a slope],[7] and dripping water are not connectives for either impurity or purity, whereas the *ʾešbōren* is a connective for both impurity and purity.

This *mishnah* states that the *niṣṣôq* and the other forms of interposing streams mentioned do not form a connection that transmits either purity or impurity, but standing pools — the *ʾešbōren* — do. Consequently, in the rabbinic view, connecting two immersion pools is possible, not because of the stream flowing through a conduit or on the ground between them, but because the status of at least one of the pools is pure; and this forms a connection with an impure pool to render it pure as well.[8] *M. Ṭoharot* 8:9 implies rejection of the application of the *niṣṣôq* to the issue of purifying a *miqweh*. Instead, the principle used by the rabbis to defend their practice was not the *niṣṣôq*, it was the *ʾešbōren*, a pool of standing water. The status of an impure pool was defined on the basis of its association with a pure pool (*ʾešbōren*) and not primarily in relation to the intermediary stream.

I propose that the Qumran community would not have accepted this rationale and viewed the connecting pipes between dual pools as *mûṣāqôt*, or at least as some form of unacceptable stream, carrying the impurity of the drawn water in the impure pool to the legitimate pool (*ʾôṣār* or *ʾešbōren*) and rendering the entire facility invalid.

Let us be perfectly clear about this: I do not suggest that the rabbinic categories or terms of discussion were precisely those of their antecedents. The protest against *mûṣāqôt* in MMT may represent an array of incipient disputes involving different types of water streams that were subsumed under this single, biblically dependent term or that were still waiting to emerge as separate issues. It cannot be said how developed such theories were at the time MMT was composed. One expects of tannaitic literature more abstract conceptualization and classification, along with further refinement in terminology,[9] and one finds it in this *mishnah*.

The best description of the ritual requirements of the Dead Sea community comes from the well-known passage in CD, recently corrected and confirmed by the 4Q fragments[10]

על הטהר במים[11]
אל ירחץ איש במים צואים ומועטים מדי מרעיל איש
אל יטהר בם כל כלי
וכל גבא בסלע אשר אין בו די מרעיל אשר נגע בו
הטמא וטמא מימיו כמימי הכלי

> Concerning purification in water. No person shall wash in foul[12] water or too little to cover a person. No one shall purify a vessel in it, and any rock pool in which there is not enough to cover,[13] which an impure person touched — its water is impure as[14] the water of a vessel (CD 10:10–13).[15]

In this passage one does not find mention of the rabbinic 40 *sĕʾâ*, but rather the more realistic requirement that there be enough water to cover a person. In fact, this is a good example of what Schwartz calls the "realistic" legal perspective of the Qumran sect vs. the "nominalist" outlook of the rabbis (Schwartz 1992a). The nominalist legal perspective is one in which legal categories possess their own life and validity and need no further reality. This is how *Sifra* explains the need for a minimum 40 *sĕʾâ* of pure water:

> 'And he shall wash in water' (Lev 15:16), even in the water of a *miqweh*. 'His whole body', [i.e.] water sufficient for his whole body. And how much is that? One cubit by one cubit by three cubits in height — you find that the volume of a *miqweh* is forty *sĕʾâ*.[16]

That this represents a nominalist outlook is indicated by the fact that 40 *sĕʾâ* is a theoretical amount, rather than the volume actually required for a person to immerse, which would in reality change with body weight and dimension. That the 40 *sĕʾâ is* a theoretical amount is made clear in *M. Miqwāʾôt* 6:3, where we find the curious case of three side-by-side *miqwāʾôt*, each containing only twenty *sĕʾâ* of water. The first two hold pure water, but the third in the row holds drawn water. According to this *mishnah*, if three people immersed in the pools, one person per pool, and thereby caused the water of the three pools to overflow and mingle, each person's immersion would be valid. The implicit reason is that the two pools of twenty *sĕʾâ* of valid water apiece would be the first to merge and would create a single valid pool of forty *sĕʾâ*. This amount would then join with the invalid water of the third pool and, in turn, purify it. The difficulty in this example rests in its assumption that a person would physically be able to immerse in twenty *sĕʾâ* of water! The *mishnah* exposes *Sifra's* fiction that forty *sĕʾâ* is the amount minimally necessary to cover a person.

Returning to CD, the phrasing "its water is impure as the water of a vessel" reinforces how tenuous was the boundary between the pool that could purify and the vessel that could contaminate, between purifying water and contaminating water. A stone pool with sufficient water did not guarantee the purity of the facility, in the Qumran perspective. Indeed, stone at Qumran did not have the same status as in rabbinic *halakhah*, and it is partly this that the Pharisees are mocking in *M. Yadayim*. The *Temple Scroll* (col. 49) included stone vessels among the types that had to be purified from corpse impurity.[17] Even the stones of the deathhouse itself had to be purified of all moisture.[18] Tannaitic law, by contrast, deemed stone vessels and materials affixed to the earth to be impervious.[19] This difference might well have added impetus to the debate about *miqwā'ōt*, which were, after all, carved in stone. If everything in the house of a decedent became impure, including the stones of the house,[20] what was the status of the family *miqweh*?

CD 12:15–17 reads: "And all wood, stones, or dust which are sullied by human impurity, having stains of oil on them, according to their impurity shall he who touches them become impure." Here, even unfinished stone can be defiled by the stains that adhere to it.[21]

Baumgarten has detailed the way in which physical stains were defiling to the Qumran community.[22] Such stains were, in Baumgarten's words, "agents of contamination," capable of transmitting impurity derived from some other source. They included oil,[23] blood,[24] and, most tellingly for our purposes, mud.[25] The judgment that mud was defiling was based on 1QS 3:2–3, which states "For he plows in the mud of wickedness (בסאון רשע) and his conversion is besmirched (וגואלים) with stains."[26] Since the text continues by telling us that no form of ablution will purify such a person, this particular usage emerges as only partly metaphoric. As far as the defiling capacity of mud in an immersion pool is concerned — this is metaphor given concrete reality.[27]

Dan 12:10, cited in the rather exclusivist document 4QFlor 2:3–4a, states that the righteous would be purified and made white. Such symbols were apparently taken quite seriously. According to Josephus, the Essenes avoided oil as defiling and *always dressed in white* (*JW* 2.123).[28] It is especially interesting that Josephus mentioned these two details together. While it is true that dressing normally followed grooming with oil, a more trenchant reason for Josephus' organization of information is that oil and other types of dirty stains on their white garb were considered defiling by the Essenes. Consequently, in the view of the Qumran covenant community, even if a purification pool was of stone and contained enough water to cover a person, if it was dirty, it was not ritually fit.[29]

By contrast, in the mishnaic view dirty water was acceptable for purifying hands *when it was connected to the ground*, but not when it was in a vessel (M. Yadayim 1:3). It should also be remembered that the water in a *miqweh* was not considered by the rabbis to be the same as חים מיים, the "living water" required for the red heifer rite (Num 19:17), purification from skin disease (Lev 14:5), or purification from abnormal discharge (Lev 15:13). Whereas *Sifra* tells us that living water had to be clear (ברורים) and not brackish (מלוחים),[30] *M. Miqwā'ōt* goes as far as to allow mud to be calculated into the total volume of a *miqweh* (2:6, 10; 7:1, 7; 9:2).

Ehud Netzer suggested that the considerable depth of some *miqwā'ōt* helped preserve the cleanliness of the *miqweh* by allowing silt to sink to the bottom.[31] Silt would especially have been an issue when water came from aqueducts,[32] as was the case at Qumran and the Hasmonaean palace at Jericho. *M. Miqwā'ōt* documents the reality of this silt layer when, as just mentioned, it leniently allows such mud to be calculated into the total volume of the *miqweh*. Even where the rabbis are concerned, however, there is some concern about the specific types of mud.[33] Rabbinic interest lay in whether the mud was thick enough to constitute an obstruction between the water and the skin of the person immersing. Interposition of any object invalidates one's immersion in the rabbinic view.[34] According to Josephus, the Essenes immersed while garbed (*JW* 2.129). Their being clothed may have been due to modesty about reciting the associated benedictions while still in the water,[35] but it also indicates that interposition was not a concern for them.[36] Whereas at Qumran the problem of mud pertained to the actual purity status of stains, in the Mishnah the subject has been entirely reframed and involves the rabbinic concept of interposition.[37]

INTERPRETING RITUAL

What can such abstruse information tell us about the ancient people who were concerned with and enacted these halakhic rules? First and foremost, it should be remembered that halakhic requirements for the *miqweh* are ritual requirements and should be understood within the framework of ritual theory. Unfortunately, Pauline perspectives on ritual *halakhah* have unduly influenced some previous inquiries, and our attendant grasp of the information has been impeded.

The social location of an investigator naturally dictates the presuppositions of any inquiry and impacts its outcome. Typically, scholarly inquiry into ancient Jewish ablution practices has been tied to Christian interest in baptism.[38] The core question usually brought to the material was whether Judaism possessed a distinct, non-purificatory form of proselyte "baptism" prior to the advent of the Christian rite. Apologetics supporting the "uniqueness" of Christian baptism and the (putatively) dubious value of Jewish purity concepts were seldom far removed from the discussion.

Initially, inquiry took place against the backdrop of rabbinic teachings, but eventually the background for John's ostensibly "once and for all" "spiritual" baptism came to be sought within the Qumran community, which supposedly possessed a precursor to the Christian initiatory rite (e.g., Brownlee 1957: 39–40). In fact, it was only with the discovery of the Qumran documents that some scholars began to entertain the notion of a possibly less "legalistic" (a false hypothesis as it turned out), and supposedly more "spiritual" form of Palestinian Judaism. The "spiritual" baptism of John was then routinely contrasted with the dry as dust "repetitive" purification rites of a "formalistic" Judaism. The latter was sometimes identified with Essenic or Qumranic Judaism,[39] but more particularly with Pharisaic/rabbinic Judaism.[40] The antipathy toward Judaism undergirding this type of argument is rendered transparent by Bell's broadly theoretical observation that repetition is merely a "frequent, but not universal strategy for producing ritualized acts" (Bell 1992: 92). After all, one does not hear about the legalistic, repetitive monotony of the Eucharist.

Bell theorizes that "ritual is never simply or solely a matter of routine, habit, or 'the dead weight of tradition'" (1992: 92). It seems that arguments to the contrary rest on the sentiment that Christian rites *really are* efficacious, while Jewish ones are not. Religious bias is overt in statements like this one by Driver (1965: 497), who wrote that Jewish water rites by the first century had "developed into an elaborate system of casuistry which had already lost itself in endless detail. These were the burdensome regulations which Jesus denounced..."[41] While increased scholarly sensitivity has reduced the number of such flagrantly offensive remarks, underlying faith confessions still can color even methodologically aware studies.[42]

Was the Qumran community the only group of Jews to have an abstract ("spiritual"), rather than a mechanical frame of reference?[43] Or rather, why is it only to Pharisaic/rabbinic rituals that abstraction, whether conscious or unaware on the part of the practitioner, has been denied? The following data are meant to indicate that John's atoning baptism should be scrutinized not in terms of a professed "uniqueness"—the agenda set by an earlier generation of scholars—but with the understanding that John's beliefs about atonement, immersion, and purification were broadly representative of the Judaism of his time.[44] More to the point, it will attempt to establish a framework for our subsequent interpretation of the *miqweh*.

In actuality, it was commonplace for actions, entities, and institutions in the Hellenistic world to be understood symbolically. There was ample classical precedent for this. Antigone, for example, was condemned not for actually burying her brother, an act which had been forbidden, but for giving the symbolic appearance of having done so.[45] In Euripides' *Iphigeneia in Tauris*, symbolic substitutions for human sacrifice occur twice: once, when a deity intervenes to substitute a fawn in place of Iphigeneia, and again when the incomplete sacrifice of Orestes by Iphigeneia results in the inauguration of a cultic practice, wherein a sword is drawn over the throat of a human victim in order to produce only token drops of blood.[46]

Within the biblical world, Ps 24:4, 73:13, and Isa 1:15–16 all indicate a *symbolic* import to washing one's hands as a way of signifying moral purity of both intent and action, a theme later carried into the Gospel of Matthew in Pilate's purported (but uncharacteristically Jewish) declaration (Matt 27:24; cf. Deut 21:1–9). The *Letter of Aristeas* and Philo also provide variations on this theme.[47] In later rabbinic texts, hand-washing serves as a symbolic substitution for ritual bathing, and, in one instance, where it is viewed as a heterodox practice, as the symbolic building of an unacceptable altar.[48]

Symbolic explanations of various facets of Judaism abound in Jewish writings of the Hellenistic Period. The biblical Tabernacle, for instance, is presented as symbolic of the universe both by Philo, representing diaspora Judaism, and Josephus, representing Judaism in the Land of Israel.[49] *Real space, in other words, was consciously conceived in symbolic terms.*

The difficulty with using either Philo or Josephus as exemplars for their time period is that in varying degrees they were writing apologies for external consumption. Judaism was presented to non-Jews in a form they could appreciate. Yet the fact that there was an object known as "the Sea" in Solomon's temple gives us some indication that cosmic signification was hardly alien to ancient Israelite ritual.[50] Certainly the eating of unleavened bread on Passover was understood symbolically (Exod 13:6–9). Moreover, Schwartz has convincingly argued that at least some of Philo's allegorical explanations probably stemmed from Judaean, priestly sources (Schwartz 1984).

We are, in fact, not entirely lacking in Second Temple Period homiletical or instructional texts capable of informing us of the motivational rationales for ancient practitioners of the Jewish immersion ritual. A number of the following texts have been rehearsed repeatedly in discussions of baptism, without a correct appreciation of their import for determining an aspect of common Jewish piety. Some of these sources are so routinely reported in studies, it is surprising that this most obvious way of interpreting them is ignored. On the other hand, several recent works, including the author's, have stressed the connection in ancient Judaism between ablutions and atonement, and the need to understand John's baptism in that light, thereby reviving an early argument by Abrahams.[51] Abrahams had launched an early protest against any distinction between moral and physical baptism, developing the theme of water as a symbol for repentance in Judaism. He observed that sin and impurity were often associated in the Bible and thereafter,[52] and offered Ps 51:4 as an example "Wash me thoroughly of my iniquity, and purify me of my sin…," on which *Gen. Rab.* 39:11 comments "Whoever commits a transgression is as though he was defiled by contact with a dead body."

The connection between immersion and atonement in the benedictions and instructions of the purity rite in 4Q512 was astutely pointed out by Baumgarten (1992: 200–201). Better known and frequently repeated is the statement in 1QS 2:26–3:12 indicating that without prior repentance and adherence to the ways and teaching of the sectarian community the rites were ineffective.[53] This latter passage is comparable to Acts 22:16, where baptismal water washes sins away, *if* one calls on Jesus' name. In neither Acts nor 1QS is the exercise automatically efficacious without the appropriate, attendant dogmatic affirmations.[54]

The association of ritual washing with repentance, or a moral cleansing, was not just to be found in sectarian or proto-sectarian texts, however. It was pervasive in ancient Judaism. Compare these comments of Philo about entry to the Temple with 1QS 2:26–3:12:

> For if we cultivate the spirit of rendering thanks and honour to Him, we shall be pure from wrongdoing and wash away the filthiness which defiles our lives in thought and word and deed. For it is absurd that a man should be forbidden to enter the temples save after bathing and cleansing his body, and yet should attempt to pray and sacrifice with a heart still soiled and spotted…. He who is resolved not only to commit no further sin, but also to wash away the past, may approach with gladness *let him who lacks this resolve keep far away, since hardly shall he be purified* [emphasis added].[55]

For Philo, one cannot properly approach the Temple without purification of body in concert with correction of soul. But already in 1 Enoch, the Flood was interpreted as purification from sinfulness.[56] In the *Life of Adam and Eve* 11 (*Apocalypse of Moses)*, Adam's exaggerated expressions of penitence include standing up to his neck in a river, a theme later repeated in the rabbinic *Pirkei de R. Eliezer* 20,[57] despite scholarly arguments for rabbinic segregation of ritual and moral purity (Baumgarten 1992: 200, 209; Klawans 1997). A complete ablution prior to a prayer for atonement figures in Mt. Athos 2:3 / 4Q213, the *Prayer of Levi:* "Then I laundered my garments and having purified them with pure water, I also washed my whole self in living water, and I made all my paths upright."[58] Ben Sira used purity as an analogue for repentance: "If one washes after touching a corpse, and touches it again, what has been gained by washing? So if one fasts for his sins, and goes again and does the same things, who will listen to his prayer?" (Ben Sira 34: 30–31). This latter idea recurs in an indisputable context of fasting and repentance in *Tosefta Ta'anit*, where a critter in the hand is worth two sins in the bush: "If a person holds an impure creature in his hand, even if he immerses in the water of the Siloam, yea in all the waters of Creation, he will never be purified. [But] if he casts the creature from his hand, immersion in 40 *sĕ'â* suffices" (*T. Ta'anit* 1:8; Urbach 1987: 464). Returning to Philo, purification of body and soul appear as necessary correlates, while time could not "wash away" (ἀπονίψει) some sins (*De Specialibus Legibus* 1.257–61; 3.89). Utilizing the puzzling Exod 38:8, Philo explains that the Tabernacle laver was made of women's mirrors, so that it could serve as a mirror to the soul (*De Vita Mosis* 2.139). His explanation embraces the "reflective" introspectiveness of the ritual as an invitation to self-scrutiny.

The fourth book of the Sibylline Oracles is one of the main sources for a putatively proto-Christian "baptism of repentance,"[59] but there is nothing extraordinary in the lustration described there.[60] The people are warned to wash their entire bodies in rivers and pray by asking forgiveness and offering words of praise. Repentance as a prelude to prayerful praise is not unique to the Sibyl and is found again in the liturgical document 4Q *Dibĕrê Ha-mĕ'ôrôt* (ca. 150 B.C.E.), where it seems that a day for the confession of sins preceded the Sabbath as a day of praise.[61] The lustration of the oracle is connected as much with prayer as with repentance, and both of these require the spiritual purity of which washing is a symbol (Abrahams 1917: 39–40).

Scholarly discussion of the baptismal issue frequently raises such questions as to whether specific references were metaphoric or denoted actual practice, and the significance of the timing of the immersion—whether before, during, or after the actual atonement, and to what extent different, organized "movements" were attached to small variations in the textual evidence. The very word "variation," however, suggests the existence of a common theme. It may be that some of these variations have had more significance for evidence-starved researchers than they did for practitioners (Lévi-Strauss 1995: 41–42).

Some years ago, word circulated in the Jewish religious community in Jerusalem that a particular Orthodox woman had, for an extended period of time, been immersing herself early every morning, regardless of the season, in the Siloam Pools, dunking a prodigious number of times on each occasion to accord with the mystical significance she attached to the event. No *halakhah* told her to do this. It was a personal act of special, solitary devotion.

The point is that purity, even more than other divine prescriptions, involves coming closer to God, and thus *intrinsically* also involves a penitential element—the desire to be worthy of being in the divine presence. Any statements of atonement associated with immersion or other purity rites surely encompass the possibility of genuine wrongdoing, but they also represent the basic feelings of unworthiness that accrue to an awareness of being human and finite.[62]

Finally, it should be stressed that the stated purpose of a ritual activity or installation does not exhaust all possible meanings or functions. From a structuralist standpoint, profound meaning can exist whether or not it is conscious. Or, to state the matter in terms of ritual theory, "to analyze practice...is...to formulate the *unexpressed* assumptions that constitute the actor's strategic understanding of the place, purpose, and trajectory of the act."[63] As explained by Bell, the actor's strategic understanding includes unspoken assumptions about the power relationships existing in a particular society. Consequently, one should not expect ritual participants to be aware of all the ways in which their actions support, and are in turn supported by, their social world. The task for scholars of ancient Judaism is to recover those assumptions, whether expressed or unexpressed, that support legal teaching and ritual practice.

THE RELATIONSHIP OF LEGAL POSITIONS TO SECTARIAN WORLD VIEWS

The individual strands of legal teaching about streams and bodies of water conform to the particular world views of the groups involved. *M. Ṭoharot* 8:9 states that the *niṣṣôq* אינן חיבור, is not a connective. It employs the language of joining. By contrast, 4QMMT emphatically states that *mûṣāqôt* אינם מבדילות ("do not separate") between the impure and the pure. It uses the language of separation. The extreme import of this concept of separation,[64] especially in priestly circles and most particularly at Qumran (cf. Newton 1985: 15–19), is to be underlined. One need hardly belabor the existence at Qumran of binary opposites of separation (בח"ר; פר"ש; בד"ל) and mixing or joining (ער"ב; בו"א; יח"ד;).

Segregationist language was highly pronounced at Qumran, where it extended into diverse areas of life. To join (ליחד) with the sect, one had to separate (להבדל) from the community of wayward outsiders (IQS 5:1–2). With full integration into the group came full integration of property (ולערב). Misbehavior resulted in distancing from the community and its lifestyle. Separation (ויבדילוהו)from the pure food of the community was a penalty for wayward sectaries (IQS 6:25). The property of the sectaries was not to mix (יתערב)with the possessions of those who had not been refined through separation (להבדל)from those wicked not having adopted the sectarian viewpoint, or who had rebelled against it.[65] Holy days were not to be mistakenly joined with profane days (Jub 6:37; 1QpHab 11:4–8; 4QCalendrical); Jerusalem was the "camp," not to be confused with the area "outside the camp;"[66] priests had to be especially wary in avoiding improper marital unions.[67]

Both concepts — separation and mingling — appear together in a single context in MMT, where the sect describes the reasons for its separation from the practices of others: "We have separated ourselves (פרשנו)from the majority of the peo[ple…] from intermingling (מהתערב) in these matters and from participating with them in these [matters]."[68] The "matters" involved were, of course, *purity* matters — MMT turns on the pivot of improper mixtures. Not surprisingly, the idea of separation is also featured in the purification rite from Cave 4, where God is blessed for separating or distinguishing between the impure and the pure.[69] It is notable that the benediction emphasizes this particular reason for immersing. By comparison, the rabbinic blessing for immersion (and most other activities) emphasizes that the reason for doing it is that God said so[70] — a nominalist justification.

The concern with maintaining categories was a priestly one, and not confined to the Qumran group alone. According to the *Temple Scroll* (11QT 45:1–7), the purity of priests arriving for their course of service in the Temple was to be ensured by their entering in such a way as to avoid the other priests who had completed their tenure. Although the *Temple Scroll* is presumed to preserve a utopian vision of Temple life, tunnels discovered under the Temple Mount have been associated by excavators with passageways (*mĕsîbot*) described in the Mishnah as providing a route by which an impure priest could retire to a *miqweh* without contaminating anyone else (Ben-Dov 1982: 147). Certain thoroughfares in Jerusalem were known to be traveled by pilgrims and priests on their way to or from their ablutions.[71] Pixner and others have observed that this principle of separation extended into the very structure of some *miqwāʾôt*, which were built with partitions to prevent the impure who entered from contacting the pure who exited.[72]

Unlike those in Jerusalem, some pools at Qumran had more than a single divider, creating three divisions. Wood posited that the third division served as a channel through which the water flowed into the pool (Wood 1984: 46–53, 58; de Vaux 1973: 8–9; Driver 1965: 41; North 1962: 110–16). It should be remembered, however, that water seldom would actually have flowed from the aqueduct that fed the pools. A central channel could have acted as a further buffer between those entering and exiting, the impure and the pure. We are reminded of the complaint voiced in Ezek 43:7–8:

> The House of Israel and their kings must not again defile My holy name by their apostasy…by the corpses of their kings…. When they placed their threshold next to My threshold and their doorposts next to My doorposts *with only a wall between Me and them*… (NJPS)

So hierarchical was the priestly structure at Qumran that an intermediate status may have been interposed to insulate the pure from the impure. Milgrom describes the existence of staged purification rites with an interim *ḥôl* ("secular") status, standing guard between the fully pure and the outright impure.[73] The gradations of holiness in literature about the Temple and Temple City also attest to the need for insulating the most pure from the most common (Maier 1989: 24, 31). A water channel interposed the entire length between the pure and the impure would have been functional, but it also conformed to the general Qumran outlook.

The Qumran sect and the Sadducees sought to uphold an absolute distinction between priestly and secular realms. To do this, according to Knohl, it was necessary to prevent the common people from mixing with the sacra. The Pharisees, for their part, emphasized that all Israel was sacred, and they endeavored to undermine the barriers that prevented the common Israelite from coming in contact with sacra.[74] It is not that the Pharisees did away with boundaries, they simply relocated them.

According to Maier, the Temple of the *Temple Scroll* was more exclusive than the Herodian Temple. The *Temple Scroll expanded* the areas that were *restricted* to particular groups of people. In contrast, the Herodian Temple *limited* the areas of high sancta, while *expanding* areas with non-cultic purposes. This allowed greater access for non-priests, women, and (perhaps) gentiles.[75] If Knohl and Maier are correct, we see *priestly circles consistently protecting their prerogatives by emphasizing absolute distinctions between boundaries.*[76] This attitude was in tension with a more inclusive tendency, which sought not to eliminate the categories,[77] but to redraw them so as to admit non-priests into more intimate contact with the core of faith and the workings of power.[78] Herod had every reason to try to circumvent priestly authority, while currying favor with the populace. Although Pharisaic efforts might, as Knohl intimates, have had genuinely populist overtones,[79] they too would have subtly served to undermine the priests in their own domain. My conclusions, however, do not rely upon a populist understanding of the Pharisees, since any concern for granting the common Israelite greater access to the sacred might have been turned inward toward their own leadership ambitions as a non-priestly, non-hereditary group.

The single-pool variety *miqwā'ôt* of the Qumran sect, like many of those found in Jerusalem, relied upon an entryway partition to prevent the impure making contact with the pure. In light of this cumulative evidence, it seems that the double pool system, involving the conjunction of a pure pool next to an impure one, with only a thin stream of water to unite or divide them, represented an uncomfortable proximity for this group of separatists. The categories were too indistinct. Merging the two pools represented an unacceptable blending of the impure with the pure.[80]

GENERAL CONCLUSIONS

The categories of vessels and storage pools were so conceptually close, that clearly delimiting their boundaries became a focus of concern in the Second Temple Period and thereafter. I have argued that, while tannaitic literature validates the use of the two-pool system by virtue of the *'ešbōren*, their argumentation probably represents the end point of a longer debate. Earlier Zadokite groups may have disputed the practice, owing to the connecting stream between the pools. Certainly they did not accept the purity of water simply on the basis of quantity and attachment to the ground. Biblical verses exist that could have promoted a preference for purifying a standing pool by means of flowing water (Ezekiel 47; Zech 13:1, 14:8),[81] such as from an aqueduct, and indeed *M. Yadayim* indicates that the Zadokites accepted use of an aqueduct, even if it flowed through a cemetery, but rejected the *niṣṣôq*. The Pharisees in this *mishnah* condemned the Zadokites for a perceived inconsistency in accepting one form of ground stream, but not the other.

The language of 4QMMT, in stating that *mûṣāqôt* do not separate between the pure and the impure, is a key to understanding the broader problem. The respective interpretations of the two main halakhic groups, Pharisaic and Zadokite, reflect their different world views. Could a pure pool be merged with an impure pool beside it? Zadokite groups enforced priestly hierarchical distinctions and said "no." Groups with Pharisaic leanings introduced a wider spectrum of the populace into the compass of elevated holiness, and they represented their agenda symbolically through the merging of pure and impure pools of water.

NOTES

1 This article is based upon the author's 1993 Duke University doctoral dissertation "Exegesis and Identity: The Hermeneutics of *miqwā'ôt* in the Greco-Roman Period," completed under the guidance of Eric Meyers, whose rigorous training and supportive mentoring made it possible. Thanks are also due to Prof. Martin Jaffee, whose clarity of thought improved mine.

2 Neusner, in his early work on ritual purity, had dated the existence of the double immersion pool principally to the Ushan period, considerably later than the archaeological evidence would now indicate. The distinction made by Neusner was that in the Yavnean level of tannaitic texts an impure pool could be purified with the water of a pure pool next to it only through removal or replacement of the impure water, while the Ushan contribution was to mingle the two bodies of water, allowing the pure to dominate the impure. I will argue that such mingling was at issue well before the Ushan period. See Neusner 1976–77: 240–41, pt. 22; but cf. 173–74, and 88–91, 127, pt. 14. My own understanding of single vs. double pools is indebted to the discussion of Sanders (1990: 214–27).

3 The positive form of this phrase appears in 11Q*Temple* 49:15 אשר יש להמה טהרה, where it means that some vessels *by nature* can be purified, whereas others cannot. The reason why *mûṣāqôt* cannot be purified is made clear in the way the verb *yuṣaq* is used in 11QT 49:7, where it replaces the biblical יבוא. The phrase in Lev 11:34 is 'all the food,' אשר יבוא עליו מים. This is replaced in 11QT with אשר יוצק עליו מים. The biblical rule states that water having been poured on food makes the food impure when it comes into contact with impurity. Water under such circumstances has a heightened receptivity to impurity and is consequently described in MMT as inherently impure. Such unrestrained water in 11QT appears as the means by which corpse impurity spreads throughout a house. A stream of water connected to an ongoing source of impurity would be analogous to the unrepentant person, who cannot be purified because he clings to the source of his impurity (i.e., sin). 1QS 3:4–5, see also 4Q512, frgs. 29–32 (García-Martínez 1994: 441). If *mûṣāqôt* cannot receive purity, they certainly cannot transmit it.

4 In Lev 11:36, a distinction is made between a spring of flowing water (מעין) and other types of catchment areas (ובור מקוה מים) where water has collected. The adversative "but" ("*but* a spring") used in the verse establishes a more significant contrast between spring or catchment water, on the one hand, which *does not* become impure under the conditions specified in the verse, and water in vessels, on the other hand, mentioned in the preceding verses and which *does* become impure under otherwise similar circumstances. It is this distinction between water in vessels and other types of water that forms the basis for later rabbinic extrapolation (*Sifra, Parašat Šĕmînî Parašah* 6, on Lev 11:32).

5 For the use of *mûṣāqôt* to indicate piping conducting fluid, see Zech 4:2.

6 Cf. *B. Giṭṭin* 16a.

7 Probably from the Greek καταπρηνής, "down-turned".

8 This might also have been the reason for so much tannaitic emphasis upon the size of the connecting conduit (*M. Miqwā'ôt* 6:7). It had to be of a specified, minimal diameter, perhaps large enough to create the fiction of a single pool.

9 That is, the creation of new terms that are not biblically dependent and which reflect some distancing from any supposed biblical basis for the traditions.

10 Underlined letters indicate portions found in 4Q266 and 4Q270. The text is derived from Baumgarten 1996 and Qimron 1992; cf. Schechter 1970 and Ginzberg 1976: 51–54.

11 CD: אל יטהד במה כלי. Emendation prior to publication of the Qumran version of the text had gone in two directions: (1) Ginzberg; Qimron: בהם or בם, i.e., do not immerse a vessel in them; or (2) Schechter: במי ,i.e., do not immerse in the water of a vessel. Orthographically it was not hard to justify the medieval copyist mistaking במי הכלי in an ancient hand; however, Ginzberg (1976: 52–53) turns out to have been correct in pointing out that טהר is used in preference to רחץ, indicating that vessels rather than people were the subject. This can now also be compared with 11QT 49:14–17, where טהר is indeed used of vessels and other items, while רחץ is used of people.

12 The word signifies not just filth but ritual unsuitability, see Zech 3:3; Meyers and Meyers 1987.

13 Widely understood as "to cover," due more to the assumption that this is what it should mean, than from any satisfactory etymology. Rejecting Schechter's (1970: xlviii) emendation of מטביל ("immerse"), Ginzberg (1976: 52–53, cf. 312) suggested reading הגעיל, with the Talmudic sense of "ritual cleansing," which for the sect involved an "actual washing clean" (This would accord with my own interest in the impurity of stains). Rabin (1958: 51 n. 11.6) offered the targumic rendering of הרעלו (*hor'ālû*) in Nah 2:4 as "wrapped (in colored garments)". Lieberman (1942: 135) proposed an association with מרחל, which he argued was a unit of measure ("no man shall wash [in water] that is less than a 'Mar'eil'...") ultimately equal to the rabbinic forty *sĕ'â*. Lieberman's proposal is compelling (Sokoloff and Qimron appear to accept it), but, even if he was correct in associating מרעיל with a large basket, this still does not mean that the unit of measurement was the equivalent of forty *sĕ'â*, which I find implausible. The passage of *Sifra* cited by Lieberman (*Šĕmînî* 6 (7), ed. Weiss 53a) to show that large baskets hold forty *sĕ'â* only means that the baskets under consideration had to hold at least that amount. See further Sokoloff 1990: 331–32, s.v. "מרעל, מרחל," and Qimron 1986: 101–2.

14 Emend במימי to כמימי in accordance with Schechter.

15 Baumgarten 1996: 66 and 159.

16 *Sifra, Mĕṣōrā' [Zābîm], Pereq* 6 (3); also *B. Yoma* 31a and *'Erubin* 4b and 14b, *inter alia.*

17 This position was presumably extrapolated from "*all* the vessels," in Num 19:18, and "*every* vessel in which work can be done," in Lev 11:32, even though stone is not among the types of vessels listed in Lev 11:32. The list of vessel types in Lev 11:32 was thus understood to be representative rather than inclusive.

18 This can be considered a "realistic" perspective, since Lev 14:40–44 records the removal of stones from a house with *ṣara'at*; see further, Pfann 1997: 15.

19 *M. Yadayim* 1:2; *M. Kelim* 10:1; and *M. 'Oholot* 5:5. Moreover, according to a tannaitic dictum (with certain exceptions), what does not have an inside is not subject to impurity, תוך טמא ואת שאין לו תוך טהור אל תוכו--את שיש לו — *Sifra, Šĕmînî, Parašah* 7 (4). For more on Pharisaic "insides" and "outsides," see the provocative article by Poirer 1996.

20 Yadin (1983, vol. I: 328–30) cited the Palestinian Targum to Num 19:14 in support of the Temple Scroll's position "And even its floor, stones and vessels are unclean for seven days," in contrast to the rabbinic position as represented in *Sifre,* Num 126 [162] "'and everything in the tent' — I might understand the straw, dried branches, wood, stones and earth are meant; therefore it is stated..."

21 In the rabbinic schema, unfinished vessels do not receive impurity, see *M. Kelim* 12:6 and Baumgarten 1972; rpt. 1977: 95.

22 Baumgarten (1972; rpt. 1977). According to *M. Makširin* 6:4, there are seven liquids that transmit impurity: dew, water, wine, oil, blood, milk, and bee honey. Oil, blood, wine, and possibly honey were singled out as objects of concern in sectarian documents and in the information about Essenes provided by Josephus, *JW*, 2.123 (oil) and the disputed comments in CD 12:12 (honey?), which in any event may pertain only to dietary regulations; see Ginzberg 1976: 78–79, *inter alia*; but also Baumgarten 1977: 93, on the question of whether diaspora Jews were unwilling to use Greek oil only for dietary purposes or for anointing also. For wine, see Baumgarten 1977: 96 n. 42.

23 CD 12:15–17, as just mentioned.

24 1QM 9:7–9; cf. Isa 59:3, 63:3; 1Sam 1:21.

25 *Temple Scroll* 49:12 adds wine and moisture.

26 The translation modifies Baumgarten towards García-Martínez 1994. See further Prov 25:26, which reads "Like a muddied spring, a [ritually] defective fountain, is a righteous person fallen before a wicked one;" and Louis Ginzberg's (1976: 14) textual notes on התגוללו in CD 3:17, where he translates "and they besmirched themselves." Ginzberg explained this usage as either a denominative from גלל, meaning "ex-

crement," or as a byform of התגאל, "to make unclean;" but if we compare התגוללו in CD 3:17 with Isaiah 9:4 (מגוללה בדמים), we can better see how the semantic range could come to encompass "besmirched with stains."

27 On the failure of scholars to recognize that seemingly metaphoric statements sometimes had concrete reality and ramifications, see Klawans 1997.

28 Compare *M. Megillah* 4:8. Goldin wrote of Essene garb: "As symbolic of their emphasis on purity they dressed in white" (1949: 116).

29 On the use of brackish water in *miqweh's*, see the debate between Eshel and Meyers (2000).

30 Or tepid, intermittent, or dripping; see *Sifra, Mĕṣōrā'*, *Pereq* 1; also *M. Para* 8:8–10. The water of the Jordan was not acceptable, although one wonders if this was a later reflex against Christian practices.

31 Netzer (1982: 117); see also North (1962: 122). A settling tank in the aqueduct would not have been acceptable by rabbinic standards, for it would render the water "drawn." Greater depth also would have allowed immersion to be performed, even when the water level fell in the dry season or in time of drought; see Sanders 1990: 217.

32 As noted by Reich (1981: 51 n. 15), who observes there would have been less of a problem in rainwater drawn from rooftops.

33 As, for example, in *B. Zebaḥim* 22a.

34 *M. Miqwā'ôt* chapter 9; also, *B. 'Erubin* 4b and *B. Baba Qamma* 82a.

35 Baumgarten (1992: 201–2) emends Baillet's reconstruction in 4Q512 of על ברכיו (while kneeling) to עומדו על (while standing). The rabbinic benediction was also said following the act of immersion, *B. Berakot* 51a and *B. Pesaḥim* 7b. See also Hippolytus' citation in *Refutatio omnium haeresium*, 9.15.3–6, of the *Book of Elchasai*, which purportedly advocated a second, clothed baptism.

36 Cf. *M. Yoma* 36, indicating that the High Priest immersed while naked. Taylor suggests that the permeability of the material worn might have been pertinent (1997: 34–39, 54–56).

37 And yet rabbinic literature may preserve an echo from Qumran. *M. Miqwā'ôt* 9:2 states that miry clay constitutes an interposition. And how do we define "miry clay"?—by use of a prooftext, Ps 40:3, ויעלני מבור שאון מטיט היון, a usage which resonates with 1QS 3:2–3.

38 To the extent that his work on purity includes pertinent data, Neusner's groundbreaking departure from this pattern should be acknowledged (1973; 1976–77).

39 For example Driver, who remarks on the Qumran water rites: "Such daily or annual ceremonies were in no way baptisms in the ordinary sense of the term, although they had a certain religious as well as a purely physical purpose." Not one to be remiss, he continues by stating that the sect's practices were not much different from those of other Jews of the time, and he then segues into a discussion of "the Rabbis." Not even John escapes unscathed, however, for "Christian baptism…added a spiritual element which that of John lacked" (1965: 498, 500, 502).

40 "Jesus showed plainly that Pharisaic ceremonial washings had no permanent claims on the conscience…" (Driver 1965: 502). I am using Driver as my straw horse, but his attitudes were typical of scholarship until recently. This kind of dubious scholarship represents the continuance of a much earlier polemic, see Heb 9:25–28; 10:10–14, 18, 22 (cf. Ezek 36:25–27). 1Peter 3:21 is actually cited by Driver (p. 503) to explain the difference between Jewish rites and Christian baptism.

41 Driver goes on to warn (1965: 498) "against attaching *undue value* to *mere rites and ceremonies*, especially to lustration as practised in contemporary Jewish society" [italics added]. Driver, by the way, saw little in common between John and the Sect, but that line of thinking undoubtedly stemmed in no small part from his relatively late dating of the scrolls.

42 See, for example, the study by Rhoads 1992, which, while seemingly well-intended, couches its Christian triumphalism in socio-cultural theory.

43 Driver actually uses the word "mechanical," when he writes that "neither Essenes nor Rabbis had *advanced* beyond the *ritual* requirements of the Pentateuch and their *mechanical* application" (1965: 505). The italics are mine, but Driver's comments speak for themselves. According to Driver, the Qumran Sect, not to be confused with the Essenes, did inject something new into Jewish lustrations, namely the requirement to repent one's sins, without which the rites were inefficacious. He claims that this demonstrates the lustration rites themselves were not really important to the Sect. Of course, it shows nothing of the kind. John, on the other hand, was "the first to make baptism a rite of initiation" (p. 505). I discussed the fallacy of dichotomizing purification and initiation in the "Introduction" to my doctoral dissertation.

44 Recent works emphasizing the need to understand John the Baptist within a Second Temple Jewish context include Webb 1991, especially chapters 4–6, and Taylor (1997), particularly pp. 8, 23, 32, and chapter 2. Neither of these fine studies was yet available

when I first formulated the ideas presented herein. I differ with Taylor in that she does not associate ritual purification with any simultaneous symbolic import (pp. 69–72), and insofar as she believes John's repentance-connected baptism was either unique to him (p. 318, cf. 86), or correlated within Judaism only with the Essenes or 1QS (pp. 79–81). As will be indicated below, I do not believe repentance-connected baptism made John "unique," only distinctive in his special emphasis, or call for re-emphasis, upon a particular aspect of immersion already known to his audience. The idea that rites are not automatically efficacious simply represents the continuation of a well-known prophetic theme, e.g. Isa 1:11–20, 58:3–14; Amos 5:21–24, as Taylor herself notes (pp. 84–86); but while acknowledging that such teachings were the heritage of all Jews, she does not fully follow through on the implications of that realization. The distinction she makes (pp. 87–88) between repenting *before* immersion (John) and *during* (*TestLevi*, *Sybll.Orac.*, and *Apoc.Moses*) only highlights John's emphasis on the sincerity of the repentance (he wants prior proof), as compared with use of immersion as part of a (potentially ostentatious) repentance process. Webb, on the other hand, appreciates that Jews other than Essenes connected penitence with immersion, but his attempt to address John's place in the Christian baptismal trajectory leads him to distinguish—I think artificially—between conversionary and penitential repentance (chapter 6).

45 Sophocles, *Antigone*. My thanks to Prof. Sheila Colwell of the Classics Department, University of Washington in Seattle, for this observation.

46 For further examples of symbolic substitutions for sacrifice, see Spiegel 1993: 64–65.

47 *Aristeas* 304–6 (cf. Josephus, *Antiq*. 12.106). Philo speaks of the correspondence between purity of soul and body (*De Vita Mosis* 2.68), and he echoes Psalms and Isaiah when he writes that the Tabernacle laver was "a symbol…of a blameless life, of years of cleanliness employed in laudable actions, and in straight travelling, not on the rough road or more properly pathless waste of vice, but on the smooth high road through virtue's land" (*De Vita Moses* 2.138, Loeb translation).

48 *B. Berakot* 15a. The altar is drawn from use of Ps 26:6 as a prooftext and is a criticism of handwashing before prayer, a practice probably attested by the presence of lavers at some ancient synagogues.

49 *Vita Mos.* 2.48–52, 80, 88, 96–108, 117, 133–35; *Antiq.* 3.180–87; see further Childs 1974: 537, 547–48. The cosmic implications of the Tabernacle are clear in the association made in Exod 40:2 between its dedication and the creation of the world, see Ibn Ezra on Exod 40:2.

50 For further information about the symbolism inherent in the architectural demarcation of the Temple, see Maier 1990: 67–82.

51 Abrahams 1917: 39–45 and 30–35, respectively; Selkin [Wise] 1993: 1–4 and chapter 7; Baumgarten 1992: 199–209; Webb 1991: 131–32; and Taylor, *The Immerser John the Baptist within Second Temple Judaism* (1997), the title of which establishes her agenda.

52 A typical counter argument dichotomizes the "spiritual metaphors" of the prophets and the spiritual purification to which they supposedly gave birth from the pentateuchal requirements and what might be termed the "purely physical," see, e.g., Driver 1965: 501 and 505.

53 Also 1QS 5:13–14. *M. Ḥagiga* 2:6 and *T. Ḥagiga* 3:2 also require proper intent, but the intention described is to become ritually pure (so as to engage in actions requiring purity), again a nominalist expression, but one countered in aggadic texts like the one cited by Abrahams above.

54 The problem of corrupt administrators of the sacraments (and hence the issue of whether the rites were automatically efficacious regardless) did not become critical within the Church until the 4th-century Donatist controversy. In a related vein, *M. Yoma* 8:9 (within a framework of atonement and purification, we might add, see below) maintains that water does not mechanically purify; it is God who causes the purification to happen.

55 *Quod Deus sit Immutabilis* 7–8 (Loeb).

56 *1 Enoch* 10:22; cf. *Jub.* 7:20–21; Nickelsburg 1986.

57 *Life of Adam and Eve*, *Pirkei de R. Eliezer*, and the fourth Sibylline Oracle were already adduced by Abrahams, "Pharisaic Baptism," 39–40. *Pirkei de R. Eliezer* probably dates to the 8th or 9th century. Although its final form is quite late, it has been described as a text under the influence of Second Temple sources, see Herr 1972 and Friedlander 1981: xxi–lvi.

58 Cited from Greenfield and Stone 1990: 155; Kugler (1996: 57–58 and 72 n. 45) plausibly associates Levi's purification with corpse contamination contracted in the attack on Shechem, but this in no way obviates the prayerful context of the purification; compare Greenfield and Stone, who disassociate the ablution from the following prayer.

59 *Sybll. Orac.* 4:163–70; Collins 1983: 388 n. e2. Collins compares this baptism with that of John and finds them both dissimilar to that of Qumran or the Essenes.

60 As noted also by Baumgarten 1992: 207–8. Baumgarten has further identified a precise parallel between the oracle and 4Q512, col. II, fr. 44, which likewise refers both to water for bathing and outstretched hands.

61 4Q504–6 in Baillet 1982: 137, as discussed by Schiffman 1987: 40–41. According to Schiffman's analysis, the prayers may be daily supplications, in which case the omission of this feature on Saturday is due to the inappropriateness of supplication on the Sabbath.

62 Investigators of fundamentalist Christian conversion are familiar with the extent to which prior sinfulness is exaggerated in order to aggrandize the degree of conversion/salvation/grace entailed.

63 Bell 1992: 85, 108–10. The emphasis is mine.

64 Although Neusner (1976–77: 37–49, pt. 22) perceived this, he was hampered in his further assessment by limited publication of the relevant Qumran materials. Consequently, despite the acknowledged importance of the concept of purity at Qumran, he found only a rudimentary system of purity regulations to support it. In retrospect, the incongruity is telling. On the priestly view of creation through separation (Genesis 1), see Fishbane 1979: 8; Houtman 1984; and Gorman 1990: 39–45, 229–30.

65 1QS 9:8, 8:23; see also 1QS 5:14, 9:5–6; and Sharvit 1980–81: 19–23.

66 11QT, e.g., cols. 46–47.

67 4QMMT, composite text B (*DJD* X), lines 48–49, 80–82.

68 Cited from Qimron and Strugnell 1985: 402; see further *DJD* X, 58–59. Rabin (1957: 28–30) discounted this meaning for the root, preferring to define it as "contact." For our purposes, the difference is not significant. Newton follows Rabin (1985: 19 n. 63, 22 n. 71, and 24 n. 84). Qimron suggests *sexual* separation is meant, but Baumgarten convincingly discounts this (1995: 5); see also Milgrom's remarks (1995: 63).

69 4Q512, fr. 40 and 41 in Baillet 1982: 274; cf. CD 6:17–18, 12:19–20; Lev 10:10, 11:47; Num 16:9 (for the word "לעבד" in fr. 40), 21. The word "impure" usually precedes "pure," often in *chiasmus* with "holy" and "profane." Specifically, the liturgical formula of the purification rite is clearly influenced by the priestly writings of Lev 10:10 and Ezek 22:26 and 42:20. The root בד"ל appears in this sense primarily in the priestly materials, and in Ezra, Nehemiah, and Chronicles. It is found also in 11QT 35:11–13 and 46:17. The affinity of the roots בד"ל and בח"ר, the latter bearing the positive association of being favored with selection and separation for a higher purpose, is seen in Deut 10:8 and 1 Chron 23:13; see further Japhet 1989: 88–91, 122–24.

70 וצונו על הטבילה *Berakot* 51a and *B. Pesaḥim* 7b.

71 *Letter of Aristeas* 106; *M. Sheqalim* 8:2; Rashi on *B. Pesaḥim* 19b; as observed by Lieberman 1967–68: 97–98; Grenfell and Hunt 1908: 12; 11QT 45:1–7; Yadin 1983, vol. 1: 271; and Reich 1980: 225–26. Baumgarten adds that Essenes would have had to avoid all crowds of outsiders, whom they considered impure (1977: 63–65). Grenfell and Hunt provide the Greek text of the Oxyrhynchus fragment with English translation and commentary. An English translation alone is available in Pixner 1976: 271 n. 54. The relevant section has a Pharisee address Jesus "I have bathed myself in the Pool of David and...I have descended...over...steps and come up over other steps..." Grenfell and Hunt (1908: 12) had considered these to be "details invented for...rhetorical effect." Lieberman was the first to associate the papyrus with the *Letter of Aristeas* and *M. Sheqalim*. Pixner (1976: 254) seems to have been the first to associate the papyrus fragment and the *Letter of Aristeas* with the ridge on the steps of some immersion pools. Prior to Pixner, there is evidence of earlier awareness of the ridges on the steps of some pools, with Dupont-Sommer (1955) already suggesting that their purpose was to prevent people with different degrees of purification from mingling. Simultaneously, Brownlee (followed by North), who was also an early supporter of the ritual use of some of the pools at Qumran, suggested that the divisions in the stairs at Qumran might have served as separate passageways. He envisioned monk-like liturgical processions to and from the pools, but remarked that de Vaux responded to him that other "cisterns" elsewhere in the country had such divisions on their steps without any indication of liturgical usage (1957: 39).

72 Pixner 1976: 270–73; Yadin 1983, vol. 1: 271; Reich 1980: 52; 1984; Benoit and Boismard 1951; Brooke 1988: 232; North 1962: 107; Avigad 1984: 142–43, fig. 149; Ben-Dov 1982, photos on 148 and 151; cf. de Vaux 1973: 131 and pl. 16, and 1956: 539–40.

73 Milgrom 1991: 162, 166–67; cf. Frymer-Kensky 1983: 404–5; and Schiffman 1990a: 147. Writes Milgrom in reference to P (1991: 524): "the notion that the same application of the blood of the purification offering can simultaneously decontaminate and consecrate is intrinsically wrong. The realms of impurity and holiness are incompatible with each other and their admixture is lethal.... Impurity and holiness must be kept apart at all costs.... Thus an object must first be emptied of its impurities before it may be sanctified. This necessitates two discrete processes first decontamination and then consecration." In a

similar vein, he discusses why the *Temple Scroll* introduced the sacrifice of a second bull into the High Priest's consecration ceremony: "it allows the altar to be decontaminated and sanctified by a discrete purification bull before the sacrificial series for the priestly consecration commenced..." (1991: 562).

74 Knohl 1991; Schwartz 1992c; cf. Saldarini 1988: 230 n. 75. Knohl was anticipated, albeit with different conclusions, by Alon 1977: 232–34; cf. Zeitlin 1924. Milgrom (1989) disagrees with Alon and sees the critical biblical distinction as resting in P's concern with holiness of the sanctuary vs. H's holiness of the land. Milgrom (1990) finds both minimalist (P) and maximalist (H) positions among the rabbis. Since Milgrom sees no populist overtones, he would presumably also disagree with Knohl on this point.

75 Maier 1989: 51; on the exclusion of gentiles, cf. Schwartz 1992b and 1990: 165–66. Maier describes three controversial occasions of boundary tampering in the Second Temple (Maier 1990: 70–71, 75). Cf. also Anderson 1992: 34.

76 The exclusionary aspects of the priestly concept of ancestry are discussed by Schwartz 1990.

77 Although, as Schwartz points out, *M. Kelim* 1:6–9 moves directly from gentiles to women to Israel without any mention of a category of proselytes.

78 According to Knohl, however, both tendencies originated within the priesthood in the form of P (exclusionary outlook) and H (inclusive), but were continued by the Sadducees/Boethusians/Qumranites on the one hand, and the Pharisees on the other.

79 Knohl 1991: 145–46; 1995, chapters 3–5, particularly p. 224; cf. Schwartz 1992c, esp. 63–66.

80 Paul's sanctification of marriage with an unbelieving partner by virtue of the believing spouse (1 Cor 7:14) bears an abstract resemblance to the purification of the impure pool. On the subject of Paul's view of mixed marriages, see Newton 1985: 105–6. Writes Newton: "through union with the believer the unbeliever is sanctified" (1985: 106) Also, Klawans' (1997) analysis of the defiling force of sin indicates that the *tannaim* compartmentalized ritual and moral impurity, whereas at Qumran the two categories were fused. If Klawans is correct, we would draw the following implications from his work: if one held the view that sinners were also ritually defiling, one would almost *have* to withdraw from society if one wanted to maintain a pure state, particularly if one also held the belief that everyone else *was* a sinner. Tannaitic compartmentalization would have meant that they could remain societally integrated, while still trying to maintain a high standard of holiness. This unifying societal perspective would find later expression in the familiar midrash (*Lev. Rab.* 30:12, commenting on Lev 23:40) concerning the *lulav* and *etrog* as a joint symbol for the four types of Jews with their varying religious strengths and weaknesses, who are nevertheless bound into one people.

81 On the importance of this passage of Ezekiel at Qumran, see Farmer 1956; Wacholder 1993; and Selkin [Wise] 1993: 156–58.

REFERENCES

Abrahams, I.

1917 *Studies in Pharisaism and the Gospels*. Cambridge: Cambridge University.

Alon, G.

1977 The Bounds of the Laws of Levitical Cleanness. Pp. 190–234 in *Jews, Judaism and the Classical World: Studies in Jewish History in the Times of the Second Temple and Talmud*, trans. I. Abrahams. Jerusalem: Magnes.

Anderson, G. A.

1992 The Interpretation of the Purification Offering in the Temple Scroll (11QTemple) and Rabbinic Literature. *Journal of Biblical Literature* 111: 17–35.

Avigad, N.

1984 *Discovering Jerusalem*. Oxford: Blackwell.

Baillet, M.

1982 *Qumran Grotte 4*. Discoveries in the Judaean Desert 7. Oxford: Clarendon.

Baillet, M.; Milik, J. T.; and de Vaux, R.

1962 *Les "Petites Grottes" de Qumran: Exploration de la Falaise, les Grottes 2Q, 3Q, 5Q, 7Q à 10Q, le Rouleau de Cuivre*. Discoveries in the Judaean Desert 3. Oxford: Clarendon.

Baumgarten, J. M.

1972 The Essene Avoidance of Oil and the Laws of Purity. *Revue de Qumran* 8: 183–93. Reprint in *Series in Judaism in Late Antiquity*, ed. J. M. Baumgarten, 1977. Leiden: Brill.

1977 *Studies in Qumran Law*. Leiden: Brill.

1980 The Pharisaic-Sadducean Controversies About Purity and the Qumran Texts. *Journal of Jewish Studies* 31: 157–70.

1992 The Purification Rituals in DJD 7. Pp. 199–209 in *The Dead Sea Scrolls: Forty Years of Research*, eds. D. Dimant and U. Rappaport. Leiden: Brill.

1995 The Laws About Fluxes in 4QTohora (4Q274). Pp. 1–8 in *Time to Prepare the Way in the Wilderness: Papers on the Qumran Scrolls*, eds. D. Dimant and L. H. Schiffman. Studies on the Texts of the Desert of Judah 5. Leiden: Brill.

1996 *Qumrân Cave 4. XIII. the Damascus Document (4Q266–273)*. Discoveries in the Judaean Desert 18. Oxford: Clarendon.

Bell, C. M.

1992 *Ritual Theory, Ritual Practice*. New York, NY: Oxford University.

Ben-Dov, M.

1982 *In the Shadow of the Temple: The Discovery of Ancient Jerusalem*, trans. I. Friedman. New York, NY: Harper & Row.

Benoit, P., and Boismard, M.-E.

1951 Un Ancien Sanctuaire Chrétien à Béthanie. *Revue Biblique* 58: 204–5.

Brooke, G. J.

1988 The Temple Scroll and the Archaeology of Qumran, 'Ain Feshkha and Masada. *Revue de Qumran* 13: 225–37.

Brownlee, W. H.

1957 John the Baptist in the New Light of the Ancient Scrolls. Pp. 33–53 in *The Scrolls and the New Testament*, ed. K. Stendahl. New York, NY: Harper.

Childs, B. S.

1974 *The Book of Exodus: A Critical, Theological Commentary*. Philadelphia, PA: Westminster.

Collins, J.

1983 Sibylline Oracles. Pp. 317–472 in *The Old Testament Pseudepigrapha*, vol. 1, ed. J. H. Charlesworth. Garden City, NY: Doubleday.

de Vaux, R.

1956 Fouilles de Khirbet Qumrân. Rapport préliminaire sue les 3e, 4e, et 5e campagnes. *Revue Biblique* 63: 533–77.

1973 *Archaeology and the Dead Sea Scrolls*. London: Oxford University.

Driver, G. R.

1965 *The Judaean Scrolls: The Problem and a Solution*. New York, NY: Schocken.

Dupont-Sommer, A.

1955 Interventions à Propos de la Communication de M. Parrot. *Revue d'Histoire et de Philosophie Religieuses* 35: 65–67.

Elman, Y.

1996 Some Remarks on 4QMMT and the Rabbinic Tradition: Or, When is a Parallel Not a Parallel? Pp. 99–128 in *Reading 4QMMT: New Perspectives on Qumran Law and Literature*, eds. J. Kampen and M. J. Bernstein. Atlanta, GA: Scholars.

Eshel, H., and Meyers, E. M.

2000 The Pools of Sepphoris – Ritual Baths or Bathtubs? *Biblical Archaeology Review* 26: 42–49, 60–61.

Farmer, W. R.

1956 The Geography of Ezekiel's River of Life. *Biblical Archaeologist* 19: 17–22.

Finkelstein, L.

1962 *The Pharisees: The Sociological Background of Their Faith*. Philadelphia, PA: Jewish Publication Society of America.

Fishbane, M.

1979 *Text and Texture: Close Readings of Selected Biblical Texts*. New York, NY: Schocken.

Friedlander, G.

1981 *Pirke de Rabbi Eliezer (The Chapters of Rabbi Eliezer the Great) According to the Text of the Manuscript Belonging to Abraham Epstein of Vienna*. New York, NY: Sepher-Hermon.

Frymer-Kensky, T.

1983 Pollution, Purification, and Purgation in Biblical Israel. Pp. 399–414 in *The Word of the Lord Shall Go Forth: Essays in Honor of David Noel Freedman in Celebration of His Sixtieth Birthday*, eds. C. L. Meyers and M. P. O'Connor. Winona Lake, IN: Eisenbrauns.

García Martínez, F.

1994 *The Dead Sea Scrolls Translated: The Qumran Texts in English*, ed. F. García Martínez, trans. W. G. Watson. Leiden: Brill.

Ginzberg, L.

1976 *An Unknown Jewish Sect*. New York, NY: Jewish Theological Seminary of America.

Goldin, J.

1949 The Period of the Talmud. Pp. 115–215 in *The Jews: Their History, Culture, and Religion*, vol. 1, ed. L. Finkelstein. Philadelphia, PA: Jewish Publication Society of America.

Gorman, F. H.

1990 *The Ideology of Ritual: Space, Time, and Status in the Priestly Theology*. Journal for the Study of the Old Testament Supplement 91. Sheffield: Journal for the Study of the Old Testament.

Grabbe, L. L.

1997 4QMMT and Second Temple Jewish Society. Pp. 89–108 in *Legal Texts and Legal Issues: Proceedings of the Second Meeting of the International Organization for Qumran Studies, Cambridge 1995, Published in Honour of Joseph M. Baumgarten*, eds. M. Bernstein, F. García Martínez and J. Kampen. Leiden: Brill.

Greenfield, J. C., and Stone, M. E.

1990 Two Notes on the Aramaic Levi Document. Pp. 153–61 in *Of Scribes and Scrolls: Studies on the Hebrew Bible, Intertestamental Judaism, and Christian Origins Presented to John Strugnell on the Occasion of His Sixtieth Birthday*, eds. H. W. Attriedge, J. J. Collins and T. H. Tobin. Lanham, MD: University Press of America.

Grenfell, B. P., and Hunt, A. S.

1908 *Fragment of an Uncanonical Gospel from Oxyrhynchus*. London: Oxford University.

Guttmann, A.

1970 *Rabbinic Judaism in the Making: A Chapter in the History of the Halakhah from Ezra to Judah I*. Detroit, MI: Wayne State University.

Herr, D.

1972 Pirkei De-Rabbi Eliezer. Pp. 558–60 in *Encyclopedia Judaica*, vol. 13. Jerusalem: Encyclopedia Judaica.

Houtman, C.

1984 Another Look at Forbidden Mixtures. *Vetus Testamentum* 34: 226–28.

Japhet, S.

1989 *The Ideology of the Book of Chronicles and Its Place in Biblical Thought*, trans. A. Barber. Beiträge zur Erforschung des Alten Testaments und des Antiken Judentums 9. Frankfurt am Main: Lang.

Klawans, J.

1997 The Impurity of Immorality in Ancient Judaism. *Journal of Jewish Studies* 48: 1–16.

Knohl, I.

1991 Participation of the People in the Temple Worship – Second Temple Sectarian Conflict and the Biblical Tradition (Hebrew). *Tarbiz* 60: 139–46.

1995 *The Sanctuary of Silence: The Priestly Torah and the Holiness School*. Minneapolis, MN: Fortress.

Kugler, R. A.

1996 *From Patriarch to Priest: The Levi-Priestly Tradition from Aramaic Levi to Testament of Levi*. Early Judaism and Its Literature 9. Atlanta, GA: Scholars.

Lévi-Strauss, C.

1995 *Myth and Meaning: Cracking the Code of Culture*. New York, NY: Schocken.

Lieberman, S.

1942 *Greek in Jewish Palestine: Studies in the Life and Manners of Jewish Palestine in the II–IV Centuries C.E.* New York, NY: Jewish Theological Seminary of America.

1967–68 Notes. Pp. 97–107 in *P'raqim: Yearbook of the Schocken Institute for Jewish Research of the Jewish Theological Seminary of America*, vol. 1, ed. E. S. Rosenthal. Jerusalem: Schocken.

Maier, J.

1989 The Architectural History of the Temple in Jerusalem in the Light of the Temple Scroll. Pp. 23–62 in *Temple Scroll Studies. Papers Presented at the International Symposium on the Temple Scroll, Manchester, December 1987*, ed. G. J. Brooke. Journal for the Study of the Pseudepigrapha Supplement 7. Sheffield: Sheffield Academic.

1990 The Temple Scroll and Tendencies in the Cultic Architecture of the Second Commonwealth. Pp. 67–82 in *Archaeology and History in the Dead Sea Scrolls, The New York University Conference in Memory of Yigael Yadin*, ed. L. Schiffman. Journal for the Study of the Pseudepigrapha Supplement 8. Sheffield: Journal for the Study of the Old Testament.

Meyers, C. L., and Meyers, E. M.

1987 Haggai, Zechariah 1–8. Pp. 187–89 in *Anchor Bible Dictionary*, vol. 3, ed. D. N. Freedman. Garden City, NY: Doubleday.

Meyers, E. M.

1976 Galilean Regionalism as a Factor in Historical Reconstruction. *Bulletin of the American Schools of Oriental Research* 221: 93–101.

Meyers, E. M., and Strange, J. F.

1981 *Archaeology, the Rabbis, and Early Christianity: The Social and Historical Setting of Palestinian Judaism and Christianity*. Nashville, TN: Abingdon.

Meyers, E. M., and White, L. M.

1989 Jews and Christians in a Roman World. *Archaeology* 42: 26–33.

Milgrom, J.

1989 The Qumran Cult: Its Exegetical Principles. Pp. 165–80 in *Temple Scroll Studies. Papers Presented at the International Symposium on the Temple Scroll, Manchester, December 1987*, ed. G. J. Brooke. Sheffield: Journal for the Study of the Old Testament.

1990 The Scriptural Foundations and Deviations in the Laws of Purity and the Temple Scroll. Pp. 83–99 in *Archaeology and History in the Dead Sea Scrolls, The New York University Conference in Memory of Yigael Yadin*, ed. L. Schiffman. Sheffield: Journal for the Study of the Old Testament.

1991 Deviations from Scripture in the Purity Laws of the Temple Scroll. Pp. 159–67 in *Jewish Civilization in the Hellenistic-Roman Period*, ed. S. Talmon. Philadelphia, PA: Trinity International.

1995 4QTohora: An Unpublished Qumran Text on Purities. Pp. 59–68 in *Time to Prepare the Way in the Wilderness : Papers on the Qumran Scrolls*, eds. D. Dimant and L. H. Schiffman. Studies on the Texts of the Desert of Judah 63. Leiden: Brill.

Netzer, E.

1982 Ancient Ritual Baths (Miqvaot) in Jericho. Pp. 106–19 in *The Jerusalem Cathedra*, vol.2, ed. L. I. Levine. Jerusalem: Yad Izhak Ben-Zvi.

Neusner, J.

1973 *The Idea of Purity in Ancient Judaism: The Haskell Lectures, 1972–1973*. Studies in Judaism in Late Antiquity 1. Leiden: Brill.

1976–77 *A History of the Mishnaic Law of Purities*. Studies in Judaism in Late Antiquity 6. Leiden: Brill.

Newton, M.

1985 *The Concept of Purity at Qumran and in the Letters of Paul*. Cambridge: Cambridge University.

Nickelsburg, G. W.

1986 1 Enoch and Qumran Origins: The State of the Question and Some Prospects for Answers. *Society of Biblical Literature Seminar Papers* 25: 349.

North, R.

1962 The Qumran Reservoirs. Pp. 100–132 in *The Bible in Current Catholic Thought*, ed. J. L. McKenzie. New York, NY: Herder and Herder.

Pfann, S. J.

1997 4Q249 Midrash Sefer Moshe. Pp. 11–18 in *Legal Texts and Legal Issues: Proceedings of the Second Meeting of the International Organization for Qumran Studies, Cambridge 1995, Published in Honour of Joseph M. Baumgarten*, eds. M. Bernstein, F. García Martínez and J. Kampen. Leiden: Brill.

Pixner, B.

1976 An Essene Quarter on Mount Zion? Pp. 245–84 in *Studia Hierosolymitana in Onore del P. Bellarmino Bagatti I. Studi Archeologici*. Studium Biblicum Franciscanum Collectio Maior 22. Jerusalem: Franciscan.

Poirer, J. C.

1996 Why Did the Pharisees Wash Their Hands? *Journal of Jewish Studies* 47: 217–33.

Qimron, E.

1986 *The Hebrew of the Dead Sea Scrolls*. Harvard Semitic Studies 29. Atlanta, GA: Scholars.

1992 The Text of CDC. Pp. 9–49 in *The Damascus Document Reconsidered*, ed. M. Broshi. Jerusalem: Israel Exploration Society.

Qimron, E., and Strugnell, J.

1985 An Unpublished Halakhic Letter from Qumran. Pp. 400–407 in *Biblical Archaeology Today*, ed. J. Amitai. Jerusalem: Israel Exploration Society.

1994 *Qumrân Cave 4. V: Miqsat Ma'ase Ha-Torah*. Discoveries in the Judaean Desert 10. Oxford: Clarendon.

Rabin, C.

1957 *Qumran Studies*. Scripta Judaica 2. London: Oxford University.

1958 *The Zadokite Documents: I. The Admonition. II. The Laws*. Oxford: Clarendon.

Reich, R.

1980 Mishnah, Sheqalim 8:2 and the Archaeological Evidence. Pp. 225–56 in *Jerusalem in the Second Temple Period: Abraham Schalit Memorial Volume*, eds. A. Oppenheimer, U. Rappaport and M. Stern. Sifriyah Le Toldot Ha Yishuv Ha Yehudi Be Erets Yisrael. Jerusalem: Yad Izhak Ben-Zvi.

1981 Archaeological Evidence of the Jewish Population at Hasmonean Gezer. *Israel Exploration Journal* 31: 48–52.

1984 A Miqweh at 'Isawiya Near Jerusalem. *Israel Exploration Journal* 34: 220–23.

Rhoads, D.

1992 Social Criticism: Crossing Boundaries. Pp. 135–61 in *Mark and Method: New Approaches in Biblical Studies*, eds. J. C. Anderson and S. D. Moore. Minneapolis, MN: Fortress.

Saldarini, A. J.

1988 *Pharisees, Scribes and Sadducees in Palestinian Society: A Sociological Approach*. Wilmington, DE: Glazier.

Sanders, E. P.

1990 *Jewish Law from Jesus to the Mishnah: Five Studies*. Philadelphia, PA: Trinity International.

Schechter, S.
1970 *Documents of Jewish Sectaries*. Reprint of 1910 edition. New York, NY: Ktav.

Schiffman, L. H.
1987 The Dead Sea Scrolls and the Early History of Jewish Liturgy. Pp. 33–48 in *The Synagogue in Late Antiquity*, ed. L. I. Levine. Philadelphia, PA: Journal of Theological Studies.
1990a The Impurity of the Dead in the Temple Scroll. Pp. 135–56 in *Archaeology and History in the Dead Sea Scrolls: The New York University Conference in Memory of Yigael Yadin*, ed. L. H. Schiffman. Sheffield: Journal for the Study of the Old Testament.
1990b The Significance of the Scrolls. *Bible Review* 6: 18–27, 52.
1992 New Light on the Pharisees: Insights from the Dead Sea Scrolls. *Bible Review* 8: 30–33, 54.

Schwartz, D. R.
1984 Philo's Priestly Descent. Pp. 165–71 in *Nourished with Peace: Studies in Hellenistic Judaism in Memory of Samuel Sandmel*, eds. F. E. Greenspahn, E. Hilgert and B. L. Mack. Chico, CA: Scholars.
1990 On Two Aspects of a Priestly View of Descent at Qumran. Pp. 157–79 in *Archaeology and History in the Dead Sea Scrolls, The New York University Conference in Memory of Yigael Yadin*, ed. L. H. Schiffman. Journal for the Study of the Pseudepigrapha Supplement 8. Sheffield: Journal for the Study of the Old Testament.
1992a Law and Truth: On Qumran-Sadducean and Rabbinic Views of Law. Pp. 229–40 in *The Dead Sea Scrolls: Forty Years of Research*, eds. D. Dimant and U. Rappaport. Studies on the Texts of the Desert of Judah 10. Leiden: Brill.
1992b On Sacrifice by Gentiles in the Temple of Jerusalem. Pp. 102–16 in *Studies in the Jewish Background of Christianity*, ed. C. Rose. Wissenschaftliche Untersuchungen zum Neuen Testament 60. Tübingen: Mohr.
1992c 'Kingdom of Priests' – A Pharisaic Slogan? Pp. 56–66 in *Studies in the Jewish Background of Christianity*, ed. C. Rose. Wissenschaftliche Untersuchungen zum Neuen Testament 60. Tübingen: Mohr.

Selkin [Wise], C. B.
1993 Exegesis and Identity: The Hermeneutics of Miqwa'ôt in the Greco-Roman Period. Unpublished Ph.D. dissertation. Duke University.

Sharvit, B.
1980–81 Impurity and Purity According to the Dead Sea Sect (Hebrew). *Beth Mikra* 26: 18–27.

Sokoloff, M.
1990 *A Dictionary of Jewish Palestine Aramaic of the Byzantine Period*. Dictionaries of Talmud, Midrash and Targum 2. Ramat-Gan, Israel: Bar Ilan University.

Spiegel, S.
1993 *The Last Trial: On the Legends and Lore of the Command to Abraham to Offer Isaac as a Sacrifice. The Akedah*, trans. J. Goldin. Woodstock, VT: Jewish Lights.

Sussmann, Y.
1989–90 The History of Halakha and the Dead Sea Scrolls: Preliminary Observations on Miqsat Ma'ase Ha-Torah (4QMMT). *Tarbiz* 59: 11–76 (Hebrew).

Taylor, J. E.
1997 *The Immerser: John the Baptist Within Second Temple Judaism*. Grand Rapids, MI: Eerdmans.

Urbach, E. E.
1987 *The Sages: Their Concepts and Beliefs*, Hebrew/English, trans. I. Abrahams. Cambridge, MA: Harvard University.

Wacholder, B. Z.
1993 Geomessianism: Why Did the Essenes Settle at Qumran. Pp. 131–38 in *Bits of Honey: Essays for Samson H. Levey*, eds. S. F. Chyet and D. H. Ellenson. South Florida Studies in the History of Judaism 74. Atlanta, GA: Scholars.

Webb, R. L.
1991 *John the Baptizer and Prophet: A Socio-Historical Study*. Journal for the Study of the New Testament Supplement 62. Sheffield: Journal for the Study of the New Testament.

Wood, B. G.
1984 To Dip or Sprinkle? The Qumran Cisterns in Perspective. *Bulletin of the American Schools of Oriental Research* 256: 45–60.

Yadin, Y.
1983 *The Temple Scroll*. Jerusalem: Israel Exploration Society.

Zeitlin, S.
1924 The Halaka in the Gospels and Its Relation to the Jewish Law at the Time of Jesus. *Hebrew Union College Annual* 1: 365–66.

Chapter 17

The Stepped Water Installations of the Sepphoris Acropolis

by Katharina Galor

One of the highest concentrations of stepped pools in Palestine has been uncovered on the Western Acropolis at Sepphoris. A total of twenty pools are spread over an area measuring approximately 3100 m^2. When discovered some fifteen years ago, this find was considered unique, both in terms of the pools' locations and their dating.[1] Since then, the discovery of similar structures in comparable contexts has proven that this site does not represent an anomaly. The use of stepped pools in domestic structures far from the Jerusalem Temple extends into the early Byzantine period at Sepphoris and beyond at other Palestinian sites. Although archaeologists are no longer surprised to encounter stepped pools, their uses and functions have caused more interpretational controversies than any other architectural element. While the excavators of the Sepphoris Acropolis have continuously referred to them as *miqva'ot*, others have disputed the pools' ritual character.[2] This recent debate on the Sepphorean pools reflects a general tendency in discussions on stepped pools: maximalists view most stepped pools as serving for ritual immersion, while minimalists oppose the pools' religious significance without offering an alternative function.[3]

MIQVEH OR STEPPED POOL — ETYMOLOGICAL CLARIFICATIONS

Without negating the possibility that most of the Sepphorean stepped pools were built and used for ritual immersion, I have chosen to replace the commonly used term of *miqveh* with "stepped pool." One of the first stepped pools was excavated at Masada by Yadin (1966: 164–67) in the 1960s. Rabbi Muntzberg's statement that this pool conformed to the halachic prescriptions of a ritual bath seemed to justify the use of the term *miqveh*. Since then, most stepped pools excavated in similar contexts (that is, most pools of the late Hellenistic, Roman and Byzantine periods in Palestine) have been designated as *miqva'ot*.[4] In my view, given the historically evolving and changing character of the word *miqveh*, this designation is problematic.

Literally translated, the word *miqveh* means "collection" or "collected mass," generally, but not always, of water. Examples can be found in Gen 1:10, Ex 7:9, Lev 11:36, and Isa 22:11. In biblical contexts, *miqveh* most frequently refers to a natural body or source of water that can eliminate impurities from people or objects. In Leviticus and Numbers, the word *miqveh* is usually associated with issues of purity and impurity. It can, however, be used in a context that is not connected with these issues. In Isa 22:1, for example, the word *miqveh* designates a pond: "You made also a pond between the two walls for the water of the old pool." It is only in Rabbinic literature that a *miqveh* designates an artificial installation built for the purpose of ritual purity. Discussions of ritual pools usually refer to Tohorot, in which an entire tractate is devoted to halachic discussions on *miqva'ot*.[5] Though the most commonly performed activity in a *miqveh* is obviously ritual immersion, it is not the only act. For example, in Miqva'ot 7:3 we read that rinsing food in a *miqveh* would not necessarily alter the ritual character of the water, provided that it stayed clear in color:

> If one rinsed in it [an immersion-pool] baskets of olives and baskets of grapes, and they changed its colors, it is valid.... If wine and olive-sap fell into it and changed its color, it is unfit. What should one do? He should wait on it until rain falls and its color returns to the color of water.

It should also be stressed that most of the qualities and rules that apply to ritual immersion pools apply to other bodies of water contained in natural depressions or containers, or built installations, such as cisterns and wells. In Miqva'ot 1:4 it is stated that

> all the same are [or in other words, the same rules apply to] (1) water of ponds, (2) water of cisterns, (3) water of ditches, (4) water of caverns, (5) water of rain-drippings which have stopped, and (6) immersion-pools which do not contain forty *seahs*: during the rainy season, all are clean.

In the Rabbinic context, the word *miqveh* can be viewed to some extent as the religious qualification attributed to a variety of depressions or constructions that can hold water and have the ability to purify. In Talmudic literature, the word *miqveh* does not exclusively designate a stepped pool.

Later definitions of *miqva'ot* are also instructive. The chronological gap in the archaeological data from Israel and the Diaspora, from the Early Islamic period (mid-seventh century C.E.) until around 1200, forces us to advance to the Middle Ages. Literary and archaeological evidence indicates that in medieval Europe the *miqveh* represented one of the most important institutions within the Jewish community.[6] In *meshib Dabar* 2:45, we learn that in urgent cases it was even permitted to sell a synagogue in order to erect a *miqveh*. Medieval *miqva'ot* were mainly built for the purposes of ritual immersion. However, in many instances they served as bathhouses, because of the order forbidding Jews to wash in the rivers together with Christians.[7]

We can, thus, conclude that only in modern times did the term *miqveh* come to designate an installation that is solely used for ritual purification of a person or an object. The functional development of this installation requires that one make a clear distinction between the modern and ancient terms and the specific installation being described.

STEPPED POOLS AND OTHER PLASTERED INSTALLATIONS

Archaeologically speaking, the stepped pools belong to a larger category of plaster-covered installations, built and used for different purposes. The relatively homogenous appearance of plaster used for different kinds of installations within any given site requires a careful cross-examination of both the plaster application and the installation in question.

Plaster

The plaster usually covers the entire installation and is applied regularly in several layers. The first, coarse layer is used to even out irregular surfaces. The last, or outer, surface layer tends to be composed of significantly smaller particles, making the texture much smoother. Unlike Reich's research (1990: 63), which suggested that *miqva'ot* or stepped pools were more frequently replastered than other plastered installations, the data from Sepphoris and other Palestinian sites indicate that the quantity of plaster layers is equally distributed among various installation types. In fact, in the Western Acropolis at Sepphoris we observed many more layers of plaster applied to installations used for industrial purposes than in the stepped pools. Stepped pools are usually covered with three layers of plaster. In contrast, the vats used for industrial purposes can be covered with up to eight successive layers. The technology of producing plaster remained relatively constant from the Hellenistic to the Late Roman period.[8] In general, the process of preparing plaster consisted of burning crushed chalk or limestone, which produced powdered quicklime. An aggregate mixture of crushed rock, sometimes sand, and, finally, water was subsequently added to this material, which, owing to chemical reactions, resulted in a lime putty or hydraulic plaster. The composition of the aggregates and, therefore, the quality and appearance of the plaster vary slightly, depending on the availability of the local material. The primary function of hydraulic plaster is to render the installation impermeable, to prevent it from deteriorating through constant or frequent contact with water, and to assure the water quality within.

Types of Installations

Installations covered with hydraulic plaster can be grouped in three different categories: (1) installations that were built to convey water from a water source to a container or reservoir, or from one container to another; (2) installations that were used for storing water fulfilling primary needs, such as drinking and irrigation; and (3) installations that contained water satisfying secondary needs, that is, leisure or luxury oriented activities, or activities of a religious nature. Installations of the first category are aqueducts and various types of channels and pipes. Examples in the Palestinian context include the aqueducts at Caesarea (Everman 1992), and the "high-level aqueduct" to Jerusalem in the Bethlehem area (Mazar 1990). Wells and cisterns, which form the second category, are illustrated by the grandiose desert installations found at the fortresses of Alexandrion, Dok, Kypros, Hyrcania, Herodion, Masada, and Machaerus (Garbrecht and Peleg 1992). The most common types of installations used to fulfill secondary needs were public nymphea and bathhouses, swimming pools, bathtubs, and, finally, stepped pools. It might appear difficult to find a common denominator for such grandiose structures as the nymphaeum of Jerash (Browning 1982: 143–47) and the bathhouses of Beth-Shean (Mazor 1988; Tsafrir et al. 1990) on the one hand, and the small and unattractive stepped pools on the other hand. It is, however, important to stress that neither type of installation was built and used to fulfill primary needs; neither was conceived to fulfill/respond to basic subsistence requirements.

The average quantity of water required to satisfy our primary needs, that is, drinking and irrigation, has obviously not changed since antiquity. Human water consumption in the Galilee, depending on the amount of physical labor, can vary between a low of 1.5 liters per day in winter and a high of 6 liters per day in summer (Schilman 2000: 74). The quantity used for satisfying secondary needs, that is, leisure or luxury oriented activities, or activities of a religious nature, is far more flexible and, therefore, more difficult to measure. The frequency of bathing, for example, was influenced not only by the availability of water, but also by social status. Generally, in the ancient Near East, most people contented themselves with washing only their faces, hands, and feet. The religious habits of the Egyptians, the Babylonians, and the Hebrews seem to have dictated more frequent bathing.[9]

Most washing and bathing activities took place in containers that were not built-in or permanent structures (Krauss 1910: 208–33; Reich 1990: 126–41). They were movable and could generally be transported easily from one place to another. Therefore, the archaeological record is biased towards stepped pools and bathtubs, since other types of containers broke and disintegrated more easily.

PLASTERED INSTALLATIONS AT SEPPHORIS

The various types of plastered installations found at Sepphoris served a wide range of different functions, reflecting the multi-faceted character of the city. An impressive system of tunnels, channels, and aqueducts, which brought fresh water to the city from the first to seventh centuries C.E. has been explored by Tsuk (1996; 2000: 35–40). The oldest aqueduct was dated to the early first century C.E., and an additional one was built during the following century. One of the channels diverted water into an open pool which, according to Tsuk, might have served as a swimming pool. Another channel debouched into a cavernous reservoir, the most impressive feature of the entire water system. At least one more plaster-lined swimming pool has been exposed as part of Strange's excavation. The public bathhouses found in Strange's and Weiss' excavations were equipped with a large number of pools and rooms, with surfaces that had to be protected by impermeable materials. Here, the mosaic or *opus sectile* techniques were well-suited to the ostentatious character of the place. Only installations of secondary importance were lined with ordinary gray plaster. The reports in progress will determine the exact dates of these installations within the context of the late Roman and Byzantine periods.

STEPPED POOLS AND CISTERNS AT THE SEPPHORIS ACROPOLIS

A high concentration of plaster-lined installations is located on the western summit of the Sepphoris Acropolis. The excavation of this primarily residential area has been conducted by the Joint Sepphoris Project (JSP) between 1985–92, and from 1993 until the present by the Sepphoris Regional Project (SRP). The JSP was directed by Carol L. Meyers, Eric M. Meyers and Ehud Netzer; the SRP by Carol L. Meyers and Eric M. Meyers until 1997. Since the last season (2000), an extension of the latter project has been conducted under the direction of Jonathan Reed.

Methodological Concerns

Prior to considering the Sepphorean installations from a technical point of view, I would like to raise two problems concerned with the study of the stepped pools, both on the Western Acropolis and in general. One concerns the difficulties associated with the proper use of the literary evidence on *miqva'ot*, and the other is connected to the problematic nature of the archaeological evidence of stepped pools.

Appropriate use of historical evidence on *miqva'ot* should consist of applying the external source as a supplement, rather than as a substitute or point of departure for the internal, archaeological evidence. The wealth of relevant literary accounts can hardly be ignored and should not be neglected in the study of contemporary evidence of plastered installations. Issues of purity and ritual immersion are treated in detail in Talmudic literature. The Mishnaic law of Purities accounts for about one quarter of Rabbinic literature—obviously an important theme to the rabbis, even after the destruction of the Temple. This written evidence should, however, not be treated as a point of departure and as a primary source for the interpretation of stepped pools. Nor should the archaeological material be treated as secondary evidence, conditioned to fit into the literary framework. Unfortunately, this approach has determined the trend of archaeological research of stepped pools ever since the identification of the Masada pools in the 1960s. Reich's typological study of "Second Temple period *miqva'ot*" laid the groundwork for this approach. This is particularly problematic in light of his exclusive consideration of post-70-C.E. textual evidence for the interpretation of pre-70-C.E. material evidence. Regardless of how appropriate using the Talmudic evidence as a point of departure appears to be, both from a chronological and thematic point of view, and particularly with respect to the Sepphorean pools, this study uses the latter as supportive, additional evidence to the primary, archaeological data.

In spite of the more careful and somewhat restricted use of the textual evidence I apply in this study, the use and interpretation of the relevant archaeological material constitutes a problem in itself. Just as with most plastered installations that are dug into rock, the archaeologist is limited when trying to establish fixed dates for the installations' times of construction and the periods they went out of use. One can only approximate the date when these pools went out of use by examining the fill, or by determining the date of a later structure that blocks access to the pool. The structural relationship between the pool and its immediate architectural context can also be helpful in answer-

Fig. 1 *Plan of the Western Acropolis at Sepphoris.*

ing chronological questions. There is no doubt, however, that the chronological data will be less precise for these pools than for other structural or architectural elements.

Technical Aspects

As the stepped pools are part of a larger group of cavities dug into the ground and tend to be confused with other installations, I have categorized them using the following nomenclature: SP for the stepped pools, C for cisterns, S for storage places, and V for vats or installations that have one step or no steps (fig. 1). Despite the fact that some of the cavities seem to have been conceived as cisterns but subsequently transformed into storage places,[10] this change in function can be almost certainly excluded from other installations. That is, not every S was originally built and used as a storage place. In contrast, each stepped and plastered pool has always belonged to the category of SP.

Chronological, Typological and Contextual Classification

A chronological, typological, and contextual classification of the stepped pools will help us to answer some of the most intriguing questions about their functional significance. The preliminary and partially incomplete state of the general stratigraphic reports will almost certainly require readjustments and corrections of this description and analysis for the final report.

The Western Acropolis excavation has uncovered a total of twenty stepped pools within an area measuring approximately 3100 m². The habitable space of the general surface, excluding roads and alleyways, is about 2900 m² (ca. 93.5 %). We can thus calculate that, on average, each pool supplies a domestic space that measures 11.23 × 11.23 m.

Chronologically, the stepped pools cover a time span of almost 700 years; the earliest pools were built around 100 B.C.E. and the latest during the

Fig. 2 *Sepphoris stepped pool 1.*

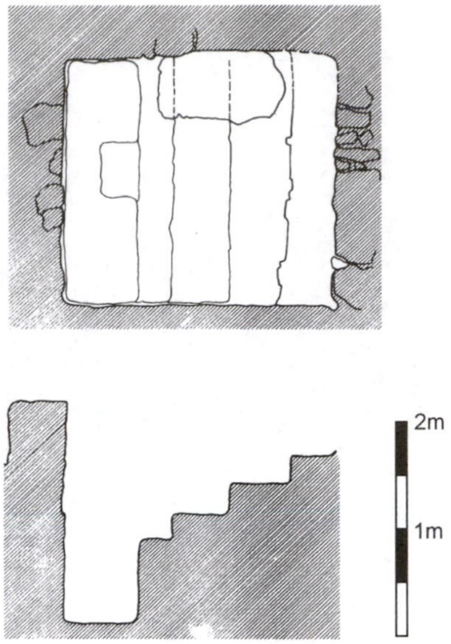

Fig. 3 *Sepphoris stepped pool 2.*

Late Roman period (that is, some time between 280–363 C.E.). Most were used until the earthquake of 363 C.E. Only two pools remained in use until the Late Byzantine or Early Islamic period. The earliest pools were uncovered in Unit I and were built within the perimeter of the fortified building. While the original Hellenistic building was constructed some time around 200 B.C.E., the additions of SP 1, SP 2 and SP 3 (figs. 2–4) fall into a refurbishing phase that took place around the year 100 B.C.E.—additions that did not alter the fortified character of the building. Historically, the construction of these pools falls into the period when Sepphoris was a Hasmonaean city. Thus, the building of the stepped pools could reflect the takeover of the Seleucid building by the Hasmonaeans. During the Early Roman period, the fortress area was transformed into a residential settlement, spreading far beyond its former limits. A two-meter-wide road led westward down the slope of the acropolis, evolving into an axis along which the residential grid on the western slope was oriented. Most of the stepped pools distributed throughout the new residential area, including Units II to VII, were built towards the beginning of the Early Roman period (during the second half of the first century B.C.E.). The complete absence of pools built during the Middle Roman period must be related to the general lack of structural remains from this period. It has been suggested that the Late Roman refurbishing activity included the clearing of Middle Roman occupational remains. Following this chronological/stratigraphical blank, an additional phase of construction of stepped pools took place during the Late Roman period. Only two pools remained in use slightly beyond the Late Roman period. The abandonment of most stepped pools after the earthquake of 363 C.E. suggests that the area was taken over by inhabitants of another cultural and, possibly, different religious orientation. Since, at this point, the aqueducts had already supplied the city with additional water for about 300 years, it is unlikely that this change in use of the stepped pools was correlated to the necessity of increasing or decreasing storage capacity for drinking or even bathing water. Chronologically speaking, the abandonment of most stepped pools coincides with the introduction of pig bones. It was after the earthquake of 363 C.E. that the latter made their appearance in this area of the city. The presence of stepped pools and the absence of pig bones during the Roman period would, therefore, suggest that the people who inhabited this particular area of the city lived according to Jewish precepts. These precepts included using the stepped pools for ritual immersion and abstaining from eating pig.

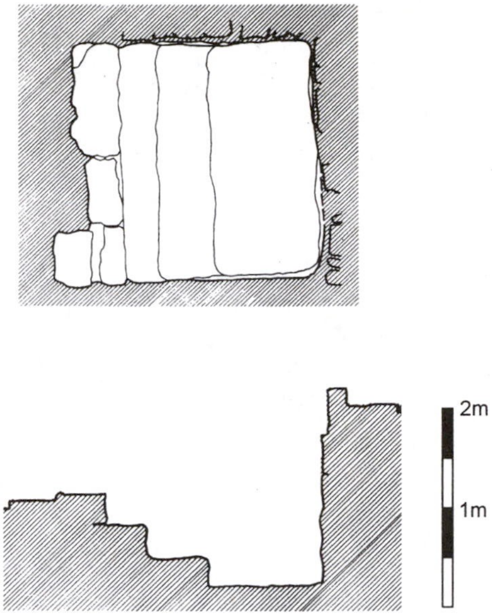

Fig. 4 Sepphoris stepped pool 3.

Fig. 5 Sepphoris stepped pool 4.

Typologically, we can subdivide the stepped pools into two main groups. One group includes pools that could hold between approximately 500 and 4000 liters of water, and the other includes pools that could hold between 4000 and 8000 liters of water. Estimates for how many liters equal 40 *seahs* vary from 250 to 1000 liters of water. Thus, even the pools of the smaller category were able to hold at least twice as much as the minimal estimation of 40 *seahs*. The smaller pools were clearly reserved for individual use, whereas the larger ones were most likely used by several people. Despite the fact that all the large pool types were built during the Hellenistic period and the smaller pool types were built during the Roman period, the chronological factor might not be the only determinant. The public nature of the Hellenistic building can hardly be compared to the private character of the domestic quarter. Other than the approximate volume and depth of the pools, the presence of steps, and the plaster applications covering the entire installation, no feature seems to follow strict rules from one pool to another. The general shape of the pools, the number of steps, whether the steps lead straight into the pools or turn (once or twice), and whether the steps cover the entire width of the installations or only part seem totally random. The general shape and appearance of these pools was obviously not confined by any aesthetic or stylistic rules. They merely had to fit into a given space and serve their purpose. It is quite likely that all the pools were originally supplied by rainwater channeled in from the exterior, possibly from the roof. Since, however, only three such channels have survived in our excavation – one channel in proximity to SP 4 (fig. 5) and C 3, one located next to SP 10 (fig. 6), and another one close to SP 18 – supply methods remain speculative.

A close examination of the location of the stepped pools within their architectural context indicates that they could be located almost randomly under a building's roof. In addition to the ceiling of the surrounding architectural space, the pool was independently protected from above. Beyond assuring privacy and preventing the water from getting dirty and overgrown with algae, the separate vaulted or flat covering structures of these installations transformed them into quasi-independent units. In Unit I, SP 2 and SP 3, as well as SP 8 (fig. 7) in Unit IV take up the entire space of the room. Sometimes, however, additional space surrounding the pool is available. This space could be either

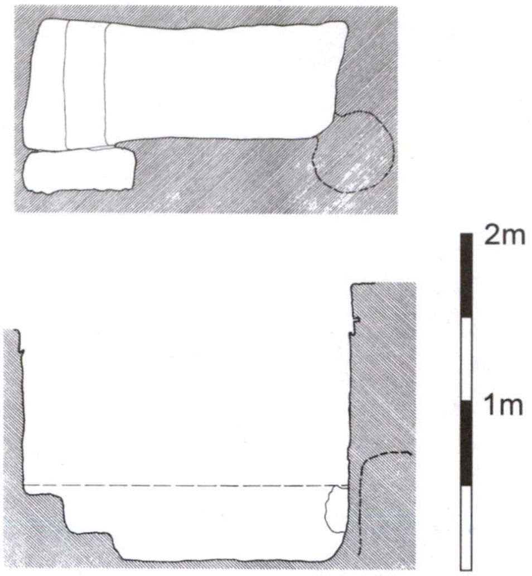

Fig. 6 *Sepphoris stepped pool 10.*

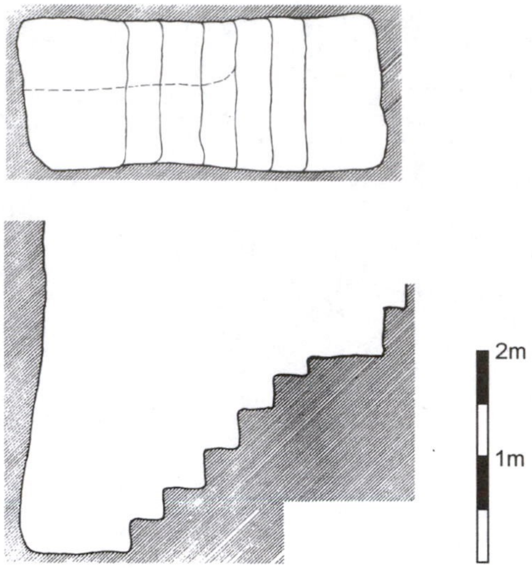

Fig. 7 *Sepphoris stepped pool 8.*

used in connection with the pool, as some sort of an anteroom (SP 9 or SP 19), or for totally unrelated purposes (in Unit II, SP 4 shares the room with a cistern and a *taboon*), suggesting that some form of divider originally separated these areas.

One of the most important factors in determining the function of the stepped pools is the presence of additional plastered installations of a totally different kind in more or less immediate proximity. In addition to the twenty stepped pools, forty — mostly bell-shaped — cisterns have been exposed on the Western Acropolis (Tsuk 1985: 40–42). In several cases, stepped pools are located adjacent or in immediate proximity to a cistern. This indicates that they were probably supplied with water by the same channel and, more importantly, were located within the same domestic unit. Given the small mouths of the cisterns, their sole function was clearly storing water. One could have easily filled a jar or bucket by reaching into the cistern opening. Bathing, however, would have been impossible.

The exposure of several enormous cisterns located on the western (C 26, C 27, C 31, and C 32A and B) and northern extremities (C 34 and C 35) of the Acropolis, adjacent to, but beyond the area of, the private domestic dwellings, suggests that the residents of the Acropolis used the latter, rather than the more distant aqueduct reservoirs. This can be substantiated by the fact that in most cities the construction of aqueducts usually complements and coincides with the construction of public baths. Thus, the water consumption in this residential quarter, though including public space, will be considered separately from the water consumption within the civic domains.

In spite of the large number of cisterns and their often impressive size, my calculations indicate that they were only used to hold drinking water. Most essential for this evaluation is to measure the cisterns' total storage capacity and to determine the average daily water consumption. Since the storage capacity does not reach its maximum potential throughout the year, and given the fact that the estimation of daily water consumption is tied to a number of factors, we can only aspire to creating a theoretical model. This model must take into account that only a certain percentage of the total precipitation was ultimately stored in the cisterns. Other factors that need to be considered are the climatic conditions (indicating precipitation and evaporation losses) and the geo-morphological features of the site being studied (determining the quantity of runoff water and water that is absorbed into the ground; Schilman 2000). This calculation, though based on hypothetical numbers, can help us to approximate the distribution of the water supply in this particular area of the city.

Since during the Roman and Byzantine periods the Western Acropolis constituted about one tenth of the total habitable space of the city (Tsuk 1985: 40) and was more densely occupied by domestic structures than the civic areas, we can speculate that it accommodated roughly fifteen percent of the total population (12,000),[11] approximately 1,800 people. In this area, forty cisterns with an average storage capacity of 47 m^3 have been located. This implies that, with an average individual daily consumption of three liters, the total drinking consumption per year for this area — which is 1971 m^3 — was slightly above the cisterns' total storage capacity of 1880 m^3.

This calculation brings us to the conclusion that, if the local inhabitants did not use any additional storage facilities or facilities outside their immediate surroundings, the cisterns could not have provided any surplus water for uses other than drinking.[12] As a result, it is unlikely that water from the cisterns would have been used to fill the stepped pools, a procedure that would have rendered the water impure from the point of view of Jewish law. The cisterns, thus, constitute the strongest evidence in support of the ritual character of the stepped pools.

STEPPED POOLS AT OTHER PALESTINIAN SITES

One of Eshel's main arguments against the identification of the stepped pools at Sepphoris as ritual baths is the absence of bathtubs (Eshel 1997: 132; 2000). Eshel compares the Sepphorean pools with the installations uncovered in the Jewish Quarter of Jerusalem. The latter were found in proximity to bathtubs, rendering the functional division between washing/bathing and ritual immersion very clear. Despite the opposite conclusions I reach regarding the functional interpretation of the Sepphorean pools, I also believe that in order to identify function and use of stepped pools, one cannot rely on the analysis of the pools independently from their context. As mentioned above, only a few features can help us distinguish the stepped pools at Sepphoris and other Palestinian sites from other plaster-covered structures. Beyond the steps and the plaster, the pools come in different shapes and sizes. Therefore, considering associated structures and examining the surrounding context can be helpful in reconstructing the intended use of the stepped pools. In the case of the Western Acropolis, examining the cisterns and their relationship to the stepped pools has proven very helpful.

A stepped pool located next to a synagogue or an oil press is easy to identify as a ritual pool, even if no other plastered installations are found in proximity.[13] The large number of stepped pools found in the vicinity of the Jerusalem Temple can be explained by the necessity of providing priests and pilgrims with ritual baths (Reich 1989; 1990: 87–93). The explicit literary documentation testifying to the necessity of immersing in a ritual bath prior to entering the Jerusalem Temple, visiting a synagogue, or using an oil press enables the functional identification of the stepped pools in these contexts. The existence of ritual pools in domestic settings, on the other hand, is barely documented in the texts. Therefore, analyzing and comparing data from similar archaeological contexts is particularly important. The most reliable control group for the Sepphorean installations would be uncovered in similar settings, that is, stepped pools found in large concentrations within domestic areas. Up to present, three other sites with analogous situations have been uncovered in the Palestinian context: the late Hellenistic palaces at Jericho (Netzer 1978; 1997: 5–31), the late Hellenistic and early Roman houses in the Jewish Quarter of Jerusalem (Avigad 1983: 139–43; Geva 2000: 29, 88, 96–97), and the Byzantine houses at Susiya (Negev 1985).[14] At Jericho, the repertoire of plastered installations includes bathtubs, cisterns, and swimming pools in addition to stepped pools. In Jerusalem, the same units that are equipped with stepped pools also have bathtubs and cisterns. Finally, the stepped pools at Susiya are found alongside cisterns. Therefore, rather than viewing a bathtub as a necessary complement to a ritual pool in the domestic context, I suggest viewing it simply as an indicator of social status. Clear indicators of social status in the domestic context can be the size and shape of the domestic unit, the quantity and quality of the decorational elements, and the nature of the small finds. That is, one has to be cautious in comparing the Jericho palaces or Jerusalem mansions that belonged to upper class residents with Sepphoris or Susiya houses that belonged to the middle or lower classes. The bathtubs at Jerusalem constitute one small element in a larger picture, including polychrome mosaic floors and frescoes, beautifully sculpted and decorated stone furniture, terra sigillata ware, marble trays, alabaster, ostraca, etc. The lack of bathtubs at Sepphoris and Susiya is merely indicative of the limited economic means of the residents. In contrast, the presence of the stepped pools in luxurious as well as more modest contexts suggests that they were not related to economic factors.

The steadily growing evidence of high concentrations of stepped pools at Sepphoris and other sites with domestic architecture indicates that this commodity was part of the Palestinian household from the late Hellenistic through the Byzantine periods. The stepped pool does not appear to indicate the socioeconomic status of its residents, but rather signals their religious affiliation.

CONCLUSIONS

The Western Acropolis at Sepphoris contains one of the highest concentrations of stepped pools of the late Hellenistic and Roman periods in Palestine. This find, a source of riches in itself, can not be examined without considering the numerous other sites that have revealed similar installations and the texts commonly associated with them. However, unlike the textual evidence, which is easily accessible to all scholars studying issues related to purity, most of the archaeological material pertaining to stepped pools is still unpublished. The single final report written on a site that includes concentrations of stepped pools (Geva 2000: 29, 88, 96–97) only briefly mentions some of them. Instead of presenting the excavated material and examining and analyzing it properly, scholars usually prioritize the textual evidence and only use the archaeological finds as supplementary evidence to their literary conclusions. This clearly undermines archaeological methodology and causes distorted representations of the material evidence. The main objective of this study is, therefore, to present and summarize the material evidence of the stepped pools and associated structures on the Western Acropolis at Sepphoris. The goal of offering a new interpretation with respect to use and function is only secondary. It is for this reason that I decided to separate these two objectives here.

The Material Evidence

The Western Acropolis excavation has uncovered a total of twenty stepped pools within an area measuring approximately 3100 m^2. In spite of the highly variegated appearance of these installations — the steps and plaster being the only constant characteristic features — they can easily be distinguished from the other plastered installations found at the site. The three largest stepped pools were built around 100 B.C.E., integrated into a pre-existing fortified building. The remaining smaller pools of the domestic complexes were built during the course of the Roman period. With the exception of the two pools that remained in use slightly beyond the Late Roman period, the earthquake of 363 C.E. put an end to both the use and construction of stepped pools. The finds at Sepphoris, together with the growing number of Late Roman and Byzantine stepped pools in other parts of the country, necessitates a reassessment of the chronological development of stepped pools in Palestine as a whole. Instead of the previously prevailing belief in a sharp decline in the use of stepped pools after 70 C.E., the Sepphorean installations suggest a continuous, if not increased, integration of this commodity within the domestic context. This situation continued throughout the entire Roman period and possibly beyond.

Interpretative Matters

The typological and chronological evaluation of the stepped pools at Sepphoris, their independent assessment within the context of the Western Acropolis, and a comparison with stepped pools from other Palestinian sites seem to indicate that these installations were used for ritual immersion.

Typologically, I have been able to show that the stepped pools were different in shape and function from other plastered installations found at the site. Given their similarity with installations identified as ritual pools at other sites, their presence at sites associated with Jewish rituals (Temple and synagogues) and residents (Jewish towns and cities), and their absence from sites lacking these associations, a purely utilitarian character, devoid of ritual significance, seems very unlikely. Chronologically, the presence of the stepped pools on the Western Acropolis coincides with the presence of Jewish residents, as attested by both the textual and material evidence (incense shovels, oil lamps decorated with Jewish symbols, absence of pig bones, etc.).

Several important considerations remain to be stressed. Regardless of the Talmudic perspective that the Sepphorean stepped pools fulfill the halachic requirements of *miqva'ot*, and despite the fact that they were likely built and used for the purposes of ritual immersion, one has to keep in mind that they were, or could have been, also used for other purposes. A number of other sites have shown that the presence of stepped pools on the Western Acropolis is not an isolated case within the boundaries of Roman–Byzantine Palestine. However, we still do not know how common it was to actually build, own, and use an installation of this type. It is not unlikely that most people continued to immerse themselves in natural, rather than artificial installations.[15]

NOTES

1 Sixteen stepped pools were uncovered during the Joint Sepphoris Project between 1985 and 1992. Four additional pools were exposed by the Sepphoris Regional Project between 1993–94 and 1996–97. During the last, 2000, season, three more pools were excavated in Unit IX. The latter will not be considered in this report.

2 After the initial careful phrasing of "stepped and plastered pools" (Meyers et al. 1985: 297), the cavities have subsequently been referred to as *miqva'ot.* See Meyers et al. 1986: 18; Meyers et al. 1995: 70; Hoglund and Meyers 1996: 40–42 and Meyers 2000: 46–49. Eshel (1997: 131–33; 2000: 42–45) has repeatedly rejected their identification as ritual pools.

3 Sanders (1990: 216) and Wright (1997: 194) discuss the criteria used by "maximalists" and "minimalists" to identify the use of stepped pools.

4 The most extensive research on stepped pools has been conducted by Reich. The title of his unpublished dissertation "*Miqva'ot* (Jewish Ritual Baths) in the Second Temple Period and the Period of the Mishnah and Talmud" (1990) and the use of the term *miqveh* in his published articles on related issues (1987; 1989; 1993; 1998) have contributed to the immediate association of stepped structures and ritual immersion baths.

5 One of the twelve tractates of Tohorot is devoted to halachic discussions on *miqva'ot.* See Neusner's translation and discussion (1976: 1–66).

6 Künzl (1992) surveys ancient and medieval ritual baths around the Mediterranean and Europe. Her study includes an analysis of both the literary and architectural evidence.

7 Through personal communications, I learned that this habit of using a *miqveh* as a bathhouse persisted well into the mid-20th century in Israel and in the Diaspora.

8 Porath (1985: 12–20) established a typological study of plaster applications indicating how to visually differentiate between plasters of different periods, beginning with the Hasmonean period and ending with the early Islamic period. His method has proven to be largely inaccurate. See Shimron et al. 2000.

9 For personal hygiene in antiquity, see Ginouvès 1962 and Laser 1983: 138–72.

10 It is impossible to pinpoint the exact date of when this transformation in usage took place. We can, however, hypothesize that this change, observed in several of the cisterns, was connected to the construction of the city's aqueducts. Despite the fact that the building of aqueducts usually takes place in conjunction with the building of bathhouses, it also relieves the cisterns from the burden of being the only storage for drinking water.

11 Given Josephus' usual habit of exaggeration when dealing with numbers, I have chosen to adopt Broshi's approach (1979) of determining the population of a city in Roman–Byzantine Palestine. According to him, the size of the urban population of Palestine at the end of the Byzantine period can be reckoned by multiplying the coefficient 400 (= persons per

ha) by the area being considered. In Jerusalem, the combined evidence of the development in area and the growth in water supply for most of the ancient periods has allowed Wilkinson (1974) to more precisely estimate populations.

12 For an alternative solution to the use of the cistern water, as not in violation of Jewish law, see Miller in this volume, chapter 18.

13 Since Reich (1990) restricted his survey mostly to Second Temple period installations, only a few examples of stepped pools found adjacent to synagogues could be listed. Updating Reich's data and including late Roman and Byzantine synagogues in the survey would, no doubt, increase the list tremendously.

14 I am grateful to David Amit for having pointed out to me the contextual similarity between the stepped pools at Sepphoris and Susiya.

15 I am particularly grateful to Eric and Carol Meyers who have made available to me all the material connected to the Western Acropolis of Sepphoris and who have encouraged me to conduct the research on the stepped pools. The examinations in the field together with Stuart Miller and our lengthy discussions on pools and ritual purity contributed greatly to my curiosity and eagerness to study the pools. I would also like to thank a number of individuals who have made valuable suggestions and comments to this paper: Melissa Aubin, Sarah Berman, Jodi Magness, Milton Moreland, Christopher Tuttle and Jürgen Zangenberg. I greatly appreciate the funds provided by the Center for Old World Archaeology and Art at Brown University to support the geochemical analysis of the plaster. A preliminary version of this article was presented at the Annual Meeting of the American Schools of Oriental Research in Nashville, TN, in November 2000.

REFERENCES

Avigad, N.
1983 *Discovering Jerusalem*. Nashville, TN: Nelson.

Broshi, M.
1979 The Population of Western Palestine in the Roman-Byzantine Period. *Bulletin of the American Schools of Oriental Research* 236: 1–10.

Browning, I.
1982 *Jerash and the Decapolis*. London: Chatto.

Eshel, H.
1997 A Note on 'Miqvaot' at Sepphoris. Pp. 131–33 in *Archaeology and the Galilee*, eds. D. Edwards and C. McCollough. Atlanta, GA: Scholars.
2000 The Pools of Sepphoris. Ritual Baths or Bathtubs: They're Not Ritual Baths. *Biblical Archaeology Review* 26, no. 4: 42–45.

Everman, D.
1992 Survey of the Coastal Area North of Caesarea and of the Aqueducts: Preliminary Report. Pp. 181–93 in *Caesarea Papers. Straton's Tower, Herod's Harbour, and Roman and Byzantine Caesarea*, ed. R. L. Vann. Journal of Roman Archaeology Supplementary Series 5. Ann Arbor, MI: Journal of Roman Archaeology.

Garbrecht, G., and Peleg, Y.
1992 The Water Supply of the Desert Fortresses in the Jordan Valley. *Biblical Archaeologist* 57, no. 3: 161–70.

Geva, H. (ed.)
2000 *Jewish Quarter Excavations in the Old City of Jerusalem conducted by Nahman Avigad, 1969–1982*. Jerusalem: Israel Exploration Society.

Ginouvès, R.
1962 *Balaneutiké: Recherches sur le Bain dans l'Antiquité Grècque*. Bibliothèque des Écoles Françaises d'Athènes et de Rome 200. Paris: Boccard.

Hoglund, K., and Meyers, E.
1996 The Residential Quarter on the Western Summit. Pp. 39–43 in *Sepphoris in Galilee. Crosscurrents of Culture*, eds. R. Nagy, C. Meyers, E. Meyers and Z. Weiss. Winona Lake, IN: Eisenbrauns.

Krauss, S.
1910 *Talmudische Archäologie*, vol. 1. Leipzig: Fock.

Künzl, H.
1992 Antike Mikwen im Mittelmeerraum und Mittelalterliche Mikwen außerhalb Deutschlands. Pp. 9–22 in *Mikwe. Geschichte und Architektur jüdischer Ritualbäder in Deutschland*, ed. G. Heuberger. Frankfurt am Main: Jüdisches Museum.

Laser, S.
1983 *Medizin und Körperpflege*. Archaeologia Homerica 3. Göttingen: Vandenhoeck.

Mazar, A.
1990 The Ancient Aqueducts of Jerusalem. *Qadmoniot* 5: 120–24.

Mazor, G.
1988 Beth Shean Project – 1988. *Excavations and Surveys in Israel* 7–8: 22–24.

Meyers, C.; Meyers, E.; and Hoglund, K.
1995 Sepphoris, 1994. *Israel Exploration Journal* 1: 68–71.

Meyers, C; Meyers, E.; and Netzer, E.
1985 Sepphoris, 1985. *Israel Exploration Journal* 35: 297.
1986 Sepphoris – "Ornament of All Galilee." *Biblical Archaeologist* 49, no. 1: 4–19.

Meyers, E.
2000 Yes, They Are. *Biblical Archaeology Review* 26, no. 4: 46–49.

Negev, A.
1985 Excavations at Carmel (Kh. Susiya) in 1984: Preliminary Report. *Israel Exploration Journal* 35: 231–52.

Netzer, E.
1978 *Mikvaot* (Ritual Baths) of the Second Temple Period at Jericho. *Qadmoniot* 11: 54–59 (Hebrew).
1997 *Die Paläste der Hasmonäer und Herodes' des Grossen*. Mainz: Zabern.

Neusner, J.
1976 *A History of the Mishnaic Law of Purities. Part Fourteen: Miqvaot, Literary and Historical Problems*. Leiden: Brill.

Porath, Y.
1985 Ancient Irrigation Agriculture in the Arid Zones of Eretz Israel. Unpublished Ph.D. Dissertation, Tel Aviv University (Hebrew).

Reich, R.
1987 More on Miqva'ot. *Biblical Archaeology Review* 13, no. 2: 59–60.
1988 The Hot Bath-House (Balneum), the Miqweh and the Jewish Community in the Second Temple Period. *Journal of Jewish Studies* 39: 102–7.
1989 Two Possible *Miqwa'ot* on the Temple Mount. *Israel Exploration Journal* 39: 63–65.
1990 Miqva'ot (Jewish Ritual Baths) in the Second Temple Period and the Period of the Mishnah and Talmud. Unpublished Ph.D. Dissertation, Hebrew University of Jerusalem (Hebrew).
1993 The Great Mikveh Debate. *Biblical Archaeology Review* 19, no. 2: 52–53.

Sanders, E.
1990 *Jewish Law from Jesus to the Mishnah: Five Studies*. London: SCM.

Schilman, B.
2000 Paleoceanography of the Eastern Mediterranean during the Late Holocene. Unpublished Ph.D. Dissertation, Hebrew University of Jerusalem (Hebrew).

Shimron, A.; Frumkin, A.; Rosenbaum, J.; Deutsch, Y.; and Dvorachek, M.
2000 The Significance of Geological Structures, Cave Sediments and Hydraulic Lime in the Interpretation of the History of the Subterranean Waterworks beneath Ancient Jerusalem: Current Research. *Geological Survey of Israel* 12: 247–56.

Tsafrir. Y.; Foerster, G.; and Mazor, G.
1990 Glorious Beth-Shean. *Biblical Archaeology Review* 16, no. 4: 26–28.

Tsuk, T.; Rosenberg, A.; and Peilstöcker, M.
1996 *The Ancient Water Reservoirs of Sepphoris. Excavations 1993–1994*. Tel Aviv (Hebrew).

Tsuk, T.
1985 The Aqueducts to Sepphoris. Unpublished MA thesis, Tel Aviv University (Hebrew).
1996 The Aqueducts of Sepphoris. Pp. 45–49 in *Sepphoris in Galilee. Crosscurrents of Culture*, eds. R. Nagy, C. Meyers, E. Meyers and Z. Weiss. Winona Lake, IN: Eisenbrauns.
2000 Bringing Water to Sepphoris. *Biblical Archaeology Review* 26, no. 4: 35–40.

Wilkinson, J.
1974 Ancient Jerusalem. Its Water Supply and Population. *Palestine Exploration Quarterly* 106: 33–51.

Wright, B.
1997 Jewish Ritual Baths – Interpreting the Digs and the Texts: Some Issues in the Social History of the Second Temple Judaism. Pp. 197–214 in *The Archaeology of Israel. Constructing the Past, Interpreting the Present*, eds. N. Silberman and D. Small. Journal for the Study of the Old Testament Supplement 237 Sheffield: Journal for the Study of the Old Testament.

Yadin, Y.
1966 *Masada: Herod's Fortress and the Zealot's Last Stand*. London: Weidenfeld.

Chapter 18

Stepped Pools and the Non-Existent Monolithic "Miqveh"

by Stuart S. Miller

The large number of stepped pools recently discovered on the western acropolis of Sepphoris, as well as similar finds at other sites, seriously challenge the notion that ritual bathing and attention to purities declined after the destruction of the Temple in Jerusalem.[1] It must be remembered, however, that the association of these newly discovered pools with the purity laws of the Jews would not have arisen to begin with, had the rabbis not provided a rich body of suggestive, roughly contemporaneous, evidence. Curiously, while talmudic sources point towards the persistence of ritual purity interests after 70 C.E., they do not at all suggest that there was a single, preferred model or design that was especially thought of as a ritual bath.[2] Indeed, the rabbis expend considerable effort in Mishnah and Tosefta *Miqvāʾôt* describing situations that would either validate or invalidate *the waters* of a ritual bath, but at no point do they actually describe one in detail. In fact, a "typical" *miqveh* would be hard to depict. Moreover, as we shall see below, the tannaitic sources clearly convey the impression that different types of "gathered waters," both natural and artificial, could be thought of as *miqvāʾôt*.[3] Thus, the various types of stepped pools have to be carefully assessed before concluding that they are, indeed, ritual baths.

To be sure, archaeologists have persuasively ruled out other uses of both pre- and post-70 C.E. stepped pools before turning to rabbinic sources for support in identifying them as ritual baths (especially Reich 1990: 62–81). Furthermore, the fact that these structures come in a variety of shapes and forms that are often difficult to understand from the standpoint of *halāḵâ* does not necessarily mean that they should *not* be identified as *miqvāʾôt*. We need only compare the history of synagogue discoveries to appreciate the extent to which archaeological finds oftentimes provide a very different picture than what is expected from the literary evidence.

With these hermeneutical concerns in mind, I would like to make some observations about the possible uses and users of such pools, particularly at Sepphoris, which will hopefully shed some light on the purpose of these installations. At the outset, it is important to recognize that the term "miqveh" had other meanings in talmudic sources, and only in later rabbinic literature is it used consistently to refer to a man-made ritual bath. This is significant, primarily because it broadens our understanding of the variety of water sources available for ritual cleansing. M. *Miqvāʾōt* (1:1, 4–8) points to several other bodies of water that are expressly regarded as *miqvāʾōt,* including a "spring" (*maʿyān*) that lacks forty *seʾāh* of rainwater, "spoiled" springwater, and *mayim hayyîm,* i.e., fresh spring water, all of which have halakhic advantages over the stationary, artificial pool of naturally collected rainwater more commonly referred to as a "miqveh."[4] These diverse meanings should come as no surprise in view of Lev 11:36, where the expression *miqvēh mayim* ("gathering of water") is used to refer to rainwater that has collected naturally into a spring *or* into a man-made cistern (*bôr).*[5] The biblical phrase certainly did not apply to a well-established institution and allowed for the wide range of meanings assumed in the Mishnah. Obviously, the *tannaim* took their cue from the biblical associations and did not think of a "miqveh" in monolithic terms, even if the term would be used increasingly to refer to a more formal, artificial structure.[6]

T. *Miqvāʾōt* 6:1–2 further establishes the varied applications of the term among the *tannaim.* This passage is primarily concerned with the ritual use of pre-existing, natural or artificial, bathing structures that are frequented by sectarian Jews or non-Jews. Thus, the Tosefta first discusses the validity of *miqvāʾōt* in the land of the Samaritans (*ʾEreṣ Ha-Kûtim*). It then considers those located in non-Jewish lands (*miqvāʾōt ha-ʿammîm she-bĕ-ḥûṣāh la-ʾāreṣ*), which are presumed to consist of drawn water. The Tosefta moves on to a discussion of ritual bathing in a cave filled with water. The same passage also considers the validity of immersion in a pool located between Usha and Shefaram, an area that was clearly Jewish. Somewhat more problematic is a pool in Rom Bet Anat to which non-Jews also had access. Next we learn from a *maʿăseh* ("case") that a late first-century sage, Rabban Gamaliel, once immersed in a "bathhouse" (*merḥāṣ*) when he was visiting Ashkelon (a decidedly Hellenistic center) with the proselyte, Onqelos. In contrast, Onqelos was said to have immersed in the sea. R. Yehoshua ben Qufsa'i then testifies that he accompanied the two sages on their trip to Ashkelon, and Rabban Gamaliel most assuredly immersed in the sea! Finally, the Tosefta discusses ritual immersion in a *merḥāṣ* of Jews that had non-Jewish attendants.[7] While the type of installation used for ritual purposes within a *merḥāṣ* is not specified, it undoubtedly resembled the other structures alluded to in the passage in one important sense: it was not designed expressly for the ritual purity needs of Jews. Stepped pools have been found in bathhouses at Masada, where they apparently served as the plunge-pools of the *frigidarium* ("cold room"). Their resemblance to stepped pools from other sites has led some to identify them as ritual baths.[8] The Tosefta suggests that such structures incorporated into bathhouses could, indeed, take on the *additional* function of a ritual bath. Obviously, the Tosefta, like the Mishnah, alludes to several types of "miqvāʾōt," none of which was designed or designated as a ritual bath from the outset; a *miqveh* in the formal sense could not have been intended. Rather, the Tosefta considers pre-existing pools to be valid "miqvāʾōt" under certain circumstances.

By the same token, rabbinic sources also resort to the phrase *bêt tĕḇilāh* or "house of immersion," to refer to a ritual bathing complex. The *bêt tĕḇilāh,* I would argue, points to a private, indeed, at times, domestic facility for ritual purification. Tannaitic sources use the phrase with reference to several such places in the environs of the Temple Mount. Thus, M. *Yômāʾ* 3:3 reports that the High Priest was required to immerse five times on the Day of Atonement in a *bêt tĕḇilāh.* According to M. *Yômāʾ* 3:2, the first of the immersions took place in a *bêt tĕḇilāh* as the High Priest entered the courtyard after the slaughtering of the daily *tāmîd* offering. This is likely the same *bêt tĕḇilāh* referred to in M. *Tāmîd* 1:1, where ordinary priests officiating in the Temple who suffered a nocturnal pollution would immerse before participating in the *tāmîd* rite.[9] The four other *Yom Kippur* immersions of the High Priest pertained more directly to the special service of that day and were to take place in a *bêt tĕḇilāh* which, according to M. *Middôt* 5:3, was situated on the roof of the *Parvāh* chamber in the "Holy" area of the Temple. This most definitely was an unusual immersion pool, at least from the point of view of later rabbinic *halāḵâ,* which required the bath to be built into the ground, so as not to resemble a "vessel" (cf. Reich 1990: 87).

While these *battê tĕḇilāh* are hardly domestic, their private or exclusive nature is certainly evident. Domestic use might be implied in M. *Shĕqālim* 8:2, which describes the bringing of utensils for immersion in a *bêt tĕḇilāh* in Jerusalem. *Midrash Tanna'îm* to Deut 6:9 takes us beyond Jerusalem and considers the possibility that a *bēt tĕḇilāh* may require the affixing of a *mezûzāh* to its entryway. The Midrash concludes that only places that people truly live in require *mezûzôt*. The Babylonian Talmud (*Yômā'* 11a) appears to be expanding upon this tannaitic tradition when it considers the same issue and explains that the question arose precisely because a *bēt tĕḇilāh* is a private, domestic complex in which an individual woman adorns herself.

The different understandings of *miqvā'ôt* and the use of the expression "bêt tĕḇilāh" are important, because they remind us not to think of the ritual bath as a monolithic institution with a single application or form. Even the artificial pools referred to by the rabbis are of different types and may not have been originally used or designed for ritual bathing. In addition, the meanings of *bêt tĕḇilāh* compel us to examine the possible domestic uses and private nature of some stepped pools. I shall return to these points.

I have already alluded to the fact that talmudic sources would not have prepared us for the rich and variegated synagogue finds uncovered over the last century. This point is worth pursuing, primarily because a comparison with synagogue discoveries can actually be helpful in appreciating the evolution of the scholarly identification of the stepped pools as *miqvā'ôt*. Although the rabbis have much to say about prayer, they convey relatively little about the structures in which it took place. Elsewhere, I have stressed that our over-preoccupation with the edifices identified as synagogues has distracted us from the origins of synagogues as communal gatherings, convened at first, perhaps, in public squares, and eventually in buildings that may not have been all that different from houses (Miller 1998; 1999a). Indeed, in many instances, these gatherings may very well have taken place in "homes." This perhaps explains the designation *bêt keneset* or "*house* of assembly." In any event, our earliest identifiable structures, those at Gamala, Masada, Herodium, and, perhaps, Jericho[10] certainly are unremarkable as gathering places for Torah reading or prayer, unlike later "synagogues," which have much more pronounced architectural and Jewish elements. More to the point, these structures could not possibly have been the only places that functioned as synagogues at the end of the Second Temple Period. It is more likely that less formal, domestic structures, now unrecognizable, were utilized as synagogues. Furthermore, even after the prominent structures that we now identify as synagogues appeared and came into more regular use, the domestic types of "houses of assembly" very likely continued to exist, much as they do today. There is no reason to assume that communal prayer and Torah reading did not continue in homes or in domestic-like structures. On the contrary, the limited size of the structures identified by archaeologists as synagogues, and the fact that no more than one or two of these oftentimes costly buildings have ever been found in relatively large sites, indicate that they were the exception, rather than the rule. Organized worship obviously occurred elsewhere as well (cf. Miller 1998: 63–66).

The point is that just as the synagogue undoubtedly evolved, so did the *miqveh*. What originally made a synagogue a synagogue was the activity that occurred therein. Once people gathered in a home or even in a "*bêt*" *midrash* to pray and read the Torah, these structures also took on the function of a "synagogue."[11] Similarly, whenever a person immersed for ritual purposes in a stream, a natural pool and, eventually, a stepped pool, these functioned as *miqvā'ôt*. It is inconceivable that a well-defined institution for ritual ablutions *suddenly* appeared when the Tanakh and Second Temple literature, including the Dead Sea Scrolls, know of no such institution. Indeed, Second Temple Greek sources from *'Ereṣ* Israel have Jews bathing for ritual purposes in natural sources, and do not allude to specially designated pools.[12] Although the Dead Sea sectarians frequently allude to ritual bathing in their writings, they, too, do not refer to the pools of different types found at Qumran by any official designation. Many of these pools undoubtedly were used for ritual purposes, but the sect had not yet come to think of them as ritual baths in a formal, institutional sense. Moreover, just as the more formal synagogue structures evolved out of familiar architectural prototypes, so the earliest identifiable, man-made "miqvā'ôt" were stepped pools that, with time, were adapted and resorted to for ritual purification.[13]

Thus, it is likely that the *miqveh,* if we may call it that, evolved over time. While it has been suggested that the great variety of stepped installations that have been discovered — those with or without reservoirs (*'ôṣārôt*) for rainwater, those with divided stairways, those that relied on rainwater from aqueducts (at Qumran), those that apparently depended on water delivered through pipes from rooftops, those with great depth (at Jericho, enough to swim in!), etc. — reflect sectarian tendencies and differences,[14] it seems equally possible that these distinctions are the product of architectural experimentation that had more to do with divergences in time and place.[15] Indeed, when the large number of stepped pools at the single site of Sepphoris is considered, at least two types are apparent: those dug into floors of homes and entered from above, and those carved into the bedrock from the side, forming cave-like structures. The excavators have suggested that the side-entry stepped pools are the earlier of the two types.[16]

Even so, a stepped pool at Sepphoris or elsewhere only functioned as a *miqveh* when the person immersing did so expressly for ritual purification. Stepped pools undoubtedly continued to be used for other purposes. M. *Miqvā'ôt* 7:3 considers the validity of a *miqveh* in which baskets that once contained either olives or grapes had been rinsed and concludes that the water remains *kāshēr* for ritual immersion even if it became discolored. While it could be claimed that this, like many other situations described in M. *Miqvā'ôt,* is hypothetical, it is not difficult to imagine that stepped pools were at times used for rinsing baskets that ordinarily contained fruits or vegetables. Particularly in domestic settings, people may very well have taken advantage of a pool of water that was always available. The rinsing of dishes and of vessels (as opposed to baskets) in a "miqveh" might be more problematic from a halakhic perspective, but this practice also should not be automatically discounted. M. *Miqvā'ôt* 4:1 is concerned about situations where vessels were used to collect rainwater from the pipe leading to the *miqveh,* thereby rendering it "drawn water" (*shĕ'ûvîn*).[17] Interestingly, much pottery, that is, earthenware that, at least according to rabbinic law, would not have required ritual immersion, has been discovered in stepped pools at Sepphoris, Jericho and elsewhere.[18] While the Mishnah only speaks of the rinsing of fruit baskets, one can surmise that stepped pools in domestic settings served as a convenient place to rinse (lightly?) soiled vessels.[19] Similarly, the cool waters of a standing, domestic pool would have been hard to resist on a particularly warm day.[20] These possible profane uses and the terminological variation found in the *Mishnah* for pools that were adapted for ritual bathing indicate an evolving, multi-use stepped pool.[21] As with the evolution of the synagogue, there is no reason to assume the spontaneous generation of the "miqveh." Nor is there any reason to assume continuity in use, especially where "private" installations were concerned. Again, the comparison with synagogue finds is instructive. In both instances, practices not foreseen or ignored by the rabbis were, undoubtedly, common.[22] In short, a "miqveh" did not always function as a *miqveh.*[23]

Still, if this assessment is correct, then many of the stepped pools at Sepphoris *were* likely to have been used for ritual bathing, regardless of their original or even primary purpose. One reason for concluding that many of these installations, whatever additional purposes they served, *also* functioned as ritual baths is precisely because of the presence of cisterns in such close proximity to many of the installations. Galor maintains that the cisterns point to a clear distinction between drinking water installations and those used for bathing.[24] She further assumes that Jews at Sepphoris would have resorted to Roman style bathtubs (which so far have not been found) or bathhouses, so the stepped pools, the purpose of which is clearly different from that of the cisterns, could only have been used for ritual applications. Perhaps a stronger case can be made that many of these pools functioned as ritual baths if it can be shown that they *were* related to or somehow dependent upon the cisterns. In other words, the presence of cisterns may serve as proof

Fig. 1 *Stepped pool installation (SP 17) from Area 84.2. The step-less pool on the left likely functioned as a reservoir/*ʾôṣār *for the stepped pool/ritual bath to its right. The channel or hole that presumably connected the two is no longer extant. An opening behind and above the step-less reservoir/*ʾôṣār *leads to a plastered container/cistern below (see n. 33.) The original date of the installation is uncertain, but it appears to have functioned into the Middle and even Late Roman periods.*

that the pools had a distinct purpose, but rather than see the two as entirely discrete installations, I would maintain that their proximity to each other suggests an interrelationship that, in turn, confirms that the pools at times could have functioned as halakhically acceptable *miqvāʾôt*.

The most easily identifiable ritual baths in *ʾEreṣ* Israel are those stepped pools that sit alongside containers of rainwater, which in more recent times have been designated *ʾôṣārôt* (sing. *ʾôṣār*, "treasury"). A pool of drawn water brought into contact by means of a channel or connecting hole with the rainwater in an adjacent *ʾôṣār* became a valid ritual bath. We have one definite installation of this type in the western acropolis at Sepphoris (fig. 1; Area 84.2). Most of the recent "great *Miqveh* debate," however, concerns the stand-alone stepped pools, precisely because it is unclear how these would have been filled with rainwater (Reich 1993; cf. Eshel 1997 and 2000). Galor and E. M. Meyers have cogently argued that pipes from the roof could easily have led to both the cisterns and the pools.[25] Perhaps, as Galor has suggested, the two were located in proximity to one another because they shared the same or adjoining pipes.[26] This seems quite reasonable, especially since we do not know how the aqueduct at Sepphoris would have provided water for the cisterns or pools in the upper city.[27]

I wonder, however, whether this fully explains the proximity of the cisterns to the stepped pools. There is an alternative explanation, one that admittedly assumes that we are dealing with installations used for ritual bathing in accordance with rabbinic *halākâ*, which, it should be kept in mind, may not have been the case. M. *Miqvāʾôt* speaks of other mechanisms, aside from the provision of rainwater from an *ʾôṣār*, for allowing drawn water to be used in ritual pools. Drawn water disqualifies a *miqveh* when it is poured directly into a bath lacking 40 *seʾāh* of rainwater. However, according to M. *Miqvāʾôt* 6:8, an unlimited amount of drawn water could be poured into a container of 40 *seʾāh* of rainwater until it overflowed into a lower container, which would thereby fill and become a valid *miqveh* of 40 *seʾāh*. This process would become known as *zĕriʿāh* ("sowing") in later halakhic sources, since the drawn water was "seeded" into the rainwater, which rendered it valid.[28]

Perhaps more relevant is the process known as *hamšāḵâ*, or "conduction." This mechanism allows for the pouring of drawn water onto the ground or into a channel attached to the ground from where it flows into the pool. The water thereby loses its "drawn" status. Biblical law actually would allow a complete *miqveh* to be formed by this means.[29] Tannaitic law appears to limit this process somewhat. According to M. *Miqvāʾôt* 4:4, if rainwater and drawn water mixed together in a courtyard, a trough (*ʿûqâ*), or on the steps of a cave leading to a *miqveh*, and then flowed into a ritual bath, the bath is *kāshēr* provided that the rainwater constituted the greater proportion of the mixture. This is usually understood in light of the amoraic discussion in B. *Tĕmûrâ* 12a–b, where the *tanna*, R. Eliezer ben Yaʿaqov, is presumed to allow 19 *sĕʾâ* of drawn water to be conducted over the ground into a pool *that already contains* 21 *sĕʾâ* of rainwater.[30] That is, the drawn water actually need not be mixed with rainwater before it arrives at the pool, but it can only be used to fill a pool that already has a majority of rainwater. The Talmud formulates this principle as שאיבה מטהרת ברבייה והמשכה, "drawn water validates with a majority [of rainwater] and conduction over the ground." However, M. *Miqvāʾôt* 4:4 appears to be more in line with R. Eliezer's opinion, as stated in T. *Miqvāʾôt* 4:2. There, Eliezer maintains that if one were to bucket 19 *sĕʾâ* of drawn water into 21 *sĕʾâ* of rainwater found on a roof, and the waters mixed "in the courtyard," i.e., the mixture of 40 *sĕʾâ* flowed on the ground before it filled the pool, the waters form a valid *miqveh*.[31] The implication here is that the *entire* pool can be filled in this manner. The amoraic perception was that R. Eliezer was concerned with drawn water that had not been mixed with rainwater prior to its conduction along the ground into the ritual bath. Thus, tannaitic sources permitted an entire *miqveh* to be filled with a mixture of drawn water and rainwater, provided that the rainwater formed at least 21 *sĕʾâ* and that the mixture underwent *hamšāḵâ* before arriving at the *miqveh*. Amoraic sources allowed drawn water to be conducted along the ground and added to a *miqveh* that already contained at least 21 *sĕʾâ* of rainwater.[32] It should also be remembered that unlimited amounts of drawn water could be added *directly* to any *miqveh* if it already contained 40 *sĕʾâ* of rainwater.

The point is that the rabbis had clever ways of utilizing drawn water to either fill or top off an existing pool of rainwater. The cisterns at Sepphoris, regardless of whether they were supplied with rainwater from rooftops or with water conveyed or transported somehow from the aqueduct to the East, could have been used not only for drinking purposes, but also for filling the stepped pools.[33] Water from the cisterns could have been "drawn" by bucket and utilized in the pools, which still could have functioned as *miqvāʾôt* even according to rabbinic *halāḵâ*, as we have just seen. The availability of drawn water would have eliminated the problem of inadequate supply of rainwater and evaporation as well as occasional removal of stale water from the stepped pool. Thus, the location of a good many of the cisterns near stepped pools suggests a relationship between the two installations and may point to the use of these pools for ritual bathing. Indeed, one of these pools (fig. 2), has a channel running through its top stair, which leads from the direction of the nearby cistern. This is very much reminiscent of the situation described in M. *Miqvāʾôt* 4:4, where drawn water flows down the stairs of a "cave" used for purification.[34] This particular pool could have been filled entirely of drawn water according to biblical law (see above) or through some combination of rainwater and drawn water *à la* the rabbis. Interestingly, a small bath that could have been used for foot washing was found in an adjoining room to the north of this same pool. While the relationship of the smaller installation to the larger stepped pool remains unclear,[35] several other similar installations have been found in close proximity to stepped pools at Sepphoris. M. *Miqvaoʾt* 9:2 explicitly speaks of the removal of dust from one's feet before immersion.[36]

Fig. 2 *Early Roman period stepped pool (SP 4) and cistern complex from Area 85.1. A channel hewn through the top stair of the pool extends under the floor of the room towards the cistern opening immediately to the east. Water could have easily been drawn from the cistern and poured into the channel. The water would then flow into the stepped pool, thereby rendering it valid according to the rabbinic principle of* hamšākâ.

Who used the stepped pools at Sepphoris and for which ritual purposes? One tendency has been to see distinct types of *miqvāʾōt* as a reflection of sectarian or group differences *vis à vis* the laws of purities. Regev claims that baths found in Jerusalem and environs with double entries and/or stairways with dividers were used primarily by the priests of the Temple. Accordingly, once these priests had immersed, they would have been careful to avoid contact with those who had not yet done so by exiting via the alternate exit or stairway.[37] Regev and Sanders claim that pools with *ʾōṣārôt* were the invention of the Pharisees, who promoted the notion that rainwater could render drawn water acceptable for purification.[38] Selkin, for similar reasons, sees the use of an *ʾōṣār* as a fundamental difference between the Pharisees, on the one hand, and the Dead Sea sect and the Sadducees, on the other.[39] Sanders also proffers that the stand-alone stepped pools in Jerusalem were used by aristocratic priests, who rejected the Pharisaic insistence on rainwater and filled them with drawn water.[40] Sawicki, for different reasons, has argued that the stepped pools at Sepphoris reflect a priestly presence already in the first century (Sawicki 2000: 125; cf. Miller 2000: 34–35).

I doubt, however, that the western acropolis of Sepphoris was populated mainly by priests, especially in view of my previous conclusion that the literary evidence only suggests significant priestly presence at Sepphoris beginning in the third century (Miller 1984: 62–132; 1999b: 152; forthcoming). All other attempts to assign ritual baths to distinct groups are equally wrongheaded and stem, once again, from an over-eagerness to find neat answers to complicated questions. At the very least, these attempts should await further clarification of the contexts and typologies of the extant installations.

Stepped pools such as those found in Jerusalem that have neither an *ʾōṣār* nor a nearby cistern, need not have been built by people who disregarded Pharisaic (rabbinic?) law. These pools could easily have been supplied via *hamšāḵâ* with rainwater from roofs to which some drawn water, admittedly not with great ease, could, from time to time, have been added. Even if they were filled directly with drawn water, as Sanders claims, aristocratic priests need not have been the only ones to use them.[41] Similarly, both the stand-alone pools and the *ʾōṣār* installation (fig. 1) at Sepphoris *may* be explained by rabbinic *halāḵâ,* as I argued above. This does not mean, however, that only rabbis or their followers used these baths.

It is important to keep in mind the manifold impurities for which ritual bathing was prescribed when considering who is likely to have used ritual baths, especially after 70 C.E. It is commonly assumed that after 70 C.E. most of the laws of purities fell into abeyance, precisely because their primary purpose was to enable access to the Temple. Accordingly, contact with a corpse no longer had any real consequences, and, in any event, there was no red cow sacrificial ceremony to remedy this impurity. The purification procedures for lepers and for those suffering from certain sexual diseases are also believed to have been suspended. Nevertheless, there are indications in the sources that priests after 70 C.E. continued to purify those who contracted leprosy or the impurity of a corpse.[42] Presumably, priests would have had a vested interest in sustaining these practices, both as a remembrance of the Temple period and in order to eat their dues in a state of purity. Indeed, T. *Ḥăgîgâ* 1:2 even explains that one immerses a child to teach him how to properly consume *tĕrûmâ.*[43]

Priests, however, are not likely to have been the only ones concerned with ritual purity, particularly when it came to eating. The Gospels testify that the consumption of everyday food was a purity concern already in the time of Jesus. Mark 7:4 singles out the Pharisees, but also says that all Jews wash their hands before eating, immerse before consuming food upon returning from the market, and wash cups, pots and vessels of bronze. The Pharisees clearly expect Jesus to immerse prior to eating in Luke 11:38 (Taylor 1997: 60; Harrington 1993: 280). Some *tannaim* fostered the eating of profane foods (*ḥûllîn*) in a state of purity, perhaps in order to extend the holiness associated with the Temple and Jerusalem to other parts of the land.[44] Thus, we hear that Rabban Gamaliel of Yavneh only ate profane foods prepared in a state of purity.[45] Similarly, the early second-century *tanna* R. Meir, who promoted the *ḥăvûrâ* ("fellowship"), reportedly insisted that one who did not eat food in purity was an *ʿam ha-ʾāreṣ.*[46] While these instances could be viewed as exceptional, supererogatory efforts on the part of the sages, there are also reports of commoners observing these laws. Thus, a disciple of R. Meir, R. Simeon ben Eleazar, comments on the extent to which "purity has spread" by referring to the maintenance of purity laws that applied to eating.[47] More revealing is an account concerning the relatively unknown fourth-generation *amora,* R. Yose ben Yose, who, while sailing on a ship, advised a person who wanted to immerse in the sea before eating that in fact he was not required to risk his life. Upon returning to shore, Yose made it clear that this was an unusual circumstance and now his fellow traveler was once again required to immerse whenever he wished to eat (P. *Bĕraḵôt* 3, 6c.). It is no wonder that metal and glass ware continued to be immersed after 70 C.E., as were other items that contracted impurities.[48] Indeed, a good proportion of the Mishnaic tractate *Kēlîm,* which is devoted to the susceptibility to impurity of all kinds of "vessels," is thought to be the work of R. Yose ben Ḥalafta, who was the most important *tanna* in second-century Sepphoris — and, incidentally, was not a priest.[49]

The immersion of food vessels would imply a domestic need for a stepped pool,[50] but purification practices associated with sexuality are even more suggestive where the home is concerned. Although it is commonly assumed that immersion following sexual relations, which is prescribed in Lev 15:18, was no longer practiced subsequent to the destruction of the Temple, when access to the sanctuary was no longer an issue, there is a wealth of evidence to the contrary.[51] During the tannaitic period, the requirement that a *baʿal qerî,* a man who had a seminal emission, required immersion before prayer or Torah study was debated.[52] Although some concluded that even nine *qabîn* (approximately four and a half gallons) of drawn water poured over a person was sufficient for purification in this instance, it is apparent that the stricter practice of full immersion in valid rainwater persisted. Certainly that would have been the case for someone meticulous about eating *ḥûllîn* in a state of purity. M. *Miqvāʾôt* 8:1 and T. *Miqvāʾôt* 6:1 do, however, specifically single out "*miqvāʾôt*" of non-Jews outside of *ʾEreṣ* Israel, that is, pools that likely consisted entirely or largely of drawn water, as suitable for immersion of a man who had a seminal emission (a *baʿal qerî*). In any event, second-century tannaitic sources indicate that men and women still practiced immersion after sexual relations, and men were considered impure even if they had a lewd dream and awoke "with warm skin" (M. *Miqvāʾôt* 8:3).

Indeed, a passage in the Palestinian Talmud (*Běrakôt* 3, 6c) has the sages express surprise that R. Yose ben Ḥalafta once immersed on Yom Kippur, when sexual relations were strictly forbidden. It is surmised that the "holy" sage must have suffered a nocturnal seminal pollution. The same passage also has the late third–early fourth-century *amora*, R. Jacob bar Avun, explain that immersion after sexual relations was instituted in order to prevent Jews from conducting their lives like fowl, "who cohabit, get up and go and eat." The *gemara* also reports that in the time of the third-century sage R. Joshua ben Levi there was interest in doing away with ritual bathing after sexual relations, because the "wives of Galilee" were becoming barren from the cold. R. Joshua ben Levi insisted, however, that the immersion "protected Israel from sin." Remarkably, another Sepphorean sage, the great R. Ḥanina bar Ḥama, who was a contemporary of R. Joshua ben Levi, is said to have objected to all those gathered early in the morning at the "gates of the baths" to wash, and sarcastically referred to them as *tôvělê šahărît*, an apparent allusion to a group of "morning bathers" who were fastidious about washing after sexual relations in Temple times.[53] Ḥanina tells them to get on with their (Torah) studies, implying that they did not have to immerse before doing so. The prevalent practice in *ʾEreṣ* Israel, however, was for one who had engaged in sexual relations or suffered a seminal emission to immerse before prayer or study of Torah.[54] It has been suggested that Ḥanina protested the practice of the "morning bathers," because he was originally from Babylonia, where the practice was not as prevalent. However, Ginzberg has shown that, although this immersion would eventually lose ground in Babylonia, the rabbis and pietists in both countries were in agreement that it was worth preserving and continued to observe it. The difference in *ʾEreṣ* Israel, Ginzberg argues, was that the practice was more widespread among commoners.[55] Ḥanina was simply protesting a common observance that some rabbis no longer insisted lay-persons perform, especially in his native Babylonia, but which remained popular in *ʾEreṣ* Israel not only among the sages and different types of pietists but also *among the masses*.

To be sure, we have already seen that there was a tendency toward leniency in the observance of this particular ritual purification. This, however, did not mean that immersion after sexual relations would be so easily eliminated. When T. *Miqvāʾôt* 6:1 has the second-century *tanna*, R. Judah ben Ilai, insist that a *baʿal qerî* could immerse "anywhere" (*bekhol maqom*), including in "miqvāʾôt" consisting of drawn water, the implication is that people indeed did just that, particularly in *ʾEreṣ* Israel. This should come as no surprise. After all, ablutions after sexual relations were common to cultures throughout the ancient world, as Milgrom has shown (1991: 932–34). As for the Jews, Philo relates that husbands and wives would not touch anything upon rising until they had bathed (*Special Laws* 3:63). While Sanders may be correct that Philo's ablution consisted of sprinklings from a basin, Josephus, whose testimony would be more relevant for *ʾEreṣ* Israel, testifies that husband and wife are required to bathe after engaging in sexual relations.[56] Perhaps Jews in the Diaspora, both in Alexandria and in Babylonia, had a more liberal understanding of "bathing." Nevertheless, Philo's assertion that these washings prevented husbands and wives from committing adultery, sounds very much like the claim attributed to Joshua ben Levi, who lived in *ʾEreṣ* Israel, that post-coital immersions "protected Israel from sin." These notions would not have been peculiar to the rabbis. Indeed, a report in the very same *sûgyā'* of the Palestinian Talmud from which so much of our evidence has been drawn, has R. Yose ben Ḥalafta warn *a donkey driver* against risking his life at night to ritually cleanse himself after sexual relations. In this instance, it is a prominent rabbi who tries to dissuade a commoner from performing the rite![57]

By now, it should be obvious that scholars who have thought of the post-70 C.E. ritual bath as primarily an institution used by women, and then only once a month after the seven-day period that followed their menses, have not fully appreciated the role this institution continued to play within domestic life. Many ritual purity practices of temple times lingered longer than scholars have cared to realize. Some were adapted and given new meaning.[58] Furthermore, the fact that the rabbinic purity laws are meticulously complex does not preclude their observance among the masses.[59] This would have been especially true with ritual immersion. After all, even a Jew who had only a superficial awareness of the biblical tradition would have understood the role water played in ritual sanctification. Hengel and Deines have pointed out that the biblical obligation "to be holy" (*qādōš*) in imitation of God (Lev 11:44–45) was readily associated with the purity laws and understood to extend beyond the Temple and the priesthood to Jerusalem, the entire land, and all of Israel (Hengel and Deines 1995: 46–47). Milgrom has further indicated that the connection of the verbal forms of *qdš* with immersion is explicit in *non-priestly* passages of the Tanakh, where the forms *qiddeš* and *hitqaddeš* are used more expressly with reference to ritual ablutions that were performed in anticipation of theophanies or demonstrations of God's presence. Moreover, the command "to be holy" in Lev 11:44 follows immediately the proscriptions regarding forbidden foods, leading to the association of sanctification with eating (Milgrom 1990: 88). The command of God to Moses in Lev 19:2, "Speak to the *whole Israelite community* and say to them, 'You shall be holy, for I, the Lord your God, am holy,'" would, therefore, have resonated in some very meaningful ways with *all* Jews. Late midrashic sources have the Yavnean Rabban Gamaliel teach that the washing of hands before meals applied to *all Israelites*, not exclusively to Priests and Levites.[60] This rabbinic teaching would not have fallen upon unreceptive ears among the masses. Moreover, the holiness of the land prescribed in the Holiness Code would also have been interpreted to mean that the people must be "holy" in more than a spiritual sense.[61] Thus, the many stepped pools found in domestic settings at Sepphoris and Jerusalem need not have belonged to Pharisees, rabbis, or Sadducaic priests.[62]

Certainly there were others who viewed water, in the words of Eliade, as a substance that "purifies and regenerates because it nullifies the past, and restores…the integrity of the dawn of things" (Eliade 1958: 194; cf. Eliade 1957: 129–32). Milgrom may be correct that the Torah strips water of its perceived magical properties and rejects its regenerative associations, but these notions would have been difficult to eradicate among the masses.[63] The rainwater of a rabbinic *miqveh*, which is thought to come directly from the heavens (cf. Neusner 1994: 147–48; Harrington 1993: 134–35), would undoubtedly have been regarded in this light. Whether the efficacy of water was rooted in magic or in God mattered little, since the person undergoing a ritual immersion did so with a realization that something would be different as a consequence. Water, in general, had other metaphoric meanings that many Jews would have appreciated. Selkin has analyzed rabbinic traditions identifying water with Torah and has demonstrated how the words of Torah were regarded as a "purifying pool" for Israel.[64] Torah study and even prayer required ritual washing beforehand, presumably because they were occasions of God's presence. Selkin observes, "…immersions, with their attendant Torah and purity symbolism, may have been part of the standard preparation for the exegetical undertaking in some circles…" (Selkin 1993: 234). Precisely because these immersions were so laden with meaning, Selkin postulates that they were opportunities for sectarian differences. She adds, "If water is Torah, and only I know correctly how Torah's depths are to be plumbed, it is to be expected that my water rites will be different from those of other Jews" (Selkin 1993: 262–63). The different exegetical approaches to which Selkin alludes need not have led to well-defined, sectarian differences. Nevertheless, the metaphoric overtones of water that she documents in detail would not have been lost on any Jew who possessed some familiarity with the Torah. The Jew who after 70 C.E. wished to remedy the impurity caused by contact with a corpse, carcasses of impure animals, bodily discharges, sexual relations, and other impurities mentioned in the Torah, would have naturally been attracted to immersion. The ubiquitous, popular perception of these impurities as things to be avoided would only have enhanced the power of water to wash them away—whether or not the rabbis insisted on such cleansing might not have even mattered.[65]

The rabbis did, however, attempt to provide renewed meaning to some of these impurities by suggesting that one needed to be pure before engaging in Torah study and prayer, but it was the home, not the synagogue, that was evidently most affected by the spiritual properties of water. True, stepped pools have been found in proximity to synagogues, but these have been the exception, rather than the rule.[66] The discovery of so many of these pools in domestic settings at Sepphoris compels us to reconsider the extent to which the home, beginning with the late Temple period, but especially after 70 C.E., became the focus of a life of sanctity.[67] Jews at Sepphoris who could afford to install or adapt existing bathing facilities in their homes may have done so precisely because these baths served a regular function that was especially personal, governing not only what they ate, on which utensils, and when, but also, and especially, their sexual lives. It is no wonder that Neusner discerns an increased emphasis upon the home and purity matters among the rabbis subsequent to 70 C.E.:

> ...the earliest stage in the unfolding of the law of Purities deals with domestic matters, not cultic ones. The points of special concern begin with the uncleanness of a woman in her menstrual period, at which point she may not prepare food which is to be kept in a state of cultic cleanness, or even sit on a chair and eat at a table at which a meal in a state of cultic cleanness is to be served. This matter brings us to the household and its hearth. The extensive early discourse of tractate Kelim on utensils susceptible to uncleanness is directed principally at domestic objects used for sleeping and eating. The principle of tractate Miqvaot, on immersion pools, concerns the restoration to cleanness of objects used in the home, exclusive of food and drink, which are beyond purification... (Neusner 1981: 68-69).

In sum, having established the role water and ritual purity played in the domestic life of Jews beyond the destruction of the Temple, we should not believe for a moment that we know all of the possible uses of the stepped pools. Nor should we assume, when these pools did indeed function as ritual baths, that their construction and use were defined exclusively by the rabbis. Indeed, evidence marshaled recently by Cohen suggests that Jewish women in 12th–13th century Spain and Byzantium frequently waited the seven days after menstruation and then immersed *in ordinary baths* (Cohen 1999).[68] Interestingly, these women claimed that what they were doing was halakhically valid. We need to keep this in mind when studying our period. Purity rituals were certainly kept after 70 C.E., yet there were probably a good number of variations on a theme. Stepped pools at Sepphoris that were situated alongside cisterns and made use of their waters may have functioned as halakhically legitimate *miqvāʾôt*. Others may have been filled entirely with drawn water and still have been used by men who had experienced a seminal pollution, or men and women who had sexual relations. At the same time, we cannot rule out profane uses for stepped pools, such as rinsing fruit baskets or dishes, or even for cooling off on a hot day. The privacy of one's home certainly would have lent itself to variation in usage and ritual applications.

In the final analysis, the identification of stepped pools in domestic settings does not come down to a choice between minimalist or maximalist positions. Wright is on the correct track, when he asserts that the lines should not be "drawn as firmly as do those who see the majority of these pools as baths having ritual uses." Wright assumes there is an alternative: some stepped pools are ritual baths and some are not (Wright 1997: 204). I agree, but there is one other possibility: that the pools were designed from the outset or ended up being used for multiple ritual and profane purposes. With time, and depending on the halakhic perspective and perhaps the means of the owner(s), many a stepped pool may have come to be used primarily or, in certain contexts, exclusively for ritual bathing. The attempt, however, to restrict most of these pools to either ritual (and then, only rabbinic) or profane uses delimits our understanding of the value and meaning of water in a traditional, ancient society. It also inhibits our appreciation of how the *miqveh mayim* of Scripture eventually encompassed the various meanings the rabbis assigned to it, and finally, by medieval times, evolved into a fixed, man-made institution known as the "miqveh."

Thus, many, if not most, of the stepped pools of Sepphoris, whether seen in their own right from the eyes of the rabbis or from what we know about immersion in antiquity, must have been used, *among other things*, for ritual ablutions. Certainly the presence in second-century Sepphoris of R. Yose ben Ḥalafta, a preeminent authority on purities, who contributed extensively to the entire Mishnaic order of *Tohŏrôt,* speaks volumes about the continued interest in ritual purity. However, only after further examination of the stepped pools and their contexts, as well as the relevant texts, will we fully appreciate the origin of each pool and its uses. While much work remains to be done, it is important to keep in mind that the Jews of the western acropolis at Sepphoris need not have been Pharisees, rabbis, or priests. They may very well have been ordinary Jews who, living in a world where ritual purity remained exceedingly important, were still at times very much doing their own thing.

ACKNOWLEDGEMENTS

I have gained much from my discussions with Katy Galor as well as with Jonathan Reed and Jürgen Zangenberg, with whom I have discussed methodological issues over the years. This article represents a preliminary discussion of the issues. A more detailed discussion will appear in the publication that Eric Meyers, Katy Galor, and I are preparing for publication.

This article actually began as a response to Katy Galor's discussion of the stepped pools of the western acropolis of Sepphoris at the Annual Meeting of ASOR, November, 2000. It is a modest but fitting recognition of the conversation between literary historians and archaeologists — between "text and spade" — that Eric Meyers has fostered so eloquently throughout his career. I am especially grateful to Eric for affording me the opportunity to be a part of this conversation, as well as for his collegiality and friendship.

NOTES

1 See Reich 1990: 143–44. Reich completed his dissertation before the full extent of stepped pool finds at Sepphoris was realized. The twenty pools excavated in the western quarter date to the Late Hellenistic (ca. 100 B.C.E.) through Late Roman/Early Byzantine periods. Some of those constructed in the Early Roman Period prior to 70 C.E. may have continued in use after the destruction.

2 For a recent attempt to differentiate between Pharisaic-Rabbinic and aristocratic/priestly ritual baths, see Sanders 1990: 222–26; cf. Regev 1996. For a response to Regev, who sees distinct Pharisaic and Sadducaic approaches to *miqveh* construction, see Grossberg 1997. Regev counters in Regev 1997; also cf. Selkin 1993: 134–61. See discussion below.

3 The term *miqveh* is derived from the root *q/v/h*, meaning "to gather." The expression *miqveh mayim* ("gathering of water") is used in Lev 11:36 with reference to purity concerns involving waters collected in either a spring or a cistern; cf. Selkin 1993: 20–22 and discussion below.

4 A *ma'yan* with less than 40 *sĕ'â* of rainwater to which drawn water is added remains fit for immersion. Similarly, "spoiled water" (*mayim mûkkim*), which according to M. *Pārâ* 8:9 is either salty or hot spring water, effects purification even if it is flowing. "Living waters" (*mayim hayyîm*), that is, fresh spring water, have the additional advantage of effecting purification of a person with a genital flux (*zav*) through immersion. In addition, *mayim hayyîm* were used in the sprinkling purification of a leper and were combined with the ashes of the red cow to form the *mê hattā't* used for the purification of someone who contracted corpse impurity. See Num 19:17 and M. *Tĕmûrâ* 1:5. M. *Miqvā'ôt* 1:4 describes the uses of water in crevices (*mê gĕvā'îm*, on which see below, n. 16), cisterns, ditches, and caves, as well as rainwater that has ceased flowing, and "miqvā'ôt" that do not contain 40 *sĕ'â*, all of which may be utilized for certain purification purposes, but not where immersion (*tĕbîlāh*) is required.

5 See above. It is clear that natural bodies of water are intended in Lev 11:36. See Levine 1989: 71 and Milgrom 1991: 680 and 923. Remarkably, the earliest source to understand *miqvēh mayim* in Lev 11:36 as a so-named structure is the Septuagint, which renders "…a spring or cistern of gathered water (*miqvēh mayim*)" as …πηγῶν ὑδάτων καὶ λάκκου καὶ συναγωγῆς ὕδατος, where συναγωγῆς ὕδατος is a discreet item introduced by the conjunction καί. *Miqveh* is repeatedly used with "water" (*mayim, mêmêhem*) in the Torah, where it always has the connotation of naturally gathered waters, whether collected in a spring or a cistern. In addition to Lev 11:36 and Gen 1:10, see Exo 7:19. Curiously, Isa 22:11 resorts to the stand-alone feminine form, *miqvâ*, to refer to a pool built by Hezekiah to collect rainwater channeled from the Gihon spring; cf. Ben Sira 50:3. Selkin (1993: 22) rightly notes that both Isaiah and Ben Sira resort to the term to refer to man-made public reservoirs or "catchment basins."

6 It should be noted that the evolution of the notion of full-body immersion and specifically of ablutions in 40 *sĕ'â* of still rainwater is subject to dispute. Neusner (1994: 145–51) sees the rabbinic system as a major departure from biblical ritual purity practices. He claims that it is rooted in the late Second Temple period, but no later than the first century B.C.E. Neusner notes that the requirement of 40 *sĕ'â* of water does not appear before Usha. Sanders (1990: 137–47; 214–15) credits the Pharisees with the extension of immersion to menstruants. Selkin (1993: 9–11; 18) questions whether the Bible knows of complete immersion. In contrast, Milgrom (1991: 667), sees the use of *yitmā' 'ad hā-'ārev* ("will be impure until evening") as implying ablution. Harrington (1993: 113–39) follows Milgrom in arguing that the rabbinic system is intricately connected to and directly derived from the biblical.

7 In contrast, the implication is that the previous case involving Rabban Gamaliel involved a non-Jewish bathhouse in Ashkelon. For the introduction of pools for ritual purposes into the bathhouses of the Jews, see Reich 1988: 102–7.

8 Netzer (1991: 94) suggests that the arrangement of the stepped pool *frigidarium* in the Large Bathhouse at the northern end of Masada permitted its use as a *miqveh*. Reich (1990: 112) identifies both this pool and one located in the bathhouse in the lower terrace of the Northern Palace (see Netzer 1991: 164–67) as ritual baths. Grossberg (1990: 169, 171) sees these and other similar installations at Masada as ritual baths that doubled as *frigidaria* (not vice versa!). Still other shallow pools at Masada, he contends (1990: 164–69), served for immersion of hands. See also Elisur 1999. Wright (1997: 196–99) acknowledges the difference between the stepped pools in the bathhouses at Masada and those found in bathhouses elsewhere in the Roman Empire, but insists that they need not be ritual baths: "They can just as easily be seen as adaptations of the Roman bathhouse to the Masada fortress." Wright's (and many others') either-or understanding of stepped pools (that is, either they are ritual baths or they are not) may not, however, be necessary. See discussion below.

9 See also M. *Middôt* 1: 6, 9.

10 A building at Jericho has recently been identified as a synagogue largely because it resembles the structure so identified at Gamala. The excavators also claim that a nearby pool is a *miqveh*, and note that in this regard, too, the configuration of the complex at Jericho is similar to that at Gamala, where a stepped pool has also been identified as a *miqveh* by archaeologists. See Netzer et al. 1999.

11 For prayer in the *bêt midrāš* and the relationship of that institution to the synagogue, see Miller 1998: 55–56 and 1999a: 60, 63–65.

12 Both *Judith* (12:7–8) and Josephus (*Ant* 3:258) allude to ritual bathing in springs. See Wright 1997: 205–10

on ritual bathing in Second Temple period sources from Israel and the Diaspora.

13 On synagogue architecture and the various views of its origins, see Levine 2000: 296–302.

14 See above, n. 2.

15 Admittedly, this remains to be proven, but the discovery of the concentration of stepped pools at Sepphoris, when just a few years ago it was assumed that such installations were peculiar to Jerusalem, and then only in Temple times, strongly suggests that the typology of these baths has a history of its own— one that is already being written.

16 See Meyers et al. 1992: 29. Selkin (1993: 83–84) posits the interesting possibility that the גבא בסלע of Damascus Document 10:12 originated with these rock hewn structures, in which case it may not have been exclusively a "*natural* rock pool." I would argue that both natural and man-made structures could have been intended, which would further reflect the multiple meanings and development suggested here. See Wright (1997: 212), who calls attention to the use of גבא at Isa 30:14 for "cistern," and at Eze 47:11 for a "swamp." See also M. *Miqvāʾôt* 1:1 and 1:4, where מי גבאים seems to allude to water in crevices in the ground. See Selkin (1993: 156–58), who translates the Mishnaic usage as "standing collections of water."

17 See especially M. *Miqvāʾôt* 4:2.

18 Netzer (1982: 110–13), maintains that pottery found in the "Cornucopia Miqveh" at Jericho was deposited there *after* the pool went out of use during "the last of the Hasmonean stages." The vessels, however, are roughly contemporaneous with the pool. Moreover, the finding of whole pottery in a pool does not necessarily mean that the pool itself had fallen out of use. Some pottery could have sunk to the bottom during rinsing or ritual immersion of the vessels (see the following note) and have been left there. Perhaps pools in which the largest quantities of whole pottery have been found were installations that were no longer used for ritual purposes, but were *still* functioning for rinsing/immersing dishes, rather than for storage; others, in which fewer and more fragmented vessels have been found, could have continued in operation both as ritual baths *and* for some of the profane applications described here. On the date of this particular pool at Jericho, see Netzer 1999: 30–31. On other pottery discoveries in stepped pools at Jericho and Sepphoris, see n. 19.

19 The other possibility, that the vessels were stored in the pools once the latter had gone out of use (see the preceding note), seems less likely. Stepped pools are not ideal places for storage. Nor does it appear that the vessels were being disposed of in defunct pools. The great many single-variety saucer-style vessels discovered recently in a stepped pool at Jericho and the many whole vessels found in some of the pools at Sepphoris hardly suggest disposal. It could, of course, be argued that some people believed, contrary to rabbinic law, that immersion of clay vessels was required. That would not, however, explain why a disproportionate number of these vessels have been found in the pools in comparison to glass vessels, which required immersion according to the *halāḵâ* and especially those composed of metal, which required ritual immersion according to *biblical* law. Interestingly, the ritual immersion of food utensils is still done today, and there are opinions that certain types of glazed earthenware require *tĕḇilāh;* see Cohen 1988: 18–19; 122–24. That some people in antiquity would have thought it was necessary to immerse earthenware, or perceived some spiritual benefit from doing so, does not seem farfetched, regardless of the view of the rabbis. In any event, rabbinic *halāḵâ* requires immersion only of metal and glass ware purchased from non-Jews. See B. *ʿAvôdâ Zarâ* 75b and P. *ʿAvôdâ Zarâ* 5, 45b. Is it likely that the amount of pottery found in stepped pools was acquired from non-Jews? Were there no Jewish potters in *ʾEreṣ* Israel? On the other hand, people who felt compelled to ritually immerse earthenware were either ignorant of rabbinic *halāḵâ* or disagreed with it. On the possible rationalization for the rabbinic practice, see Alon 1977a: 181–82.

20 Could swimming explain the depth of some of the pools at Jericho, as Netzer (1982: 117) has suggested? The rabbis were primarily concerned with the discoloration of the water used for ritual purification, not necessarily with how clean it was. Apparently, M. *Miqvāʾôt* 7:3 allows the rinsing of baskets that once contained fruit precisely because whatever fruit debris adhered to the unclean baskets was too insignificant and would not have discolored the water. See the comments of R. Ovadiah of Bartenoro and R. Yom Tov Lipmann Heller to M. *Miqvāʾôt* 7:3. M. *Yadayim* 1:3 allows for the ritual washing of hands in water that was "unfit for animals to drink," as long as the water was collected on the ground, rather than in a vessel. The same Mishnah continues that if the water had been discolored by ink, gum or vitriol—all of which suggest industrial use—it was invalid. The concern throughout appears to be that the water retain its character as water. Again, see the commentary of R. Ovadiah of Bartenoro *ad loc.* Thus, swimming, bathing or rinsing of dishes in a ritual bath may not have rendered the bath invalid according to rabbinic law. Interestingly,

the Damascus Document (10: 10–13) may have been stricter with regard to the use of foul water for ritual purification. See Selkin 1993: 140–41.

21 This approach obviates the concern of Eshel (1997: 131–33 and 2000: 45), who argues that stand-alone stepped pools were more likely to have been bathing installations. The point here is that these pools could very well have been built as such *or* with multiple uses in mind.

22 See the discussion of Levine (2000: 357–86, 446–47) on the "Communal Dimension" of the synagogue and on the disparity between the archaeological finds and the rabbinic perception of this institution.

23 Cf. Selkin 1993: 32: "Certainly there was a tremendous time differential between the biblical priestly materials and the Talmudic period. It would be naïve to suppose that no development, modification, dispute, or advance had occurred with the passage of time." Selkin argues that the artificial pools were non-existent in the pre-exilic period and only emerged in the Hellenistic period. Be that as it may (see above, n. 6), once they did appear, there is no reason to assume that their purpose and design did not evolve further over time. Are we dealing here with the sudden materialization of fully developed "miqvaot?" I doubt it. To be sure, Selkin (1993: 257, 264) seems to sense the likelihood of ongoing development and suggests that the *tannaim* eventually attempted to arrive at a compromise between the various purification systems available in their time.

24 See Galor's article in this volume, chapter 17.

25 See Galor's article in this volume, chapter 17, and Meyers, 2000: 49. Cf. Meyers 2002: 212–13.

26 See Galor's article in this volume, chapter 17.

27 See, most recently, Tsuk 2000: 41. The precise function of the water wheels at Sepphoris referred to as *galgalya' dĕ-Ṣippôri* in *Ecclesiastes Rabbâ* 12:6 and *Leviticus Rabbâ* 18:1 is unclear, despite recent speculation that these brought water from the aqueduct to the upper city.

28 See B. *Pĕsāḥîm* 34b, where the concept is explained, although there it applies to impure water that was intended for use in Temple times for the libation on the festival of *Sûkkôt*. This water could be seeded into valid rainwater, which would render it pure. See the comments of Rashi to B. *Niddāh* 17a. The term *zĕri'āh* frequently appears in later halakhic literature in reference to drawn water poured into a valid *miqveh*.

29 See comments of *Tôsafôt* to B. *Bāḇā' Batrā'* 66b.

30 There were two *tannaim* called Eliezer ben Ya'aqov, one belonging to the first generation of *tannaim*, the other to the post-Bar Kokhba period.

31 The *Tôsefta'* implies that the drawn water was added to the rainwater on the roof itself. See Maimonides, *Hilḵôt Miqvā'ôt* 4:8 and cf. Reich (1990: 27–28), who explains how this could have been done. The point seems to be that the waters had to mix before undergoing conduction along the ground to the pool; cf. Avramsky (1986: 28).

32 For a detailed discussion of the various ways in which M. *Miqvā'ôt* 4:4 can be understood, see Kehati 1977: 253–55. Also, see the comments of Horowitz 1991: 13, 87–89, where *hamšāḵâ* is described.

33 Galor (chapter 17 in this volume) argues that the water contained in the cisterns would barely have met the consumption needs of the population, making it unlikely that it would have been used in the stepped pools. However, it is just as unlikely that the stepped pools would have been solely filled with rainwater. Additional water would have been needed, depending upon the season and amount and types of use of any given pool. While water was precious, the amount needed periodically from the cisterns would not have taxed the overall system, except in the driest of spells, but then conservation measures would undoubtedly have applied to both the cisterns and the stepped pools. The location of the cisterns in such close proximity to these pools at Sepphoris, Sussiya (see Galor, chapter 17 in this volume) and Yodfat (Adan-Bayewitz and Aviam 1999: 150–51) remains suspicious and implies an organic relationship, one that easily can be discerned in SP 4 (fig. 2) and, for that matter, in SP 17 (fig. 1) as well. Right behind and above the *'ôṣār* in fig. 1 is an opening to a plastered container/cistern that extends south and eastward underneath the separation wall visible at the top of the photo. Beyond the wall and the cistern is a stairway (not visible in fig. 1) that leads down into a plastered niche and, three steps below, through an archway that opens into the container/cistern. The stairway/niche/archway may have been a later adaptation of the container/cistern installation resulting in another stepped pool (SP 16), this one directly supplied with water by the cistern. In any event, a clearly visible channel at the base of the wall in fig. 1 leads to the opening of the container/cistern and may have brought rainwater from the rooftop not only to the cistern and SP 16, but also to the reservoir/*'ôṣār* of SP 17.

34 The "cave" or a pit therein constituted an actual *miqveh*. See R. Ovadiah of Bartinoro, *ad loc.* and cf. the use of *mĕ'ārâ* at M. *Miqvā'ôt* 7:7. Interestingly, Reich (1990: 28) has identified a small basin near some stepped pools that may have been the trough (*'uqâ*) that is also referred to in M. *Miqvā'ôt* 4:4.

35 According to Jonathan Reed, the context and architecture of this particular installation remains unclear (personal communication). The suggestion made here must, therefore, remain tentative.

36 Immersion of hands is perhaps another possibility; see above, n. 8.

37 Regev 1996. Also, see Regev (1997: 169–72) where he responds to the objections of Grossberg (1997: 151–56). Grossberg maintains that these baths were meant to accommodate the great many pilgrims to Jerusalem, whether priests, Levites or Israelites, and that they were designed so that one could exit to the right and towards the east, which, according to B. *Yômāʾ* 17b and B. *Zĕvāḥim* 62b, was the preferred protocol. Reich (1980: 225–56) was the first to elaborate the theory that the divided stairways were intended to separate those who had already bathed from those who were still impure. Grossberg discounts this possibility as well. For other pools with partitioned stairs, see Amit (1997; 1999).

38 See Sanders 1990: 218–19; Regev 1996: 12–21. Also, see Regev 1997: 172–76, where he responds to Grossberg 1997: 159–63.

39 Selkin 1993: 147–49, 160–61.

40 Sanders 1990: 222–25. Sander's contention that these aristocrats used drawn water in their *miqvāʾôt* is partially premised on his understanding of M. *Zāḇîm* 5:12. This Mishnah precludes the eating of *tĕrûmâ* by an impure person who has immersed their head and most of their body in drawn water and by a person who happens to be "pure," but upon whose head and most of their body three *lûgin* of drawn water has fallen. While Sanders presumes that this means people actually immersed in drawn water, the commentators understand these two rulings as *related.* According to R. Ovadiah of Bartinoro, *ad loc.,* for example, one who immersed in smelly waters in a cave (not a plastered pool!) might be tempted to bathe in drawn water afterwards, which could lead to the mistaken use of drawn water altogether. In order to further ensure that this was not done, the rabbis ruled that a person who was *tāhôr* upon whom drawn water fell would also be unfit for eating *tĕrûmâ.* The commentators, at least, do not see this as a rejection of some sectarian practice. Rather, the Mishnah seems to be primarily concerned with *washing* in drawn water *after* one has immersed properly in rainwater. The further restriction was simply intended as a *gĕzērâ* to ensure that this was not done. It was not necessarily a response to a common practice of immersing in drawn water. Sanders may be correct that some people did just that (see below), but this passage requires too much reading into to support his argument.

41 Sanders (1990: 224) argues that only aristocrats, who could afford servants to bucket the considerable volume needed to fill the pools, would have owned them! Again, at least during the rainy season, rainwater could have gathered upon the rooftops and flowed through pipes to the pools. During the drier seasons, drawn water could have supplemented whatever was left of the rainwater. To be sure, Sanders (1990: 356–57, n. 63) considers this possibility, but rejects it both because, to date, archaeological evidence for rooftop "reservoirs" does not exist and, in any event, such structures would be impractical. In fact, however, a "reservoir" was not needed. As already discussed, talmudic sources refer to waters collected on roofs that flowed into *miqvāʾôt* (see n. 31). Several stepped pools at Sepphoris appear to have had pipes leading from above. Cf. Meyers 2000: 49.

42 See T. *Nĕgāʿîm* 8:2 and parallels, where R. Tarfon is said to have purified some lepers. On the preservation after 70 C.E. of ashes of the red cow for the preparation of "water of purification" for those who contracted corpse impurity, see T. *Pārâ* 5:6 and the comments of Safrai 1958: 206–7. Also, cf. Oppenheimer 1977: 64.

43 The practice is presented among other matters taught to minors, and not as an obsolete custom only applicable to Temple times. The passage includes a gloss by R. Judah ben Ilai, who was a second-century *tanna.* Cf. T. *Tohŏrôt* 3:10.

44 See Alon 1977b: 205–34. The view that the Pharisees ate everyday meals in a state of purity, promoted especially by Neusner 1979: 83, and in much of his other work on the Pharisees, has been challenged by Sanders (1990: 131–254). For recent discussions of the issue and bibliography, see Harrington 1993: 267–81; Hengel and Deines 1995: 41–51; Taylor 1997: 60, n. 21; and Maccoby 1999: 209–13.

45 See T. *Ḥăgîgâ* 3:2–3 where we also hear that Onkelos the proselyte did the same. See Oppenheimer 1977: 64.

46 T. *ʿAvôdâ Zarâ* 3:10 and parallels. See Safrai 1972: 74–76 and cf. Oppenheimer 1977: 83, 145.

47 T. *Šabbāt* 1: 14; P. *Šabbāt* 1, 3b and B. *Šabbāt* 13a. On the expression "purity has spread," which is often incorrectly translated as "purity has broken out," see Miller 2003: 403, n. 7 and 412.

48 See especially P. *ʿAvôdâ Zarâ* 5, 45b, where late third- and early fourth-century *amoraim* of *ʾEreṣ* Israel discuss issues that arose pertaining to the immersion of vessels purchased from Gentiles. See Alon 1977a: 181.

49 On Yose's contribution to the Mishnah, see Epstein 1957: 126–47 and Miller 1999b: 153–54. Not surprisingly, Yose's opinions also frequently appear in the tractate *Miqvāʾôt.* On Yose at Sepphoris, see Miller 2006: 36–38, 289 n. 235, and 443.

50 Cf. discussion of *bēt tĕbilâ* above, and see M. *Shĕqālim* 8:2.

51 A tradition preserved in both *Talmûdîm* ascribes this immersion to Ezra. See P. *Yômaʾ* 8, 44d; P. *Taʿănît* 1, 64c; P. *Mĕgillâ* 75a; B. *Bĕrakôt* 22b; and B. *Bābāʾ Qammāʾ* 82a. For discussions of the evolution of this ablution, see Alon 1977b: 191–97 and Ginzberg 1941: 272–76.

52 See B. *Bĕrakôt* 22b and discussion in Ginzberg 1941: 274.

53 On the *tôvĕlê šahărît* see Ginzberg 1941: 238–39.

54 Note how the book of Judith (12:7) reports that the heroine would immerse daily before prayer.

55 Ginzberg 1941: 236–38, 274–76. See also the objections *of the Pharisees* to the morning bathers in *T. Yādayim* 2:20.

56 *Against Apion* 2:202–3. On Philo, see Sanders 1992: 268–70.

57 Again see P. *Bĕrakôt* 3, 6c. The donkey driver appears to have been a transgressor who had adulterous relations with a menstruating woman, but this piece of data may have been meant to be taken facetiously. In any event, he pays a price for not listening to the prominent rabbi — he drowns! For a fuller discussion, see Ginzberg 1941: 255–56 and Miller 1999c: 547–48. See, in the same *sûgyāʾ*, the already cited story involving Yose ben Yose and a fellow traveler on a ship who wanted to immerse before eating. The intention there also seems to have been that the person was sexually impure.

58 That scholars frequently overlook these practices is particularly fascinating since the ritual bath continues to be used for some of the same purposes even today. Thus, aside from its use by women who have completed the waiting period after their menstrual flow, the ritual bath is still used for immersion of eating utensils (see n. 19). It is also used by some men, primarily Kabbalists, once a week before the Sabbath, and by many others before festivals, especially Yom Kippur. A bride and groom each immerse before their wedding. In addition, although not a full immersion, washing of hands is required in the morning in preparing for prayer, as well as before meals at which bread is eaten. While some of these practices are later developments, they all testify either to the ongoing, if vestigial, significance of purity in Jewish life or to the persistence of the symbolism and meaning of water, on which, see below. Converts, too, are required by *halākâ* to undergo immersion, much as the Israelites did in anticipation of the revelation at Sinai, according to the traditional understanding of the forms of *q/d/š* in Exo 19:10, 14. See Schiffman 1985: 19–21, 25–30. Proselyte immersion may also have been a purification rite, as the derivation from Exodus 19 would suggest. See Taylor 1997: 64–69 and Selkin 1993: 3.

59 Goodman (1983: 94–96) collects rabbinic case studies to examine the interest in purities in Roman Galilee. He concludes (p. 102) that the purity laws were "those most likely to be ignored because of their complexity." Nevertheless, he admits that the sexual purity laws were observed,and suggests (p. 107) this was "because these laws were securely in the control of the women and could be used by them for psychological advantage over their husbands." In contrast, the point made here is that *both* men and women had ritual obligations where sexuality was concerned and that the ritual bath was not solely used for immersion after a woman's menstrual flow. More importantly, there were other applications of ritual purity that involved the ritual bath after 70 C.E., and, in any event, purity and immersion practices had much more compelling motivations that resulted in their widespread observance. The minutiae of rabbinic law should not be seen as an overwhelming obstacle to the observance of ritual purity laws, since the basic practices would have had a life of their own. I would agree with Sanders (1992: 229), who claims that the biblical purity laws had much influence in the last century before the destruction of the Temple. I further argue here that such influence would not have waned and instead would have found renewed expression after 70 C.E. Non-observance of purity laws or their limitation to menstrual laws would have been strange.

60 *Yalqût Kî Tiśāʾ* 386 and *Elîyahû Rabbâ* 16.

61 Cf. Milgrom 1990: 88. On the ritual purity-land nexus, see Maccoby 1999: 199–208, 212–13.

62 See Milgrom (1990: 96–97, n. 17), who maintains that Sadducees would have shared with the Pharisees an interest in purity matters beyond the Temple. Their real difference with the Pharisees was that they thought of themselves as "the master pedagogues," authorized by the Torah and especially its Holiness Code to demonstrate how one lives a life of sanctity.

63 According to Milgrom, water is only "purificatory" and not regenerative in the Torah. See, especially, Milgrom 1991: 957–68, where he considers the view of Eliade.

64 Selkin 1993: 233–34. See especially *Siprê* Deut 48 (ed. Finkelstein, 110.12–111.5) and *Tannāʾ de-Bê Eliyāhû* 18 (ed. Ish Shalom, 105).

65 In his *Dialogue with Trypho* (14:1), Justin Martyr insists that the Jews dig cisterns that only cleanse the flesh and body. He also (46:2) has Trypho allude to washing after coming into contact with things prohibited by Moses and after sexual relations as an important law. Sanders (1990: 360 n. 11) suggests that *baptizesthai* may not mean full immersion here. In contrast, Selkin (1993: 230) thinks the cisterns Justin refers to are actually allusions to ritual baths.

66 Noted already by Reich 1995: 289–97, where he discusses the evidence. See Levine (2000: 310–11), who sees the inclusion of stepped pools in synagogue complexes as primarily a pre-70 C.E. phenomenon and maintains that there was a diminished interest in ritual purity observance after that time.

67 The earliest pools at Sepphoris date from the Hellenistic period and are the largest, intended to accommodate more than a single person. These more likely belong to public buildings, such as the fortified building in area 85.3. See Galor, chapter 17 in this volume. With the onset of the Roman period, domestic pools become more prevalent, suggesting a new perception of their various applications that only grew with time, particularly after 70 C.E.. It is at least curious that this very much parallels the development of the synagogue, which also first appeared, in its rudimentary but formal form, in the Hellenistic period and became increasingly more multifaceted and ubiquitous with time.

68 On the development of rabbinic understandings of menstruation, see Fonrobert 2000.

REFERENCES

Adan-Bayewitz, D., and Aviam, M.

1999 Iotapata, Josephus and the Siege of 67: Preliminary Report on the 1992–94 Seasons. Pp. 131–65 in *The Roman and Byzantine Near East*, ed. J. Humphrey. Journal of Roman Archaeology Supplementary Series 31. Ann Arbor, MI: JRA.

Alon, G.

1977a The Levitical Uncleanness of Gentiles. Pp. 146–89 in *Jews, Judaism and the Classical World: Studies in Jewish History in the Times of the Second Temple and Talmud*, trans. I. Abrahams. Jerusalem: Magnes.

1977b Bounds of the Laws of Levitical Cleanness. Pp. 190–234 in *Jews, Judaism and the Classical World: Studies in Jewish History in the Times of the Second Temple and Talmud*, trans. I. Abrahams. Jerusalem: Magnes.

Amit, D.

1997 Jerusalem-Style Ritual Baths from the Time of the Second Temple in Mt. Hevron. Pp. 35–48 in *Studies in the History of the Land of Israel dedicated to Professor Yehuda Feliks*, eds. Y. Friedman, Z. Safrai and J. Schwartz. Ramat Gan: Bar Ilan (Hebrew).

1999 A *Miqveh* Complex Near Alon Shevut. *Atiqot* 38: 75–84.

Avramsky, Y.

1986 *Tosefta with the Commentary Ḥāzôn Yehezqel, Masek̲tta' Miqvā'ōt.* Jerusalem (Hebrew).

Cohen, S. J. D.

1999 Purity, Piety, and Polemic: Medieval Rabbinic Denunciations of 'Incorrect' Purification Practices. Pp. 82–100 in *Women and Water: Menstruation in Jewish Life and Law*, ed. R. R. Wasserfall. Hanover, NH: Brandeis / University Press of New England.

Cohen, Z.

1988 *Tevilath Kelim, A Comprehensive Guide.* Southfied, MI: Targum.

Eliade, M.

1957 *The Sacred and the Profane: The Nature of Religion*, trans. W. R. Trask. San Diego, CA: Harcourt.

1958 *Patterns in Comparative Religion.*, trans. R. Sheed. New York, NY: Sheed and Ward.

Elisur, Y.

1999 Miqvā'ōt for the Immersion of Hands. *Cathedra* 91: 169–72 (Hebrew).

Epstein, J. N.

1957 *Introduction to Tannaitic Literature, Mishna, Tosephta and Halakhic Midrashim.* Tel Aviv: Devir (Hebrew).

Eshel, H.

1997 A Note on 'Miqvaot' at Sepphoris. Pp. 131–33 in *Archaeology and the Galilee*, eds. D. R. Edwards and C. T. McCollough. Atlanta, GA: Scholars.

2000 They're Not Ritual Baths. Featured debate on: The Pools of Sepphoris, Ritual Baths or Bathtubs? *Biblical Archaeology Review* 26, no. 4: 46–49.

Fonrobert, C. E.
2000 *Menstrual Purity: Rabbinic and Christian Reconstructions of Biblical Gender.* Stanford, CA: Stanford University.

Ginzberg, L.
1941 *A Commentary on the Palestinian Talmud, a Study of the Development of the Halakhah and Haggadah in Palestine and Babylonia,* vol. 2. New York, NY: Ktav.

Goodman, M.
1983 *State and Society in Roman Galilee, A.D. 132–212.* Totowa, NJ: Rowman & Allanheld.

Grossberg A.
1990 Ritual Baths for the Immersion of Hands at Masada. *Cathedra* 95: 164–71.
1997 The *Miqva'ot* in Jerusalem during the Second Temple Period and Methods for their Ritual Preparation. *Cathedra* 83: 151–68 (Hebrew).

Harrington H. K.
1993 *The Impurity Systems of Qumran and the Rabbis.* Atlanta, GA: Scholars.

Hengel, M., and Deines, R.
1995 E. P. Sander's 'Common Judaism', Jesus, and the Pharisees. *Journal of Theological Studies* (n.s.) 46, no. 1: 1–70.

Horowitz Z.
1991 *Seder Tohoros Vol. IV(b), Tractate Mikvaos.* Artscroll Mishnah Series. Brooklyn, NY: Mesorah.

Kehati, P.
1977 *Mishnāyôt, Sēder Tohŏrôt,* II. Jerusalem: Hekhal Shelomo (Hebrew).

Levine, B. A.
1989 *The JPS Torah Commentary: Leviticus.* Philadelphia, PA: JPS.

Levine, L. I.
2000 *The Ancient Synagogue, The First Thousand Years.* New Haven, CT: Yale University.

Maccoby, H.
1999 *Ritual and Morality, The Ritual Purity System and its Place in Judaism.* Cambridge: Cambridge University.

Meyers, E. M.; Netzer, E.; and Meyers, C. L.
1992 *Sepphoris.* Winona Lake, IN: Eisenbrauns.

Meyers, E. M.
2000 Yes, They Are (Response to H. Eshel, The Pools of Sepphoris, Ritual Baths or Bathtubs? —They're Not Ritual Baths). *Biblical Archaeology Review* 26, no. 4: 46–49.
2002 Aspects of Everyday Life in Roman Palestine with Special Reference to Private Domiciles and Ritual Baths. Pp. 193–220 in *Jews in the Hellenistic and Roman Cities,* ed. J. R. Bartlett. London: Routledge.

Milgrom, J.
1990 The Scriptural Foundations and Derivations in the Laws of Purity of the Temple Scroll. Pp. 83–99 in *Archaeology and History in the Dead Sea Scrolls, The New York University Conference in Memory of Yigael Yadin*, ed. L. H. Schiffman. Journal for the Study of the Pseudepigrapha Supplement Series 8. Sheffied: JSOT.
1991 *Leviticus 1–16. A New Translation with Introduction and Commentary.* New York, NY: Doubleday.

Miller, S. S.
1984 *Studies in the History and Traditions of Sepphoris.* Leiden: Brill.
1998 On the Number of Synagogues in the Cities of 'Eretz Israel. *Journal of Jewish Studies* 49, no.1: 51–66.
1999a The Rabbis and the Non-Existent Monolithic Synagogue. Pp. 57–70 in *Jews, Christians and Polytheists in the Ancient Synagogue,* ed. S. Fine. London: Routledge.
1999b New Perspectives on the History of Sepphoris. Pp. 145–59 in *Galilee through the Centuries: Confluence of Cultures,* ed. E. Meyers. Winona Lake, IN: Eisenbrauns.
1999c Those Cantankerous Sepphoreans Revisited. Pp. 543–73 in *Ki Baruch Hu: Ancient Near Eastern, Biblical, and Judaic Studies in Honor of Baruch A. Levine,* eds. R. Chazan, W. W. Hallo and L. H. Schiffman. Warsaw, IN: Eisenbrauns.
2000 Review of D. R. Edwards and C. T. McCollough, eds., *Archaeology and the Galilee.* Atlanta: Scholars Press, 1997. In *Jewish Quarterly Review* 91, no. 1–2: 33–38.
2003 Some Observations on Stone Vessel Finds and Ritual Purity in Light of Talmudic Sources. Pp. 402–19 in *Zeichen aus Text und Stein: Studien auf dem Weg zu einer Archäologie des Neuen Testaments*, eds. S. Alkier and J. Zangenberg. Tübingen: Francke.
2006 *Sages and Commoners in Late Antique 'Ereẓ Israel: A Philological Inquiry into Local Traditions in Talmud Yerushalmi.* Tübingen: Mohr Siebeck.
forthcoming Priests, Purities, and the Jews of Galilee. In *Ancient Galilee in Interaction, Religion, Ethnicity and Identity*, eds. H. W. Attridge, D. B. Martin and J. Zangenberg. Tübingen: Mohr.

Netzer, E.
1982 Ancient Ritual Baths (*Miqvaot*) in Jericho. Pp. 106–19 in *The Jerusalem Cathedra, Studies in the History, Archaeology, Geography and Ethnography of the Land of Israel* 2, ed. L. Levine. Detroit, MI: Wayne State.

1991 *Masada III: The Yigal Yadin Excavations 1963–1965, Final Reports.* Jerusalem: Israel Exploration Society.

1999 *The Palaces of the Hasmoneans and Herod the Great.* Jerusalem: Yad Izhak ben-Zvi (Hebrew).

Netzer, E.; Kalman, Y.; and Luries, Y.

1999 A Synagogue from the Period of the Hasmoneans at Jericho. *Qadmoniyot* 32, no. 1: 17–24.

Neusner, J.

1979 *From Politics to Piety: the Emergence of Pharisaic Judaism.* New York, NY: Ktav.

1981 *Judaism: The Evidence of the Mishnah.* Chicago, IL: University of Chicago.

1994 *Purity in Rabbinic Judaism, A Systematic Account: The Sources, Media, Effects, and Removal of Uncleanness.* Atlanta, GA: Scholars.

Oppenheimer, A.

1977 *The Am Ha-Aretz, A Study in the Social History of the Jewish People in the Hellenistic-Roman Period.* Leiden: Brill.

Regev, A.

1996 Purification Baths of Classes and Sects in Israel during the Second Temple Period,. *Cathedra* 79: 3–21 (Hebrew).

1997 More on Ritual Purity Baths of Classes and Sects: The Methodology of Scholarly Research and the Archeological Finds—A Response. *Cathedra* 83: 169–76 (Hebrew).

Reich, R.

1980 Mishnah *Sheqalim* 8:2 and Archaeological Discovery. Pp. 225–56 in *Jerusalem in the Second Temple Period, Abraham Schalit Memorial Volume,* eds. A. Oppenheimer, U. Rappaport and M. Stern. Jerusalem: Yad Izhak Ben-Zvi (Hebrew).

1988 The Hot Bath House (*balneum*), the *Miqweh* and the Jewish Community in the Second Temple Period," *Journal of Jewish Studies* 39, no.1: 102–17.

1990 Ritual Purity Baths in the Second Temple Period and the Period of the Mishnah and Talmud. Unpublished Ph.D. dissertation, Hebrew University.

1993 The Great Mikveh Debate. *Biblical Archaeology Review* 19, no. 2: 52–53.

1995 The Synagogue and the *Miqweh* in Eretz-Israel in the Second-Temple, Mishnaic, and Talmudic Periods. Pp. 289–97 in *Ancient Synagogues, Historical Analysis and Archaeological Discovery,* eds. D. Urman and P. V. M. Flesher. Leiden: Brill.

Safrai, S.

1958 Bet She'arim in Talmudic Literature. *'Eres-Israel* 5: 206–12 (Hebrew).

1972 The Holy Congregation in Jerusalem. *Scripta Hierosolymitana* 28: 62–78.

Sanders, E. P.

1990 *Jewish Law from Jesus to the Mishnah.* Philadelphia, PA: Trinity International.

1992 *Judaism: Practice and Belief 63* BCE*–66* CE. Philadelphia, PA: Trinity International.

Sawicki, M.

2000 *Crossing Galilee: Architectures of Contact in the Occupied Land of Jesus.* Harrisburg, PA: Trinity International.

Schiffman, L. H.

1985 *Who Was a Jew: Rabbinic and Halakhic Perspectives on the Jewish-Christian Schism.* Hoboken, NJ: Ktav.

Selkin, C. B.

1993 Exegesis and Identity: The Hermeneutics of *Miqwa'ot* in the Greco-Roman Period. Unpublished Ph.D. dissertation, Duke University.

Taylor, J.

1997 *The Immerser: John the Baptist within Second Temple Judaism.* Grand Rapids, MI: Eerdmans.

Tsuk, T.

2000 Bringing Water to Sepphoris. *Biblical Archaeology Review* 26, no. 4: 34–41.

Wright III, B. G.

1997 Jewish Ritual Baths—Interpreting the Digs and the Texts: Some Issues in the Social History of Second Temple Judaism. Pp. 190–214 in *The Archaeology of Israel, Constructing the Past, Interpreting the Present,* eds. N. A. Silberman and D. Small. JSOT Supplement Series 237. Sheffield: Sheffield Academic.

Chapter 19

Jewish Ossuaries of the Early Roman Period: Continuity and Change in Death Ritual

by Byron R. McCane

The rise of the Jewish ossuary during the Early Roman period has long been puzzling to archaeologists and historians of Syria-Palestine.[1] Amid the rich ferment of Jewish culture in Palestine under the Greeks and Romans, the emergence of these limestone chests for individual secondary burial stands out as a striking — and elusive — development. Completely unknown before about 30 B.C.E., Jewish ossuaries proliferate in and around Jerusalem during the first century C.E. and persist in various locations across Palestine until at least the mid-third century C.E. What were the factors behind the rise of the Jewish ossuary? What forces prompted Jews in this part of the world to begin practicing this new form of secondary burial? In particular, what moved them to alter their long-standing pattern of collective secondary burial, a custom with deep roots in local history and culture?

More than thirty years ago, Eric M. Meyers proposed that parallels to the Jewish ossuary could be found in similar types of ancient Near Eastern containers for secondary burial (Meyers 1971a: 92–96). Drawing upon examples from as far away as Persia and Crete, Meyers interpreted the ossuary as a Jewish adaptation of a widespread ancient Near Eastern funerary practice. Since then Prof. Meyers' distinguished work as an archaeologist and biblical scholar has had the effect of dramatically expanding our understanding of the history and culture of Syria-Palestine. In particular, he has helped to bring to light with subtle clarity the practical contours of the confluence between Judaism and Hellenism during the Hellenistic and Roman periods. This chapter argues that the rise of the Jewish ossuary also belongs to the story of the encounter between Judaism and Hellenism. In particular, I maintain that it was the increasing influence of Hellenistic cultural norms valorizing the human individual, which led Palestinian Jews to develop a form of secondary burial that preserved individual identity. The ossuary is best understood, in other words, as an artifact of the intersection between Judaism and Hellenism, and, as such, it exemplifies what Prof. Meyers has described as Hellenism's ability to "serve as a framework for preserving and promoting local Semitic culture" (Meyers 1998: 29).

DEFINING THE JEWISH OSSUARY

A Jewish ossuary from the early Roman (ER) period is a chest or box, usually made of stone, but occasionally of clay or wood, used for secondary burial, i.e., the reburial of human bones after the flesh of the corpse has decayed. Hollowed out from blocks of the soft limestone that is so common in Syria-Palestine, ossuaries are proportionate in size to the large and long bones of the body (e.g., skull and femur). Thus the average size for an adult's ossuary is approximately 60 × 35 × 30 cm, with smaller measurements for children. In keeping with their function, ossuaries have removable lids, most of which are flat, although some are domed or gabled. The majority of ossuaries are plain and undecorated, but many are ornamented with decorations typical of artistic motifs in the Early Jewish culture of Syria-Palestine (Figueras 1983; Rahmani 1994: 28–52). Geometric designs, for example, appear very frequently, the most common being a six-petalled rosette that was chip-carved into the side of the ossuary using a chisel and compass (Rahmani 1988). Representations of Jewish religious themes also appear, including palm branches, *menoroth*, and Torah shrines. Inscriptions, when present, are scrawled with charcoal or scratched with a nail or sharp object and may be found virtually anywhere on the ossuary, including the sides, ends, lid, or even along the inside edge. These inscriptions typically include only the name of the deceased and sometimes a nickname, patronymic, or place of origin. Occasionally, a distinguishing fact about the deceased may also be added. Since my argument is that ossuaries emerged from the engagement of Judaism with Hellenism, it is of interest to note here that slightly more than forty percent of inscriptions on Jewish ossuaries from the ER period are in Greek.[2]

Ossuaries are found in Jewish tombs from ER Palestine, most often in tombs within the vicinity of Jerusalem.[3] The typical cave is a nearly square chamber (approximately 3.5 m on a side) cut from bedrock, with a shallow rectangular pit in the floor creating a low shelf around the walls. Several *loculi* (Heb. *kokhim*) — i.e., deep narrow niches for the primary burial of a single body — are usually carved into the walls. The openings of *loculi* that contained human remains are often found to have been covered with flat stone slabs. Ossuaries may be found in whole or in part in several locations around such a tomb, including on the shelf, in niches, and on the floor. Other typical finds include human bones on the shelf and in the niches, perfume bottles (piriform *unguentaria*), juglets, cooking pots, and lamps. Coins, by contrast, are quite rare (McCane 2003).

SECONDARY BURIAL

The archaeological evidence from tombs of this sort, along with contemporaneous literary references to death and burial, indicates that the ritual process of secondary burial in ossuaries took place in two stages. At the time of death, bodies were placed in the tomb, either on the shelf or in niches. The presence of human skeletal remains — often still articulated — on the shelves or in niches confirms this practice of primary burial. Literary sources agree, depicting primary burial in a rock-cut tomb as a public ceremony that occurred as soon as possible after death, often on the same day (Mk 5:21–43; Jn 11:1–44; *m. Sanh.* 6.5). Shortly after death had occurred, the body was washed, wrapped in linen, placed on a bier, and carried to the tomb. Literary sources describe this ceremony of primary burial as a public occasion, a ritual moment during which the family of the deceased experienced significant social visibility. Josephus (*War* II.1) goes so far as to assert that many families were reduced to poverty by the expense of providing a socially acceptable funeral. Josephus exaggerates, of course, but his remark does underline the social prominence of the ritual of primary burial.

Secondary burial, by contrast, was performed much later when decomposition of the flesh was complete — or nearly so. In a private ceremony that took place entirely within the confines of the family burial cave, the bones of the deceased were taken from their resting place on the shelf or in a niche and were collected in an ossuary. The ossuary was then marked with the name of the deceased and positioned in its final resting place, either on the floor, on the shelf, or in a niche. When ossuaries were placed in *loculi*, the openings of the niches were frequently sealed over with stone slabs. Literary depictions of secondary burial are consonant with this archaeological evidence. The sources describe a private ceremony, attended perhaps by as few as one or two close relatives of the deceased. *Sem.* 12.9, for example, describes the rite of secondary burial rather poignantly:

> Rabbi Eleazar bar Zadok said: Thus spoke my father at the time of his death: "My son, bury me first in a niche. In the course of time, collect my bones and put them in an ossuary; but do not gather them with your own hands." And thus did I attend him: Johanan entered, collected the bones, and spread a sheet over them. I then came in, rent my clothes for them, and sprinkled dried herbs over them. Just as he attended his father, so I attended him.

Other sources (e.g., Q 9:59–60) also emphasize the connection between secondary burial and the nuclear family group.

Individual secondary burial of this sort had virtually no history in Syria-Palestine prior to the ER period. On the contrary, the dominant pattern throughout the region for centuries had been *collective* secondary burial, in which the bones of the deceased were piled together in a common heap along with the bones of all previously deceased family members. In the Late Bronze Age, for example, bones were gathered together to one side of a roughly circular underground tomb. By the Iron II, this simple LB tomb architecture had evolved into the Israelite "bench tomb," in which a low bench ran along three sides of a roughly square cave. At the time of primary burial, bodies were laid on the shelf to decompose, and when decomposition was complete, the bones were gathered into a recess hollowed out beneath the bench. Over time, these recesses came to hold the bones of all family members long dead, so that the material culture of Iron Age secondary burial is vividly captured in the familiar biblical expression, "he slept and was gathered to his fathers" (Meyers 1971b: 96; cf. Bloch-Smith 1992). Collective secondary burial of this sort persisted into the closing decades of the first century B.C.E., when charnel rooms are common in many Jewish tombs of the Late Hellenistic and ER period. In these tombs, bones of family members were piled together in a separate chamber prepared and reserved exclusively for that purpose (see Rahmani 1958; 1967; Kloner 1980). It is important to observe that at the conclusion of this kind of collective secondary burial, the remains of the deceased would have been rendered completely indistinguishable from the remains of the "fathers." The identity of the individual would have been thoroughly dissolved into an ancestral collective. In the common heap of bones beneath the bench of an Iron II tomb or in a charnel room of the Late Hellenistic period, it would have been impossible for surviving relatives to identify the remains of any individual deceased family member. With the ossuary, by contrast, the identity of the deceased was preserved even after death and secondary burial, because the individual container — often marked with the name of the deceased — protected his or her individuality.[4]

THE RISE OF THE JEWISH OSSUARY

Previous attempts to account for the rise of the Jewish ossuary have been generally unsatisfactory, largely because they have sought to explain the ossuary primarily as an expression of Jewish theological convictions and religious beliefs. A particularly common view has held that the ossuary arose from Jewish convictions about death and the afterlife, especially belief in the bodily resurrection of the dead.[5] Drawing upon late rabbinic sources, including some that suggest that decomposition of the flesh could expiate sin (*BT Shabb.* 13b; *BT Kidd.* 31b; *BT Sanh.* 47b; *BT Berakh.* 18b), this view has maintained that individual secondary burial in ossuaries served as a ritual preparation of the dead for the day of resurrection. Gathering the bones of the deceased in an ossuary supposedly gave symbolic representation to the fact that the deceased was purified from sin and ready to be raised. The rise of the ossuary, in other words, was driven by the rise of belief in bodily resurrection. The weakness of this argument is plain to see and does not need to be belabored here. Suffice it to say that no sources from the ER period associate the ossuary with belief in the resurrection, and talmudic sources are simply too late to be used as uncorroborated evidence for Jewish religious beliefs in the first century C.E.

THE OSSUARY AND SOCIAL STRUCTURE

It is a striking fact that academic discussion of the Jewish ossuary has not made use of an insight that has become a commonplace in the anthropology of death ritual, namely, that death ritual is intimately related to social structure. Ever since the early 20th century, when Robert Hertz first traced the extent of social determination in funerary practice, it has become increasingly clear that ritual disposal of the dead is laden with symbolic representations and ceremonial performances which express, celebrate, repair, and reinforce a social system (Hertz 1960; cf. Metcalf and Huntington 1992). The performance of death ritual is driven not primarily by the psychological needs of individuals, nor even by the religious convictions of groups, but by tasks and conflicts that confront society as a whole. For death hardly confines itself to ending the physical life of a mortal body; certainly it does that, but it also does much more, tearing a hole in the fabric of a society, slashing through bonds that have tied people together, and knocking the social equilibrium off balance. Death forcibly removes a member of a social network, and in so doing, calls into question the ongoing viability of the network as a whole. Death ritual, Hertz argued, is a social process that meets the threat of death head on; it is society's way of ensuring that "the last word must be with life" (Hertz 1960: 97). In other words, social structure is established through death ritual, and changes in death ritual, when they occur, usually are associated with developments in social structure. As Ian Morris has succinctly put it, "In rituals people use symbols to make social structure explicit" (Morris 1992: 1). A compelling account of the rise of the Jewish ossuary, then, should connect the emergence of these bone containers with changes in the social structure of Jerusalem during the late first century B.C.E. and the early first century C.E.

HELLENISM AND THE RISE OF INDIVIDUATION IN DEATH RITUALS

Fine has recently taken a step in this direction by proposing that the rise of the ossuary reflects "a general pattern of individuation within the Greco-Roman world" (Fine 2000: 76). Citing both economic and cultural factors, he argues that economic prosperity in Jerusalem under Herod the Great, along with "developing notions of the individual's place within the family unit" (Fine 2000: 75), provided the means and the motive for Jews in Jerusalem to begin practicing a form of secondary burial that preserved individual identity. "Clearly there were Jews in first-century Jerusalem for whom the identity of each individual was important" (Fine 2000: 74). This is the beginning of a good argument. Certainly the building programs of Herod the Great did bring economic prosperity in general, and a thriving stone-carving industry in particular, to Jerusalem. Some ossuaries — such as the "Caiaphas" ossuary with its richly ornamented rosettes — betray an unmistakable level of affluence. Prosperity alone, however, is not sufficient to account for the rise of the Jewish ossuary. Some ossuaries are ornately decorated and elegantly crafted, but many (if not most) are of quite crude construction — roughly hewn, unevenly formed, and lacking any kind of decoration. Such artifacts are certainly not products of skilled workmanship, nor monuments of material affluence. In addition, while economic prosperity may be able to explain the rising quality of some burial goods in ER Jerusalem, it does not account for the change in the *form* of burial ritual during this time. Rising standards of living in and of themselves do not demand a shift from *collective* secondary burial in charnel rooms to *individual* secondary burial in ossuaries. Prosperous Jews in first-century Jerusalem could equally well have hired skilled stone-carvers to construct elaborately ornamented charnel rooms for their family tombs. Of course, they did not — they began to use ossuaries instead. Economic developments in first-century Jerusalem do not, therefore, provide a sufficient background for the rise of the Jewish ossuary. The anthropology of death ritual, by contrast, suggests that the most likely source for the social energy that produced the ossuary was a change of some sort in the role of the individual in family and society in ER Jerusalem.

Certainly, Jewish society in Jerusalem had undergone profound changes in the centuries immediately prior to the ER period, and during this time no influence was more substantial or long-lasting than the culture of Hellenism. Even before Alexander the Great had conquered the eastern end of the Mediterranean, traders and mercenaries from the Aegean had already made their way to Palestine, bringing with them the Attic coins and black-figured wares that regularly surface in Persian-period strata of archaeological excavations. As early as the middle of the fifth century B.C.E., "the handwriting was already on the wall, and it was in Greek" (Meyers 1992). Later, under the auspices of Roman political and military authority, the cultural streams of Judaism and Hellenism came to terms with each other more fully and in specific and creative ways. All Jews in Palestine (indeed, all Jews in the ancient world) became "hellenized" to one degree or another, as every area of life — language, politics, education, architecture, literature, religion, and material culture — absorbed a cultural imprint whose origins were in Greece. While the depth of this imprint varied from place to place, by the ER period its breadth covered most of Syria-Palestine. It is important to observe that among the areas of culture which Hellenism had touched was death ritual. Even before the ER period, the process of Hellenization had already begun to introduce recognizable changes into Jewish death ritual in Palestine. Primary burial in sarcophagi, for example, increased during the Early Hellenistic period, and the *loculus* niche — a Hellenistic form of tomb architecture — also came into Palestine during the first century B.C.E. (McCane 1997; Ilan 1997). Even the Greco-Roman custom of putting a coin in the mouth of the deceased (to pay Charon, the ferryman across the river Styx) eventually came to be practiced by some Jewish families, including the family of Caiaphas the High Priest. All of these burial customs are of Hellenistic origin, showing that the ossuary would certainly not have been the first aspect of Jewish death ritual to be affected by the interaction of Judaism with Hellenism.

It is particularly significant to note that these changes in Jewish death ritual all valorize the human individual in ways that had been consistently celebrated in Hellenic society and culture. Greek politics had long valued the voice of the individual in the democratic process, and Greek theater was steeped in the tradition of tragedians who had dramatized the psychological strengths and weaknesses of individual human beings. Greek sculptors of the Hellenistic period had pursued an artistic quest for the ideal human form, and Greek educators took up that quest on an individual level through the exercises that were a staple of training in the *gymnasium*.

The emergence of Hellenistic burial practices in ER Jerusalem strongly suggests that by the end of the first century B.C.E. the structure of Jewish society in Jerusalem was beginning to make more room for the human individual. Cohen has aptly described the development of post-biblical Judaism as the "democratization" of traditional Israelite religion, pointing out that while the piety of pre-exilic Israel centered on the group, "the piety of second temple Judaism centered on both the group and the individual" (Cohen 1989: 22). This observation aptly fits the developments we are following here. The rise of the Jewish ossuary indicates that in the ER period, democratization was beginning to reach into the internal structure of Jewish families in Jerusalem. Individual secondary burial in an ossuary symbolically represented and celebrated individual identity and dignity, even after death and burial. In the privacy of the family tomb, usually with only one or two close relatives present, the social structure of the family was established and reinforced in a way that protected and defended the individual. The persona of the deceased did not dissolve into an ancestral collective, but was symbolically preserved for all time. Those who could afford to do so supplemented this symbolic preservation through ornamentation and decoration, and those who were literate inscribed it with a name, patronymic or other epithet; but even the use of a roughly-hewn, uninscribed, and undecorated ossuary served to affirm the lasting value and eternal destiny of a discrete human being. The piety of ossuary burial in ER Jerusalem, like much of the piety in early Judaism, was centered upon both the group and the individual.

Of course, this emergent valorization of the human individual was circumscribed by deeply rooted cultural norms and social patterns that had long structured Jewish life in Jerusalem. Thus, it is not surprising that Peleg has recently demonstrated that the Jewish practice of secondary burial in ossuaries evinces a preference for males over females. In a sample of seventy ossuaries excavated in Jerusalem and Jericho, close observation of gender in both inscriptions and skeletal remains showed that the bones of females were more likely to be gathered in ossuaries not by themselves, but along with the bones of someone else, usually their husband and/or children. Ossuary inscriptions are more likely to record the names of males than females. As Peleg puts it, in ER Jerusalem "the identity of the male person was more individualized than that of the female" (Peleg 2002: 65).

CONCLUSION

Bowersock has written that in the ancient Mediterranean world, Hellenization did not so much extinguish or overwhelm local customs, as it provided fresh energy for their expression in new and innovative ways (Bowersock 1990). Meyers has agreed, and under his direction the ongoing excavations at Sepphoris have clearly documented the rich confluence of cultural traditions that came to expression in the Lower Galilee during the Roman period (Meyers 1999). In this historical context, the rise of the Jewish ossuary in ER Jerusalem furnishes an exemplary case study in the power of Hellenism to influence a local culture, and in the resilience and creativity of a local culture in resisting it. By continuing to gather the bones of their dead, Jewish families of ER Jerusalem honored one of their most deeply-rooted ancestral traditions, and by gathering bones in individual containers, those same families also welcomed an emerging new pattern in their social system.

Yet there should be no mistake about which way the wind was blowing: Hellenism, a world culture, was certain to have the last word, and it did. The preservation of individual identity after death would eventually, during the Byzantine Period, become the foundation for the early Christian cult of the dead. But that is a story for another occasion.

NOTES

1 For the course of the discussion see Meyers 1971a; 1971b; Figueras 1983; Hachlili 1988; Rahmani 1994; Teitelbaum 1998; Kraemer 2000; for representative and important excavation reports see Avigad 1962; Hachlili 1979; Greenhut 1992.

2 Rahmani 1994, where 93 of 231 (40.2%) are in Greek.

3 Ossuaries do not appear in Galilee, for example, until the early second century C.E., as at Huqoq; cf. Ravani 1961.

4 It is important not to overstate the degree to which ossuary burial preserved individual identity, since analysis of skeletal remains shows that many ossuaries held the remains of more than one person. The famous "Caiaphas" ossuary, for example, held the partial remains of six individuals; cf. Zias 1992: 78. Rabbinic discussions considered the possibility that more than one individual's bones might be collected in the same ossuary. Intermingling of bones was to be avoided, said Rabbi Akiba, but Rabbi Judah is reported to have allowed persons who could share a bed in life to share an ossuary in death (*Sem.* 12.6; 12.9). Thus, the Jewish ossuary was not always associated with *strictly* individual secondary burial. Yet it certainly preserved individual identity to a greater degree than previous forms of collective secondary burial.

5 For representatives of this view see Lieberman 1965; Rahmani 1994: 53–55; Figueras 1984; and Hachlili 1988. Meyers was a lone dissenter: "It is an oversimplification to suggest that the custom of Jewish ossuaries reflects only the Pharisaic community of Jerusalem, which adhered to a rather literal conception of resurrection" (1971: 85).

REFERENCES

Avigad, N.
1962 A Depository of Inscribed Ossuaries in the Kidron Valley. *Israel Exploration Journal* 12: 1–12.

Bloch-Smith, E.
1992 *Judahite Burial Practices and Beliefs About the Dead*. Sheffield: JSOT.

Bowersock, G. W.
1990 *Hellenism in Late Antiquity*. Ann Arbor, MI: University of Michigan.

Cohen, S. J.
1989 *From the Maccabees to the Mishnah*. Philadelphia, PA: Westminster.

Figueras, P.
1983 *Decorated Jewish Ossuaries*. Leiden: Brill.
1984 Jewish Ossuaries and Secondary Burial. *Immanuel* 19: 42–57.

Fine, S.
2000 A Note on Ossuary Burial and Resurrection of the Dead in First-Century Jerusalem. *Journal of Jewish Studies* 51: 69–76.

Greenhut, Z.
1992 The 'Caiaphas' Tomb in North Talpiyot, Jerusalem. *'Atiqot* 21: 63–71.

Hachlili, R.
1979 The Goliath Family in Jericho: Funerary Inscriptions from a First Century AD Jewish Monumental Tomb. *Bulletin of the American Schools of Oriental Research* 235: 31–65.
1988 *Jewish Ornamented Ossuaries of the Late Second Temple Period*. Haifa: University of Haifa.

Hertz, R.
1960 *Death and the Right Hand*, trans. R. and C. Needham. Aberdeen: The University Press.

Ilan, D. Y.
1997 Tombs. Pp. 218–21 in *The Oxford Encyclopedia of Archaeology in the Near East*, vol. 5, ed. E. M. Meyers. New York, NY: Oxford University.

Kloner, A.
1980 A Tomb of the Second Temple Period at French Hill, Jerusalem. *Israel Exploration Journal* 30: 99–108.

Kraemer, D.
2000 *The Meaning of Death in Rabbinic Judaism*. London: Routledge.

Lieberman, S.
1965 Some Aspects of After-Life in Early Rabbinic Literature. Pp. 495–532 in *Harry Austryn Wolfson Jubilee Volume on the Occasion of His Seventy-Fifth Birthday*. Jerusalem: American Association of Jewish Research.

McCane, B. R.
1997 Sarcophagus. Pp. 481–82 in *The Oxford Encyclopedia of Archaeology in the Near East*, vol. 4, ed. E. M. Meyers. New York, NY: Oxford University.
2003 *Roll Back the Stone: Death and Burial in the World of Jesus*. Harrisburg, PA: Trinity International.

Metcalf, P., and Huntington, R.
1992 *Celebrations of Death: The Anthropology of Mortuary Ritual*, 2nd ed. Cambridge: Cambridge University.

Meyers, E. M.
1971a *Jewish Ossuaries: Reburial and Rebirth. Secondary Burials in Their Ancient Near Eastern Setting*. Rome: Biblical Institute.
1971b The Theological Implications of an Ancient Jewish Burial Custom. *Jewish Quarterly Review* 62: 95–119.
1992 The Challenge of Hellenism for Early Judaism and Christianity. *Biblical Archaeologist* 55: 84–92.
1998 Jesus und Seine Galiläische Lebenswelt. *Zeitschrift Für Neues Testament* 1: 27–39.

Meyers, E. M. (ed.)
1999 *Galilee Through the Centuries: Confluence of Cultures*. Winona Lake, IN: Eisenbrauns.

Morris, I.
1992 *Death-Ritual and Societal Structure in Classical Antiquity*. New York, NY: Cambridge University.

Peleg, Y.
2002 Gender and Ossuaries: Ideology and Meaning. *Bulletin of the American Schools of Oriental Research* 325: 65–73.

Rahmani, L. Y.
1958 A Jewish Tomb on Shahin Hill, Jerusalem. *Israel Exploration Journal* 8: 101–5.
1967 Jason's Tomb. *Israel Exploration Journal* 17: 61–100.
1988 Chip-Carving in Palestine. *Israel Exploration Journal* 38: 59–75.

1994 *A Catalogue of Jewish Ossuaries in the Collections of the State of Israel*. Jerusalem: Israel Antiquities Authority.

Ravani, B.

1961 Rock Cut Tombs at Huqoq. *'Atiqot* 3: 128–43.

Teitelbaum, D. E.

1998 The Relationship between Ossuary Burial and the Belief in Resurrection during the Late Second Temple Period Judaism. Masters thesis, Carleton University, Ottawa. Ann Arbor, MI: University Microfilms.

Zias, J.

1992 Human Skeletal Remains from the 'Caiaphas' Tomb. *'Atiqot* 21: 78–80.

Chapter 20

Attitudes Toward the Dead: Protective Measures Employed Against the Desecration of Tombs, Coffins and Ossuaries

by Rachel Hachlili

In ancient times, the desecration of tombs for secondary usage or for the purpose of plunder was a frequent occurrence. Ancient tombs, especially those of prominent or rich people, were supposed to contain valuable objects buried with the dead. During the Roman period, an Imperial law (Avigad 1976: 256 n. 15; *Supp. Epig. Graecum* III 1929: 13) was enacted to prevent the violation of tombs and the removal of bones from tombs in order to bury other bodies instead.

In Jewish tombs of the Second Temple period, various measures were employed to seal wooden coffins and ossuaries. Wooden coffins were closed and fastened with ropes. Some ossuaries have pairs of drilled holes through the rim and lid that served to secure the lid to the chest with rivets, strings or ropes. Some ossuaries have direction marks — incised or charcoal-drawn lines, usually in pairs — on the lid and on the chest to indicate the position of holes (Rahmani and Sussman 1994: 18; cf. Sem. 12:8, 13:8). This step of securing the wooden coffins and ossuaries probably resulted from the wish to protect the remains of the deceased and the desire to prevent the mixing of their bones with those of others. In some 3rd–4th-century C.E. lead coffins (some from Beth She'arim), the lid is soldered with lead to the chest's rim or to both long sides of the chest, or the closure is implemented with lead tongues (Rahmani 1999: 12–13).

Another preventive measure were Hebrew, Aramaic, and Greek inscriptions, which included curses and threats, with the affirmation that nothing of value was within the tomb. In addition, some of the epitaphs contain curses and warnings against tomb robbers or against secondary use of the tomb (Avigad 1953: 147; van der Horst 1991: 54–60). The curse or threat was supposed to deter the tomb-violators, often depicting the outcome of violation as horrible death, bodily sufferings, punishment after death, and sometimes financial penalty. These inscriptions are common among pagans, Jews, and Christians throughout the ancient Near East.

Preventive measures employed against the desecration of tombs could be demonstrated by physical and symbolic evidence, as well as by inscribed curse and warning formulae (Hachlili 2005: 489–507).

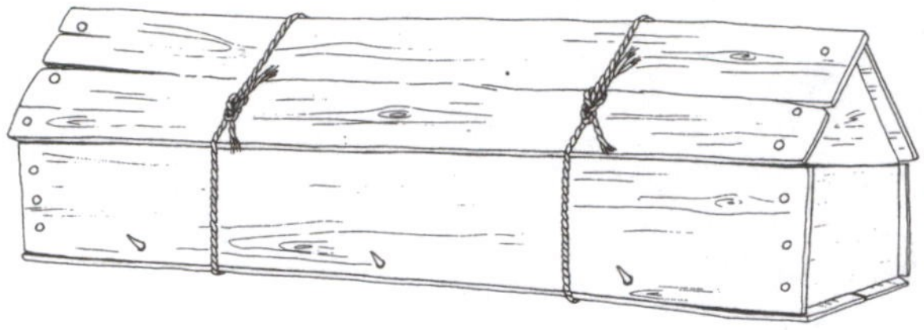

Fig. 1 *Wooden coffin from En Gedi, wound around with rope.*

Fig. 2 *Ossuary with holes, Jericho (Hachlili and Killebrew 1999: III.45).*

Fig. 3 *Ossuary with holes, Jericho (Hachlili and Killebrew 1999: III.49).*

PHYSICAL EVIDENCE

Ropes Binding Wooden Coffins

- A rope fragment, made of palm fiber, was discovered with wooden coffin 85, tomb D12, Jericho (Hachlili and Killebrew 1999: 22, cat. no. 151).
- At Jericho, a leather string was found associated with coffin 78 (Hachlili and Killebrew 1999: 22).
- In Jericho Tomb G.81, a string was found with one well preserved reef knot across the lid of a coffin, presumably to hold it together (Bennett 1965: 532).
- At 'En Gedi, triple braided ropes (1 cm thick) made of date-palm fibers were wound around almost all the closed wooden coffins. The rope was wrapped around once or more and tied in an overhand knot (fig. 1; see coffins 5 and 8 from tomb 1; coffin 7 from tomb 5: Hadas 1994: 4,* fig.4, coffin 8; fig. 12, coffin 5; figs. 33, 42, coffin 7).

Holes and Direction Marks on Ossuaries

Some ossuaries from Jerusalem and Jericho have direction marks, that is, lines incised or drawn with charcoal on the rim and lid to indicate the position of holes. These pairs of drilled holes through the rim and lid of an ossuary were evidently intended as a means to secure the lid to the ossuary chest with strings, rivets, or ropes and to prevent its opening.

- Three ossuaries (nos. II, XV, XXII) from Jericho Tomb H (the 'Goliath' family tomb) had drilled holes with incised lines or crosses as direction marks on the rim and lid, apparently to indicate the place for the holes (Hachlili and Killebrew 1999: 93, figs. III.45, 49, 51). Ossuary II (fig. 2) has six holes in the lid, corresponding to six holes in the ossuary chest (two in each long side, one in each short side; ossuary XV (fig. 3) has double drilled holes on the front, sides and back and double holes on all four sides of the lid. Small ossuary XXII (fig. 4) has four holes in each side of the lid and one hole in each side of the ossuary (Hachlili and Killebrew 1999: 93, 102, 108, 111, figs. III.45, 49, 51). The sealing of these ossuaries was secured with

Fig. 4 *Ossuary with holes, Jericho (Hachlili and Killebrew 1999: III.51).*

Fig. 5 *Ossuary with two lids, Jericho (Hachlili and Killebrew 1999: III.47).*

rope, iron or lead rivets that have disintegrated since.

- Similar direction marks, usually in the shape of crosses, appear on Jerusalem ossuaries and were once erroneously thought to be an early record of Christianity (Sukenik 1947: 12–15, 21–26, 30; refuted by Tzaferis 1970: 27; Smith 1974: 65; Rahmani and Sussman 1994: 19–21, figs. 8–12).

Three ossuaries from Jerusalem have iron or lead rivets; one ossuary from a double-chambered acrosolium tomb on the south slope of Talbiyeh (Rahmani and Sussman 1994: no. 70) has iron rivets through the outer edge of the lid and the corresponding narrow side of the chest. This ossuary also had the Aramaic inscription, "Dostas, our father, and not to be opened" (see below). Another ossuary (Rahmani and Sussman 1994: no. 77) has incised marks and unfinished and unused holes in its upper outer corners; an iron rivet is secured through the rim of the chest and narrow outer edge of the lid. Fragments of lead rivets, which fastened the lid to the rim of the chest, appear on an ossuary from Arnona (Rahmani and Sussman 1994: no. 196).

The Jericho examples support the contention that the marks served to indicate the position of the lids on the ossuaries, since on the marks or next to them were the holes that served to fasten the lid to the ossuary with ropes or metal pieces. The sealing was ostensibly intended to protect the remains of the deceased.

The various measures employed to bind the wooden coffins and to facilitate closure of the ossuaries with strings or iron rivets were probably prompted by the wish to secure the coffin's or ossuary contents on the journey to the tomb, to guard the remains of the deceased, and to avoid the mixing of their remains with those of others (Rahmani and Sussman 1994: 18; cf. Sem. 12:8, 13:8). However, it is also possible to interpret the closure practices as a form of defensive "magic," restraining hostile powers by preventing anything from leaving or entering the coffin or ossuary (also White 1997: 11; 1999: 87). Nevertheless, it is quite difficult to explain why these sealing practices occurred so rarely. Were these measures employed especially for children? In Jericho, the ossuary sealing was used only in Tomb H (the 'Goliath' Tomb); the inscriptions and the skeletal remains indicate that the ossuaries with the holes contained a child, an infant, and a single 40-year-old unmarried woman[1] (Hachlili and Killebrew 1999: 93, 102, 108, 111); the 'En Gedi wrapped coffins also contained children, as well as a male.

SYMBOLIC EVIDENCE

Some symbolic implications could be observed on a double lid, graffiti on ossuaries, and a wooden coffin's iron lock, possibly designated as signs to protect the remains of the deceased and to prevent the ossuaries or coffins from being reopened.

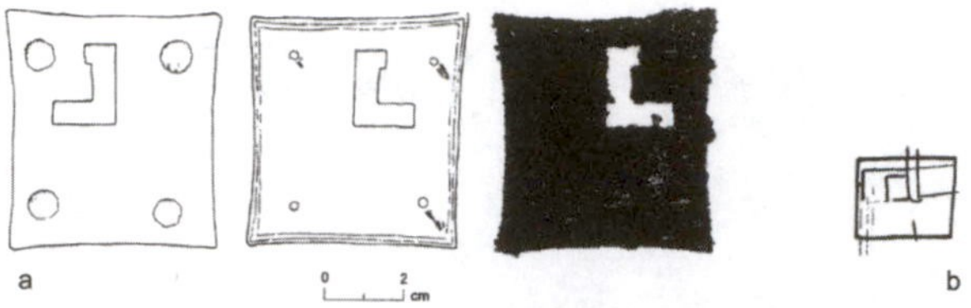

Fig. 6 *a) An iron lock plate of a wooden coffin, Jericho (Hachlili and Killebrew 1999: III.8); b) Iron lock graffito on ossuary, Jerusalem (Rahmani and Sussman 1994: no. 403).*

Fig. 7 *Lid of lead coffin with rope design (after Rahmani 1999: pl. 38:77).*

- An ossuary from Jericho (Hachlili and Killebrew 1999: 102, ossuary VIII, fig. III.47 = Rahmani and Sussman 1994: no. 789) was found with two lids (fig. 5): a lower flat lid and, placed on top of this, an upper vaulted lid. These double lids are unique.
- An iron lock plate was found with Jericho wooden coffin 113 (fig. 6a); the lock has a perforated L-shaped opening and was probably attached to the long side of the coffin (Hachlili and Killebrew 1999: 67, fig. III.8).
- A rough graffito of a similar lock (fig. 6b) appears on the flat sliding lid of an ossuary from Jerusalem; it was depicted next to a rivet, which firmly affixed the lid to the rim of the chest (Rahmani and Sussman 1994: 20, no. 403). Both these locks may have implied that the coffin and the ossuary had been sealed. They could have been meant as symbolic protective marks.

Lead coffins (some from Beth She'arim) dated to the 3rd–4th century C.E. were found with the lid soldered with lead to the chest's rim or to both long sides of the chest. Many of the Jerusalem lead coffins were sealed shut with lead tongues. Some lead coffins were encased in wooden casings or, rarely, in a stone sarcophagus (Rahmani 1999: 12–13, 17, 65–67, 79, figs. 11–14; White 1999: 77–80, figs. 12–15). Many of the lead coffins found in Jerusalem have a decorative element of running braided rope, twisted rope, cord, or cable in parallel horizontal or intersecting lines (fig. 7); twisted cords and straps seem to appear tied down, with broad crossing straps arranged diagonally and horizontally along the coffin's central axis. The bound coffin motif signifies a well-secured container. These decorative and technical measures may have expressed a local concern for the security of the deceased's resting place.

The rope symbolizes the act of tying up and binding the coffin. The peculiar decoration on the Jerusalem lead coffins of crisscrossing ropes on the lid and on the long sides create the impression that the coffin was tied up with cord (Rahmani 1987: 136; 1999: 65; White 1997: 9, fig. 10). The ropes decorating the lead coffins seem to be symbolic bonds, providing the coffin with the appearance of a firmly bound box.

The motif of the roped lead coffin could be clarified by the curse tablets made of lead or lead alloys, many of which were buried in graves from the 5th–4th centuries B.C.E. onwards (White 1999: 85). The figurine-like effigy (made of lead, mud, clay, or wax) of the victim was dropped into a grave as another way of targeting a curse. They may be shown mutilated or/and with their hands trussed up behind their back (Faraone 1991: 190, 200–91; Gager 1992: 15–16, 127–29, figs. 2–3; White 1997: 10, fig. 13; 1999: 86 nn. 65–66). Examples include a lead figurine with bound hands placed in a lead coffin set in an Athenian grave dated to the 5th century B.C.E. (Kurtz and Boardman 1971: 217, pl. 46). Several figurines of later date were discovered: a lead figurine of a headless naked man with tied hands was found in a tomb in Ketef Hinnom, Jerusalem. The dating is not clear and estimates range from Hellenistic to late Roman (Barkay 1994: 92–93). Sixteen similar lead figurines were discovered at Marissa (Bliss 1900: 332–34 and pl. 85; Zissu 1995: 162) and at Tel Anafa, a clay figurine of a man with hands tied on his back was found (Weinberg 1971: pl. 19, D–E). A fragmentary folded lead plaque was discovered in the wooden coffin in Tomb D14 at Jericho (Hachlili and Killebrew 1999: 141, cat. 220).

Rope decoration on lead coffins symbolizes the act of binding or tying up the coffin. It might reflect a memory of the symbolic act of tying up and securing the coffin's contents. Avi-Yonah (1930: 310) associated the motif of the rope loop on lead coffins with a symbol of immortality and resurrection, with an added significance of the binding of evil spirits. The lead coffins decorated with cord and rope, the curse tablets, and the curse figurines represented a way to avert something from either escaping or entering the coffin. The purpose might have been to prevent the ghost of the deceased from escaping its chest to harm the living, as well as to protect the spirit of the dead from the powers of evil (Rahmani 1987: 136; 1992: 82, n. 3; White 1997: 9; 1999: 77–80, 87–91).

INSCRIPTIONS AND EPITAPHS WITH CURSES AND WARNINGS

Warnings and curses against tomb robbers or against reuse of the tomb appear frequently in inscribed epitaphs throughout the ancient Near East in various languages. Ancient tombs, in particular those of prominent people, were assumed to contain valuable objects buried with the dead. Hence, as a deterrent measure, tomb inscriptions sometimes included curses and threats against would-be robbers, hostile spells, or spirits, and also affirmed that nothing of value was to be found within the tomb (Avigad 1953: 147).

The term *defixiones (katadesmoi* in Greek) is used by Gager (1992: 3 n. 1) in the generic sense to designate curses, spells and warnings inscribed on a variety of media in formulaic language. They "illustrate the long and difficult debate about 'magic' and 'religion' in Western culture.... Unlike ancient literary texts...they are intensely personal and direct." At present, surviving examples exceed the number of 1,500. They are primarily inscribed on thin sheets of lead, but also on ostraca, wax tablets, and gemstones (Gager 1992: 25–26).

These curses were also common among Phoenician-Aramaic (Palmyrean and Nabatean) funerary inscriptions from the 11th to the 4th century B.C.E. and are similar in structure and wording. Curses stated that, other than the dead body, no valuables were present in the tomb. Sometimes there is a warning against opening or plundering the tomb or sarcophagus, with the inclusion of a curse. The following are formalized expressions, with cursing and warning apparently installed for protection against robbers or hostile spells. Several examples are noted (Avigad 1953: 147–48):

- The "Ahiram" Phoenician tomb inscription (11th century B.C.E.) contains: "...curses upon the man who lays bare the sarcophagus."
- A 7th-century B.C.E. Aramaic inscription of Agbar, priest of Sahar in Nêrab (Syria), states: "...Whosoever thou art that shalt injure and plunder me, may Sahar and Nikal make his death miserable, and may his posterity perish!"
- In a 5th–4th-century B.C.E. Phoenician inscription on a sarcophagus from Sidon, Tabnit, the priest of Ishtar, declares: "Do not, do not open me nor disquiet me, for I have not indeed(?) silver, I have not indeed(?) gold nor any jewels of...only I am lying in this coffin.... And if thou do at all open me and at all disquiet me, mayest thou have no seed among the living under the sun, not resting-place among the shades!"
- A formula of woe and oath appears on the 5th-century B.C.E. Phoenician sarcophagus inscription of Eshmanezer (son of Tabnit), the king of Sidon: ממלכת וכל אדם אל יפתח אית משכב ז' קנמי את כל... "For every prince and every man who shall open this resting-place...may they have no resting-place with the shades, nor be buried in a grave, nor have son or seed in their stead.... (Avigad 1953: 148; Naveh 1992: 199).
- A Nabatean funerary inscription from Heger dated to 1 B.C.E. (Cooke 1903: 217–20; Naveh 1992: 198).
- An Aramaic epitaph from Palmyra (2nd–3rd century C.E.) reads לא יפתח עלוהי גומחה דנה עד עלמא ואנש "And let no man open over him this niche forever" (Sukenik 1935: 194; Avigad 1953: 149; 1967: 235).

Similar inscriptions with curse formulae against those who do not leave the tomb untouched were also common in Asia Minor, dating to the 5th–4th century B.C.E. in Lycia (Bryce 1986: 116–20) and to the 2nd–3rd century C.E. in Phrygia (van der Horst 1991: 54-60).

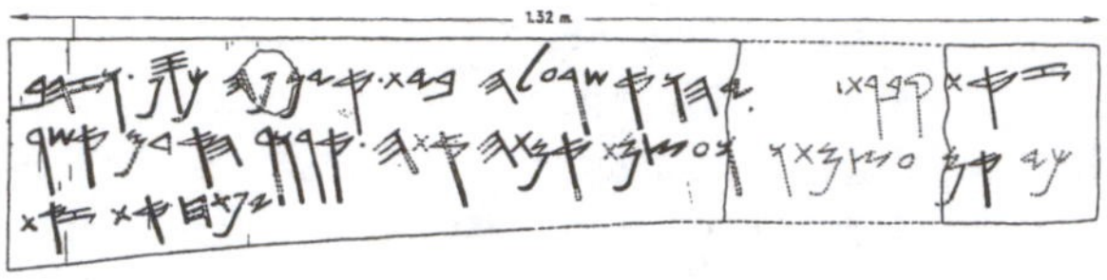

Fig. 8 *Inscription 1 (after Avigad 1953: pl. 9B).*

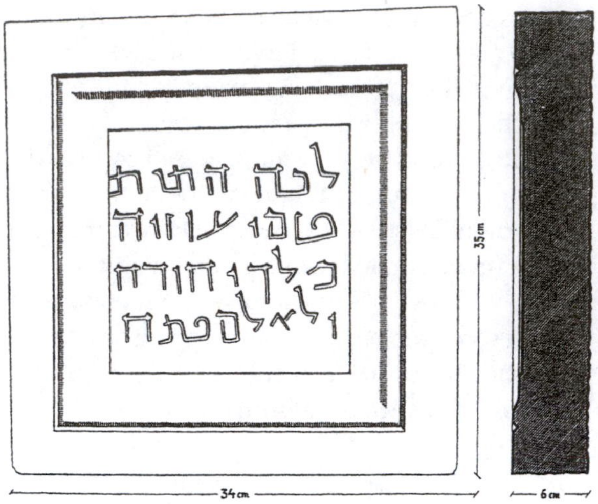

Fig. 9 *Inscription 2 (after Sukenik 1931: pl. II,2).*

JEWISH ARAMAIC, HEBREW AND GREEK PROTECTIVE INSCRIPTIONS AND CURSE FORMULAE

The following protective inscriptions with curse formulae for violations appear on Jerusalem's ancient tombs and on ossuaries; early inscriptions, such as no. 1, perhaps inspired the use of protective formulae on ossuaries. Some of the inscriptions were probably intended to prevent further handling of the remains in an ossuary, especially the burial of additional remains (Avigad 1953; 1967: 235; Rahmani and Sussman 1994: 18–21).

The inscriptions are engraved or painted. Their locations are as follows: above the door of a monolithic monument (no. 1), on a sealing stone (no. 2), on a stone slab (nos. 3, 15), above a tomb *loculus* (no. 4), on a stone coffin lid (no .7). Eight of them (nos. 3, 5–6, 8–12) are carved on ossuaries, and six are painted on catacomb walls (nos. 15–16, 18–21). The inscriptions are dated to the 8th–7th century B.C.E. (no. 1), the 1st century C.E. (nos. 2–14), and the 3rd–4th century C.E. (nos. 15–22).

1. A Hebrew burial inscription above the door of a small monolithic monument with rock façade from Silwan, Jerusalem, is worded as a curse (fig. 8):

   ]יהו אשר על הבית אין פה כסף וזהב [כי] אם [עצמתו
   ...זאת [קברת
   ועצמת אמתה אתה ארור האדם אשר יפתח את זאת

   "This is [the sepulchre of...]yahu who is over the house. There is no silver and no gold here but [his bones] and the bones of his slave-wife with him. Cursed be the man who shall open this (i.e., burial)" (Avigad 1953).

   The owner of the tomb was, no doubt, one of the king's ministers, and the inscription contained a formula common in sepulchral inscriptions.

2. On the sealing stone of a tomb *loculus* an Aramaic inscription of King Uzziah is engraved (fig. 9; Sukenik 1931; Fitzmyer and Harrington 1978, no. 70; Naveh 1992: 194): יהודה ולא למפתח לכה התית טמי עוזיה מלך "Hither were brought the bones of Uzziah, king of Judah, and not to be opened." The inscription, apparently belonging to the tomb of King Uzziah, forbids the opening of the tomb. Avigad (1958: 78) dates the inscription to the mid-1st century C.E.

3. An Aramaic epitaph on a stone slab from the Kidron Valley in the collection of the Dormition Museum, Jerusalem, is inscribed with the formula [אבהתנ ולא למפתח לעל[ם "Our fathers, (it is) not (permitted) to be opened [forever]," the last word being a new ending here (Spoer 1907: 358, no. 11; Sukenik 1935: 195; Frey 1952: 1334; Fitzmyer and Harrington 1978: no. 71).

4. A dipinto, a red painted Aramaic inscription above the third *loculus* on the west wall of a tomb in the Kidron Valley, dated to the mid-1st century C.E., reads:

   ארך אמין תרתין / ולא למפתח עליהון
   כוכה דנה עביד / לגרמי אבהתנה

   "This sepulchral chamber was made for the bones of our fathers. (In) length (it is) two cubits. (It is) not (permitted) to open them! (or Not to be opened!)."

   The inscription requests that the bones in

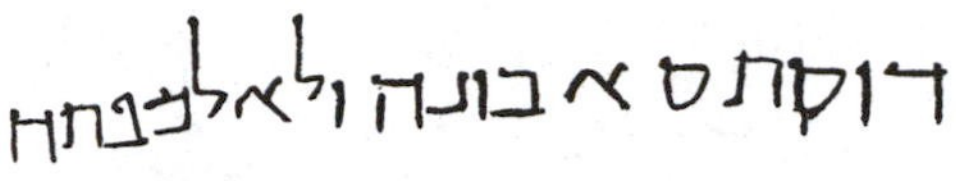

Fig. 10 *Inscription 5 (after Rahmani and Sussman 1994: no. 70).*

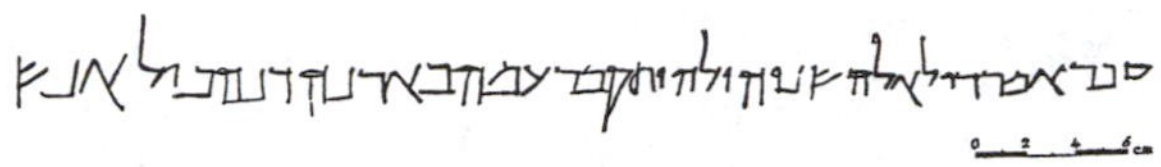

Fig. 13 *Inscription 8 (after Puech 1989: fig. III.1).*

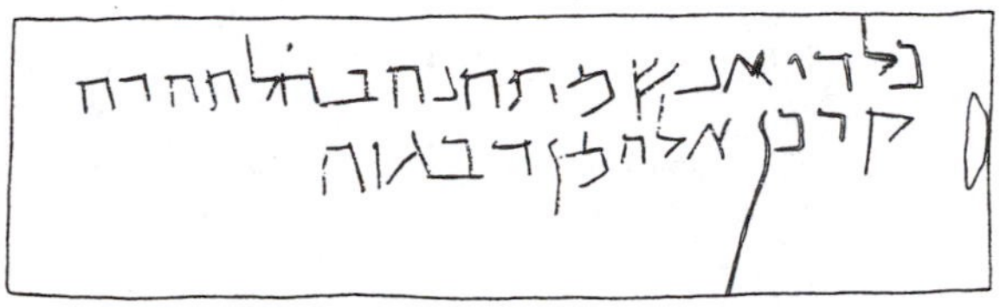

Fig. 11 *Inscription 6 (after Milik 1956: figs. 2–3, Inscription A1).*

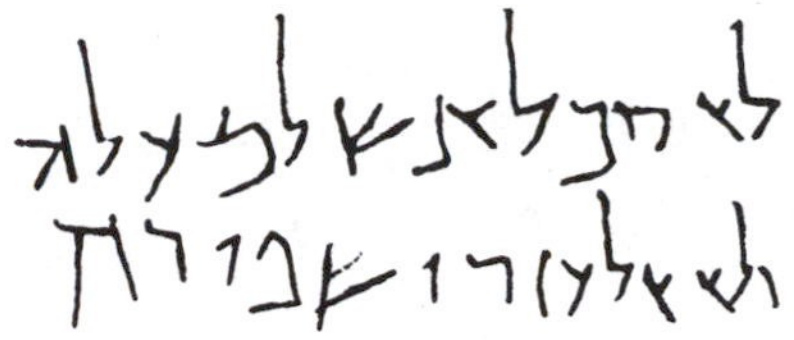

Fig. 14 *Inscription 9 (after Rahmani and Sussman 1994: no. 455).*

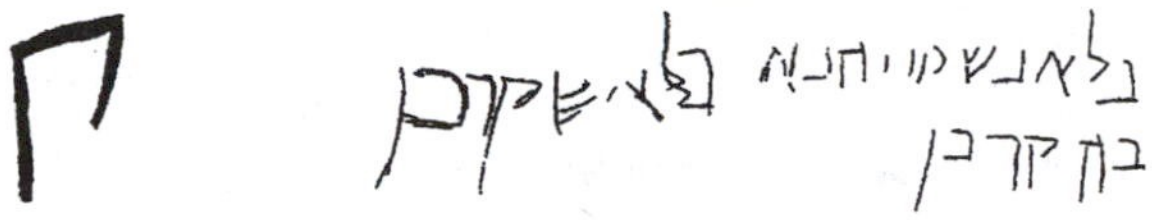

Fig. 12 *Inscription 7 (after Bilig 2000: fig. 3).*

the ossuary or the *kokh* not be moved again (Sukenik 1935: 192–95, fig. 3; Frey 1952: no. 1300; Avigad 1967: 235; Fitzmyer and Harrington 1978, no. 67; Naveh 1992: 194, fig. 133).

5. A brief Aramaic inscription (fig. 10) on an ossuary from Talbiyeh, Jerusalem, reads דוסתס אבונה ולא למפתח "Dostas, our father, and not to be opened." The inscription prohibits the opening of an ossuary (Sukenik 1928: 113–21; Savignac 1925; Frey 1952: no. 1359b; Fitzmyer and Harrington 1978, no. 95; Rahmani and Sussman 1994: no. 70).
6. An Aramaic protective formula (fig. 11) on an ossuary lid from Jebel Hallat et-Turi (Milik 1956: 235, Inscription A1, figs. 2–3; Fitzmyer 1959; Fitzmyer and Harrington 1978, no. 69; Naveh 1992: 198–99; Rahmani 1994: 18, n. 89; Benovitz 1995) reads

   כל די אנש מתהנה בחלתה דה קרבן אלה מן דבגוה

   "Everything that a man will find to his profit in this ossuary (is) an offering to God from the one within it."

   This inscription does not follow the identification of the deceased person. The inscription has been discussed widely, and it seems that it is a formula that warns against secondary use of the ossuary and that anything of value in the ossuary is an offering to God and is not intended for any profane use. The word קרבן, *Qorban,* is probably used in the inscription in the meaning of "an offering to God," rather than "a curse of God" (Fitzmyer 1959: 65). The language and formula of this inscription are comparable to nos. 7 and 8.
7. On an ossuary from a tomb in Arnona, Jerusalem (Bilig 2000), a bilingual inscription (fig. 12) in Aramaic and Hebrew was carved:

   כל אנש מתהנא בה קרבן   כל אש קרבן

   "Everything that a man will find to his profit in this ossuary (is) an offering to God."

   The inscription and interpretation are similar to inscription no. 6 (above).
8. An Aramaic inscription (fig. 13) on a stone coffin lid reads

   סכר אמר די לא להשניה ולה יתקבר עמה בארנה
   דנה כול אנש

   "Closed by the ram (or lamb): It may not be changed and none entombed with him in this coffin" (Puech 1989; translation Rahmani and Sussman 1994: 18 n. 89). The inscription means: the ossuary is closed, and by no means is it permitted to damage or open it or to bury anybody else in it. Naveh (1992: 197, fig. 137) compares this phrase to similar expressions on Nabatean burial inscriptions and proposes that אמרא, "ram, lamb," refers to the daily burnt offering, here invoked as a binding conjuration.

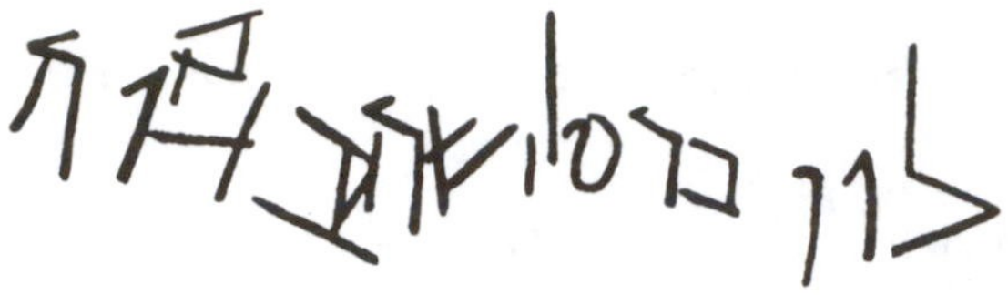

Fig. 15 *Inscription 10 (after Rahmani and Sussman 1994: no. 610).*

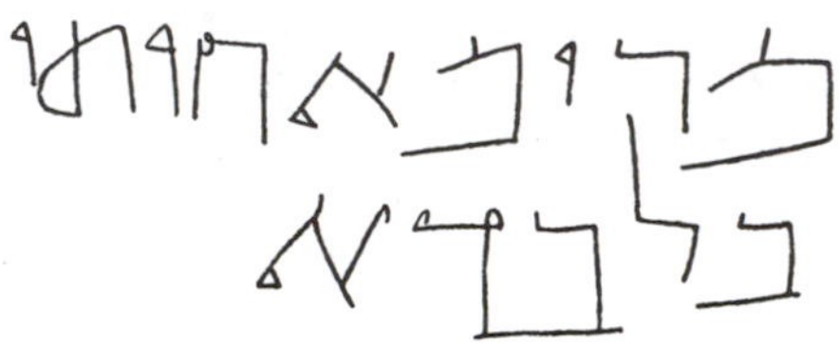

Fig. 16 *Inscription 11 (after Avigad 1961: fig. 1).*

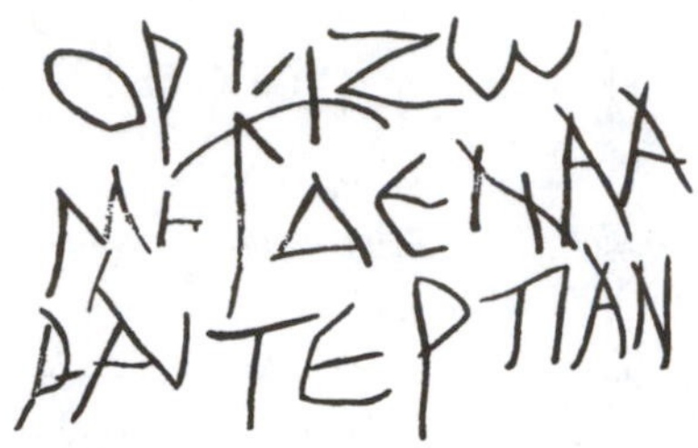

Fig. 17 *Inscription 12 (after Rahmani and Sussman 1994: no. 259).*

Fig. 18 *Inscription 13 (after Rahmani and Sussman 1994: no. 142).*

Fig. 19 *Inscription 14 (after Rahmani and Sussman 1994: no. 559).*

9. On an ossuary lid from a tomb at Mt. Scopus, eastern slope, Jerusalem, the Aramaic inscription (fig. 14) reads
לא סכל אנש למעלה ולא אלעזר ושפירה
"Nobody has abolished his entering, not even Ele'azar and Shappira" (Rahmani and Sussman 1994: no. 455, pl. 66). Cross (1983: 245–46) interprets it in the sense of "can lift himself from the grave;" Puech (1989: 164*) understands it as forbidding any additional remains to be buried in this ossuary, except for those of the persons mentioned, Eleazar and Shappira. Naveh (1980; 1992: 206–7) rejects both these interpretations and argues that the inscription is an Aramaic epigram, a consolatory burial inscription, only expressing loss and grief.
10. An inscription (fig. 15) on an ossuary from Ben Shemen, reads לוי בר מלשה בגפיה "Levi, son of Malosha, by himself" (Rahmani and Sussman 1994: 18, no. 610).
11. On the lid of an ossuary, the Hebrew inscription (fig. 16) reads מרימ אחותי בלבדא "Miriam, my sister, by herself" (Avigad 1961).
Such words as בגפיה or בלבדה, meaning "himself" or "herself," might indicate that the ossuary was possibly intended for a single person's remains or conceivably that it contained nothing worth taking.
12. A Greek formula (fig. 17) on a Jerusalem (?) ossuary reads Ὀρκίζω/μηδένα ἀ/ραι Τερτιάν, "I adjure: let no one take away (of) Tertian" and is an admonition not to disturb the remains of the deceased (Rahmani and Sussman 1994: no. 259).
13. A Greek protective inscription (fig. 18) with a threat on an ossuary from Qiryat Shemuel, Jerusalem, reads Ρούφου ός δ άν/μετενένκη πα[ρ(έβη?)]/τόν όρκ/ον/αύ(του), "of Rufus, whoever/moves it/breaks his vow" (Rahmani and Sussman 1994: no. 142).
14. A Greek inscription (fig. 19) on an ossuary from French Hill, Jerusalem, reads: Μαριεάμη Μαθίας/γυνή ὑ ἀντισκινής(ας)/αὐτά πάταξε αὔτου/ουρουν, "Maryame, wife of Mathia; who(soever) moves these (bones) away, may blindness strike him." This formula is intended to protect the remains of the deceased with a threat against transgressors (Rahmani and Sussman 1994: no. 559).

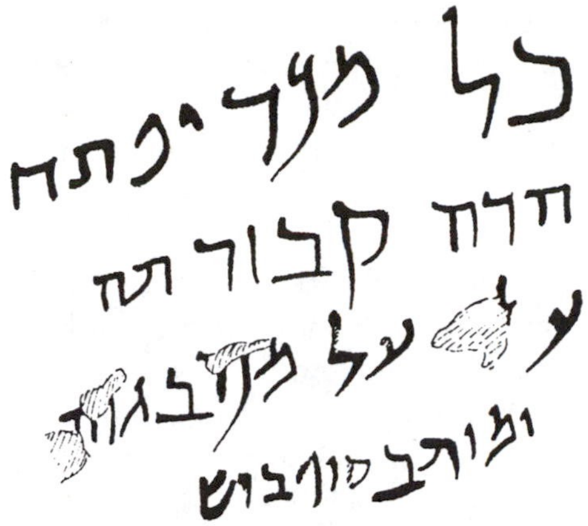

Fig. 20 *Inscription 15 (after Avigad 1976: fig. 104).*

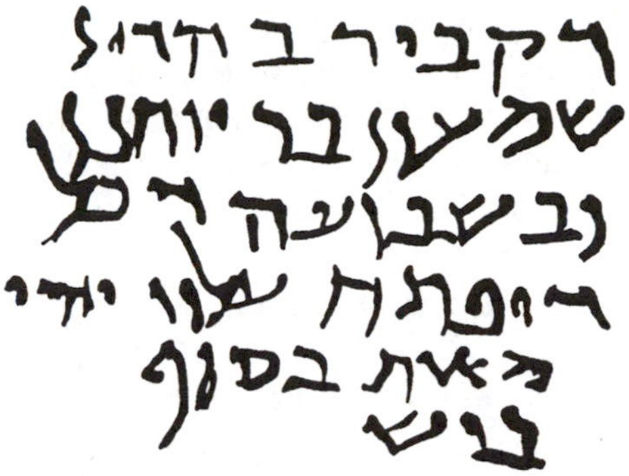

Fig. 21 *Inscription 16 (after Avigad 1976: fig. 105).*

Fig. 22 *Inscription 17 (after Avigad 1976: fig. 106).*

The language of the Greek inscriptions (nos. 12–14) articulates woe and oath formulae. A similar type of formula was inscribed on Hellenistic tombs of Marissa (Peters and Thiersch 1905: 48, no. 17; Rahmani and Sussman 1994: 18).

Similar Aramaic and Greek curse-formula inscriptions were discovered at the necropolis of Beth She'arim, dated to the 3rd–4th century C.E. The Aramaic inscriptions (nos. 15–18) contain versions of explicit threats and retribution against transgressors; Nos. 15 and 16 are unique in Aramaic epigraphy in the exceptional wording of their curses. The Greek inscriptions (nos. 18–19) express the protection of the tomb and include threats and belief in the immortality of the soul and the resurrection of the dead (Schwabe and Lifshitz 1974: 223–24).

15. On the back wall of arcosolium 3, room III, Hall A, Catacomb 12, an Aramaic dipinto (fig. 20) in red reads

    בסוף ביש כל מן דיפתח הדא קבורתה על מן דבגוה ימות

    "Anyone who shall open this burial whoever is inside shall die of an evil end." The Aramaic warning was apparently not sufficient and it was repeated in Greek as well, in a slightly altered formula: "Nobody shall open, in the name of the divine and secular law" (Avigad 1976: 23–25, 233; inscription 1, fig. 104, pl. III.3, 4; Schwabe and Lifshitz 1974: 223, no. 134). The prohibition in this inscription to open the tomb is based on the law of the Torah and of the state. Avigad notes, "the expression at the end of the inscription is unique and has no parallel in Aramaic or Hebrew epigraphy." This unique inscription demands protection for the deceased and issues a warning in the name of both religious and secular law. Schwabe explains that the famous imperial edict discovered in Galilee (SEG, VIII,13) is the only known epigraphic evidence that threatens punishment for the violation of graves, especially prohibiting the removal of the dead and their transfer elsewhere (Schwabe and Lifshitz 1974: 124, n. 12).

16. An Aramaic painted inscription (fig. 21) above the opening of the right *kokh* in the southern wall, room VIII, Hall A, Catacomb 12, states

    דקביר בהדין שמעון בר יוחנן ובשבועה דכל יפתח עלוי יהי
    מאית בסוף ביש

    "He who is buried here is Shimon the son of Yohanan; and on oath whoever shall open upon him shall die of an evil end" (Avigad 1976: 234–35; inscription 2, fig. 105, pl. IV.4). This inscription mentions the deceased and invokes the curse on whoever disturbs his rest; the wording is comparable to Greek inscription no. 129 from catacomb 11 (see below, no. 18). These two inscriptions are written in a formula "devised to warn people against touching the grave and disturbing the rest of the deceased and to threaten them with punishment otherwise…and threaten offenders with God's judgment or exclusion from eternal life. They are the only ones threatening a death penalty" (Avigad 1976: 235).

17. An Aramaic painted inscription (fig. 22) on a fragment of a stone slab, Hall A, room VIII, Catacomb 12, reads כל מן דיפתח "Anyone who shall open…." The stone slab either served to close a *kokh* or to cover one of the trough graves (Avigad 1976: 235; inscription 3, fig. 106).
18. A Greek inscription painted on the front of arcosolium 2, room V, Catacomb 11, reads
 οιύμύρ[ι] Ἐγώ Ἡσύχις ἐνθάδε κϊμε σύν τή ἐμή συνβίω πάς τολμών ἀνύξε ἐφ [ἡ]μάς μή ἔχη μέρος είς τον [βίον] ἀόνιο[ν].
 "I, Hesychios, lie here with my wife. May anyone who dares to open (the grave) above us not have a portion in the eternal life" (Schwabe and Lifshitz 1974: 113–14, no. 129; pl. IV.4).
 The curse on this inscription is unusual and "is the only example to date in which the share in eternal life is explicitly threatened…. The importance of this inscription is in the fact that it gives expression to the belief in eternal life…it is not mere chance that explicit evidence of this belief is found in an inscription whose function is to protect a tomb" (Schwabe and Lifschitz 1974: 113–14).
19. A Greek inscription incised and painted red above the arch of arcosolium 1 in room II, Catacomb 13, reads
 Ος ἐάν μεταθή ταύτην ό ἐπανγιλάμενος ζωποιησε τούς νεκρούς αύτός κρινε(ί).
 "Anyone who changes this lady's place [i.e., the woman buried in this grave], He who promised to resurrect the dead will Himself judge (him)" (Schwabe and Lifshitz 1974: 139, no. 162; pl. VI.1). The inscription warns against violation of the tomb and the peace of the dead. Punishment by God Himself will befall those who do not obey. The inscription's formula is unique; it constitutes definite evidence of the contemporary belief in the resurrection of the dead; it has no parallel at Beth She'arim or other places in the country.
20. A 4th-century C.E. Aramaic inscription carved above the tomb entrance of Hirbet Gomer reads

 אנה אלעזר בר אבה מארי עבדת הדה קבורתה
 לאבה מארי בר בתה
 חש[י]שתה שבועה

 "I, Elazar son of Abah Mari made this tomb for Abah Mari son of Batha, warn against touching the tomb with a vow."
 This inscription conveys a warning and a vow prohibiting the opening of the tomb (Kloner 1985: 97–98; Naveh 1992: 196, fig. 136).

The Beth She'arim and Hirbet Gomer inscriptions (Avigad 1976: 234–35; Schwabe and Lifshitz 1974: 162; also van der Horst 1991: 124–25) are written in a formula that serves as a warning to people against touching the tomb and disturbing the rest of the deceased, as well as threatening them with punishment; it is also meant to frighten offenders with God's judgment or exclusion from eternal life. Two of the inscriptions (nos. 15–16) also include a threat of the death penalty. These warnings against tomb violation comprise belief in a judgment or post-mortem punishment.

A popular belief along the coastal Levant under Roman administration was that near the graves of persons whose lives had been cut short by violence or accident, ghosts hovered and sought retribution from the living. Tombs, graves, and burial places were also believed to be the potential haunt of ghosts and other evil spirits (Cumont 1962: 62–63; Toynbee 1971: 34–42; White 1999: 87). The ghosts of the dead were regarded as evil spirits that might harm the living; they were feared especially at funerals and thereafter, when their evil powers had to be guarded against. The ghost of the dead was envisioned as a hostile and dangerous spirit, hovering with malicious intent, making demands or harming its living kin. It had to be dealt with sensibly and watchfully, so that the living might be safe from its anger and malice. The attacks by these ghosts of the dead must be warded off by various means and formulae; they must be appeased and their hostility placated (Morgenstern 1966: 141, 147, 185–86).

Binding up the coffin and sealing the ossuary are associated with securing the coffin's or ossuary's contents on the journey to the tomb; they were also preventive measures against the desecration of tombs for the purpose of plunder or secondary usage. The wish to protect the remains of the deceased and the need to prevent the mingling of the remains probably stimulated the various measures employed to bind the coffins, seal the ossuaries, and carve the inscriptions prohibiting the opening of a tomb or receptacle.

The protective inscriptions reflect several types of formulae and probably various objectives: prohibiting the opening of a tomb, *loculus*, or ossuary, protecting the remains of the deceased against reburial and secondary use, and explicitly threatening transgressors and those who disturb the bones of the dead with curse formulae and retribution. Threats against transgressors and belief in the immortality of the soul and the resurrection of the dead are expressed in the Greek inscriptions of Beth She'arim. Some of the inscriptions are general warnings and do not mention the deceased's personal name.

The careful protective treatment of the dead (though only in some instances) was realized by means of securing coffin and ossuary chests and lids, and special protective inscriptions, marks, and symbols. Additionally, sealing possibly also reflected symbolic bonds, which may imply a desire to prevent something from leaving or entering the coffin. The ropes or straps could also have represented symbolic tying and sealing to keep out evil spirits. Protective and curse inscriptions regularly include threats of bodily sufferings, a terrible death, and punishment after death of the tomb disturber and his relatives; sometimes a financial penalty is threatened as a further deterrent.

NOTES

1 This ossuary had an inscription of a woman named Mariah relating that she was the daughter of Natanel and the granddaughter of Shelamsiyon (Hachlili and Killebrew 1999: inscription 7b). Mariah's inscription attests that she was the third generation to be interred. Examination of her remains showed that she died at age 40. Her inscription mentions her father, the manumitted Theodotos/Nath[an]el and uniquely is citing her grandmother Shelamsiyon. The interment of Mariah in her father's and grandmother's family tomb (instead of in her husband's family tomb, as was customary) evidently means that she was unmarried, a widow with no children, or a divorcee who returned to her father's house and was then buried in her father's family tomb. It is suggested that a woman on the death of her husband was forced (by his heirs) or chose to return to her father's house and was then buried in the family tomb and inscribed by her original name "X daughter of Y" (Hachlili 2005: 320).

REFERENCES

Avigad, N.
1953 The Epitaph of a Royal Steward from Siloam Village. *Israel Exploration Journal* 3: 137–52.
1958 The Paleography of the Dead Sea Scrolls and Related Documents. *Scripta Hierosolymitana* 4: 56–87.
1961 A Hebrew Ossuary Inscription. *Bulletin of the Israel Exploration Society* 25: 143–44 (Hebrew).
1967 Jewish Rock-Cut Tombs in Jerusalem and in the Judean Hill-Country. *Eretz-Israel* 8: 119–42. (Hebrew).
1976 *Beth She'arim III: Report on the Excavations during 1953–1958. Catacombs XII–XXIII.* New Brunswick, NJ: Rutgers University.

Avi-Yonah, M.
1930 Three Lead Coffins from Palestine. *Journal of Hellenic Studies* 50: 300–12.

Barkay, G.
1994 Excavations at Ketef Hinnom Pp. 85–110 in *Ancient Jerusalem Revealed*, ed. H. Geva. Jerusalem: Israel Exploration Society.

Bennett, C.
1965 Tombs of the Roman Period. Pp. 516–45 in *Excavations at Jericho II*, eds. K. Kenyon and T. A. Holland. London: British School of Archaeology in Jerusalem.

Bilig, Y.
2000 An Ossuary from Jerusalem bearing 'Korban' Inscriptions. *Cathedra* 98: 49–60.

Bliss, F. J.
1900 Report on the Excavations at Tell Sandahannah. *Palestine Exploration Fund Quarterly Studies* 32: 319–41.

Bryce, T. R.
1986 *The Lycians in Literary and Epigraphic Sources*. Cambridge: Museum Tusculanum.

Cooke, G. A.
1903 *A Text-Book of North-Semitic Inscriptions: Moabite, Hebrew, Phoenician, Aramaic, Nabtaean, Palmyrene, Jewish*. Oxford: Clarendon.

Cross, F. M.
1983 A Note on a Burial Inscription from Mount Scopus. *Israel Exploration Journal* 33: 245–46.

Cumont, F.
1962 *After Life in Roman Paganism*. New York, NY: Dover.

Faraone, C.
1991 Binding and Burying the Forces of Evil: The Defensive Use of 'Voodoo Dolls' in Ancient Greece. *Classical Antiquity* 10, no. 2: 165–205.

Fitzmyer, J. A.
1959 The Aramaic Qorban Inscription from Jebel Hallet et-Turi and Mark 7,11; Matt. 15,5. *Journal of Biblical Literature* 78: 60–65.

Fitzmyer, J. A. and D. J. Harrington
1978 *A Manual of Palestinian Aramaic Texts*. Rome: Biblical Institute.

Frey, J. B.
1952 *Corpus Inscriptionum Judaicarum* II. Rome: Pontificio Istituto di Archeologia Cristiana.

Gager, J. G.
1992 *Curse Tablets and Binding Spells from the Ancient World*. Oxford: Oxford University.

Hachlili, R.
2005 *Jewish Funerary Customs, Practices and Rights in the Second Temple Period*. Leiden: Brill.

Hachlili, R., and Killebrew, A.
1999 *Jericho—The Jewish Cemetery of the Second Temple Period*, Chapters I–VI. IAA Reports 7. Jerusalem: Israel Antiquities Authority.

Hadas, G.
1994 Nine Tombs of the Second Temple Period at 'En Gedi, *'Atiqot* 24: 1–8 (English Abstract).

Kloner, A.
1985 New Jewish Inscriptions from the "Darom." *Qadmoniot* 18: 96–100.

Kurtz, D. C., and Boardman, J.
1971 *Greek Burial Customs*. London: Thames and Hudson.

Milik, J. T.
1956 Trois tombeaux juifs récemment découverts au sud-est de Jerusalem. *Liber Annus* 7: 232–67.

Morgenstern, J.
1966 *Rites of Birth, Marriage, Death and Kindred Occasions among the Semites*. Cincinnati, OH: Hebrew Union College.

Naveh, J.
1980 An Aramaic Consolatory Burial Inscription. *'Atiqot* 14: 15–59.
1992 *On Sherd and Papyrus: Aramaic and Hebrew Inscriptions from the Second Temple, Mishnaic and Talmudic Periods*. Jerusalem: Magnes (Hebrew).

Peters, J. D., and Thiersch, H.
1905 *Painted Tombs in the Necropolis of Marissa*. London: Palestine Exploration Fund.

Puech, E.
1989 Une Inscription Araméenne sur un Couvercle de Sarcophage, *Eretz-Israel* 20: 161–65.

Rahmani, L. Y.
1987 More Lead Coffins from Israel. *Israel Exploration Journal* 37: 135–36.
1992 Five Lead Coffins from Israel. *Israel Exploration Journal* 42: 81–102.
1999 *A Catalogue of Roman and Byzantine Lead Coffins from Israel*. Jerusalem: Israel Antiquities Authority.

Rahmani, L. Y., and Sussman, A.
1994 *A Catalogue of Jewish Ossuaries in the Collections of the State of Israel*. Jerusalem: Israel Antiquities Authority.

Savignac, M. R.
1925 Nouveaux ossuaries juifs avec graffites (Mélanges). *Révue Biblique* 34: 253–66.

Schwabe, M., and Lifshitz, B.
1974 *Beth She'arim* II. *The Greek Inscriptions*. Jerusalem: Israel Exploration Society/Massada.

Smith, R. H.
1974 The Cross Marks on Jewish Ossuaries. *Palestine Exploration Quarterly* 106: 53–66.

Spoer, H. H.
1907 New Ossuaries from Jerusalem. *Journal of the American Oriental Society* 28: 355–59.

Sukenik, E. L.
1928 A Jewish Hypogeum near Jerusalem. *Journal of the Palestine Oriental Society* 8: 113–21.
1931 Funerary Tablet of Uzziah, King of Judah. *Palestine Exploration Fund Quarterly Studies* 64: 217–21.
1935 A Jewish Tomb Cave in the Kidron Valley. *Tarbiz* 6: 190–96.
1947 *The Earliest Records of Christianity: A Special Abstract from the American Journal of Archaeology, Volume LI, Number 4*. Menasha, WI: Banta.

Toynbee, J. M. C.
1971 *Death and Burial in the Roman World.* London: Thames and Hudson.

Tzaferis, V.
1970 Jewish Tombs at and near Giv'at Ha-Mivtar, Jerusalem. *Israel Exploration Journal* 20: 18–32.

van der Horst, P. W.
1991 *Ancient Jewish Epitaphs: An Introductory Survey of a Millennium of Jewish Funerary Epigraphy (300 BCE–700 CE)*. Kampen: Kok Pharos.

Weinberg, S.
1971 Tel Anafa, The Hellenistic Town. *Israel Exploration Journal* 21: 86–109.

White, D.
1997 Of Coffins, Curses and Other Plumbeous Matters: The Museum's Lead Burial Casket from Tyre. *Expedition* 39, no. 3: 3–14.
1999 The Eschatological Connection between Lead and Ropes as Reflected in a Roman Imperial Period Coffin in Philadelphia. *Israel Exploration Journal* 49: 66–90.

Zissu, B.
1995 Kh. Aleq and Kh. Abu Haf - Two Herodian Columbaria Towers. Pp. 56–69 in *The Roman and Byzantine Near East,* ed. J. Humphrey. Journal of Roman Archaeology Supplementary Series 14. Ann Arbor, MI: Journal of Roman Archaeology.

Chapter 21

Khirbet Qana's Necropolis and Ethnic Questions

by Peter Richardson

Khirbet Qana (ancient Cana; Arabic: Gana; map reference 1786.2475) lies on the north side of the Beth Netofa valley (el-Buttauf), directly across from Sepphoris (Zippori), one of the major sites associated with Eric Meyers' work.[1] Cana commands a strategically wide-angle view of the whole valley at the mouth of the Wadi Yodefat, about two km southeast of the village of Yodefat (Jotapata), which played a major role in the Jewish Revolt against Rome in 66–74 C.E.[2] When Yodefat was destroyed after a 47-day siege in 67 C.E., Cana apparently suffered no damage.[3] Vespasian and his army must have bypassed Cana on their way between Yodefat and Sepphoris; the absence of evidence of military action at Khirbet Qana suggests that Cana was not involved in the Revolt.[4]

Excavations at Khirbet Qana set it within its regional context as an integral part of the Beth Netofa valley and have shown its long occupation, perhaps from the Bronze Age through early modern periods.[5] The peaks of occupation seem to be the late Hellenistic, early Roman, and late Byzantine periods, in ascending order of occupational intensity, with smaller peaks in the Iron Age and the Arab period. The evidence of continuity in occupancy of the site is relatively strong, though clearly there are transition periods and rebuilding. Houses on the east and west slopes, whose walls survive to heights of 2–3 m, show stratified occupational levels with evidence of residential alterations and structural changes, but without evidence of destruction and rebuilding.

Although Cana became a major Christian pilgrimage site because of Jesus' water-to-wine incident, it was an obviously Jewish site prior to and overlapping that stage for the majority of the half millennium from the 2nd–1st century B.C.E. through the 4th–5th century C.E. From then until the Persian invasion, Christianity may have been a dominant force. Judaism and Christianity must have overlapped as competing or complementary entities at Cana in somewhat the same way as at Capernaum and Nazareth, so that the Khirbet Qana excavations should ultimately shed light on Jewish/Christian relationships in Galilee. The question of the relationship of Judaism and Christianity at the site is still just a little uncertain, since there is no evidence of Christian burials at Khirbet Qana. But a very clear sign of the vigor of Judaism is the necropolis.

CANA NECROPOLIS

Thirteen Tombs

A survey has identified a substantial necropolis of thirteen tombs; another has been identified subsequently, making fourteen in all, though I have not yet examined this latest find. There are a minimum of eighteen chambers in the thirteen tombs, in four separate locations in a roughly oval pattern around the village; the number could be larger since there is some uncertainty about the number of chambers in some shafts. Five tombs are located on the lower southwest slope, four on the lower southeast slope, and three to the northwest of the site, near a steep but minor water course taking runoff water down to the Wadi Yodefat. Here I concentrate on these twelve typologically similar tombs; the one tomb on the east slope differs from the others in its design. The farthest are situated ca. 500 m from the center of the built-up area; the closest dwelling units are ca. 100 m from the nearest graves, in a kind of suburb on the southern hillside, which dates from a period later than the tombs.[6]

All tombs are in closely related seams of hard limestone, sloping from northwest to southeast, good for quarrying, with cisterns nearby, though the cisterns are not architecturally integrated with the graveyards. Twelve of the thirteen tombs are entered by vertical shafts, none with steps or indications of ladders to give access to the "courtyards." None of the tombs is decorated; several, however, include surface features that may suggest architectural embellishment of the tombs. The tombs' locations are visible from nearby roads, perhaps deliberately so. The southwest and northern tomb groups are close to the Sepphoris–Cana–Yodefat road; the southeast group and the east tomb are visible from Cana's main approach road, which was on the east.[7] Table 1 summarizes the main internal and external features of shafts, chambers, and loculi.

Since no excavations have been conducted in or around the tombs, the following analysis is based on surface examination and partial information. We entered twelve of eighteen chambers and made drawings and took photographs of those twelve (in a couple of additional cases, we could reach into the openings to take photographs). Sometimes it was impossible to do more than ascertain that there was a chamber; sometimes we were uncertain even of the number of chambers. The analysis is thus incomplete (Table 2).

Group 1, the southwest complex, is carved into a relatively flat, bare, low-sloping section of bedrock. Five shafts are organized informally into a southwest graveyard, somewhat above the valley bottom, oriented approximately northeast–southwest following the contours. We could enter five of the eight chambers, with a total of twenty *loculi*. There are several large ancient bell-cisterns nearby.

Group 2, the southeast complex, is similarly located in an area of bare, flat, sloping bedrock, about the same height above the valley bottom, with the tombs distributed over a larger area. They are oriented approximately northwest–southeast, following the contours. One shaft is either completely filled flush with the bedrock or was merely begun but never finished. Of the five discernible chambers, the three we could enter had twenty-three *loculi*. Here, too, there were cisterns nearby.

Group 3, the northwest complex, is located in front of a vertical face in the limestone bedrock. Though a *dromos*-type entrance would have been simpler and more convenient, the tombs are still of the shaft type. The shafts are all oriented approximately northeast–southwest, following the bedrock seam's orientation. We entered three of the four chambers (of three shafts) with sixteen *loculi*. There were major cisterns in the same limestone seam.

Group 4 is a single tomb on the lower east slope, with no shaft or formally defined *dromos*; its opening is cut into a vertical face of bedrock. It is, thus, typologically different from the other tombs externally; its chamber and eleven loculi, however, are generally similar to the others.

Shafts

The tombs in Groups 1–3 all have shaft entrances, which function as small "courtyards," even in the case of the northwest group, which more logically might have had *dromos*-style entrances. The

Table 1 Khirbet Qana Necropolis.

Tomb	Chamber	Loculi	External features	Internal features
Group 1 Southwest				
1	A	?	Door to chamber arched in arched field, offset to south; ledge on 3 sides	Established existence of chamber; not entered
	B	?		
	C	1		Poor rock, *loculus* collapsed
2	A	3	Large shallow rock-cutting to N, with water channel, above chamber; small shallow recess to S of shaft; door to chamber arched in square field	*Loculus* 3 is only 30 cm long; two *loculi* arched in square field; one *loculus* arched
3	A	7	Narrow shaft, 3 prominent ledges; door to chamber arched in arched field	Two *loculi* rotated in plan; *loculi* arched
4	A	?	No obvious external features	Not entered
	B	7		*Loculi* 2, 5, 6, 7 slightly rotated; *loculi* 3, 4 joined (bone room?) and tapered; *loculus* 1 partly under shaft; *loculi* arched
5	A	2	Portions of ledges on three sides of shaft; door to chamber arched in arched field, small portion of arch on upper right not completed	One short *loculus*; one bone room (?); *loculi* arched
Group 2 Southeast				
6	A	?	Two round "pots" at SW and SE; doors to chambers arched in arched field, with very deep recesses	Not entered
	B	?		Not entered
7	A	9	Two small round "pots" on NE bedrock; very wide roughly rectangular door (ca. 2 m) in high arched field; plastered	*Loculus* 1 rotated in plan; *loculus* 4 barely begun; *loculi* arched; interior of *loculi* plastered
8	A	5	Large, deep, round "pot" on E bedrock connects with shaft; ledge on two or three sides; door to chamber rectangular in arched field; shallow recess	*Loculus* 2 slightly rotated; *loculus* 1 short; rectangular *loculi*
9	A	9	Wide square door (1.2 m) in arched field, with deep recess; small shaft, with little evidence of ledges	*Loculi* 1-5 rotated; *loculus* 7 unusually large; *loculi* arched, the largest one most noticeably
Group 3 Northwest				
10	A	5	Information incomplete	*Loculus* 1, to left, 1.2 m deep; two *loculi* in other two walls
11	A	9	Information incomplete	Three *loculi* on each side
12	A	2	Information incomplete; doors to chambers rectangular in arched field	Arcosolia (? uncertain)
	B	8 or 9?		Not entered; photos suggest perhaps 8–9 *loculi*
Group 4 East				
13	A	11	No shaft or other external features; door to chamber very roughly arched opening in vertical bedrock	Rectangular *loculi*; 1, 2 & 8 rotated; 4 double width (bone repository?); slight modulation of ceiling

Table 2 Summary of Tombs.

	GROUP 1 – SW	GROUP 2 – SE	GROUP 3 – NW	GROUP 4 – E	TOTALS
SHAFTS	5	4	3	None	12 + 1
CHAMBERS	8	5	4	1	18
LOCULI	20 in 5 chambers	23 in 3 chambers	16 in 3 chambers	11 in 1 chamber	70 in 12 chambers
EXTERNAL	2 with ledges and 1 with water installation	1 with ledges and 3 with round "pots"	Small niche in one shaft opposite door	No shaft, dromos, or external features	
INTERNAL	All *loculi* arched	Some arched, some rectangular	Arcosolia in one chamber (?)	All *loculi* rectangular	
BONE ROOMS	2	None	None	1	3
OSSUARIES	None	None	None	None	None
ESTIMATED LOCULI	32	38	21	11	102 *loculi* total estimated

shaft-design must have been deliberately chosen, despite the fact that it was neither regionally common nor, in Group 3, logical. The shafts share several important features: none is monumental in scale; all are 1–2 m deep, with vertical sides and rectangular plan; none showed evidence of benches in the shafts, though it is not certain that there were none, since no fill was removed from the courtyards; and none has any visible means of descent from bedrock to the courtyard floor. Hewn stairs in a corner or on a side could have been designed not to interfere with entry into the chambers, but there are none, nor is there evidence of supports for wooden stairs. Presumably short ladders were used as occasion demanded.[8] There is no evidence of tomb closures, whether basalt or limestone doors, rolling stones, or sealing stones,[9] so there is some uncertainty how they prevented carnivores from molesting the corpses. One shaft had a small rectangular niche opposite a doorway; it is possible that this took the end of a beam spanning the shaft to seal the stone door of a chamber in place of a "buttressing stone" (cf. *m. Oholoth* 15.8). The rest were unelaborated except for the doorways, which took the form of recessed openings, usually arched, with a (usually arched) door within the recess. The most deeply recessed opening created a kind of porch, 1.9 m deep, with a further half meter of bedrock for the doorway (Tomb 7); this was the only entrance that was plastered.

The shafts vary in area from 4.62 m^2 to 15.54 m^2.[10] Several shafts have badly weathered or damaged ledges around the opening just below the level of the bedrock that ranged from 15–30 cm wide. The ledges had been leveled in some cases; others followed the contours of the bedrock. There was no surviving evidence of the purpose of the ledges.

Chambers

It is impossible to stand in any of the chambers; without excavation, heights are only approximate, but all appear to be between 110 and 170 cm. They vary in size and number. One tomb has three chambers, three tombs have two chambers, and nine tombs have only one chamber.[11] No tomb has four chambers, nor does any have a chamber opening off another chamber. The layouts of *loculi* within the chambers vary, but the designs are generally similar; in several cases *loculi* were rotated or splayed, creating an almost radial plan.

The chambers are roughly though not carelessly hewn; chisel marks are evident. All ceilings are relatively flat, some following the bedrock seam. There are no moldings around doors or *loculi* or at the intersection of walls and ceilings. The chambers

Table 3 Dimensions of shafts, chambers and *loculi.* * indicates shafts exceeding the area of 6 × 6 cubits; † indicates chambers exceeding the area of 4 × 6 cubits. Only tombs 5 and 7 have dimensions exceeding the *Mishnah's* courtyard and chamber size.

Shaft	Shaft size	Chamber	Chamber size	Max. Loculus Size W × H × D	Min. Loculus Size W × H × D
1	2.5 × 2.3 m = 5.75 m^2	A	?		
		B	?		
		C	2.2 × 2.2 m = 4.84 m^2	50 × 100 × 190 cm	
2	1.9 × 2.6 m = 4.94 m^2	A	†2.4 × 2.2 m = 5.28 m^2	50 × 90 × 190 cm	60 × 80 × 180 cm
3	1.4 × 3.3 m = 4.62 m^2	A	†2.5 × 2.5 m = 6.25 m^2	70 × 90 × 180 cm	50 × 90 × 180 cm
4	*2.9 × 3.0 m = 8.7 m^2	A	?		
		B	†2.8 × 2.8 m = 7.84 m^2	140 × 90 × 200 cm	50 × 70 × 200 cm
5	*3.3 × 3.7 m = 12.21 m^2	A	†2.7 × 2.5 m = 6.75 m^2	150 × 90 × 125 cm	50 × 90 × 40 cm
6	*2.8 × 3.0 m = 8.4 m^2	A	?		
		B	† 2.3 ×. 2.5 = 5.75 m^2	?	
7	*4.2 × 3.7 m = 15.54 m^2	A	†3.5 × 2.8 m = 9.8 m^2	60 × 90 × 220 cm	50 × 80 × 190 cm
8	1.8 × 2.9 m = 5.22 m^2	A	†2.7 × 3.3 m = 8.91 m^2	80 × 90 × 180 cm	75 × 90 × 110 cm
9	2.0 × 2.9 m = 5.8 m^2	A	†3.4–4.0 × 2.9–3.5 m, irregular = ca. 11 m^2	90 × 100 × 200 cm	60 × 80 × 210 cm
10	Information incomplete	A	Information incomplete		
11	Information incomplete	A	Information incomplete		
12	Information incomplete	A	Information incomplete		
		B			
13	No shaft	A	†2.6–3.5 × 3.4–3.6 m, irregular = ca. 10.5 m^2	140 × 90 × 210 cm	55 × 90 × 210 cm

are a rural and poorer form of chambers, similar to those in Jerusalem, but lacking all embellishments appropriate to larger, elite, urbanized, and wealthier settings. I do not recall seeing niches for lamps.

Loculi *and Bone Rooms*

The *loculi* (*kokhim*) are similar in form and type to those found in other locations, such as Jerusalem and other Galilean sites.[12] Tombs 8 and 13 have niches with rectangular cross-sections; all others had arched openings and arched cross-sections. Variations in width, height and length are listed in Table 3. Only in Tomb 2—with arched openings inside rectangular fields—is there decorative embellishment around the *loculi*. Other than a few short *loculi* (for children? bone rooms?), most are between 180 and 210 cm long. Though no ossuaries were found, there is one extra-wide *loculus*, one with two joined *loculi*, and another "room,"[13] all plausibly functioning as repositories for secondary burials.[14]

Decorative Features

Decoration, whether inside or outside, is almost entirely absent at Khirbet Qana. Some tombs have surface features that may suggest monuments or other kinds of functional features.[15] Tomb 2, for example, has on the uphill (north) side of the shaft a shallow water-related rock-cut installation, with a channel or drain leading beyond the corner of the shaft, possibly to take water away so that it did not run into the shaft and from there into the chambers (an unresolved problem in all the tombs) or alternatively for decorative reasons; the same tomb has a smaller installation on the south side of the shaft. This is the only tomb where the features are integrally related with the shaft and chamber: the larger depression is precisely above the chamber, and both depressions are on the same axis as the chamber and shaft. Tombs 6, 7, 8, and perhaps 3, have circular pits of varying diameters and depths in no discernible pattern. None seem to have had channels or drains, and the purpose seems not for water, but for some other burial-related function (offerings? pestles for preparing spices?). I find no relevant discussion of these issues in the *Mishnah*.

The ledges around Tombs 1, 3, 5, and 8 could be for simple decoration, to dress up the opening. It is also plausible that the ledges originally supported some kind of "monument," though the monument would likely to have had to be wood rather than stone, given the narrowness of the ledges. Another possibility, suggested by *m. Erubin* 2.1 (marking wells to protect against injury), is that the ledge was designed to support a low wall of upright boards or thin stone panels around the shaft.[16]

ANALYSIS

Typology

In most respects, Cana's necropolis presents no mysteries.[17] Courtyards, chambers, and *loculi* fit neatly late Hellenistic through Second Temple tomb design, as it is known from a large number of sites, especially in Jerusalem. Cana tombs relate to Jerusalem's generally pre-70 C.E. tombs as rural, peasant tombs relate to urban, wealthy tombs. Typologically, the rural *loculi* and chambers are virtually identical to the *loculi* and chambers of the city. Their dimensions are usually smaller, they are unembellished, and they do not advertise their presence with monuments, as compared with those in the city. But functionally they are similar, and they indicate rather clearly that rural village burial practices correlated closely with Jerusalem practices. The Cana tombs fit comfortably within the range of design features, dimensions, and customs of the 1st–2nd century C.E., as those are considered in the *Mishnah*. These are Jewish tombs of the Second Temple period or just after, and they suggest that there are not great differences in burial practices between south and north, between city and countryside, between rich and poor.

In some respects, however, the Cana tombs raise questions:

- There is little presently visible external embellishment and none suggestive of other ethnic influences (cf. the Egyptian pyramid motif at the Tombs of Zechariah, Jason, Absalom, and Queen Helena of Adiabene; the late-Hellenistic conventions at the Tomb of Absalom; the early Roman features in Herod's family tomb, as reconstructed by Netzer), for which there are Galilean analogies at Beth She'arim, Khirbet Shema, Tiberias, Sepphoris, and other places. Is this decorative restraint a function of poverty, rural location, or religion?
- Some pre-70 C.E. Jerusalem tombs, especially the Aceldama Tombs, have internal embellishments with some decorative features resembling the Herodian temple (e.g., mimicking the monolithic ceiling panels at the Huldah gates, suggesting the masonry of the podium, and hinting at the façade of the Holy Place).[18] Why are Jerusalem motifs absent at Cana?
- Most Jerusalem tombs contained ossuaries for secondary burial, but, to date, there are none at Cana, though there are bone repositories. Is this merely an alternative form of secondary burial or is the simplest explanation that the ossuaries have been robbed over the years?
- A *dromos* entrance is typical in Jerusalem (e.g., Jason, Sanhedrin and Aceldama Tombs), while no Cana tomb has one. Shaft tombs are known in Jerusalem (Queen Helena's Tomb, with its impressive shaft and stair). Why is there a difference in courtyard designs between Jerusalem and Cana?
- Some tombs in Jerusalem (e.g., Tomb of the Bene Hezir, of Jason, of Abba) had inscriptions (and ossuaries with inscriptions). Why are there no inscriptions at Cana?

A thorough study would necessarily involve comparisons with other nearby tombs (Yodefat, Nazareth, Meiron, Achziv, Hanita, Sepphoris and Beth

She'arim, to name but a few), though the paucity of extensive simple Galilean graveyards makes rural comparisons difficult.[19] Here at Khirbet Qana it may be that some features noted can be accounted for on the basis of Cana's lower status, lesser wealth, and simpler cultural influences.

The peculiarity of the shaft entrance is particularly noteworthy. Phoenician tombs sometimes had small, deep shaft entrances, some up to 30 m deep, though, in fact, most Phoenician tombs had steps and were of the *dromos* type.[20] It has been suggested that the Cana shafts might recall Phoenician influence, a not implausible proposal that would be more persuasive if the Galilean shafts were deeper and if other sites in Lower and Upper Galilee had such shafts. The evidence leaves us with a conundrum: we know of Phoenician tombs with shafts of a different design and we know of Jewish tombs without shafts but with a *dromos* of a similar design. The Cana tombs seem to be a genuinely variant design.

Several functional problems arise from considering the Cana necropolis: (a) Protection of the corpses from carnivores was necessary, and the *Mishnah*'s references to "stones that seal a grave" provide the likeliest general solution, confirmed by tombs in Jerusalem and elsewhere. The Cana necropolis has not provided any explicit evidence that helps to understand this local solution. (b) Runoff water, especially in the two main groups of tombs in the southwest and the southeast, must have been a very serious problem during the winter rains, when much water would naturally drain into the closed shafts, and from there into the chambers and the *loculi*. Only one shaft has a design feature that might reasonably be interpreted as a solution to this problem, and even this is at best a partial solution. (c) The absence of niches for lamps—needed while the tombs were being hewn and during burials—is a minor question. Perhaps more careful inspection of the tomb chambers will disclose evidence of such niches. (d) Related to the burials themselves are other questions: how to carry corpses into the chambers when there were no stairs; what provision was made for spices; why were there no formal indications of mourners' benches; how was the whiting of tombs done when virtually all features were below ground level; did the soil washed off the bedrock pose problems of ritual contamination on the fields below?[21]

Chronology

Without the stratigraphic precision and material evidence that excavation of the tombs would provide, it is impossible to establish a chronology of Cana's necropolis. Its close typological similarities to pre-70 C.E. Jerusalem tombs suggest that the tombs span the late Hellenistic through Roman periods, especially the Early Roman period. The coherence with the *Mishnah* also suggests this same general period. This hypothesis is consistent with the evidence of peaks of occupation at Khirbet Qana in the late Hellenistic and Early Roman periods and also with the possibility of resettlement of the area following the conquest of the Galilee, with some of the population deriving from Judea.

The tombs were probably hewn mainly in the Early Roman period (late 1st century B.C.E. through 2nd century C.E.), with the possibility that some may be late Hellenistic and that others could be middle Roman. It is likely that the tombs were hewn over a period of time, but that must remain uncertain. Were embellished tombs, the rectangular *loculi*, and the better built tombs earlier or later? The following overall picture might be hypothesized: the earliest tombs were probably those in the southwest and the southeast, followed by the ones in the northwest, with the lone tomb on the east likely the latest.

Ethnicity

Though *loculi* were widely used in surrounding cultures, their use at Khirbet Qana reflects Jewish burial patterns, as the various references to the *Mishnah* suggest. The evidence of the site coheres closely with usual reconstructions of Jewish history in the region, especially a Hasmonean reconquest of Galilee ca. 100 B.C.E. An expansion of the village at this period is consistent with the archaeological evidence of Jewish culture (Hasmonean coins, stoneware, mikvaoth, GCW pottery). Since no other tombs from obviously earlier or later periods have been found — not even from the Christian period — the necropolis must derive from a major period of occupation; none fits as well as the Jewish occupation during the Early Roman period.

Population Estimates

The Cana necropolis offers a possible test of population estimates, since it is a large necropolis connected to a relatively small village over a limited chronological period. It seems reasonable to imagine that the tombs from a given period should be sufficient for the burial needs of that same period, perhaps with a factor thrown in for oversupply. The maximum population the necropolis could serve might be calculated as follows: If we assume 100 *loculi*, an average life expectancy of 30 to 35 years, an evenly distributed death rate (though this is obviously unlikely), and primary burial lasting one year in a *loculus* (prior to secondary burial), the necropolis could serve 100 (*loculi*) times 30–35 (life expectancy) times one (year of interment), or about 3000 persons. This maximum is considerably too generous for Khirbet Qana even at peak population periods. The population was probably a third or a quarter of that, raising yet another question, about the overbuilding of tombs.

CONCLUSION

This preliminary report has emphasized the unusual shaft entrances, but has reached no conclusion about ethnic influence at Khirbet Qana. I hope that its data and questions will serve as an appropriate homage to Eric Meyers, whose own investigations have been so meticulously reported, acutely analyzed, and imaginatively reconstructed. The direction in which this survey of the Cana necropolis tends can be summarized in the following propositions: (a) Khirbet Qana offers one of the largest rural village necropolises in the Galilee; (b) the overall design of the tombs, the social historical reconstructions of the village itself, together with textual evidence from the *Mishnah*, suggest that the tombs derive from the 1st century B.C.E. through the 2nd century C.E., or a more limited portion of that period; (c) the shaft entrances to twelve of the thirteen tombs need further consideration to ascertain the origin of this unusual feature that seems reflected poorly in the presently known data; (d) the design of the shafts may plausibly be interpreted as an influence from Phoenician practice; if that suggestion is supported by subsequent examination, it will be a factor of considerable importance in discussions of the cultural matrix of western Lower Galilee.

NOTES

1 Eric M. Meyers' work is a model for Galilean excavations, both urban and rural. It is a pleasure to acknowledge both his archaeological and institutional contributions.

2 On Yodefat, see Richardson 2004, part 2; on Galilean walled villages, Aviam and Richardson 2001.

3 The excavations have found no early Roman destruction, arrowheads, *ballista* stones, or catapult bolts.

4 Sepphoris and most neighboring towns stayed quiet early in the revolt (Josephus, *War* 2.511), but rebels and brigands fought Romans on Mount Azmon, adjacent to both Cana and Yodefat. On brigands, Edwards and Richardson 2004, chap. 2.

5 Excavations by the University of Puget Sound, under the direction of Douglas R. Edwards, began in 1998. See Edwards 2002.

6 *Mishnah Baba Bathra* 2.9 says graves are to be 50 cubits (ca. 23 m) from dwellings; *m. Oholoth* 16.3 (cf. 17.1, 18.2) suggests a maximum of 20 cubits (ca. 9 m) between graves within graveyards.

7 Aaro Söderlund and Byron McCane wrote a preliminary report (1999) considering the tombs; both have been helpful in preparing this chapter.

8 The *Mishnah* does not explicitly mention such a problem when discussing burial practices.

9 *Mishnah Oholoth* 2.4 (cf. 15.9; *m. Erubin* 1.7; *m. Nazir* 7.3) mentions stones that seal graves, with a "buttressing stone." This may sometimes refer to a rolling stone, at other times to a stone fitting the chamber entrance with another stone holding it in place (in *m. Oholoth* 15.9 a "jar" or even a "living beast" can be used to seal a tomb!).

10 According to *m. Oholoth* 6.8 the "courtyard" was to be 6 × 6 cubits, large enough for the bier and bearers (ca. 7.6 m^2 in area). Five shafts are less than this area, four are larger.

11 *Mishnah Baba Bathra* 6.8 says the chamber is to be 4 × 6 cubits (ca. 5 m^2), with eight niches, three on the sides and two opposite the door. Rabbi Simeon said 4 × 8 cu (ca. 6.7 m^2), with 13 niches, four on each side, three opposite the door, and one on either side of the door. Courtyards could have three chambers; R. Simeon said up to four; R. Simeon ben Gamaliel said "All depends on the nature of the rock."

12 *Mishnah Baba Bathra* 6.8 discusses niche dimensions: 4 cubits long (ca. 1.85 m), 6 handbreadths wide and 7 high (ca. 54 by 63 cm). Table 3 shows that the minimum niche sizes hover around these dimensions.

13 In Tomb 5 the "bone room" is the only functional *loculus*, since the only other *loculus* seems incomplete.

14 On secondary burial, see *m. Pesahim* 8.8; *m. Moed Katan* 1.5; *m. Sanhedrin* 6.6. Two styles of ossuaries are presumed in *m. Oholoth* 9.15, those with lids that fit within the sides and those with lids overhanging the sides: see Meyers 1971; Rahmani 1994.

15 Several passages in the *Mishnah* presuppose monuments or decoration: *m. Oholoth* 7.1 (a solid monument); *m. Erubin* 5.1 (a monument in which is a "dwelling chamber" or hollow); *m. Shekalim* 2.5 (building a monument with excess money).

16 The need to mark graves by whiting them is well known: *m. Maaser Sheni* 5.1; *m. Moed Katan* 1.2; *m. Shekalim* 1.1 (on 15 Adar).

17 Hachlili 1988, chap. 4; Stern 2001: 470–77; Bloch-Smith 1992; Pearson 1999; Chapman et al. 1981.

18 Richardson 2004, chap. 17.

19 The door design, in particular, has similarities at Achziv and Hanita; Frankel and Getzov 1997: 45*–47*.

20 On Phoenician tombs, see Ward 1997: 316; Markoe 1997: 329–30; 2000: 141; Baramki 1961: 97–99; Harden 1980: 96–104; Lipinski 1992: 457–61; Moscati 1988: 267–83.

21 Washed-down soil, *m. Oholoth* 17.4; areas for mourners, *m. Oholoth* 18.4 (cf. also 18.7; 2.3); *m. Megillah* 4.3; *m. Ketuboth* 2.10; *m. Baba Bathra* 6.7; whiting, see above; carrying the bier, *m. Baba Bathra* 6.7–8.

REFERENCES

Aviam, M., and Richardson, P.
2001 Josephus's Galilee in Archaeological Perspective. Pp. 177–209 in *Flavius Josephus*, ed. S. Mason. Life of Josephus, vol. 9. Leiden: Brill.

Baramki, D.
1961 *Phoenicia and the Phoenicians*. Beirut: Khayats.

Bloch-Smith, E.
1992 *Judahite Burial Practices and Beliefs About the Dead*. Sheffield: Journal for the Study of the Old Testament.

Chapman, R.; Kinnes, I.; and Randsborg, K. (eds.)
1981 *The Archaeology of Death*. Cambridge: Cambridge University.

Edwards, D.
2002 Khirbet Qana: From Jewish Village to Christian Pilgrim Site. Pp. 101–32 in The *Roman and Byzantine East*, vol. 3, ed. J. Humphrey. Journal of Roman Archaeology Supplementary Series 49. Portsmouth, RI: JRA.

Edwards, D., and Richardson, P.
2004 Jesus and Palestinian Social Protest in Archaeological and Literary Perspective. Pp. 17–38 in *Building Jewish in the Roman East*, ed. P. Richardson. Waco, TX: Baylor University.

Frankel, R., and Getzov, N.
1997 *Maps of Akhziv (1) and Hanita (2)*. Jerusalem: Israel Antiquities Authority.

Hachlili, R.
1988 *Ancient Jewish Art and Archaeology in the Land of Israel*. Leiden: Brill.

Harden, D. B.
1980 *The Phoenicians*. Harmondsworth: Penguin.

Lipinski, E. (ed.)
1992 *Dictionnaire de la Civilization Phénicienne et Punique*. Turnhout: Brepols.

Markoe, G.
1997 Phoenicians. Pp. 329–30 in *Oxford Encyclopedia of Archaeology in the Near East*, vol. 4, ed. E. M. Meyers. New York, NY: Oxford University.
2000 *Phoenicians*. London: British Museum.

Moscati, S.
1988 *The Phoenicians*. New York, NY: Abbeville.

Pearson, M. P.
1999 *The Archaeology of Death and Burial*. Stroud: Sutton.

Rahmani, L.
1994 *A Catalogue of Jewish Ossuaries in the Collections of the State of Israel*. Jerusalem: Israel Antiquities Authority.

Richardson, P. (ed.)
2004 *Building Jewish in the Roman East*. Waco, TX: Baylor University.

Stern, E.
2001 *Archaeology of the Land of the Bible*, vol. 2. New York, NY: Doubleday.

Ward, W. A.
1997 Phoenicia. Pp. 313–17 in *Oxford Encyclopedia of Archaeology in the Near East*, vol. 4, ed. E. M. Meyers. New York, NY: Oxford University.

Chapter 22

Monumental Changes: Architecture and Culture in Late Roman and Early Byzantine Sepphoris

by C. Thomas McCollough

Libanius, the well-known orator of the fourth century C.E., took note of signs of the decline of the ancient city and was appalled by the inattention given to this crisis. Libanius acknowledges that cities of his era had been ravaged by any number of internal and external problems and catastrophes, but he argues the decline is not inevitable or uncorrectable: as he observed, "Considering also that the destinies of cities are not identical with those of men, for man's end is irrevocable while they — the cities — can be revived" (*Orations* 12.50–51). As Libanius goes on to observe, to do otherwise risked not only barbarian takeover, but also the onset of melancholy, "Failure to found a non-existent city is no shame, but to ignore the destruction of a previously existing town involves the double penalty of disgrace and damage. The occurrence of such a disaster is an invitation to the barbarians...and to our people an inevitable cause of despondency...."(*Orations* 12.50–51).

Sepphoris, a large city in lower Galilee, could well have been one of the cities for which Libanius grieved. As was true of other cities in Roman Palestine, Sepphoris underwent changes, and in some cases dramatic changes, in its urban landscape beginning in the mid-fourth century C.E. The excavators of the site have all noted evidence of destruction in the mid-4th century and accounted for the destruction layer either in terms of the Gallus revolt of 352 and/or the earthquake of 363. From that point forward, the city evolved in ways that show signs of continuity and discontinuity with its former self. This study focuses on two major urban structures — a basilica and a theater — and, in terms of the excavation results, offers some observations about the city and its population as it entered the Byzantine period.

Recent studies on changing patterns of urbanism in the late antique world have demonstrated both the complexity of the endeavor as well as the potential for such studies to truly allow archaeology to give back a voice to the people of the past. The latter has been especially true in studies that have emphasized a more postmodernist perspective on urbanism. This perspective has located in the archaeology and architecture evidence of a multiplicity of forces operative in the urban setting at its point of transition from the classical cities of the Hellenic east to the pragmatic cities of Byzantium. This approach opens the analysis to a greater sense of the active role of the urban resident in determining his/her world. The urban context is no longer seen simply as the setting for the manipulative strategies of the elite, but as the context in which individuals adapted and in some cases radically transformed their urban space for a host of reasons, ranging from economic to religious to environmental. It is in this way that studies of urban archaeology can openly converge with the concerns of the archaeology of difference in the ancient world.

Over the last fifteen years, several excavation teams have worked at uncovering the ancient city of Sepphoris. I have been affiliated with the University of South Florida Excavations at Sepphoris. Our excavations have opened five fields and two of those have centered upon monumental structures from the urban landscape of Sepphoris: the theater and a basilica-type building. While an important goal of the excavations was, of course, the question of foundation, the excavations fully exposed the depositional history of the later occupation and use of the structures. This stratigraphical history gave important insight into the city in transition. The theater and the basilica, classic features of a Roman city, were transformed as the city entered the early Byzantine (meaning the mid-4th century C.E.) period. Previous assessments of Sepphoris in this period have noted some changes in the city's landscape, but have tended to characterize the late fourth century as witnessing an almost immediate restoration or rebuilding of the city. In fact, one scholar has contended that after the Gallus revolt of 352 "the city was immediately rebuilt. . . ." (Strange 1999), while others noted that after the earthquake of 363, "In certain parts of the city, damaged buildings were restored and in other parts, new buildings were erected" (Weiss 1997: 123). The impression given by these sorts of assessments is one of rapid recovery and only modest change in the urban landscape. What I would argue is that in light of the excavations of the two monumental structures, these sorts of impressions need modification. For in each case, these buildings — flagship structures of the Roman *polis* — are not restored, but rather in both cases there is spoilage and a radical reuse of space. The archaeological record of these two buildings signals the dawn of a new phase in the character of this city, a phase that points in a direction away from the Roman *polis* and in the direction of a *medina*, away from a city focused upon and held together by the central buildings of the *polis* and in the direction of a city broken into neighborhoods and clustered around other centers of loyalty and identity.

It has become a truism, but a truism built on a substantial body of evidence, that urban architecture in the Empire in late antiquity — meaning the mid-3rd and through to the 4th centuries C.E. — was being transformed by shifts in political, economic and cultural (more specifically, religious) forces. These forces significantly disrupted the urban pattern inherited from the Hellenistic period and continued (and one might say perfected) during the period of the Roman Empire's hegemony over the Mediterranean basin. The urban patterns that emerged in the midst of this disruption had been cast as indicators of decay on the eve of the invasions from Persia and, in time, the massive takeover by the Islamic invaders. More recent studies have rejected such pessimistic evaluations and instead characterized this period as a time "not of decay and barbarism but a creative tension between old and new, between a compelling tradition of urbanism inherited from the past and new spiritual and social realities" (Holum 1993: 698).[1] One goal of this study is to test this paradigm shift in the characterization of the late antique city. Have the excavations given us a city in decay or one recasting itself in accordance with a changed view of the city? And how might the transitional data be used as well for capturing the multifaceted forces driving the changes?

There is widespread agreement that late-third- and fourth-century imperial policy regarding the cities had a significant impact on urban architecture, as it disrupted, and in some cases destroyed, the fiscal sources for building and maintaining public structures and relocated the sources for social status and stature from municipal office to imperial office (e.g., Saradi-Mendelovici 1988). The fiscal resources for building and maintaining public buildings in the city appear to have been three-fold. The largest source of funds came from private benefactors. Public spending by a rich man displayed the virtue of *magnanimitas,* and on the more mundane level, it both showed off wealth and brought status. As Ward-Perkins quipped, "Social pressures, not written constitutions, set the pace for public buildings" (1984: 8).

A second source for funds was what may be called civic patronage. These were funds administered by town administrators, secured by taxation and by way of fees paid by the aristocracy for the honor of holding civic offices, such as decurion and magistrate. Finally, there were the funds made available by the imperial administration and these most often were for the building and repair of city walls. The erosion of these sources was a gradual and complex process, but one can certainly point to the reorganization of the imperial administration, begun under Diocletian in the late third century, as a critical juncture in the process. Diocletian's and Constantine's efforts to create a far more centralized and autocratic polity and to supply badly needed funds to the imperial treasury struck at the foundation of the cities' resources. A series of imperial laws make evident the imperial fiscus' efforts at subverting the revenues of the cities (Saradi-Mendelovici 1988: 372; see also Jones 1964: 732–34 and Liebeschuetz 1972: 149). Moreover, the re-centering of the polity on the imperial house redefined the route to status. Real power and status were no longer garnered by lavishing buildings or other gifts on one's hometown, but rather was derived from holding imperial posts and imperial honors. The parvenus of the fourth century sought out imperial service rather than local office or local prestige. Imperial legislation shows that the class of decurions, in particular, was depleted by movements into senatorial rank, by way of seeking exemptions from the office and/or moving to country estates, or by conversion to Christianity.[2] On top of this savaging of funds and private resources, there were natural and man-made calamities that put at risk what meager resources might be available.

And finally, and, some have argued, most fatally, there was the assault by Christianity on certain public buildings of the ancient city, such as the theater, as they were connected with encouraging frivolous behavior and, thus, distracting from a life of virtue.[3] In a work from somewhat later in the Byzantine era, under the title *Peira,* there is an intriguing collection of judicial decisions of the Byzantine judge Eustathius Romaeus, wherein the neglect and disappearance of the traditional public institutions is explained by specifically referring to the new attitude towards life introduced by the Christian religion:

> The ancient custom was that those who died left behind money to build, for instance, a Thessalonian hippodrome, or a bath, or to contribute in any other way to the enjoyment of the people; since Christianity was established, however, all theses practices were abolished, and diligence for one's soul became more important than that for one's body.[4]

To be sure, the "demise of the ancient city" and Christianity's role therein does not adhere to a linear or universal pattern. Indeed, it is important to differentiate a transformed sense of the makeup of the urban landscape from the question of urban prosperity. As Mark Whittow (1990) has argued, the flight of the decurions and the collapse of the *curiales* as sources of urban financial stability should not be taken as sure indicators of urban collapse. Rather, we have in the archaeological record signs of continuing prosperity, much of which was made possible and ultimately overseen by the Church and its clergy. In a number of provincial cities, Christianity took up the mantle of private benefaction, not only in terms of providing funds for another sort of monumental structure — the Church — but also asserting its stature and role as the new source of influence and power in the city by patronizing the building or rebuilding of at least some of the more innocuous public structures, like colonnaded sidewalks.[5] Thus, there is a case to be made for continued prosperity, but as the quote from Eustathius Romaeus makes evident, this fiscal renewal did not insure the continuation of the classical city and its monumental structures. As Haldon noted,

> Archaeological surveys and excavations show an almost universal tendency for cities to lose by neglect many of the features familiar from their classical structure. Major public buildings fall into disrepair…major thoroughfares and public spaces are built on, and so on. These changes may not necessarily have involved any substantial reduction in economic or exchange activity in cities, of course. On the other hand, the undoubted decline in the maintenance of public structures…is suggestive of a major shift in the modes of urban living: of both the object of the investment of wealth, and of finance and administration in particular (Haldon 1999: 4).[6]

These are the observations that have been made about the broad patterns of change which gave shape to the urban landscape in the Byzantine period. We turn now to the provincial city of Sepphoris to test these claims against the archaeological record as it has been recovered to this point.

The archaeological record is, in fact, the key resource for recovering a history of the city of Sepphoris in the Byzantine period. The literary and epigraphic resources for Sepphoris in this era are limited and those that are available are difficult to use for recovering a social or economic history of the city. As Stuart Miller has shown in his several studies of the Talmudic traditions regarding Sepphoris, the effort to construct an urban history from these sources is bound to be problematic, if not impossible. As he notes,

> The interest of the Jews of the Late Second Temple and Talmudic Periods in urban matters does not compare to the interest in urban matters taken by their Greco-Roman contemporaries or later by Christians and Muslims…. Indeed, Jacob Neusner may well be right when he characterizes the city as "a useless symbol in Late Antique Judaism." The Jews may have formed distinct communities in the metropolises of the Mediterranean world and may also have constituted the majority in large towns such as Tiberius and Sepphoris, but by and large, as Neusner says, "they entered no encounter with the city either as an abstraction, or as something concrete and ominous in their lives." Indeed, for the Pharisees and later the rabbis, the internalization of the Halakah may have provided the Jew with a sense of *politeia* that transcended the physical parameters and idea of the city, as Ellis Rivkin claims (Miller 1999: 145–46; cf. Neusner 1983: 29; Rivkin 1966).

The literary sources do allow for some general observations about the city in the fourth and fifth centuries. For one, Sepphoris was perceived as an important center for rabbinic thought even after Tiberius eclipsed Sepphoris as the center of rabbinic authority in the fourth century. The presence of several synagogues is mentioned in the rabbinic texts and a synagogue inscription found in the rubble of the Crusader church may refer to a synagogue in Sepphoris. Tomb inscriptions from burials near the city make reference to a Hoshayah bar Tanhum, a Rabbi Yaakob, and a Rabbi Nahum (Strange 1999: 1092). I think we can say with some confidence that the population of the city remained predominantly Jewish even into the fifth century. The sources outside of the rabbinic corpus witness to the resistance of Sepphoris to a Christian presence in the city in the fourth century.[7] That there were non-Jews in residence in the city is also very likely and the local elite population must have been a mix of Jews and non-Jews. Our first textual reference to a Christian presence comes in 374, with the peculiar report of the Arian Emperor Valens exiling orthodox Christians from Egypt to the territory of Sepphoris (Diocaesarea).[8] A record of the bishops in attendance at the Council of Chalcedon in the mid-fifth century includes a reference to a Doretheus from Sepphoris (Diocaesarea) and there is a reference to a Marcellinus, a bishop of Sepphoris (Diocaesarea), who intervenes in a matter before the Council of Jerusalem in the early fifth century.[9] We also have an inscription that places a bishop in Sepphoris in the fifth century (see below).

The archaeological record of late Roman and Byzantine Sepphoris has been greatly enhanced by the excavations of Hebrew University under the direction of Zeev Weiss and Ehud Netzer.[10] These excavations have exposed, in particular on the eastern flank, evidence of a city that by the early fifth century was in full recovery from the disasters of the mid-fourth century. As anticipated by the discussion above, the Church seemed to have played a major role in this recovery. Traces of two churches have been found to either side of the *cardo* near its intersection with the *decumanus*. Dedicatory inscriptions in the mosaics of the sidewalk near the churches date to the mid-fifth century and mention the *Episcopus* Eutropius, who is given a role in the renovation of the stoas.[11] Further south on the *cardo,* the excavations uncovered a large public building that they note was "most probably built at the end of the fourth or at the beginning of the fifth century." The excavators suggest this was "a municipal basilica, which in Byzantine sources is mentioned as a place where regional meetings, lectures and the like were held." The floors of the rooms of the building were carpeted with polychrome mosaics, one of which had a scene from a Nile River festival, and thus the building has been named the Nile festival building.

Still on the eastern flank, but to the north of the center of the main focus of Byzantine renewal, the Hebrew University excavations exposed a synagogue dated to the sixth century. The synagogue floor was paved with a mosaic that included scenes of biblical stories, Temple ritual items, as well as a zodiac (Weiss and Netzer 1996).

Weiss and Netzer describe a very different pattern of urban development exposed in their excavations on the acropolis. Buildings damaged by the mid-fourth-century earthquake were largely left in ruins. The "mansion," which housed the *triclinium* with a floor covered by the Dionysiac mosaic, is for the most part not restored and "poorly planned buildings constructed out of stones in secondary use were erected above the rest of the ruined mansion" (Weiss and Netzer 1996: 81). In the center of the acropolis, the space is transformed into a storeroom in which twelve large *pithoi* were found *in situ.* In terms of their excavations of the theater, Weiss and Netzer comment that it is presumed that the structure was damaged by the earthquake of 363, but that it continued to be used "in the late fourth and fifth century but was abandoned later in the Byzantine period, when most of its building stones were looted for other construction projects as well as for the production of lime" (Weiss and Netzer 1996: 82).

In sum, Weiss and Netzer give us a portrait of a city experiencing uneven development after the mid-fourth century. Some elements of the classical city are retained (the *cardo* and *decumanus*), but significant aspects are lost—in particular the Roman theater. With the possible exception of the Nile festival building, the urban monuments are now primarily those constructed by religious communities and funding for urban construction appears to be shifted to these same religious communities. As suggested above, the pattern of "demise" in this provincial city is a complicated matter that requires an equally complex interpretative approach. Before offering such an interpretation (however tentative), I add the archaeological evidence recovered by our excavations of two of the most important structures of the classical city, the theater and the basilica. Our carefully stratified excavation of these structures offers another sort of evidential resource, as it allows for a more microcosmic study of structures as they pass through the transition from Roman to Byzantine period of occupation.[12] The depositional history of these structures opens the window more fully on the urban dwellers and their perceptions of space and its use.

We turn first to the theater. The questions of who built the theater and when are still being argued.[13] For this paper, the founding date is not an issue that needs to be revisited. For our purposes, the point is that certainly by the beginning of the second century, Sepphoris included in its architectural statements a Roman theater. The theater was a ubiquitous and defining feature of the specifically Roman urban landscape, one of the several public buildings that, as McDonald notes, "were essential to a distinctive architectural creation, the specifically Roman town...these robust objects were instruments of architectural colonization, symbols of the claims and ways of Rome" (McDonald 1982:

101). In terms of theaters in the Roman Near East, the theater at Sepphoris was a medium-size structure with seating for approximately 5000. It was located on the acropolis and the archaeology gives evidence of one or possibly two renovations. The theater in a provincial city like Sepphoris served several purposes, from providing the setting for entertainment and spectacles to public displays of local and foreign authority and social rank. The provincial elite and the municipality put their funds to work, building a theater because it was a recognized symbol of affluence and civic pride. As Segal noted, the elite citizens of provincial cities of Palestine, "...knowing that political and military avenues were barred to them, the citizens of these cities turned their energies and funds to construction activities which could satisfy their desire for recreation and ostentation, i.e., colonnaded streets, triumphal arches, nymphae, and theaters" (Segal 1995: 12).

Our excavations opened areas within the *cavea* and around the external face of the stage. In terms of the Byzantine phase of occupation of these areas, our conclusions, in general, coincide with those of the Hebrew University excavations. The excavation in the *cavea* was centered over the upper row of seats in the *imma cavea* and the interior corridor. The excavation produced evidence of continued use through the end of the fourth century and in the fifth century abandonment and the introduction of fill. In the corridor a layer of soil 85 cm deep just above the bedrock foundation for the corridor yielded forty-two coins dating from 364 to 402 in conjunction with pottery that dated consistently to the Byzantine period. The soil loci above this layer (95 cm deep) were consistent in having very few artifacts, pottery that dated the layers to the late fourth–early fifth century and the consistency of gravity sorted fill. The excavations along the exterior face of the stage wall gave us a similar depositional history. There was evidence of repair and reinforcement of walls and drains until the end of the fourth century. Beginning in the early fifth century, there were signs of a terracing and preparation of the area to the rear of the theater for agriculture. Moreover, we were able to locate a portion of the large retaining wall that had been constructed across the orchestra floor for the purpose of filling the theater's *cavea*. The latest date for the ceramics and coins collected from the soil layers against this wall of foundation was fifth century.[14]

In sum, the evidence we recovered gave us a picture of continued use into the late fourth century and then abandonment and intentional fill beginning in the early fifth century. As noted, these conclusions agree with the Hebrew University (and the University of Michigan) excavations, with one exception:[15] the University of Michigan excavators suggested the "retaining wall" was constructed in the Crusader period (Waterman 1937: 31). We found no evidence of Crusader construction, but rather find the wall to be part of the reconfiguration of the acropolis area that took place beginning in the late fourth century. Our excavations of the areas immediately to the south of the theater and around the base of the citadel (now used as the site's museum) have given evidence of the transformation of this space into a military fortress in the mid-fourth century. The transformation of the acropolis into a military fortress is typical of the reallocation of resources in the Byzantine period. That is, the building of the retaining wall and the reuse of the space immediately to the south of the theater appears to have been for the sake of a military enclave, which is consistent with the pattern of the infusion of imperial resources from the late fourth century on. Resources made available to the city from the imperial treasury were given to the cities for the sake of fortification, rather than the restoration of civic structures. This decision to invest in fortifications would be especially appropriate in the aftermath of the Gallus revolt. The decision to fill the theater should then be seen as part of this transformation of the classical city for military ends.

The fate of classical theaters in the Eastern provinces is uneven and for that matter not well documented, as excavations of these structures were more often than not driven by the issue of foundation, meaning that later stratigraphy was handled sloppily, if at all. Where there is usable evidence, we have an uneven history. For example, at Scythopolis/Bet Shean, one of the other major urban centers of the lower Galilee, the theater suffered significant damage in the earthquake of 363 C.E., when, according to the excavators, the upper cavea was ruined and the façade of the *scaenae frons* was badly damaged. But in this case, again according to the excavators, there was a major restoration in the late fourth century (Tsafrir and Foerster 1997: 109). On the other hand, the fate of the theater at Pella in the Decapolis was much like that of Sepphoris, as it was filled and invaded by small-scale structures in the early Byzantine period (Smith and Day 1989: 28–29). What would account for the decision to abandon the theater and how does this decision reflect the urban population of Sepphoris in the early Byzantine period? These are the key interpretative questions, but the answers need be held until we examine the fate of the other major structure of the classical city, the basilica.

The basilical building is located in the 'lower city' on the eastern flank. It is a large building, approximately 60 × 40 m, and is bound on its east and south by what we take to be the city's *cardo* (perhaps the *cardo maximus*) and *decumanus*. We have evidence that it was at least partially covered with a roof and had a second floor. Small rooms, probably shops, lined the outer margins of the building, while the central space was divided by columns, marble screens and, we presume, a stairway that joined the entrance and its foyer with the main hall. The interior space was enlivened with polychrome mosaic floors, wall frescoes, and decorative pools or gardens. This sort of municipal building became, like the theater, "indispensable to a proper town" (McDonald 1982: 111). It was, as John Carter notes, "the one building which stands out as peculiarly Roman type…a large covered hall which performed the function of the ubiquitous stoas of Hellenistic architecture…and became, along with the great bath-buildings of the Empire, a major vehicle of Roman originality and development in architecture" (Carter 1989: 32). Our excavations of this building have exposed foundations that date to the early decades of the first century C.E. We interpret it as one of the buildings (along with the theater) built by Herod Antipas as a defining structure of Sepphoris as a Roman *polis*. The middle and late Roman phase — the second through the third centuries C.E. — is perhaps the most propitious of times for Sepphoris and witnessed the installation of elegant mosaics. As with the theater, by the mid-fourth century a dramatic change, a monumental change, was exposed.

Unlike the theater, there are obvious signs of the building being badly damaged by earthquake or revolt in the mid-fourth century. For example, we exposed second-floor collapse that is clearly dated to this period. What is important, is that the building from this point enjoys only uneven efforts at restoration. We found that small portions of the western half of the building were repaired (e.g., mosaics were repaired, but not with polychrome mosaic *tesserae* — less expensive large white *tesserae* were used instead), and from the large number of coin finds appear to have been used for commercial transactions until the mid-fifth century. After this point, even this portion of the building was no longer maintained and silt from the acropolis covered the mosaic floors and animal troughs and transient habitation became prevalent. In the eastern portion of the building, there was, in the later part of the fourth century, an immediate and dramatic transformation of space. In the northeastern corner, the floors of the building were completely torn out and a bath complex was installed. Along the eastern façade, the space was transformed into small industrial installations, including one for the production of glass. In the center area of the eastern part of the building, the floor again was removed and a large lime kiln was installed. In sum, the monumental structure that was so critical to defining the Roman city of Sepphoris was not incorporated into the Byzantine city. Instead, it was either abandoned or transformed into discrete space to accommodate the desires of the "neighborhood" or for the sake of the newly arrived urban industry.[16]

We can now return to the question that we posed in the discussion of the abandonment of the theater. Why, in the case of these monumental structures that so obviously defined the ancient city, is there spoilage and reuse rather than reconstruction or renovation? On the one hand, as noted, the law codes show a pattern of reduced revenues, as resources were shifted to the emperor's *res privata*.

Moreover, the epigraphical evidence reveals a dramatic decrease in the role of the city council (ἡ βουλή) and of private φιλοτωία in providing for public construction.[17] Added to these broad patterns of shifting of funds, we noted the Gallus revolt, the ascendance of Tiberius as the center of the rabbinic movement in lower Galilee, and the resistance to Christianization as factors specific to the situation at Sepphoris that account for the demise of parts of the ancient city. The buildings that we have focused on, the theater and the basilica, were both likely to have suffered considerable damage by way of the Gallus revolt and/or the earthquake of 362 C.E. The decision to leave these structures in rubble or to reuse the space was surely a matter of lack of financial resources, at least until the arrival of a new civic patron, the Church.

In addition to the shift in financial resources, we should take into account some demographic variables for the period of the late fourth–early fifth centuries. As Tsafrir and Foerster note, "In the first part of the sixth century, Palestine reached its peak in terms of population and the number and size of settlements" (Tsafrir and Foerster 1997: 99). Given the rather high concentration of the population in urban centers in Palestine, one would expect an impact on Sepphoris. The incomplete state of the excavations does not allow us at this point to fully track this impact, but in terms of these two buildings, I think we can say that this variable manifests itself as an increased demand for urban space for pragmatic structures, at the cost of the monumental public structures of the Roman *polis*. The evidence from Scythopolis/Beth Shean is similar and instructive. Foerster and Tsafrir see in the archaeology from 363 C.E. on a pattern of selective rebuilding and restoration that "meets demographic demand by the addition of new monuments and institutions of purely utilitarian character (e.g., industrial installations and bath complexes)." In terms of the basilica, in particular, they note, "the large Roman basilica went out of use in the 4th century (perhaps after the earthquake of 363) and on its site were built rooms, lanes and porticoes, probably for utilitarian or even industrial purposes...the grandeur of the Roman urban planning deteriorated...and the pragmatic Byzantine approach became more explicit" (Tsafrir and Foerster 1994: 105). The transformation of the basilica in Sepphoris into space for industry and a bath is a sign of a new sort of city in the making—one in which industrial activity is now housed inside the city itself and not allocated to the villages.

Finally, in accounting for the transformations of the classical city, I would offer some observations that respond to the challenge of the postmodernist perspective on urban evolution posed at the outset of this study. That is, can we use the archaeology to go beyond the notion of a passive urban population being manipulated by greater forces (e.g., the Emperor's fiscal policy)? At the risk of over-interpreting the evidence of mute stones, I suggest that the city of Sepphoris that emerges after the mid-fourth century is one in which the urban dweller has a new vision of urban space and is actively involved in the transformation. These are urban dwellers that have relocated their identity from the *polis* to discrete communities residing within the *polis*. The new identity is primarily one shaped by religious authorities that increasingly emphasize the particularities of the religious communities. These are urban dwellers no longer enchanted by the vision of Libanius and his deep love of public space. In the fourth century, Libanius waxed eloquent about the joys to be found wandering among the public structures of the city and mingling in the public places with other citizens of the city, "isn't it more pleasant to walk through merchandise rather than through gardens, aren't the meetings in the agora more pleasant than residing at home? Doesn't the view of the crowd which flows through the city bring joy?" (Libanius, *Oration* 11.266). The archaeology suggests the future of the city was not to be true to Libanius' hopes or visions, but rather more that of the Christian orator John Chrysostom, who, on the eve of the fifth century, inveighed against the city, its spectacles, its public monuments, and its social links, arguing instead that men's and women's lives need to be centered on the family, on the Church. For Chrysostom, the ideal life is one in stark contrast to that offered by the city, "In the city, baths make people voluptuous, taverns make them indulgent, markets and festivals make them hasty. In the fields, virtue reigns supreme, free from licentiousness, drunkenness, and daintiness, it looks like heaven."[18]

The city that has emerged from the archaeological excavations of the monumental structures of the classical city of Sepphoris offers intriguing evidence of a moment of transition that contains elements of continuity as well as significant manifestations of a departure from the classical ideal of the urban landscape. It is a transition that points away from the classical city of the Roman world and toward the *medina* of the Arab period. The city continued to serve as a social and political center for the region. Bishops are to be found embedded in the cities and the town plan of Hippodamus continued to provide the visual map for the ordering of the city structures. But there is change, significant change — monumental change — that points forward and not back. The public structures that defined the city architecturally and in terms of values were replaced by other structures and by other values. On the one hand, Libanius is wrong, as this shift does not signal a sort a malaise of a melancholy sort. There is every reason to believe that Avi-Yonah was right to characterize Palestine in the late fourth and early fifth centuries as a locale witnessing economic vigor and manifesting heady confidence in the future (Avi-Yonah 1976). And yet, it is a confidence that has been re-centered and refocused off the classical institutions of the past. As Peter Brown observed, in this period of transition, "on every level of life the institutions that had seemed capable of receiving the awesome charge of permanence and divinity in classical times either declined or exploded" (Brown 1971: 85). The monumental structures that defined the Roman *polis* are left for spoilage, and the space is reconfigured and the city begins a gradual transition that will witness the dissolution of the *polis* and a shift toward fragmentation and greater social atomization. It is a dissolution that will ultimately also manifest itself in an urban landscape evolving into a *medina*. And so I end with a quote from Hugh Kennedy whose observations regarding the cities in Byzantine Syria wonderfully captures the dynamics of this city in lower Galilee:

> ...the broad, colonnaded streets were invaded and divided up by intrusive structures, both houses and shops, and became more like winding lanes than the massive thoroughfares of classical antiquity; and the extensive, open agora, scene for markets and meetings was gone. The other main features of the ancient city, the monumental buildings, disappeared almost entirely, to be replaced by the small industry or bathhouse" (Kennedy 1985: 5).

NOTES

1 As Holum notes, Claude's study of the Byzantine city (*Die Byzantinische Stadt im 6. Jahrhundert*. Munich, 1969) was critical for identifying the Byzantine phase as a distinct phase of urban development, as was Kennedy (1985) for correcting Claude and showing that the 6th-century phase of the Byzantine city was "just one phase in a gradual transition from classical polis to Muslim *medinah*...."

2 The transformation of the ruling elite of the cities has been studied in detail by a number of scholars including Jones (1964: 42–52, 366–75, 687–89) and Liebeschuetz (1972: 186–92).

3 See, for example, the discussion in Brown 1988, especially chapter 1.

4 I. and P. Zepos, *Jus Graecoromanum*, vol. 4.67.1, cited in Saradi-Mendelovici 1988: 391.

5 The role of Christianity in the financial stability of the Byzantine city has been discussed in a number of publications. See, for example, Whittow's discussion of the wealth of the Late Roman cities in the Near East (1990: 13–20) and Haldon 1999; for Palestine in particular, see Dan 1984.

6 In this same vein, see also Dagon 1977 and Saradi-Mendelovici 1988: 365–401.

7 See, e.g., the reference to Joseph of Tiberius in Ephiphanius, *Adv. Haeres.* 1.30 and *Panarion* 30, 12:1–10.

8 Palladius, *h. Laus.* ch. 117.

9 Mansi, 6.1091E and 8.1071C. Cited in Strange 1999: 1092–93.

10 The results of these excavations have been described briefly in several sources including Nagy et al. 1996: 29–38; Weiss 1997; Netzer and Weiss 1994.

11 The dedicatory inscription does mention Marianus, the "father of the city" (πατηρ πόλεεως), who "provided" for the construction. Another reference to a 'father of the city' for Sepphoris is in an inscription first edited by Avi-Yonah in 1961 and retranslated by Di Segni (1995: 325). Di Segni describes the role of the *pater civitatis* to be that of an imperial officer, who "administered the city's revenues and was responsible for the upkeep of the public streets and buildings" (p. 325). These administrators were not, however, the source of the funding.

12 The excavations of Sepphoris have, in fact, offered a good test case of the value of somewhat different approaches to archaeological method. The Hebrew University excavations have moved more rapidly, not at the total sacrifice of stratigraphy, but certainly with an emphasis on architecture over depositional history. Our excavations have "erred" in the other direction.

13 The disagreement is between the later publications of the Joint Sepphoris Project/Hebrew University Excavations and the publications of the University of South Florida Excavations at Sepphoris. The initial field reports of the JSP and the USF excavations, published in the *Israel Exploration Journal*, agreed on a dating of the early first century C.E. The JSP and then Hebrew University changed their mind in later publications and argued for a date of late first or early second century C.E. The University of South Florida is preparing a publication of its excavations of the theater.

14 See the field reports in *Israel Exploration Journal* 34, no. 1: 51–52; 35: 297–95; 38, no. 3: 188–90; and 39, no. 12: 104–10.

15 In 1931, Leroy Waterman of the University of Michigan excavated a portion of the theater. In his remarks about the occupational history of the theater, Waterman's assistant Samuel Yeivin concluded that the theater had gone out of use in the mid-fourth century. Yeivin reached this conclusion, in part, from evidence recovered from a cistern uncovered near the theater. The cistern contained architectural fragments from the theater and "large amounts of Byzantine but not later, shards so that one must conclude that at the latest, the theater was destroyed in the Byzantine period." Yeivin goes on to observe, that, "A confirmation of the Byzantine date may be seen in a few badly ruined walls found over the lowest seats...the construction of these walls seem to belong to the 4th–6th centuries and so it follows that the theater was likely to have been destroyed some time during the first half of the 4th century perhaps during the sack of the city under Gallus (351 C.E.)." (Waterman 1937: 30).

16 See the field reports in *Israel Exploration Journal* 49 (1999) 122–26.

17 On the epigraphy, see Di Segni 1995

18 PG 60, coll. 147–48; cited in Saradi-Mendelovici 1988: 390.

REFERENCES

Avi-Yonah, M.

1976 *The Jews of Palestine: A Political History from the Bar-Kochba War to the Arab Conquest.* Oxford: Blackwell.

Brown, P.

1971 The Rise and Function of the Holy Man. *Journal of Roman Studies* 61: 80–101.

1988 *Body and Society.* New York, NY: Columbia University.

Carter, J.

1989 Civic and Other Public Buildings. Pp. 31–66 in *Roman Public Buildings,* ed. I. M. Barton. Exeter: Exeter University.

Dagon, G.

1977 Le christianisme dans la ville Byzantine. *Dumbarton Oaks Collected Papers* 31: 1–26.

Dan, Y.

1984 *Urban Life in the Land of Israel at the End of Ancient Times.* Jerusalem: Yad Ishak Ben Zevi (Hebrew).

Di Segni, L.

1995 The Involvement of local, municipal, and provincial Authorities in Urban Planning in Late Antique Palestine and Arabia. Pp. 313–22 in *The Roman Byzantine Near East: Some Recent Archaeological Research,* ed. J. Humphrey. Journal of Roman Archaeology Supplementary Series 14. Ann Arbor, MI: University of Michigan.

Haldon, J.

1999 The Idea of the Town in the Byzantine Empire. Pp. 1–23 in *The Idea and the Ideal of the Town Between Late Antiquity and the Early Middle*

Ages, eds. G. P. Brogiolo and B. Ward-Perkins. Leiden: Brill.

Holum, K.
1993 Caesarea Maritima in the Byzantine Period: Continuity and Change. Pp. 699–703 in *Biblical Archaeology Today, 1990: Proceedings of the Second International Congress on Biblical Archaeology.* Jerusalem: Israel Exploration Society.

Jones, A. H. M.
1964 *The Later Roman Empire, 284–602,* vol. 1. Oxford: Oxford University.

Kennedy, H.
1985 From *Polis* to *Medina. Past and Present* 106: 3–27.

Libanius
1904 Oration 12 in *Libanii Opera,* vol. 2, ed. R. Foerster. Leipzig: Teubner.

Liebeschuetz, J. H. W. G.
1972 *Antioch: City and Imperial Administration in the Later Roman Empire.* Oxford: Oxford University.

McDonald, W.
1982 *Architecture of the Roman Empire: Volume II, An Urban Appraisal.* New Haven, CT: Yale University.

Miller, S.
1999 New Perspectives on the History of Sepphoris. Pp. 145–60 in *Galilee Through the Centuries,* ed. E. Meyers. Winona Lake, IN: Eisenbrauns.

Nagy, R.; Meyers, C.; Meyers, E.; and Weiss, Z.
1996 *Sepphoris in Galilee: Crosscurrents of Culture.* Raleigh, NC: North Carolina Museum of Art.

Netzer, E., and Weiss, Z.
1994 *Sepphoris.* Jerusalem: Israel Exploration Society.

Neusner, J.
1983 *Major Trends in Formative Judaism I: Society and Symbol in Political Crisis.* Chico, CA: Scholars.

Rivkin, E.
1966 The Internal City: Judaism and Urbanization. *Journal for the Social Study of Religion* 5: 225–40.

Saradi-Mendelovici, H.
1988 The Demise of the Ancient City and Emergence of the Medieval City in the Eastern Roman Empire. *Echos du Monde Classique/Classical Views* 33, no. 7: 365–401.

Segal, A.
1995 *Theaters in Roman and Provincial Palestine and Provincia Arabia.* New York, NY: Brill.

Smith, R., and Day, L.
1989 *Pella of the Decapolis. Volume 2.* Wooster, OH: University of Wooster.

Strange, J. F.
1999 Sepphoris. Pp. 1090–93 in *Anchor Bible Dictionary,* vol. 5, ed. D .N. Freedman. New York, NY: Doubleday.

Tsafrir, Y., and Foerster, G.
1994 From Scythopolis to Baysan – Changing Concepts of Urbanism. Pp. 95–116 in *The Byzantine and Early Islamic Near East, II: Land Use and Settlement Patterns,* eds. G. King and A. Cameron. Princeton, NJ: Princeton University.
1997 Urbanism at Scythopolis–Bet Shean in the Fourth to the Seventh Centuries. *Dumbarton Oaks Papers* 51: 85–146.

Ward-Perkins, B.
1984 *From Classical Antiquity to the Middle Ages. Urban Public Building in Northern and Central Italy AD 300–850.* Oxford: Oxford University.

Waterman, L.
1937 *Preliminary Report of the University of Michigan Excavations at Sepphoris.* Ann Arbor, MI: University of Michigan.

Weiss, Z.
1997 Architectural Development of Sepphoris During the Roman and Byzantine Periods. Pp. 117–30 in *Archaeology and the Galilee: Texts and Contexts in the Greco-Roman and Byzantine Periods,* eds. D. Edwards and T. McCollough. Atlanta, GA: Scholars.

Weiss, Z., and Netzer, E.
1996 *Promise and Redemption: A Synagogue Mosaic from Sepphoris.* Jerusalem: Israel Exploration Society.

Whittow, M.
1990 Ruling the Late Roman and Early Byzantine City: A Continuous History. *Past and Present* 129: 3–29.

Chapter 23

The Butchers of Sepphoris: Archaeological Evidence of Ethnic Variability

by Bill Grantham

Because of its potential for "describing and explaining culture change in prehistory" (Santley et al. 1987), ethnicity has increasingly become an interest to archaeologists focusing on complex societies (Schuyler 1980; Shennan 1989). Archaeologists have attempted to isolate patterns in the archaeological record that might be useful as indicators of the ethnicity of those responsible for the creation of the record. Through ethnicity, archaeologists have attempted to understand how culturally different people interact in complex societies, the relationship between ethnicity and subsistence strategies, and how material culture may reflect ethnicity.

Food remains, ceramics, and architecture have been the foci of most attempts to evaluate ethnicity archaeologically (McGuire 1982: 162) and some of the more successful attempts have focused on food remains and food related technology (Crabtree 1990). McGuire (1982) asserts that food refuse and artifacts associated with food are particularly good criteria for examining ethnic differences. Referring to his work in the American southwest, he asserts that ethnic food practices have varied greatly between American ethnic groups and that, since food refuse and ceramics are very common in material remains, they should provide sufficient information to make ethnic identifications (McGuire 1982: 163). Hesse (1986: 17) suggests that foodways are conservative elements of culture that can be distinctive markers of ethnicity. He further suggests:

> Moreover, people tend to resist change in their ways of getting and consuming foods. The choice of what animal to slaughter, the procedures for butchering the selected victim, and the methods for cooking or otherwise making use of the carcass can constitute a cultural pattern potentially as distinctive in the archaeological record as other more traditional forms of artifactual debris (Hesse 1986: 17).

Similarly, McKee (1987: 32) suggests that foodways are an important expression of ethnicity:

> What people eat, and how they eat it, is an important aspect of the process of ethnicity. Most people are rather particular about what they eat, and foodways often rival

> ideology and religion in terms of cultural conservatism (McKee 1987: 32).

He further suggests that "food is one of the primary symbols manipulated by people seeking to maintain their cultural identity and group solidarity."

Thus, most scholars agree on the importance of foodways in expressing and maintaining ethnicity. They also agree that ethnic identifiers should be recoverable from archaeological food remains. McGuire (1982: 163) asserts that because food refuse is a class of archaeological data common to most archaeological sites, it could provide a data base suitable for an examination of ethnicity. Many studies also seem to isolate subsistence related technology, such as butchering practices or methods of obtaining wild foods, as a basic detectable difference between the subsistence strategies of different ethnic groups.

ROMAN-BYZANTINE PALESTINE

Roman-Byzantine Palestine is an ideal area to test archaeological models of ethnicity. The region was inhabited by an ethnically diverse population. There is also a rich historical accounting of life in Roman-Byzantine Palestine (e.g., Josephus [Whiston 1987]; the Mishnah [Neusner 1989]; the Talmud [Steinsaltz 1993]), which suggests marked differences in dietary practices (e.g., avoidance of certain species for religious reasons [Hecker 1982; Hesse 1988; 1990]).

Epigraphic evidence provides a useful source for establishing archaeological expectations. While the accuracy of the documentary evidence with respect to the ethnic nature of a population should not be blindly accepted, if the two sources of information, documentary and archaeological, support each other, a strong argument can be made for the reliability of both.

The Archaeological Site of Sepphoris

The site of Sepphoris is located approximately five km northwest of the modern town of Nazareth, Israel, and is an excellent site for testing hypotheses regarding the recognition of ethnicity in the archaeological record. Though little is known about the nature of the earliest occupation of Sepphoris, the city served as the political capital of the Galilee in the Hasmonean period (first century B.C.E.) and in the Herodian period (late first century B.C.E. through first century C.E.). During the second century C.E., the Sanhedrin, the Jewish high court, was located at Sepphoris and the city became a center of Jewish law and learning (Netzer and Weiss 1992: 37). In about 200 C.E., Judah ha-Nasi compiled the Mishnah (the earliest rabbinic text) in Sepphoris and the city was known for its many great sages, who taught in the *beth midrashim,* or houses of study (Netzer and Weiss 1992: 37).

Batey (1992: 52) describes Sepphoris as "a Greco-Roman metropolis" with a multi-ethnic population of around 30,000. The city also served as a commercial and agricultural center for the region (Netzer and Weiss 1992: 37). Sepphoris' urban character, its role as a capital of Roman Galilee and its role as a center for Jewish legal and spiritual thought during the Roman and Byzantine periods are indicative of a multi-ethnic, urban society (see Batey 1992 and Crossan 1992).

Excavations at Sepphoris

Excavation first began at Sepphoris in 1931. Yeivin (1937: 17) described the site at the time of excavation:

> The ancient town of Sepphoris (Sippori), four miles northwest of Nazareth, is buried to a great extent under a large modern Arab village, Saffuriyye, a name which preserves the old name of the place.

The 1931 excavation focused on the citadel hilltop and parts of the northern slope. Yeivin (1937: 26) reports the recovery of the remains of two buildings—the citadel (which was in use as the village school at the time of excavation) and the theater (which Yeivin speculates was built by Herod Antipas). In 1985, the Joint Sepphoris Project was launched by the Hebrew University and Duke University. After five seasons of excavation of a residential district of Sepphoris, the excavation was discontinued. In 1991, Duke University, Wake Forest University, and the University of Connecticut formed the Sepphoris Regional Project and have continued the excavations in the residential district of Sepphoris. Four field seasons (1993, 1994, 1996 and 1997) have recovered several structures in the residential area.

Areas 84.1 and 85.1 consist of domestic structures. From Area 85.1 a Late Roman floor, Early Roman water installations, pottery dumps, and two *miqwā'ôt* were recovered. One of the *miqwā'ôt* apparently was used as a dump. It contained extensive bone and ceramic remains (Meyers, personal communication).

Area 84.4 consists of the remains of a Byzantine structure plus a Late Roman floor. The function of the building appears to have been non-domestic/production oriented (Meyers, personal communication). Areas 84.4 and 84.5 also appear to have been used for non-domestic/production oriented buildings.

Area 85.3 consists of a large Hellenistic structure. The function of this building is not entirely understood, but non-domestic use, possibly military housing, seems likely. The remains of the building were used as a dump or intentionally filled in probably before the first century C.E. (Meyers, personal communication).

Area 84.6 was likely public space, consisting of a large water reservoir and its associated architecture (three large walls dividing plaster floors in use during the Late Roman period). This area was probably constructed during the Early Roman period and was in use during the Late Roman period until the earthquake of 363 C.E.

From these six areas a total of 16,349 identifiable animal bone fragments were recovered, which represent a total of thirty-two species or analytical categories of animals used by the inhabitants of these structures. Of these bone fragments 13,968 represent domestic species, 722 fragments wild species, and 1,659 could only be identified as animal bone fragments.

Sepphoris in Historical and Cultural Perspective

Little is known historically about Sepphoris prior to the Hellenistic period. Unfortunately, archaeological evidence is also scarce, owing to a leveling off of previous remains, probably during the time of rebuilding by Herod Antipas (Yeivin 1937: 22). There is also little documentary evidence with respect to the ethno-cultural nature of Sepphoris during the Persian period. Meyers (1993a: 739) reports the existence of Attic black wares at Sepphoris during the fifth century B.C.E. He suggests that, while this alone does not necessarily mean that there were Greek mercenaries at Sepphoris during this time, "in view of many other considerations, an interpretation favoring a military presence may ultimately be the best explanation" (Meyers 1993a: 739).

Sepphoris is first mentioned historically by Josephus (*Antiq.* 13.12.5), a Jewish historian, who tells of a failed attempt (ca. 100 B.C.E.) by Ptolemy Lathyrus, governor of Cyprus, to take the city during the reign of Alexander Jannaeus (Yeivin 1937: 19). Most scholars agree that Sepphoris became militarily strategic early in its history, but there is little evidence that any military group, other than Jewish, occupied Sepphoris before the arrival of the Romans.

Yeivin (1937: 27) reports that the masonry of the citadel built by Herod Antipas included some slightly larger blocks of stone typical of the Hasmonean and Herodian buildings in the country. Yeivin further suggest these blocks could be the remains of an old citadel built by the early Hasmoneans.

Traditional, ritualized food behavior practiced among Jews in the region is attested to historically as early as the fourth century B.C.E. In this regard, the Letter of Aristeus, written around 285 B.C.E., notes:

> Jewish delegates dined with the pagan Ptolemaic king Ptolemy II Philadelphus, but here it is explicitly stated that the food was chosen and served in accordance with the habits of the Jews and that no pagan acts of worship took place (Aristeas 181–86, cited in Borgen 1994: 6).

After the Maccabean Revolt (ca. 166–63 B.C.E.), a tyrannical dynasty was established. In 164 B.C.E., Judas Maccabaeus took Jerusalem and "cleansed the Temple," establishing Hasmonean (Jewish) control over much of the region (M. Miller 1982: 148). Meyers (1992: 85) describes the dynasty as

> …more like that of the Hellenistic tyrants than of the former rulers of Israel. In their public demeanor and style they were just

> like their non-Jewish counterparts. But attachment to Hebrew tradition among the general population was undiminished.

During much of the first century B.C.E. and first century C.E., Sepphoris served as the capital of the Galilee. In 55 B.C.E., under Gabinius, one of the five Sanhedrins or Jewish high courts was assigned to Sepphoris, where it remained until Vespasian occupied the city early in the Great Revolt (Yeivin 1937: 19).

It was also early in the Roman period that Sepphoris' importance as a Jewish religious and political center began to grow. Herod the Great captured Sepphoris during the winter of 39–38 B.C.E. and used it as his northern command post (Meyers 1993b: 30). At Herod's death (4 B.C.E.), an insurrection broke out and Varus, legate of Syria, sent two legions to subdue the region. Sepphoris was burnt and many of its inhabitants were taken as slaves (Josephus *War* II.68; *Ant.* XVII.289).

During Herod Antipas' first reign (4 B.C.E.–19 C.E.), he reconstructed the city and made it his capital. In 19 C.E., Antipas founded Tiberias and moved his capital there (Meshorer 1979: 159). Under Felix (52–60 C.E.), Sepphoris again became the capital of the Galilee, but only after the fall of Jerusalem (70 C.E.) did the city become a real center of Jewish life and a center for Jewish study (Meshorer 1979: 163).

During the reign of Trajan (98–117 C.E.), a Jewish revolt erupted against Romans in North Africa, Egypt, Cyprus, and Mesopotamia (Meshorer 1979: 164). The revolt was suppressed during the reign of Hadrian (117–139 C.E.) and, according to Meshorer (1979: 165), Sepphoris "being one of the very few places inhabited only by Jews" was singled out for punishment by the Romans.

According to Meyers (1992: 88), first-century-C.E. Sepphoris was "full of priests," "had a patrician character," and "an overwhelming majority of the inhabitants were Jewish." The significant number of *miqwāʾôt* discovered there and evidence of "strict Jewish burial practices outside of the city" support Meyers' assertion (Meyers 1992: 88).

There is also epigraphic evidence of the ethnic nature of Sepphoris during the first century C.E. S. Miller (1987: 9) reports from Rabbinic literature that

> In a discussion of the *kashrut* of a slaughtered animal that has been found, it is decided that the area of the find is determinative. That is, if the animal was found in a place known for its Jewish settlement, such as the area between Sepphoris and Tiberias, it is permitted for consumption.

Miller (1987: 9) cites as further evidence:

> ...where, with regard to the validation of witnesses in a murder case, Rabbi Yohanan explains that the witnesses are not required to identify the victim as Jew or non-Jew if the killing took place between Tiberias and Sepphoris; it is assumed that the territory between the two cities is predominantly Jewish (B. *Baba Mezia'* 24b. Cf. P. *Sanhedrin* 5, 22c).

During the reign of Hadrian (117–38 C.E.), a gentile administration was installed at Sepphoris and the city became known as Diocaesarea, or the City of Zeus, and Hadrian adopted the title of Zeus Olympios (Meyers 1992: 88). Meyers (1993b: 33) maintains that, "despite the urbanization policies of Rome," the Galilee remained "predominately Jewish throughout the Roman Period, especially in the first century C.E.," though he suggests that "by the mid-second century the pluralistic nature of Sepphoris, and hence its Hellenistic ambiance, was greatly heightened" (Meyers 1992: 88).

There is also archaeological evidence of the changing cultural nature of Sepphoris during the second century C.E.:

> ...all manner of Roman decorated lamps can be found, including ones with mythological figures and a variety of erotic themes. Many are found in Jewish domestic areas, indicating their sense of being at home in a physical environment in which pagan themes and symbols came to dominate (Meyers 1992: 89).

Meyers (1992: 89) suggests that while "the actual trappings of Hellenistic culture" were welcomed by the Jews, their "expressions of Judaism" survived and prevailed."

That the Jewish population of Sepphoris should take on some of the trappings of Hellenistic culture while maintaining a separate ethnic identity is not an isolated occurrence. Jewish sarcophagi from Rome often exhibit pagan imagery (Rutgers 1992: 104). In Rome, Jews and Christians bought lead sarcophagi cast from the same mold, but bearing stamped images of menorahs or crosses according to one's belief.

Rutgers (1992: 106) suggests that Jewish, Early Christian, and Mithriac art were all influenced by Roman-pagan artistic traditions. He reports that at Rome an amulet depicting Medusa was discovered along with other amulets of undisputed Jewish origin in a "seemingly undisturbed grave in the Jewish Vigna Randanini catacomb." Jewish literature from the fourth century or later often contains incantations to Helios, Aphrodite, Hermes, and the moon.

Despite abundant evidence that Jews incorporated pagan images and themes into their art and that they were not opposed to the use of mass produced pagan goods such as lead sarcophagi, history suggests they maintained a strong sense of ethnic identity. Tacitus noted in the second century that Roman households "comprise nations with customs the reverse of our own, with foreign cults or with none" (Rutgers 1992, citing Tacitus). Rutgers suggests the Jews were one such group who maintained a strong ethnic identity, an observation also made by Augustine in the early fifth century (Rutgers 1992: 117).

Jerome (ca. 380 C.E.) and other Christian chronographers beginning with Socrates (ca. 380–450 C.E.) maintain that a Jewish uprising against the Romans in Sepphoris resulted in the destruction of the city by Gallus around 352 C.E. Historical accounts suggest that the uprising was pacified by Aracsinus, who is reported to have burned the city (Yeivin 1937: 21). Archaeological evidence (Yeivin 1937) supports the accounts that the city was at least partially destroyed, but it is unlikely that the city was subjected to complete ruin. Travelers' reports from Christian pilgrims, such as the Piacenza Pilgrim, who visited the city around 570, continue throughout the Byzantine Period, suggesting that the city continued to be a viable urban center (S. Miller 1992: 80).

A distinct Christian presence was not evident in Sepphoris during the fourth century C.E., but was experienced throughout the region. During the early fourth century (ca. 307–337 C.E.), many of the laws of Constantine were directed specifically at such ethnic situations as socially separating Jews from Christians (Geller Nathanson 1986: 27–28), and conversion to Judaism also became unlawful. Geller Nathanson (1986: 30) asserts that

> ...from the time of Constantine massive church-building projects were undertaken to create a visible manifestation of the legitimacy and preeminence of Christian rule, which in turn was understood to be an outward sign of the truth of Christianity.

Sepphoris was not, however, totally unaffected by the spread of Christianity and the regional changes in the social relations between Jews and Christians. Evidence from Rabbinic literature (mostly the Palestinian Talmud) suggests that at least those Jews directly involved may have been persecuted in the aftermath of the uprising discussed in the preceding section. Geller Nathanson (1986: 33) cites a passage from the Palestinian Talmud (PT Sota 9.3,23c):

> (It came to pass) in the days of Ursicinus the king that the people of Sepphoris were sought. And they had placed plasters on their noses and no one recognized them. But in the end an evil tongue informed on them and all of them were captured because of the information against them.

Although it is unlikely that the inhabitants of Sepphoris wore masks, it is reasonable to interpret this passage to mean

> ...that in the days of Ursicinus—perhaps in the days of Gallus—some portion of the population of Sepphoris hid from the authorities, most likely the Romans (Geller Nathanson 1986: 33).

Other cities in the region were affected by the uprising as well, and the pattern of destruction in the region may be a reflection of the social relations between Jews and Christians within the region, and the evidence would suggest that the revolt was both limited and selective (Geller Nathanson 1986: 34). For example, Nabratein and Meiron, Jewish centers of population, were abandoned around the time of the revolt whereas the nearby sites of Khirbet Shemaʿ and Gush Halav continued to thrive. The limited and seemingly selective destruction of some cities and towns and the abandonment of others suggests that

> …the revolt was caused not by actual economic or political hardship, but perhaps by feeling of cultural and political deprivation on the part of the rebels [Jewish], relative to what they had enjoyed under pagan Rome and, possibly, relative to the enhanced status of the growing Christian population and church in Palestine (Geller Nathanson 1986: 34).

Though the Gallus Revolt and the following destruction indicate an impact of the growing Christian presence in the Holy Land or Sepphoris during the fourth century, there is evidence that a Jewish population continued to thrive there for some time. S. Miller (1992: 80) reports that Epiphanius, Bishop of Salamis (315–403 C.E.), and Theodoret, Bishop of Cyrus (393–460 C.E.), commented on the "Jewish character of the city." Theodoret relates that

> …eleven bishops of Egypt were banished around 373 C.E. by the Arians "to a place named Diocaesarea [Sepphoris], inhabited by Jews" (S. Miller 1992: 80).

Thus, by the end of the fourth century, there was at Sepphoris a truly plural society with strong Jewish and Roman and a more limited Christian cultural presence.

Summary of Cultural Influences at Sepphoris

From the historical and archaeological data, the relative impact of various cultural influences on the population of Sepphoris can be summarized. Owing to minimal historical evidence, it is difficult to evaluate the cultural nature of the population of Sepphoris during the Persian and Hellenistic periods. Meyers (1993: 739) suggests a military presence at Sepphoris was likely during the Persian period, but the cultural composition of the population remains unclear. Both Meyers (1992: 85) and Yeivin (1937: 27) suggest a Hasmonean presence at Sepphoris during the Hellenistic period, but Meyers adds that, in his opinion, the general population of the region maintained "Hebrew tradition."

The cultural nature of Sepphoris during the early Roman period was unmistakably Jewish, although there was likely a small Roman military presence in the city. By the mid-Roman period, Roman influence at Sepphoris was considerable, although the Jewish nature of the city persisted. A growing Christian population began to assert its influence during the Byzantine period, and by the late fifth century C.E., Christian influence in the city was strong. Historical evidence seems to suggest that, while Christian influence continued during the later part of the Byzantine period, the city was still known for its Jewish nature.

EPIGRAPHIC EVIDENCE

Epigraphic evidence suggests that butcher shops at Sepphoris were regulated in accordance with Jewish religious law. Miller (personal communication) cites several references to "the butchers of Sepphoris" in Rabbinic literature. These butchers were well known, not only for their skill and ability at their trade, but also as reputable and knowledgeable of the Jewish religious laws that govern the slaughtering of animals. One such butcher, Natan bar Shila, is known from Rabbinic literature as the head butcher of Sepphoris, who was not only an expert on the anatomy of cattle, but could quote Jewish sages.

Seemingly not all butchers at Sepphoris were as reputable as bar Shila. Two incidents reported in Rabbinic literature suggest that some Jewish butchers were not particularly concerned with religious regulation of their trade. One such incident concerns a butcher who, because of his refusal to sell meat to a Jew, was suspected of selling *nevalot* (meat of an improperly slaughtered animal or of one that met a violent death — neither are acceptable under Jewish religious laws). Having been refused meat from the butcher, the Jew sent a Roman to buy meat. According to Miller (personal communication), the Roman was either sold *nevalot* or the butcher agreed to sell him meat only after the Roman provided him with *nevalot*.

In another such incident, a butcher known to have sold improper meat to Jews in Sepphoris "got drunk on the eve of Yom Kippur and fell to his death from a rooftop." When asked if it would be religiously proper to move the body on a holiday, a rabbi replied: "This one who stole dogs and fed Israel *nevalot* and *terefot* [the meat of an animal that died from a fatal disease or injury] — Allow them (the dogs) to eat of him as they are eating of their own flesh" (Miller, personal communication).

Whether reputable or not, these passages clearly associate "the butchers of Sepphoris" with the Jewish population there. Interestingly, butchers, along with tanners, smiths, craftsmen, shopkeepers, and others of similar occupation, were despised by the upper classes in the Roman Empire (Miller, personal communication).

ARCHAEOLOGICAL DATA

At least one class of artifacts recovered from Sepphoris — butchery remains — supports the epigraphic descriptions of the changing cultural nature of the city. Evidence of standardized butchering procedures at Sepphoris suggests a highly developed commercial butchery industry that may be reflective of the ethnic nature of the population. A total of 650 bone fragments exhibit saw cuts, which suggests a standardized method of butchery that likely was commercial.

Almost 39 percent of the specimens that were sawn were either *Bos* (cow) or large mammal bones. Almost 58 percent were either *Ovis-Capra* (sheep-goat) or medium size mammal bones. An additional 18 *Sus* (pig), and three *Cervid* (deer) bones were sawn. Of both the *Bos*/large mammal and *Ovis-Capra*/medium mammal specimens, the most commonly recovered sawn bones were from the axial skeleton. Axial bones (primarily vertebrae) account for 51 percent of the sawn *Bos*/large mammal remains and 61 percent of the sawn *Ovis-Capra*/medium mammal remains (fig. 1).

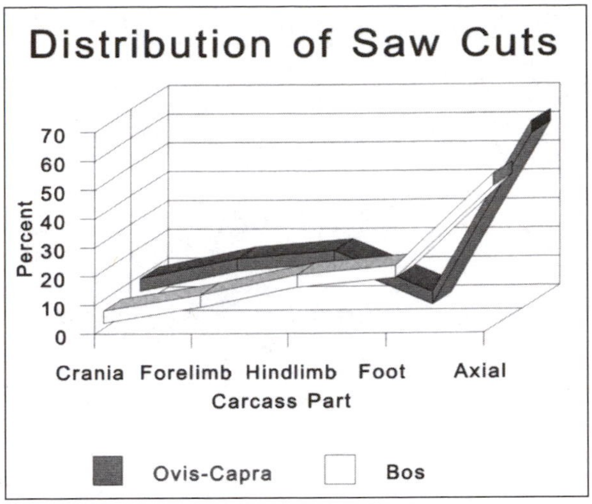

Fig. 1 *Distribution of saw cuts.*

Placement of Cuts with Respect to Bone Density

The method of butchery seems highly standardized. Bone density codes were assigned to each sawn bone fragment following Lyman (1984). The distribution of these codes was divided into three equal categories, representing "soft" bones, "medium density" bones, and "hard" bones. Of the sawn *Ovis-Capra*/medium mammal bones, over 68 percent were "soft" bones. Of the *Bos*/large mammal bones, 44 percent were "soft" density bones. Not surprisingly, this suggests that bone density was a significant variable in the dismemberment of carcasses.

Standardization of Meat Cuts

It is also apparent that many of the cuts were standardized. For example, 84 or 62 percent of the cuts on *Ovis-Capra*/medium mammal vertebrae are variations of only two saw angles. A similar frequency, 54 percent, of the same saw angles occurs on *Bos*/large mammal.

Evaluation of Butchery Evidence

Having associated the butchers of Sepphoris with Jewish ethnicity, an evaluation of the frequency with which sawn bones were recovered from the different archaeological periods may reveal something of the changing ethnic nature of the population of the city. For this evaluation only specimens

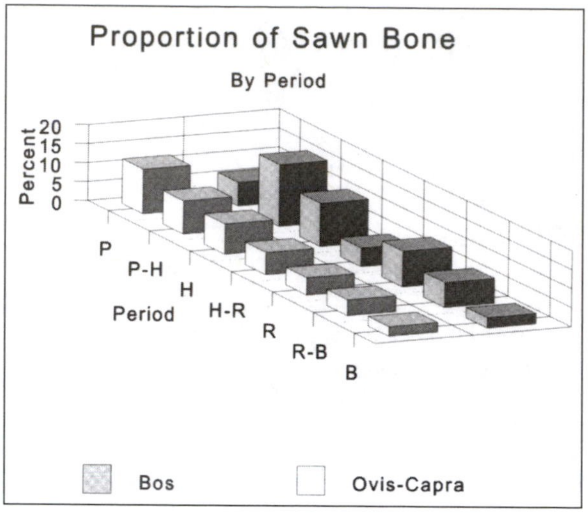

Fig. 2 *Proportion of sawn bone by period.*

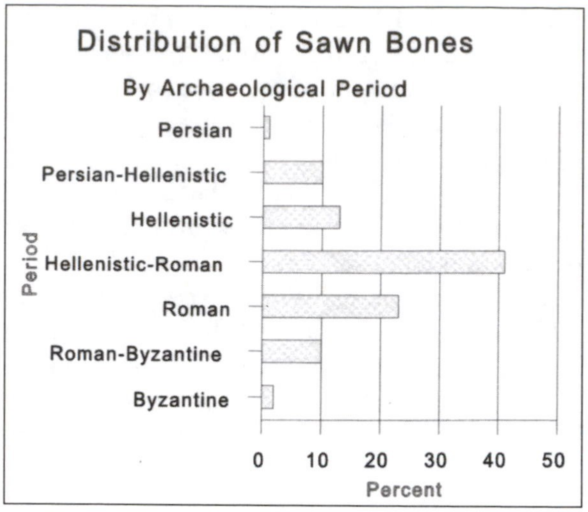

Fig. 3 *Distribution of sawn bones by archaeological period.*

that could be identified as either *Bos* or *Ovis-Capra* were used. The proportion of the samples represented by sawn bones from each period and the distribution of sawn bones by archaeological period were calculated (figs. 2–3).

Sawn bones were far more frequent during the Hellenistic and Hellenistic-Roman periods. Their frequency declines rapidly through time until by the Byzantine period their occurrence was relatively rare. This suggests that the importance of meat provided by the butchers declined through time, which was likely the result of increasing ethnic diversity at Sepphoris. Little pattern in the spatial distribution of these sawn bones was apparent, except that they occurred most often in Area 85.3 during the Hellenistic and Hellenistic-Byzantine periods (Table 1).

Butchery Evidence and Species

It is also important to note that almost all of the butchery remains were either *Ovis-Capra, Bos,* medium, or large mammal (the bulk of which were likely *Ovis-Capra* and *Bos,* respectively). Less than three percent of remains identified as "standardized" butchery remains were from *Sus* (pig), a species forbidden by Jewish religious law. The scarce *Sus* remains at the site accounted for less than four percent of the sample from each period, except for the Byzantine period, in which they accounted for 20 percent (215) of the sample. However, the huge increase in the frequency of *Sus* in the Byzantine period is not accompanied by a proportional increase in "standardized" butchery remains. In fact, the lowest proportional occurrence of sawn *Sus* remains was observed for the Byzantine Period. Two *Sus* bones were recovered from the Persian period and three from the Persian-Hellenistic period. No evidence of butchery was observable on these specimens. Saw marks were observed on 3.3 percent of the 30 *Sus* specimens recovered from the Hellenistic period, 2.4 percent of the 127 specimens from the Hellenistic-Roman period, 12 percent of the 25 specimens from the Roman period, 9 percent of the specimens from the Roman-Byzantine period, and only 1.9 percent of the 215 specimens from the Byzantine period. Although *Sus* played a more important role in the diet of the inhabitants of Sepphoris during the Byzantine period, *Sus,* along with *Ovis-Capra* and *Bos* specimens that exhibit evidence of standardized butchery, become, proportionally, more scarce.

CONCLUSIONS

The epigraphic evidence suggests a strong Jewish presence at Sepphoris that reached its zenith during the Roman period and became diluted with an influx of Roman and Christian influences toward

Table 1 Distribution of sawn bones by area and chronology.

PERIOD ↓ AREA→	84.1	84.4	84.5	85.1	85.3
			Bos / LARGE MAMMAL		
Persian	2	–	–	–	–
Persian-Hellenistic	–	–	–	–	26
Hellenistic	–	–	–	–	40
Hellenistic-Roman	2	–	1	19	119
Roman	22	7	1	10	9
Roman-Byzantine	13	1	–	3	8
Byzantine	5	3	1	–	–
Total	44	11	3	32	202
			Ovis-Capra / MEDIUM MAMMAL		
Persian	–	–	–	1	–
Persian-Hellenistic	–	–	–	–	21
Hellenistic	–	–	–	1	24
Hellenistic-Roman	1	–	1	3	54
Roman	46	1	3	7	7
Roman-Byzantine	7	3	3	4	5
Byzantine	2	–	–	2	–
Total	56	4	7	18	111

the end of the Roman period and during the Byzantine period. The historical evidence also suggests the presence of religiously regulated butcher shops associated with the Jewish population at Sepphoris. Archaeological evidence in the form of butchery remains strongly supports the epigraphic evidence of regulated or standardized butchery practices at the site. The frequency of specimens that exhibit butcher marks decreases through time until they are relatively scarce during the Byzantine period. The decrease in demand for religiously regulated butchery products parallels the diminishing Jewish influence in the city suggested by the epigraphic evidence.

A significant increase in the occurrence of *Sus* remains, forbidden to the Jews by religious law, also occurs during the Byzantine period, a time for which the epigraphic evidence suggests an increasing Christian presence in the city. The data suggest that these *Sus* remains were not a product of the regulated butcher shops.

To summarize, regulated butcher shops offering *Ovis-Capra* and *Bos* products, religiously acceptable to the Jews, existed in Sepphoris, but became increasingly unimportant through time. At the same time as the importance of the butcher shops decreased, the occurrence of *Sus* remains, religiously unacceptable to the Jews, increased. The archaeological evidence strongly supports the epigraphic suggestion that toward the end of the Roman period and during the Byzantine period Jewish influence at Sepphoris diminished, as possibly Roman and certainly Christian influence grew.

REFERENCES

Batey, R. A.
1992 Sepphoris: An Urban Portrait of Jesus. *Biblical Archaeology Review* 18, no. 3: 52–62.

Borgen, P.
1994 Yes, No, How Far? The Participation of Jews and Christians in Pagan Cult. *Explorations* 8: 5–6.

Crabtree, P. J.
1990 Zooarchaeology and Complex Societies: Some uses of Faunal Analysis for the Study of Trade, Social Status, and Ethnicity. *Archaeological Method and Theory* 2: 155–205.

Crossan, J. D.
1992 *The Historical Jesus: The Life of a Mediterranean Jewish Peasant.* San Francisco, CA: Harper

Geller Nathanson, B. G.
1986 Jews, Christians, and the Gallus Revolt in Fourth-Century Palestine. *Biblical Archaeologist* 49, no. 1: 26–36.

Hecker, H.
1982 Zooarchaeological Inquiry into Pork Consumption in Egypt from Prehistoric to New Kingdom Times. *Journal of the American Research Center in Egypt* 19: 59–71.

Hesse, B.
1986 Animal Use at Tel Miqne-Ekron in the Bronze Age and Iron Age. *Bulletin of the American School of Oriental Research* 264: 17–27.

Lyman, R. L.
1984 Bone Density and Differential Survivorship of Fossil Classes. *Journal of Anthropological Archaeology* 3: 259–99.

McGuire, R.
1982 The Study of Ethnicity in Historical Archaeology. *Journal of Anthropological Archaeology* 1: 159–78.

McKee, L. W.
1987 Delineating Ethnicity from the Garbage of Early Virginians: Faunal Remains from the Kingsmill Plantation Slave Quarter. *American Archaeology* 6, no. 1: 31–39.

Meshorer, Y.
1979 Sepphoris and Rome. Pp. 159–63 in *Greek Numismatics and Archaeology,* eds. O. Morkholm and N. M. Waggoner. Wetteren: Cultura.

Meyers, E.
1992 The Challenge of Hellenism for Early Judaism and Christianity. *Biblical Archaeologist* 55: 84–91.
1993a Identifying Religious and Ethnic Groups Through Archaeology. Pp. 738–45 in *Biblical Archaeology Today, 1990,* eds. A. Biran and J. Aviram. Proceedings of the Second International Congress on Biblical Archaeology. Jerusalem: Israel Exploration Society.
1993b Aspects of Roman Sepphoris in the Light of Recent Archaeology. Pp. 29–36 in *Early Christianity in Context: Monuments and Documents. Essays in Honour of Emmanuel Testa,* eds. F. Mann and E. Alliata. Studium Biblicum Franciscanum Collectio Maior 38. Jerusalem: Franciscan.

Miller, M.
1982 *Introducing the Holy Land.* Macon, GA: Mercer University.

Miller, S.
1987 Intercity Relations in Roman Palestine: The Case of Sepphoris and Tiberias. *Association for Jewish Studies Review* 12: 1–24.
1992 Sepphoris, the Well Remembered City. *Biblical Archaeologist* 55: 74–83.

Netzer, E., and Weiss, Z.
1992 New Mosaic Art from Sepphoris. *Biblical Archaeology Review* 18: 36–43, 78.

Neusner, J.
1989 *Oral Traditions in Judaism: The Case of the Mishnah.* New York, NY: Garland.

Rutgers, L. V.
1992 Archaeological Evidence for the Interaction of Jews and Non-Jews in Late Antiquity. *American Journal of Archaeology* 96:101–18.

Santley, R. C.; Yarborough, C.; and Hall, B.
1987 Enclaves, Ethnicity, and the Archaeological Record at Matacapan. Pp. 85–100 in *Ethnicity and Culture,* eds. R. Auger, M. Glass, S. MacEachern, and P. MacCartney. Calgary: Archaeology Association of the University of Calgary.

Schuyler, R. L.
1980 Preface, Pp. vii–viii in *Archaeological Perspectives on Ethnicity in America,* ed. R. Schuyler. Farmingdale, NY: Baywood.

Shennan, S. (ed.)
1989 *Archaeological Approaches to Cultural Identity.* London: Unwin Hyman.

Steinsaltz, A.
1993 *Talmud.* New York, NY: Random House.

Whiston, W. (trans.)
1987 *The Works of Josephus.* Peabody, MA: Hendrickson.

Yeivin, S.
1937 Historical and Archaeological Notes. Pp. 1–86 in *Preliminary Report of the University of Michigan Excavations at Sepphoris, Palestine,* ed. L. Waterman. Ann Arbor, MI: University of Michigan.

Chapter 24

Sepphoris and the Earliest Christian Congregations

by James F. Strange

Nowhere in the records of Christianity from 35–70 C.E. are Sepphoris or Tiberias mentioned as Christian centers. On the other hand, Capernaum, a much smaller locality, was a kind of headquarters for Jesus according to the gospels. We might expect early Christian congregations to have developed at Capernaum. Yet the curse on Capernaum in Luke 10:15 suggests that early Christian communities did *not* develop at Capernaum.

Is Sepphoris a likely candidate to have become a Christian center? From the Jewish sources we can infer that Sepphoris was a stronghold of Judaism in the early centuries (Miller 1984). Manns developed the thesis, relying on certain Talmudic texts, that Sepphoris was a bastion of Jewish Christianity (Manns 1977: 12). He was apparently unaware that Scholem had already articulated a similar thesis (Miller 1993).

If we turn from texts to archaeological evidence, do the excavations at Sepphoris reveal enough of the early material culture to argue to what extent early Christian communities might have thrived at Sepphoris or in its administrative territory? It depends, of course, on what the criteria might be for inferring the probable or even plausible Christian presence at Sepphoris from said remains. Since we have no developed criteria as yet, the question, as stated, remains moot.

Be that as it may, we have not yet declared what archaeology tells us about the layout of Sepphoris, the presence of public buildings, the type of housing available, or the relative abundance of luxury goods. What are the results, specifically, of the excavations of the University of South Florida at Sepphoris and others that help us draw a context for the earliest Christian congregations in its territory?

The results of the USF Excavations at Sepphoris tend to contribute to a view of a walled city that exhibits some Roman (not necessarily "Hellenistic") elements in public space, but less so in private space, which in fact appears to be Jewish. If so, then the development of a Jewish-Christian community at Sepphoris is not ruled out. In fact, since archaeology seems to document both accommodation of and resistance to Roman institutions, Sepphoris may have been an ideal environment for the development of a Jewish-Christian presence meeting in homes until 70 C.E. That the author of

Mark has a geographical viewpoint from the west and north of the country tends to support such a hypothesis.

THE EXCAVATIONS AT SEPPHORIS 1983–2000

In 1983, when USF first entered the field, the objective was simply to probe the stratification beside the "Citadel," or Fortress, at Sepphoris (Strange and Longstaff 1985). There was little from previous excavations from which one could formulate preliminary hypotheses, but the hope was that enough remains of the ancient city would persist in the stratification to eventually reconstruct architecture, living patterns, and economic life, but also to make certain comparisons to village life in the Galilee. We also hoped to be able to determine whether Sepphoris was a Jewish city, as many maintained, or a mainly Gentile city, as others thought.

Another important objective was to check the findings of Waterman, who had dug one season at Sepphoris in 1931 under the aegis of the University of Michigan. Waterman had excavated a structure that he had interpreted as a church. In fact, he thought that Christians had built it before Christianity was a *religio licita*, which had implications for the course of Christianity in Palestine in general and in the Galilee in particular (Waterman 1937). We set out to test the hypothesis of Avi-Yonah, who suggested that the structure was more than likely a villa (Avi-Yonah 1975).

The findings were, first, that the tower on top was not Crusader in its founding. It appears that it was certainly used and renovated in the Crusader or Fatimid periods, but its founding was mid-fourth century C.E. It appears to have been a Roman military tower. Those who built it first destroyed houses and other buildings down to their foundations. In the cleared area of about 90 × 180 m, they built the tower in the center and built other structures nearby, apparently all for military reasons. They paved the whole with a layer of lime and clay on top of as much as a meter of mixed debris from the destruction of the city.

In terms of the archaeological aims of the expedition up to 1988, the finds were scant. Nevertheless, it was clear that the Sepphoreans had built all the foundations of all the houses that USF investigated on bedrock during the second century B.C.E. There was a second major period of rebuilding in the transition from the first century B.C.E. to the first century C.E. In other words, on or about the birth of Christ, following the usual chronologies, the Sepphoreans rebuilt their city directly on the foundations of the earlier city. This seems to accord with the history of Sepphoris as read in Josephus, who wrote that Varus destroyed the city when it revolted at the death of Herod the Great (*Ant* 17.289; *War* 2.56; Strange and Longstaff 1985).

This occupation sequence tends to be confirmed by the history of some underground chambers cut beneath the remains of houses. The earliest accumulations on the floors of the cisterns (dipping jars and cooking pots lowered on strings to dip water) were from the Late Hellenistic period or the late second century B.C.E. We propose that this is a remnant of the Hellenistic city. In the course of the first century B.C.E.–C.E., workmen associated with one house cut two new cisterns. They did not know by this time of the earliest cistern, which had gone out of use.

This picture of building in the Late Hellenistic period and rebuilding at the turn to the first century C.E. tended to emerge everywhere USF dug on top of the hill of Sepphoris. Later, USF would find the same pattern at the bottom of the hill next to the *cardo*. The character of life in these buildings was everywhere the same also. That is, USF found intense domestic use with storage of foodstuffs, but also storage of ceramics, olive oil and perhaps wine, and impounding of water in cisterns. The economic level of the people was not poor, but neither was it necessarily rich (Strange 1992).

All the houses that USF probed came equipped with *miqwāʾôt*, or ritual baths, beneath their floors. Users entered each bath by a narrow staircase that usually turned to the right or left, perhaps to save room for the footprint in cutting the feature out of bedrock. The baths were small, only large enough for one person at a time. The builders plastered the interior on all surfaces, even the ceiling, with a strong white plaster suitable for holding water. The plasterers took care to round off all corners so that no user would injure himself or herself when entering and leaving the chamber.

Why is USF so convinced that these are ritual baths and not simply baths? The answer is not complicated. First, in the large villa that Waterman first uncovered and which USF re-excavated, there do exist at least three rectangular stepped basins cut into bedrock that are most easily interpreted as baths or even bathtubs. Waterman interpreted one of them as a baptismal font, but he did not mention the other two, though they appear in his plans and in the plans of Makhouly. That one type is simple and the second type more complex itself suggests separate uses. Only the fully plastered chambers cut with staircases fulfill the requirements for immersion.

We also noticed that there was a type of limestone vessel that appeared in the early Roman strata but never in the later strata. The exception is when well-worn fragments that clearly stem from earlier occupation appear in Late Roman strata. In other words, the inhabitants of the city used some small and some large stone vessels, all cut from the local limestone of the hills of Lower Galilee.

We now know the source of these vessels, namely, at ancient Abila, which also happens to be the origin of one of the aqueducts that serviced Sepphoris. These vessels appear in recent archaeological and historical literature as veritable markers of the practice of Judaism (Deines 1993). This is because these vessels are not subject to impurity, according to the Mishnah, *Kelim* 10:1, "These vessels afford protection with a tightly-stopped up cover: vessels of dung, vessels of stone, vessels of earth, vessels of clay, and vessels of alum." A similar sequence appears in M *Yedayim* 1:2: "With all sorts of utensils do they pour [water] for hands, even with utensils made of dung, utensils made of stone, and utensils made of clay." It is apparently the firing that makes vessels of clay or earth susceptible to uncleanness, as witnesses M *Kelim* 4:5: "Clay vessels, from what time do they receive uncleanness? When they are fired in the furnace. And that is the completion of their manufacture." It appears that the rabbis classified stone vessels as natural vessels, since firing was not part of their manufacture (Magen 1994; Strange 1997).

The presence of *miqwā'ōt* under the floors of all houses so far excavated at Sepphoris, coupled with the presence of limestone vessels in the Early Roman strata, tends to confirm that the majority of the population at Sepphoris was Jewish during that period, even if we do not know precisely what kind of Judaism they practiced. This was true as early as 103 B.C.E., when Ptolemy Lathrys besieged the city unsuccessfully on a Sabbath (*Ant.* 13.338). Presumably, Ptolemy thought that the Jewish inhabitants would not defend themselves on a Sabbath. He did not know that this issue had been settled since the Maccabean War.

Is there more evidence to suggest the character of this city during the Early Roman period? The answer is, of course, "yes", and I turn to this evidence now.

Waterman had discovered a Roman theater at Sepphoris in 1931. We approached the theater with some curiosity. There are not that many Roman theaters in ancient Palestine proper, so the matter of its founding date and history of usage remained an intriguing problem. Waterman had suggested that Herod Antipas had built the theater. Albright, after a visit to the site, later published a comment that the stones looked second-century to him (Albright 1938: 148).

The dating of the theater remains a bone of contention between the Hebrew University and ourselves, but USF remains relatively certain that it was indeed Antipas who founded the theater. Our finds in the foundations of the west end of the stage showed us extensive rebuilding after the Early Roman period, but set the founding of the theater in the first century C.E. This was determined from pottery in the foundation trenches and in drains beneath the foundations, which is exactly parallel to pottery of period Ib from Qumran. The date also rests upon the feature of engaged columns built into the façade of the theater, a feature known otherwise only in the combination hippodrome and theater built at Jericho by Herod the Great (Netzer 1993).

This date also accords with what we know of Antipas. He had lived all his life in Rome as a Roman, undergoing the education of a prince. He knew the first century theaters of Rome and perhaps of other localities, such as Pompeii. It seems clear that the first appearance of a theater that early at Sepphoris would have required royal patronage, and specifically patronage of the Herodian family, who were romanophiles.

In 1987, the USF Excavations at Sepphoris examined the surface of the ground on the eastern slopes of the hill of Sepphoris. No digging took place. While forcing a path through thistles nearly two meters tall and through thorns up to our knees, we stumbled upon the bottom of a heart-shaped column still *in situ*. Because of its size, it was clear that the building we were standing in had to be very large. Of course, none of us knew its date. Hardly five meters away another staff member dusted off the remnant of a white mosaic floor at the modern surface. The combination of heart-shaped column (or corner column) and mosaic floor bespoke major architecture (Strange et al. 1988; 1989).

In the years of excavation since then, our expedition has determined that there was a very large building on this spot, which measured about 40 × 60 m overall. It was rectangular in plan, with roughly half the plan occupied by three or perhaps four porches. Two rows of columns graced the interior, but it was not the case that there was one entrance at either end, nor was there a single entrance on one broad side, except perhaps on the north. Rather, the enclosed building was a more or less square enclosed and roofed space with rooms on either side of the longitudinal axis. On the east end, at the *cardo,* the simplest architectural solution from the traces of walls is that there were four porches, each with its colonnade of columns.

There was second story collapse at the west end of the building, which told us that there were offices upstairs at least in that part of the building. The materials found in the collapse of the second story included intact storage jars from the last use of the building. We do not know what the jars contained, but one may infer that there was at least some storage upstairs.

In the excavations in 1993, USF discovered that the corridor on the north side of the building was much wider than that on the south side. In the 1999 and 2000 excavations, USF discovered that there was an enormous vaulted cistern exactly underneath the wide corridor, which explained its width. The cistern held up to 60 m^3 of roof run-off, though USF has not yet found where it emptied or what the use of the water was. The vaulted cistern was original to the building.

The interior of the building in its first, that is, Early Roman phase was plastered everywhere on the walls in white. The floors were also white mosaics. Everywhere USF could check beneath the white mosaics, they dated to the Early Roman period. Everywhere USF could check in the foundations of the building, it was clearly early Roman, though to the north some of the foundations were reused by Hasmonean period structures.

We also discovered that there were three interconnecting rooms beneath the mosaic floor on the north side of the building. Someone used this basement apartment, as it were, for centuries right up to the middle of the fourth century C.E., when the entire structure was destroyed. Even in the second half of the fourth century, someone was using the room at the northeast corner of the enclosed building, accessing it from the street to the north. In the next century, when more than a meter of material had washed in from the upper hill, workers dug down into these rooms and used part of the space again.

On the north side of the building stood one entrance from the street. This entrance was not directly opposite an entrance on the south. Rather, the traffic pattern includes entry near the southeast corner of the building into the corridors and entry in the middle of the north side into the corridors. The colonnaded corridors invite one to walk around the two central spaces. Each of the two central spaces featured rows of columns around all four sides.

Is it possible to deduce the nature of the interior space of the building and, therefore, the use of the building? We shall start with the plan itself. We noticed that there are five rooms along the south side of the building and five on the north, but the builders took no care to place them symmetrically. One enters the rooms to the south only from inside the building, as far as we know, for there are no thresholds for doorways in the south sides of any of these rooms. On the other hand, there are at least five entrances into a narrow corridor from the street on the south side of the building. This is odd, for we expected a line of entrances to let directly into space for shops or offices.

One of the south entrances is a main entrance into the building. In this case, visitors walked through a double-leaf doorway into a vestibule. To the right one saw a decorative pool, whose top stood higher than the mosaic floor. From that point one was guided into a rectangular corridor that traversed the east end of the building with columns around a central space and connected with a second central space to the west. The central space to the east was about five centimeters higher than the space of the corridor. Two parallel black bands, seven centimeters wide, in the floor of the corridor directed traffic around the space and through a north–south corridor between two rows of columns and between two spaces. The north–south corridor apparently led to a doorway that exited to the north street.

The second central space to the west was surrounded by columns and furnished with two pools to the north and south. One entered the shops or offices directly from this inner space. A beautiful mosaic with birds, fishes, and animals decorated the western space in the Late Roman period, while geometric colored mosaics decorated the eastern space in the same period. Neither space was provided with a tribunal or *bema*.

One of the most interesting features of the western rectangular space, aside from the birds and fishes mosaic, is the beautifully cut threshold that lay between two larger columns. The stones are among the most beautifully cut, finished, and placed stones that I have seen anywhere. It was not until the summer of 2001 that our architectural team discovered that there are wear marks on this threshold from some kind of door. The reason that I say "some kind" is that there is no provision for doorjambs on either side, as in an ordinary entrance. There is one finely cut, square mortise hole on the side end of this threshold, but no doorjamb, unless some kind of a narrow jamb had a tenon on its bottom that fit into this hole.

About the only kind of door that would fit this feature would be one which pivoted on a single hinge in the south, as determined by the circular scrape marks on the threshold. This door could not reasonably have been very tall, if there are no jambs. I propose that this was a special kind of door no more than a meter high that formed a kind of low barrier to enter into the eastern space from the central corridor. Since the threshold is almost devoid of wear from walking upon it, I would suggest that it was, in fact, rarely used as a doorway, but when it was, the bottom of the door scraped the relatively soft stone enough to leave its marks.

There may well have been inscriptions in the floor that named a donor or gave the name of a governor or Caesar, but none has come to light. Three times in the eastern rectangle of the Late Roman mosaic one reads the word EYTYXWC, once on each of three sides of the rectangle. This is most easily read as an adverb derived from εὐτυχέω. In that case, the inscription is wishing the viewer good fortune. This is not recognizably Jewish, Christian, or necessarily pagan, but more or less a generic greeting. It may be quite deliberate, so that citizens of any religious persuasion might use the building.

We have not discussed the streets on four sides of the building, but they have an interest in themselves. The street on the west side of the building was no more than a sidewalk and narrow street, each about 2 m wide. The sidewalk, paved with stones, stood about 20 cm above the street, itself also paved with stones. The street had an Early Roman founding.

Workers paved the north street with crushed limestone, not with cut stone. Next to the building there was a curbing made sometimes of the same crushed limestone and sometimes of cut stones about 25 cm high. This curb effectively protected the building from the water that rushed down the street to the east during the rainy season.

The street on the east side of the building, apparently the *Cardo Maximus*, was originally paved with the same crushed limestone, as presumably was the south street. The *cardo* was provided with stones cut into blocks for a sidewalk in the early Roman period. This raised sidewalk kept citizens from the wet and dirty street. In the second century c.e., renovations at Sepphoris included adding cut-stone paving stones to the *cardo* above its original pavement of crushed limestone.

The building stood at the intersection of the *cardo* and the d*ecumanus*, which is ordinarily understood to be an honored or high-status space. Thus, the USF expedition was sure that it was an important public building. Is it possible to deduce what the building was used in the first century?

Given the description of the inner space, we can deduce at least three uses. First, the four porches or stoas on the east side of the building bespeak public space very powerfully. In some ways, the porch, or stoa, and the basilica, the descendent of the stoa, are quintessential statements of Roman public space in the sense that citizens stroll together, pass the time of day, or transact business out of the weather. Vitruvius understood this aspect of public space very well (*De Arch* 5.9 and following).

A second use of the space is for economic activity. From the last use of the building many coins — small bronzes — were found directly upon the mosaic floor. These coins must have had little monetary value to their owners, for no one bothered to seek them out in the relative gloom of an architectural volume illuminated by shafts of light from high above the floor. Since small nails also appeared on the floor, then presumably frames or shelves may also have stood in this space. Admittedly, this inferred economic usage is dated to the middle of the fourth century C.E., but it is an activity that could have occurred at any time during the life of the building, including the first century.

Since offices or shops line the north and south sides of the building, it is possible that the building housed administrative offices. I think this unlikely, for the simple reason that the administrative offices excavated elsewhere are very small rooms. On the contrary, the sheer size and grandness of this buildings suggests that those who rented these offices used them for special purposes, perhaps for some kind of services such as banking, money lending, amanuensis offices, legal archives, or others.

A fourth possible use of the building is for government purposes. In this case, some high official of the realm met with his retainers and suppliants in one of the rectangular spaces surrounded by columns and walkways or corridors. Such a state of affairs suggests intermittent use of the birds and fishes mosaic with its threshold as a special gathering place. Many gatherings could qualify for this imprint in the archaeological record, but I favor judicial uses or for high officials, perhaps for the governor of the toparchy.

If the building was owned by the city of Sepphoris, then it may even have served for the *boulé* or city council from time to time. This will remain hypothetical until other excavated details tend to confirm or disconfirm this usage. This is an attractive hypothesis, for it helps us to understand why such grand space was built at all, much less renovated so stylishly in the second century. At that time the owners replastered the interior and painted the plaster with panels of primary colors, but some also with plants and birds. Such painted plaster is well-attested in Roman structures elsewhere in the Empire.

In sum, USF discovered housing of the first century at Sepphoris that is surely Jewish in nature. We have investigated primarily one villa, but our finds cohere nicely with the finds of the other expeditions, all of which have excavated houses. We have also satisfied ourselves that the first phase of the theater comes from the time of Herod Antipas, though we must leave open the possibility that Herod the Great initiated building of this specifically Roman building.

Finally, USF has provided evidence for a large building, perhaps a civil basilica, that served special needs of the people of Sepphoris for 350 years. That is, an enormous structure with a tiled roof dominated the intersection of the two main streets of Sepphoris. It was large enough to be visible from the top of the ridge above Nazareth, about four miles to the south.

SEPPHORIS AND THE EARLIEST CHRISTIAN CONGREGATIONS

Let us now turn to the Galilee in general and the place of Sepphoris within it to garner a broader picture of the context of the earliest Christian congregations. May I first point out that Sepphoris stands more or less in the center of Lower Galilee, midway between the Mediterranean coast and the western coast of the Sea of Galilee, or the Kinneret, to use its Hebrew name. Yet, the territory I am speaking of at

1300 km^2, or about 505 square miles, is only slightly larger than Los Angeles at 467 square miles. This tiny hilly country is nestled between non-Jewish territories. It stands sandwiched between Phoenician territory to the west, Itruria to the north, and Samaria and the territory of Beth Shean-Scythopolis to the south. To the east the border is more permeable, since it is formed by the lake, which provides access to city territories to the east.

Sepphoris, then, stands as a Jewish city in the center of a more or less non-Jewish circle. The citizens of Sepphoris and all Galilee faced daily the problem of maintaining Jewish identity in this state of affairs. We have commented that the Galileans used certain elements of the material culture to maintain their identity, namely, stone vessels and ritual baths. This is surely correct, but there must be other elements as well.

Although Galilee was quite small, as was the ancient province of Judea, it was marked by several major economic and political disruptions between 103 B.C.E. and 70 C.E.: (1) the Annexation of Galilee as Jewish territory solidified by Alexander Jannaeus at the beginning of his reign, (2) the coming of Rome in 63 B.C.E., (3) the installation of the Council at Sepphoris by Gabinius in 55 B.C.E., which marks the advent of an official Roman institution in Galilee for the first time, (4) the Civil War between Antipater and Herod, itself punctuated by the incursion of the Persians in 43 B.C.E., (5) the death of Herod the Great and the crowning of Herod Antipas about 4 B.C.E. Accompanying this change of the reigns of power was the destruction of Sepphoris at the hands of Varus and its rebuilding by Antipas using craftsmen from all Galilee, (6) the building and founding of Tiberias about 21 C.E. by Herod Antipas, again using craftsmen from all Galilee, (7) the banishment of Herod Antipas about 39 C.E. and the passing of Galilee into the hands of King Herod Agrippa I until 44 C.E., (8) the passing of the rulership to Roman procurators in 44 C.E., (9) the First Revolt against Rome from 66–73 or 74 C.E. In this revolt Sepphoris had the distinction of being a city of peace, while the other localities of Galilee, at least according to Josephus, were strongly pro-revolt. This string of disruptions and changes in administration must have left its imprint on the population, though precisely what this means for understanding the emergence of early Christianity is problematic.

I am making the assumption, by the way, that the earliest Christian congregations were likely completely participant in Galilean life: in the languages, trade, manufacturing, agriculture, social gatherings, giving and receiving brides, and the consumption of public goods, including the legal and other services that the cities and the territory of Galilee offered.

Were there public buildings, such as synagogues, in the first century where the nascent Christian congregations could gather? This question still undergoes debate, but I am convinced that there were. Even though we do not have a candidate for a first-century synagogue at Nazareth or Sepphoris yet, one may emerge. So far, for the entire country candidates for first-century synagogue buildings are to be found at Capernaum (the black basalt building beneath the Byzantine synagogue of white limestone), Gamla, Herodium, Masada, Kiryat Sefer, Modi'in, and NT Jericho. All follow the same pattern or template, if you will, in which the builders mark the interior rectangular floor space by architectural features within features. One finds columns all around or on two or three sides, then walkways between the columns and the walls on three or all four sides, and finally benches between the walls and the walkways. The result of such a design is that participants had to look between the columns to see what was going on. Although this feature is known from Nabatean mortuary temples, it is otherwise virtually unknown in the Roman world (Strange 1995; 1999).

The vast network of roads connecting villages, towns, and cities suggests that Christians had access to a communication network just as their neighbors who were not Christians. This gave the earliest Christians no advantage, but it does mean that the Christian urge to communicate the Gospel was helped by this existing road network. This may help us explain the assumption in the *Didaché* that traveling evangelists and prophets might drop in from time to time. The Christian communities were obligated to offer them hospitality. That is, by the time of the *Didaché*, the Christian communities of Galilee had managed to move into southern Syria with their message, following established trade routes.

As an aside, may I respond to Crossan and Reed, who believe that there is an anti-city stance in Galilee, quoting Josephus' *Life* (Crossan and Reed 2001)? Such a view is also found in the Hebrew Bible, which tends to support the hypothesis that the anti-city view would appear in Judaism of the first century. But this view is not an ideology that was amalgamated with Christianity, for the earliest missionary strategy that we know is that of Paul, which was an urban strategy. Therefore, it seems reasonable to speculate that there will likely be both city-Christians and country-Christians in the first century in Galilee, both exhibiting some anti-city views and feelings.

CONCLUSIONS

The above remarks amount to preliminary observations. There are as yet no firm conclusions, even from the relatively hard evidence of excavation. This is very simply because archaeological evidence requires interpretation in the same way that texts do, and conscientious scholars can disagree on what archaeological evidence means. This is especially true when one moves from inference of technology, which is relatively straightforward, to inference of social patterns, beliefs, and values. We are not yet at the stage of some kind of consensus about inferring such patterns of belief and values from material culture. This latter challenge will continue to occupy us for some time to come.

REFERENCES

Albright, W. F.
1938 Review of Waterman's Preliminary Report on the 1931 Excavations. *Classical Weekly* 21: 148.

Avi-Yonah, M.
1975 Sepphoris. Pp. 1051–55 in *Encyclopedia of Archaeological Excavations in the Holy Land*, vol. 4, eds. M. Avi-Yonah and E. Stern. Jerusalem: Israel Exploration Society/Masada.

Crossan, J. D., and Reed, J. L.
2001 *Excavating Jesus: The Key Discoveries for Understanding Jesus in His World.* San Francisco, CA: Harper.

Deines, R.
1993 *Jüdische Steingefässe und pharisäische Frömmigkeit: ein archäologisch-historischer Beitrag zum Verständis von Joh 2,6 und der jüdischen Reinheitshalacha zur Zeit Jesu.* Tübingen: Mohr.

Magen, I.
1994 *Purity Broke Out in Israel.* The Ruben and Edith Hecht Museum Catalogue 9. Haifa: University of Haifa.

Manns, F.
1977 *Essais sur le Judéo-Christianisme.* Jerusalem: Franciscan Printing.

Miller, S.
1984 *Studies in the History and Traditions of Sepphoris.* Leiden: Brill.
1993 The Minim of Sepphoris Reconsidered. *Harvard Theological Review* 86: 377–402.

Netzer, E.
1993 Tell es-Samarat. Pp. 691–92 in *The New Encyclopedia of Archaeological Excavations in the Holy Land*, vol. 2, ed. E. Stern. Jerusalem: Israel Exploration Society.

Strange, J. F.
1992 Six campaigns at Sepphoris: the University of South Florida Excavations, 1983–1989. Pp. 339–55 in *The Galilee in Late Antiquity*, ed. L. Levine. New York, NY: Jewish Theological Seminary of America.
1995 The Art and Archaeology of Ancient Judaism. Pp. 64–114 in *Judaism in Late Antiquity*, vol. 1, ed. J. Neusner. Leiden: Brill.
1997 First Century Galilee from Archaeology and the Texts. Pp. 39–48 in *Archaeology and the Galilee: Texts and Contexts in the Greco-Roman and Byzantine Periods,* eds. D. Edwards and C. T. McCollough. Atlanta, GA: Scholars.
1999 Ancient Texts, Archaeology as Text, and the Problem of the First Century Synagogue. Pp. 27–45 in *Evolution of the Synagogue: Problems and Progress,* eds. H. Kee and L. Cohick. Harrisburg, PA: Trinity International.

Strange, J. F., and Longstaff, T. R. W.
1985 Sepphoris (1984). *Revue Biblique* 92: 429.

Strange, J. F.; Groh, D.; and Longstaff, T. R. W.
1988 Sepphoris (Sippori), 1987. *Israel Exploration Journal* 38, no. 3: 188–90.
1989 Sepphoris (Sippori), 1988. *Israel Exploration Journal*, 39, no. 1–2: 104–6.

Waterman, L.
1937 *Preliminary Report of the University of Michigan Excavations at Sepphoris/Diocaesarea, Palestine in 1931*. Ann Arbor, MI: University of Michigan.

Chapter 25

The Lives of Glass-Workers at Sepphoris

by Alysia Fischer

In this article, the physical ramifications of glass-blowing in antiquity are considered. By using archaeological and ethnographic evidence related to glass-working, it is possible to hypothesize about the lives of the glass-blowers working at the site of Sepphoris during the Byzantine period (363–640 C.E.). Creating a possible life history for these craftsmen not only highlights the differences between modern and ancient glass-blowers, but also offers a case-study for future comparison with other social groups. The glass data derive from two separate excavations at the site: the University of South Florida's Excavations at Sepphoris (USF), led by James F. Strange, and the Sepphoris Regional Project (SRP), led by Eric Meyers of Duke University.

The majority of the glass artifacts and virtually all of the evidence for glass-working at Sepphoris come from two workshop areas that operated during the Byzantine period (363–640 C.E.). These workshops primarily produced goblets, cups, bowls, and hanging lamps, with a variety of each type. A full report and discussion of the glass vessel assemblages from the two excavations will be published with the final excavation reports. Here, I use this data alongside ethnographic material to develop an in-depth picture of the life of a glass-worker in antiquity.

Ethnographic research I undertook with traditional glass-blowers in Jordan and Egypt in 1996 and 1999 demonstrated that those workmen were exposing themselves to carcinogens in the fumes from the motor oil they burned as a fuel (Fischer 2001: 128). This pattern of behavior led me to question whether substances or practices employed by glass-workers in antiquity may also have impacted their bodies, and subsequently their quality and length of life. Archaeological evidence clearly indicates that most of the body would have been affected in some way by working with glass, largely in adverse ways. The following discussion of such adverse effects on the body of glass-workers in antiquity, and at Sepphoris in particular, pays special attention to the lungs, kidneys and heart, reproductive organs, eyes, muscle and skin.

LUNGS

As a result of their craft, glass-workers are at risk for chronic bronchitis, emphysema, and silicosis, a form of pneumoniconiosis. This heightened risk is primarily due to silica exposure, although wood smoke can also be a factor in some cases. According to Rossol, "a large percentage of glassblowers develop lung problems and significantly decreased lung capacities" (1990: 219). These conditions are primarily the "bio-accumulative effects" of inhaling silica over a number of years (Bray and Dobing 1978: 16). While the particles used to make glass are too large to inhale, silica that is crushed into a fine powder can become airborne and be inhaled. There is potential for airborne silica at all stages of glass-manufacture; glass-making, glass-melting, glass-blowing and working with finished vessels. These activities took place in two different types of workshops in antiquity, thus a glass-blower would not have come into contact with the raw materials in the same way as a glass-maker. At the site of Sepphoris, there is evidence for two glass-blowing workshops. This evidence consists of glass droplets, tooled glass bits, furnace waste, and other by-products of glass-blowing. Glass-making evidently took place at peripheral sites, such as Bet She'arim (Freestone and Gorin-Rosen 1999) and Hadera (Gorin-Rosen 1993).

Glass-makers would have been at the highest risk for silica inhalation among the glass-workers of antiquity. While mixing the ingredients for the glass melts, the glass-makers would have been exposed to large amounts of silica as well as other potentially harmful glass constituents; if the glass-makers ground the sand to a finer grit to aid in the melting process, their exposure would have been even greater. Being around broken glass vessels and poorly stored raw materials also increases the risk of silica inhalation.

Not only would the glass-workers have been affected by silica, but their families would have also faced the risks of inhaling silica. Many of the safety guidelines for glass-workers today recommend the removal of clothes worn when in contact with silica, to avoid bringing silica into the home and exposing other family members (Rossol 1990: 225). Lawrie also recommends frequent washing of work clothes so they do not "harbour dust which will be right under your nose" (1984: 28). It is unlikely that these activities were practiced in antiquity, and therefore likely that family members who did not work in the glass workshop were still exposed to silica.

Silica inhalation can lead to silicosis, an irreversible condition. When silica enters the lungs it cannot be absorbed. Once in the lungs, silica collects on the walls of the alveoli, irritating the alveoli and causing them to form scar tissue (McCann 1992: 99). This scar tissue prevents the passage of oxygen into the bloodstream. The scar tissue also causes the lungs to become rigid, rather than elastic, making the physical act of breathing more difficult (Barazani 1983). Silicosis takes ten to twenty years to become apparent in an individual under modern exposure rates of forty hours per week who began at age eighteen or later, so glass-blowers in antiquity may not have been immediately aware of the risks to which they were exposing themselves (McCann 1992: 99). As Barazani points out, "most hazardous dusts [including silica] are so fine they can't be seen," which further underscores the probability that ancient glass-workers were unaware of this threat (1983: 4).

Glass-workers in antiquity generally had shorter life spans than their modern counterparts, but that does not necessarily mean that they would not have experienced the effects of silicosis. Ethnographic studies suggest that traditional glass-workers typically began work at an early age and work daily for longer periods, increasing their exposure. Research with traditional glass-workers in Afghanistan, conducted by the Corning Museum of Glass in the 1980s, showed that involvement in the glass-working process began at a very young age. In the family they studied, the eight-year-old son of the glass-blower spent his days stoking the glass furnace with fuel, thus exposing his young lungs to the silica and other harmful substances that a western glass-worker would not experience until later in life (Corning: The Glassmakers of Herat). Young glass-workers were also recorded by Burra (1995: 43) in India during the 1980s, where twenty-five percent of the workers in the glass factories of Firozabad were under the age of eighteen. In like manner, the exposure to silica was likely to have begun before the age of eighteen in antiquity, increasing the exposure time significantly and making it necessary to adjust the date of onset of silicosis. In addition, traditional glass-workers also worked more than 40 hours per week. Glass-blowers in Cairo reported working approximately forty-five hours a week, while Burra interviewed glass-workers in India who worked twelve-hour days (1995: 35). A combination of similar factors would have impacted the Galilean glass-workers at Sepphoris much as it does in these traditional situations.

Silica causes other physical problems in addition to silicosis. Silica is considered a carcinogen by the International Agency for Research in Cancer (IARC; Rossol 1992: 102). The carcinogenic label has been applied to silica based on experiments with animals as well as "limited evidence for the carcinogenicity of crystalline silica in humans" (Rossol 1992: 102). It has been difficult to link many specific cases of cancer to glass-working because of the latency period between exposure and manifestation of the cancer in the body. This situation is further complicated by the prevalence of cigarette smoking among glass-workers in the 1970s and 1980s. Personal testimonials concerning the formation of tumors following a lifetime of glass-working do, however, point towards the higher risk of cancer in this population (Kristel 1981).

Appropriate safety equipment can significantly lower the risk of developing debilitating lung conditions. The glass-blowers I visited in the Near East, however, do not use such safety equipment. Glass-workers in antiquity did not have this type of safety equipment and would certainly have had substantive exposure to silica with possible resultant damage to the lungs.

Wood Smoke

Silica would not have been the only damaging substance entering the lungs of glass-workers in antiquity. Wood smoke from the firebox of their furnace, as well as from the possible use of wood tools, would have also been inhaled. Wood has long been used as a material for shaping glass. As long as the wooden tool is kept wet, it will burn very slowly. If the tool dries out, it will catch fire upon contacting hot glass. In both scenarios, varying amounts of wood smoke forms and, in the first, steam is also produced. Assuming that the ventilation in the ancient workshops was no better than that seen in traditional Near Eastern glass workshops today, it is likely that a significant amount of smoke was present in the work area. This would have been particularly true when the furnace was stoked, especially if improperly dried wood was in use.

The craft of glass-working clearly has negative effects on the tissue of the lungs. Depending on an individual's exposure to silica and other irritants, his or her symptoms can range from mild discomfort to silicosis, emphysema, or cancer. These same conditions may have been prevalent among the glass-workers of the Byzantine period in the Galilee, particularly among the glass-makers. Because there is a latency period between exposure and the appearance of symptoms, the glass-workers may not have recognized the link between their activities and their health.

KIDNEYS / HEART

Heat emitted from glass furnaces places significant stress on the kidneys and the heart. The body works to maintain an internal temperature of 98.6°F, which is difficult in front of a 2500°F furnace containing molten glass. In order to see what internal temperatures can be reached in a glass studio during the summer, the body temperatures of four glass-workers, including the author, were monitored on August 3rd and 5th of 2001. While this small sample size and the use of an ear thermometer make any conclusions anecdotal, it is noteworthy that all individuals started with body temperatures ranging from 96.5–98.4° F, and during the glass-blowing process reached between 99.6 and 100.6°F. The glass-blower with the most years of experience began with the lowest temperature and ended with the highest, a situation that warrants further study.

High temperatures are stressful for the body, causing the heart and kidneys to work harder, circulating blood and water (Waller 1985: 41). Overworking these organs can sometimes lead to their collapse (Barazani 1980a: 46). Organ damage typically occurs as the result of a heat stroke when the body temperature is over 104°F.

Glass-blowers are more likely to suffer episodes of heat exhaustion than to suffer from heat stroke. It is difficult for the body to maintain its optimum temperature while working with glass because most glass workshops are quite hot, hovering around 104°F and are even hotter around the furnace, where the glass is held at 2500°F. The work area in front of the glass furnace in Cairo, for example, was 140°F. The temperatures are even hotter during the summer months. Glass furnaces in antiquity probably only reached approximately 2000°F, yet they would have produced sufficient heat to contribute to the necessary conditions for heat-related illnesses (Fischer 2001: 178), such as heat exhaustion, and related symptoms, such as "weakness, headache, and nausea" (Finkel 2001: 1).

The primary method of heat loss utilized by glass-blowers' bodies is evaporation through sweating and exhalation. When subjected to constant heat stresses, the body reacts by sweating. When the ambient temperature is above 35°C, or 95°F, the body loses ninety percent of its heat by evaporation of water on the skin and from the lungs during exhalation (Frisancho 1996: 35). This excessive sweating puts stress on the heart and kidneys, which must work hard to process and move fluids through the body.

Sweat cools the body as a result of the energy lost during the evaporation of the liquid on the skin (Frisancho 1996: 36). The human body has between two and five million sweat glands and thus this part of the cooling system is rather efficient (Frisancho 1996: 36). Over a period of repeated exposure to heat, the body becomes more efficient at sweating (Barazani 1980a: 46). For the majority of the history of glass-working current evidence suggests that the craft was practiced primarily in the warm climate of the Near East. Individuals, such as those at Sepphoris, would have already developed some tolerance to heat as a result of the hot dry summers they experienced and may have more easily adapted to the high temperatures of glass-working. Such tolerance could be gained over a few weeks. Frisancho describes the first four days of new exposure to heat stress as a period of "increased heat and circulatory strain," during which "an increase in blood flow from the internal core to the shell may increase the peripheral heat conductance from five to six times its normal value" (1996: 55). The individual will also sweat profusely but not efficiently, because "only a small proportion of this sweat is evaporated" (Frisancho 1996: 55). Often this initial period is enough to deter individuals from pursuing glass-working. It has been suggested that the best way to get acclimated to the heat in a glass-blowing studio is to do so slowly, "increas[ing] your work load gradually over several days" (McCann 1992: 229).

Frisancho also states that, as a result of long-term exposure, "acclimation to heat stress is attained through the continued maintenance of high peripheral heat conductance" (1996: 55). This heat conduction is a result of an "increase in vasodilation," "an increase in plasma volume and total circulating protein," and "a more complete and even distribution of sweat over the skin" (Frisancho 1996: 55). Thus, it is not surprising that glass-workers develop the ability to withstand very hot working conditions. However, the acclimated heat tolerance only "lasts two months beyond the end of the exposure," and necessitates reacquisition of the tolerance if leaving the craft for an extended period of time (Waller 1985: 41).

The accumulated ability to lose heat efficiently does not come without potential long-term costs to the body. Because blood is diverted to the skin during periods of heat stress, an individual can suffer from acute kidney and heart problems, in part because these organs are not receiving an adequate blood supply (McCann 1992: 228). When the body is working at its peak heat-shedding efficiency, it is still taxing the heart and kidneys because of the higher volume of fluids that must be filtered and pumped through the body. Waller has pointed out that acclimation to stressful amounts of heat also "produces a variety of harmful reactions such as skin disorders, water and salt imbalance, heat exhaustion, cramps, edema" (1985: 41). The body can even reach a point where it can no longer adjust to the heat, where further exposure may result in death (Waller 1985: 41).

In order to work efficiently in hot conditions, glass-workers must reduce their risk of heat absorption by covering their bodies with appropriate clothing and maintaining a constant supply of water with which to replenish their bodies. Glass-blowers in antiquity, then, were likely to have taken periodic breaks throughout the day during which they ingested liquids.

The glass-blowers may have taken further steps to protect their bodies from the furnace's heat.

Fig. 1 *Glass-blower with protective padding in Cairo.*

Figure 1 shows a glass-blower in Cairo who created additional protection in the abdominal area by folding up fabric and placing it beneath his shirt as a heat shield. A second way that glass-workers protect their body from the heat of the furnace is to build walls of the same materials used in the furnace, located between the opening to the furnace and the glass-worker's station, as can be seen in the modern Jordanian glass workshop shown in figure 2.

Being able to adapt to high temperatures may have been a prerequisite for becoming a glass-worker in antiquity. This heat tolerance could also have been a factor in the dominance of men in the glass craft. Women cannot endure as much heat stress as men (Frisancho 1996: 57). Their inability to shed heat as quickly may be one reason they were excluded from many of the pyrotechnic crafts. While this may have been a factor in the historical exclusion of women from glass-working, it is more likely that safety and socio-economic concerns were to blame. Glass-working was probably considered an arduous and dangerous profession unsuitable for women. Glass-working would also have carried the potential for earning enough money to support a family, again keeping it out of the female arena, as males have historically retained control over such professions.

REPRODUCTIVE ORGANS

Another potential area of concern for glass-workers deals with reproduction. Studies have shown that a number of the materials used in glass production today can adversely affect reproductive success. Three of these substances were also in use in the Galilean glass industry of the Byzantine period: Antimony (Sb), Copper (Cu), and Manganese (Mn). An earlier study of glass from Sepphoris shows that Sb and Mn were used as decolorants in some of the glass vessels at the site, while Cu was added to others in order to impart a blue hue (Fischer and McCray 1999: 901).

It is unclear whether decolorants and colorants were added by the glass-maker or the glass-blower in antiquity. There is some evidence for either scenario. Certainly, glass-makers made a variety of different colors of glass, which would have exposed them to a variety of harmful substances. Glass-blowers may also have added colorants to the glass they purchased, especially if the desired colors were not available. It seems possible, therefore, that both could have been exposed to Sb, Cu, and Mn. These three substances can enter the body through ingestion of small quantities or inhalation of vola-

Fig. 2 Glass-blower with brick heat-shield in Na'ur, Jordan.

tilized gases. While Barazani points out that "trace amounts of many metals are present in the body and necessary in the diet," she goes on to say that "very small variations in quantity can cause harmful cumulative effects, particularly over a prolonged period" (1980b: 56). The glass-workers in Egypt, Jordan, and Turkey were all seen drinking beverages in their workshops. Figure 3 shows a kettle on top of the furnace that was used for making tea. Drinking beverages in the studio is a useful way to combat heat exhaustion but is also a potential avenue for the ingestion of harmful materials. While in Cairo, I saw the glass-blowers using their furnace to heat vegetables, in this case eggplant and garlic, that they would later consume. It is possible that glass-workers at Sepphoris also used the heat from their furnace to prepare food and beverages, which would have created another avenue for harmful substances to enter their bodies.

The adverse reproductive effects of these materials are significant. Antimony, in particular, has been shown in both human and animal studies to have dire reproductive consequences. In addition to affecting the fertility of both men and women, it also has the potential to induce "miscarriage, stillbirth and spontaneous abortion" and to negatively affect newborns (Jossy 1985: 28). Animal studies have suggested that copper has similar effects, while both human and animal studies show manganese to have negative effects on male and female fertility (Jossy 1985: 28).

The Galilean glass-makers were certainly exposed to these materials, and the glass-blowers may have been. Like silica exposure, Sb, Cu, and Mn exposure could have affected the health of a glass-worker's entire family. Future work with particular glass-working lineages could indicate the extent of reproductive problems among traditional glass-workers, making it possible to hypothesize further about the fertility of glass-workers in the past.

EYES

Glass-workers also had to worry about slowly going blind. Molten glass emits infrared (IR) and ultraviolet (UV) radiation. Infrared radiation, in particular, affects the eyes during glass-working. While it may seem that ultraviolet radiation would also cause problems for the eyes, Layton claims "only negligible amounts are produced at glass-

Fig. 3 *Glass-blowers using their furnace to heat water kettle in Görece, Turkey.*

working temperatures" (1979: 20). Kerkvliet and Dunham suggest, however, that ultraviolet exposure can cause an irritation that "feels like sand in your eyes" (1997: 98). Mild exposure to IR and UV radiation can result in conjunctivitis, also known as pink eye, and chronic exposure to IR can result in cataracts (McCann 1992: 215). These conditions result because "the lens of the eye is poorly protected against overheating" (Layton 1979: 20).

As Layton describes, cataracts develop as a result of glass-working because "continual or repeated overheating can cause the lens to become cloudy or opaque rather than clear" (1979: 20). Historically, cataracts have been so common among glass-blowers that they have been called "glass-blower's cataracts" (McCann 1992: 218). As with silicosis, the damage to the eyes is cumulative and in antiquity would have been irreversible.

Byzantine period glass-workers would have been unaware of the constant infrared radiation because the eye is ill-equipped to send messages of pain. Kerkvliet and Dunham have pointed out that, while the skin "provides its own warning mechanism by having a pain threshold below that of the burn threshold," there "is no such adequate warning mechanism in the eye" (1997: 98). A glass-worker would move away from the furnace due to skin irritation long before he would realize that damage is being done to his eyes. There seems to have been some knowledge about the effects of glass-working on the eyes, as Kazhdan mentions a Byzantine period text where "Moschos mentions a *hyalopsos* [glass-blower] who was blinded by the flame" (1991: 853).

Infrared-resistant eyeglasses, widely available in the United States and Europe, are not within the price-range of the traditional glass-workers in the Near East. The only traditional glass-workers I encountered who wore any sort of eyeglasses were five older men whose eyesight had clearly begun to experience the negative effects of years of glass-working. The four remaining glass-workers did not wear eyeglasses of any sort. Certainly, glass-workers in antiquity had no such eye protection, which left them at high risk for developing cataracts.

Modern glass-workers can also reduce the risk of exposure to heat and glare by building shielding, like that mentioned earlier, around the furnaces (Barazani 1980a: 47). The traditional glass workers in Jordan employed this strategy, having constructed a small brick wall between the glass-blower and the furnace opening, as shown in figure 2. While the short wall was built to protect the glass-blower's body from the heat of the furnace, it would also provide some protection for the eyes. These traditional approaches suggest that a similar strategy may have been employed in antiquity. While we currently lack any evidence of such heat-shielding walls archaeologically, we also lack evidence for any upper furnace structures. Hopefully, future excavation and publication of glass furnaces can help to answer this question.

MUSCLES

Glass-working also causes immediate discomfort. Some glass-blowers today go through a series of stretches to avoid the "neck, back, and shoulder stiffness and pain" that result from their craft (Spencer 1997: 95). This discomfort results from carrying hot glass around the workshop on the end of a blowpipe or pontil. Moreover, while the length of the blowpipe serves to distance the glass-blower from the heat of the glass, it also multiplies the weight of the glass.

Another physical ramification of glass-working is carpal tunnel syndrome, often caused by the constant rotation of molten glass on the end of a blowpipe. This rotation is necessary to keep the glass object symmetrical and avoid slumping. The repetitive nature of rotating the blowpipe can directly contribute to the development of carpal tunnel problems. Sitting can also have negative physical repercussions, especially while working on the floor, which can cause further aches in the lower body and possibly lead to arthritis in the knees or other joints. Approximately half of the traditional glass-workers that were observed sat on the floor. All of the bead-makers in Turkey and half of the glass-blowers in Egypt chose to sit cross-legged on the floor while working.

THE SKIN: BURNS AND CUTS

The final part of the body affected by glass-working is the skin, which can be burned and cut by glass. Of the afflictions related to glass-working, these are the most avoidable, although burns are common, due to the temperature of the glass when it is being worked. Metal tools also present a danger when they come in contact with hot glass. These tools become very hot and need a sufficient time to cool down before the portion that was in contact with the glass is handled. Many glass-blowers in the United States bear the scars of accidental contact with either hot glass or a hot hand tool, which can cause burns ranging from first to third degree.

Hot glass and tools can burn not only the skin, but also clothing. Experts suggest glass-workers wear natural fibers that will not melt to the skin and heavy-duty shoes that cannot be penetrated by molten or broken glass (Barazani 1980a: 47; Bond 1976: 28; Rossol 1990: 225). At Sepphoris, the glass-blowers could have been wearing linen, wool, or leather clothing, which has the potential to catch fire. As for footwear used by the traditional glass-workers I met, most did not wear shoes while working; the same may have been true in the past. Working in a hot glass studio while barefoot exposes the workers to the possibility of being burned by hot glass, or stepping on sharp shards of glass and getting cut.

Feet are not the only body part that can be cut by glass. Glass wounds often occur in the upper body after a glass object is broken and a person handles it in an unsafe manner. Rossol (1990: 220) has underscored that there are many points in the glass-working process where "sharp glass splinters and shards are created," including "when pieces are discarded, transferred to the pontil, or knocked off the pontil into the annealing oven." These accidental glass wounds can be severe, and there are modern glass-workers in the United States who have severed a tendon in the hand/wrist region as a result of working with panes of glass. Poor annealing would increase the probability of getting cut by broken glass, as the stresses created under those conditions are unpredictable. Poorly annealed glass can shatter at any time, potentially injuring someone either nearby or handling the object.

Glass can also have long-term effects on the skin. The ultraviolet light and IR radiation mentioned earlier can also affect the glass-workers' skin. UV radiation can cause damage to the skin that ranges from sunburn to melanoma (McCann 1992: 218).

Traditional glass-blowers ignore this potential threat because sunburn fades, removing the damage visible to the naked eye; moreover, skin cancers take 20–40 years to develop. Because these skin conditions disappear or lie dormant, traditional glass-workers may not be aware of the risks they are taking. It may seem that wearing less clothing would make an individual's body temperature lower, but in cases of exposure to extreme heat, the body ends up gaining more heat from exposure than it is losing by evaporation (Frisancho 1996: 33). Glass-blowers in antiquity would have faced the same exposure and long-term effects.

CONCLUSION

Looking at the physical effects of glass-working in traditional workshops in Jordan and Egypt provides important insights into the lives of glass-workers in antiquity, especially in regards to their bodies and their quality of life. Glass-working could and probably did contribute to a variety of physical ailments, including chronic cough, loss of eyesight, and even death through the inability to absorb oxygen. Ironically, beautiful or utilitarian objects were not the only products of glass-working; a host of physical ailments would have also permeated ancient glass workshops. These workshops were full of dangerous items that could harm craftsmen and their families both immediately and over time.

One might suppose that glass-workers in antiquity were sickly as a result of the dangerous practices of their craft. This probably overstates the situation, since most of the glass-workers in traditional settings that I encountered appeared healthy. But the appearance of health on a macroscopic level can mask internal problems. In addition to the many physical effects discussed above, Schwind has pointed out that in Early American glasshouses "infections of any sort spread rapidly because the blowpipe passed from mouth to mouth in the manufacturing process" (1984: 178). Blowpipes would have also been shared in antiquity, although the passing of infections in this manner would not have been as significant a problem for the glass-blowers at Sepphoris, as the workshops only seem to have employed a few workers. Once infections were present in the population, however, the silica in the lungs of the glass-workers would have probably aggravated colds, allergies, asthma, bronchitis, and other respiratory conditions (Bond 1976: 27).

Of the two glass professions mentioned here, glass-making and glass-blowing, glass-making was the most hazardous in antiquity. Exposure to airborne silica and various colorants would have been present, although this exposure occurred in bursts and was not constant. Glass-blowers, in contrast, would also have been under almost daily assault from the heat and UV and IR radiation coming from their furnaces.

The glass-blower's family would have been significantly impacted as well, notably in regards to potential reproductive problems and with children who were introduced to the craft at an early age. Glass-blowers in Cairo said that they would retire when they died; Galilean glass-blowers would probably have retired out of physical necessity, when they could no longer see the glass they were working. This was certainly the case in the family of glass-blowers interviewed in Afghanistan by the Corning researchers. In the resulting film, the youngest glass-worker described how his father and grandfather "were crippled and blind when they died" (Corning: The Glassmakers of Herat).

One wonders why, with such a variety of physical ailments, anyone would have wanted to become a glass-worker in antiquity. The adverse physical effects would have been noticed, even if the life-spans were somewhat shorter than today. Indeed, in modern day India even the poorest in the population know that glass-working will "cut short" the life of a worker by ten to fifteen years (Burra 1995: 39). And glass-workers in the Near East have a hard time convincing their sons to follow in their footsteps because of such concerns. The strength of the tradition of passing the craft from father to son certainly played a significant role in antiquity. A 14th-century manuscript about Jerusalem illustrates this practice when describing the occupations of the servants of the Noble Sanctuary (Haram al-Sharif), which included glass-workers, each of whom was, as Engle notes, "cast into his role before he was born" (Engle 1984: 73). In antiquity one did not choose to be a glass-worker, but was rather born into the craft.

REFERENCES

Barazani, G.

1980a Health Hazards. *The Glass Art Society Journal* 1980: 46–48.

1980b Hazards of Glass Manufacturing. *Glass Studio* 12: 52–58.

1983 Protecting Your Health. *The Crafts Report* 9, no. 89: 4.

Bond, J. R.

1976 Occupational Health Hazards. *Glass Art* 4, no. 4: 26–29.

Bray, C., and Dobing, T.

1978 Safety. *British Artists in Glass Newsletter* 4: 16–26.

Burra, N.

1995 *Born to Work: Child Labour in India*. New Delhi: Oxford University.

The Corning Museum of Glass

1979 *The Glassmakers of Herat*. Benchmark Films, Briarcliff Manor, NY.

Engle, A.

1984 *1,000 Years of Glassmaking in Ancient Jerusalem*. Jerusalem: Phoenix.

Finkel, M.

2001 Heat Wave Dangers. Pp. 1–4. http://www.abcnews.go.com/sections/living/Healthology/heatwave_dangers.html/. July 25, 2001.

Fischer, A.

2001 *Integrating Anthropology in Pursuit of the Byzantine Period Glass Industry in Northern Israel*. Ph.D. Dissertation. UMI number: 3040159. Ann Arbor, MI: University Microfilms.

Fischer, A., and McCray, W. P.

1999 Glass Production Activities as Practised at Sepphoris, Israel (37 BC–AD 1516). *Journal of Archaeological Science* 26: 893–905.

Freestone, I., and Gorin-Rosen, Y.

1999 The Great Glass Slab at Bet She'arim, Israel: An Early Islamic Glassmaking Experiment? *Journal of Glass Studies* 41: 105–16.

Frisancho, A. R.

1996 *Human Adaptation and Accommodation*. Ann Arbor, MI: University of Michigan.

Gorin-Rosen, Y.

1993 Hadera, Bet Eli'ezer. *Excavations and Surveys in Israel* 13: 42–43.

Jossy, P.

1985 Reproductive Hazards in the Arts and Crafts. *Glass Studio* 46: 26–28.

Kazhdan, A.

1991 Glass, Production of. P. 853 in *The Oxford Dictionary of Byzantium*, vol. 2, eds. A. P. Kazhdan, A.-M. Talbot, A. Cutler, T. E. Gregory and N. P. Ševčenko. New York, NY: Oxford University.

Kerkvliet, B., and Dunham, B. S.

1997 Eye Protection for Glassworkers. *The Glass Art Society Journal* 1997: 97–100.

Kristel, D.

1981 Silicosis: Beyond Repair. *Glass Studio* 17: 39.

Lawrie, J.

1984 Safety Sense. *Craft Work: Scotland's Craft Magazine* 6: 28.

Layton, P.

1979 Eyes and Safety. *British Artists in Glass Newsletter* 9: 20–21.

McCann, M.

1992 *Artist Beware*. New York, NY: Lyons and Burford.

Rossol, M.

1990 *The Artist's Complete Health and Safety Guide*. New York, NY: Allworth.

1992 Glassmaking Health and Safety Update 1992. *The Glass Art Society Journal* 1992: 99–104.

Schwind, A. P.

1984 The Glassmakers of Early America. Pp. 158–89 in *The Craftsmen of Early America*, ed. I. M. G. Quimby. New York, NY: Norton.

Spencer, J. E.

1997 The Prevention and Care of Neck, Back, and Shoulder Pain Syndromes in the Glassworker. *The Glass Art Society Journal* 1997: 95–97.

Waller, J. A.

1985 *Safe Practices in the Arts & Crafts: A Studio Guide*. New York, NY: College Art Association of America.

Chapter 26

Two Terracotta Figurine Fragments from the Sepphoris Acropolis

by Melissa Aubin

In the course of the Sepphoris Regional Project's excavation of the Hellenistic fortress on the western summit of the Sepphoris acropolis, two fragments of separate terracotta figurines were recovered (85.3031.3x and 85.3100.1x), each of differing character and manufacture. One fragment displays the head and shoulders of an anthropomorphic subject, the other shows the right arm and right side of the torso of what appears to be a clothed masculine subject.

DESCRIPTIONS AND MANUFACTURE

Fragment 1, 85.3031.3x, Recovered in 1993

The fragment (fig. 1) is rather small, measuring 8.1 cm long, 4 cm wide at the head, 5.7 wide at shoulders, and 4 cm deep at the chest. All that remains of the figurine are the head, shoulders, and top half of the torso. Judging by the proportions of the figurine, if it were a standing figure, it would have been approximately 16 cm tall. The clay color is Munsell 10YR 7/3 (dull yellow orange).

The most detailed portion of the figurine is the front of the head, where facial features, head adornments, and hair are clearly displayed. The almond-shaped eyes were formed by incising the outline of the eye within two small lumps of clay that had been smoothed into the rest of the face. The result is a depressed outline of protruding eyes. No pupil, iris, or lashes are indicated. The eyes are not precisely symmetrical; the left eye is larger and its outside corner is slightly more down-turned than that of the right eye. The bridge of the nose emerges high on the face, level with the top of the outline of the eyes. The tip of the nose is broken off, though it appears that the nostrils were broad and the entire nose was pronounced. The mouth was formed in a similar fashion to the eyes. An incision as thick as the outline of the eye separates the lips, and the corners of the mouth are slightly upturned. The chin juts out slightly just below the lower lip. The ears are visible but not clearly defined at the level of the eyes. Each ear is marked only by an outline surrounding a gentle depression. The ears themselves do not protrude, but rather blend into an ill-defined border of the contour of the head. Except for the nose, the face is rather flat.

The forehead stretches up to a clearly defined band spanning the front of the head only. Just

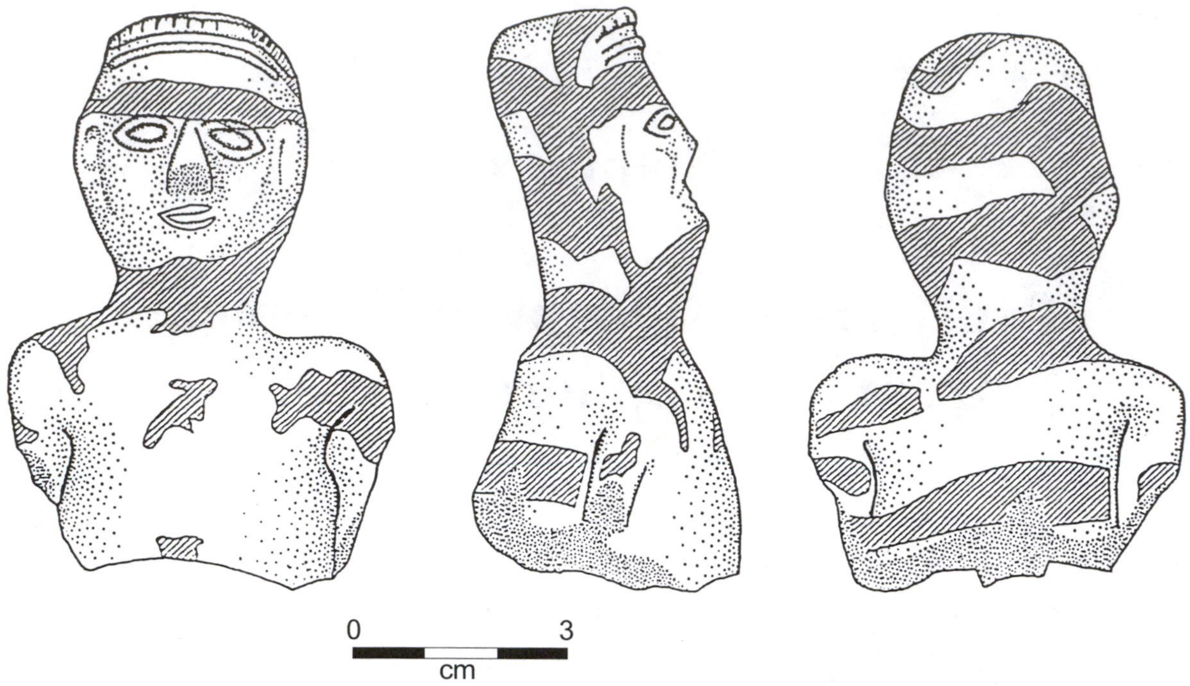

Fig. 1 *Sepphoris terracotta fragment 85.3031.3x.*

above the band, hair is represented by intermittent, short incisions paralleling the width of the band. Hair is not represented on the crown, sides or back of the head.

The head meets the shoulders at a thick, short neck. The chest itself resembles in the shape of a half oval. Although the shoulders are prominent, the arms are narrow and thin, and would have been vulnerable to breakage.

Aside from the headband, there is no clothing on the torso. The back of the figurine fragment displays no incised features. The most notable embellishment on the figurine is red striping (10R 4/6, red). Painted after firing, the striping (average width 0.8 cm) is visible on the top if the head, and on the front, back, and sides of the head and torso. Though the paint has survived more clearly on the back of the figurine, the striping seems to roughly spiral around the figure.

The three-stage manufacture of this piece is worthy of note. The head, torso, and arms were each formed separately and later joined. None of these components were mould-made: the irregularity, slight asymmetry, and uneven surface of the figurine all indicate that the parts were fashioned by hand. In the first step, the hollow torso was formed, with a 0.6 cm thick layer of clay forming the exterior. A hole was left at the center top of the torso so that the neck and head could be attached. In the second step, the solid head was formed atop a conical base of clay that was then inserted into the neck hole of the torso.[1] This conical clay base is visible from the inside of the broken torso. The joining of the head and torso is very smooth, so that no seam is apparent at the neck of the figurine. Limbs were attached in the third step. The arms were simply rolled coils of clay joined to the torso at the shoulder and then pinched along the surviving length of the arms to form flat, narrow limbs falling at the sides. The face was incised with a narrow, pointed tool to form the eyes, headband, mouth, and ears. The regularity of the pattern in the representation of the hair indicates that this feature was incised with a comb.

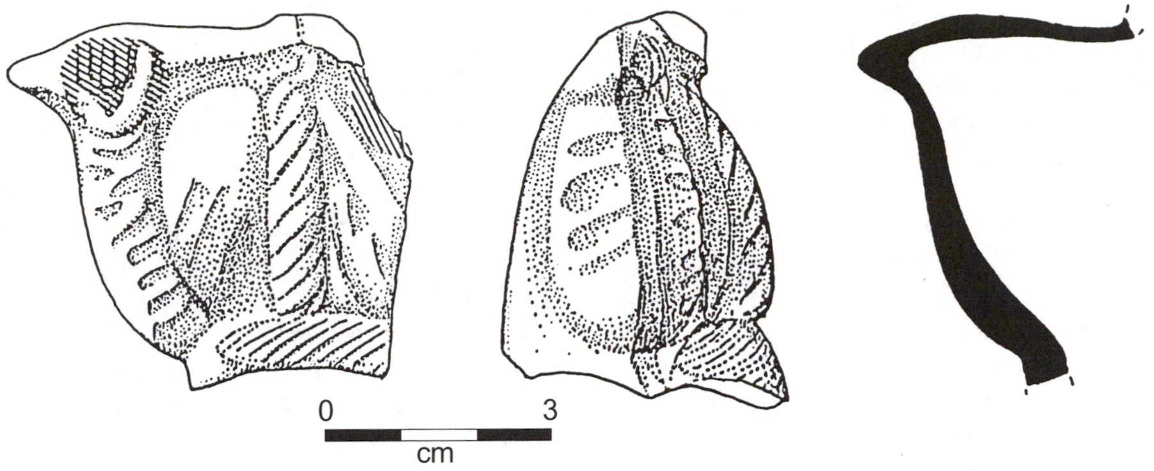

Fig. 2 Sepphoris terracotta fragment 85.3100.1x.

Fragment 2, 85.3100.1x, Recovered in 1994

The second fragment (fig. 2) measures 4 cm high and 5 cm wide, with a depth of 3 cm. Although it only survives as a fragment, it is clear that its production and appearance differ greatly from Fragment 1. The clay color is slightly more orange (5YR 7/4, dull orange). The fragment depicts the right side of a torso and the right arm of a masculine subject. The figure is clothed with a garment covering the torso and arm. Folds of a long-sleeved garment are apparent on the front of the arm. There are also shallow folds on the back of the arm, though the arm itself is not defined at the back, and there is no other decoration on the back of the fragment. There appears to be a second, short-sleeved garment, with draping folds below the neck, over the top of the long-sleeved garment. One thick cord surrounds the waist and another extends from the right shoulder to the waist. The arm is raised up at the elbow, carrying some sort of tool or other object that rests on the right shoulder. The hand encloses the tool so that the lower palm, fingers, and thumb are visible.

Traces of red paint, likely red ochre (10R 4/8, red), remain in the depressions at the hand and around the neck. The coroplast selected a plastic clay, porous enough so that moisture easily evaporated from it, and vitreous enough to harden in firing, with sufficient inert matter to mitigate the shrinkage that occurs during drying and firing.

This fragment was certainly part of a larger, mould-made figurine. Thumbprints are still visible inside the hollow figurine in places where the coroplast pressed the flat (0.3 cm thick) sheets of clay against each mould, one for the front of the figurine, and another for the back. After placing the clay in the moulds, the two sides of the figurine were pressed together, and the edges were scored and brushed with slip.[2] The spot where the two halves were joined is still visible; here, a flat tool smoothed any irregularities in the seam, leaving a 0.3 cm mark along the border where the moulds met. No projections were attached to the fragment after the moulds were removed, though it appears that there were minor modifications. The coroplast added definition to the hand by clearly incising the outline of the fingers and to the waist cord by adding incised diagonal lines, perhaps where the clay had not been fully depressed into the mould.

CONTEXT

Both fragments of figurines were discovered in the course of excavating the remains of a fortress on the western summit of the Sepphoris acropolis. Fragment 1 was recovered in 1993 from a soil locus (85.3031) within the stratigraphic level known as Stratum VII/Phase 2, subphase A: "Seleucid" (ca. 200–150 B.C.E.).[3] This locus was located over bedrock at the base of one of the walls of the fortress (85.3052), and thus can be associated with the construction or earliest periods of the use of the fortress (elevation 284.08 m above sea level; 1.48 m below ground level). One should note that it is certainly possible that the figurine pre-dates this stratum. Persian and Iron Age period pottery fragments have been excavated from the cracks in the bedrock, indicating ephemeral occupation of the area before the construction of the fortress. So it is conceivable that the figurine, which was also recovered just above bedrock, was dropped there in an earlier period and somehow not displaced during the construction of the fortress wall. Other materials recovered from the same locus include a metal fibula and fragments of pottery dating from the Persian and Early Hellenistic periods.

The second fragment was recovered in 1994 during the excavation of the E–W balk separating excavation squares G and H within the fortress. The fragment was discovered at an elevation of 284.68 m above sea level, 1.02 m below ground level, along the uppermost remaining course of wall 85.3118. This context belongs to the level known as Stratum VI/ Phase 1: Early Roman sub-phase C, 50/70–135 C.E., initiated by the destruction of the upper courses of the walls and in-filling of the fortress during the early Roman period. The massive fill generally consists of loose rubble with scattered spots of compacted white and yellowish soil. It contained many cobbles, many bones, very often with butcher marks,[4] and a very large quantity of pottery, mostly plain wares. Interestingly, the pottery sherds could very rarely be reconstructed into whole vessels, so the vessels were not destroyed on the spot where their remains have been found. The orientation of sherds was not uniform; they were not found spread out horizontally on a surface or similar architectural features. All these features, including a considerable amount of faunal remains, suggest that the fill largely consisted of domestic waste that was intentionally brought in, in order to fill and level the whole area without regard to any of the existing architecture. Thus, Figurine Fragment 2 was brought to the spot from a place elsewhere in the city, and it is difficult to determine its context of use.

Though the figurine fragments were broken, it is clear that neither findspot was a *favissa*. The figurines were likely not redeposited from disturbed *favissae*, since no sanctuary or temple has been found in the area. It is also clear that neither fragment belonged to a domestic under-floor deposit, nor does it appear to be production waste. It is possible that either fragment served secular or sacred purposes, but there is unfortunately no evidence to indicate specifically the figurines' uses.[5]

Although both of these figurine fragments were recovered in close proximity to one another, the contexts from which they were recovered are separated by a time span of 150–200 years. The very coarse quality of Fragment 1, recovered from a clearly Hellenistic stratum, is markedly less skillfully produced than Fragment 2, which may date as late as the early Roman period. Fragment 1 bears no obvious resemblance to the much finer terracotta figurines exported from Alexandria in the Hellenistic period, nor does it display the workmanship of the finer terracottas discovered from *favissae*, cemeteries and other deposits along the Israeli and Phoenician coast (Lunand 1944–45; Riis 1979; Stern 1978; 1982a; Pritchard 1975; Rosenthal-Hegginbottom 1995; Linder 1973; Culican 1969; 1976; Messika 1996; 1997; Chéhab 1951–52). The closest parallel in form appears to be a terracotta head from the coastal site Tel Michal, dated to the Persian period (5th–4th centuries B.C.E.), though it should be noted that this piece is not painted (Stern 1982b: 174, photo 295:2).[6] Another comparandum appears in the finds from Makmish (Avigad 1958: 90–96, pl. 11:D). Avigad has suggested that the style of this head is Cypriot influenced (Avigad 1958: 94). Given the fact that Fragment 1 is painted with red striping, a motif that was current in Cyprus (see, e.g., Karageorghis 1995: pl. IV:6–7), it is possible to suggest that Cypriot style influenced the manufacture of Fragment 1, whether it was created in Cyprus or Palestine.

It is certainly possible that this figurine was made locally, since it lacks the refined artistry of urban workshops. In addition, it exhibits a technique of construction that had existed in Palestine since the sixth century (Negbi 1966: 8, n. 58). In comparison to other published Hellenistic terracotta figurines from inland Syro-Palestine, Fragment 1 exhibits low quality (McNicoll et al. 1982: pl. 15a; Derfler 1981; Iliffe 1934; Crowfoot et al. 1957: 83–84), though another unsophisticated figurine at Tel Anafa might attest to local production of figurines elsewhere in Northern Israel.[7] Nonetheless, we cannot reject the possibility that it was brought in from an outside source, such as Cyprus[8] or elsewhere in the eastern Mediterranean, since the area of the Bet Netofa valley would have hosted commercial and military traffic during the Hellenistic period and before (Weiss and Netzer 1996: 21–28). Negbi has ably shown that one cannot determine place of production based on stylistic grounds alone, since several of the so-called "western" types she has studied originate in Syro-Palestine (Negbi 1966; see also Shenhav 1966).

Fragment 2, however, does exhibit more advanced workmanship, and if it was indeed produced in the early Roman period, it dates to a time of increased international traffic in the Lower Galilee, when imported pottery and lamps stand (albeit in a minority) alongside fine locally made goods. Without provenience testing, we should not hasten to presume that Fragment 2 is necessarily an import, since Sepphoris would have provided a hospitable environment for producing crafts that were suitable for distribution within the city and region. To be sure, the Syro-Palestine region produced its own terracotta figurines in the Roman period, including provincial reinterpretations of western types. Nonetheless, the consanguinity of the clothing indicated on Fragment 2 with broader Greco-Roman representations of clothed figurines militates against any determinations of provenance on stylistic grounds alone (see Weber 1986; another comparandum appears in the finds from Makmish: Avigad 1958: pl. 11:D).[9]

NOTES

1 An earlier version of this type of head attachment is clearly apparent at Beit Mirsim (Albright 1941–43: 154, pl. B:6).

2 On the manufacture of terracotta figurines, see Uhlenbrock 1990: 89–92.

3 Jürgen Zangenberg and Melissa Aubin, "The Stratigraphy of the Late Hellenistic Fortress on the Acropolis of Sepphoris, Preliminary Notes on Four Seasons of Excavation," forthcoming.

4 I am indebted to Dr. Bill Grantham for providing us with preliminary results of his investigations.

5 Bronze figurines, one depicting Pan and another depicting Prometheus, have also been recovered from later contexts (ca. 2nd–3rd centuries C.E.), and seem to have served decorative, rather than votive, purposes (Nagy et al. 1996: 171–72, cat. nos. 17 and 18).

6 In addition, another earlier, unpainted head resembles the head of Fragment 1, inasmuch as the headband and eyes are similar; see Crowfoot et al. 1957: pl. XI:2. Avigad has suggested that the style of this head is Cypriot influenced.

7 See Weinberg 1971: 105, pl. 19:D–E; but see also the better crafted early Hellenistic heads from Tel Anafa in Weinberg 1973: 116, pl. 30:C–D.

8 Negbi 1966: 8 also indicates that the mode of production exhibited in Fragment 1 is evidenced in 6th-century B.C.E. Cyprus. Figurines painted with red striping are certainly attested during that period.

9 See also the production of terracottas in first- and second-century Petra (Parr 1993; Parlasca 1993; Horsfield and Horsfield 1941).

REFERENCES

Albright, W. F.
1941–1943 *The Excavation of Tell Beit Mirsim III, The Iron Age*. Annual of the American Schools of Oriental Research 21–22. Cambridge, MA: American Schools of Oriental Research.

Avigad, N.
1958 Excavations at Makmish 1960. Preliminary Report. *Israel Exploration Journal* 11: 90–96.

Chéhab, M. H.
1951–1952 Les Terres cuites de Kharayeb: Texte. *Bulletin du Musée de Beyrouth* X: 5–184
1953–1954 Les Terres cuites de Kharayeb: Planches. *Bulletin du Musée de Beyrouth* XI: v–xxviii.

Crowfoot, J. W.; Crowfoot, G. M.; and Kenyon, K. M.
1957 *Samaria Sebaste III: The Objects from Samaria*. London: Palestine Exploration Fund.

Culican, W.

1969 Dea Tyria Gravida. *Australian Journal of Biblical Archaeology* 2: 35–50.

1976 A Votive Model from the Sea. *Palestine Exploration Quarterly* 108: 119–23.

Derfler, S.

1981 A Terracotta Figurine form the Hellenistic Temple at Tel Beer-Sheba. *Israel Exploration Journal* 31: 97–99.

Horsfield, G., and Horsfield, A.

1941 Sela Petra, the Rock of Edom and Nabatene: The Finds. *Quarterly of the Department of Antiquities in Palestine* 9: 105–206.

Iliffe, J. H.

1934 A Nude Terra Cotta Statuette of Aphrodite. *Quarterly of the Department of Antiquities in Palestine* 3: 106–11.

Karageorghis, V.

1995 *The Coroplastic Art of Ancient Cyprus IV: The Cypro-Archaic Period. Small Male Figurines.* Nicosia: Imprinta.

Linder, E.

1973 A Cargo of Phoenicio-Punic Figurines. *Archaeology* 26: 182–87.

Lunand, M.

1944 –1945 Les sculptures de la favissa du temple d'Amrit. *Bulletin du Musée de Beyrouth* VII: 99–107.

McNicoll, A.; Smith, R. H.; and Hennessy, B.

1982 *Pella in Jordan I: Plates and Illustrations.* Canberra: Australian National Gallery.

Messika, N.

1996 The Terracotta Figurines form the Persian and Hellenistic Periods in 'Akko. Unpublished M.A. Thesis, Hebrew University, Jerusalem.

1997 Excavation of the Courthouse Site at 'Akko: The Hellenistic Terracotta Figurines from Areas TB and TC. *'Atiqot (English Series)* 31: 121–28

Nagy, R. M.; Meyers, C.; Meyers, E.; and Weiss, Z.

1996 *Sepphoris of Galilee. Crosscurrents of Culture.* Winona Lake, IN: Eisenbrauns.

Negbi, O.

1966 A Deposit of Terracottas and Statuettes from Tel Sippor. *'Atiqot (English Series)* 6: 1–22.

Parlasca, I.

1993 Terrakotten aus Petra: Ein neues Kapitel nabatäischer Archäologie. Pp. 87–105 in *Petra and the Caravan Cities*, ed. F. Zayadine. Amman: Department of Antiquities.

Parr, P. J.

1993 A Commentary of the Terracotta Figurines from the British Excavations at Petra, 1958–64. Pp. 77–86 in *Petra and the Caravan Cities*, ed. F. Zayadine. Amman: Department of Antiquities.

Pritchard, J. B.

1975 *Sarepta: A Preliminary Report on the Iron Age.* Philadelphia, PA: University Museum, University of Pennsylvania.

Riis, P. J.

1979 *Sukas VI: The Graeco-Roman Phoenician Cemetery and Sanctuary at the Southern Harbour.* Copenhagen: Munksgaard.

Rosental-Heginbottom, R.

1995 Terracottas from the Hellenistic Period. Pp. 456–58 in *Excavations at Dor: Final Reports*, Vol. 1B, *Areas A and C: The Finds*, ed. E. Stern. Qedem Reports 2. Jerusalem: Institute of Archaeology, Hebrew University of Jerusalem.

Shenhav, H.

1966 Mineralogical Analysis of Terracottas from Tel Sippor. *'Atiqot (English Series)* 6: 23–24.

Stern, E.

1978 *Excavations at Tel Mevorakh 1970–1976.* Vol. 1: *From the Iron Age to the Roman Period.* Qedem 9. Jerusalem: Institute of Archaeology, Hebrew University of Jerusalem.

1982a A Favissa of a Phoenician Sanctuary from Tel Dor. *Journal of Jewish Studies* 33: 35–54.

1982b *Material Culture of the Land of the Bible in the Persian Period 538–332 BC.* Warminster: Aris and Phillips.

Weber, T.

1986 A Group of Roman Terracotta Appliques from Abila of the Decapolis. *Annual of the Department of Antiquities of Jordan* 30: 211–17.

Uhlenbrock, J. P. (ed.)

1990 *Hellenistic Alexandria, The Coroplast's Art.* New Paltz, NY: College Art Gallery, The College at New Paltz, SUNY.

Weinberg, S. S.

1971 Tel Anafa: The Hellenistic Town. *Israel Exploration Journal* 21: 87–107.

1973 Tel Anafa. *Israel Exploration Journal* 23: 113–17.

Weiss, Z., and Netzer, E.

1996 Hellenistic and Roman Sepphoris: The Archaeological Evidence. Pp. 21–28 in *Sepphoris in Galilee: Crosscurrents of Culture*, eds. R. Nagy, C. Meyers, E. Meyers and Z. Weiss. Winona Lake, IN: Eisenbrauns.

Chapter 27

The Archaeology of Bethsaida and the Historical Jesus Quest

by Rami Arav

Bethsaida presents perhaps the best example of a New Testament town in which, on one hand, most scholars believe Jesus had been active, and which, on the other hand, is accessible to archaeological investigation. According to the New Testament, three apostles were born there, Peter, Andrew and Philip, and it was at Bethsaida that Jesus performed his mighty works (Appold 1995; Kuhn 1995; Rousseau 1995). Byzantine traditions add to this list two more apostles, James and John, the sons of the fisherman Zebedai. Some other traditions attribute three more apostles to this number, which means that between three to eight apostles were born in one small place (Arav 1999b: 79–80).

Josephus mentions Bethsaida more often than he mentions the Pharisees. He asserts that the place was situated near the Jordan River estuary and in lower Gaulanitis and that Philip, the son of Herod the Great, elevated it to the status of a city and "named it after Julia, the emperor's daughter" (*Ant.* 8:28). Philip's coins indicate that this change was made in 29/30 C.E. and that Julia, who gave her name to the city, was no other but Livia-Julia, the wife of Augustus and the mother of Tiberius, the reigning Emperor in that year. Julia-Livia died in 29 (January) C.E., and the renaming of the place can be explained as a part of Philip's endeavor to participate in the Roman imperial cult.[1] Jewish and Roman sources indicate that the place still existed during the Late Roman period. It is from the 4th century C.E. on that the information about the town is perplexing and misleading. It seems that the town was lost during this period (Freund 1995).

Modern scholarship, beginning in the 19th century, attempted to locate the site without much success. A few contenders were proposed for Bethsaida. One of them was e-Tell, a very large mound on the Sea of Galilee, situated about 1.5 km from the seashores, and the second one was el-Araj, a shallow ruin at the estuary of the Jordan River. Probes and surveys carried out in 1987 yielded Hellenistic and early Roman remains only in e-Tell, while the other contenders yielded only Late Roman and Byzantine remains.[2] Ground penetration radar tests carried out in the stretch from the Sea of Galilee through the ruins of el-Araj confirm what archaeological sounding revealed: that el-Araj consists of one occupation level only.[3] This level has been dated to the Byzantine period. The ground below the Byzantine

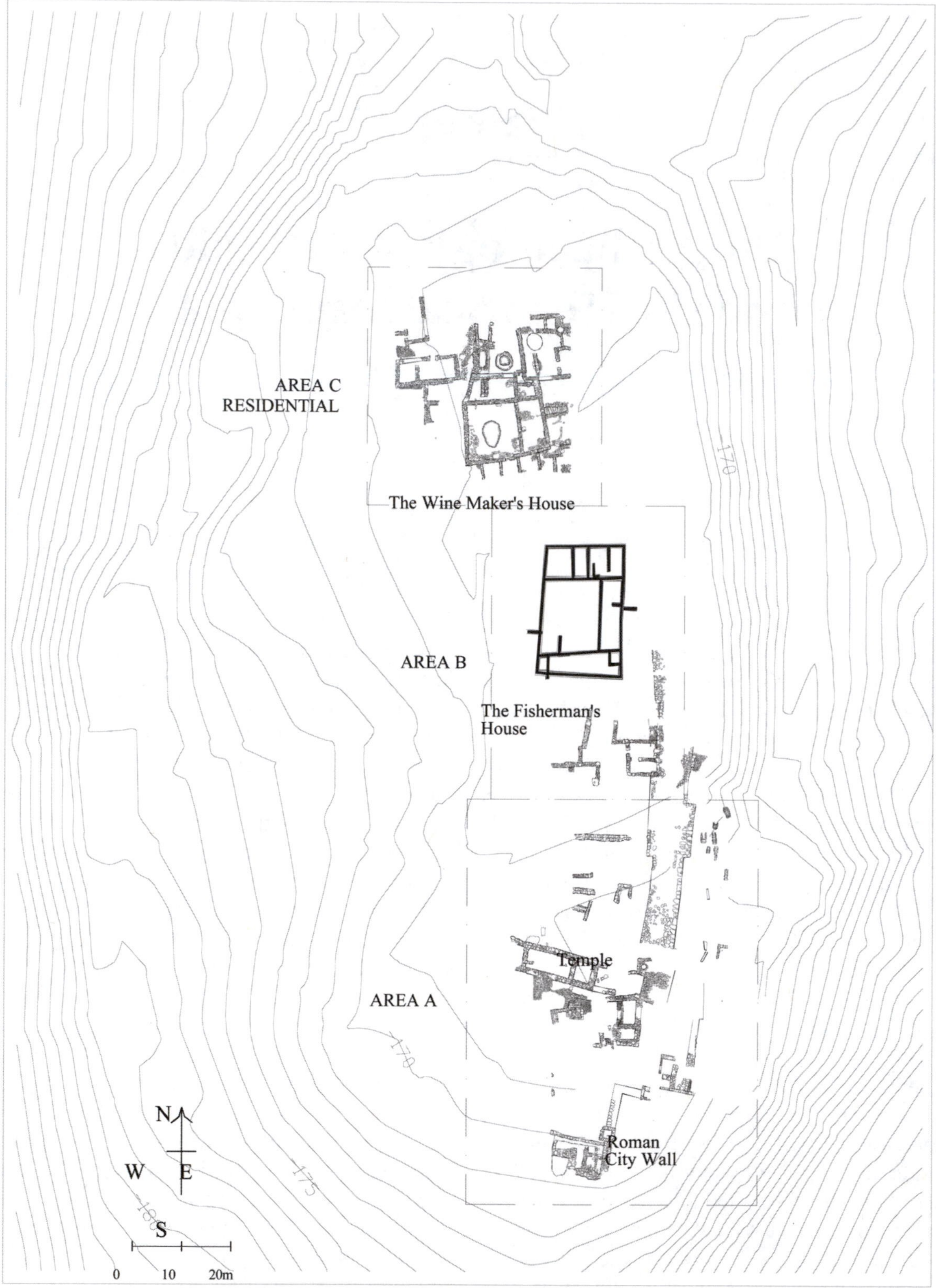

Fig. 1 *Map of Bethsaida.*

level was found to be beach sedimentary layers with no remains of inhabitation. Further geological and geomorphological research carried out on the plain of Bethsaida explains what had happened to the plain in the past 15,000 years: the plain was created by silt that was shifted from the banks of the Jordan River gorge and, at times of geological catastrophes, the shift of silt increased (Shroder and Inbar 1995; Shroder et al. 1999). The fisherman settlement of the third century C.E. was too far away from the body of water it needed to sustain its livelihood and eventually was deserted for an alternative site close to the water. This is not an unusual phenomenon in the history of settlements.

Excavations at e-Tell, now identified as Bethsaida, began in 1988 and still continue (2007). The finds help to enhance our understanding of the environment of Jesus and elucidate the physical and social circumstances of the society surrounding Jesus.[4]

THE ARCHAEOLOGICAL DISCOVERIES

Archaeological research discovered that the city of Bethsaida (fig. 1) was founded in the tenth century B.C.E. on a basalt extension that descended from the lava flow of the Golan Heights. The lava flow created strong foundations for construction and provided extensive construction material for the settlers. However, large boulders and uneven terrain compelled the founders to carry out large-scale earthworks, which filled the gaps and created an even plateau on which the city was constructed. The city thrived during the Iron Age (Arav 1995; 1999a). The fortifications of the city are almost without parallels. They consisted of two city walls, two gates and a spacious plaza extending between the gates. The outer city wall measures 2–3 m wide and the inner 6–8 m. The city gate is the largest of its kind ever discovered. The plaza was flanked by a palace known in the Aramean-Assyrian architecture as Bit Hilani (Arav and Bernett 1997; 2000). Most probably Bethsaida was the capital of the petty kingdom of Geshur, which is mentioned often in the Old Testament (Kokhavi 1996).

The city was destroyed several times during the Iron Age. It was first destroyed in the first half of the ninth century B.C.E., perhaps by the Aramean king Hazael of Damascus who consolidated, by means of conquest and annexation, the Aramean petty kingdoms in southern Syria. A much more severe destruction occurred during the end of the eighth century B.C.E. and was observed at several places at Bethsaida. It is undoubtedly the result of the campaign of the Assyrian king Tiglath Pileser III in this area in 732 B.C.E. (Tadmor 1994: 232–82). The conquest of the town resulted in the destruction of the Iron Age city gate, which created a shallow mound on the flat surface of the upper city. This mound was prominent enough in the first century C.E. to arrange it as a platform on which a temple was built. The habitation at Bethsaida did not cease in the period between the Iron Age and the Hellenistic period, as small finds such as cylinder seals and stamps dating from the Persian period testify. No meaningful structures, however, were added to the existing buildings.

Ironically, a major change occurred after the conquest of Alexander the Great, when central government seemed to be by far more imposing and tighter than the ethnical freedom that nations maintained during the Persian period. It is reasonable to think that the new markets in Greece and Rome served as catalysts for the primary mercantile economy of the Phoenician cities, which rapidly seized the new commercial opportunities (Markoe 2000: 63–67). At Bethsaida, a larger influx of new settlers arrived, presumably from the thriving Phoenician coast, in a movement that can be interpreted as expansion of their hinterland. The new settlers rebuilt the ruins and were engaged in trade with the coastal cities. Pollen analysis shows that flax was becoming a major growth industry and it is reasonable to assume that linen garments were traded with the coast for fine wares and other luxury items (Schoenwetter and Geyer 2000).

The architecture of Bethsaida in this period demonstrates a major change from the Iron Age city. Although the Iron Age city wall still existed and rose to a considerable level and was used as a back wall for the Hellenistic private homes, the Hellenistic city bears rural features, as opposed to the urban features of previous periods. It is interesting to note that all through the Hellenistic and Roman periods these features remain the same, in spite

Fig. 2 *Reconstruction of a house in Area B – the "Fisherman's House."*

Fig. 3 *An iron fish hook.*

of the population change. On top of the Iron Age public buildings, a cluster of private rural houses was built. The new houses made use of the old walls that were still protruding above the ground. The walls of the new houses were thinner, generally 70 cm wide, as opposed to wall widths between 1.5 and 2.5 m during the Iron Age. Segments of old structures and particularly the old palace in the Bit Hilani style were reinhabited. Parts of the city wall were rebuilt, as is indicated in the southern section of Area A. It was, however, not to the same extent and width as the Iron Age city wall.

It seems that the settlement spread from the northern city walls to the south within these centuries. During the third century B.C.E., densely populated areas existed next to the northern city walls, but by the first century C.E. and later there was very little activity near the northern city wall, while more activity was concentrated towards the southern sections of the mound.

Some of the houses dating from the Hellenistic and Early Roman periods were built in the style of courtyard houses (figs. 2–8). This type of house is built around a large open courtyard. The courtyard is flanked by a kitchen to the east and a dining room (triclinium?) and residences in the north. This type of house is typical for Mediterranean civilizations and is found almost everywhere and in all periods (Robertson 1969: 297–321; Arav 1989). The courtyards were developed into an elaborate atrium in the Greek and the Roman world, although at Bethsaida we do not observe this development. The houses remain humble, and the courtyards were not adorned with columns, fountains, mosaic or marble floors as lavish dwellings elsewhere were, nor did Bethsaida homes have stucco and other decorations, which were present in rural homes at Tel Anafa, north of Bethsaida. The impression one gets from the ruins of the Hellenistic-Early Roman periods is similar to that of the humble houses of Gamala and Capernaum of the first centuries B.C.E.–C.E. Pig bones, large numbers of Tyrian and other Phoenician coins, and fine wares from the Phoenician coast indicate that the population either originated from these areas or kept close contact with the cities there through the third and second centuries B.C.E.

A major change in the population can be observed in the period following the conquest of Alexander Jannaeus in 84 B.C.E. (fig. 9). A drop in Phoenician coins versus a rise in Hasmonean coins, together with pottery produced in Kefar Hanania and Kefar Shikhin and limestone vessels, indicate that the new inhabitants were Jewish. The conquest of Alexander Jannaeus caused a change in the ethnicity of the population from Phoenician to Jewish. How exactly this change was achieved is a matter for further study. Was it a conversion of the

Fig. 4 A room in the "Roman House" in Area B. Note that there is no paving on the floor.

Fig. 5 A "Herodian" oil lamp from the "Roman House" in Area B.

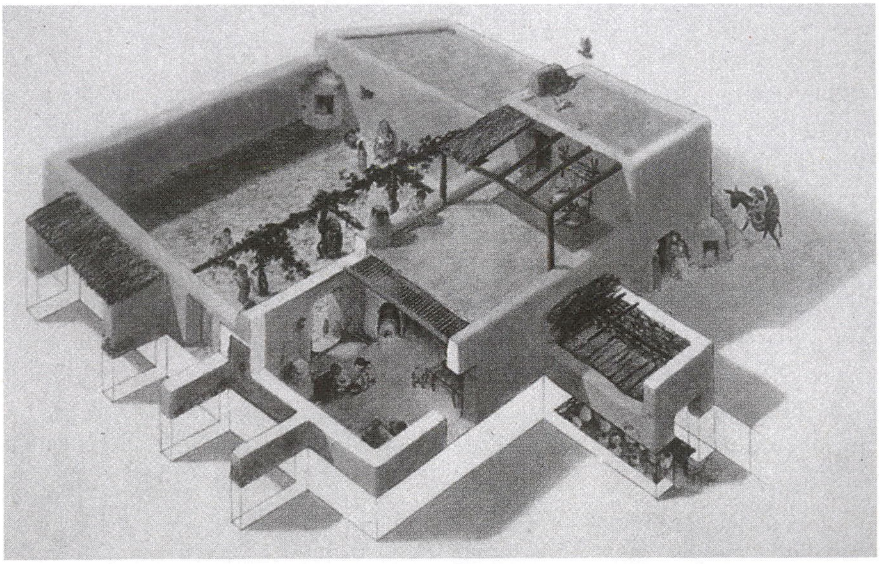

Fig. 6 Reconstruction of a house in Area C – the "Wine Maker's House."

Fig. 7 *A wine cellar in the "Wine Maker's House."*

Fig. 8 *A Rhodian wine jar.*

Phoenician population to Judaism, or the arrival of Jewish veterans and settlers who replaced the local population? At present this is unclear.

This picture did not last long. Two decades later, the Romans under Pompey the Great invaded Judea, captured Jerusalem in 63 B.C.E., and put an end to the independence of the Hasmonean kingdom (Berlin 1997). The new settlement wave Pompey brought to the area, in which the Ithureans got back Gaulanitis, resulted in a short-term decline of the Jewish population of Bethsaida. This can be discerned from the absence of pottery and coins from the period following Pompey's conquest until the accession to power of Herod the Great in 37 B.C.E. Jewish coins reoccur during the reign of Herod the Great and indicate the return of the Jewish population. Herod was granted back the territories of the Gaulanitis, Hauranitis and Batanea from Augustus and resettled the Jewish population therein. No change in habitation occurred until the geological catastrophes of the mid-third century C.E., which pushed the northern shores of the Sea of Galilee farther south and caused the fishermen to desert their homes on the ancient mound and to move to a new location closer to the shoreline. E-Tell – Bethsaida is the village into which the apostles were born and where Jesus visited and performed his "mighty works."

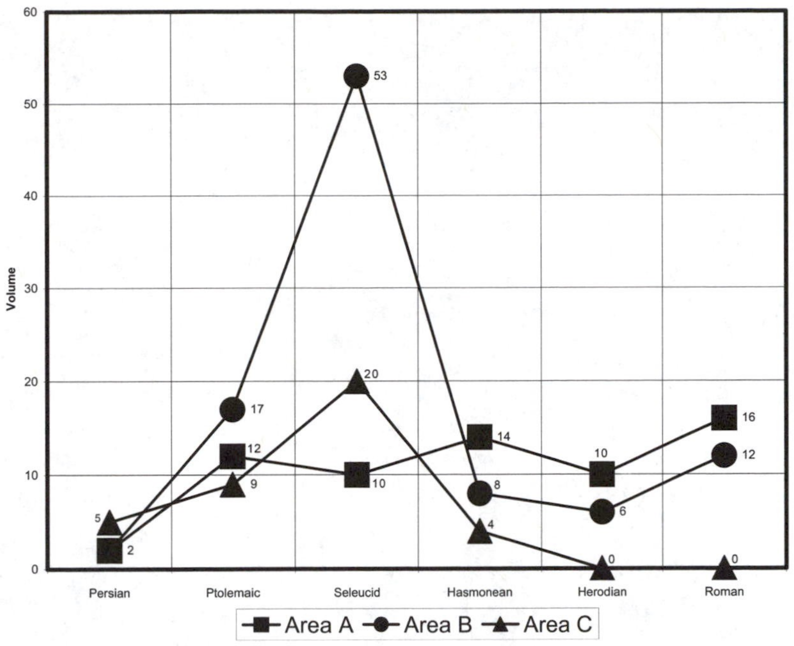

Fig. 9 *Bethsaida coin chart.*

THE ROMAN TEMPLE

Analysis of the historical, archaeological, and numismatic accounts leads to the conclusion that Bethsaida was elevated to the status of a Greek city-state, a "polis," during the year 29/30 C.E., just a few months after hearing the news that Julia-Livia had died (January 29). Analogy with other foundations that bore the emperor's name, or that of members of his family, indicates that the naming or renaming of a city was only one of the things done by client kings and local rulers in an effort to participate in the Roman imperial cult. This interesting cult developed, from its inception, features very similar to traditional religion. Lacking only a mythological past, it was developed almost instantly into a large-scale project from the time when Octavian was given the title Augustus (27 B.C.E.). Within time the cult was observed as a means to demonstrate loyalty to the emperor. The cult developed a special calendar, in which a series of practices and annual festivals were celebrated. The most important event was New Year's Eve, which was the birthday of the Emperor, on September 23rd. The last celebration of the year was Livia-Julia's adopted birthday, September 21 (she was not born on this day), leaving one day, September 22nd, off for preparations for the New Year's Eve (recorded only in Pergamon). The celebrations took place at institutions and installations built for this purpose. Well-to-do benefactors and local rulers (who could afford it) erected temples and facilities that were used in the gathering of worshippers to celebrate musical, drama, and athletic competitions. Such constructions were theaters, amphitheaters, stadia, and hippodromes. This is how we should interpret the lavish institutions Herod the Great erected in Sebaste and Caesarea Maritima. Lesser benefactors were happy with one or two installations, or, at least, with an altar in an existing temple. The temples would vary from lavishly decorated huge temples, clad in marble and adorned with statues, to a modest distyle temple built of local materials.[5]

While his father was able to erect magnificent edifices to facilitate the imperial cult, Philip Herod was perhaps more financially limited and could not afford such lavish establishments. The temple that Philip built at Bethsaida was so modest, so small, and so severely destroyed in the Byzantine period that without the testimony of Josephus regarding the elevation of the village to a "polis" and the renaming of the place, it would have been almost

Fig. 10 *Aerial photograph of Area A. Note the remains of the temple in the center of the picture.*

impossible to reconstruct it.[6] The physical evidence of the temple is very scarce and circumstantial (fig. 10).[7] No inscriptions were found and even the ground plan of the building is badly preserved. However, through evidence retrieved from excavation, along with the testimony of Josephus, we may likely conclude that the building excavated at the summit of the mound is the temple, although we are still in the process of study. The main arguments and the initial results of this research are briefly presented as follows:

1. A rectangular building was discovered on the highest place of the mound on top of a shallow mound, which covered the ruins of the Iron Age monumental city gate. There was no podium to this temple, but a retaining wall, which was built in the Iron Age, served to create a large elevated infrastructure for the temple.
2. The temple presents an oblong building (20 × 6 m), which is oriented east–west. Two antae in the east create a porch. Foundation remains of a column base were discerned between the antae. The threshold to the building was removed from its original location. The "naos" was an empty rectangular room. An opening in the west wall led to another porch, which was interpreted as an adyton. The walls of this building are of unusual width and construction. They average 1 m in width and are of good masonry, as opposed to 0.7 m-wide walls for a regular house from this period.
3. No dressed stones were found in the walls of this building, although the only dressed stones found at Bethsaida were found around this building, mostly reused in Bedouin tombs.
4. Four decorated stones were the only remains of this building, and they were all found in a secondary context. One was a lintel block decorated with a meander flanked by two rosettes. Two other fragments show floral motifs in scrolls, and another large slab also depicts a floral motif (figs. 11–12).

Fig. 11 *Frieze of floral scroll decoration from Area A.*

Fig. 12 *Frieze of floral scroll decoration from Chorazim. Note the similarity to the Bethsaida frieze.*

5. The floor of the building was completely looted, but remnants of the infrastructure were discovered. They consist of beaten earth embedded with small shards of pottery and small pebbles (fig. 13).
6. The finds inside and in close vicinity of the building were also remarkable and indicate special religious purposes. Among these were two bronze incense shovels of a type associated with religious ceremonies (fig. 14). A similar shovel was found by Yadin in the Cave of the Letters in 1960. It is particularly important to notice that the Cave of Letters shovel was found together with eighteen bronze vessels, which most likely formed a collection of religious objects, known also as "Instrumenta Sacra".[8] The objects included a *patera*, two bowls, and a number of jugs.
7. Several pits were discovered in the vicinity of the temple. In these pits, jugs similar to the jugs of the "Instrumenta Sacra" deposit in the Cave of Letters were found. It is possible that the jugs at Bethsaida were used in the service of the temple (fig. 15).
8. Five coins of Philip Herod were found in the vicinity of the temple. Three of them were minted in commemoration of the renaming of Bethsaida: perhaps not a coincidental discovery.
9. Female figurines were also discovered. One depicts a woman wearing curls and a veil, and the other figurine is a woman wearing a diadem over a tiara covered with a veil. Although these types of figurines are common in the Hellenistic-Roman world, they clearly indicate cultic practices and may be associated with the cult of Livia-Julia.
10. Several basalt pumice stones in the shape of a pyramid were found near the temple. These small objects recall large stone anchors and are usually interpreted as votive anchors. They could have been either given to the fishermen by the temple as a talisman or given to the temple by the fishermen as a gift (fig. 16).
11. Similarly, a clay stamp, pyramidal in shape was also recovered; it depicts a somewhat illegible scene that has no parallel in ancient art: the stamp shows one or two persons on a boat of the "hippos" type. A round object flanked by a semicircular object is at the top of the scene, and a reed plant is in front of the boat. Possibly this seal served as an amulet either given by the temple or given to the temple. The pyramidal shape associates it with the other votive anchors and indicates a similar purpose.
12. The Mishnah preserves a tradition that "foreign worship/idolatry" was practiced at Bethsaida (Mishna, *Aboda Zara* 3:7). Might this be the Roman imperial cult?
13. Although the evidence is circumstantial, one may add the reconstructed pediment that

Fig. 13 *The floor of the temple.*

Fig. 14 *Incense shovel from the temple area.*

Fig. 15 *A juglet from the* favissa *of the temple.*

Fig. 16 *A basalt votive anchor.*

Fig. 17 *The pediment from Chorazim. Note the floral decoration similar to the frieze in Bethsaida.*

was discovered in the Byzantine synagogue of Chorazim (fig. 17). The podium is 6 m long and depicts an eagle in three-dimensional Roman style. The eagle is seen with wide-open wings at the top of the gable (fig. 18; Hachlili 1988). Several characteristics suggest that this pediment was looted from the temple at Bethsaida: the fact that the depiction is three-dimensional and not in low relief would make it more plausibly Roman, rather than Byzantine, which was the date of the synagogue. Although eagles also occur in Jewish art, they are primarily a symbol of the Roman imperial cult. The width of the pediment fits perfectly the width of the temple at Bethsaida. Fragments of a similar pediment were discovered in the ruins of the synagogue of ed-Dikke, 3 km north of Bethsaida, and it is possible that these originated at Bethsaida as well.

14. Interestingly, the Byzantine synagogue at Chorazim presents floral-in-scrolls ornaments, carved in basalt stone, similar to the Bethsaida finds. These stones were likely transferred from Bethsaida to Chorazim. It is impossible to argue the opposite simply because there is no Byzantine level at Bethsaida.
15. Among the ornaments of Chorazim there is a depiction in basalt of a scene, which is very mutilated and is usually interpreted as a grape harvest. This scene can also be interpreted as a soldier bringing an offering to an altar. If this is correct, then it is obviously a Roman imperial cult scene.

Our assumption is that the Roman imperial temple at Bethsaida was dismantled and removed to be used in the construction of the synagogue at Chorazim. Such practice was very common in the Roman period and was done in private and public building alike, both Jewish and Roman.

Fig. 18 *The top of the Chorazim pediment. Note the Roman eagle.*

SOCIOLOGICAL ASPECTS

Although we observed a shift in population from Gentiles to Jewish during the first century C.E., trade and occupations perhaps did not change very much during the Hellenistic-Early Roman periods. The size of the population at Bethsaida during the time of Jesus is not yet fully clear. A common model of population estimation is 100 people per built acre. The site of Bethsaida, which extends over 20 acres, therefore would have been inhabited by 2000 people (Broshi 1984). However, it is clear from our research thus far that not all 20 acres were densely populated. An estimate of several hundred people during the time of Jesus would perhaps be closer to the truth.

Investigating the remains of fauna and flora, together with working tools found at the site, provides a wealth of information pertinent to the occupation and trade of the inhabitants of Bethsaida during the Hellenistic and Early Roman periods. The final statistics of the finds are not conclusive, but they may indicate that the inhabitants of Bethsaida were busy in more than one trade. The name Bethsaida means "fisherman's house." Artifacts discovered at the site show, indeed, that the occupation of the inhabitants was primarily fishing. Dozens of fishing net lead weights were found across the site, indicating that fishing was shared by all. Other implements found include a few basalt anchors, basalt and limestone line sinkers, and bronze and iron fish hooks. The discovery of an extremely rare fishhook that had not yet been curved and made ready for use indicates that there was also a small fishhook industry at the site, which supported the local fishermen. In addition, there were long bronze and iron needles to sew and repair the sails of boats. An interesting find was an anchor incised on a jar handle, which may indicate fishing activities.

Faunal remains do not indicate a maritime focus for obvious reasons. Fish bones are much more difficult to detect than those of large mammals. However, about eight percent of the entire corpus of bones discovered at the site was fish. Among the fish, it is interesting to note the presence of a large number of the non-Kosher catfish that are abundant in this area.

Animal husbandry was practiced at Bethsaida as well. Most of the livestock were bovines, horses, donkeys, and mules. Herding of sheep and goat was common, but to a lesser degree. About five percent of the bones collected were those of pigs. However, due to stratigraphical difficulties in most of the loci excavated, it seems that the pig bones belong to the pre-Hasmonean occupation, and the final site report will certainly reflect a critical analysis of the evidence.

Another occupation attested by archaeological remains is viticulture. A private house in Area C, the only one excavated entirely, yielded, in addition to fishing implements such as lead fishing net weights and boat anchors, three pruning hooks for grape harvesting and an unusual corbel roof cellar, which contained four jars and a casserole possibly indicating a wine cellar. Shards of Rhodian wine amphorae were discovered in almost all areas. However, only a single complete wine amphora was found on a fragmentary floor of a house in Area B. Whether the Rhodian wine amphorae arrived at Bethsaida with their original contents is uncertain, and their presence is still the subject of debate.

Another profession found at Bethsaida was textile manufacture. Garments were produced at Bethsaida from flax and wool, as indicated by a large number of flax pollen that dominated the round structure in Area A. A wool industry could be identified by the large number of spindle whorls that were discovered. Most were made of hard, dark stone and some were glass. Small pyramidal loom weights were found, as well, in Area A, close to the structure identified as a temple.

Olives were the main planting crops at Bethsaida, as testified by the large amount of olive pollen discovered all over the examined area. With the exception of one threshing stone, which could be used for grapes and olives alike, no remains of olive presses were discovered at the site. Usually, these jobs were carried out in the fields or in the groves. The groves and cultivated fields were evidently towards the east and the north side of the city, because of the presence of the remains of ancient agricultural terraces and lanes winding between the terraces.

Evidence of the growing of grain was also found at Bethsaida. Pollen research shows that barley was more prevalent than wheat in all areas examined. Remains of flour mills were found in the private houses, and public flour mills, powered by water from the Jordan River, were just at a short distance northwest of the mound. Such mills are still seen today. A segment of a round grinding water mill was discovered in a secondary use on the mound.

Tannery was another occupation practiced at the site. This was evidenced by tannery implements found in Area A. A large amount of cows, versus sheep and goats, were observed in the zooarchaeological record and probably provided the raw material for this craft.

The landscape of Bethsaida in the first century B.C.E. and the first century C.E. was different from that of today. Pollen analysis indicates that the trees around the site were oak and tamarisk. High grass, good for grazing animals, was also abundant.

BETHSAIDA AND HELLENISM

The finds at Bethsaida do not support the conclusion of a thoroughly Hellenistic presence at the site all through the Hellenistic and Roman periods. There are no remains of Hellenism reflected in the architecture of the houses, not one single Greek capital or any Hellenistic fashion, in the way it is present at the nearby site of Tel Anafa, and no mosaic floors. Hellenistic imports from the Phoenician coast, the Greek islands (especially Rhodes) and mainland Greece are numerous and appear up to the Hasmonean conquest, which may indicate a Jewish population. Among the few Hellenistic imports, most telling is an iron strigil normally used in baths and gymnasia, Rhodian wine amphorae and oil lamps, a small number of vases known as "Megarian" vessels, and fine-ware pottery. An architectural feature is the building proposed as a temple, noting the "instrumenta sacra" found associated with it. Although this building was a prominent one and was located at the highest point of the site, it seems that the structure was imposed by the Herodian dynasty and did not evolve from the local population. It is reasonable to expect a correlation between the capabilities of the local community and the public buildings that are erected. Certainly, a wealthy community can support elaborate public structures whereas a poor community would have difficulty doing so. At Bethsaida it seems that the discrepancy between the temple with its decorations and the rest of the rural settlement is great. The temple at Bethsaida was most probably endowed and imposed by the Herodians and was not erected by the local inhabitants.

It is reasonable, therefore, to assume that the ministry of Jesus took place at Bethsaida while the Roman imperial cult temple was erected. With a temple like that in the background, Jesus' address to the Gentiles is far better understood.

NOTES

1 Kindler was first to notice this after a long debate on the dating of this transition. Previously Schuerer proposed that the renaming took place between 4 B.C.E., the accession of Philip to power, and 2 B.C.E., the date when Julia, the daughter of Augustus, was banished. See detailed treatment on this issue in Kindler 1989 [Hebrew]. This idea was presented by Kindler in a conference on Herod at Haifa University on 9–10 April 1989. Kindler 1999: 245–49. See also Kuhn and Arav 1991; Strickert 1995.

2 The problem of the identification of the site was resolved in a series of probes in 1986–78 and the finds were published in Kuhn and Arav 1991.

3 The GPR tests were carried out by Dr. Harry Jol of the University of Wisconsin at Eau Claire. The results will be published in the forthcoming Bethsaida volumes.

4 For general descriptions of the excavations see Arav 1999a: 45–56.

5 I would like to thank M. Bernett for discussing this matter with me. See more detailed research on this topic in Bernett 2007.

6 The temple was first reported in Arav 1999a: 18–24.

7 Kuhn has studied the temple remains and the artifacts, and has concluded that the temple was built already in the Hellenistic period. This conclusion ignores the stratigraphy of the structure, which suggests that the temple utilized secondary earlier walls. See Kuhn 2000: 222–29.

8 See Siebert 1999. Incense shovels are only rarely depicted in Roman art. There is only one depiction I know of from North Africa (I would like to thank M. Bernett for bringing this to my attention). This is perhaps the reason why Siebert does not present an incense shovel in her study.

REFERENCES

Appold, M. L.

1995 The Mighty Works of Bethsaida: Witness of NT and Related Traditions. Pp. 229–42 in *Bethsaida: A City by the North Shore of the Sea of Galilee*, vol. 1, eds. R. Arav and R. A. Freund. The Bethsaida Excavations Project Reports and Contextual Studies 1. Kirksville, MO: Thomas Jefferson University.

Arav, R.

1989 *Hellenistic Palestine: Settlement Patterns and City Planning, 337–31 B.C.E.* British Archaeological Reports 485. London: Hadrian.

1995 Bethsaida Excavations: Preliminary Report 1987–1993. Pp. 3–63 in *Bethsaida: A City by the North Shore of the Sea of Galilee,* vol. 1, eds. R. Arav and R. A. Freund. The Bethsaida Excavations Project Reports and Contextual Studies 1. Kirksville, MO: Thomas Jefferson University.

1999a Bethsaida Excavations: Preliminary Report 1994–1996. Pp. 3–113 in *Bethsaida: A City by the North Shore of the Sea of Galilee,* vol. 2, eds. R. Arav and R. A. Freund. The Bethsaida Excavations Project Reports and Contextual Studies 2. Kirksville, MO: Truman State University.

1999b New Testament Archaeology and the Case of Bethsaida. Pp. 75–99 in *Das Ende der Tage und die Gegenwart des Heils: Begegnungen mit dem Neuen Testament und seiner Umwelt. Festschrift für Heinz-Wolfgang Kuhn zum 65. Geburtstag,* eds. M. Becker and W. Fenske. Leiden: Brill.

Arav, R., and Bernett, M.

1997 An Egyptian Figurine of Pataekos at Bethsaida. *Israel Exploration Journal* 47: 198–213.

2000 The Bit Hilani at Bethsaida: Its Place in Aramean/Neo-Hittite and Israelite Palace Architecture in the Iron Age II. *Israel Exploration Journal* 50: 47–81.

Berlin, A.

1997 Between Large Forces: Palestine in the Hellenistic Period. *Biblical Archaeologist* 60, no. 1: 2–51.

Bernett, M.

2007 *Der Kaiserkult in Judäa unter den Herodiern und Römern: Untersuchungen zur politischen und religiösen Geschichte Judäas von 30 v. bis 66 n. Chr.* Tübingen: Mohr Siebeck.

Broshi, M.

1984 The Land of Israel in the Middle Bronze Age II: Settlements and Population. *Cathedra* 31: 3–24.

Freund, R. A.

1995 The Search for Bethsaida in the Rabbinic Literature. Pp. 267–311 in *Bethsaida: A City by the North Shore of the Sea of Galilee,* vol. 1, eds. R. Arav and R. A. Freund. The Bethsaida Excavations Project Reports and Contextual Studies 1. Kirksville, MO: Thomas Jefferson University.

Hachlili, R.

1988 *Ancient Jewish Art and Archaeology in the Land of Israel.* Leiden: Brill.

Kindler, A.

1989 The Coins of the Tetrarch Philip and Bethsaida. *Cathedra for the History of Eretz Israel and Its Yishuv* 53.

1999 The Coins of the Tetrarch Philip and Bethsaida. Pp. 245–49 in *Bethsaida: A City by the North Shore of the Sea of Galilee,* vol. 2, eds. R. Arav and R. A. Freund. The Bethsaida Excavations Project Reports and Contextual Studies 2. Kirksville, MO: Truman State University.

Kokhavi, M.

1996 The Land of Geshur: History of a Region in the Biblical Period (Hebrew). *Eretz Israel* 25: 184–201.

Kuhn, H. W.

1995 Bethsaida in the Gospels: The Feeding Story in Luke 9 and the Q Saying in Luke 10. Pp. 243–56 in *Bethsaida: A City by the North Shore of the Sea of Galilee,* vol. 1, eds. R. Arav and R. A. Freund. The Bethsaida Excavations Project Reports and Contextual Studies 1. Kirksville, MO: Thomas Jefferson University.

2000 Jesu Hinwendung zu den Heiden im Markusevangelium im Verhältnis zu Jesu historischem Wirken in Bethsaida, mit einem Zwischenbericht zur Ausgrabung eines vermuteten heidnischen Tempels auf et-Tell (Betsaida). Pp. 204–40 in *Die Weite des Mysteriums: Christliche Idenitität im Dialog. Festschrift für Horst Bürkle*, eds. K. Kraemer and P. Ansgar. Freiburg: Herder.

Kuhn, H. W., and Arav, R.

1991 The Bethsaida Excavations: Historical and Archaeological Approaches. Pp. 77–106 in *The Future of Early Christianity: Essays in Honor of Helmut Koester*, ed. B. A. Pearson. Minneapolis, MN: Fortress.

Markoe, G. E.

2000 *Phoenicians*. Berkeley, CA: University of California.

Robertson, D. S.

1969 *Greek and Roman Architecture,* 2nd edition. Cambridge: Cambridge University Press.

Rousseau, J. J.

1995 The Healing of the Blind Man at Bethsaida. Pp. 257–66 in *Bethsaida: A City by the North Shore of the Sea of Galilee,* vol. 1, eds. R. Arav and R. A. Freund. The Bethsaida Excavations Project Reports and Contextual Studies 1. Kirksville, MO: Thomas Jefferson University.

Schoenwetter, J., and Geyer, P. S.
2000 Implications of Archaeological Palynology at Bethsaida, Israel. *Journal of Field Archaeology* 27, no. 1: 63–73.

Shroder Jr., J. F.; Bishop, M. P.; Cornwell, K.; and Inbar, M.
1999 Catastrophic Geomorphic Processes and Bethsaida Archaeology, Israel. Pp. 115–73 in *Bethsaida: A City by the North Shore of the Sea of Galilee,* vol. 2, eds. R. Arav and R. A. Freund. The Bethsaida Excavations Project Reports and Contextual Studies 2. Kirksville, MO: Truman State University.

Shroder Jr., J. F., and Inbar, M.
1995 Geologic and Geomorphic Background to the Bethsaida Excavations. Pp. 65–98 in *Bethsaida: A City by the North Shore of the Sea of Galilee,* vol. 1, eds. R. Arav and R. A. Freund. The Bethsaida Excavations Project Reports and Contextual Studies 1. Kirksville, MO: Thomas Jefferson University.

Siebert, A. V.
1999 *Instrumenta Sacra: Untersuchungen zu Römischen Opfer-, Kult- und Priestergeräten.* Berlin: de Gruyter.

Strickert, F.
1995 The Coins of Philip. Pp. 165–89 in *Bethsaida: A City by the North Shore of the Sea of Galilee,* vol. 1, eds. R. Arav and R. A. Freund. The Bethsaida Excavations Project Reports and Contextual Studies 1. Kirksville, MO: Thomas Jefferson University.

Tadmor, H.
1994 *The Inscriptions of Tiglath Pileser III, King of Assyria.* Jerusalem: Israel Academy of Science.

Chapter 28

Caesarea Philippi (Paneas) in the Roman and Byzantine Periods

by Vassilios Tzaferis

The establishment of the city Caesarea Philippi-Paneas by the Tetrarch Philip, the son of Herod the Great, in the year 3 B.C.E. was undoubtedly an historical event of great significance for the regions of Gaulanitis (Golan), Ituraea (northern Golan Heights), and Ulatha (northern Hula and southern Beka'a valleys). The region of Ituraea in the north also included the district of Paneas, first mentioned by Polybius as Paneion (Polybius, *Historiae,* XVI, 18.2). During Hellenistic and early Roman times, all these areas had been in the process of Hellenization for almost two centuries, quite before Philip the Tetrarch founded his capital Caesarea. Since 200 B.C.E., when Antiochus the III took political control over Palestine and southwest Phoenicia, the Seleucid regime exercised in these newly conquered areas an intense and consistent policy of Hellenization.

The district of Ituraea attracted special attention due to its demographics. Already from the Persian period on and throughout the third century B.C.E., the region of the present Golan Heights, notably its northern areas as well as the northern parts of the Hula Valley, was ravaged by hordes of nomadic tribes, mostly Arabs, whom the Seleucid regime sought to subdue and control, incorporating them into the Hellenistic political regime and gathering them under the aegis of Greek culture by creating urban centers and sedentary settlements. These approaches, which later on were also employed by the Romans, were very effective. In the course of the first century B.C.E., the nomadic way of life was replaced with permanent settlements and by a political and social organization under the framework of tributary kingship (Schürer 1973: 564). That was the prevailing political and cultural situation in Ituraea, when the Romans, for their own reasons granted Herod the Great the Paneion district, ca. 20 B.C.E. (Josephus, *Ant.* XV, 360; *War* I, 404–6).

The impact of hellenization among the tribes, known in the literary sources as Ituraeans (Strabo, *Geog.* XVI, 2, 18.775), related mainly to external forms, such as architectural patterns, artistic models, use of the goods and chattels of the Hellenistic culture, or use of the Greek language and names of deities. Under the cultural, linguistic, and artistic layers of assimilation existed the traditional attitude of the indigenous population, who were, for the most part, not Greeks. The significance, therefore, underlying the foundation of Caesarea by Philip

Fig. 1 *General view of the archaeological site of Banias.*

consists in the fact that an urban center, based on the main principles of a real Greek *polis* with almost all of its civic and cultural institutes, was created in the frame of which the expectancies of Greek life could be practiced and be accomplished.

CAESAREA PHILIPPI, CAPITAL OF THE KINGDOM

Literary Sources

Philip's decision to found his capital near the springs of the Jordan in the Paneion region was not without good reasons. The location was endued with topographical and strategic virtues, which, along with its congenial natural landscape, rendered it peculiar importance (fig. 1). In addition, it possessed an abundance of fertile lands—the whole northern part of Hula valley—and affluent water. It also controlled one of the main routes connecting the coast of Phoenicia in the west with Damascus and other important towns in the east. But above all, it was affined with an age-long worship, that of the god Pan, from whom it attained its name Paneion, and of an ulterior worship, that of Augustus established by Philip's father, Herod the Great (Josephus, *War* I, 404–5).

Josephus' testimony in his *Antiquities* (XVIII, ii, 1,28), "Φίλππος δέ Πανεάδα τήν πρός ταῖς πηγαῖς τοῦ Ιορδάνου κατασκευάσας ὀνομάζει καισάρεαν," is brief and ambiguous. The English translation of the paragraph by Feldman in the Loeb Classical Library, "Philip too made improvements at Paneas, the city near the sources of the Jordan, and called it Caesarea," does not convey correctly the original Greek text. The verb κατασκεναζω in Greek has different meanings; one of them is *to erect* or *to build,* which very probably has to be applied in the above Josephus version. Consequently, the translation should be: "Philip too built Paneas, near the springs of Jordan, and called it Caesarea." On the other hand, Josephus' statement in his *War,* "καί ὁ Φίλιππος ὁ μέν πρός ταῖς τοῦ' Ιορδάνου πηγαῖς ἐν Πανεάδι πόλις κτίζει Καισάρειαν—Philip built Caesarea near the sources of the Jordan in the district of Paneas" (*War* II, ix, 1,168), is much more explicit, leaving no doubts at all that he (Philip) was the founder of the city.

Equally brief are Josephus' references on Paneas, the city, under Agrippa II (54–96 C.E.). Josephus says almost nothing about the city itself, how it looked, what public or cultural buildings were there or what was its layout in Agrippa's reign. He mentions, however, that Agrippa "embellished it at great expense" (*War* III, 514), and that he changed the name from Caesarea to Neronias (*Ant.* XX, 211). The above statements of Josephus, and especially in his *War,* may conceal serious structural activities, both in buildings and in town planning, carried out at Paneas under Agrippa II. It is, therefore, very probably during Agrippa's reign that Paneas took on its final urban form, similar to contemporary Greco-Roman cities in the east. Paneas, in the half-century-long reign of king Agrippa II, was the acknowledged capital of the kingdom and the official abode of the king, though he himself used to stay for long intervals elsewhere. It was in the royal courts that he built at Paneas where he hosted Vespasian during the years of the great Jewish revolt (Jos. *War* III, 443–44). It was there, too, where Titus, after the conquest of Jerusalem, enjoyed Agrippa's generous hospitality, which included all kinds of spectacles (*War* VII, 23–24).

Josephus mentions Caesarea Philippi (Paneas) several other times, but in none of his statements are descriptions or allusions of the visage of the city or its monuments and structures given. Similarly, other contemporaneous literary sources, such as the New Testament books (Matthew 16:13–16; Mark 8:27–28), that refer to Caesarea Philippi do not provide any description about the visual appearance of the city during the first century C.E. What, however, the literary sources fail to provide, archaeological research, though incomplete, can help complete and visualize.

Archaeological Evidence

Since 1967, several salvage excavations, soundings, and surveys have been conducted in different places at the site of Banias, exposing remains of several monumental constructions, Roman-Byzantine villas, medieval fortifications, and Roman-Byzantine tombs.[1] In addition to the salvage excavations, several intensive surveys were carried out by various scholars, which established the limits of Caesarea Philippi at the height of its expansion in the late Roman and Early Byzantine periods.

In 1988, when the site was officially designated as a nature reserve, the Israel Department of Antiquities, now the Israel Antiquities Authority, decided to initiate methodical excavations in order to expose Banias' archaeological treasures and put the site on the archaeological map of the country. Three large-scale excavations were organized. The first, headed by M. Hartal, explored the ancient aqueduct that supplied water to the northwestern residential quarters in the Roman and Byzantine city. The second, placed under the direction of Zvi Maoz, excavated the sanctuary of Pan above the springs and near the cave. The third, the Joint Archaeological Expedition, directed by the writer, explored the central area of the site, from the cave and the springs in the north to the stream Sa'ar in the south and the stream Hermon in the west.

On the basis of the results of all archaeological excavations, soundings, and surveys carried out on the site we can now delimit not only the urban expanse of Caesarea Philippi throughout all its historical periods, but also mark out the religious, civic and residential districts organized within it. Thus, the first-century town founded by Philip and enlarged by Agrippa II extended from the springs in the north to the streams Sa'ar and Hermon in the south and west, respectively. Within this area, occupying almost 200 *dunams*, were found the religious, cultural and administrative buildings that existed during the reigns of Philip and Agrippa II. So far, no remains of residential quarters have been discovered within the boundaries of this area. Until new evidence comes to light, we may assume that this area was the civic and religious center of Caesarea Philippi during the Roman and Byzantine periods. Moreover, since absolutely no remnants of private houses dated to the first century C.E. have been discovered so far anywhere in the archaeological site areas, we conclude that the Caesarea Philippi of Philip and Agrippa II contained only the Temenos, i.e., the Sanctuary of Pan with all its ceremonial and praying spaces, and the admin-

Fig. 2 *The springs and the cave of Pan.*

istration center, where all the public buildings of the capital were found (fig. 2). Private housing was virtually non-existent or limited to the minimum necessary for public service and the maintenance of the buildings.

Private dwellings in the town start appearing from the second century C.E. onwards and only in areas extended beyond the above mentioned streams (Sa'ar and Hermon). Very likely the initial intention of the founder, Philip the Tetrarch, was not to build a populous city, but rather to create an effective administrative center, a capital from which he could administer the affairs of his kingdom. Agrippa II, too, by embellishing and enlarging the capital by new monumental buildings, continued the policy of Philip. The population lived not within the urban limits of the city, but in the neighboring villages, the κωμαις Καισαριας της Φιλιππου — "in the villages of Caesarea Philippi," as they are mentioned in Mark 8:27–28. Extensive habitation within the urban boundaries of Caesarea Philippi began only after the death of King Agrippa, when the city ceased to function as the capital of the kingdom.

With regard to the town plan, applied first by Philip and later on by Agrippa II, the archaeological evidence provides an outline. Utilizing the topography at hand, the city planners included all the essential elements of a standard Greco-Roman town, which generally possessed dedicated areas for temples, a forum, colonnaded streets, cultural and entertainment centers, such as theaters and bathhouses, public monuments, such as nymphaea and administration buildings. Paneas, which from the beginning was designed as the capital of the kingdom, in addition to the abovementioned complexes also included a palace or a respectable residence to accommodate the royal family and a royal court.

Hitherto, the archaeological excavations of all three expeditions have detected the sacred area (*temenos*) of the city, the main colonnaded street (*cardo*; fig. 3), the ruins of a monumental structure, very probably a nymphaeum, the aqueducts, which supplied sufficient quantities of water to the city from the nearby springs, and an impressive monumental structure, undoubtedly the royal residence of king Agrippa II (fig. 4).

The colonnaded street (*cardo*), a twenty-meter-long section of which was discovered in area K, bisected the center of the city from the stream Sa'ar in the south as far as close to the sacred area and the springs in the north (fig. 3). The two colonnades, western and eastern, are set nine meters apart, measured from the center of the columns. Nine meters was therefore the width of the central passage of the street. The sidewalks and shops flanking the main street are not yet excavated. Assuming that the colonnaded street of Paneas maintained the customary proportions in regard to the width of the central passage and the sidewalks, the entire width of the colonnaded street could be between eighteen and twenty meters. As such, the colonnaded street of Paneas is among the widest *cardos* discovered in Greco-Roman cities in the East so far (Segal 1995: 16–17; 1996: 25).

Fig. 3 *The western colonnade of the* cardo.

At the south end of the site, just above the northern bank of the stream, is one of the main gates of the city, a location that continued in importance in later periods up to nineteenth century. To the north, the street stopped some distance from the stream. There it intersected with a colonnaded monument, probably a nymphaeum, located within the space of the forum. The total length of the colonnaded street was about 300 meters. The east–west colonnaded street, the *decumanus,* as yet undiscovered, probably began at the Hermon stream in the west and, like the *cardo,* terminated at the forum. The remains of the so-called "Roman Bridge" preserved above the stream of Hermon may indicate the western starting point of the street.

The wide area that extended from the "colonnaded building" in the forum as far as the sanctuary of Pan in the north was probably a public open space, serving both as a place for cult celebrations and for pleasant walks. The beautiful landscape, the springs, and the temples comprising the Sanctuary of Pan crested by the white and elegant Augustaeum, all framed by the dramatic cliff side in the background, undoubtedly made this the most pleasant and impressive quarter of the city. In the southwest corner of the city in areas D and I, the excavations of the Joint Expedition brought to light one of the most interesting structures of Caesarea Philippi, apparently the royal palace erected by Agrippa II (fig. 5). The final form of the structure was completed during Agrippa's reign, but we suggest that its foundations were already laid during the thirty-six years of Philip's reign (3 B.C.E.–33 C.E.).

Four years of excavation have thus far exposed only parts of its southern wing, which extends for more than 40,000 square meters. The length of the exposed portion, from east to west, exceeds 100 m, while its width measures more than forty m. The structure's northern sections are as yet unexcavated. However, based on probes conducted in a number of places, we may estimate that the dimensions of the northern wing were as large as the southern wing. If our suppositions are correct, the structure consists of four wings flanking an open courtyard set at the center. Such an arrangement would make the royal palace of Paneas the largest and most magnificent Roman edifice ever constructed in Palestine and one of the largest in the eastern part of the Roman Empire.

The structure is impressive not only because of its grand dimensions. but also for its sophisticated building style, unique plan, and creative use of the natural topography upon which it was built. Its spacious courtyards are arranged in wonderful symmetry. The apsidal halls, the magnificent basilica, the vaulted passageways (fig. 6), and the impressive interior entrances and exits all suggest

Fig. 4 Remains of the palace in Area D.

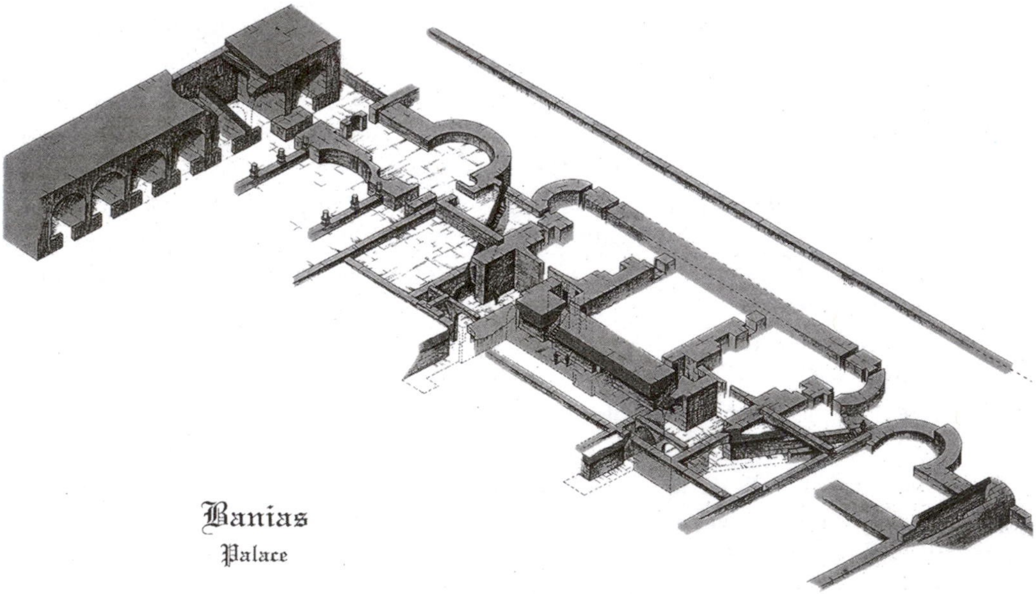

Fig. 5 The palace of Agrippa II.

architectural and engineering planning and skill, with attention to the finest details. Its planners obviously intended to provide facilities for events requiring stateliness and formality, recreation, pleasure, and, apparently, defense against potential threats to security. The structure is situated in one of the most beautiful locations at the site. To its west, Nahal Hermon carries water from the springs in a dramatic torrent, and to the south is Nahal Sa'ar, equally impressive in all its beauty. The wings of the building were constructed in an area that is lower than the level of the springs near the cave, thus enabling the planners to ensure a constant supply of water for the use and pleasure of those who resided within it. Beneath its floors, an elaborate system of large water channels of finest construction conveyed water from the springs to the palace gardens and fountains, and then carried away the excess into Nahal Sa'ar.

This structure, with all its stateliness and luxury, incorporated within its various wings a wide range of functions, making maximum use of the natural elements around it. In particular, the plan demonstrates a concern for the efficient control of the movement of people, both as they entered and exited the building, and as they moved about within it. This edifice cannot be an ordinary public building. It is quite literally a structure fit for a king. There are a number of sound reasons for our assumption that it was built during the second half of the first century and served as the palace for King Agrippa II. For instance, the plan of the building, the masonry, which is typical early Roman, and above all the luxurious character of the structure, if not used for public space certainly served as a palace. Future excavations, we hope, will shed more light on this unique building, so far unparalleled in the archaeological chronicles of Roman Palestine.

As noted earlier, first-century Caesarea Philippi possessed a theater where the Roman troops of both Vespasian and Titus were entertained with breathtaking spectacles. Excavations have not yet found the theater at Paneas; however, its location might be at the northeastern corner of the city, next to the southern gate. There, the ground, which gently slopes down towards the east side of the colonnaded street or *cardo*, very probably hides its ruins for future discoveries. Apparently, the various civic and social institutes, such as the *boulé,* or halls for general assembles of the citizens, requisite for the administration of the city, were not erected in first-century Paneas as independent structural units, but rather as components of the royal courts. During the reigning years of Philip and Agrippa II the administration of the city, and the kingdom as well, was carved out within the palace by commissaries appointed by the king (Jos. *Life*, 52–55).

Fig. 6 *One of the vaulted passages of the palace.*

Just as the city plan of Paneas from the day of its foundation by Philip at the end of the first century B.C.E. was based on the principles of a standard Greco-Roman city, so was the composition of its population. Most inhabitants and civil officers were pagans. Among them were many Hellenized Ituraeans and Syrians, Greek immigrants from Greece, Syria and Phoenicia, and veteran mercenaries. Although numerous, the Jewish community, very probably recognized as a *politeuma* within the urban frame of the city (Jos. *Life* 54, 61, 74), was ineffective at least in matters of religion and in the official pagan cults exercised at Paneas. Neither the literary sources nor the archaeological evidence hint at the existence of a synagogue in the city. On the other hand, archaeological, epigraphic, numismatic, and literary sources clearly confirm that Caesarea Philippi was replete with sanctuaries, temples, and cult statues. In such a city, privileged by the status of being an autonomous *polis*, the temples dedicated to the patron gods were the most significant and indispensable. Yet, the pagan inhabitants of Paneas did not have many alternatives in choosing their own gods. The place already had its patron god, Pan, as well as its official politico-religious cult, that of Augustus, long before the city was founded. The impressive natural cave hanging over the springs (fig. 2) had been dedicated to Pan and had become a well-accepted cult site as early as the late third or early second century B.C.E. (Polybius, *Historiae* XVI, 18–19). Later on, probably in 19 B.C.E., Herod the Great erected a magnificent temple of white marble to Augustus, known as the Augustaeum (Jos. *War* I, 404; *Ant.* XV, 364). The cults of Pan and Augustus continued to function well after the foundation of Caesarea Philippi. Moreover, there are good reasons to believe that the heathen inhabitants accepted both cults as the official worship in the newly founded city. The city was filled with statues and many pagan deities were worshipped there in addition to Pan and Augustus. One can even suggest that, at least up to the years of king Agrippa II's reign (end of the first century C.E.), these two cults remained the principal forms of worship practiced in the city.

The sanctuary of Pan, thoroughly excavated by Zvi Maoz, occupied the entire terrace across the cliffs above the springs (Maoz, forthcoming; Berlin 1999). The Augustaeum, on the other hand, must be located on another terrace found to the south of the springs and not, as Maoz suggested, at the very entrance of the cave. Ehud Netzer's excavations in 1977 on that terrace exposed sections of retaining walls built in *opus reticulatum* pattern, characteristic to Herodian times. It is within these walls that Herod the Great apparently set up the magnificent temple dedicated to Augustus.

Neither the literary sources nor the archaeological excavations provide evidence for the existence of city walls or of any other kind of fortification in Paneas during the first century. Nevertheless, some sort of walls delimiting the urban space of the city very probably existed. We cannot imagine that the Tetrarch Philip or King Agrippa II would have built a capital city with all the distinctive rights of a *polis* without enclosing it in a city wall or at least setting certain landmarks, such as gates or towers indicating its urban limits. The location and extent of the walls are directly tied to the topography of the city's site. As we have already mentioned, during the reign of Philip and Agrippa II the urban limits of Paneas did not extend beyond the gorge of Sa'ar in the south or the stream of Hermon in the west. To the north, the city boundaries extended almost as far as the springs and the high cliff above them. This space, totaling less than 200 *dunams* (200,000 square meters), seems to have been the area that was delimited by walls. It is quite certain that the architects and engineers employed by Philip and Agrippa II were able to build these walls in an aesthetically pleasing way. The southern and western walls were thus constructed, the first along the northern bank of the Sa'ar, and the second along the eastern bank of the Hermon. In the east, the wall could have run from the bend in the Sa'ar up to the foot of the mountainside. The northern wall, if there was one, remains problematic. However, it is evident that the springs and the cliffs mark the northern boundary of the city.

Apparently three main gates served the city; two were situated at the eastern and western terminations of the *decumanus*, and one was at the southern terminal of the *cardo*. Access to the *cardo* was gained by means of a bridge built across the Sa'ar, a pattern that continued from medieval Banias up to the nineteenth century. A similar bridge, which survives to this day and is known as the "Roman Bridge," was built above the Hermon stream to give access to the western gate. The northern gate was very probably located close to the forum where both the *cardo* and the *decumanus* met. The arrangement of the city gates as described above

Fig. 7 *Bath installations (hypocausts) in one of the courts of the palace.*

corresponds to the roads approaching the city from west, south, and north. The main west–east road, which crossed the northern Huleh valley and climbed up to the Golan Heights, divided into two distinct routes west of Banias. The southern route traversed the Huleh along the northern edge of its marshes and entered the city through the *cardo.* The northern route entered the city through the western gate of the *decumanus.* The two routes met in the center of Paneas at the intersection of the *cardo* and the *decumanus,* and exited the city through its northeastern gate. From there the road began its relatively easy climb toward the western approaches of the Golan Heights.

CAESAREA PHILIPPI IN THE LATE ROMAN PERIOD

After the death of Agrippa II in 96 C.E., Caesarea Philippi was converted from a capital to a common town/*polis,* maintaining all the juristic and social privileges acknowledged by the Roman regime. As before, the city continued to issue its own coins and run its internal affairs like any standard Greco-Roman town. Paneas was shortly annexed to the province of Syria and soon after that permanently to the province of Phoenicia. The transition from capital to common town did not result in any serious change to the city's outward appearance. It did, however, necessitate modifications in the functions of some of the public buildings and perhaps even the partial destruction of some of them.

Modifications in the City

The "colonnaded building" discovered in area B was partially or totally demolished following the construction of an aqueduct, built to bring fresh water from the springs to the center of the city. The aqueduct, however, was probably constructed to supply adequate quantities of water to the area of the palace, which now was converted to bathhouse (fig. 7).

We may assume that the *cardo* remained unchanged, as did other public buildings of the town. The "palace" in the southwest corner of the city (Areas D and I) was preserved in its entirety, but its function changed. Extensive remodeling, accessions and blockings were done in all the halls

Fig. 8 *Wall mosaics covering the arch of the basilica.*

and the courts of the palace. The entire southern wing with all its halls, rooms, and courts seems to have been converted to *caldaria;* in most areas we excavated we found hypocausts. During our excavations, structural adaptations were observed everywhere. Judging by the ceramic and the numismatic evidence found in one of the vaulted passages blocked intentionally and subsequently filled up with debris, the conversion of the palace to a bath took place sometime in the second half of the second century or the first half of the third.

The most significant development, which occurred during the Late Roman period, concerns the urban layout and demographic apportionment of the city. Whereas in the first century the city limits were confined to the area bounded by the springs and the Sa'ar and Hermon, now, for the first time, the habitable areas were extended far beyond. Intensive archaeological surveys, salvage excavations and soundings done in the past twenty years by M. Hartal and others have proved beyond doubt that dense residential quarters were erected beyond the aforementioned streams. The expansion of the city limits into new areas located on a level higher than the springs meant that new sources of water needed to be located. The city exploited one of the water sources found near the modern Druze village of En Kanta, located at a higher altitude than Paneas. From there, a ca. three-kilometer-long aqueduct was constructed, which brought water to the new suburbs of the town (Hartal, forthcoming; 1998). The prosperity characterizing most cities of the second and third centuries in the eastern Roman Empire did not bypass Paneas. The completion of the new and relatively long aqueduct demanded formidable financial resources. Similarly, the conversion of the huge palace complex into a bath required both considerable funds and skilled personnel.

The significant financial base of the town during the Late Roman Period was displayed not only through impressive building activities, but also by various artistic accomplishments. The secular basilica, originally part of the royal palace, was now remodeled for the new needs of the bath; the interior of the basilica's apse was covered with colorful wall mosaics (fig. 8). Beautiful marble statues representing various deities of the Greco-Roman pantheon enriched the sanctuary of Pan (Friedland 1999).

The sanctuary itself was enlarged by additional cult installations, worship spaces and small temples dedicated to different deities, including Pan, Hermes, Echo, Maia, and Nemesis. These deities constituted a company of associated gods through either genetic lineage or common religious concepts (Tzaferis 1992). In addition, numismatic evidence confirms that gods other than Pan and his associates were present at Paneas in the second and third centuries. The cult of Tyche was active at Caesarea Philippi, very probably, during the reign of Agrippa II; but she acquired her first temple only during the second or at the beginning of the third century. The numismatic evidence for this is conclusive. Coins issued at Paneas during the time of Agrippa II represent Tyche without any architectural element, whereas on those issued in the first half of the third century the goddess is shown within a tetrastyle temple and sometimes within a distyle one. The different structures accompanying Tyche on the coins may even indicate the existence of more than one temple dedicated to her in Caesarea Philippi. Finally, Zeus-Jupiter, god and father of gods and men alike, was present in Paneas. Greek and Roman cities competed for the honor of erecting the most magnificent temple or earning the favor of the supreme god, and Caesarea Philippi was no exception. During the second half of the second century, probably under the reign of Marcus Aurelius (161–180 C.E.), the first temple to Zeus was erected in the city, a fact positively attested by the numismatic evidence (Meshorer 1984).

The territorial expansion of the city and the great structural projects accomplished in the sanctuary of Pan and in the conversion of the palace to a bath leave no doubt that Paneas in the Late Roman period enjoyed prosperity and peace. Its location on the main road connecting the two provincial capitals Damascus and Tyre enhanced the fame and importance of the city and increased its economy. An abundance of financial resources was directed to the welfare of the citizens and to activities embellishing the town with statues and works of art, and the constitution of new cults. There is no doubt at all that the second and third centuries were the golden age of Caesarea Philippi.

CAESAREA PHILIPPI IN THE BYZANTINE PERIOD

Excavation at this point seems to suggest that the overall Roman city plan and the external appearance of the city were not drastically altered in the Byzantine period. The civic area, as it was designated in the Roman period, continued to function in the same manner. In none of the areas of our excavation were houses for private habitation found. We may only assume that some of the buildings, such as temples or monuments of pagan character, were intentionally demolished or replaced by others that accommodated the Byzantine administration and the new religious needs of the citizens. The colonnaded street (*cardo*) remained essentially unchanged with only minor modifications. To the west of the *cardo* and parallel to it another street was constructed, the "Byzantine Street," which contained commercial activities, according to the archaeological evidence. The suburbs beyond the streams continued to be attractive for private habitation at least up to the first half of the fifth century. Sometime in the course of the fourth century or the beginning of the fifth, a new enclosure wall was erected to protect the city from unexpected raids and bandits. Remains of the enclosure wall were detected in the surveys done by M. Hartal beyond the stream Sa'ar.

Serious alterations, however, were executed within the civic center on the monuments and some of the public buildings. The bathhouse that had been installed within the rooms and courtyards of the "palace" in the late second century continued to function and to serve the city's Byzantine residents, but not without internal structural interventions and functional modifications. The Byzantines demolished the magnificent basilica, which had served the city for more than two hundred years, first as an essential part of the palace and then in the bathhouse. Its architectural elements, pedestals, and columns were recycled in another basilica, erected for the newly established Christian cult. The pagan temples probably met a similar fate, though archaeologically this is not yet attested. Even if they were not demolished immediately after the emergence of Christianity, in the first half of

Fig. 9 *Area B with the remains of the Christian basilica.*

the fourth century, they certainly fell into neglect and by the end of the fourth century into ruin. The decline of the cult of Pan had already begun in the first half of the 4th century (Eusebius, *Eccl. Hist.* VI, 16–17). The structures, prayer and ceremonial spaces, as well as the statues of gods set up on the worship terrace next to the cave were all in ruins by the end of the fourth century.

The excavations in Area B have revealed the most convincing evidence attesting to the dramatic collapse of paganism at Caesarea Philippi and the triumph of Christianity. There, the "colonnaded building," erected in the first century by Philip or Agrippa II, was entirely demolished down to its foundations. The remaining ruins of the pagan structure were filled up with soil in order to create a high and spacious platform. On top of the platform was erected a large Christian basilica, the builders of which recycled all possible structural elements used in the pagan monument, such as fragments of columns, decorated architectural elements, and ashlars (fig. 9). The rest, such as complete columns and pedestals used within the church, were spolia from the secular basilica of the palace.

Judging from what has survived, we may assume that the Christian basilica was undoubtedly a large and grandiose building standing close to the springs and just opposite the sanctuary of Pan. Only the northeastern corner of the church has been preserved; it included a northern room with fragments of a mosaic pavement, the northern *pastophorium* (*prothesis*) with most of its mosaic pavement, almost all of the central apse, and about 35 m of the northern outer wall. The rest of the structure was destroyed, partly during the Fatimid or Crusader Periods and partly by later building projects undertaken by the Mamluks and Ottomans. About half a dozen white hard-stone pedestals and a similar number of granite columns used in the church as spolia from the palace basilica were found scattered in the area or incorporated into nearby buildings built in later periods. None were *in situ*. These were obviously reused as construction materials after the church had been destroyed and was lying in ruins.

As already noted, the only surviving parts of the church were its northeastern corner and a section of its northern outer wall; yet, there is no doubt that it was an ordinary timber-roofed Christian basilica. Like most Christian basilicas, it included all the essential elements: an apse with *bema* and chancel, two rectangular rooms flanking the apse (*pastophoria*), a central nave, aisles and a western court (*atrium*) or some sort of inner court (*narthex*).

The width of the basilica measured 21 m, while its length, if the common average ratios of 4:5, 3:4, 2:3, or 1:2 were kept, was about 35 to 40 m in the interior (Orlandos 1992: 202–6; Ovadia 1970: 203–4). The width of the aisles, based on what has been preserved in the northeastern corner, was 5.50 m and that of the nave about 10 m, i.e., a ratio of 1:2, the normal average ratio in early Christian basilicas. No signs of a stylobate were preserved, though several pedestals of local white stone and several columns of granite were scattered in the area as building materials reused in various later structures. Assuming that the builders of the church arranged the columns at the maximum possible distance of 4 m, each of the two rows contained between eight to ten columns.

The mosaic pavements found in the northern *pastophorium* (*prothesis*), and a fragment of mosaic preserved in the northeastern corner of the northern aisle (both at +350.80 m) are sufficient evidence that all parts of the basilica, apart from the area of the apse, were paved with mosaics. The pavement of the semicircular apse, which was about 20 cm higher than those of the *pastophoria* and the aisles, used square, 20 × 20 cm, marble or stone slabs. The slabs themselves were not preserved; only their negative impressions confirmed their existence.

Thus, the church at Paneas was built in the shape of a standard tripartite basilica with an inscribed apse. The outside of the building may have appeared rather clumsy and unattractive. The interior, on the other hand, with its dark-colored granite columns, sitting on high white stone pedestals, with its colored mosaic pavements and rich wall ornamentation must have been quite pleasing from an aesthetic point of view.

The location of the church, directly in the line with the *cardo,* near the springs, and at a distance of less than 150 m from the sanctuary of Pan is also worthy of note. No doubt the Christians of Paneas chose such a prominent place for their church deliberately. Its location, size, and magnificence symbolized both the decline of the old pagan sanctuary and the triumph of the new faith — developments that occurred during the fourth century. In addition, the enormous Christian basilica was probably constructed at the springs of Paneas specifically to house and exhibit the famous "Statue of Jesus" mentioned by Eusebius and other church fathers. Eusebius was the first of the church fathers to tell the story of the statue at Banias. His description is an eyewitness report. "I saw it (the statue) with my own eyes," he says, "when I resided in the city" (Eusebius. *Eccl. Hist.* VI: xviii). Originally, the monument consisted of two figures, one standing and the other kneeling, believed by the Christians to be Jesus and the woman whom he healed of hemorrhaging (Luke 8:43–48). Christian tradition made her a citizen of Banias and claimed that she had placed the monument in front of her house as a mark of gratitude and respect to Jesus. When Eusebius visited Paneas, sometime in the first half of the fourth century, he saw the statue standing in its original place — "at the gates of her house." A century later another church father, Philostorgius, who wrote his *Ecclesiastical History* between 425 and 433, tells another version of the same story (Philostorgius, *Hist. Eccl.* VII.3). According to him, the statue originally stood in a most prominent place in the city of Paneas and only much later, after the reign of Julian the Apostate, it was moved into the *diaconicon* of the church. Actually, only fragments of it were displayed there, the rest having been destroyed by order of Julian. After Julian's death (363), the Christians of the city rescued the remaining fragments of the statue and stored them in the church, Philostorgius says. The story of the "Statue of Jesus" in Paneas appears frequently in the writings of the church fathers and in early Christian itineraries during the following centuries (Sozomen, *Eccl. Hist.* V, XXII; Malalas John, 237–39; John of Damascus, *De Imaginibus Oratio* II, PG [Migne], 94 cols. 1369–74). The story may have an historical kernel. A statue was certainly displayed in the city, and was seen by Eusebius. Whatever its actual origin, the

Christians believed it to be an actual statue of Jesus. In fact, early Christian art presented in relief the miracle of the Bleeding Woman. In 1591, near the basilica of St. Peter in Rome, was found a christian sarcophagus (now in the Lateran Museum, inv. no. 176) from the time of Constantine the Great; on one side was depicted the standing figure of Jesus with the kneeling figure of the bleeding woman as described by Eusebius. The scene is shown on a building-style background representing gabled structures similar to early Christian basilicas. One cannot exclude the possibility that the depiction of the miracle on the Lateran sarcophagus in fact replicated an original relief statue that existed at Paneas (Von Matt 1961: pls. 36–38; *H. Dict. D'Arch. Chr.*, vol. 8, cols. 1737–41).

Our present interest in the story is the relation it may have to the date of the erection of the basilica. Whereas Eusebius, in the first half of the fourth century, saw no church building connected with the statue, Philostorgius, less than a hundred years later, describes it as stored in a church built close to the springs. This suggests that the church was erected sometime between the writing of Eusebius' *Ecclesiastical History*, around 316 C.E., and that of Philostorgius, written between 425 and 433 C.E.

The above-mentioned activities undertaken in Paneas in the Byzantine period relate to the first two hundred years of the Byzantine period. Surprisingly, no substantial finds (architectural, ceramic or numismatic) from the last two centuries of the Byzantine period (6th–7th centuries) have been found so far. All the architectural remains attributed to the Byzantine stratum at Paneas, without exception, are dated to the fourth and fifth centuries alone. At the beginning of the fifth century, some calamitous blight may have fallen upon the city, causing all occupation to cease abruptly. Perhaps such absence may also be due to the accidental character of archaeological evidence from the areas we excavated. Yet, there remains the real possibility that the apparent death of the city at the beginning of the fifth century was the result of social decay, a destructive earthquake, or some malignant epidemic. Whatever the case may be, the great days of Caesarea Philippi as the capital of a kingdom in the first century C.E. and a prosperous Greco-Roman town of the Late Roman period were long-distant memories. In the ensuing historical periods life continued at Paneas, as a small Arabic town, Medina, as a formidable Crusader fortress, Bellinas, as an Ayyubid-Mamluk fortified small town, and as an insignificant Ottoman and Syrian village, Banias, preserving under its houses the ruins and memories of a most glorious past and the original name Paneas.

NOTES

1 Salvage excavations and soundings at the archaeological site of Banias were first conducted in 1973 by D. Amir in the area west of stream Hermon, where he uncovered mosaic floors and remnants of a magnificent residence (1974). Additional salvage excavations were conducted by M. Hartal to the south of the same stream, uncovering another Roman-Byzantine villa (1985), and Idan Saked in 1999, discovering a colorful mosaic pavement of a private house (1999). In 1977, E. Netzer conducted a sounding on a terrace to the south of the springs, cleaning and exposing the remains of the so called *opus reticulatus* terraces (1978). The site of ancient Banias was also systematically surveyed, first by the late D. Olami in the years 1967–68, and later in 1989 by M. Hartal and Z. Maoz.

REFERENCES

Amir, D.
1974 Banias. *Hadashot Arkheologiyot* 51–52: 24, nos. 48–49 (Hebrew).

Berlin, A. M.
1999 The Archaeology of Ritual: The Sanctuary of Pan at Banias/Caesarea Philippi. *Bulletin of the American Schools of Oriental Research* 315: 27–45.

Dictionnaire d'Archéologie Chrétienne et de Liturgie
1907–50 Ed. Henri Leclercq. Paris: Letouzey & Ané.

Friedland, E. A.
1999 Graeco-Roman Sculpture in the Levant: The Marbles from the Sanctuary of Pan at Caesarea Philippi (Banias). Pp. 7–22 in *The Roman and Byzantine Near East,* vol. 2, ed. J. H. Humphrey. Journal of Roman Archaeology Supplementary Series 31. Portsmouth, RI: Journal of Roman Archaeology.

Hartal, M.
1985 Banias. *Hadashot Arkheologiyot* 86–87: 2, no. 76 (Hebrew).
1998 The Aqueduct to Banias. *Qadmoniot* 31, no. 115: 26–29 (in Hebrew).
forthcoming *Banias I: The Aqueduct and the Northern Cemetery*. Israel Antiquities Authority Reports. Jerusalem: Israel Antiquities Authority.

Maoz, Z.
forthcoming *Paneion I: Excavations at the Sanctuary of Pan at Caesarea Philippi 1988–1993*. Israel Antiquities Authority Reports. Jerusalem: Israel Antiquities Authority.

Meshorer, Y.
1984 The Coins of Caesarea Paneas. *Israel Numismatic Journal* 8: 42–43.

Netzer, E.
1978 Banias. *Hadashot Arkheologiyot* 59–60: 6, nos. 103–4 (Hebrew).

Orlandos, A. K.
1992 Χυλοστεγὸ Παλαιοξριστιανικη Βασιλικη Τὴ Μεσογειακὴ Λεκανὴ *(The Wood-Roofed Early Christian Basilica in the Mediterranean Basin),* in Greek. Athens: The Archaeological Society at Athens.

Ovadia, A.
1970 *Corpus of the Byzantine Churches in the Holy Land*. Theophaneia 22. Bonn: Hanstein.

Saked, I.
1999 Banias. *Hadashot Arkheologiyot* 109–10: 7, no. 90 (Hebrew).

Schürer, E.
1973 *The History of the Jewish People in the Age of Jesus Christ (175 BC–AD 135),* vol. 1, revised by G. Vermes and F. Millar. Edinburgh: T & T Clark.

Segal, A.
1995 *Monumental Architecture in Roman Palestine and the Eastern Provinces of the Roman Empire*, in Hebrew. Haifa: Haifa University.
1996 City Landscape in Roman Palestine. *Eretz Israel* 25: 456–62 (in Hebrew with English summary).

Tzaferis, V.
1992 Cults and Deities Worshipped at Caesarea Philippi-Banias. Pp. 190–201 in *Priests, Prophets and Scribes: Essays on the Formation and Heritage of Second Temple Jerusalem in Honor of Joseph Blenkinsopp*, eds. E. C. Ulrich, J. Wright, R. P. Carroll and P. R. Davies. Journal for the Study of the Old Testament Supplemental Series 149. Sheffield: Sheffield Academic.

Von Matt, L.
1961 *Early Christian Art in Rome. Commentary by Enrico Josi*. New York, NY: Universe.

Chapter 29

Rabbis, Romans, and Rabies: Religion, Disease, and the "Other" A Case Study

by Barbara Geller

This chapter is a study of the talmudic texts on the etiology, transmission, symptoms, and treatment of rabies in the comparative context of the roughly contemporary Greek and Latin texts that address the same subjects.[1] The questions posed by these texts require the examination of rabies as a cultural artifact in the rabbinic constructions of reality, as reflected in the Mishnah and in the Palestinian and Babylonian Talmuds, which were completed in approximately 200, 400, and 550 C.E., respectively. The passages on rabies reflect a constellation of rabbinic views on sickness and healing, including the ill-defined and interconnected relationships among what would today be loosely described as medicine, magic and religion. They are also yet another illustration of the ways in which the rabbinic systems of belief were both shaped by, and differed from, the larger environments in which the canon of rabbinic literature evolved.

An overview of the modern understanding of rabies may be helpful. The disease, which is invariably fatal following the onset of clinical symptoms, is an acute viral infection of the central nervous system. It is characterized by a variable incubation period, typically one to three months, which, however, can range from seven days to as long as a year. The virus is found in the saliva of infected animals and is transmitted to humans by the bite of a rabid animal, usually a dog—the focus of most of the ancient sources on rabies. A standard medical textbook summarizes:

> The onset of the disease [in humans] is usually signalized by pain or numbness in the region of the bite, soon followed by apathy, drowsiness, headache and anorexia. This period of lethargy passes rapidly into a state of excitability in which all external stimuli are apt to produce localized twitchings or generalized convulsions. There may be delirium with hallucinations. There is a profuse flow of saliva and spasmodic contractions of the pharynx and larynx occur. The latter are precipitated by any attempt to take liquid or solid food. As a result the patient violently

> refuses to accept any liquids, hence the name hydrophobia. The body temperature is usually elevated and may reach 105 to 107 F in the terminal stages. The stage of hyperirritability gradually passes over into a state of generalized paralysis and coma. Death results from paralysis of respiration (Merrit 1975: 78–79).

Rabies is pathogenic for all warm-blooded animals. However, in mammals, only the orders *carnivora* and *chiroptera* (bats) serve as important reservoirs for the disease.[2] Among the *carnivora*, rabies is found worldwide in *canidae* (dogs, jackals, foxes, and wolves). Infected animals exhibit both "dumb" and "furious" forms of the disease. The latter, characteristic of twenty-five percent of rabid dogs, has given rise to the common impression of the "mad" dog — wild, excitable, aggressive, and prone to the uncontrollable biting of other animals that it encounters (Bedford 1976: 161). Between five and twenty-five percent of the bitten hosts will develop rabies. The likelihood increases with facial and neck bites and in the absence of clothing or thick fur. Both because the typical mode of transmission is through biting, resulting often in the immediate death of the host, and the fact that the virus is so lethal, rapidly destroying both reservoir and host populations, rabies epidemics are self-limiting. Thus, rabies differs from such viral diseases as smallpox, influenza, measles, and yellow fever in that it has never killed large numbers of people, nor has it devastated and, in a sense, shaped human societies as, for example, bubonic plague in fourteenth-century Europe. However, from the time of Xenophon (*Anabasis* 5. 7. 26) and Aristotle (*Historia Animalium* 8. 22) until Pasteur's development of an anti-rabies vaccine in 1885, the disease received a disproportionate amount of attention in both medical and non-medical literature relative to its actual incidence in humans.[3] For example, at a time, contemporary with Pasteur, when according to public health data, fewer than twenty-five people died annually in France from rabies, many French publications dwelt on its dangers and speculated widely concerning its possible causes and cures, some even suggesting that canine rabies might arise spontaneously from the insalubrious effects of French pet culture, which forced would-be hunters' and shepherds' companions into small Parisian apartments and too intimate an association with humans (Kete 1988: 89–99). Other publications discussed the propensity of rabies to bring out the "beast" in man. In an 1886 essay, a Dr. Fredet described a patient of Pasteur:

> The wretched victim attacks his surroundings. Laughing at things, he crushes them, breaks them into a thousand pieces. He beats his head against the wall, as if to split it open. He bites himself. Seizing the flesh of his arms with his teeth, he devours himself. His convulsions become more forceful and generalized. Fits begin in earnest. His voice turns hoarse and convulsive, sounding like the barking of a dog, the howling of a wolf — Is this an animal? Is this a man? (G. E. Fredet, quoted in Kete 1988: 91).

Similarly, several studies commented on the behavioral similarities among victims of rabies, satyriasis, and nymphomania (Kete 1988: 92-95).

To be sure, as Kathleen Kete has noted in an excellent article on nineteenth-century French perceptions of rabies, such studies reflect in large part the constraints and particulars of French bourgeois society. However, they are also illustrative of a seemingly widespread and long-time interest in the disease. This intense interest is a function of the fear and uncertainty concerning the onset of rabies following an animal bite, its visually striking symptomatology, which can include a wild and frenzied form of behavior that "civilization" is supposed to keep in check, its rapid and devastating course and fatal outcome, and, finally, its intimate association with the dog, who for millennia has lived in close proximity to and association with humans, earning in most human societies a reputation for fidelity, devotion, and protectiveness. The dog's ties to both "nature" and "culture" have resulted in its unique role in the epidemiology of rabies. Thus, A. D. Irvin, a veterinary epidemiologist, concluded:

> [The domestic dog] frequently acts as a link host between rabies in wildlife and rabies

> in man and other domestic animals; Steck for example recorded frequent instances of dogs fighting with rabid foxes. Domestic dogs can interbreed with jackals and wolves, they are not limited in their distribution by natural geographical barriers, since they frequently accompany man, and they can revert to a semi-wild state. In this feral condition they usually live a peri-domestic existence, scavenging off man, but they are nonetheless frequently in contact with wildlife and can act as links between wildlife and domestic dogs transmitting the disease in both directions (Irvin 1976: 336).

In Israel today, the occurrence of rabies in humans is very rare. In 1997, three people died of the disease, the first deaths from rabies in Israel in more than thirty years. The source of their exposure is uncertain (Awerbuch et al. 1998). However, every year a growing number of people in Israel seek treatment for possible exposure to rabies, primarily from dog bites. In 1991–92, the incidence of rabies among dogs increased. Veterinary and public health authorities speculated that this may have been a result of the Gulf War, as people sought temporary refuge from urban centers such as Tel Aviv, with a subsequent increase in the stray and unvaccinated dog population. This was an exception to the pattern of a declining percentage of rabies among dogs, following the introduction of mandatory vaccination of owned dogs in 1957 (Awerbuch et al. 1998; Shimshony 1997).

Among documented cases of rabies in Israel in recent years, the largest number have occurred in foxes, followed, among wildlife, by jackals (Shimshony 1997). The close linkage between rabies in dogs and jackals is suggested by epidemiological studies, such as those carried out on the spread of rabies in Zimbabwe (Cumming 1982). Elsewhere, foxes serve as important reservoirs and vectors for the disease (Irvin 1976: 336).

Returning to the ancient world, although it is not possible to definitively determine the epidemiology of rabies in Roman and Byzantine Palestine or in neighboring Persia, it seems likely that the complex relationships and interactions among wolves, foxes, jackals, dogs and wild dogs created reservoirs for the disease, allowing the dog, at times, to serve as a vector for the transmission of the disease to humans. These animals are well attested in Biblical and post-Biblical literature, including the Mishnah and Talmud. Interestingly, one mishnaic text comments that the wolf *(z'b̲)* and the dog (*klb̲*), and the wild dog (*klb̲ kp̲ry*) and jackal/ fox (*shw'l*) are like each other, yet are to be accounted as different kinds (M. Kilaim 1.6). It should be noted that whereas *shw'l* is usually translated as fox, and is distinct from *tn,* jackal, several Biblical and talmudic texts seem to confuse or blur the distinction (Shoshan 1971: 76, citing M. Avot 2.10; TB Kilaim 1.6; Brown et al. 1968: 1043, citing Ju 15:4; Ez 13:4; La 5:18; Ps. 63:11). Thus, Danby (*Mishnah* 1933: 29) translates *shw'l* as jackal, whereas Jastrow (1950: 624, 1538) translates it as both fox and jackal. However, linguistic ambiguities notwithstanding, the Mishnah text reflects the rabbinic authors' awareness of the presence of and connections among a group of canids which, modern science informs us, could serve as both reservoirs and vectors for the introduction of rabies to human populations. It is worth noting that modern Hebrew uses the term *klb̲t*, a derivative of *klb̲* (dog), to designate rabies. The mishnaic and talmudic term for a rabid or "mad" dog is *klb̲ sth. Swth* and related forms of the root, *sth,* are used in other contexts to designate madness, wildness, and insanity (Jastrow 1950: 1531–32). For example, the Babylonian Talmud comments that "no man sins unless the spirit of madness, *rwh sth*, enters him" (TB Sotah 3a).

The centuries of Roman rule in Palestine witnessed an increase in population and urbanization and the development of an elaborate road system. However, it is almost certainly the case that sufficient habitat remained for the maintenance of sizable sylvatic canid populations. Domestic or quasi-domestic dogs would have had ample opportunities to interact with their sylvatic relatives at the margins where towns and cultivated land met the less densely inhabited and uncultivated hilly and low-grade mountainous terrains characteristic of Upper and Lower Galilee, the latter serving as the heartland of the Palestinian Jewish population in the aftermath of the War of Bar-Kochba (132–135 C.E.), and the locale of the rabbinic academies in which the Mishnah and Palestinian Talmud took shape.

The earliest extant rabbinic reference to a rabid animal, Mishnah Yoma 8.5, forms part of a chapter on the laws of the fast for the Day of Atonement. The chapter cites instances in which these laws can be overridden, as in the cases of pregnant women and those suffering from an illness who crave food. The passage reads as follows:

> Whoever is seized by a ravenous hunger, they feed him even unclean things until his eyes are enlightened. Whoever was bitten by a mad dog, they do not feed him the lobe of its liver; but Rabbi Mattiah ben Harash permits it. Moreover Rabbi Mattiah ben Harash said: The one who has a pain in his throat, they drop medicine into his mouth on the Sabbath, because there is doubt concerning danger to life, and every matter of doubt concerning danger to life overrides the Sabbath.

The above, consistent with the rest of the chapter, is illustrative of a rabbinic dictum that allows the prohibitions of the Sabbath to be suspended in all cases where there is a question concerning danger to life. By analogy, this applies also to the Day of Atonement (Yom Kippur, Yoma), described in Leviticus 23:32 as a "sabbath of complete rest." Moreover, the text goes even further in allowing a presumably healthy individual "seized by a ravenous hunger (*blmws*, derived from the Greek *boulimos*)," but lacking understanding, to break the mandated fast for Yom Kippur and even to eat foods that violate the rabbinic dietary laws. The man who is "unenlightened" is, perhaps, like a child who also is not compelled to fast (M. Yoma 8.4). Thus, the ruling that a victim of a rabid dog is not to be given the lobe of the animal's liver is not a function of the "unclean" status of the dog or the commandment to fast on Yom Kippur, for both laws of diet and fasting can be overridden where life is in danger. Rather, this probably reflects a prevailing belief that such treatment would be ineffective. Rabbi Mattiah ben Harash, a second-century figure who is described as neither a physician nor a healer, disagrees. Curiously, according to a talmudic *baraita*, Mattiah moved from Palestine to Rome and there established a rabbinic academy, conferring with other sages when they visited the city (TB Sanhedrin 32b; Yoma 53b). Unlike the rabbis behind the mishnaic ruling, physicians and medical authorities from Rome and elsewhere in the Empire advocated the consumption of the liver of a mad (Latin *rabidus*, from *rabere*, to rage) dog for the treatment of rabies. Thus, Pliny the Elder, who wrote his *Natural History* in the first century C.E., commented:

> Under the tongue of a mad dog is a slimy saliva, which given in drink prevents hydrophobia, but much the most useful remedy is the liver of the dog that bit in his madness to be eaten raw, if that can be done, if it cannot, cooked in any way, or a broth must be made from the boiled flesh (*Natural History* 29.32.99, trans. Jones, p. 247).

Similarly, Pliny's contemporary, Dioscorides, who compiled an encyclopedia of plant and animal medicaments, stated, "The liver of a mad dog, being roasted by those which have been bitten by him, is thought to keep them safe from fear of water" (*Greek Herbal* 2.49, trans. Gunther, p. 103). Dioscorides' work was highly valued by Galen a century later and was also cited by many later Byzantine physicians (Scarborough 1969: 128; Théoridès 1985). In the mid-fourth century, Oribasios, physician to Emperor Julian (361–363 C.E.), recommended the consumption of the liver of the rabid dog as part of a larger regimen for the treatment of rabies (fr. *Synopsis*, cited in Théoridès 1985: 152), as did Aetios of Amida, a sixth-century physician who composed a text on the diseases of the head and brain (Théoridès 1985: 155).

At first glance, the belief in the value of the consumption of the liver of a rabid dog for the treatment of its victims seems out of place with the overall understanding of rabies among Roman and Byzantine authors. They typically liken the "mad" dog to the venomous serpent, both of which transmit lethal poison to their victims, typically through a bite. Indeed, rabies was often discussed in treatises on poison and poisonous animals, such as the opening section of Philumenos' book, *Poisonous Animals* (Théoridès 1985: 149–51).[4] Most medical texts recommended treatments that included cauterizing the wound from the bite and placing on it various plant and animal based dressings and poultices to absorb the poison and to prevent its penetration into the body's organs. Purgatives were also administered to rid the patient of the rabid dog's "venom." Thus, for the bite of a rabid dog, Celsus advised:

> The poison must be drawn out by a cup; next, if the wound is not among sinews and muscles, it must be cauterized; if it cannot be cauterized, it is not amiss to bleed the man. After cauterizing, applications are to be put on as for other burns; if the wound is not cauterized, such medicaments as are powerful corrosives. After this the wound should be filled in and brought to healing, not by any new method, but as already described above. After the bite of a mad dog some send the patients at once to the bath, and there let them sweat as much as their bodily strength allows, the wound being kept open in order that the poison may drop out freely from it (*De Medicina* 5.27.2, trans. Spencer, p. 113).

Given the understanding of rabies as evolving out of a poisonous bite, these remedies make sense in a modern medical context. However, the ingestion of the rabid dog's liver reflects a different approach, which, to quote Dioscorides, was recommended in conjunction with the preceding as part of "the whole art of healing" (*Greek Herbal*, Introduction to Book One, Gunther pp. 2–3). Those authors who believed that the "mad" dog's liver was an effective treatment consistently recommend that it be given to the bite victim to prevent the onset of symptoms; it was not recommended following any visible signs of the disease process.

The consumption of the liver seems to be a form of sympathetic "magical" healing and was sometimes advised in conjunction with such related practices as carrying the tooth or heart of a rabid dog or drinking the blood of a healthy puppy. For example, Dioscorides followed his mention of the prophylactic value of the "mad" dog's liver by adding, "For a precaution they also use the dog tooth of that dog which did bite, putting it into a bag, and so tying it to the arm" (*Greek Herbal* 2.49, trans. Gunther, p. 103). Elsewhere, he recommended drinking dog's blood to treat the bite (*Greek Herbal* 2.96; see also Kee 1986: 41–46). Pliny recommended not only the "mad" dog's liver, but also noted that some prescribe the consumption of a dog's head, the application of ash made from the burnt head of a healthy dog, or the tail of a rabid dog, and the wearing of an amulet made of a worm from a dead dog (*Natural History* 29.32.98–99). Pliny also noted that, "Dogs run away from one who carries a dog's heart, and indeed do not bark if a dog's tongue is placed in the shoe under the big toe" (*Natural History* 29.32.99, trans. Jones, p. 247).

The role of the liver, rather than some other organ, was probably connected to the widely held belief that it was the body's source of blood, a view expressed also in the Babylonian Talmud (TB Berachoth 55a; see also Preuss 1983: 95–98). The ingestion of the blood-laden liver, according to some Byzantine physicians, would overcome the effects of the hydrophobia associated with rabies, would nourish the veins, and induce the patient to drink (e.g., Aetios of Amida: Théoridès 1985: 155).

In considering the long duration of such remedies, one must note the great strength of tradition in the handing down of remedies through generations of Roman and Byzantine medical authorities. Thus, the medical historian Owsei Temkin characterized Byzantine medicine as shaped between the interplay of tradition and empiricism (Temkin 1977).

Both the Palestinian and Babylonian Talmuds comment on M. Yoma 8.5, discussed above. The phrase in the Mishnah, "whoever was bitten by a mad dog," provides the basis for the editors of the Talmuds to present diverse materials on the symptoms of the rabid dog, and the treatments for the victim of its bite. The *g'mara* of both Talmuds begin with a description of the signs of a "mad" dog: its mouth is open, its ears are flapping, its tail is hanging between its thighs, it walks on the sides of the roads, if it barks, its voice is not heard. The Palestinian Talmud adds that other dogs bark at it (Y. Yoma 8.5; TB Yoma 83b). The passage is a general representation of the visible symptoms of some rabid dogs. The "silent bark" probably reflects the difficulty in swallowing and the pharyngeal and laryngeal spasms and progressive paralysis associated with the advanced stages of the disease.

Both texts continue with a discussion attributed to two prominent third-century sages, Rav and Samuel, of whom the latter is one of the few talmudic rabbis described as a physician (TB Baba Mezia 85b, cited in Rosner 1977: 158). The discussion focuses on the etiology of the "mad" dog's affliction. One sage attributes it to an (evil, TB) spirit/wind resting on the dog; the other to a woman (Y), or women (TB), engaged in witchcraft, and penetrating (Y) or playing (TB) with the dog (Y. Yoma 8.5; TB Yoma 83b). The Palestinian Talmud concludes with the story of a German servant of Judah the Patriarch who, having been bitten by a rabid dog, was given the lobe of its liver to eat. The treatment was unsuccessful, and the man died—validating the majority ruling in the Mishnah passage concerning the ineffectiveness of this regimen and exemplifying a statement found here and, similarly, in Y. Berachoth 8.5, "Let no man say to you that he was bitten by a mad dog and lived." The Babylonian Talmud follows Rav's and Samuel's dispute with a passage that reads as follows:

> Where does [the dog's madness] come from?—Rab said: Witches are having their fun with it. Samuel said: An evil spirit rests upon it. What is the practical difference between these two views?—This is the difference as to killing it by throwing something at it. It was taught in accordance with Samuel: When one kills it, one does so only with something thrown against it. One against whom it rubs itself is endangered; one whom it bites, dies. 'One against whom it rubs itself is endangered.' What is the remedy?—Let him cast off his clothing and run. As it happened with R. Huna, the son of R. Joshua, against whom one mad dog rubbed itself in the market-place: he stripped off his garments and ran, saying: I fulfilled in myself, 'Wisdom preserveth the life of him who hath it [Ecclesiastes 7:12.1.] 'One whom it bites, dies.' What is the remedy?—Abaye said: Let him take the skin of a male hyena, and write upon it: I So-and so, the son of that-and-that woman, write upon the skin of a male hyena: Kanti, kanti, kloros. God, God, Lord of Hosts, Amen, Amen, Selah. Then let him strip off his clothes, and bury them in a grave for twelve months of a year. Then he should take them out and burn them in an oven, and scatter the ashes. During these twelve months, if he drinks water, he shall not drink it but out of a copper tube, lest he see the shadow of the demon [*shyd'*] and be endangered. Thus the mother of Abba b. Martha, who is Abba b. Minyumi, made for him a tube of gold (TB Yoma 83b–84a, trans. Jung).

The preceding is an amalgam of views concerning the disease and its treatment, a feature it shares with other talmudic passages on the etiology of sickness in general, and on the symptoms of and remedies for specific illnesses. As noted above, both Talmuds include the dispute, attributed to Rav and Samuel, on the causes of the "mad" dog's affliction. Rav and Samuel are often paired, especially in the Babylonian Talmud. Their discussions range widely and include medical topics—for example, the proper procedures for the widespread practice of bloodletting, which was employed both prophylactically and as a remedy for many illnesses (TB Shabbat 129a–b). Elsewhere, Rav and Samuel discuss the nature of disease (TB Baba Mezia 107b). In commenting on Deuteronomy 7:15, "And the Lord will take away from you all sickness," Rav argues that this is the evil eye from which ninety-nine of one hundred people die. Samuel says that it (sickness) is *rwh*. The word is used in both Talmuds to mean wind or air and also spirit or demon (Jastrow 1950: 1458). Preuss maintains that it should be read here as demon, whereas Kottek suggests that it probably means wind or air (Preuss 1983: 141; Kottek 1985: 15–16). As such, he continues, it exemplifies one of the talmudic concepts of disease, which holds that illness can emanate from climatic and environmental factors including wind, *sharav* (sirocco), and hot and cold (Kottek 1985: 16). The meaning of *rwh* in this passage remains unclear. However, the parallels between this text and the Yoma texts on rabies are striking. In the latter, Rav attributes rabies to the activities of witches, a concept of disease similar to the belief in the evil eye, which he expresses in Baba Mezia. Samuel, on the other hand, attributes the "mad" dog's ailment to a *rwh* in Y. Yoma, and, in TB Yoma, to an evil *rwh*, just as he attributes disease to *rwh* in TB Baba Mezia. To be sure, the passages on rabies state also that the *rwh* rests or is seen upon the dog, an image that is more suggestive of demons than of winds or miasmas. Nevertheless, it is possible that Rav and Samuel are disputing over quite different concepts of disease in their discussion of the "mad" dog: a "demonological" theory of sickness versus a belief in the climatic and contagious origin of illness. However, it seems more likely that they are debating two variations — witches and demons — of the "demonological" theory of disease, which, in this instance, may have been connected with the frenzied (seemingly "possessed") behavior of some rabid dogs. Both concepts of disease are found elsewhere in the Talmuds, as are other theories on the etiology of sickness, including its origin in bile, secretions, blood, fever, and obsession (see especially TB Baba Mezia 107b; Baba Batra 58b; Y. Shabbat 14.3; Kottek 1985: 16–21; Preuss 1983: 139–50).

It is interesting to note that both Yoma passages depict Rav as stating that the doing of witchcraft/sorcery by women caused "madness" in dogs. The linkage between women and witchcraft is common in the canon of rabbinic literature and is illustrated by such passages as M. Avot 2.7, "more women, more witches," and the story of Simeon b. Shetah's execution of eighty female witches in Ashkelon (Y. Hagigah 2.2; Sanhedrin 45b–46a). In all of these passages, the words used for witch and witchcraft are derived from the root *kshf*, a form of which also appears in the Biblical injunction, "Thou shalt not allow a witch [female] to live (Ex 22:17)." *Kishuf*, unlike other forms of sorcery, is defined neither in the Bible nor in rabbinic literature, although it is described as a capital offense in both. Its lack of definition allows it to become associated with a variety of activities (usually by women) and phenomena loathsome to the rabbis, including canine "madness."

Samuel's admonition concerning the necessity of killing a rabid dog by throwing a stone at it in order to avoid physical contact with the animal may reflect a belief in the contagious character of the disease, a contagion which could possibly be inflicted, even indirectly, through clothing. It may also indicate that the talmudic authors shared the view, common to Byzantine medical authorities, that the bite of the "mad" dog, like that of a serpent, transmitted a lethal poison to its victim. Some Byzantine physicians held that the poison could also be transmitted in other ways. Thus, Caelius Aurelianus, the Byzantine era authority who wrote most extensively and carefully on "hydrophobia," commented:

> The antecedent cause of the disease is the bite of a mad dog.... But some cases of hydrophobia arise merely from the wafting of an odor from a mad dog, when normal breathing is vitiated by a chance emanation; poisonous air is then breathed in and distributed to the vital parts.... And once when a seamstress was preparing to patch a cloak rent by the bites of a rabid animal, she adjusted the threads along the end, using her tongue, and then as she sewed she licked the edges that were being joined, in order to make the passage of the needle easier. It is reported that two days later she was stricken by rabies (*Acute Diseases* 3.9.99–100, trans. Drabkin, p. 363).

Caelius Aurelianus probably lived in the fifth century. However, his *Treatise on Acute Diseases* is a Latin translation of a lost work of the second-century physician Soranus, so that the dating of the above passage is uncertain. In any case, the Yoma passage reflects, perhaps, a belief in the potency of the "mad" dog's poison, which might be transmitted through the animal's breath or such secretions as saliva or sweat, to an individual's clothing, and then to the individual. That the bite of a dog was believed to convey poison is also suggested by several talmudic texts that link the bites of mad dogs with those of serpents. Especially clear is a passage in TB Hullin, which states that it was taught that it was forbidden to eat the meat of an animal who was bitten by a "mad" dog or a snake, not because the animal was rendered unfit, but because it was a matter of danger to life (TB Hullin 55a).

After presenting Samuel's statement on the lethal character of the bite of a "mad" dog, the Yoma text follows with a remedy attributed to Abaye, a third/fourth-century Babylonian sage. As described above, Abaye's cure begins with the writing of an incantation on the skin of a male hyena. Notwithstanding Biblical and talmudic prohibitions against "magic," the canon of rabbinic literature depicts prominent rabbis engaged in magical practices, and, indeed, demonstrating their authority through their ability to master and manipulate it. These practices included incantations to heal the sick, several of which, including another attributed to Abaye, are found in TB Shabbat 66b–77a. Of course, the use of incantations was widespread both in Babylonia and in the Roman world throughout the Roman and Early Byzantine periods, the era of the formation of the Mishnah and Talmuds. Even Galen concluded that:

> Some people believe that incantations are equivalent to fairy tales of old women. I, too, thought this way for a long time. As time passed, however, I became convinced of the value of incantations, because of their apparent efficacy. I learned of their use for scorpion bites, and also for bones which remained stuck in the throat, and which became immediately dislodged following the enunciation of an incantation.... The incantation formulas fulfill their purpose (fr. *Alexander of Tralles*, quoted in Preuss 1983: 145–46).

Curiously, one of the incantations mentioned in TB Shabbat was to be used to dislodge bones that were stuck in the throat. Abaye's incantation against rabies begins with the victim writing his name and that of his mother on the skin of a male hyena. Elsewhere, Abaye, in a general comment on incantations, states that his mother told him that incantations which are to be repeated should contain the name of the patient's mother (TB Shabbat 66b). The incantation against rabies follows this dictum and then continues with the writing of the "magical" words, "kanti, kanti, klyros." Although it is not clear in the above translation, the text repeats the efficacious words, with the slight variation, "kandi, kandi, kloros," followed by the name of God, "Yah, Yah, Lord of Hosts" (TB Yoma 84a).

Just as the use of incantations for the remedying of disease was common, so, too, apparently, was the use of hyena skin and meat in the treatment of rabies. Thus Caelius Aurelianus wrote:

> Others [physicians] think the patient should drink from a cup covered with a linen cloth or the skin of a hyena; [in the latter case] they are obviously led astray by a superstition that the natural power of hyenas, opposed as it is to dogs, will dispel the patient's fear. But these notions, which are popularly thought to have been proved sound in actual practice, are obviously quite out of keeping with the medical art (*Acute Diseases* 3.16.137, trans. Drabkin, pp. 387–388).

Timotheus of Gaza, who also lived in the fifth century, commented:

> They who are bitten by a rabid dog fear water [and] seldom live [that is, survive]. Drinking a pill with the right [side] of a hyena, they escape [death] [or] those who sacrifice a puppy and drink the curdled milk from its stomach with water (fr. *On Animals*, trans. F. S. Bodenheimer and A. Rabinowitz, quoted in Théoridès 1985: 153; see also Wellmann 1927).

Approximately four hundred years earlier, Pliny had remarked that the Magi say that eating the meat of the hyena, especially the liver, counteracts the effects of the bites of rabid dogs (*Natural History* 28.27.104, cited in Théoridès 1985: 153).

As described above, according to Abaye, the patient, after committing the incantation to the hyena skin, was to remove his clothes, bury them in a grave for a year, and then burn them in an oven and scatter the ashes. Here, Abaye's remedy is linked with Samuel's statement that an individual should remove his clothes if he rubs against a rabid dog, an act then carried out by Rabbi Huna who encountered a "mad" dog in the market place. However, the motivation for the patient's removal and burial of his clothes is probably not only to prevent the communication of the rabid animal's contagion that is embedded in his garments. This act may also be a form of sympathetic magic. The patient does not die. He is not buried; rather his clothes are laid to rest in a grave for a year, the period after which, for example, the flesh was to have turned to dust and the bones could be removed if they were to be transported for secondary burial. The clothing is removed, heated, and destroyed; the ashes are scattered. The disease, transferred to the clothing, has disappeared.

This interpretation finds support in additional examples of sympathetic healing in the Babylonian Talmud. Indeed, again in TB Shabbat 66b, in a passage attributed to Abaye, he states that his mother told him that for a daily fever

> One must take a white *zuz,* go to a salt deposit, take its weight in salt, and tie it up in the nape of the neck with a white twisted cord. But if this is not [possible], let one sit at the cross-roads, and when he sees a large ant carrying something, let him take and throw it into a [copper] tube and close it with lead, and seal it with sixty seals. Let him shake it, lift it up and say to it, 'Thy burden be upon me and my burden be upon thee' (trans. Freedman).

In the Yoma text, Abaye tells the victim that during the twelve months in which his clothes are buried in the grave he is to drink only through a copper tube, lest he see the shadow of the demon and be endangered. *Shyd'*, the word used here for demon, differs from *rwh,* discussed above, in that it is unambiguous. *Shyd'* and its variants always designate demons. A "demonological" etiology for rabies is consistent with the Yoma material attributed to Abaye. The concern that the patient might see the shadow of the demon may reflect a belief that the patient's reaction might induce illness, perhaps the difficulty in swallowing and concomitant hydrophobia associated with rabies (Ebstein 1903: 258; Rosner 1977: 51). However, it seems more likely that the fear is that the "rabies demon" might seek to possess the patient at a time when he is still vulnerable and, thereby, negate Abaye's remedy. The mention of the drinking tube probably reflects the employment of such devices to aid or compel the patient with rabies to take water, following the onset of difficulty in swallowing. Such tubes are described by Caelius Aurelianus (*Acute Diseases* 3.16.137). Again, Abaye's treatment is reminiscent of Timotheus of Gaza's observations on victims of rabid dogs. The latter commented that if an individual who was bitten by a "mad" dog saw in a mirror the image of the dog, then he would die (Théoridès 1985: 153).

The *g'mara* concludes with a discussion of the diseases and associated remedies for which the rules of the Sabbath, and, by analogy, the Day of Atonement can be overridden. The text follows the Mishnah's ruling in noting that whereas Mattiah ben Harash advocated the suspension of the rules of the Sabbath to give the lobe of the rabid dog's liver to its victims, the sages forbid it. They explain their decision by adding that they do not regard the consumption of the liver to be a cure for the bite of a "mad" dog.

Finally, the danger posed by the "mad" dog is reflected in yet another talmudic text on the Sabbath. The sage, Joshua ben Levi, argued that all animals that cause injury can be killed on the Sabbath. Rabbi Joseph disagreed, stating that it is permitted to kill only five: an Egyptian fly, a Ninevah hornet, an Adiabene scorpion, a snake in Palestine, and a "mad" dog anywhere (TB Shabbat 121b, cited in Rosner 1977: 52).

CONCLUSION

In the introduction to his study of the Graeco-Roman context of the phenomena of healing in the New Testament, Kee defined medicine, miracle, and magic as follows:

> Medicine is a method of diagnosis of human ailments and prescription for them based on a combination of theory about and observations of the body, its function and malfunctions. Miracle embodies the claim

> that healing can be accomplished through appeal to, and subsequent action by the gods, either directly or through a chosen intermediary agent. Magic is a technique, through word or act, by which a desired end is achieved, whether that end lies in the solution to the seeker's problem or in damage to the enemy who has caused the problem (Kee 1986: 3).

As suggested by the above, both the rabbinic and the Greek and Latin texts on rabies reflect a commingling of medicine and magic, two intertwined and often indistinguishable facets of "the whole art of healing" (Dioscorides, *Greek Herbal*, Introduction to Book One, Gunther pp. 2–3). Thus, while the rabbis of the Mishnah and Talmud, the physicians of the Roman and Byzantine periods, and such chroniclers of healing practices as Celsus and Pliny generally disavowed magicians and magical practices, their understandings of disease and recommended remedies often included aspects of magic and suggest how very fluid and interdependent were the categories of medicine and magic.

Interestingly, Galen and other Roman physicians complained in their writings that some patients would more readily follow the advice of the priest at the Asklepieion than they would the physician's prescriptions. At the same time, Galen, for example, acknowledged the importance of dream-visions from Asklepios for diagnosis and treatment. Indeed, Asklepios was both the patron of physicians and the focus of a method of healing in which physicians and medicine were not necessarily involved (Jackson 1988: 138–69; Kee 1986: 34–60).

However, at least one recorded Byzantine practice for the treatment of the bite of the "mad" dog entailed a clear blending of the "medical" with the "miraculous." Beginning in the eighth century, chapels were built in France in honor of Saint Hubert, an eighth-century French bishop, who, many believed, could cure rabies by placing his stole on the forehead of the victim of the "mad" dog. Many shrines of Saint Hubert included his statue as well as that of a dog. In his hand, he held a cauterizing ring that was often shaped in a cross. Those who sought his aid would offer prayers for his intervention and would also have their bite wound cauterized, which, as noted above, was the common Byzantine medical practice employed to eliminate the lethal "venom" of the "mad" dog's bite (Théoridès 1980b). The present study suggests also that the authors and editors of the Mishnah's and Talmuds' texts on the bite of a "mad," that is, rabid, dog were familiar with at least some of the remedies against rabies and the understanding of the disease process, common to many of the roughly contemporary Greek and Latin authors who wrote about rabies. The rabbinic texts are probably representative both of the rabbinic understandings of disease and healing and the reality of the presence of rabies in Roman and Early Byzantine Palestine, together with its treatment.[5]

It is likely that the apparent rabbinic familiarity with the Graeco-Roman understanding and treatment of rabies was rooted in the opportunities for contact between Palestinian Jewry and Graeco-Roman medical and veterinary practitioners. This would have been facilitated not only by the increasing possibilities of travel between Palestine and other regions of the Roman Empire, but, more importantly, by the presence of multi-ethnic populations both in coastal cities, such as Caesarea, and also in such centers of rabbinic learning as Sepphoris/Diocaesarea and Tiberias. Ongoing archaeological excavations and regional studies of Roman and Byzantine Palestine have provided further evidence of the following:

> Many a Hellenistic *polis* [in Palestine] had a well-established Jewish community (Caesarea, Scythopolis, Ptolemais, Gadara, Hippos, Gerasa, and others), while in Roman times, most predominantly Jewish towns included Gentiles among their inhabitants (Tiberias, Diocaesarea, Diospolis and others). In the Roman-Byzantine period there was a growing tendency toward a mixed urban population due to economic and other factors (Maoz 1985: 64).

So, too, the Roman army may have been a conduit of medical and veterinary information. Literary, legal, and epigraphic sources provide ample evidence of the presence, and, indeed, importance of a range of medical and veterinary specialists who were responsible for the well-being of the soldiers, and, in the case of the latter, the cavalry horses and draught and other animals that were essential to the functioning of the army.[6]

Of course, the Mishnah and Talmuds, the sources in which the rabbinic texts on rabies are embedded, differ greatly in content and purpose from the types of literature in which the Greek and Latin texts on rabies are found.[7] The latter are located primarily in treatises on diseases, medicaments, poisons, and animals, and were written by physicians or such Roman aristocratic "gentlemen-scholars" as Celsus and Pliny, both of whom were very interested in medicine. The Mishnah and Talmuds reflect the interests and worldviews of a male scholar class of holy men for whom medicine was largely an incidental interest on those occasions when it served to address an issue that was of concern to them — for example, as it pertained to questions concerning the menstruant, circumcision, the proper slaughtering of animals who were deemed fit for consumption, and, in the case of the texts on rabies, Sabbath observances. As Kass remarked, medical matters that are raised in the Talmud are "a handmaiden to the study of the law" (Kass 1987: 494).

NOTES

1 It is a delight to have this study included in a volume in honor of Professor Eric Meyers, mentor, colleague, and friend. I met Professor Meyers more than thirty years ago. His erudition, intellectual passion, work ethic, warmth, and generosity remain an inspiration.

2 One must note also that the epidemiology of sylvatic rabies is not well understood. Indeed, zoologists and veterinarians increasingly believe that rabies may occur in "silent epidemics" among bats, *mustelidae* (weasels, martens, etc.) and *viverridae* (mongooses, etc.), thereby contributing to the maintenance of the disease. It is likely that the disease is transmitted among maintenance hosts by methods other than or in addition to biting, such as airborne transmission to animals in caves that are densely inhabited by infected bats (Kaplan and Koprowski 1980: 128; Irvin 1976: 333, 344).

3 It is interesting to note that Aristotle confounded later commentators (Wilkinson 1977: 17) in asserting that all animals, with the exception of humans, were susceptible to rabies (*Historia Animalium* 8.22). The Greek term for rabies, *lussa*, means raging madness or frenzy and is used not only of rabid animals but, for example, is also employed in texts that describe martial or Bacchic events. References to rabies may not antedate the fifth century B.C.E. The Code of Eshnunna, which is dated to ca. 2000 B.C.E., describes the penalties to the owner of a vicious dog whose bite results in the death of an individual. However, the text, sometimes cited as the earliest reference to rabies, may describe only ill-tempered canines (*Laws of Eshnunna* 1958: 138). Adamson has gathered several Old Babylonian texts which, he suggests, may describe rabies in dogs and other animals. Again, the texts are ambiguous, and may well refer to "vicious" animals or to ailments other than rabies. However, it is clear that Old Babylonian texts assume the domestication of the dog. For example, Adamson cites four tablets from the Ur III period that mention rations for dogs: BM 15149, 15170, 15185, 14562, and 13495 (Adamson 1977: 143). For an overview of the major recorded episodes of rabies epidemics in Europe and in the Americas, see Steele 1975: 5–19 and Ackerknecht 1966: 746–47. On eighteenth and nineteenth-century theories concerning the etiology and treatment of rabies, many of which, prior to Pasteur's landmark research, were similar to and no more accurate than those advanced, for example, by Celsus (*De Medicina* 5.27.2) and Pliny (*Natural History* 29.32.97–103; 32.17.45–48) in the first century C.E., see Théoridès 1976; Carter 1982: 68–77; Théoridès 1974: 1253–56; Wilkinson 1977: 19–22. To illustrate the preceding, one need only note the practice, still widespread in the late nineteenth century, of "worming" the tongue of the dog to prevent rabies. The "worm" is, in fact, a normal anatomical structure of the dog (*Modern Veterinary Practice* 1981: 962). Pliny had written, "There is a little worm [*vermiculus*] on the tongue of the dog which the Greeks call *lytta*, and if this is taken away when they are baby puppies they neither go mad nor lose their appetite" (*Natural History* 29.31.100, trans. Jones, p. 247). On Pasteur's breakthrough discovery of an anti-rabies vaccine and its subsequent refinements for the treatment of rabies, see Kaplan and Koprowski 1980: 122–31 and Malkin 1986: 40–45.

4 The renowned Jewish physician, philosopher, and rabbinic commentator Maimonides discussed the symptoms of, and treatment for, rabies in this *Treatise on Poisons,* which was composed in 1198. He stated:

> The early physicians already noted the varied character of a mad dog's symptoms.... The mad dog always wanders about by himself, in a roundabout way, leaning on walls and never barking.... Everything mentioned in the literature against the bites of a mad dog is useful, if at all, only when applied before rabies sets in. When such is the case I have as yet seen nobody who escaped with his life.... The dangerous symptoms indicating rabies appear as a rule only after eight days, sometimes even much later. It therefore follows that anybody bitten by a stray dog should adhere to the general rules, that is, bandaging, incision, sucking out, copious blood-letting from the affected spot by means of cupping glasses, vomiting, and treatment by theriac (quoted in Rosner 1977: 52; see also Shoshan 1967: 285).

On the treatment of rabies in medieval Arab medical texts, see Théoridès 1980a.

5 Kottek summarizes his study of the concepts of disease in the Talmuds with a helpful chart (1997: 23):

I.	Magical Aspects:	Evil Eye
II.	Humors:	Blood, Bile (Secretions)
III.	Climate:	Air (wind), Sharav, 'Cold and Warm'
IV.	Specific Agents:	Fever, Obsession, Carelessness
A.	Popular Beliefs:	Evil Eye, Carelessness, 'Cold and Warm'
B.	Empirical Medicine:	Bile, Fevers, Secretions, Obsession
C.	Theoretical Medicine:	Blood, Bile, Climate

6 On the medical service of the Roman army, see, for example, Davies 1989: 209–36. On veterinary medicine in Greek and Latin sources, for both civilian and military contexts, see, for example, Scarborough 1969: 171–73, and R. E. Walker, "Appendix Roman Veterinary Medicine" in Toynbee 1973: 301–43.

7 The earliest Jewish medical book, the *Book of Asaph,* is of uncertain date. Rosner dates it to between the third and seventh centuries (Rosner 1977: 119). It includes Hebrew translations of portions of the works of Dioscorides and Galen. It is also important to note that the authors of the Mishnah and the Talmuds were not particularly interested in dogs, the animal that is most closely associated with rabies in Roman and Byzantine sources. The canon of rabbinic literature mentions dogs infrequently and only in passing. They are depicted in close proximity to people—in towns, marketplaces, and homes. However, this literature does not include lengthy discussions on the breeding and care of dogs and how they can be utilized best in agriculture and hunting—topics that were addressed by many Greek and Roman authors. For example, Varro and Columella discuss the breeding and care of dogs in their works on farming (Varro, *On Agriculture* 2.9.1–15; Columella, *On Agriculture* 7.12.1–13.3). The latter mentions rabies atop a section on canine diseases (*On Agriculture* 7.12.14). Other Roman authors in the tradition of Xenophon (*On Hunting*) wrote books on hunting in which they discussed both the breeding and the care of dogs, and the ways in which dogs that were properly raised and trained could aid the hunter. Ovid's friend Grattius composed one such book in which he mentioned rabies as part of a section on canine diseases (*Cynegticon* 408–66, cited in Anderson 1985: 44). Grattius and others wrote for an audience that regarded hunting both as a means to acquire food and as a sport—one in which dogs played an important role. In contrast to the preceding, references to hunting in rabbinic literature suggest that it was regarded as acceptable only as a means of food acquisition. For some of the important literary, artistic, and epigraphic sources on the roles of the dog in Roman society, see Toynbee 1973: 102–24. These roles included not only aids to hunting, farming, and shepherding, but also roles as draught animals, circus performers, watchdogs, and beloved pets. Dogs were also seemingly linked with some healing deities (Toynbee 1973: 122–24; Jackson 988: 142–48). This study was completed before the publication of Joshua Schwartz's article, "Dogs in Jewish Society in the Second Temple Period and in the Time of the Mishnah and Talmud," *Journal of Jewish Studies* 55, no. 2 (2004): 246–77, a very thoughtful and informative examination of the varied roles of, and attitudes toward dogs. On "mad" dogs, see pp. 270–72.

REFERENCES

Ackerknecht, E. H.
1966 Zur Geschichte der Tollwut. *Journal Suisse de Médecine* 96: 746–48.

Adamson, P.
1977 The Spread of Rabies Into Europe and the Probable Origin of This Disease in Antiquity. *Journal of the Royal Asiatic Society of Great Britain and Ireland* 2: 140–44.

Anderson, J. K.
1985 *Hunting in the Ancient World*. Berkeley, CA: University of California.

Aristotle
1970 *Historia Animalium I–III*, trans. A. L. Peck. Loeb Classical Library. Cambridge, MA: Harvard University.

Aurelianus, C.
1950 *On Acute Diseases and On Chronic Diseases*, ed. and trans. I. E. Drabkin. Chicago, IL: University of Chicago.

Awerbuch, T.; Bader, K.; and Greenbalt, C. L.
1998 Ecological Continuum and Disease Transmission Across Political Borders Between Israel and Its Neighbors. In *The Fourth Nordic Conference on Middle Eastern Studies: The Middle East in a Globalizing World*. Oslo, 13–16 August. Http://www.hf.uib.no/smi/pao/awerbuch.html.

Babylonian Talmud (Talmud Bavli)
1972 Jerusalem.

Babylonian Talmud: Hebrew-English Edition of the Babylonian Talmud – Shabbath I
1972 Trans. H. Freedman. London: Soncino.

Babylonian Talmud: Hebrew-English Edition of the Babylonian Talmud – Yoma
1974 Trans. L. Jung and I. Epstein. London: Soncino.

Bedford, P. G. C.
1976 Diagnosis of Rabies in Animals. Pp. 160–62 in *The Veterinary Record*, vol. 93. London: The Association.

Brown, F.; Driver, S. R.; and Briggs, C. A.
1968 *The Brown-Driver-Briggs Hebrew and English Lexicon: With an Appendix Containing the Biblical Aramaic*. Oxford: Clarendon.

Carter, K. C.
1982 Nineteenth-Century Treatments for Rabies as Reported in the Lancet. *Medical History* 26: 67–78.

Celsus, A. C.
1953 *De Medicina II*, trans. W. Spencer. Loeb Classical Library. Cambridge, MA: Harvard University.

Columella, L. J. M.
1954 *On Agriculture II*, trans. E. S. Forster and E. H. Heffner. Loeb Classical Library. Cambridge, MA: Harvard University.

Cumming, D.
1982 A Case History of the Spread of Rabies in an African Country. *South African Journal of Science* 78: 443–47.

Davies, R. W.
1989 *Service in the Roman Army*. New York, NY: Columbia University.

Dioscorides
1959 *The Greek Herbal of Dioscorides*, trans. R. T. Gunther. New York, NY: Hafner.

Ebstein, W.
1903 *Die Medizin im Neuen Testament und im Talmud*. Stuttgart: Enke.

Irvin, A.
1976 The Epidemiology of Wildlife Rabies. Pp. 333–48 in *The Veterinary Record*, vol. 87. London: The Association.

Jackson, R.
1988 *Doctors and Diseases in the Roman Empire*. Norman, OK: University of Oklahoma.

Jastrow, M.
1950 *A Dictionary of the Targumim, the Talmud Babli and Yerusahlmi, and the Midrashic Literature*. New York, NY: Pardes.

Kaplan, M. M., and Koprowski, H.
1980 Rabies. *Scientific American* 242: 120–34.

Kass, N.
1987 The Place of Medicine in the Talmud. *Koroth* 9: 494–502.

Kee, H. C.
1986 *Medicine, Miracle and Magic in New Testament Times*. Cambridge: Cambridge University.

Kete, K.
1988 La Rage and the Bourgeoisie: The Cultural Context of Rabies in the French Nineteenth Century. *Representations* 22: 89–107.

Kottek, S.
1981 The Last Word: Rabies Control in Olden Times. *Modern Veterinary Practice* 62: 962.

1985 Concepts of Disease in the Talmud. *Koroth* 9: 7–33.

Laws of Eshnunna
1958 In *The Ancient Near East: An Anthology of Texts and Pictures*, ed. J. B. Pritchard, trans. A. Goetze. Princeton, NJ: Princeton University.

Liddell, H. G., and Scott, R.
1968 *A Greek-English Lexicon*. Oxford: Clarendon.

Malkin, H.
1986 Louis Pasteur and 'Le Rage' – 100 Years Ago. *Perspectives in Biology and Medicine* 30: 40–46.

Maoz, Z.
1985 Comments on Jewish and Christian Communities in Byzantine Palestine. *Palestine Exploration Quarterly* 117: 59–68.

Merritt, H. H.
1975 *A Textbook of Neurology*. Fifth Edition. Philadelphia, PA: Lea and Febiger.

Mishnah
1933 Trans. H. Danby. Oxford: Oxford University.

Mishnah
1935 Ed. C. Albeck. Jerusalem: Bialik Institute.

Palestinian Talmud (Talmud Yerushalmi)
1948 Vienna, Cracow, Krotoschin Edition. Jerusalem: Shulsinger.

Pliny
1963 *Natural History VIII*, trans. W. H. S. Jones. Loeb Classical Library. Cambridge, MA: Harvard University.

Preuss, J.
1983 *Biblical and Talmudic Medicine*, ed. and trans. F. Rosner. New York, NY: Hebrew Publishing Company.

Rosner, F.
1977 *Medicine in the the Bible and the Talmud: Selections from Classical Jewish Sources*. New York, NY: Ktav and Yeshiva University.

Scarborough, J.
1969 *Roman Medicine*. Ithaca, NY: Cornell University.

Shimshony, A.
1997 Epidemiology of Emerging Zoonoses in Israel. *Emerging Infectious Diseases* 3. Http://www.cdc.gov/ncidod/eid/vol3no2/shimshon.htm.

Shoshan, A.
1967 Rabies and Leptospirosis in Ancient Hebrew Sources. *Koroth* 4: 283–90 (in Hebrew).
1971 *Animals in Jewish Literature: The Jew and His Animal* (Hebrew). Rehovot: Shoshanim.

Steele, J. H.
1975 History of Rabies. Pp. 1–29 in *The Natural History of Rabies*, ed. G. M. Baer. New York, NY: Academic.

Temkin, O.
1977 Byzantine Medicine: Tradition and Empiricism. Pp. 202–22 in *The Double Face of Janus and Other Essays in the History of Medicine*, ed. O. Temkin. Baltimore, MD: John Hopkins University.

Théoridès, J.
1974 Some Remarks on the History of Rabies. Pp. 1252–57 in *Proceedings of the XXIII International Congress of the History of Medicine, London 2–9 September 1972*. London: Wellcome Institute of the History of Medicine.
1976 Quelques Aspects de la Rage au 18e Siècle. *Clio Medica* 11: 95–109.
1980a Rabies in Arabian Medicine. *Studies in the History of Medicine* 4: 13–22.
1980b Saints in Medical History: A Complement. *Clio Medica* 14: 269–70.
1985 Rabies in Byzantine Medicine. Pp. 149–58 in *Symposium on Byzantine Medicine*, ed. J. Scarborough. Washington, DC: Dumbarton Oaks Research Library and Collection.

Toynbee, J. M.
1973 *Animals in Roman Life and Art*. Ithaca, NY: Cornell University.

Varro, M. T.
1954 *On Agriculture*, trans. W. D. Hooper and H. B. Ash. Loeb Classical Library. Cambridge, MA: Harvard University.

Wellmann, M.
1927 Timotheos von Gaza. *Hermes* 62: 179–204.

Wilkinson, L.
1977 The Development of the Virus Concept as Reflected in Corpora of Studies on Individual Pathogens: 4. Rabies – Two Millenia of Ideas and Conjecture on the Aetiology of a Virus Disease. *Medical History* 21: 15–31.

Xenophon
1922 *Anabasis*, trans. C. L. Brownson. Loeb Classical Library. New York, NY: Putnam's.
1925 *On Hunting*, trans. E. C. Marchant. Loeb Classical Library. New York, NY: Putnam's.

Chapter 30

Celsus of Pergamum: Locating a Critic of Early Christianity

by Stephen Goranson

Alēthēs Logos of Celsus, preserved in large part with Origen's response in *Contra Celsum*, is the most significant extant second-century literary attack on Christianity. Celsus attacked Christianity not only for philosophic reasons, but also because he was alarmed about social consequences of the spread of Christianity. His book was occasioned by Christians refusing to honor the cults of the Roman Empire, avoiding military service, and even seeking martyrdom (for Greek text, see Borret 1967–76; for English translation, see Chadwick 1953). To understand fully Celsus' experience of Christians and his view of this threat to society as he perceived it, one would need to know where he lived. Rome, Alexandria, and Caesarea Maritima have all been proposed as Celsus' residence. But, as this paper will show, these three cities are quite improbable; the evidence strongly indicates that Celsus lived in Pergamum in Asia Minor.

In the following sections, first, we briefly consider whether and how it matters where Celsus lived. Then, we show that Rome, Alexandria, and Caesarea as proposed homes for Celsus are each highly improbable. Finally, the converging evidence points to Pergamum.

WHY LOCATE CELSUS?

Celsus wrote *Alēthēs Logos* most probably during the reign of Marcus Aurelius, 161–180 (Borret 1967: I, 15–21; Chadwick 1953: xxiv–xxviii; Rosenbaum 1972: 102–11; Burke 1981: 49–57; Grant 1988: 136), perhaps in 178, near the end of the Stoic-influenced emperors. Origen responded with his *Contra Celsum*, which he wrote in 248 or 249 in Caesarea (Nautin 1977: 375–76). Celsus and Origen wrote at different times and in different places. In various passages Origen depicted a different social reality than Celsus. Consider the following example: Celsus delivered some of his condemnation of Christianity via a fictitious Jewish character. Because this Jewish interlocutor of Celsus quoted from a play of Euripides, Origen declared that Celsus' Jew was an unpersuasive creation, because "Jews are not at all well read in Greek literature" (Origen, *Contra Celsum* [hereafter cited as *Cels.*] II, 34). Probably, in this case, both Celsus and Origen honestly related their experience. While the Jews Origen knew may not have attended such theatre productions, clearly in some times and locations Jews did, as shown, for instance, by an inscription in the theatre in

Miletus in Asia Minor, designating certain seats for the Jews. The inscription, located on good fifth-row seats, dates from the late second or early third century (Schürer 1986: III, 167–68) — that is, a time between Celsus and Origen. Another inscription in the odeum at Aphrodisias in Caria identifies the seats of certain Jews (Seager and Kraabel 1983: 181). The question whether Jews would know such a play as Euripides' *Bacchae* was also a matter of discussion among various excavators of Sepphoris, where a mosaic of Dionysius was uncovered near the theatre. For instance, Batey (1991) suggested that Jesus of Nazareth saw in Sepphoris a production of *The Trojan Women* by Euripides; but I am skeptical of his claim (Goranson 1992).

In another instance, Origen also criticized Celsus for failing to note that some Christians still observe Jewish law, and, in a manner of speaking, informed the deceased Celsus, as if he should have known, that they are called Ebionites; again, what Origen assumed as common knowledge may not have applied in the time and location of Celsus (*Cels.* II, 1). Though the term gradually evolved from a generic Hebrew usage, Irenaeus of Lyon is the first Greek writer known to use the term "Ebionite" as a heresy name (e.g., in *Adver. Haer.* V, 13), writing in ca. 190, that is, between the time of Celsus and Origen.

A recent study makes an interesting case for a later date (circa 200) for the book by Celsus (Hargis 1999: 20–24). I mention it here not because I found that argument persuasive (I did not), but because, though this study stresses the possible importance of dating the work, it ignores the geography of Celsus, hence missing the possible importance of regionalism — a concept explored in the Galilee by Eric Meyers. It may be worth noting that Origen himself, though he tried to place Celsus philosophically and theologically, also ignored the geographic location of Celsus, offering no explicit speculation about this matter which might have been helpful to historians.

CELSUS OF ROME?

Rome has been presented in several studies as the home of Celsus. For instance, Williams declared, "He was, as it seems, a Roman lawyer," whose residence in the city of Rome is "almost certain" (Williams 1935: 79; further arguments for Rome: Keim 1873; Chadwick 1953: xxviii; Borret 1976: V, 137–39; Patrick 1892: 3–9). According to Bauer, because Celsus wrote of "the great church" (*Cels.* V, 59) and "those of the multitude" (*Cels.* V, 61), Celsus could not have learned about the orthodox Christian church "anywhere but in Rome" (Bauer 1971: 50, nn. 30 and 148). However, Bauer offers no other supporting evidence for Rome (Burke 1981: 15–16). Rome may have been a convenient place to learn of such groups as Marcellians, Valentinians, and Mithraists, but this provides only a weak argument, as these groups are all found elsewhere as well.

There were some Roman officials named Celsus, e.g., Celsus Iulius Aquilla, another Asia Minor native (Friesen 1993), who became governor of Asia Minor, and for whom the Library of Celsus in Ephesus is named. But our Celsus, unusually, provides no fuller name nor title; so this provides no help. If Celsus were an employee of the emperor, he surely would have named his benefactor. Below, we will consider the hypothesis that our Celsus can be identified with another contemporary Celsus — who is also known only by that single name.

The main argument for Rome seems to be the patriotism of Celsus. Celsus did appeal to Christians to "help the emperor...and cooperate with him..." (*Cels.* VIII, 73). Yet Celsus demonstrates no firsthand knowledge of Roman realia. Though highly literate, he never quotes any Latin authors nor shows any interest in Latin culture. In fact, Celsus is a Hellenist to a chauvinist degree. He asked Christians to cooperate with the Romans and "their" — note, not "our" — "customary honors" (*Cels.* VIII, 69). Celsus did not bother to distinguish between "the Persian or Roman emperor" in his explanation of the importance of the hierarchy of daemons who help maintain civilization if they are not "insulted" (*Cels.* VIII, 35). Christians, Celsus recommended, "ought to pay formal acknowledgement to them, in so far as this is expedient" (*Cels.* VIII, 62). It becomes apparent that Celsus regarded the Romans as useful in preventing barbarians from destroying "true" — that is, Hellenistic — culture.

We are allowed a rare glimpse of Celsus' emotions, as he seems to sigh: "Would that it were possible to unite under one law the inhabitants of Asia, Europe and Libya, both Greeks [Hellenes] and barbarians even at the furthest limits" (*Cels.* VIII, 72). Celsus is no enthusiast for Rome; Hellenes, not Romans, serve as the antithesis to the barbarians. In his geographic list, the priority of Asia, I suggest, is not without significance. It is not Europe, with Rome (and Greece itself!), that Celsus regarded as the source of this imagined spread of Hellenic civility, nor is it Libya (i.e., Africa), including Alexandria. Rather, his pleasant dream began in Asia. That this dream did not begin in Greece accords with Glucker's conclusion that Celsus was "most unlikely to have been an Athenian" (Glucker 1978: 144). For a parallel case where the order of terms appears to be significant, compare Hippolytus of Rome, writing ca. 225:

> Such is the true doctrine [*alēthēs logos*] I regard to the divine nature. O ye men, Greeks and Barbarians, Chaldeans and Assyrians, Egyptians and Libyans, Indians and Ethiopians, Celts and ye Latins who lead armies, and all ye that inhabit Europe and Asia and Libya (*Refutation of All Heresies* X, 30; trans. Roberts and Donaldson 1886: V, 152; Greek text, numbered X.34.1, in Marcovich 1986).

Hippolytus, writing in Rome, placed Europe first; Celsus, of whose location we inquire, placed Asia first.

Keim argued that Celsus lived in Rome. Chadwick argued against Keim's presentation that our Celsus was the same individual as the Celsus mentioned by Lucian, dismissively writing, "...cannot one picture Origen's opponent arm in arm with [Lucian] the Samosatene? They lived at the same time, and even in the same place." (Chadwick 1953: xxv). Though Chadwick does not explicitly name this proposed place, it is not the one Keim intended. As we shall see, our Celsus may, indeed, have walked together with Lucian, not in Rome, but in Pergamum. Celsus was not a resident of Rome.

CELSUS OF ALEXANDRIA?

"Kelsos von Alexandreia" — such is the listing for Celsus in the reference work, *Der Kleine Pauly: Lexikon der Antike* (Dörrie 1969; additional arguments for Alexandria, Chadwick 1953: xxix; Borret 1967–76: 139–40). Though no ancient writer refers to him this way, many modern scholars have sought his home there. He could have learned of Gnostic groups in Alexandria — though, again, not only there. He shows some interest in Egyptian religion, but what he described was available from historians, and Herodotus in particular. Celsus never claimed that he visited Egypt, and he provides no eyewitness accounts of Egypt. In fact, in the extant text of Celsus, he nowhere claims to have traveled at all and may have been disinclined or unable to travel; in any case, nothing requires his presence outside Pergamum. Celsus is aware of Jewish Logos theology (*Cels.* II, 31), which may suggest the name of Philo of Alexandria to modern readers, but Celsus shows no acquaintance with Philo or Aristobolus, as Origen noticed (*Cels.* IV, 51). Celsus had read Aristo of Pella, who could be his source in this case (*Cels.* IV, 52). Celsus mentioned an Egyptian musician named Dionysius, who tells him philosophers are immune to effects of magic (*Cels.* IV, 41). That Celsus identified this acquaintance as an Egyptian suggests that he was *not* his neighbor in Egypt.

Williams remarked that Celsus' book must have been well known, since he imagined the text traveling from Rome to Alexandria, where Origen would encounter it (Williams 1935: 80). In fact, Origen did *not* encounter it there. Origen did not know of *Alēthēs Logos* until he had moved to Caesarea, where his patron Ambrose sent it to him (*Cels.* Preface, 1 and VIII, 76, the latter asking if Ambrose will "search out and send" an additional treatise of Celsus; on Ambrose, see Trigg 1983 and Nautin 1977). Apparently, neither had Clement of Alexandria heard of it, which would be difficult to conceive if Celsus had attacked Christianity in his city. Origen had already written *Exhortation to Martyrdom* at Ambrose's request when Ambrose — who Origen had converted from Valentinian Gnosticism — was still in Alexandria. But it was only *after* Ambrose moved to Nicomedia in Bithynia in Asia that he wrote to Origen that Celsus' book was a threat to the faith of his Christian neighbors. Celsus' book is first attested not in Alexandria, but in Asia.

CELSUS OF CAESAREA?

According to Frend, during the reign of Marcus Aurelius "the Christians were being challenged on their own ground, by Celsus, probably in Caesarea in Palestine…"(Frend 1965: 268). Again, it is necessary to recall that Origen was unaware of the book *Alēthēs Logos* and uncertain about the identity of Celsus when he was sent the book. If Celsus had lived in Caesarea, Origen was a sufficiently diligent student that he would have learned about him.

Palestine is suggested as Celsus' home primarily because he wrote of prophets in Phoenicia and Palestine who "wander about begging and roaming around cities and military camps" and

> pretend to be moved as if giving some oracular utterance…'. Blessed is he who has worshipped me now! But I will cast everlasting fire upon all the rest' … they then go on to add incomprehensible, incoherent, and utterly obscure utterances, the meaning of which no intelligent person could discover; for they are meaningless and nonsensical, and give a chance for any fool or sorcerer to take the words in whatever sense he likes (*Cels.* VII, 9).

(By the way, it may be noted that usage of Hebrew in some amulets, not limited to Palestine, may have appeared to some as especially opaque). But Celsus rhetorically linked these prophets with the earlier prophets in Judaea (*Cels.* VII, 8). Origen questioned whether Celsus really had first-hand knowledge of these prophets, especially because Celsus claimed that, upon examining them, the prophets supposedly admitted that they were frauds, and thereafter Celsus gave no details elaborating on such a coup (*Cels.* VII, 11). According to Burke, "all [Celsus] is trying to do is characterize the OT prophets by contemporary examples from the same geographic area. This becomes clear if one follows his argument from the beginning of book VII…" (Burke 1981: 183–85). Even though Burke correctly perceived the literary nature of this description, he then reverted to the widely-held but misconceived view that the passage indicated Celsus was familiar with the area. In this case, Origen's protest of ignorance of Celsus most likely is valid. Furthermore, Celsus certainly demonstrates no knowledge of Semitic languages, which would make long-term residence in Palestine, or any lands eastward, unlikely. In any case, no other evidence supports Caesarea.

CELSUS OF PERGAMUM

As it happens, the disdain Celsus felt for such "begging priests" and "scoundrels" appeared earlier and more believably when Celsus specified, as especially unreasonable people,

> begging priests of Cybele and soothsayers, worshippers of Mithras and Sabazius, and whatever else one might meet, apparitions of Hecate or of some other daemon or daemons (*Cels.* I, 9).

This conglomeration of groups would more likely be encountered in Asia Minor than in Palestine.

Additionally, other groups and places mentioned by Celsus were found in Asia. Celsus refers to places where "gods are to be seen in human form" (*Cels.* VII, 35); they are in Boeotia, Greece, and Cilicia. Celsus also refers to miracles of Aristeas the Preconnesian, in northern Asia, and "a certain Clazomenian," (i.e., from near Smyrna; *Cels.* III, 3). In a favorable reference to Asclepius foretelling the future, Celsus named cities dedicated to him (*Cels.* III, 3); these cities are in Greece and Asia Minor, e.g., Pergamum. Angel worship plays a prominent role in Celsus' condemnation of Jews and Christians; this practice is attested in Asia Minor (*Cels.* I, 26 and V, 6; see Burke 1981: 139–40; Johnson 1975; Kraabel 1968). Celsus is the only source for a group of Sibyllists (*Cels.* V, 61); since such a group is otherwise unattested, they cannot be surely located, but Phrygia (the birthplace of Montanism) was home to many "wandering prophets," who expected, and hoped for, an end to the world — the sort of people that worried Celsus.

Celsus knew of Christian martyrdoms (*Cels.* VIII, 6 and 52; Frend 1965: 268–302). During his time Polycarp was martyred in Smyrna. In Pergamum, Carpus and his companions were burned alive. After Carpus refused to honor the emperor, according to the *Acta Carpi*, a woman named Agathonike rushed forward and joined him. According to this account, the crowd cried, "It is a terrible sentence; these are unjust decrees" (Musurillo 1972: 29). While this account cannot be considered entirely reliable, it may be sufficiently accurate to help us understand the occasion for Celsus' book. As Bigg observed, while Marcus Aurelius was wondering at the dogged persistence of the Christians, Celsus was asking whether the breech could be healed (Bigg 1913: 314).

A contemporary of Celsus, Melito of Sardis, wrote an apology to Marcus Aurelius. As excavations at Sardis have shown, particularly at the large synagogue, the Jewish community there prospered, having been settled in Sardis for many generations. Many of the synagogue donor inscriptions proudly refer to their status as citizens of Sardis, along with other titles indicating various government offices. Melito spoke quite harshly of the Jews, and he clearly fought an uphill battle in his attempt to show his minority community of Christians as good citizens. This is the sort of conflict between Jews and Christians that Celsus reflects (Seager and Kraabel 1983; Wilken 1976). Though Celsus shows no great affection for Judaism, he apparently was familiar with a society in which Jews played a role he found acceptable — unlike the Jews in Palestine (and North Africa and Cyprus), who seemingly had not given up revolution. Celsus' view of Christianity makes sense in Asia Minor. Pergamum, in particular, presents a highly plausible home for Celsus; it was a cultured city and seaport that once had a famous library. As noted by Josephus (*Antiquities* XVI.10.22 [247–55]), the Jewish community there had good relations with Rome since Hasmonean times.

An important question is whether our Celsus is identical with the Celsus to whom Lucian dedicated *Alexander the False Prophet*, a story about a false oracle in Abonoteichus in Asia. Alexander is presented as abusing the honorable Asclepius cult. In favor of the identification is the fact that the two are contemporary writers named Celsus, whose interests included oracles, magic, and Christianity. The only difficulty in the identification is that our Celsus appears to be a middle Platonist, whereas Lucian commends Epicurus to his friend, making Celsus appear to some readers to be an Epicurean. Clay, however, cautioned that Lucian modifies actual characters in these works (Clay 1992); and, in any case, Lucian imputes no more Epicureanism to Celsus than to himself. Further, Celsus may have changed his philosophic preferences since his earlier book on magic (Lucian, *Alexander*, 21; *Cels.* I, 68, a book with evident parallels in book 4, 28–42 of Hippolytus, *Refutation of All Heresies*), perhaps written in the time of Hadrian (*Cels.* I, 8.). Galen of Pergamum also corresponded with a Celsus, listed as an Epicurean in the account of Galen's library (Mueller 1891: 124). Many writers have argued against identity (e.g., Chadwick 1953: xxiv–xxvi; Burke 1981: 60–67; Frede 1994). Many others have argued for identification (e.g., Keim 1873: 275–93; Hoffmann 1987: 30–32; Schwartz 1973; for further bibliography, see Pichler 1980).

Schwartz alluded to the possibility (in a note, within parentheses, and with a question mark) that Celsus could have lived in the province of Asia or Syria (Schwartz 1960: 144, n. 2). Stern made a similar brief observation (Stern 1980: 2, 224–5). If the two contemporary authors named Celsus are identical, this would provide additional indication of the residence of our Celsus in Pergamum. Though he spent years in Rome, Galen was born and died in Pergamum and had served as physician in the Pergamene Asclepius temple. And Lucian shows interest in the Asclepius cult in *Alexander*, the book dedicated to Celsus.

Pergamum was dedicated to Asclepius, which Celsus notes; in fact, his most favorable comments concerning any cult pertain to Asclepius (*Cels.* III, 3; III, 24; III, 43; VII, 53). In accord with the hypothesis mentioned above, our Celsus may have been acquainted with Galen of Pergamum, who had served at the Asclepius temple. The book that Lucian dedicated to Celsus — our Celsus — was precisely about the abuse of an Asclepius cult in Asia, and this type of abuse by soothsayers was what our

Celsus had written about in his book on magic — a book acknowledged by Origen and Lucian. Like both Galen and Lucian, Celsus berated Christians for privileging faith over reason (Wilken 1984).

Pergamum experienced a cultural renaissance and rebuilding, financed by Hadrian, in the second century. Besides the above-mentioned martyrdoms, Pergamum had a theatre, a Panathenaea observance when the "robe of Athena ... is seen by every spectator" (*Cels.* VI, 42), numerous Cybele statues (*Cels.* I, 9), and many other features reflected in Celsus' attack on Christianity (Koester 1998). Celsus' patriotic viewpoint on Pergamum is practically the opposite of that found in the anti-Roman *Apocalypse of John,* which is starkly disapproving of the mainstream Pergamene society. Much more so than Rome, Alexandria, or Caesarea, Pergamum is the plausible setting for Celsus. On the geographic location of Celsus, the evidence presented here certainly suggests we can better understand the concerns of Celsus, given recognition of his place in the society of Asia Minor. Surely, Celsus provides one of the most important sources on second-century Christianity. The realization that he encountered Christianity in Asia Minor will help clarify that history.

REFERENCES

Batey, R. A.
1991 *Jesus & The Forgotten City: New Light on Sepphoris and the Urban World of Jesus.* Grand Rapids, MI: Baker.

Bauer, W.
1971 *Orthodoxy and Heresy in Earliest Christianity,* eds. R. Kraft and G. Krodel. Philadelphia, PA: Fortress.

Bigg, C.
1913 *Christian Platonists of Alexandria.* Oxford: Clarendon.

Borret, M.
1967 -1976 *Origène. Contre Celse,* 5 vols. Sources Chrétiennes 132, 136, 147, 150, 227. Paris: Cerf.

Burke, G. T.
1981 Celsus and Late Second Century Christianity. Unpublished Ph. D. Dissertation. University of Iowa.

Chadwick, H.
1953 *Origen. Contra Celsum.* Cambridge: Cambridge University.

Clay, D.
1992 Lucian of Samosata; Four Philosophical Lives (Nigrinus, Demonax, Peregrinus, Alexander Pseudomantis). Pp. 3406–50 in *Aufstieg und Niedergang der römischen Welt* II.36.5, eds. H. Temporini and W. Haase. Berlin: de Gruyter.

Dörrie, H.
1969 Kelsos von Alexandreia. Cols. 179–181 in *Der kleine Pauly: Lexikon der Antike.* Stuttgart: Druckenmüller.

Frede, M.
1994 Celsus philosophus Platonicus. Pp. 5183–213 in *Aufsteig und Niedergang der römischen Welt* II.36.7, eds. H. Temporini and W. Haase. Berlin: de Gruyter.

Frend, W. H. C.
1965 *Martyrdom and Persecution in the Early Church.* Oxford: Blackwell.

Friesen, S.
1993 *Twice Neokoros: Ephesus, Asia, the Cult of the Flavian Imperial Family.* Leiden: Brill.

Glucker, J.
1978 *Antiochus and the Late Academy.* Gőttingen: Druckenműller.

Goranson, S.
1992 Review of *Jesus & the Forgotten City*, by R. A. Batey. *Ioudaios Review* electronic journal. Ftp://ftp.lehigh.edu/pub/listserv/ioudaios-review/2.1992/batey.goranson.006.

Grant, R. M.
1988 *Greek Apologists of the Second Century.* Philadelphia, PA: Westminster.

Hargis, J. W.
1999 *Against the Christians: The Rise of Early Anti-Christian Polemic.* Patristic Studies 1. New York, NY: Lang.

Hoffmann, R. J.
1987 *Celsus on the True Doctrine.* New York, NY: Oxford University.

Johnson, S. E.
1975 Asia Minor and Early Christianity. Pp. 77–145 in *Christianity, Judaism and Other Greco-Roman Cults*, vol. 2, ed. J. Neusner. Leiden: Brill.

Keim. T.
1873 *Kelsos'* Wahres Wort. Zürich: Orell, Füssli.

Koester, H.
1998 *Pergamon, Citadel of the Gods: Archaeological Record, Literary Description, and Religious Development.* Harvard Theological Studies 46. Harrisburg, PA: Trinity.

Kraabel, A. T.
1968 The Jews of Western Asia Minor under the Roman Empire. Unpublished Ph. D. Dissertation. Harvard University.

Marcovich, M. (ed.)
1986 *Hippolytus. Refutatio omnium haeresium.* Patristische Texte und Studien 25. Berlin: de Gruyter.

Mueller, I. (ed.)
1891 *Claudii Galenii Pergameni. Scriptora Minora.* Leipzig: Tuebner.

Musurillo, H. A.
1972 *The Acts of the Christian Martyrs.* Oxford: Clarendon.

Nautin. P.
1977 *Origène: Sa Vie et son Oeuvre.* Paris: Beauchesne.

Patrick, J.
1892 *The Apology of Origen in Reply to Celsus.* Edinburgh: Blackwood.

Pichler, K.
1980 *Streit um das Christentum: Der Angriff des Kelsos und die Antwort des Origenes.* Regensburger Studien zur Theologie 23. Frankfurt am Main: Lang.

Roberts, A., and Donaldson, J. (eds.)
1886 *The Refutation of All Heresies,* trans. J. H. McMahon from Greek. Pp. 9–153 in *Fathers of the Third Century.* Ante-Nicene Fathers, vol. V. Buffalo, NY: Christian Literature.

Rosenbaum, H.-U.
1972 Zur Datierung von Celsus' *Aléthés Logos. Vigiliae Christianae* 26: 102–11.

Schürer, E.
1986 *The History of the Jewish People in the Age of Jesus Christ,* eds. G. Vermes, F. Millar, M. Goodman, P. Vermes and M. Black. Edinburgh: Clark.

Schwartz, J.
1960 Du Testament de Lévi au Discourse véritable de Celse. *Revue d'Histoire et de Philosophie religieuses* 40: 126–45.
1973 Celsus redivivus. *Revue d'Histoire et de Philosophie religieuses* 53: 399–405.

Seager, A. R., and Kraabel, A. T.
1983 The Synagogue and the Jewish Community. Pp. 168–90 in *Sardis from Prehistoric to Roman Times: Results of the Archaeological Exploration of Sardis, 1958–1975,* ed. G. M. A. Hanfmann. Cambridge, MA: Harvard University.

Stern, M.
1980 *Greek and Latin Authors on Jews and Judaism,* vol. 2. Jerusalem: Magness.

Trigg, J. W.
1983 *Origen: The Bible and Philosophy in the Third-Century Church.* Atlanta, GA: Knox.

Wilken, R. L.
1976 Melito, the Jewish Community at Sardis, and the Sacrifice of Isaac. *Theological Studies* 37: 53–69.
1984 *The Christians as the Romans Saw Them.* New Haven, CT: Yale University.

Williams, A. L.
1935 *Adversus Judaeos: A Birds-eye View of Christian* Apologiae *until the Renaissance.* Cambridge: Cambridge University.

Chapter 31

Marketing Religious Difference in Late Antique Syria-Palestine: Clay Oil Lamps as Clientele Indicators

by Eric C. Lapp

It is generally impossible to determine the religious affiliation of the manufacturer, trader, and owner of an ancient clay oil lamp. Archaeological evidence, for example, suggests that North African lamps portraying menorahs—an indisputable Jewish motif—may, in fact, have originated from a pagan workshop (Hachlili 1998: 448). Only on occasion might a lamp actually hint at the religious affiliation of its manufacturer or owner. For example, an inked Hebrew graffito ("Yehoḥanan") on the shoulder fragment of a "Herodian" lamp recovered at Masada suggests that the lamp owner was a Jew (Barag and Hershkowitz 1994: 71, no. 125).[1]

By the fourth century C.E., motifs and/or inscriptions linked to specific religious groups became more common on lamps of select classes manufactured at local Syro-Palestinian workshops. Chief among these motifs were the Jewish (and Samaritan) menorah and the Christian cross. Inscriptions quoting either Samaritan scriptures or Greek passages associated with the liturgies of specific Christian holy sites (e.g., Church of the Nativity) occur on clay lamps belonging to select classes, primarily the Samaritan and slipper "candlestick" forms, respectively. Yet, despite the difficulty of identifying the religious affiliation of either the lamp maker or the customer of any given lamp found (e.g., on an excavation or in a museum collection), such motifs and inscriptions do reveal the probable religious affiliation of the clientele to whom the lamp maker had intended to market his or her lamps.[2]

This chapter examines the use of clay lamps as indicators of clientele and as instruments that reflect the religious differences in Syro-Palestinian society in Late Antiquity. It argues that economic reasons, rather than solely religiously inspired ones or artistic self-expression, influenced the types of iconography and inscriptions artisans chose to carve into lamp moulds which, in turn, lamp makers purchased to manufacture a product that would best appeal to his or her clientele. The diverse motifs and/or inscriptions found on select Syro-Palestinian lamps reflect the different religious communities in society, differences that were deliberately exploited by the lamp mould carver and the lamp maker for financial profit.

MARKETING

The ultimate objective of the lamp maker was to sell lamps. The successful sale of a lamp depended in part on its durability, ease of use, affordability, and, most importantly, its capacity to carry out its intended task of providing light. But aside from these practical concerns, the lamp's general aesthetic qualities (e.g., decoration, design, motifs, and slipping) may also have played a pivotal role in its sale. Depending on the customers' aesthetic tastes, he or she may have been attracted to lamps that, for example, were highly ornate or merely plain. Clay lamps without decoration or with only geometric or floral designs generally would have appealed to any customer, regardless of religious affiliation. Because such lamps do not portray motifs and/or inscriptions linked to a specific religious group, their sale could be aimed at all customers (i.e., mass marketed). And given the rich repertoire of motifs and patterns depicted on clay lamps of various classes manufactured in Roman and Byzantine Syria-Palestine, regional workshops provided customers with a wide variety of lamps from which to choose. By doing so, the lamp maker could increase the chance of selling his or her products by satisfying the different aesthetic or religious preferences of a culturally diverse clientele. In Late Antique Syria-Palestine, the numerous types of locally manufactured lamps, made available to the consumer in substantial quantities, indicate a competitive lamp market in a region where rival workshops were driven to diversify their products in design, decoration, and form.

Lamp advertisements further indicate that lamp makers had a financial motive for selling their manufactured goods. Although evidence for advertising is scarce among lamp makers operating in the Mediterranean and Near East, it is nonetheless explicit in the graffiti found on select lamps requesting and encouraging the public to buy the product. A lamp maker from Carthage, for example, inscribed advertisements on some lamps with the exhortation, "Please buy our lamps, only one cent; they are the best" (Smith 1966: 17, n. 28). A North African coroplast further advertised himself as a maker of "fine lamps and statuettes" (Smith 1966: 17, n. 27). Advertisements on other lamps take on a slightly intimidating tone: "Buy me" and "May it be for his good who shall buy it" (Walters 1905: 422). Inscriptions on two Cnidian lamps are presumably exhortations to buy the lighting devices for votive purposes (Bailey 1988: 118, Q2783 and Q2727 ["Take this for the gods"]). An inscription on a ship-shaped lamp unearthed at Jerash reads "Take this as a thank-offering for the gods" (Bailey 1988: 118); the lamp dates to the second century C.E. and probably originates from Cnidus, too (Bailey 1988: 118). A lamp maker's mark on the base of a Tunisian lamp reads "from the workshop of Victoris" (Knowles 1994: 33–34, no. 64, fig. 2.3), and advertises the lighting device's place of manufacture. In the Levant, the closest example of this kind of advertisement occurs on the Byzantine-period, slipper-shaped Jerash lamp type with a zoomorphic or tongue handle. Arabic inscriptions found on select examples follow a formula that identifies the lamp maker and the place of manufacture — Jerash (Rosenthal and Sivan 1978: 139, no. 574). One such lamp was recovered as far north as Qafr Boutna, a suburb south of Damascus, Syria (Al-Khouly 2001: 194–96, *lampe* 4, fig. 4).

CLIENTELE INDICATORS

The types of motifs and/or inscriptions occurring on lamps reflect the religious diversity of the clientele to whom the lamps were marketed. When purchasing lamp moulds, the lamp maker did so with a specific target market, a homogenous religious group in mind. A useful example of a Jewish and Christian clientele heralds from the Shephalah, where a substantial quantity of locally manufactured Beit Nattif lamps depicting either menorahs or crosses indicates a large Jewish and Christian lamp market in the area of Beth Guvrin, Beit Nattif, and the surrounding region, where some of the heaviest concentrations of these forms occur (Lapp 1997: 66–70, 338, fig. 49; Magness and Avni 1998: 92–100).

In the Diaspora, a similar example of this can be found in Greece, where archaeological evidence attests to a substantial Christian clientele in Athens.

The impressive quantity of locally manufactured clay lamps portraying moulded images of crosses found during the "metro" excavations in Greece's capital city indicates that a local production center had supplied lamps to a sizable, urban Christian community. A number of these Christian lamps have been published recently (Stampolidis and Palarma 2000: 86, no. 63; 195, pl. 6, lower left and upper right; Karivieri 1996: pl. 7:82; pl. 8:83–86, 88, 90; pl. 9:89, 91, 104–5). In Cyprus, a fourth-century lamp class of local production (Vessberg Type 18) attests to a Jewish and Christian clientele on the island; select lamps of this Cypriot group bear images of crosses or menorahs (for examples with crosses, see Bailey 1988: pl. 71:317–18, Q2608 MLA, Q2609, Q2610, and Q2613; and with menorahs, see Hachlili 2001: 456–57, L6.25–29, Corpus pl. p. 89*). The widespread distribution of the African red slip ware lamps (also referred to as "Carthaginian") decorated with crosses or menorahs indicates that they were manufactured and marketed aggressively to satisfy the high consumer demand of a local and an international Christian and Jewish clientele (for examples, see Knowles 1994: 38–39, nos. 111–13, fig. 2.4; Hachlili 2001: 458–63, L7.1–33, pl. II:88, Corpus pl. p. 89*).

With the introduction of motifs and/or inscriptions closely associated with specific religious groups to lamp design beginning in the late third century C.E., the Syro-Palestinian lamp maker intended to persuade members of one or more religious groups to buy his or her lamps. For example, the artisan who had carved a cross into a lamp mould did so with the knowledge that it would be sold to a lamp maker who, in turn, by selecting the mould, had made a deliberate choice to which target market he or she intended to sell the cross-bearing lamp — to members of the Christian community. The lamp maker made a conscious decision to direct the lamp sale to a more restricted market of a specific group of customers.

I doubt the fourth-century lamp maker who manufactured lamps with images of the cross had intended to market them to members of the local Samaritan or Jewish community: lamps depicting the cross — an indisputable Christian motif — would have appealed exclusively to a Christian clientele. By choosing lamp moulds that would produce clay lamps depicting this Christian motif, the lamp maker was knowingly targeting a select group of customers. Similarly, lamps portraying a seven-branched menorah flanked by additional Jewish motifs (e.g., *shofar, lulav, etrog,* and incense shovel)[3] would certainly have appealed more to a Jewish clientele. Thus, the lamp maker who manufactured oil lamps with menorah images had made a deliberate and conscious decision to narrow lamp sales to Jewish customers. Granted, I am not arguing that Jews only bought lamps with Jewish motifs, Christians only lamps with Christian images, and Samaritans only lamps with Samaritan inscriptions; one must not rule out the possibility that an occasional lamp customer, regardless of religious affiliation, may not have cared at all about the kind of motifs that were represented on the lamps purchased.

In Syria-Palestine, local workshops manufactured clay oil lamps portraying pagan images until as late as the third century C.E. A proliferation of lamps depicting Jewish, Christian, and Samaritan motifs began roughly in the fourth century C.E. The most common lamps with Jewish and non-Jewish images generally belong to the Syro-Palestinian discus, the Beit Nattif, Caesarea round, slipper "candlestick", and Samaritan classes. That motifs and/or inscriptions linked to specific religious groups occur on lamps belonging to these classes is itself evidence for religious difference in Syria-Palestine, and for target marketing whereby the lamp maker produced lamps to appeal to one or more distinct bodies of customers. Thus, depending on the types of motifs (e.g., the menorah, the cross, the Torah shrine, and the Gospel aedicula) and inscriptions (e.g., Greek, Hebrew, and Samaritan) portrayed on examples of these locally manufactured classes (Lapp 2001a: 294), the lamps help us identify the lamp makers' intended clientele (i.e., target market): members of the Jewish, Christian, Samaritan, and pagan communities.

The geographic distribution of the lamps belonging to the classes under discussion indicates that they were not traded on an international scale, but rather on a local and regional level generally confined to areas in Syria-Palestine and Transjordan, where pagan, Jewish, Christian, and/or Samaritan communities existed (Lapp 1997: Caesarea round type, 47–49, fig. 28; Beit Nattif type, 66–70, fig. 49; and Samaritan type, 60–66, fig. 46; Magness 1993: large slipper "candlestick" type, 173–77, fig. 12). The examples that do occur at find spots outside of Syria-Palestine are too few to suggest trade, and may instead represent souvenirs brought home by tourists, traders, and other visitors. For example, only two Syro-Palestinian discus lamps and a Northern Stamped lamp have been found at Athens (see Perlzweig 1961: 84, pl. 5:132–33, of Syro-Palestinian discus type; 103, no. 376, pl. 11, a version of Sussman Northern Stamped Type 6a).

Syro-Palestinian Discus Class

A diverse repertoire of pagan images occurs on Syro-Palestinian discus lamps (a version of Broneer Type 25, not to be confused with discus lamps of the Beit Nattif type) manufactured from the second half of the first century through the third century C.E. (Rosenthal and Sivan 1978: 85). By the fourth century, the depiction of a single menorah became more common on the later versions of this lamp type. A fourth-century version of a discus lamp portraying a seven-branched menorah was found at Sepphoris (Lapp 1996: 222, no. 117; for additional examples of discus lamps with menorah images, see Hachlili 2001: 448–51, L4.2–16, pl. II:82–84). By the fourth century, the Beit Nattif with bow-shaped nozzle, Caesarea round, and slipper lamp classes surpassed the discus lamp as the types *par excellence* for depicting Jewish and Christian iconography. With the broader nozzles and shoulders of the Beit Nattif and slipper forms, and the wide central discus of the Caesarea round class, these morphological improvements enabled lamps to carry more sophisticated motifs and/or inscriptions. For example, not only was the slipper lamp's nozzle wide enough to accommodate an image of a cross or menorah, the shoulder, too, was sufficiently spacious to carry an inscription.

Although the predominant pagan motifs occurring on discus lamps of the second and third centuries would have appealed to pagan customers, archaeological evidence indicates that such lamps bearing images of Helios also attracted a Jewish clientele. Pictorial representations of Helios occur on synagogue mosaics at Beth Alpha, Na'aran, Hammath Tiberias and Sepphoris (Hachlili 1988: pls. 76– 78; Weiss and Netzer 1996: 26–29). A further image of Helios in carved relief decorates a synagogue lintel at Chorazim (Hachlili 1988: pl. 46). Jewish magical texts also allude to Helios (Morgan 1983: 71). Since a close Jewish association with Helios is substantiated in the archaeological and literary record, it is reasonable to presume that Jews did not take offense to lamps bearing depictions of Helios. Thus, it should not be considered surprising that a discus lamp decorated with an image of Helios was recovered from a synagogue context at Nabratein (Lapp 1996: 221, no. 115).

The discovery of a Syro-Palestinian discus lamp fragment depicting an erotic scene in Catacomb 20 of the Jewish necropolis at Beit She'arim in Lower Galilee (Avigad 1976: 185, pl. 70:3) further indicates that Jews were not necessarily offended by such "pagan" imagery. That the second- to third-century-C.E. lamp was found among a group of lamps dating to the "burial phase" of the catacomb suggests that it could very well have been deposited by a Jewish or pagan member of the funeral party (Lapp 2001c: 66). Discus lamps with erotic images have been recovered from additional Jewish archaeological contexts, including the residential quarter at Sepphoris and in the Akeldama Tomb in the Kidron Valley (see Lapp 1997: 94, n. 34, figs. 74 and 77; sample DS9, 238–39, 257, fig. 98, table 2; Lapp 1996: 220–21, no. 114). It is possible that ancient lamp owners in Syria-Palestine were indifferent to the erotic scenes depicted on oil lamps and other media; perhaps they viewed erotic imagery no more differently than the depiction of an acanthus leaf, gladiator, or rosette (Lapp 2001c: 66).

All said, the widely popular discus lamp class appealed to both pagans and Jews, especially in the second and third centuries C.E. The introduction of the menorah on late third- and fourth-century versions of this group suggests that Syro-Palestinian lamp makers were refining their marketing practices by designing products to appeal to members of a specific religious group or target market: Jews and Samaritans. Similarly, Egyptian workshops of the Loeschcke Type VIII discus lamps target marketed their products with menorah images (see

Bailey 1988: 251, Q2061–62 MLA, pl. 44, fig. 38) to a Jewish clientele and those with cross motifs (see Bailey 1988: 251, Q2066, pl. 44, fig. 34) to a Christian one.

Beit Nattif Class

In 1934, Baramki recovered moulds and unused lamps from two cisterns at Beit Nattif that represent evidence for a workshop (Baramki 1936: 3–10). Three shape types were manufactured at the Beit Nattif facility: round lamps with decorated discus of Beit Nattif type (ca. 250–350 C.E.), lamps with bow-shaped nozzle (second half of the third century to the fifth century C.E.), and ovoid lamps with large filling hole (third to fifth centuries C.E.; Magness and Avni 1998: 93–99). Numerous examples of Beit Nattif lamps with bow-shaped nozzles are decorated with only geometric and floral designs (for examples, see Rosenthal and Sivan 1978: 105–10, nos. 423–47). This suggests that the lamp maker intended to sell products to a wide market: the non-religious decoration would have appealed to any customer, regardless of religious affiliation. Several such Beit Nattif lamps were recovered from the *sacellum* in the amphitheater at Beth Guvrin (Kloner and Hübsch 1996: 101–3, fig. 25:1–6, 10–12). The shoulder decoration of a Beit Nattif lamp with a bow-shaped nozzle belonging to the Archaeological Collection of the Johns Hopkins University is reminiscent of set stones in metal jewelry.[4]

Beit Nattif ovoid lamps, too, are covered in geometric patterns that would have appealed to any clientele (see, for example, an ovoid lamp unearthed in the Ahinoam Cave Cemetery at Beth Guvrin in Magness and Avni 1998: 98, fig. 6, lower right), and thereby represent further evidence for mass marketing. One example is the shoulder of a Beit Nattif ovoid lamp, found in the collection of the Royal Museum of Art and History in Brussels, decorated with an ornate geometric pattern of circles positioned between consecutive radial lines in moulded relief (Skinkel-Taupin 1980: 10, 35b; compare with Israeli and Avida 1988: 129, no. 371).

Select Beit Nattif lamps with religious motifs also indicate the existence of two target markets: Jewish and Christian. For example, cross images found on the bow-shaped nozzles of select Beit Nattif lamps suggest target marketing to members of the Christian community. For instance, a cross decorates the bow-shaped nozzle of a Beit Nattif lamp recovered from the Ahinoam Cave Cemetery at Beth Guvrin (Magness and Avni 1998: 95 and 97, fig. 5, upper right; see also Sussman 1982: 11, top middle).

The discovery of Beit Nattif lamps with Jewish motifs at archaeological sites represents evidence for a second target market for this class, namely one restricted to Jewish customers. Such lamps were explicitly manufactured to appeal to a Jewish clientele, and have been found in Jewish archaeological contexts. For example, a menorah decorates the bow-shaped nozzle of a Beit Nattif lamp recovered from Tomb N.III of the Southern Cemetery at Beth Guvrin (Avni et al. 1987: 73, fig. 1; Lapp 1997: 420, fig. 150), and of another found in the treasury of the synagogue at Hammath Tiberias in Lower Galilee (Lapp 1997: 202–3, 416, fig. 144; for additional Beit Nattif examples with menorah images, see Hachlili 2001: 442–48, L2.3–26, L3.1–5, Corpus pls. pp. 86*–88*, pls. II:80–81).

Caesarea Round Class

In 1960, Negev conducted excavations at Caesarea Maritima on the coast of northern Israel, where he recovered several limestone moulds for lamp and figurine manufacture. The moulds were found in a deposit above the apse of a fourth-century-C.E. building located south of the city wall (Sussman 1980: 76–79). Similar to the lamps belonging to the Beit Nattif class, the lamp makers of the Caesarea round type intended to market their product to both a Jewish and Christian clientele. Until recently, Caesarea round lamps—known for their rich repertoire of Christian images (e.g., the cross, a Gospel aedicula, a fisherman, and a peacock) fashioned in a freehand linear style on the lamps' wide central discs—were considered to be made exclusively for a Christian population (Sussman 1980: 77, n. 4; 78). Most Caesarea round lamps recovered from archaeological sites in Israel bear Christian motifs, thereby suggesting that their chief target market was the Christian community. But the recent discovery of a Caesarea round lamp fragment portraying a menorah flanked by a *lulav* (palm frond) in the residential quarter at Sepphoris

(Lapp 1996: 222, no. 118), and the recovery of a lamp belonging to the same class depicting an image of a Torah shrine with a drawn *parochet* from a tomb near Caesarea Maritima (Siegelmann 1992: 65, fig. 4:11; Fine 1996: 171, cat. no. 69),[5] indicates that select lamps belonging to this class were also manufactured with Jewish customers in mind (Lapp 2001b: 297). Other Caesarea round lamps decorated with geometric or floral designs were manufactured to appeal to a wider market (for examples, see Israeli and Avida 1988: 112, nos. 322–23). For example, a Caesarea round lamp decorated with a non-religious floral pattern was found in the synagogue at En-Gedi (Lapp 1997: 205 and 419, figs. 148–49), indicating that its mass-market appeal also included members of the En-Gedi Jewish community.

Slipper ("Candlestick") Class

The slipper lamp class (also referred to as the "candlestick" type) is closely associated with early Christianity. Christian motifs, such as the cross or peacock, decorate the nozzles of select Magness Form 2 small slipper lamps (for examples with cross images, see Rosenthal and Sivan 1978: 113, nos. 453–62; Bailey 1988: 288–89, Q2337 PRB, pl. 60). At Tel el-Ful, two types of crosses appear on several slipper lamps recovered from a burial cave at the site: (1) a Greek cross roughly square in shape with bifurcated ends (Lapp, in press: nos. 20, 83, 88, and 93), and (2) a rectilinear cross with bifurcated ends and an elongated central shaft (Lapp, in press: no. 137). The Magness Form 2 lamps date from the second half of the fourth to the mid-sixth century C.E. (Magness and Avni 1998: 99, n. 24). Greek inscriptions associated with liturgies of specific Christian holy sites also occur in moulded relief on the back shoulders of select Magness Form 3 large slipper lamps (Magness 1998: 42–43, 46–47, 70). These inscriptions occasionally include mention of Christian historical figures, such as "Christ" (or "Jesus") and the "Mother of God" (referring to "Mary;" Saller 1957: 178–79, n. 97; Magness 1993: 176–77). The Magness Form 3 lamps range in date from the mid-sixth century to the late seventh or early eighth century C.E. (Magness and Avni 1998: 99). The consistent recovery of slipper lamps from Christian burial contexts further substantiates this type's strong Christian association (e.g., Macalister 1912: Tomb 124, Pl. CI). The abundant images of the cross found on church mosaics, architectural features, and the material culture of the Jerusalem area and throughout Byzantine Palestine (e.g., Tsafrir 1993: 45, lower left, 51, upper left, 195, upper left, 237, upper right) provided a rich repertoire of examples of this exclusively Christian motif for the mould makers and the lamp makers of the slipper class to copy.

There is no reason to assume, however, that slipper lamps only appealed to Christians. Representations of multiple-branched menorahs with either bi- or tripod bases occur on select slipper lamps (see, for example, Sellers 1951: 42, 44, no. 1; Rosenthal and Sivan 1978: 118, nos. 484–86; Magness 1998: 42, lower right; Hachlili 2001: 468–69, L10.11–13, pls. VII:4–6), thus suggesting that lamps of this class were also manufactured with a second target market in mind—a Jewish clientele. Although missing a base, the multiple-branched lampstand image depicted on the nozzle-top of a slipper lamp closely resembles a menorah with a cross-bar (Loffreda 1993: 427, fig. 58). However, as far as I am aware, no examples of slipper lamps with representations of a menorah flanked by a *shofar, lulav*, and/or *etrog* have been found. Additional slipper lamps bearing depictions of multiple-branched menorahs were unearthed in Cave 44 at Tel el-Ful (Lapp, in press: nos. 5, 9, and 108). Their occurrence in this Christian burial complex suggests Christian borrowing of Jewish iconography, and thus underscores the complexities involved with the interpretation of motifs in Late Antiquity.[6]

Samaritan Class

Samaritan lamps are most commonly decorated with geometric patterns (for an explanation of the "Samaritan" nomenclature adopted for members of this lamp class, see Sussman 1978: 238–240 and 243). The Samaritan lamps belonging to Sussman Types 1 and 2 found at Apollonia-Arsuf exhibit the rich variety of patterns made available to the lamp customer (Sussman 1983: 77, 87–95, fig. 3, also pls. 2:1–10, pl. 3:11–18, and pl. 4:19–26; for additional examples, see Israeli and Avida 1988: 137–41, nos.

389–406). That geometric designs on these examples dating to the early third to fourth century, and on Sussman Type 3 and 4 lamps ranging from the fifth to seventh century (Sussman 1983: 73–74 and 85), are abundant suggest that the lamp makers of this class had generally intended to sell their products to a wider, more diverse clientele and not strictly to Samaritan customers. As is the case with other lamp types with simple geometric patterns (e.g., Beit Nattif), the non-religiously specific decoration would have appealed to members of any religious group, and therefore suggests manufacture intended for a mass market.

Samaritan lamps that incorporate a menorah into their design, however, are less common and would have appealed more to a workshop's Samaritan and Jewish customers (for examples, see Hachlili 2001: 470–76, L.11.1–27, pls. VII:2–3, Corpus pl. p. 91*). A significant example of a Samaritan lamp (Sussman Type 1), portraying both a menorah and Torah shrine, was uncovered at Samra (Magen 1992: 88, lower right). Additional examples of Samaritan lamps decorated with menorah images were found at Apollonia-Arsuf (Sussman 1983: 78, 90, pl.5, lamp no. 29, fig. 4:4) and at Caesarea Maritima (Holum et al. 1988: 197, fig. 144). The rare Samaritan class lamp with a Samaritan inscription (see, for example, Naveh 1988: 38, pl. 8:G; Lapp 1997: 61, n. 94) may represent evidence that the lamp maker had intended to restrict the sale of this inscribed product to a Samaritan market only. The absence of Christian motifs on Samaritan lamps suggests that lamp sales for this class were not specifically targeting a Christian clientele.

CONCLUSION

Archaeological, epigraphic, and literary evidence indicates religiously diverse populations in several major Syro-Palestinian cities, such as Caesarea Maritima, Beth Shean, and Sepphoris (Tsafrir et al. 1994: 94–96, 223–25, and 227–28). Lamp workshops operating in these cities manufactured lamps to appeal to that diversity. The lamp makers of the Beit Nattif, Caesarea round, slipper, Samaritan, and fourth-century-C.E. versions of the Syro-Palestinian discus classes exploited religious difference to sell their product. The various religious motifs and/or inscriptions depicted on lamps belonging to these classes reflect this difference in religious belief, practice, and custom.

Clay lamp decoration was not inspired solely by the artistic tastes of the lamp mould carver: one must not ignore both the mould carver's and the lamp maker's need to sell their respective products. Thus, lamp decoration, too, offered the lamp maker an additional means by which to entice customers to buy the product. Plain lamps or examples decorated with simple geometric and/or floral patterns (e.g., select Beit Nattif, Samaritan, and Syro-Palestinian lamps) would have appealed to a wide, general clientele regardless of the customers' religious affiliation. By appealing to a broad customer base, such varied decoration would have aided in the sale of the lamp makers' products in a competitive lamp market.

Lamps bearing motifs and/or inscriptions linked to a specific religious group indicate that the lamp maker had a specific target market in mind for the sale of his or her product, and had manufactured lamps to appeal to that market. By doing so, the lamp maker was restricting lamp sales to a narrower body of customers. Thus, by manufacturing a slipper lamp replete with a cross and an inscription associated with, for example, the Church of the Holy Sepulchre (Magness 1998: 43; for examples of slipper lamps associated with this sacred site, see Lyon-Caen and Hoff 1986: 132, nos. 172–73), the lamp maker did so deliberately, realizing full well that such a lamp would appeal exclusively to a Christian clientele.

In the end, the lamp maker's chief objective was to sell lamps. To do so, he or she needed to produce lamps that would appeal to the widest market possible, and purchased moulds with which lamps could be made with a variety of patterns, motifs, and inscriptions that would best attract customers. Syro-Palestinian lamp makers knew their audience and catered to their customers' varied aesthetic tastes and religious differences in order to sell their product. The choice of manufacturing lamps with any given religious motif or inscription was as much market-driven as it was influenced by diverse religious beliefs and artistic expression.

NOTES

1 A second lamp fragment recovered at Masada belongs to the moulded floral class; the name "Joseph" stamped on the lower portion of its nozzle suggests the manufacturer was Jewish (Barag and Hershkovitz 1994: 66, no. 111).

2 With the use of "her," I consider the possibility that in Late Antique Syria-Palestine, women, too, were involved in the crafts of carving lamp moulds and of manufacturing clay lamps. That women are mentioned in literary and epigraphic sources as active participants in a variety of trades and crafts in antiquity supports this argument (Peskowitz 1997: 62–66; for women in pottery manufacture, see Freestone and Gaimster 1997: 15, 87, 166). Further, a glass beaker of probable Syro-Palestinian origin may have been manufactured by a woman (Stern 1995: 100–2, no. 5; Kondoleon 2000: 193–94, no. 80), and if so, would represent concrete archaeological evidence suggesting the involvement of women in such industrial activities.

3 See, for example, the lamps found at Sepphoris, Beit Nattif, and Beth Guvrin in Lapp 1996: 222, no. 118; Baramki 1936: 7, pl. X:24; Kloner and Hübsch 1996: 101–2; fig. 25:9.

4 E. C. Lapp, *Clay Lamps of the Ancient Near East in the Archaeological Collection of the Johns Hopkins University*, forthcoming, inventory no. 646; similar to nos. 349–51 in Israeli and Avida 1988. I thank Eunice Dauterman Maguire for her astute identification of the jewel-like pattern on this lamp.

5 Torah shrine images also occur on lamps from the Diaspora. For example, Torah shrines of the aedicule type with closed paneled doors are portrayed on two clay lamps from Miletus and Kalymnos (Lapp 1991: 156–58, pl. 8a–d; Hachlili 1998: 364; 2000: 154, n. 82).

6 No find better exemplifies the borrowing of religious images than the marble chancel screen found at Pella, which depicts a mixing of motifs associated with Christianity — a cross — and Jewish motifs — a *shofar*, a *lulav*, and a possible menorah (McNicoll et al. 1982: 55, 111, pl. 39a).

REFERENCES

Al-Khouly, M.
2001 Nouvelles lampes inscrites de la période omeyyade. Pp. 193–95 in *La Céramique Byzantine et Proto-Islamique en Syrie-Jordanie (IVe–VIIe Siècles apr. J.-C.)*, eds. E. Villeneuve and P. M. Watson. Bibliothèque Archéologique et Historique 159. Beyrouth: Institut Français d'Archéologie du Proche Orient.

Avni, G.; Dahari, U.; and Kloner, A.
1987 Beth Guvrin: The Ahinoam Cave Cemetery. *Israel Exploration Journal* 37: 72–74.

Avigad, N.
1976 *Beth She'arim*, vol. III: *The Catacombs 12–23*. Jerusalem: Masada.

Bailey, D. M.
1988 *A Catalogue of the Lamps in the British Museum III: Roman Provincial Lamps*. London: British Museum.

Barag, D., and Hershkovitz, M.
1994 Lamps. Pp. 107–24 in *Masada IV: The Yigael Yadin Excavations 1963–1965. Final Reports*, eds. J. Aviram, G. Foerster and E. Netzer. Jerusalem: Israel Exploration Society.

Baramki, D. C.
1936 Two Roman Cisterns at Beit Nattif. *Quarterly of the Department of Antiquities in Palestine* 5: 3–10.

Broneer, O.
1930 *Corinth IV, Terracotta Lamps, Part II*. Cambridge, MA: Harvard University.

Fine, S.
1996 *Sacred Realm: The Emergence of the Synagogue in the Ancient World*. Oxford: Oxford University.

Freestone, I., and Gaimster, D.
1997 *Pottery in the Making: World Ceramic Traditions*. London: British Museum.

Hachlili, R.
1988 *Ancient Jewish Art and Archaeology in the Land of Israel*. Leiden: Brill.
1998 *Ancient Jewish Art and Archaeology in the Diaspora*. Leiden: Brill.
2001 *Menorah, The Ancient Seven-Armed Candelabrum: Origin, Form and Significance*. Leiden: Brill.

Holum, K. G.; Hohlfelder, R. L.; Bull, R. J.; and Raban, A.
1988 *King Herod's Dream: Caesarea on the Sea*. New York, NY: Norton.

Israeli, Y., and Avida, U.
1988 *Oil-Lamps from Eretz-Israel: The Louis and Carmen Warschaw Collection at the Israel Museum Jerusalem*. Tel Aviv: Sabinsky.

Karivieri, A.
1996 *The Athenian Lamp Industry in Late Antiquity*. Papers and Monographs of the Finnish Institute at Athens 5. Helsinki: Finnish Institute at Athens.

Kloner, A., and Hübsch, A.
1996 The Roman Amphitheater of Bet Guvrin: A Preliminary Report on the 1992, 1993, and 1994 Seasons. *'Atiqot* (English Series) 30: 85–106.

Knowles, K.
1994 The Lamps. Pp. 23–41 in *Excavations at Carthage*, vol. II, 2: *The Circular Harbor, North Side: The Pottery*, eds. M. G. Fulford and D. P. S. Peacock. British Monographs in Archaeology 5. Oxford: Oxford University.

Kondoleon, S. E.
2000 80. Barrel-Shaped Cup Signed by Neikais. Pp. 193–94 in *Antioch: The Lost Ancient City*, ed. C. Kondoleon. Princeton, NJ: Princeton University.

Lapp, E. C.
1991 Zwei spätantike jüdische Tonlampen aus Kleinasien. *Jahrbuch für Antike und Christentum* 35: 156–58.
1996 Clay Oil Lamps. Pp. 217–24 in *Sepphoris in Galilee: Crosscurrents of Culture*, eds. R. Nagy, C. Meyers, E. Meyers and Z. Weiss. Raleigh, NC: North Carolina Museum of Art.
1997 The Archaeology of Light: The Cultural Significance of the Oil Lamp from Roman Palestine. Unpublished Ph.D. diss., Duke University.
2001a Lamps. Pp. 292–94 in *Archaeological Encyclopedia of the Holy Land*, eds. A. Negev and S. Gibson. New York, NY: Continuum.
2001b Lamps—Israel/Palestine. Pp. 295–97 in *Archaeological Encyclopedia of the Holy Land*, eds. A. Negev and S. Gibson. New York, NY: Continuum.
2001c Les lampes à huile érotiques en Terre Sainte. *Archéologia* 377: 62–66.
in press The Late Roman and Byzantine Clay Lamps from a Christian Burial Cave at Tel el-Ful. *'Atiqot.*

Loffreda, S. P.
1993 Motivi Decorativi Nelle Lucerne Del Tipo 17A. *Liber Annuus* 43: 411–37.

Lyon-Caen, C., and Hoff, V.
1986 *Musée du Louvre: Catalogue des lampes en terre cuite grecques et chrétiennes*. Paris: Musée du Louvre.

Macalister, R. A. S.
1912 *The Excavation of Gezer*, vols. I–III. London: Murray.

Magen, Y.
1992 Samaritan Synagogues. *Qadmoniot* 25: 66–90 (Hebrew).

Magness, J.
1993 *Jerusalem Ceramic Chronology: Circa 200–800 CE*. JSOT/ASOR Monograph Series 9. Sheffield: Sheffield Academic.
1998 Illuminating Byzantine Jerusalem: Oil Lamps Shed Light on Early Christian Worship. *Biblical Archaeology Review* 24, no. 2: 41–47, 70–71.

Magness, J., and Avni, G.
1998 Jews and Christians in a Late Roman Cemetery at Beth Guvrin. Pp. 87–114 in *Religious and Ethnic Communities in Later Roman Palestine*, ed. H. Lapin. Studies and Texts in Jewish History and Culture V. College Park, MD: University of Maryland.

McNicoll, A.; Smith, R. H.; and Hennessy, J. B.
1982 *Pella in Jordan 1: An Interim Report on the Joint University of Sydney and The College of Wooster Excavations at Pella 1979–1981*, vol. 2. Canberra: Australian National Gallery.

Morgan, M. A. (trans.)
1983 *Sepher Ha-Razim. The Book of the Mysteries*. Society of Biblical Literature Pseudepigrapha Series 11. Chico, CA: Scholars.

Naveh, J.
1988 Lamp Inscriptions and Inverted Writing. *Israel Exploration Journal* 38: 36–43.

Perlzweig, J.
1961 *The Athenian Agora, VII: Lamps from the Roman Period.* Princeton, NJ: American School of Classical Studies at Athens.

Peskowitz, M. B.
1997 *Spinning Fantasies: Rabbis, Gender, and History*. Berkeley, CA: University of California.

Rosenthal, R., and Sivan, R.
1978 *Ancient Lamps in the Schloessinger Collection*. Qedem 8. Jerusalem: Israel Exploration Society.

Saller, S. J.
1957 *Excavations at Bethany*. Jerusalem: Franciscan.

Sellers, O. R.

1951 The Candlestick Decoration on Byzantine Lamps. *Bulletin of the American Schools of Oriental Research* 122: 42–45.

Siegelmann, A.

1992 Roman and Byzantine Remains in the Northern Central Plain. *'Atiqot* 21: 63–67.

Skinkel-Taupin, C.

1980 *Lampes en Terre Cuite de la Méditerranée Grècque et Romaine*. Brussels: Musées Royaux d'Art et d'Histoire.

Smith, R. H.

1966 The Household Lamps of Palestine in New Testament Times. *Biblical Archaeologist* 29: 2–27.

Stampolidis, N. C., and Palarma, L.

2000 *Athens: The City Beneath the City*. Athens: Kapon.

Stern, E. M.

1995 *Roman Mold-Blown Glass: The First through Sixth Centuries*. Toledo, OH: Toledo Museum of Art.

Sussman, V.

1978 Samaritan Lamps of the Third-Fourth Centuries A.D. *Israel Exploration Journal* 28: 238–50.

1980 Moulds for Lamps and Figurines from a Caesarea Workshop. *'Atiqot* (English Series) 14: 76–79.

1982 *Ornamented Jewish Oil-Lamps: From the Destruction of the Second Temple through the Bar-Kokhba Revolt*. London: Aris and Phillips.

1983 The Samaritan Oil Lamps from Apollonia-Arsuf. *Tel Aviv* 10: 71–96.

1989 Northern Stamped Oil Lamps and Their Typology. *Michmanim* 4: 22–58.

Tsafrir, Y. (ed.)

1993 *Ancient Churches Revealed*. Jerusalem: Israel Exploration Society.

Tsafrir, Y.; DiSegni, L.; and Green, J.

1994 *Tabula Imperii Romani: Iudaea-Palaestina. Maps and Gazetteer*. Jerusalem: Israel Academy of Sciences and Humanities.

Vessberg, O.

1953 Hellenistic and Roman Lamps in Cyprus. *Opuscula Atheniensia* I: 115–29.

Walters, H. B.

1905 *History of Ancient Pottery*, vol. II. London: Murray.

Weiss, Z., and Netzer, E.

1996 *Promise and Redemption: A Synagogue Mosaic from Sepphoris*. Jerusalem: Israel Museum.

Chapter 32

"Set the Showbread on the Table Before Me Always" (Exodus 25:30): Artistic Representations of the Showbread Table in Early Jewish and Christian Art

by Zeev Weiss

Several showbread tables were made in the course of history for the Wilderness Tabernacle and for the First and Second Temples in Jerusalem. Moses built a table for the Tabernacle (Exodus 25:23–30; 37:10–16), Solomon built one for the First Temple in Jerusalem (I Kings 7:48), those returning from Babylon fashioned one for the Second Temple, Ptolemy donated an impressive table (Letter of Aristeas 52–72), later looted by Antiochus Epiphanes (I Mac. 1:22), and the last was built by the Hasmoneans following the purification of the Temple in Jerusalem (I Mac. 4:49; II Mac. 1:8, 10:3). During the Second Temple period the showbread table and the *menorah* were removed together with other sacred vessels from the sanctuary and displayed before the people on the festivals.[1]

Although the various showbread tables used in the Wilderness Tabernacle and in the First and Second Temples in Jerusalem were different from one another in their details, it is clear that the biblical archetype mentioned twice in Exodus (25:23–30; 37:10–16) was a source of inspiration and imitation for all. In both passages, a rectangular table built of *shittim* wood and overlaid with gold is described; on top was a gold border, and rings were placed in its four corners to hold staves that bore the table. Twelve loaves of showbread were laid in two rows on the table, sprinkled with frankincense, and changed once a week.

The showbread table, which Josephus describes as being one of "three most wonderful works of art universally renowned," was placed in the Tabernacle and in the Temple, on the north side, opposite the *menorah,* so that its length paralleled the long axis of the building (*War* 5.216–17). It is only briefly described in several sources dated to the Second Temple period, but talmudic literature provides valuable information regarding this piece of furniture.[2] Few artistic representations of the table were made during the time of the Second

Fig. 1 The Showbread Table on a coin of Mattathias Antigonus from the second half of the first century B.C.E. *(after Meshorer 2001: 54).*

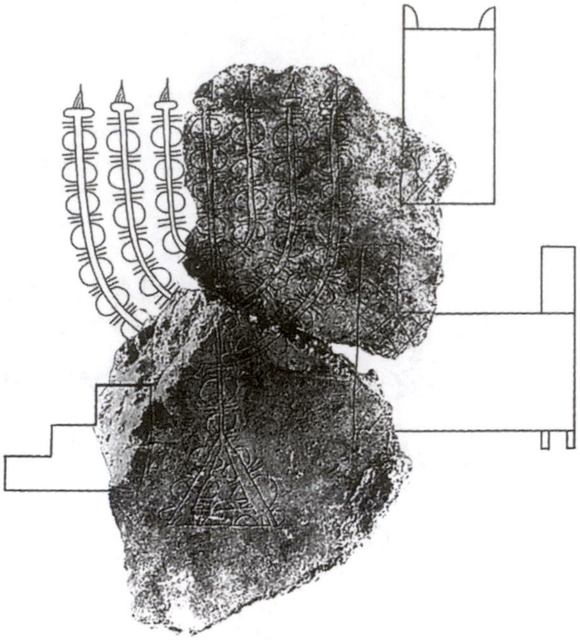

Fig. 2 Showbread Table incised on a plaster fragment from the Herodian period, found ex situ *in the Jewish Quarter, Jerusalem (after Habas 2003: 332, photo 12:4).*

Temple; most belong to the period following its destruction, when the artists had only written sources and the historical memory of the Temple and its artifacts to inspire them.

In the following, I will attempt to examine various artistic representations of the showbread table, addressing the manner in which the assorted iconographic traditions crystallized, and the extent to which written texts may have inspired the pictorial representations of the table.

The first two representations appeared prior to the destruction of the Temple. The earliest is depicted on a coin from the days of Mattathias Antigonus, dated to the second half of the first century B.C.E. (fig. 1; Meshorer 1982a: 94–97; 2001: 54-57). The small dimensions of the coin do not enable us to determine the precise details of the table, but it is evidently a rectangular, four-legged piece of furniture, on which rounded loaves of bread are placed, one on top of the other in two equal piles.

The second representation is incised on a plaster fragment from the Herodian period found *ex situ* in the Jewish Quarter excavations in Jerusalem (fig. 2; Avigad 1980: 147–49; Narkiss 1974: 6–14; Habas 2003: 335–36). The showbread table is depicted there beside representations of the *menorah* and the altar of incense. According to Narkiss, their relative location on the plaster reflects their original positions within the Tabernacle and Temple. The table has raised borders at either narrow end and four short legs. It is possible that the two raised borders represent the *senifim*, or props, which, according to the Mishnah, supported the loaves of bread on the table (M. Mena'ot 11, 6), but it is probable that they are only a schematic representation of the props together with the piles of loaves, which is reminiscent of the depiction in the Spanish illuminated manuscripts.[3]

Subsequent to the destruction of the Temple, the showbread table was depicted on the arch of Titus in Rome (fig. 3; Knight 1896: 91–99; Pfanner 1983: 53; Yarden 1991: 71–88). The relief has been damaged over the years, but the table there appears to be rectangular, rather than octagonal, as suggested by Yarden (Yarden 1991: 81). The border of the table is decorated with a simple relief, and its legs are shaped like lions' feet. Two small vessels, identified as the censers of frankincense, are placed on its surface, and between its legs are two trumpets. According to Barag, the table reappears on coins of Bar-Kokhba minted during the years 132–135 C.E.; on the large coin, the tetradrachm, it is seen from the side, whereas on the smaller didrachm, the longer front of the table is depicted (Barag 2000: 272–76). If the proposed identification is correct, then this is a rectangular table with raised borders, similar to the engraving from the Jewish Quarter, except for its borders, which are rounded at the top.

Fig. 3 *Close-up of the Showbread Table depicted on the Arch of Titus in Rome (after Pfanner 1983: plate 59:3).*

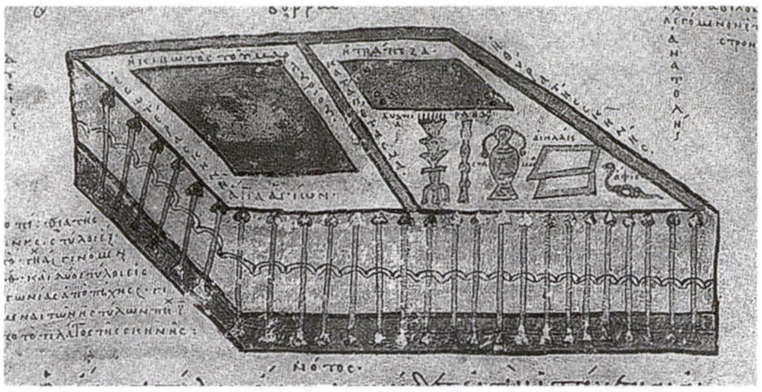

Fig. 4 *The Tabernacle,* The Christian Topography *of Constantine of Antioch. Sinai, St. Catherine's Monastery, MS 1186, 77v. The Showbread Table with the loaves of bread on the four corners is depicted on the upper right side of the miniature (after Weitzmann and Galavaris 1990: I, 56, pl. LXVI).*

A rectangular showbread table also appears in Christian art, mainly in late Byzantine manuscripts illustrating the Tabernacle and its holy vessels. These are later than the examples described above, but it is customary to suppose that they are based on earlier models, incorporating themes borrowed from ancient Jewish art. The table in Codex Amiatinus, for instance, is placed within the *qodesh*, opposite the *menorah,* and is seen from a three-dimensional perspective.[4] In *The Christian Topography* of Constantine of Antioch (fig. 4) and in the Octateuchs, the table is in a similar position, but this time it is depicted as a two-dimensional rectangular plane, seen, as it were, from above.[5] The twelve loaves of bread are shown as round objects placed on the table in groups of three at its four corners, in a manner reminiscent of the twelve months and the four seasons.

In the depiction of the rectangular showbread table, one may point to several iconographic traditions that are not particularly dependent on each other, but seem to have the common desideratum to depict it in accordance with the literary sources and as it existed in the Tabernacle or Temple. The table is described in early depictions in frontal or even three-dimensional view, at least in one case including the loaves of showbread placed upon it. This trend is repeated in Byzantine illuminated manuscripts, but there, for the first time, we have a different type of depiction, symbolic and general, including only enough details to clearly identify it as the showbread table.[6] Some of the details in the depictions of the rectangular showbread table allude to what is known from the written sources, such as the way in which the loaves of bread are piled on the table on the coin of Mattathias Antigonus, the props for the piles of bread in the engraving from the Jewish Quarter and perhaps also on a Bar-Kokhba coin, as well as the two censers sitting on the table, a detail appearing only on the Arch of Titus. Closer examination reveals that no one representation is similar to the other, and that the details do not always correspond to descriptions from the written sources, making it difficult to conclude the exact form of the showbread table as it was in the Tabernacle or in the Temple.

Another artistic tradition describes the showbread table as being round. A round three-legged table already appears on coins of King Herod, but Meshorer's opinion that it is not intended to depict the showbread table, but rather represent one of the other tables in the Temple mentioned in the Mishna (Sheqalim 6:4), seems plausible (Meshorer 1982b: 23–24; 2001: 66–67).

A depiction of a round showbread table first appears in the synagogue at Dura Europus, in the mid-third century C.E., on a panel depicting the miraculous well of Be'er (fig. 5).[7] The yellowish table with three curved legs stands in front of the Tabernacle, before the menorah.

Another round table appears in a mosaic found in a synagogue at Sepphoris, dated to the early fifth century C.E. (fig. 6; Weiss 2005: 95–96). This depic-

Fig. 5 *Dura Europos, Miraculous Well of Be'er. The round Showbread Table stands in front of the tabernacle, at the foot of the menorah (after Kraeling 1956: pl. LIX).*

tion, richer in details than the previous example, is included in a group of panels presenting various aspects of the Tabernacle or Temple, located above the zodiac. The showbread table at Sepphoris is round, with three legs, visible beneath the cloth covering the table. The cloth is decorated with circles containing a crisscross pattern placed in its four corners and has fringed edges. The twelve loaves of bread, shown as round objects, are arranged on the table in three rows, with six loaves in the central row and three in each of the others. Two censers containing frankincense are depicted above the table to either side of it.

A round showbread table is also depicted in a fourth-century mosaic discovered in the Samaritan synagogue at el-Khirbē (fig. 7; Magen 1993: 198–200; 2002: 404–8, 438). There, it is shown at the front of the Tabernacle together with other holy vessels. It is presented as a metal tripod, on which various vessels are laid, including three round loaves of bread. The shape of the table, the assortment of vessels on it and the number of loaves are different from those represented at Sepphoris, but it seems nevertheless to belong to a similar iconographic tradition, common to Jewish and Samaritan art, which presents the showbread table as round, rather than rectangular, as described in the Bible and other written sources.

A round showbread table is apparently depicted also in the ninth-century Marginal Psalter of Mt. Athos (fig. 8).[8] Here, the Tabernacle containing the holy artifacts is depicted to the side of the text of Psalm 113. Three objects are arranged in a row beyond the entrance, which is covered by the curtain (*parochet*) in the front of the structure. To the left is the seven-branched *menorah*; to the right is the jug of manna. Between the two is a round table with three legs, on which round objects are placed. Dufrenne identifies this as the altar of incense, but it is unclear on what this identification is based, especially in light of the fact that the altar was square and not round, and that it had horns in each of its corners, evidently absent from the representation before us. The similarity to the Sepphoris mosaic, as in the case of the depiction from Dura Europus, suggests that the round table from the Marginal Psalter of Mt. Athos represents the showbread table. In both cases we have a three-legged round table bearing the loaves of bread, but whereas at Sepphoris the correct number of loaves appears, here it is difficult to determine their number, owing to the minute size of the illustration in the manuscript.

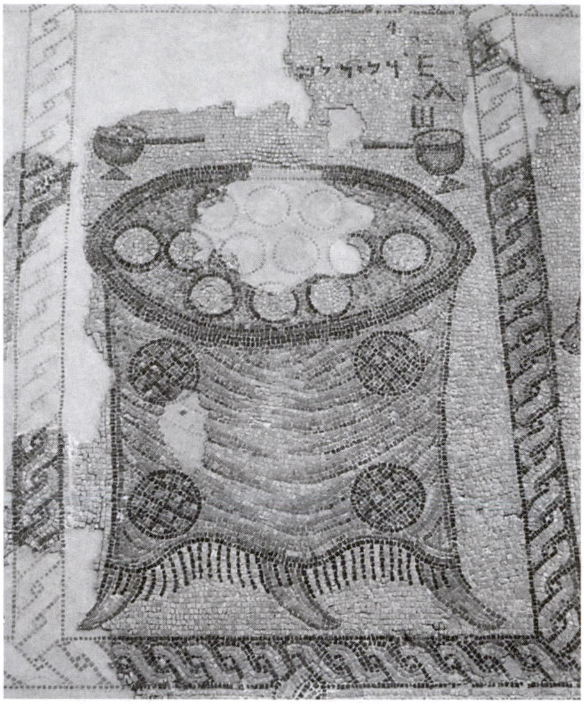

Fig. 6 *Sepphoris: The Showbread Table (Sepphoris Expedition, The Hebrew University of Jerusalem. Photo by G. Laron).*

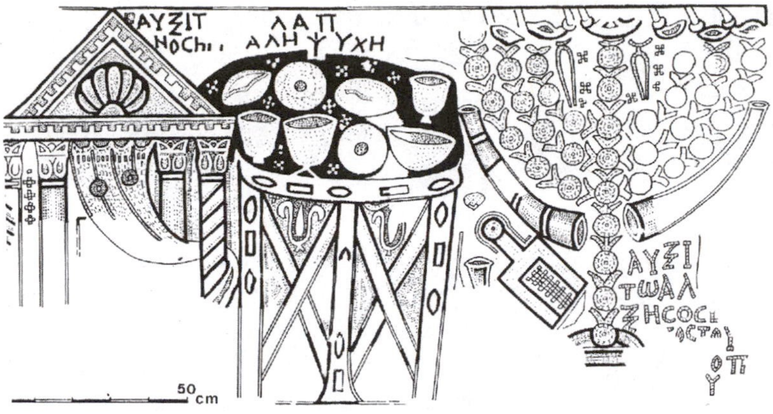

Fig. 7 El-Khirbē, detail of a panel from the Samaritan synagogue depicting the Tabernacle and several of its utensils (courtesy of Y. Magen).

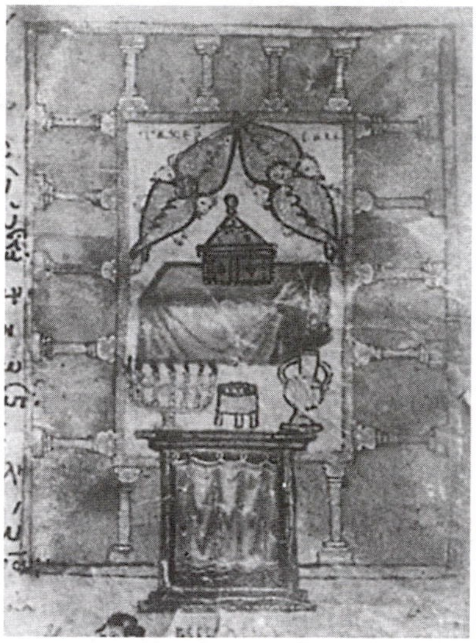

Fig. 8 Marginal Psalter of Mount Athos, Pantocrator 61, fol. 165r. The round Showbread Table is depicted above the curtained entrance, between the menorah and the manna vessel (courtesy of H. L. Kessler).

The examples above indicate a new, separate artistic tradition for the description of the showbread table in the Tabernacle and the Temple. It is difficult to determine precisely where and when this tradition originated, but it would seem, in light of the available data, that this occurred after the destruction of the Temple, possibly as late as the third century C.E. One cannot argue that this iconographic tradition, completely different from the previous examples, aims to give another version of what the table in the Tabernacle or Temple actually was, since it contradicts descriptions from the written sources. It is also difficult to prove that the artist intentionally depicted a table different from the one at the Temple, following the ruling that

> A man may not make a house in the form of the Temple, or an *exedra* in the form of the Temple hall, or a courtyard corresponding to the Temple court, or a table corresponding to the [sacred] table, or a *menorah* corresponding to the [sacred] *menorah*, but he may make one (a menorah) with five or six or eight lamps, but with seven he should not make.[9]

Why should the artist have gone so far, depicting a table so different from the actual reality and the textual evidence? It would have been enough to change one or two details in the shape of the original table in order to abide by the law, as was the custom in depictions of the *menorah,* which frequently appears in ancient Jewish art (Barag 1999: 71–75; Levine 2000: 144–53). We also can not accept the possibility suggested recently, that the round form of the tables in the mosaics at Sepphoris and in the Samaritan synagogue was chosen in order to distinguish it from the church altar on which the Eucharist was offered (Talgam 2000: 104). This iconographic tradition developed, as suggested above, at a time when the Christian community still played a minor role in the area, and long before the shape of the church altar crystallized into its traditional form. Furthermore, even if the rectangular altar was more widespread in the church, there are still a fair number of instances in which it was round or semicircular; this claim, therefore, does not resolve the problem (Trombley and Bouras 1991: 71).

It would seem, then, that the round shape of the table did not result from either a lack of information or a consistent mistake, but rather a conscious choice of familiar themes, through which the artists wished to illustrate the nature of the showbread table, even if its shape contradicted the accepted written sources. Certain details were sometimes represented according to written tradition; however, the entire depiction was intended only to symbolize the table, rather than precisely describe its actual appearance in the Tabernacle or Temple. It should also be borne in mind that neither the artists nor their audience were acquainted with the holy vessels of the Temple and had no visual memory of their actual appearance. Therefore, the artist or his iconographic sources used a simple language of symbols that was familiar to all, and by means of which they intended to illustrate the Temple implements that neither they, nor the members of their community had ever seen.[10]

The round table, termed a *mensa delphica,* was a well-known piece of furniture in Roman times, often represented in Roman and early Byzantine art.[11] The diners sat around this table, on which vessels with food were laid. A three-legged table is called a *delphica* in talmudic literature, and was probably a familiar piece of furniture to the Jewish community as well.[12] Placing a round table of this type beside the *menorah*, or combining it with other themes, such as the loaves of showbread or the censers of frankincense, formed the necessary impression. This use of familiar symbols with the addition of unique attributes stressed the fact that the object described was no commonplace piece of furniture, but the showbread table, which had been in the Tabernacle or in the Temple.

A similar trend is apparent in pictorial representations of the loaves of bread and their arrangement on the table. The loaves of showbread in the Temple were rectangular and of a uniform size, as stipulated in the Mishnah:

> The [loaves of the] showbread were ten [handbreadths] long and five wide and their horns were seven fingerbreadths [high].[13]

The twelve loaves were placed on the table in two equal piles, and above them the frankincense, as described in Lev. 24:6–7:

> Place them on the pure table before the Lord in two rows, six to a row. With each row you shall place pure frankincense, which is to be a token offering for the bread, as an offering by fire to the Lord.

The Tosefta further explains:

> How is the showbread to be arranged? Six loaves are placed in this setting and six loaves in this setting.... How are the censers arranged? One censer is placed on this setting and one censer on this setting.[14]

The loaves depicted on the coin of Mattathias Antigonus were laid in two rows on the table as described, and their roundish shape possibly alludes to the shape described in the Mishna. All the other depictions, however, show the loaves spread out on the table. At Sepphoris and in the Marginal Psalter of Mt. Athos they are laid out on the table, whereas in the Christian topography of Constantine of Antioch and in the Octateuchs, they appear in groups of three, in the corners of the table. It should be noted that in all, the loaves are round rather than rectangular, as described in the Mishna.

The depiction of the bread as a round object is not intended to contradict the written sources; loaves of bread were round in antiquity (Gusman 1900: 242–43; Ziehr 1984: 86–87). In Talmudic sources, bread is sometimes called an *iggul,* a circle or rounded loaf,[15] and in Roman and Byzantine art bread is often depicted as being round.[16] Moreover, Targum Pseudo-Jonathan to Exod. 40:4 ("Bring in the table and lay out its due setting....") elaborates upon the description of the showbread table in the Tabernacle, referring explicitly to the loaves of bread that were laid on the table as *iggulim* (round loaves):

> Bring the table on the northern side ... and lay them out in two settings of showbread, six *iggulim* per setting, symbolizing the tribes of Jacob.

Apparently, the translator adopted this term, since it was commonly used for bread at the time. Artists used the same method, choosing to present the bread in a shape familiar to all, although representing the showbread. The exact number of loaves originally placed in the Tabernacle and the Temple was emphasized, rather than their original shape. If he had represented the loaf of bread as a rectangular object, the depiction may not have been understood by everyone. For the same reason, the artist scattered the loaves of bread over the table—not because it was difficult to create the correct perspective for the two piles on the table, but because the number of loaves, he believed, served as another indicator for interpreting the entire motif.

The censers at Sepphoris, also appearing on the Titus Arch and, probably, in the depiction at el-Khirbē, are another detail that aids the decipherment of the picture. Here, too, artists used vessels well known to their audience, although they did not necessarily correspond to the reality in the Tabernacle or the Temple. The number of censers and their position on the table are the marks whereby the artists achieved their identification.

To conclude, two major iconographic traditions describing the showbread table existed in antiquity. The first presented it as a rectangular table, whereas the other depicted it as round. The earlier tradition originated in the days of the Temple, whereas the later one only appeared following its destruction. Both traditions developed within Jewish circles, and were later borrowed or imitated by Christian art. Whereas the first tradition aimed to present the table as it actually was, the second did not attempt to do so at all. A lack of correspondence between the table's pictorial representations and its description in written sources is common to both traditions; nevertheless, the artists in each case took care to emphasize some details that identify the furnishing under discussion as the showbread table in the Tabernacle and Temple. Although the final representations may differ widely, all symbolize the showbread table in the Tabernacle or the Temple—a symbol with deep meanings, which, however, must be discussed elsewhere.

NOTES

1 M Hagigah 3, 8; B Hagigah 26b; see also J Hagigah 3 8, 69d, which notes that the Showbread Table, with the showbread on it, was displayed before the pilgrims. For details regarding such ceremonies held during festivals in the Second Temple period, see Knohl 1992: 601–9.

2 Rectangular proportions recur in the detailed description of the table in the Letter of Aristeas (56–72). They also emerge in a reconstruction of the text missing in the Temple Scroll describing the Showbread Table; see Yadin 1983: II, 31; M Mena'ot 11, 5 and parallels; Baraita d'Melekhet Hamishkan 8 (ed. Friedman, pp. 58–59).

3 Narkiss 1974: 11, and parallels there.

4 Florence Bibl. Laur. Codex Amiatinus I, fols. 2v–3r; see also Revel-Neher 1982: 6–8.

5 Cosmas Indicopleustès, Roma, Biblioteca Apostolica Vaticana, cod. gr. 699, fol. 46v, W. Wolska-Conus, *La Topographie Chrétienne de Cosmas Indicopleustès*, Paris 1968–73, II, 45. This depiction, which illustrates only the table next to the menorah, has been preserved in a miniature in a manuscript from St. Catherine's monastery; see Weitzmann and Galavaris 1990: I, 56, Pl. LXVI. The depiction in the Octateuchs appears in all manuscripts, but with slight differences; see Weitzmann and Bernabò 1999: I, 177; II, nos. 763–765. On the shape of the Showbread Table according to Constantine of Antioch and its comparison to the depiction in the Octateuchs, see Mouriki-Charalambous 1970: 101–7, 118–26; Hahn 1979: . 38–39; Brubaker 1981; Lowden 1992: 88–89.

6 Unlike the four-legged table appearing in the Tabernacle in a number of depictions from the Byzantine period, where it actually represents the church altar there and has no connection to the Showbread Table. See, for example, the panel in St. Maria Maggiore presenting the stoning of Moses; Karpp 1966, fig. 118. The depiction of the Temple in the mosaic of the Theotokos Chapel on Mt. Nebo contains a rectangular object, which Piccirillo identifies as the "offering table;" see Piccirillo and Alliata 1998: 302. Saller, in contrast, opines that this was the entrance to the Holy of Holies; see Saller 1941: I, 236.

7 Kraeling 1956: 119. Weitzmann, in contrast, believes that this was the incense altar, albeit not in its original form but "as a piece of elegant furniture of Graeco-Roman tradition;" see Weitzmann and Kessler 1990: 67.

8 Pantocrator 61, fol. 165r; and see Dufrenne 1965.

9 B Rosh Hashanah 24a–b; B Avodah Zarah 43a; B Mena'ot 28b.

10 The similarity of the round showbread tables from Dura, Sepphoris, and el-Khirbē indicates, according

to Hachlili, that "most probably they were all based on images appearing in a Jewish pattern book (see Hachlili 1998: 345–46). The existence of a pattern book is questionable and unverifiable, however, the appearance of depictions in the three locales may be reminiscent hints of model(s) that existed within the Jewish realm which were utilized differently by each artist while sharing similar perceptions.

11 Richter 1926: 139–40; 1966: 111–12; Moss 1988: I, 37–43. Similar tables are depicted in mosaics and wall paintings; see Levi 1947: II, pl. 42b; Février 1977: 29–45. A round three-legged table is depicted in the Orpheus mosaic discovered in Sepphoris; see Weiss and Netzer 1997: 9, Pl. 1.

12 M Kelim 25, 1; Avodah Zarah 5, 5; J Demai 6 10, 25d. On the form of the table and its parts in Talmudic literature, see Krauss 1929: 13–15; Tabory 1979.

13 M Mena'ot 11, 4. Two sages in the Babylonian Talmud dispute the question regarding the form that the rectangular showbread should take: did it have the shape of a "chest" with two raised borders, or the shape of a "boat" with a triangular section?; see B Mena'ot 94b.

14 T Mena'ot 11, 14–15 (ed. Zuckermandel, p. 530). This description recurs in Josephus as well; see *Ant.* 3.142–43, 255–56 — in contrast to the tradition found in the Temple Scroll, wherein it may be assumed that the frankincense was placed directly on the bread and not in a vessel, as prescribed in the Bible; see Yadin 1983: II, 30–38.

15 See Targum Pseudo-Jonathan to Exod. 29:22; J Hagigah 22, 77d; Genesis Rabbah 49, 4 (ed. Theodor-Albeck, p. 503), and elsewhere; see Sokoloff 1990: 402, s.v. עיגול; Krauss 1929: 185.

16 Goodenough 1964: XI, fig. 247; Levi 1947: II, pl. CLIIa–b. The round loaves of bread depicted in a Christian context are sometimes decorated with a cross; see Schneider 1937: 56–58; Deichmann 1958: fig. 315. On the production of bread and bread stamps in the Roman and Byzantine world, see Galavaris 1970: 3–39.

REFERENCES

Avigad, N.

1980 *Discovering Jerusalem.* Jerusalem: Shikmonah.

Barag, D.

1999 The Menorah as a Messianic Symbol in Antiquity. Pp. 71–75 in *In the Light of the Menorah: Story of a Symbol,* ed. Y. Israeli. Jerusalem: The Israel Museum.

2000 The Table of the Showbread and the Façade of the Temple on Coins of the Bar Kokhba Revolt. Pp. 272–76 in *Ancient Jerusalem Revealed,* ed. H. Geva. Jerusalem: Israel Exploration Society.

Brubaker, L.

1981 The Tabernacle Miniatures of the Byzantine Octateuchs. Pp. 73–92 in *Actes du XVe Congrès International d'Études Byzantines (Athènes 1976),* vol. II.

Deichmann, F. W.

1958 *Frühchristliche Bauten und Mosaiken von Ravenna.* Wiesbaden: Steiner.

Dufrenne, S.

1965 Une illustration 'historique' inconnue du Psautier du Mont-Athos, Pantocrator No. 61. *Cahiers Archéologiques* 15: 81–95.

Février, P. A.

1977 A propos du repas funéraire: Culte et sociabilité. *Cahiers Archéologiques* 26: 29–45.

Galavaris, G.

1970 *Bread and the Liturgy.* Madison, WI: University of Wisconsin.

Goodenough, E.

1964 *Jewish Symbols in the Greco-Roman Period.* New York, NY: Pantheon.

Gusman, P.

1900 *Pompei: the City, its Life and Art.* London: Heinemann.

Habas, L.

2003 An Incised Depiction of the Temple Menorah and Other Cult Objects of the Second Temple Period. Pp. 229–42 in *Jewish Quarter Excavations in the Old City of Jerusalem Conducted by Nahman Avigad 1969–1982,* vol. II, ed. H. Geva. Jerusalem: Israel Exploration Society.

Hachlili, R.

1998 *Ancient Jewish Art and Archaeology in the Diaspora.* Leiden: Brill.

Hahn, C.

1979 The Creation of the Cosmos: Genesis Illustration in the Octateuchs. *Cahiers Archéologiques* 28: 29–40.

Karpp, H.

1966 *Die frühchristlichen und mittelalterlichen Mosaiken in Santa Maria Maggiore zu Rom.* Baden Baden: Grimm.

Knight, W.

1896 *The Arch of Titus and the Spoils of the Temple.* London: The Religious Tract Society.

Knohl, I.

1992 Post-Biblical Sectarianism and the Priestly Schools in the Pentateuch: The Issue of Popular Participation in the Temple Cult on Festivals. Pp. 601–9 in *The Madrid Qumran Congress: Proceedings of the International Congress on the Dead Sea Scrolls*, eds. J. T. Barrera and L.V. Montaner. Leiden: Brill.

Kraeling, C. H.

1956 *The Synagogue—The Excavations at Dura Europos.* New Haven, CT: Yale University.

Krauss, S.

1929 *Talmudic Antiquities.* Tel Aviv: Devir (in Hebrew).

Levi, D.

1947 *Antioch Mosaic Pavements.* Princeton, NJ: Princeton University.

Levine, L. I.

2000 The History and Significance of the Menorah in Antiquity. Pp. 131–53 in *From Dura to Sepphoris: Studies in Jewish Art and Society in Late Antiquity*, eds. L. I. Levine and Z. Weiss. Journal of Roman Archaeology Supplementary Series 40. Portsmouth, RI: Journal of Roman Archaeology.

Lowden, J.

1992 *The Octateuchs: A Study in Byzantine Manuscript Illustration.* University Park, PA: Pennsylvania State University.

Magen, Y.

1993 Samaritan Synagogues. Pp. 193–230 in *Early Christianity in Context: Monuments and Documents*, eds. F. Manns and E. Alliata. Jerusalem: Franciscan Printing.

2002 Samaritan Synagogues. Pp. 382–443 in *The Samaritans*, eds. E. Stern and H. Eshel. Jerusalem: Yad Yitshak Ben-Tsevi (in Hebrew).

Meshorer, Y.

1982a *Ancient Jewish Coinage*, vol. I. New York, NY: Amphora.

1982b *Ancient Jewish Coinage*, vol. II. New York, NY: Amphora.

2001 *A Treasury of Jewish Coins from the Persian Period to Bar Kokhba.* Jerusalem: Yad Yitshak Ben-Tsevi.

Moss, C. F.

1988 Roman Marble Tables. Unpublished Ph.D. dissertation, Princeton University.

Mouriki-Charalambous, D.

1970 The Octateuch Miniatures of the Byzantine Manuscripts of Cosmas Indicopleustes. Unpublished Ph.D. dissertation, Princeton University.

Narkiss, B.

1974 A Scheme of the Sanctuary from the Time of Herod the Great. *Journal of Jewsih Art* 1: 6–14.

Pfanner, M.

1983 *Der Titusbogen.* Mainz: von Zabern.

Piccirillo, M., and Alliata, E.

1998 *Mount Nebo: New Archaeological Excavations 1967–1997.* Jerusalem: Franciscan Printing.

Revel-Neher, E.

1982 La double-page du Codex Amiatinus et ses rapports avec les plans du Tabernacle dans l'art juif et dans l'art byzantin. *Journal of Jewish Art* 9: 6–17.

Richter, G. M. A.

1926 *Ancient Furniture: A History of Greek, Etruscan and Roman Furniture.* Oxford: Clarendon.

1966 *The Furniture of the Greeks, Etruscans and Romans.* London: Phaidon.

Saller, S. J.

1941 *The Memorial of Moses on Mount Nebo* I. Jerusalem: Franciscan Printing.

Schneider, A. M.

1937 *The Church of the Multiplying of the Loaves and Fishes at Tabgha on the Lake of Gennesaret and Its Mosaics.* London: Ouseley.

Sokoloff, M.

1990 *A Dictionary of Jewish Palestinian Aramaic of the Byzantine Period.* Ramat Gan: Bar Ilan University.

Tabory, J.

1979 The Household Table in Rabbinic Palestine. *Association for Jewish Studies Review* 4: 211–15.

Talgam, R.
2000 Similarities and Differences between Synagogue and Church Mosaics in Palestine during the Byzantine and Umayyad Periods. Pp. 93–110 in *From Dura to Sepphoris: Studies in Jewish Art and Society in Late Antiquity*, eds. L. Levine and Z. Weiss. Journal of Roman Archaeology Supplementary Series 40. Portsmouth, RI: Journal of Roman Archaeology.

Trombley, F. R., and Bouras, L.
1991 Altar. *The Oxford Dictionary of Byzantium* 1: 71. New York, NY: Oxford University.

Weiss, Z.
2005 *The Sepphoris Synagogue: Deciphering an Ancient Message in its Archaeological and Socio-Historical Contexts*. Jerusalem: Israel Exploration Society.

Weiss, Z., and Netzer, E.
1997 The Hebrew University Excavations at Sepphoris. *Qadmoniot* 30, no. 113: 2–21.

Weitzmann, K., and Bernabó, M.
1999 *The Byzantine Octateuchs*. Princeton, NJ: Princeton University.

Weitzmann, K., and Galavaris, G.
1990 *The Monastery of Saint Catherine at Mount Sinai*. Princeton, NJ: Princeton University.

Weitzmann, K., and Kessler, H. L.
1990 *Frescoes of the Dura Synagogue and Christian Art*. Washington, DC: Dumbarton Oaks Research Library and Collection.

Yadin, Y.
1983 *The Temple Scroll*. Jerusalem: Israel Exploration Society.

Yarden, L.
1991 *The Spoils of Jerusalem on the Arch of Titus: A Re-Investigation*. Stockholm: Svenska Institutet i Rom.

Ziehr, W.
1984 *Das Brot: Von der Steinzeit bis Heute*. Lucerne: Herrsching.

Chapter 33

Christians Among Jews in En-Gedi

by Anna de Vincenz

The church fathers Eusebius (early fourth century) and Jerome (late fourth–early fifth centuries) refer to En-Gedi as "a very large village of Jews" *(Onom.* 86:16). Archaeological excavations conducted in the 1970s at the site revealed a large synagogue, with Hebrew and Aramaic inscriptions on its floors (Barag et al. 1981). The Byzantine-period village around the synagogue was excavated by Hirschfeld, and dwellings dated to the Roman period have been excavated by Hadas on the slope opposite the village. This essay argues that, despite the statement that "En-Gedi was a very large village of Jews," there was coexistence of some kind between Jews and Christians in the village during the Byzantine period.

JEWISH AND CHRISTIAN ARTIFACTS

During the excavation of the synagogue, artifacts that can be assigned to Jews were found; these include a *menorah*, a ceramic basin, and the above-mentioned inscription. The large synagogue itself, standing in the middle of the village, was certainly in use during the Byzantine period. During the recent excavations of the Roman dwellings, many stone vessels dated to the Roman period have been found, among them a complete measuring cup, clearly indicating Jewish presence. On the other hand, the Byzantine-period village also yielded a number of artifacts that bore cross decorations. These items include 'Candlestick' lamps (fig. 1) and Late Roman Fine Ware vessels (fig. 2), all of which come from different locations in the village and date to the fifth and sixth centuries C.E. Two fragmentary lamps with cross decorations have to be added to this list, but are unique in their representation of the cross. The first one (fig. 3) has a *crux gemmata,* or bejeweled cross, on its discus, while the second one is decorated with a cross above an edicule (fig. 4).

The presence of these artifacts, both Jewish and Christian, indicate clearly that there were Jewish and Christian inhabitants in En-Gedi during the Byzantine period.

DESCRIPTION OF THE LAMPS

Both lamps are mould-made, flat and elongated in shape, with a bow-shaped nozzle, broken in the *crux gemmata* lamp (fig. 3). This one has a stump-handle without a perforation and a central, rather small filling hole. It is made of a particularly fine ware (Munsell Chart 7.5YR 7/4 pink, with many black and white inclusions). The rim is decorated

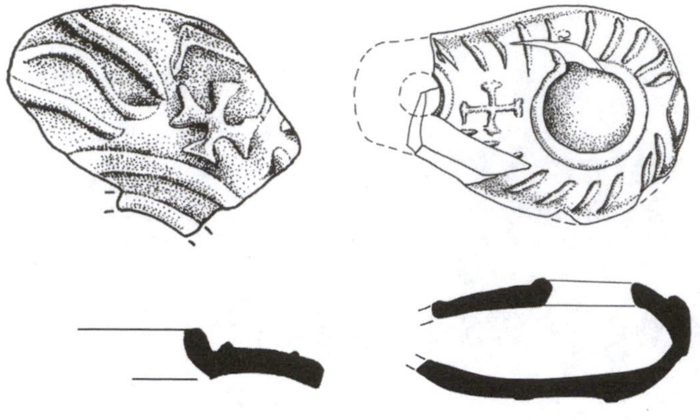

Fig. 1 *Candlestick lamps from En-Gedi.*

Fig. 2 *Crosses on Late Roman C platters from En-Gedi.*

with an intertwining zigzag line. The area of the discus is surrounded by a band filled with dots. This band continues towards the wick-hole, which it probably originally surrounded. The discus itself is decorated with a bejeweled cross standing on an indeterminate structural feature. The filling hole forms the center of the cross. Four circles are positioned between the arms of the cross.

The other lamp (fig. 4), of which only the burnt nozzle and part of the body are preserved, is made of fine ware (Munsell Chart 2.5YR 6/6 light red, no inclusions visible). Its nozzle is decorated up to the filling hole with a cross; the cross branches are made of three lines. Under the cross, towards the nozzle, are two double columns with an arch on top. The rest of the lamp is not preserved. Both lamps have been found in a Byzantine context in close proximity to each other.

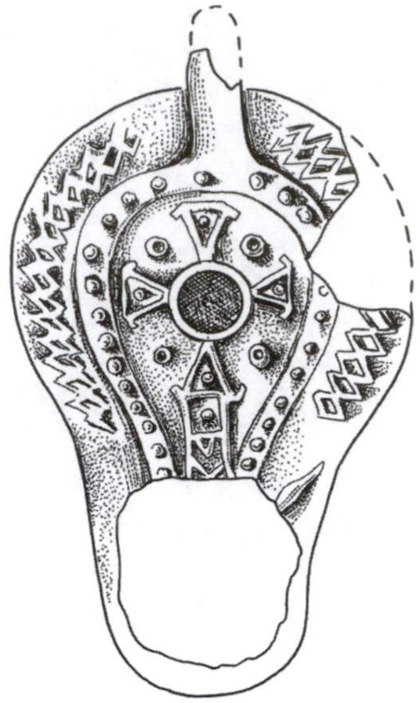

Fig. 3 *Lamp with* crux gemmata *from En-Gedi.*

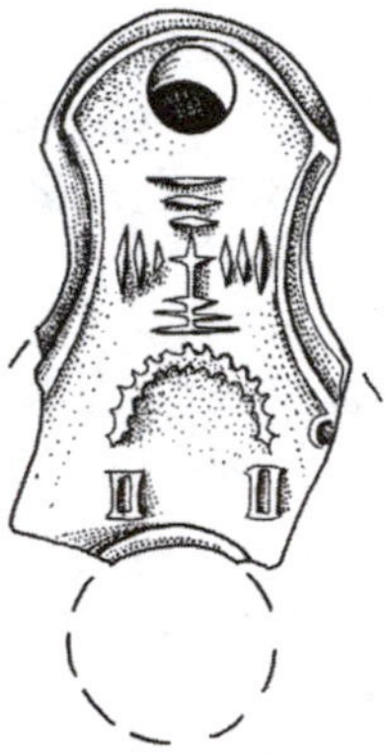

Fig. 4 *Lamp with edicule from En-Gedi.*

SYMBOLISM AND THE BEJEWELED CROSS

The iconography of the bejeweled cross has been discussed by the author in a recent article (de Vincenz 2003). Here, it should suffice to say that the cross is a "Greek" cross (a cross with arms of the same length). On a sculptured slab from the Armenian Garden excavations in Jerusalem, published by Tushingham (1985: 498, pl. 124), there is a bejeweled cross depicted standing on a pedestal

Fig. 5 Glass pilgrim flask (after Barag 1970: 59, fig. 2c).

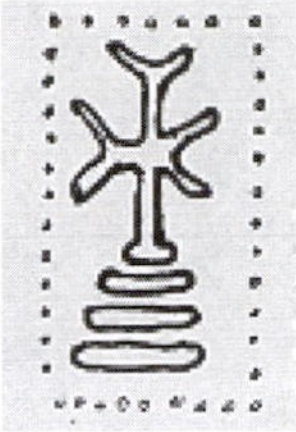

Fig. 6 Cross from glass pilgrim flask (after Barag 1970: 52, pl. IV, first cross).

Fig. 7 Cross from glass pilgrim flask (after Barag 1970: 52, pl. V, second cross).

Fig. 8 Monza flask with Golgotha (after Grabar 1958: pl. 10, ampoule 4 re.).

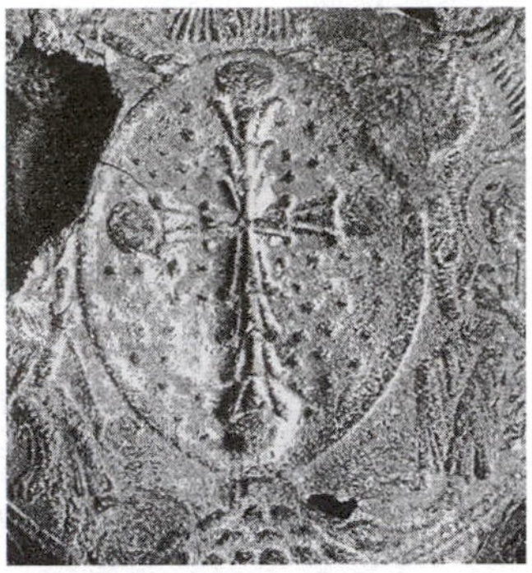

Fig. 9 Monza Flask with Golgotha (after Grabar 1958: pl. 32, ampoule 1).

or a column. The Armenian Garden cross was dated to the sixth century, according to existing parallels (Tushingham 1985: 100). On glass pilgrim flasks the cross is sometimes shown standing on steps seen from above (fig. 5; Barag 1970: 52, fig. A:3 second cross; 59: fig. 2:c). In one instance the cross stands on steps represented by three lines (fig. 6; Barag 1970: 52, fig. A:4, first cross) and in another it stands on a feature that may be a mound (fig. 7; Barag 1970: 52, fig. A:5, second cross). These glass pilgrim vessels date, according to Barag, no earlier than the sixth century (Barag 1970: 45). Depictions of crosses standing on steps or mounds are also known from the Monza Pilgrim Flasks (Grabar 1958), showing the cross standing on the three steps (fig. 8 and Grabar 1958: pl. 10, ampoule 4 revers) or on rocky mounds (fig. 9 and Grabar 1958: pl. 11, ampoule 5 avers and pl. 32, ampoule 1). The Monza flasks also date to the sixth century.

A marble panel from Tabgha (fig. 10), dated to the fifth–sixth centuries, shows a cross on top of a mound represented by three circles (Bagatti and Testa 1978: 50, fig. 3). The same way of representation of the mound with circles can be seen on a lead weight from the Franciscan Museum of the Flagellation (fig. 11). The cross on top is bejeweled (Bagatti and Testa 1978: fig. 7). Greek type crosses also appear on ceramic vessels of the Late Roman C type. A bowl depicting three stamped crosses on a pedestal (fig. 12) was found at the Athenian Agora and seems to relate directly to the scene of the crucifixion (Hayes 1972: 349, 366, fig. 79:76n).

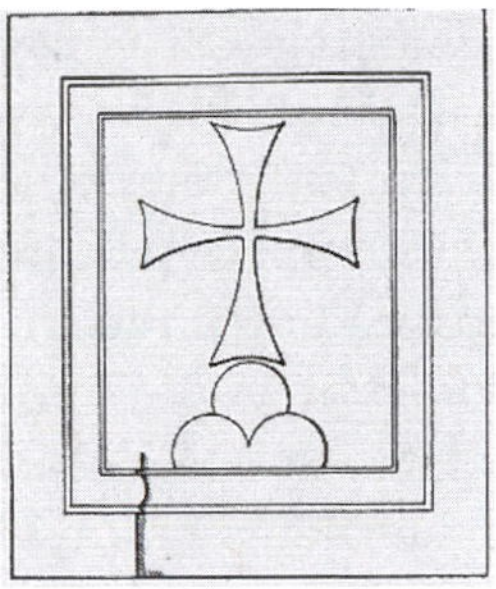

Fig. 10 Marble panel from Tabgha (after Bagatti and Testa 1978: 50, fig. 3).

Fig. 11 Lead weight with Golgotha (after Bagatti and Testa 1978: 54, fig. 7).

Fig. 12 Stamped cross on LRC vessel (after Hayes 1972: 366, fig. 79:76n).

Of particular interest on all these vessels is what the cross stands on, which appears to represent a pedestal, a column, or steps. There are numerous examples in Byzantine art of crosses shown on

Fig. 13 *Monza flask with edicule (after Biddle 1999: 23, fig. 18).*

Fig. 14 *Monza flask with edicule (after Grabar 1958: pl. 11,* ampoule *5, re.).*

Fig. 15 *Pewter medallion (after Biddle 1999: 23, fig. 19).*

pedestals or positioned on top of rocky mounds; these refer specifically to the cross on Golgotha in Jerusalem. Historical sources dating back to the late fourth century mention that a replica of the cross was set on top of the actual rock of Golgotha in the area of the present Church of the Holy Sepulchre (Hunt 1984: 12). Indeed, steps leading up to the rock of Golgotha are mentioned by visiting pilgrims in the sixth century, notably by Theodosius and the Piacenza Pilgrim. Archaeological excavations there have revealed remains that may have been part of some plastered structure on which a replica cross would have been placed (Gibson and Taylor 1994: 80–81). According to an account by Theophanes *(Chron.* 86:28), a gold and bejeweled cross was placed on the Rock of Calvary. It seems, therefore, that the bejeweled cross from En-Gedi is a representation of a cross standing on the Golgotha mound.

Fig. 16 *Ceramic* ampulla *(after Biddle 1999: 23, fig. 20).*

Fig. 17 *Edicule from glass pilgrim flask (after Barag 1970: 52, pl. VII, second cross).*

Fig. 18 *Edicule from glass pilgrim flask (after Barag 1970: 52, pl. VII, first cross).*

SYMBOLISM AND THE EDICULE

The second lamp has a cross above double columns and an arch (fig. 4). These double columns with the arch on top look like an edicule. They can be found on the above-mentioned Monza Pilgrim Flasks dated to the sixth century (figs. 13–14; Biddle 1999: 23, fig. 18; Grabar 1958: pl. 11, ampoule 5 revers). On a pewter medallion conserved in Stuttgart (fig. 15), the edicule is shown as a small roofed building with doors; a cross is positioned on the roof (Biddle 1999: 23, fig. 19). A ceramic *ampulla* in the Franciscan Museum of the Flagellation shows an edicule very similar to the one on our lamp (fig. 16). The edicule consists of two columns with an arch on top (Corbo 1988: 420–22, fig. 5). On the above-mentioned glass pilgrim flasks, the edicule is represented either by two columns surmounted by an arch (fig. 17), or by two columns surmounted by a pointed roof (fig. 18). In both cases a cross is situated inside the edicule (Barag 1970: fig. A:7, first and third cross). Of particular interest is an edicule in the mosaic from Umm al-Rasas (fig.

19); the edicule is represented by three columns surmounted by a pointed roof (Biddle 1999: 25, fig. 23).

Representations of the edicule are frequent in Byzantine art and symbolize the tomb of Jesus. As has been shown by the examples above, their representation can be stylized or more naturalistic. The representation of the edicule symbolizing the tomb of Jesus is certainly meant for Christians and, thus, the stylized representation of the edicule would be of special meaning to a Christian.

Fig. 19 *Mosaic from Umm al-Rasas (after Biddle 1999: 25, fig. 23).*

CONCLUSION

The specific symbolism inherent in the representation of both the lamp with the bejeweled cross and the lamp with the edicule must suggest that its owner was a Christian. It is hardly likely that a Jew or a pagan would have owned such lamps, especially one with a depiction of the replica cross on Golgotha, representing not just the symbolism of the crucifixion of Jesus but also the adoration of the True Cross. The second lamp, with the depiction of the tomb of Jesus, symbolizes the adoration of that tomb and, perhaps, as the edicule is empty and the cross is positioned on top of it, the resurrection of Jesus. As noted above, additional artifacts (primarily bowls and lamps) ornamented with common crosses were found at various locations in the village. While these common crosses could have been regarded as ornamental signs devoid of any symbolical meaning by non-Christians, the same cannot be said for the lamp with the bejeweled cross and the lamp with the edicule.

What does this imply in terms of the ethnic makeup of the village of En-Gedi in the fifth and sixth centuries and the religious beliefs that were held by its inhabitants? The presence of these two special lamps with a depiction of a bejeweled cross and the edicule, with the strong Christian symbolism connecting it to the crucifixion and the Rock of Golgotha and the tomb of Jesus and the resurrection, undoubtedly indicates some Christian presence at En-Gedi. Further support for this comes from the array of other artifacts from the site bearing crosses. Does this, therefore, suggest a mixed Jewish/Christian village at the site and what would have been the size of the Christian component amongst its inhabitants? Mixed Jewish/Christian villages have existed as Dauphin points out (Dauphin 1998: 320–30) and, thus, it would not be surprising if En-Gedi was one of those mixed villages. The fact that Eusebius and Jerome refer to it as "a very large village of Jews" *(Onom.* 86:16) suggests that the proportion of Jewish inhabitants was larger than that of Christians.

ACKNOWLEDGMENTS

I wish to thank the late Professor Yizhar Hirschfeld for allowing me to publish these lamps. A technical report on the lamps will also appear in the chapter on the ceramics in the Final Report of the En-Gedi excavations. The drawings are the work of Helena Bitan and Julia Rudman, whom I thank. I wish to thank also Gideon Hadas for allowing me to mention the stone measuring cup. This cup is going to be published in the report on ceramic and stone vessels from the En-Gedi Oasis excavations prepared by the author. In addition, I wish to thank my friend and colleague Shimon Gibson for useful comments and long discussions on the subject.

REFERENCES

Bagatti, B., and Testa, E.
1978 *Il Golgota e la Croce. Ricerche Storico-Archeologiche*. Jerusalem: Franciscan Printing.

Barag, D.
1970 Glass Pilgrim Vessels from Jerusalem: Part 1. *Journal of Glass Studies* 12: 35–63.

Barag, D.; Porat, Y.; and Netzer, E.
1981 The Synagogue at En-Gedi. Pp. 116–19 in *Ancient Synagogues Revealed*, ed. L. I. Levine. Jerusalem: Israel Exploration Society.

Biddle, M.
1999 *The Tomb of Christ*. Stroud: Sutton.

Corbo, V. C.
1988 Il Santo Sepolcro di Gerusalemme. Nova et Vetera. *Liber Annus* 38: 391–422.

Dauphin, C.
1998 *La Palestine Byzantine: Peuplement et Populations*. BAR International Series 726. Oxford: Archaeopress.

de Vincenz, A.
2003 A Crux Gemmata Representation on a Lamp from Ein Gedi. *Bulletin of the Anglo-Israel Archaeological Society* 21: 39–43.

Gibson, S., and Taylor, J. E.
1994 *Beneath the Church of the Holy Sepulchre, Jerusalem: The Archaeology and Early History of Traditional Golgotha*. London: Palestine Exploration Fund.

Grabar, A.
1958 *Ampoules de Terre Sainte (Monza, Bobbio)*. Paris: Klincksieck.

Hayes, J. W.
1972 *Late Roman Pottery*. London: British School at Rome.

Hunt, E. D.
1984 *Holy Land Pilgrimage in the Later Roman Empire AD 312–460*. Oxford: Clarendon.

Tushingham, A.
1985 *Excavations in Jerusalem 1961–1967*. Toronto: Royal Ontario Museum.

Chapter 34

Nomad Settlement in Palestine During the Late Byzantine–Early Moslem Period

by Ze'ev Safrai and Ofer Sion

Types of settlement are one of the most conservative and uniform components of any society. Societies designed the types of settlement appropriate to them and continued them for long periods, even after basic circumstances had changed. Settlement type is a compromise between various constraints — security needs, social needs, privacy, connection with the group, family, agricultural and other economic needs, among others. The design of settlement types is influenced by the conjunction of "objective" physical conditions and social structure. All these components should have led to frequent changes in settlement types, since we would have thought that every significant social change would find expression in the type of settlement. In fact, this did not happen. Thus, for example, the penetration of Christianity into the East did not cause a drastic change in the character of settlements. Even the rise of Islam did not cause a change in settlements, although changes did take place as a result of the conditions of the new era. This is because the structure of settlements is influenced, first and foremost, by traditional-conservative factors. In a period where there are no official guidelines, it is difficult for an individual to initiate changes in settlement types, and human society has difficulty in "inventing" (developing) new types.

A change in settlement type often occurs during a period of migration and in the area where there is a meeting between the new settlers, the veteran settlers, the conditions of the new land, and the country of origin as remembered by the new settlers. The new land presents the immigrants with new challenges and new conditions. The new settlers re-form their society in accordance with the conditions of the country and the society. Research on migration movements has found that immigrants design settlement types as one of their strategies in adjusting to the conditions of a new world. Some immigrants are partially released from the bonds of the past, which leads to open re-examination of settlement types. Other immigrants typically choose from two basic options:

1. To continue the type of settlement familiar to them from their country of origin.

2. To adopt the type of settlement existing in the new country.

Between these two extremes there are many intermediate solutions. In this chapter, we focus on a little-treated historical episode, i.e., the penetration of nomadic tribes (of Arab origin) into Palestine during the late Byzantine and early Islamic periods.[1]

The years 637–640 C.E. are considered the years of "The Arab Conquest." Modern research casts doubt on the degree to which this was a military campaign of conquest, rather than a largely "peaceful" wave of settlement, accompanied by military conflicts, which were of secondary importance (Whitcomb 1988; 1995; Magness 2003). In either case, the desert nomad tribes were apparently greatly strengthened in the late Byzantine period (the sixth and early seventh centuries). On the borders of the settled areas of the country, the nomads gradually turned into permanent residents — in the northern Negev, in Trachon, and in northern Trans-Jordan (Bowersock 1983, esp. 123–47; Shahid 1995, esp. xxv–xxx). Of course, this process was only one component of a mosaic of settlement that we do not understand completely. For instance, a process of domestication, or permanent settlement, took place in the territory of the Nabatean kingdom during the first century C.E. and in the territory or the kingdom of the Itureans in the Byzantine period. This process will be discussed briefly below.

PENETRATION OF NOMADS INTO THE AREA OF PERMANENT SETTLEMENT — HISTORICAL EVIDENCE

The many inscriptions from the Byzantine period found in the Negev reveal a mixed society, containing a mixture of names of Greek and Semitic — mainly Arab — origin. (It is not always easy to distinguish between names of Aramaic origin and those of Arab origin.). We may assume that many of the bearers of Greek names are of Arab origin. Evidence of this phenomenon is seen in members of "mixed" families, in which the father had an Arabic name and the son a Greek one, and vice versa. The papyri in Nessana reveal this aspect of settlement. According to the inscriptions, settlers of Arab origin lived in the settlement. In addition, we hear of tribes encamped or living in the area. The domestication of the nomads was apparently one of the main components of the flowering of the Negev from the fourth to the seventh centuries, or perhaps even the main motivation for civilian settlement in this region.[2]

A similar phenomenon took place in the Trachon and the Hauran, but there it began earlier. Already in the first century we hear of nomadic tribes that settled permanently in the Hauran. Beginning in the second and third centuries, there is increased evidence of this process of settlement. These nomadic settlers built traditional villages (see below), but numerous inscriptions disclose their Semitic and Arabic origins. This area developed a unique pagan religion, which had a mixture of gods of different ethnic origins (Dar 1993), and later, in the Byzantine period, there was a special brand of Christianity present in this area. This phenomenon of Christianity differs from that in areas of established settlement, and is a recurring one that deserves separate study. There is far less evidence of the penetration of nomadic tribes into the settled parts of the country.

Cyril of Scythopolis, who wrote biographies of monastic leaders in the Judean Desert, tells of one tribe of Saracens that emigrated to Judea. The tribe was transferred to the land by the Byzantine procurator in the aftermath of wars in the Syrian desert. This tribe was a "Khamula" (extended family) that aided the Byzantines in the war against the Persians and was pushed out of its area of settlement.[3] The tribe was transferred to the Judean Desert in the fifth century and here was aided by St. Euthymius (*Vita Euthemii*, 10). As a result, the tribe led by Asuebtus converted to Christianity, and the monk even helped the tribe to build a church and a cistern (*Vita Euthemii*, 51). Two possible sites have been suggested for the encampment of the tribe, both in the plain of Adumim. In both sites (Bir az-Zara'a and Khirbet Hinma), a cistern and a church were found. At Bir az-Zara'a, piles of stones were also found, which are apparently remains of the encampments that were scattered around the structures (see below; Federlin 1907; Sion 1992; 1997a; Hirschfeld 1984:

80–82). It was suggested that the tribe was located at one of these sites.

One generation later, Thalabas, one of the leaders of the tribe, is described as a resident of Lazarium (present-day Azariyah, a village in the suburbs of Jerusalem). The tribe, in full or in part, moved from the desert, ceased to be nomadic, and settled in a village on the desert fringe. In the time of Justinian, another Christian tribe, headed by one Arethas, moved to Palestine (*Vita Euthemii*, 52).

Another group of Christian Saracens built the Martyrium of St. Salome on the Judean plain (Kloner 1990). According to the Inscriptions and the Arabic names, it is clear that the holy cave was built in the sixth century by a Christian group of Arabic origin. We cannot find other archaeological evidence for the settlement of those Christian Arabs in the area of the Judean plain. It is important to note the special character of the group, which sanctified "Salome," a Christian martyr who is almost unknown in established Christian tradition (Kloner 1990).

In the Golan lived another Christian Saracen tribe between "Mount Harib" (today's Kefar Haruv) and Jabiye (Shahid 1989: 258–62). The Golan is located at the margins of the Hauran area, which was, as we have stated, undoubtedly an area of nomadic settlement. Migrations into the area took place mainly in the sixth and seventh centuries. In an imperial edict included in the Beersheba inscriptions, a tribal chief is mentioned, apparently in connection with the Gerar area (Alt 1921: 12). Corroborating evidence for the claim for Arab penetration into this area can be found in the inscription in the church in Kissufin, in which the name of a Christian church official named Abba is mentioned; the name is certain evidence of his Semitic origin (Meimris 1986, no. 869). Units of Limes soldiers camped in this area, some of whom were of Arabic origin (Avi Yonah 1977: 162–64). It may be that these soldiers are the ones responsible for the appearance of an Arabic tribe in the area. The name of another donor of Arabic origin appears in the inscription of the church in Bet Loya, further north in the area of Eleutheropolis (Patrick and Zafrir 1985).

Sozomenos states that Arabs participated in the fair of Terebinthos (in Alonei Mamre, north of Hebron; Sozomenos, *Church History* II, 4, 6) already in the time of the Emperor Constantine (in the middle of the fourth century), but this may reflect commercial ties and cultural influences, rather than the settlement of Arabic tribes. The fair attracted traders from remote areas, and those Arabs could have been traders rather than immigrants.

Talmudic evidence of Arab settlement is only moderately relevant. The Talmudic material reflects the situation in Palestine up to the end of the fourth century, whereas we are discussing later phenomena. Arabs are, of course, mentioned in the Rabbinic literature, but usually it is difficult to determine whether they were permanent residents, merchants who happened to come to the settlement (e.g., T. Berachot 4:16; M. Shabat 6:6; Y. Kilayim 6:30c), or, perhaps, nomads who operated outside the boundaries of the permanent settlement. This is the extent of our discussion regarding the image of the Arab in Rabbinic literature; suffice it to say that we have no evidence of contact with them inside the boundaries of the permanent settlement.

The situation is somewhat different towards the end of the Talmudic period. One source reports that a fire broke out in R. Yonah's neighborhood (Tiberias, in the middle of the fourth century) and one "Naptai" wanted to put it out (Y. Yoma 8:45b; Y. Shabbat 15:15d). This "Nabatean" is apparently a nickname for an Arab, who is a resident of Tiberias. In contrast, the mention of the Nabateans (Naptai) or the "Arabs" in other sources are likely descriptions of foreigners who live far away, or even a term describing Jews living in Arabia (e.g., Y. Baba Batra 8:16b; Sanhedrin 9:27b; Shabbat 14:14b). After the Arab conquest, there is increased evidence of Arabic settlement; but this is beyond the scope of the present study.

Shahid found some other evidence of Ghassanid settlements in Palestine Prima (the Ghassanids were one of the Arab tribes beyond the border of Palestine), and even two villages that preserve this traditional Arabic name until today. In neither case do we know when this name was given(Shahid 1995: 652–56)

Fig. 1 *Um Rihan (after Dar et al. 1986: 10–11).*

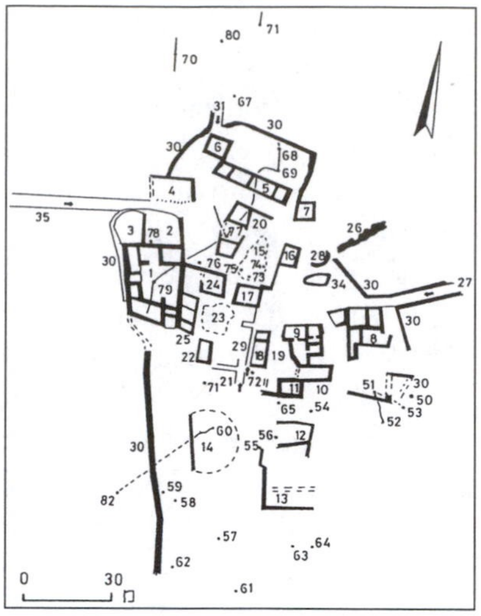

Fig. 2 *Khirbet Qerumit, an ordinary centralized village in the Judean plain (after Safrai 1997: 13).*

In summary, there is little direct evidence supporting the mass penetration of nomadic tribes into the area of settlement; rather, the situation appears to be, at most, a wave of settlement in the desert areas of the Negev and the Hauran.

THE TYPICAL SETTLEMENT OF NOMADIC TRIBES

For the purpose of our discussion, we list the types of rural settlement common in the area of Palestine during the Byzantine period and at the beginning of the Islamic period. These types of settlement have been common in the East for generations and continue be so to this day.

1. A nucleated densely populated village — this is the traditional Eastern village, familiar until today (figs. 1–2). The village varies in size from a few to many dozens of *dunams*; sometimes it is preferable to call the village a rural township in order to express its size. The nucleated village is the dominant model in most parts of the country, including the northern Judean Desert ,where seven such sites have been found (Sion 1994a: 138–41).
2. Single structures surrounding the village, or placed far away from it — these houses were the cause of a debate in the past years. Appelbaum claimed that these were villas in the imperial Roman style, whereas Hirschfeld claimed that they were the buildings of ordinary residents without any special economic status. Safrai has demonstrated that some of the buildings were Roman villas, and some belonged to ordinary residents, most of whom were wealthier than average.
   In any case, they are a phenomenon that is one of the components of the nucleated village (Hirschfeld 1996: 3–18; Appelbaum 1987; Safrai 1994a: 82–99).

In the border areas, we have evidence of three additional settlement types, which are the main subject of our discussion:

3. Small scattered villages — a concentration of buildings a few dozen meters apart. Usually there is only a small number of up to six buildings (figs.3–6).
4. A small number of buildings — they are separated from each other by a distance of a few dozen or even a few hundred meters. In fact, this is an area of simple farm homes. These are not buildings surrounding a nucleated village, but rather a series of farms — and the farms are the focal point of the distribution of the local settlement (see Avni 1996: 62–63 for numerous examples).

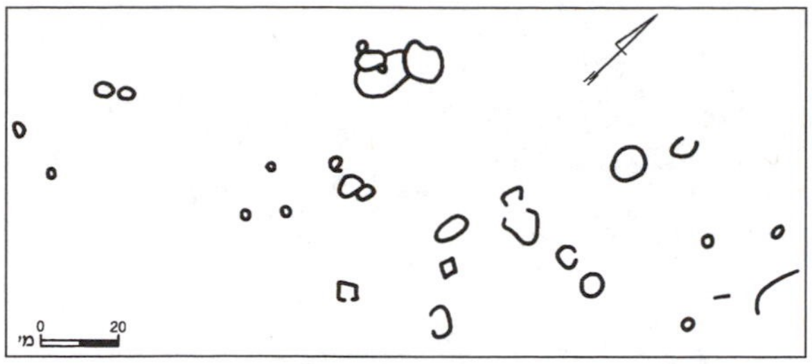

Fig. 3 *Nomadic settlement in the Mizpe Ramon area (after Haiman 1991: 73).*

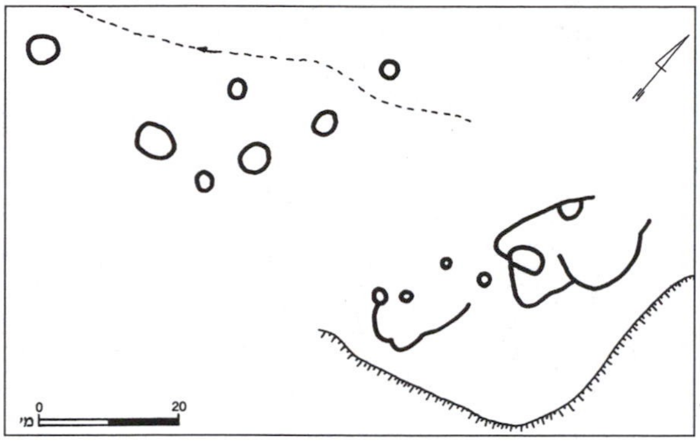

Fig. 4 *Nomadic settlement in the Mizpe Ramon area (after Haiman 1991: 62.*

5. Encampments — an area in which one or two buildings were found, in addition to vestiges of tent sites. Sometimes there is a public building surrounded by tents.

The last three types, which are very similar, are typical of nomadic settlement. Dozens of farm buildings like these have been discovered all over the northern Negev. The typical building includes a number of living rooms, sheep pens, and an agricultural drainage or water system. On rare occasions, there is a concentration of four or five such farm buildings, which heralds the beginning of a scattered village according to type 3 listed above.

Another area of scattered villages in the Hermon region was researched and excavated by Dar. The villages were mostly small and consisted of scattered isolated buildings, such as at Bir As-Sobah, Magaar Taba, and Mazraat Zabdine, in addition to other sites (figs. 7–9; Haiman 1992: Avni 1996).

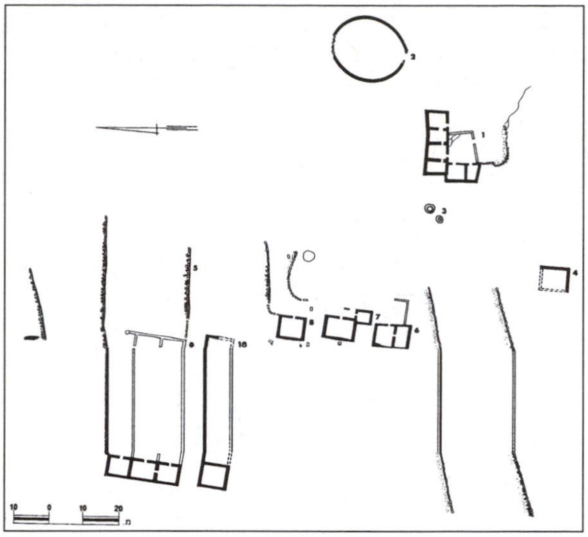

Fig. 5 *The Sede Boker site, a hamlet in the Negev (after Cohen 1981: 68).*

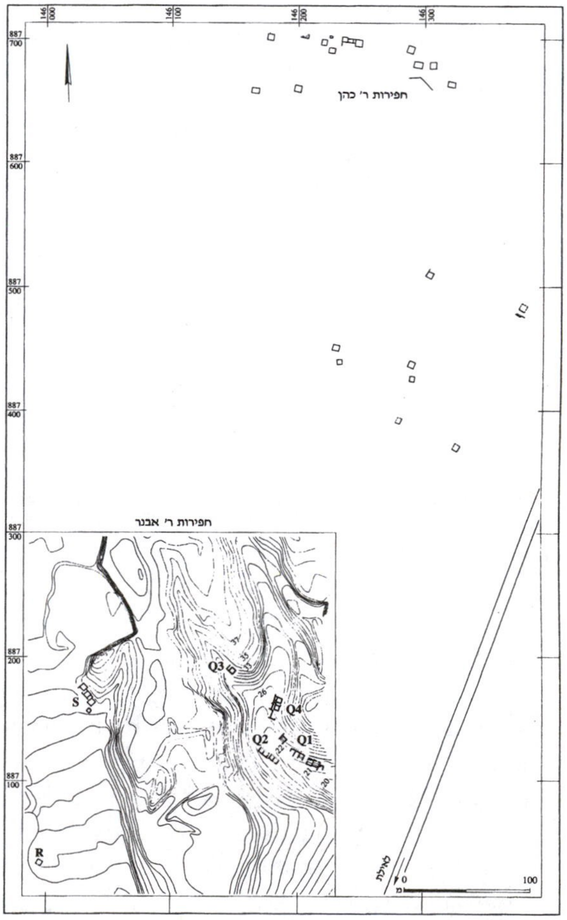

Fig. 6 *A scattered hamlet in the southern Negev (after Avner 1998: 22*).*

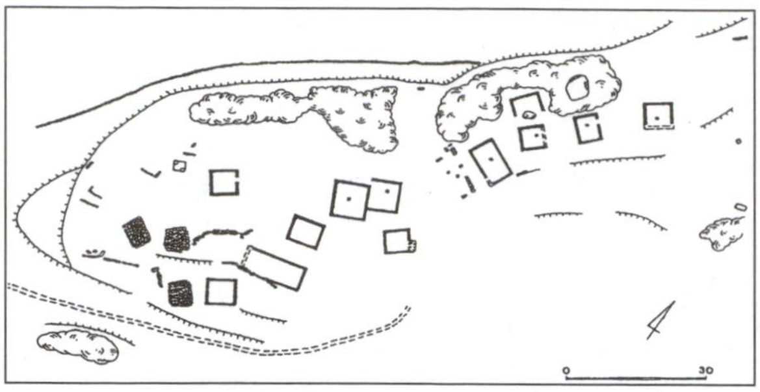

Fig. 7 A hamlet on the Hermon (after Hirschfeld 1997: 80).

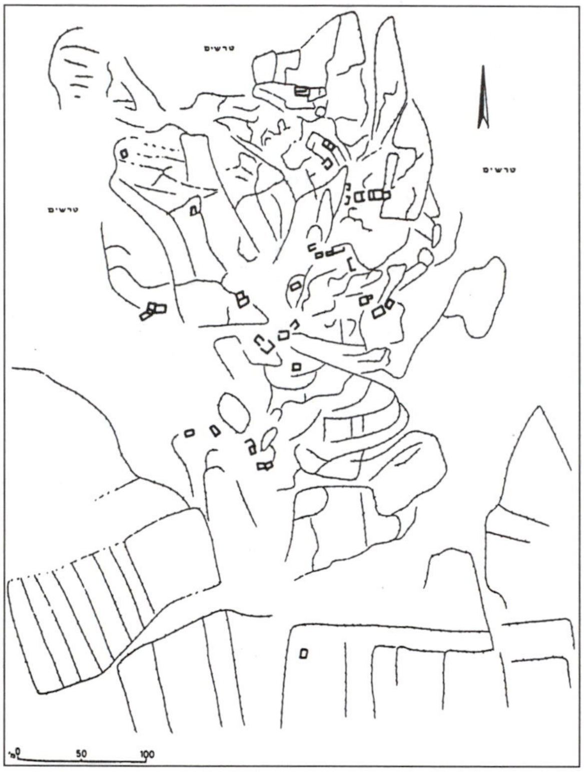

Fig. 8 Mag'ar Tbbaa, settlement plan (after Dar 1978: 110).

Fig. 9 Mazzrat Zabdin, settlement plan (after Dar 1978: 111).

The Besor region can be joined to the Negev area. Gazit found more than twenty sites that were defined as campsites, all from the Byzantine period; at some, pottery shards from an earlier period were found as well (Gazit 1996). For this study, sites were chosen that lacked signs of building and could stretch over a broad area, sometimes hundreds of *dunams*; it is difficult to assume that there was a large permanent settlement there.[4] In addition, scattered hamlets were identified by the site surveyor (e.g., site 116 and, perhaps, site 217). Further north, a few churches without surrounding settlements were found. Apparently, judging by the vestiges, these are not monasteries. Possibly, they are sites of churches that served nomads.[5]

This type of settlement may well be typical of the permanent residence of nomads in desert areas. One must ascertain what factors were responsible for the formation of the scattered settlement typical of the nomads. In this article, we compare ancient patterns to the type of settlement apparent in fixed residence patterns of nomads in modern times. The domestication of the Bedouin in modern times is characterized by a gradual transition from an encampment to a building (from a hut to a house), while retaining the pattern of a scattered village with great distances between the buildings (figs. 10–11; Shmueli 1970: 83–97). Shmueli, who studied this pattern, emphasized the need to preserve individualism in the crowded "Khamula," the need for a place to keep the sheep around the house, and the small number of community services. The scattering of houses also reflects, of course, the self-confidence of the settlers who have no need of a wall.

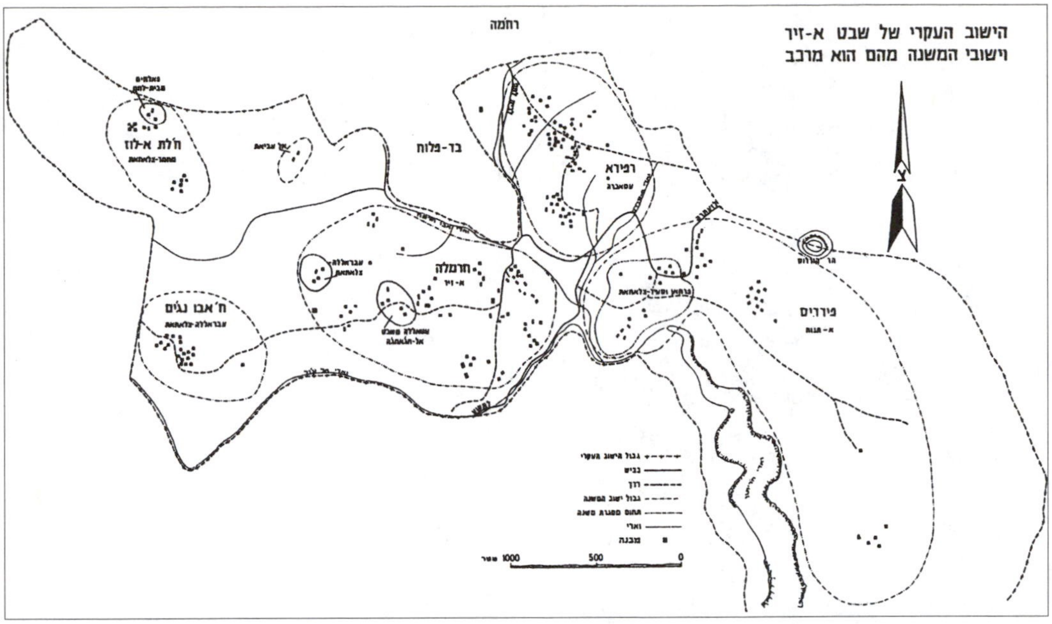

Fig. 10 *The settlement of the tribe of Taʿamra in the Judean Desert (after Shmueli 1970: 84).*

There are other reasons for the scattered settlement as well. The residential areas are exposed to neighbors, and it is difficult to preserve privacy in tents or huts. A certain distance between houses protects privacy to some extent. In addition, the "Khamula" (extended family) includes a small number of seminal units. Thus, it is possible to preserve family cohesion despite the distance between the houses. In more developed settlements containing hundreds of families this becomes impossible. The settlement then becomes too large and stretches over a broad area, which does not allow for a communal life. Settlements were greatly influenced by the cultural tradition and the historical heritage of all the Bedouin tribes.

As has been determined above, research has suggested the penetration of nomadic tribes in areas of permanent settlement in the Roman province of Syria-Palaestina. Since the usual types of settlement in the area where nomads settled permanently ("the area of domestication") have been identified, we must ascertain if we can identify a similar type of settlement in the settled parts of the country. Scattered settlements in the eastern region, in Trans-Jordan, or in the Hauran are known to exist (fig.

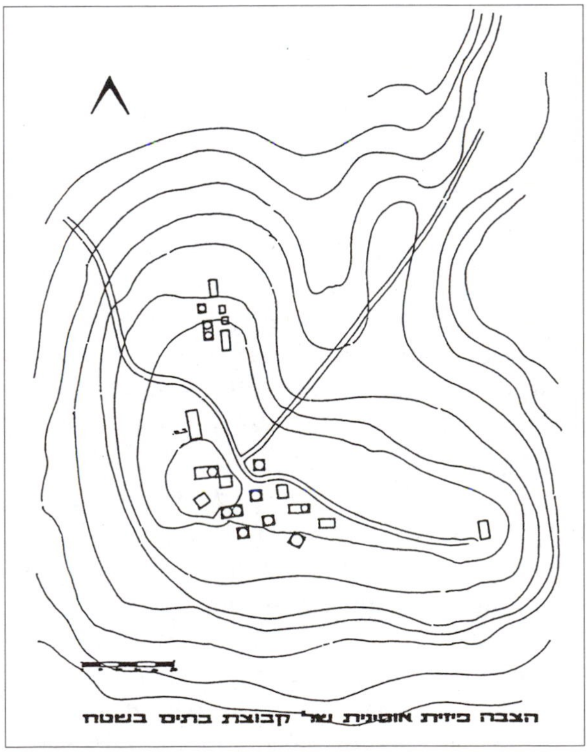

Fig. 11 *A group of houses in a contemporary Bedouin settlement (after Shmueli 1970: 91).*

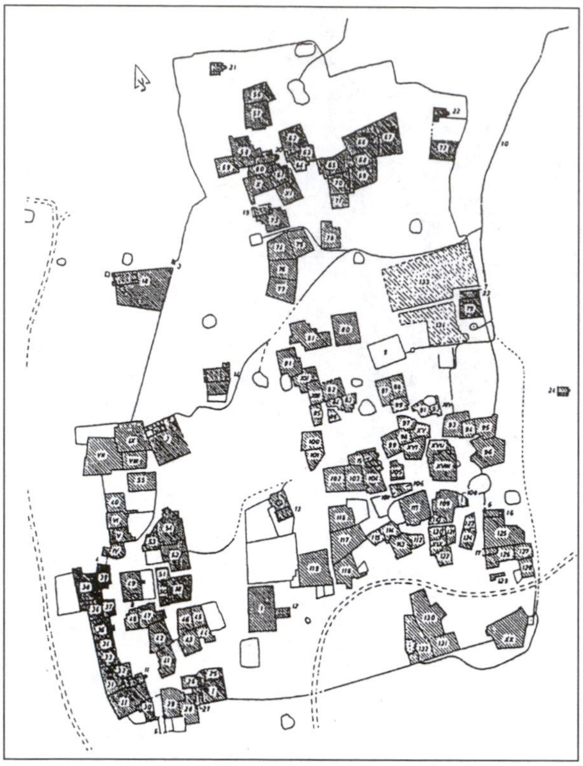

Fig. 12 Umm al Jimal, a military settlement in northern Transjordan. Note the blocs of buildings and the empty areas. This was a scattered settlement, the intermediate areas of which were gradually built up (after De Vries 1981: 58–59).

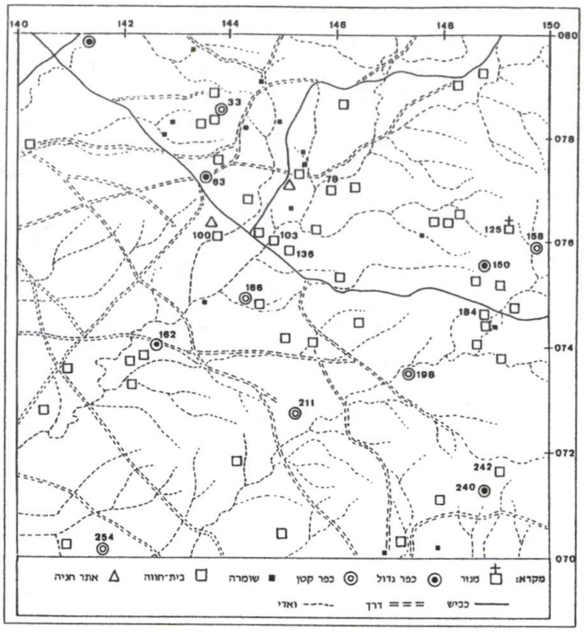

Fig. 13 The settlements in the Yatir region, a settlement area without a defined village center (after Hirschfeld 1997: 102).

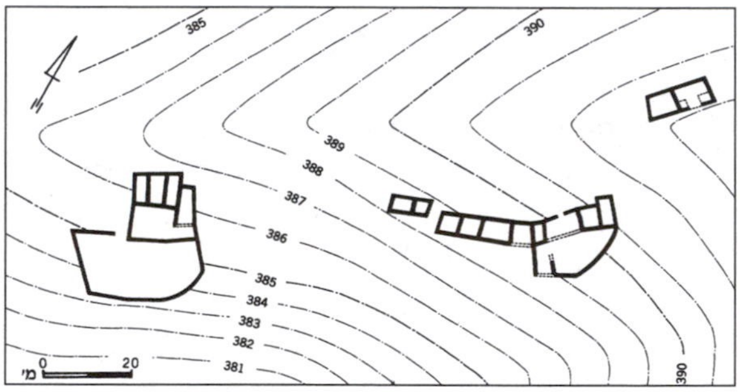

Fig. 14 Site no. 166 at Nahal So'a, settlement plan (after Guvrin, 1992: 109).

12).[6] Therefore, evidence of scattered settlements as far west as possible must be sought.

The question is whether it is possible to find evidence of this type of settlement even in the crowded areas of settlement. If the answer is positive, this type of settlement will show the dispersion of Arab tribal settlement in the inhabited part of the country. If not, one must conclude either that the penetration of the nomads was limited or that the Arabs adopted types of settlement common to the countries of immigration that they had chosen (model 2).

The Yatir region is apparently an area of scattered settlement during the Byzantine period. The term "Yatir region" refers to the slopes of the Judean Hills towards the Beersheba valley. During the Second Temple period, the region was included in the area of Jewish settlement — mikvehs and hidden caves from the Bar Kokhba Revolt were found there. The area, surveyed by Guvrin, is in a good state of preservation, which enables us to understand the nature of the settlement (Guvrin 1992). During the Byzantine period, this was an area of farms, characterized by a series of single structures at a distance of dozens or hundreds of meters from each other (fig. 13). There are villages in the area as well, e.g., Khirbat Sawa, Khirbat Hura, Qaryatein (Qerayot), among others. The single structures, however, do not encircle a central town but create independent units. Moreover, in the Yatir region small scattered villages were found as well and Guvrin measured

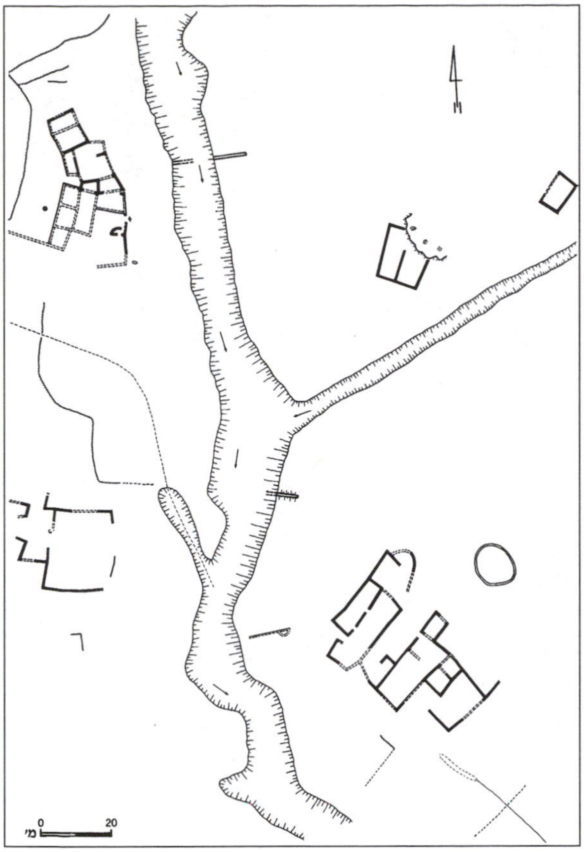

Fig. 15 *Site no. 158 at Nahal 'Anim, settlement plan (after Guvrin, 1992: 103).*

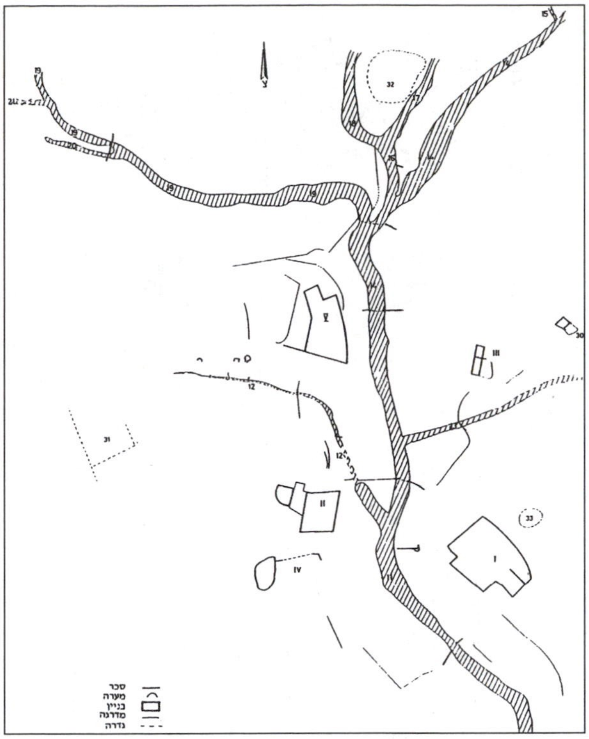

Fig. 16 *Terrace lines and agriculture dams (after Safrai 1997: 23).*

several of them. Site 166 is an example of such a small village or hamlet (fig. 14). In the same area, Guvrin identified another hamlet containing five structures in an area of approximately twenty-five *dunams* (fig. 15; Guvrin 1992: 101–3), surrounded by agricultural cultivation. Each of the five structures was composed of living rooms and open pens. More important is the evidence of agricultural cultivation. The wadis were dammed by a series of dams that allowed limited use of floodwaters and also prevented the erosion of the soil. On the slopes a system of agricultural terraces was built, allowing some agricultural activity around the houses (fig. 16). Two sizable nucleated villages were also found in the region.

In light of the above, one can assume that nomads coming from the area of the northern Negev settled in the Yatir region. These nomads became domesticated and created a type of village familiar to them. Since the Yatir region is located between the Negev and the hilly region, the penetration of nomads from the desert is a "natural" phenomenon that still occurs today, albeit under very different circumstances.

Another area where there is evidence of nomadic penetration is the northern Judean Desert. In Khirbat Abu Suwwana, Sion excavated a village, and in the eastern part he excavated four scattered residential structures and associated installations (fig.17; Sion 1997b). The site was built in the seventh century and was apparently a small Moslem village of 5 *dunams* with a population of about 200. The village is further evidence of the settlement of "Khamulot" who became domesticated in the wake of Arab immigrants.

In the area between Jerusalem and the western border of the northern Judean Desert, there are another seven sites where early Islamic ceramics were found (Sion 1994b; Finkelstein 1993: 78–80, sites 76, 79, 81; Feldstein et al. 1993: 164–67, sites

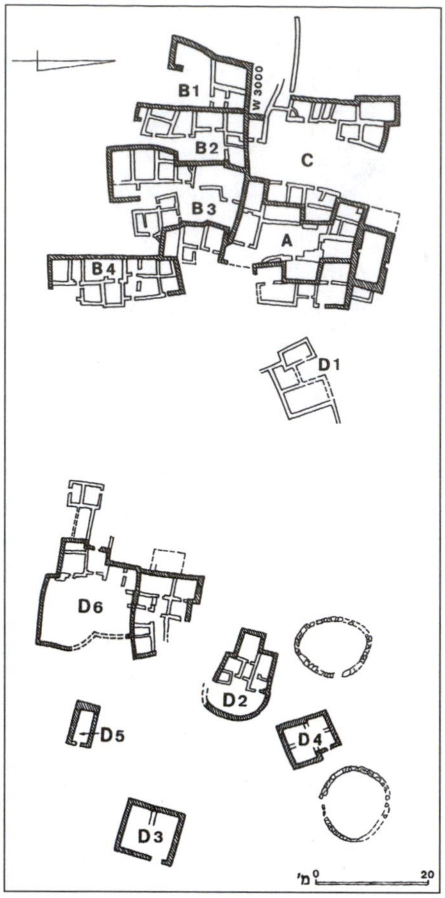

Fig. 17 *Khirbet Abu Suwwana, a small scattered village in the Judean Desert (after Sion 1997b: 184).*

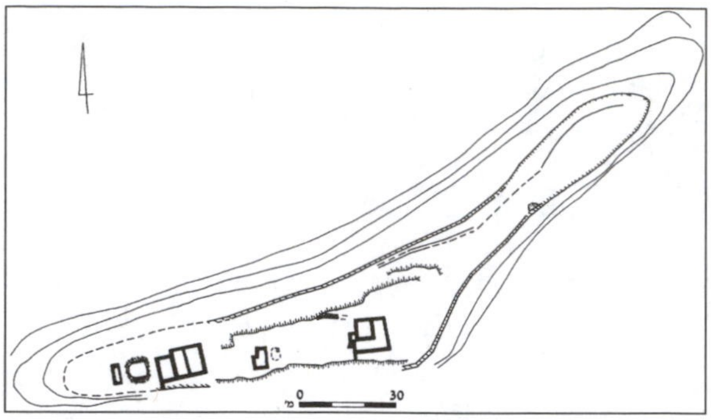

Fig. 18 *Wadi el Baqquq, a monastery or small scattered village (after Patrich 1994: site no. 85).*

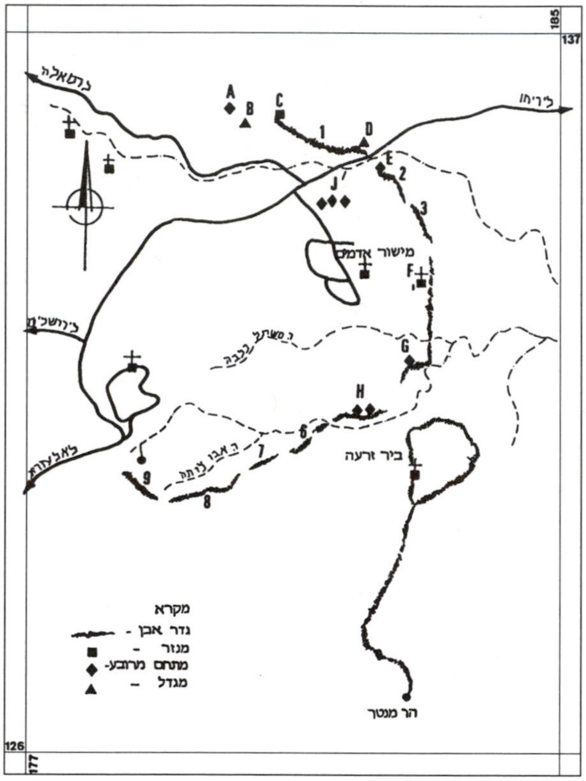

Fig. 19 *Fence around Misshore Addumim (after Sion 1994b: 223).*

181, 183–85). Six of the seven surveyed sites can be defined as encampments. Three of them were linked to cisterns and a few agricultural features, including terraces and field towers. Only one site, Khirbet Deir Shabab el Qiblia, was potentially a nucleated village, judging from the number of structures, the size of the site, and the architectural similarity to Khirbet Abu Suwwana.

In a survey south of Khirbet Abu Suwwana, twelve sites were surveyed, among them three from this period. Two of them can be defined as encampments. Khirbet al Rabini was found to be very similar to Khirbet Zuna in terms of size, architecture, and surrounding sheepfolds (Sion, unpublished).

In all of the sites mentioned above, there was no evidence of a wall. Surrounding a settlement with a wall is a reflection of security problems in the region. In the Judean Desert, one site surrounded by a wall was surveyed, but this might have been a monastery (fig. 18). As has been already pointed out, the encampment of the Asuebtus tribe was surrounded by a fence, and on the site itself there were encampments surrounding public buildings (figs. 19–20, a church and a cistern; Sion 1994b).

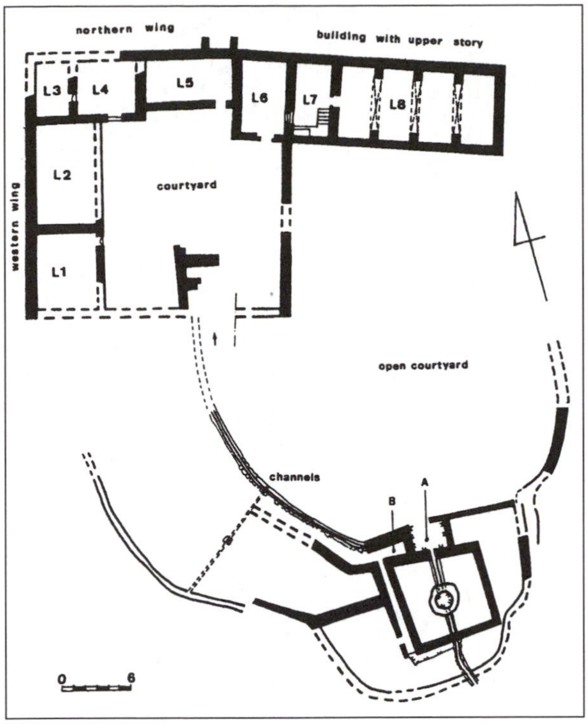

Fig. 20 *Khirbet Handuma (after Sion 1997a: 150).*

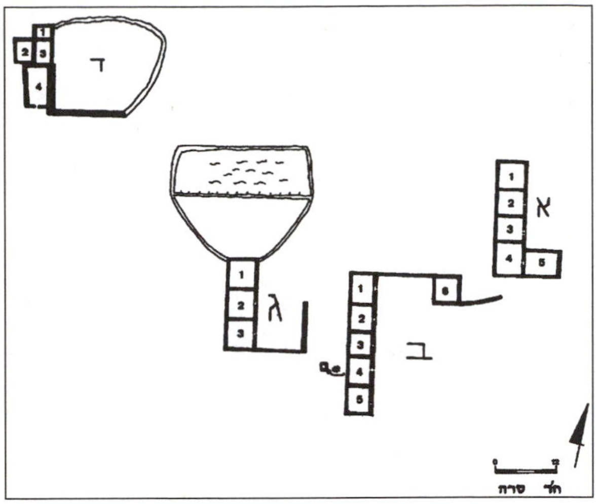

Fig. 21 *Khirbet Sara (Sion, unpublished).*

Material remains from these sites date only from the beginning of the Arabic period and there is no evidence of previous permanent settlement. The circumstances suggest evidence of settlement of families of Arab origin, who then became domesticated in the wake of Arabic domination.

Further to the east, in the Wadi Kelt, a number of encampments were found scattered in two areas. One area was to the north, along the Roman road from Jericho to modern Ramallah, and includes Tariq "Abu Hindi" and Tariq "Abu George." Another concentration of scattered encampments was found south of the Jerusalem–Jericho road. These are sites that "penetrate" deep into the desert, almost up to the eastern desert border. Altogether, twenty-four sites were found; eleven of them were protected from the wind, a factor that does not seem to have been important to their location. Water sources and partial terraces that were not used for agriculture were found in three of them. Sheepfolds (sometimes more than one) were found in seventeen sites. In most cases, the encampments stretched over an area of two *dunams,* although, in rare instances, they covered an area of only seven *dunams*. Their small size testifies to a family migration, rather than a migration of larger groups.

A number of scattered sites were found in the eastern border area of Samaria. In Khirbet Sara, east of Shilo (Israel Ref. 17930/16240), a small village was surveyed; four farm structures containing a pen/courtyard and a row of rooms facing south were identified (fig. 21). Two other scattered villages were Khirbet Iraq El Hamra in the desert of northern Samaria (fig. 22) and Khirbet Ghadbane in the northern Al Buqeia (fig. 23; Zertal 1996: 451–53, fig. 356).

These sites are all located in the eastern part of the settled area of the country. The Yatir region and the eastern regions of Judea and Samaria are border areas next to the desert, although the Judean Desert is also very near to the center of the settled part of the province of Palaestina. In the Yatir region, the settlements date from the Byzantine period, whereas the Judean Desert sites date only from the beginning of the Arabic period. The latter represent nomadic settlement after the expulsion of the Byzantine government. In addition, in the area of the northern Judean Desert a quantitatively marginal phenomenon is present. Other than these examples, scattered hamlets or encampments (types 3–5) are a rare phenomenon in Palestine.

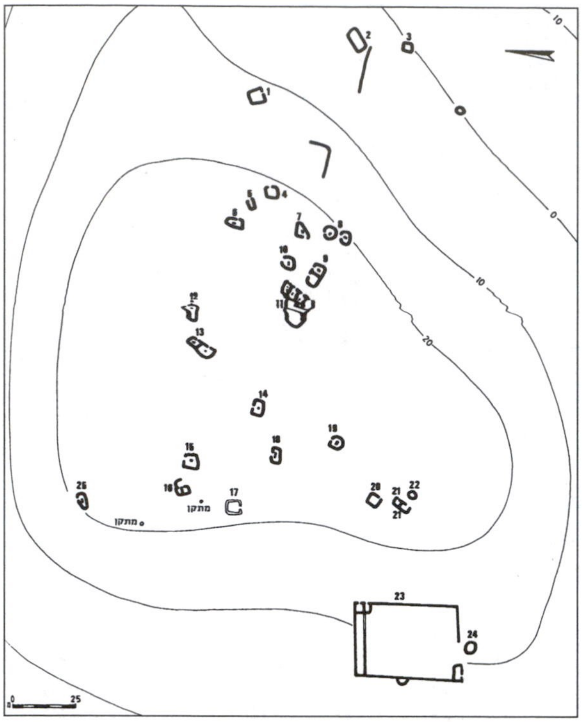

Fig. 22 *Iraq el-Hamra, site plan (after Zertal 1996: fig. 356).*

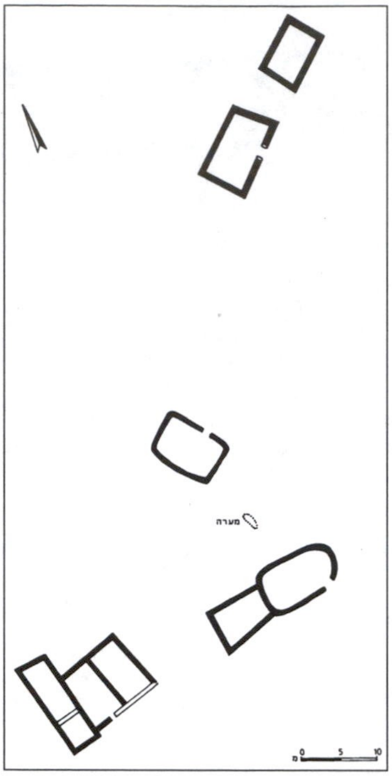

Fig. 23 *Khirbet Ghadbane, site plan (after Zertal 1996: fig. 366).*

CONCLUSION

- In the desert areas a process of partial and complete domestication of the nomads took place during several periods, although this study deals with only the Byzantine–early Moslem periods.
- During the process of domestication, nomads created new types of settlement that suited their nature and the kinds of agricultural problems they faced.
- Nomads penetrated the borders of the settled areas of the country and there continued their familiar settlement tradition (the above-mentioned option 1).
- Historical evidence indicates sparse nomadic settlement on the margins of the settled area of the country and nomadic types of settlement have been found only in such places (the Yatir region and the northern desert in Judea and Samaria).

With the available evidence, one can conclude either that nomadic settlement in the Byzantine period was very limited in scope or that the nomads adopted the types of settlement existing in the settled areas (the above-mentioned option 2). Only in the desert areas did they continue to build settlement types that they were familiar with from the desert, whereas in the settled areas they adopted a centralized type of settlement. Additional research may reveal more small scattered villages and there may be increased evidence of nomad villages.[7] It is also possible that nomads penetrated existing villages, and even if they populated them in a scattered manner, it may not be possible to document this. Therefore, the conclusions presented here are preliminary and merit further investigation.

If, in fact, nomadic settlement in the settled areas of the country was limited in its scope, this has implications for the debate as to whether there was an Arab conquest or a peaceful process of settlement in the settled regions. At this point, there is not enough evidence for the massive settlement of Arabic tribes in Palestine before the Arab "conquest." Even after the conquest, there is no evidence of a wave of settlement of Arabic tribes in the country. Of course, this does not end the debate about the Arab "conquest" or the Arab "settlement." There is simply too little evidence of a conquest in the historical literature and in the archaeological findings. One might define the phenomenon as a "trickle" of settlers, but there is no evidence of a massive wave of settlement. In contrast, the Negev, the Hauran, and eastern Syria were flooded with Arabic tribes already towards the end of the Byzantine period; here the kingdoms of Arabic tribes were also established. Although this study does not completely answer how the Byzantine government was expelled from the East, the facts presented do contribute to the important debate about the end of Byzantine rule in the Middle East.

NOTES

1 The term "Palestine" in this context is imprecise and an anachronism; we refer to the area of permanent settlement in what the Romans called Syria Palaestina.

2 The flowering of the Negev is evident from archaeological surveys in the Negev hills. For a summary see Haiman 1989; 1992.

3 A similar historical story from the first century is the transference of the tribe of Zamaris from Babylon to the border of Judea and their settlement in the Golan and in the Hauran (Jos. *Ant.* 17:29).

4 They include the following:

Site Number	Area of site in *dunams*
161	500
163	Broad
164	50
165	100
167	200
169	Broad
170	Broad
174	100
189	40
191?	2000
192	50
194	Broad
195	150
196	100
205	50
211	40
220	100
234	50
255	40

5 For example, the church in Khirbat Shellal and the one in Beikatt Abu-Radi near Kissufim (Gazit 1986: 144). An additional site that is perhaps connected to a nomadic settlement is site 190 in the Urim Map survey (Gazit 1986). Located nearby is a large cemetery from the Moslem period with no link to a defined settlement. The adjacent site (128) is a small, one-*dunam* "campsite." About half a kilometer from the cemetery there is another site (189), which is a campsite or an agricultural plot of 2000 *dunams*; it certainly was not a regular settlement.

6 Only one example from Transjordan is provided: the famous town of Umm al-Jimal, northeast of the River Jordan, where comprehensive research is being carried out; although as yet unpublished, it is already clear that this was a military settlement consisting of many units, many of whose soldiers were of Arab origin. The settlement was built as a set of closely built blocks of houses with wide open areas between them. Large pools were built in the open area and these areas may have served as sheep pens as well (De Vries 1982; see also fig. 12).

7 It is possible that nomads who penetrated and dominated an ancient scattered village lived in some of the existing structures. Without careful excavations, there is no chance of revealing this.

REFERENCES

Alt, A.
1921 *Die Griechischen Inschriften der Palestina Tertia westlich der 'Araba*. Berlin: Vereinigung Wissenschaftlicher Verleger.

Appelbaum, S.
1987 The problem of the Villa in Eretz Israel. *Eretz Israel* 19: 1–5 (Hebrew).

Avi-Yonah, M.
1977 *The Holy Land, from the Persian to the Arab Conquests, 536 B.C. to A.D. 640: a Historical Geography*. Grand Rapids, MI: Baker.

Avner, R.
1998 A Village from the Early Islamic Period. *Antiquities* 36: 21*–39* (Hebrew).

Avni, G.
1996 *Nomads, Farmers and Town-Dwellers*. Jerusalem: Israel Antiquities Authority (Hebrew).

Bowersock, G. W.
1983 *Roman Arabia*. Cambridge, MA: Harvard University.

Cohen, R.
1981 *Archeological Survey of Israel, Map of Sede Boqer East (168)*. Jerusalem: Archaeological Survey of Israel (Hebrew).

Dar, S.
1978 A Survey of Early Settlements on the Hermon Shoulder. Pp 110–11 in *The Hermon and its Foot*, ed. S. Applebaum. Tel Aviv: United Kibbutz.
1993 *Settlements and Cult Sites on Mount Hermon, Israel*. British Archaeological Reports, International Series 589. Oxford: British Archaeological Reports.

Dar, S.; Safrai Z.; and Tepper, Y.
1986 *Um Rihan – A village of the Mishnah*. Tel Aviv: United Kibbutz (Hebrew).

De Vries, B.,
1981 The Umm Jimal Project, *Bulletin of the American Schools of Oriental Research* 244: 53–72.
1982 The Umm el-Jimal project 1972–1977. *Annual of the Department of Antiquities of Jordan* 26: 97–116.

Federlin, R. P.
1907 Les Campements des Arabes Chrétiens des Paremboles, Au Desert de Jérusalem. *La Terre Sainte* 24: 177–84.

Feldstein, A.; Kidron, G.; Hanin, N.; Kamaisky, Y; and Eitam, D.
1993 Southern Parts of the Maps of Ramallah and el-Bireh and Northern Parts of the Map of Ein Kerem. Pp. 164–67 in *Archaeological Survey of the Hill Country of Benjamin*, eds. I. Finkelstein and Y. Magen. Jerusalem: Israel Antiquities Authority.

Finkelstein, I.
1993 Northern Parts of the Maps of Beit Sira, Ramallah and el-Bireh. Pp. 78–80 in *Archaeological Survey of the Hill Country of Benjamin*, eds. I. Finkelstein and Y. Magen. Jerusalem: Israel Antiquities Authority.

Gazit,D.
1986 *The Besor Region*. Tel-Aviv: Archaeological Survey of Isael (Hebrew).
1996 *Archeological Survey of Israel, Map of Urim (125)*. Jerusalem: Israel Antiquities Authority (Hebrew).

Guvrin,Y.
1992 *Archeological Survey of Israel, Map of Nahal Yattir (139)*. Jerusalem: Israel Antiquities Authority (Hebrew).

Haiman, M.
1989 *Shepherds and Farmers in the Kadesh Barnea Area*. Sdeh Boker: Society for the Protection of Nature (Hebrew).
1991 *Archeological Survey of Israel, Map of Mizpe Ramon Southwest (200)*. Jerusalem: Israel Antiquities Authority (Hebrew).
1992 Early Settlement Patterns the Negev Highlands. Unpublished Ph.D. dissertation. Hebrew University, Jerusalem (Hebrew).

Hirschfeld, Y.
1984 Monastery of St. Euthymis. Survey and Excavation. *Excavation and Surveys in Israel* 3: 2–82.
1996 Changes in Settlement Patterns of the Jewish Rural Populace before and after Rebellions against Rome. *Katedra* 80: 3–18(Hebrew).
1997 Villages, Estate Houses and Farmhouses in Byzantine Israel. Pp. 75–129 in *The Ancient Village in the Land of Israel*, eds. S. Dar and Z. Safrai. Tel Aviv: Tel Aviv University (Hebrew).

Kloner, A.
1990 The Cave Chapel of Horvat Qasra. *'Atiqot* 10: 129–37 (Hebrew series).

Magness, J.
2003 *The Archaeology of the Early Islamic Settlement in Palestine*. Winona Lake, IN: Eisenbrauns.

Meimris, Y. E.
1986 *Sacred Names, Saints, Martyrs, Church Officials*. Athens: Research Centre for Greek and Roman Antiquity.

Patrich, J.
1994 *Archeological Survey of Israel, Map of Deir Mar Saba (109/7)*. Jerusalem: Israel Antiquities Authority (Hebrew).

Patrick, Y., and Zafrir, Y.
1985 A Byzantine Church and Agricultural Installations of the Byzantine period at Khurbat Bet Loya. *Qadmoniot* 71–72: 106–11 (Hebrew).

Safrai, Z.
1997 The Judean Village. Pp. 11–73 in *The Ancient Village in the Land of Israel*, eds. S. Dar and Z. Safrai. Tel Aviv: Tel Aviv University (Hebrew).

Shahid, I.
1989 *Byzantion and the Arabs in the Fifth Century*. Washington, DC: Dumbarton Oaks.
1995 *Byzantium and the Arabs in the Sixth Century*. Washington, DC: Dumbarton Oaks.

Shmueli, A.
1970 *The Beduin Settlement of the Judean Desert*. Tel Aviv: Security Office (Hebrew).

Sion, O.
1992 A monastic Precinct in Khirbet Handuma. *Liber Annuus* 42: 179–287.
1994a Settlement distribution in the northern Judean desert during the 7th and 8th centuries CE. Unpublished M.A Thesis, Hebrew University Jerusalem (Hebrew).
1994b The Roman-Byzantine Period in the Map of the Wadi Kelt Survey. Pp. 221–32 in *Judea and Samaria Research Studies III*, ed. Y. Eshel. Ariel: Judea and Samaria College (Hebrew).
1997a Mishor Adumin (Khirbet Handoma). *Antiquities* 32: 149–58 (Hebrew).
1997b Khirbet Abu Suwwana. *Antiquities* 32: 183–94 (Hebrew).

Sozomenos, H.
1983 *Ecclesiastical History, Historia Ecclesiastica*, eds. J. Bidez and G. Hanson. Paris: Garnier.

Whitcomb, D.
1988 Khirbet al-Mafjar Reconsidered: The Ceramic Evidence. *Bulletin of the American Schools of Oriental Research* 271: 51–67.
1995 Islam and the Socio-cultural Transition of Palestine – Early Islamic Period (638–1099 CE). Pp. 488–501 in *The Archaeology of Society in the Holy Land*, ed. T. Levy. London: Leicester University.

Zertal, A.
1996 *The Manasseh Hill Country B*. Tel Aviv: Haifa University (Hebrew).

Vita Euthemii
1991 Pp. 1–92 in Cyril of Scythopolis, *Lives of the Monks of Palestine: Life of Euthmius*, trans. R. M. Price. Collegeville, MN: Cistercian.

Index

Subject Index

Author Index